THEORIES OF HUMAN COMMUNICATION

EIGHTH EDITION

Stephen W. Littlejohn
*Adjunct Professor, University of New Mexico, Albuquerque,
and Domenici Littlejohn, Inc., Albuquerque, New Mexico*

Karen A. Foss
Professor, University of New Mexico, Albuquerque

THOMSON

WADSWORTH

Australia • Canada • Mexico • Singapore • Spain • United Kingdom • United States

THOMSON

WADSWORTH

Publisher: *Holly J. Allen*
Acquisitions Editor: *Annie Mitchell*
Development Editor: *Renée Deljon*
Assistant Editor: *Aarti Jayaraman*
Editorial Assistant: *Trina Enriquez*
Technology Project Manager: *Jeanette Wiseman*
Marketing Manager: *Kimberly Russell*
Marketing Assistant: *Andrew Keay*
Advertising Project Manager: *Shemika Britt*
Project Manager, Editorial Production: *Matt Ballantyne*
Art Director: *Maria Epes*

Print/Media Buyer: *Karen Hunt*
Permissions Editor: *Stephanie Lee*
Production Service: *Scratchgravel Publishing Services*
Compositor: *Scratchgravel Publishing Services*
Text Designer: *Jeanne Calabrese*
Copy Editor: *Sara Wilson*
Cover Designer: *Scott Ratinoff*
Cover Image: *Wassily Kandinsky, "Struttura Angolare"*
  © 2004 Artists Rights Society (ARS),
  New York/ADAGP, Paris
Text and Cover Printer: *Webcom*

Printed in Canada

1 2 3 4 5 6 7 08 07 06 05 04

For more information about our products, contact us at:
Thomson Learning Academic Resource Center
1-800-423-0563

For permission to use material from this text or product, submit a request online at
http://www.thomsonrights.com.
Any additional questions about permissions can be submitted by email to
thomsonrights@thomson.com.

Library of Congress Control Number: 2004106592

ISBN 0-534-63873-2

Thomson Wadsworth
10 Davis Drive
Belmont, CA 94002-3098
USA

Asia
Thomson Learning
5 Shenton Way #01-01
UIC Building
Singapore 068808

Australia/New Zealand
Thomson Learning
102 Dodds Street
Southbank, Victoria 3006
Australia

Canada
Nelson
1120 Birchmount Road
Toronto, Ontario M1K 5G4
Canada

Europe/Middle East/Africa
Thomson Learning
High Holborn House
50/51 Bedford Row
London WC1R 4LR
United Kingdom

Latin America
Thomson Learning
Seneca, 53
Colonia Polanco
11560 Mexico D.F.
Mexico

Spain/Portugal
Paraninfo
Calle Magallanes, 25
28015 Madrid, Spain

BRIEF CONTENTS

Detailed Contents

PREFACE

With this eighth edition, *Theories of Human Communication* turns twenty-seven years old, and with it come many changes. The first major change is in terms of authorship: We have decided to become coauthors on this project. As a married couple, we have always been conversational partners on this book, and now Karen has become a formal contributor. We started discussing this revision last summer in Italy, and we hope the flavor of those early brainstorming sessions can still be found here in a creative new format and approach to communication theory.

While the book is different in many ways, we have retained features of the book that the field has always appreciated—a strong discussion of theory and the nature of inquiry, a high-level survey of theories across the communication discipline, the continued addition of new materials and sources, a useful bibliography for further exploration of specific theories, and an accessible writing style.

To these features, we have added a metatheoretical framework that we hope will provide coherence for students seeking to understand the relationships among theories. We have framed communication theory around two intersecting elements—contexts and theoretical traditions—and show, across the chapters of the book, how various theoretical traditions have added to our knowledge of eight communication contexts. We believe that this new framework more accurately presents the nuances of the communication discipline and the way in which various theories can be part of various traditions. Rather than thinking of critical theory, for example, as a unitary set of theories in the discipline, there is in fact a critical component to many of the traditions—and this new approach allows us to reflect that. Similarly, feminist scholarship has threads in many of the traditions of the communication discipline, and we present it as such here. We hope this new framework will provide a useful organizing scheme for professors around which to develop the course and for students seeking to understand connections, trajectories, and relationships among the theories.

We have also added a section at the end of each chapter called *Applications & Implications*. This section is designed to remind students that the theories presented have implications for their own lives as communicators. We hope it also provides a way of stepping back from the particular theories and remembering the dimensions that give each set of theories its coherence. We hope you find these changes useful as you make your way through the theories in this new edition.

In writing this book, we have many people to thank. First, we offer our deep appreciation to our adopters, who have kept the project alive, and to students from around the world, who have told us over the years that the book was helpful and sometimes even invaluable in their education. We would also like to thank Robert Craig for his essay on communication traditions that provided the model for this approach. We wish also to thank the following who reviewed various chapters or responded to surveys for this edition:

Karen Lee Ashcraft, University of Utah

Kevin Barge, University of Georgia

George A. Barnett, University of Buffalo, The State University of New York

Vincent L. Bloom, California State University, Fresno

David M. Bollinger, University of North Carolina at Wilmington

Jon Braddy, University of Tennessee

Brant Burleson, Purdue University

John Chetro-Szivos, Fitchburg State College

Janet Cramer, University of New Mexico

Benita Dilley, Huntingdom College

Qingwen Dong, University of the Pacific

Don Ellis, University of Hartford

Stephanie Evans, California State University, Los Angeles

Lisa Flores, University of Utah

Kathleen Galvin, Northwestern University

Deb Geisler, Suffolk University

Dirk C. Gibson, University of New Mexico

Mark Gring, Texas Tech University

Susan Hafen, Weber State University

Alan D. Heisel, University of Missouri—St. Louis

Sandra Herndon, Ithaca College

Jerry Jordan, Wittenberg University

Pamela Kalbfleisch, University of Wyoming

Peggy Kendall, Bethel College

Igor Klyukanov, Eastern Washington University

Clifford Kobland, State University of New York, Oswego

Maureen Amber MacLeod, University of Hawaii at Manoa

Marie Mater, Houston Baptist University

Theodore Matula, University of Illinois, Springfield

Virginia McDermott, University of New Mexico

Dan McDonald, Ohio State University

Tom Mickey, Bridgewater State College

Dennis Mumby, The University of North Carolina at Chapel Hill

Darrin S. Murray, Loyola Marymount University

John Oetzel, University of New Mexico

Shara Toursh Pavlow, University of Miami

Sandra Petronio, Wayne State University

David Roskos-Ewoldsen, University of Alabama

Erin Sahlstein, University of Richmond

Kristi Schaller, University of Hawaii at Manoa

Mary M. Step, Case Western Reserve University

William N. Swain, University of Louisiana at Lafayette

Karen Tracy, University of Colorado at Boulder

Kyle Tusing, University of Arizona

Jill Tyler, University of South Dakota

Michelle Violanti, The University of Tennessee

Heather Walters, Southwest Missouri State University

Lynne M. Webb, University of Arkansas

David Weinandy, Aquinas College

Jennifer Willis-Rivera, Southern Illinois University

Bruce Winston, Regent University

Peter Wollheim, Boise State University

Weiwu Zhang, Austin Peay State University

This combination of reviews led to a dialogue that led to a much improved project. We wish especially to thank Phola Mabizela, our bibliographical assistant, without whose thoroughness and efficiency we could not have finished this project on time. Finally, our thanks to each other, for a collaboration that continues to delight every aspect of our lives.

Stephen W. Littlejohn
Karen A. Foss

THEORIES
OF HUMAN
COMMUNICATION

FOUNDATIONS

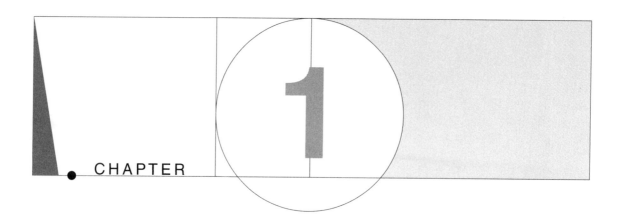

COMMUNICATION THEORY AND SCHOLARSHIP

As long as people have wondered about the world, they have been intrigued by the mysteries of human nature. The most commonplace activities of our lives—the things we take for granted—can become quite puzzling when we try to understand them systematically. Communication is one of those everyday activities that is intertwined with all of human life so completely that we sometimes overlook its pervasiveness, importance, and complexity. In this book, we treat communication as central to human life. Every aspect of our daily lives is affected by our communication with others, as well as by messages from people we don't even know—people both near and far, living and dead. This book is designed to help you better understand communication in all of its aspects—its complexities, its powers, its possibilities, and its limitations.

We could proceed with this book in several ways. We could provide a set of recipes for improving communication, but such an approach would ignore the complexities and ambiguities of the communication process. We could offer some basic models, but this too offers a limited view of communication. Instead, we will focus on theories of communication, because theories provide explanations that can assist us in understanding all parts of the phenomenon we call communication. By developing an understanding of a variety of communication theories, we can be more discriminating in our interpretation of communication, will gain tools to improve our communication, and will better understand what the discipline of communication is about.[1] Our guiding question is how scholars from various traditions have described and explained this universal human experience.

Studying communication theory will help you see things you never saw before. One writer put it this way: "The paradigm observer is not the man who sees and reports what all normal observers see and report, but the man who sees in familiar objects what no one else has seen before."[2] This widening of perception, or unhitching of blinders, helps us transcend habitual thinking and become increasingly adaptable and flexible. To borrow some analogies from philosopher Thomas Kuhn, "Looking at a contour map, the student sees lines on paper, the cartographer a picture of a terrain. Looking at a bubble-chamber photograph, the student sees confused and broken lines, the physicist a record of familiar subnuclear events."[3] Theories, then, provide a set of useful tools for seeing new and useful things.

◖ THE ACADEMIC STUDY OF COMMUNICATION

Although communication has been studied since antiquity,[4] it became an especially important topic in the twentieth century. W. Barnett Pearce describes this development as a "revolutionary discovery," largely caused by the rise of communication technologies such as radio, television, telephone, satellites, and computer networking, along with industrialization, big business, and global politics.[5] Clearly, communication has assumed immense importance in our time.

Intense interest in the academic study of communication began after World War I, as advances in technology and literacy made communication a topic of concern.[6] The subject was further promoted by the popular twentieth-century philosophies of progressivism and pragmatism, which stimulated a desire to improve society through widespread social change. This trend is important because it grounds communication firmly in the intellectual history of the United States during the twentieth century. During this period, the nation was "on the move" in terms of efforts to advance technology, improve society, fight tyranny, and build capitalism. Communication figured prominently in these movements and became central to such concerns as propaganda and public opinion; the rise of the social sciences; and the role of the media in commerce, marketing, and advertising.

After World War II, the social sciences became fully recognized as legitimate disciplines, and the interest in psychological and social processes became intense. Persuasion and decision making in groups were central concerns, not only among researchers but in society in general. Communication studies developed considerably in the second half of the twentieth century.

Most universities and colleges now have departments of communication, speech communication, or mass communication, although the subject remains largely eclectic and multidisciplinary.[7] University courses related to communication are found in many departments, just as the theories described in this book represent a wide range of fields. As Dean Barnlund observes, "While many disciplines have undoubtedly benefited from adopting a communication model, it is equally true that they, in turn, have added greatly to our understanding of human interaction."[8] When people tell you they are communication experts, their primary interests may be in the sciences or the arts, mathematics or literature, biology or politics.[9]

Researchers in most fields consider communication as a secondary process. For example, psychologists study individual behavior and view communication as a particular kind of behavior. Sociologists focus on society and social process, seeing communication as one of many social factors. Anthropologists are interested primarily in culture, and if they investigate communication, they treat it as an aspect of a broader theme. In recent years many scholars have recognized that communication is central to all human experience and have emphasized it above other topics. Some of these scholars were trained in traditional disciplines, and others studied in academic departments of communication, speech communication, or mass communication.

Regardless of their original academic homes, however, these scholars have formed the new field called communication.[10] This field is characterized by its focus on communication as the central topic and by its attention to the entire breadth of communication concerns. The work of such organizations as the International Communication Association and the National Communication Association, along with numerous journals devoted to the topic, typify what is happening in the field. Indeed, the communication field is now producing fresh theories, many of which are covered in this textbook.

The approaches to the study of communication have taken different turns in various parts of the world. Communication theory has had a different history in Europe than in the United States.[11] In the United States, researchers have tended to study communication quantitatively to try to achieve objectivity. Although these researchers were never in complete agreement on this objective ideal, quantitative methods were the standard for many years. European investigations, on the other hand, were influenced more by historical, cultural, and critical interests and were shaped to a large extent by Marxism. Considerable influence has flowed both ways as scientific procedures have developed a toehold in Europe and critical and other qualitative perspectives have been developed and taken seriously in North America.

Communication scholars have also begun to attend to distinctions between Western and Eastern forms of communication theory.[12] Some scholars are interested in comparing the characteristics of a variety of Western and Eastern perspectives. Eastern theories tend to focus on wholeness and unity, whereas Western perspectives sometimes measure parts without always integrating these parts into a unified process. Second, much Western theory is dominated by a vision of individualism. People are considered to be active in achieving personal aims. Most Eastern theories, on the other hand, view communication outcomes as unplanned and natural consequences of events. Even the many Western theories that share the Asian preoccupation with unintended events tend to be individualistic and highly cognitive, whereas most Eastern traditions stress emotional and spiritual convergence as communication outcomes.

A third difference deals with language and thought. Most Western theories are dominated by language. In the East, verbal symbols, especially speech, are downplayed and viewed with skepticism. Western-style thinking is also mistrusted in the Eastern tradition. What counts in many Asian philosophies is intuitive insight gained from direct experience. Such insight can be acquired by not intervening in natural events, which explains why silence is so important in Eastern communication. Finally, relationships are conceptualized differently in the two traditions. In Western thought, relationships exist between two or more individuals. In many Eastern traditions, relationships are more complicated, evolving out of differences in the social positions of role, status, and power.

Some scholars seek to develop larger theories that are culture-specific. Molefi Asante's work on Afrocentricity and Yoshitaka Miike's efforts to describe an Asiacentric theory of communication are two examples. By outlining theoretical concepts and constructs, research materials, and methodologies, such scholars seek to introduce alternatives to the Eurocentric paradigm in the field of communication.[13]

Like all distinctions, however, the Eastern–Western division should be viewed with caution. Although general differences can be noted, similarities abound. We could take each of the aforementioned characteristics of Eastern thought and show how they are manifest in Western thinking as well. Communication is so broad that it cannot be confined within any single paradigm. In this text, we focus on communication theories as they have emerged in the Western discipline called communication or communication studies. This is not to say other perspectives are not important, but they simply cannot all be treated comprehensively in one text.

◖ INTRODUCING COMMUNICATION THEORY

Before taking this course, you may not have given much thought to the definition of a theory. Perhaps you saw it as an explanation or an educated guess about how something works. To a certain extent, this is accurate, but in this book, you will learn to understand theory in a more sophisticated way. A theory is not just an explanation; it is a way of packaging reality, a way of understanding it. Human beings always represent reality symbolically, and we are always operating in the realm of theory. A theory is a system of thought, a way of looking. We can never "view" reality purely. Instead, we must use a set of concepts and symbols to define what we see, and our theories provide the lenses with which we observe and experience the world.

The term *communication theory* can refer to a single theory, or it can be used to designate the collective wisdom found in the entire body of theories related to communication. Much disagreement exists about what constitutes an adequate theory of communication. Reading the chapters of this book will give you a glimpse of this world of communication theory. As you read this book, you will make your own judgments about which theories are most helpful to you and will consider how to package reality given your preferences.

The theories included here vary in terms of how they were generated, the kind of research used, the style in which they are presented, and the aspect of communication they address. These theories are different because they come from various academic communities within the field, each of which has its own standards of excellence. What is judged valuable in one group may not be considered very interesting or rigorous within another. That's just the way it is in the world of scholarship. Indeed, huge debates rage about which community's methods and standards should prevail, but these debates will never be settled.

In the end we need to realize two things about theory: (1) Theory is the product of human judgment and discussion; and (2) different people prefer different ways of knowing. You might think that this state of affairs is problematic. Instead, we see it as a rich resource for developing a more thorough and complex understanding of the communication experience. Each theory looks at the process from a different angle, and each provides insights of its own. We encourage you, then, to welcome and appreciate a multi-theoretical orientation that is the nature of communication theory.[14]

A body of theory is really just a snapshot in time. It provides a brief glance at a moment in the evolving history of ideas within a community of scholars. The body of theory helps members of the community identify their primary areas of interest and work; it pulls them together as a community and provides a set of standards for how scholarly work should proceed. The "body" metaphor is good because it captures the qualities of growth, change, development, aging, and renewal. A community of scholars, like any community, changes over time, and one way to see this change is to note what happens to its theories during particular periods. For example, the theories a scholar comes to respect and use in graduate school will not be the same set of theories he or she uses in mid-career and will probably not resemble closely what is most valued within the field later in the scholar's career. Scholars are often bemused by these changes when they read old journal articles they have written, cull their libraries, or prepare to teach new courses.

What, then, makes for an important or leading theory? Although leading theories change over time, they share certain important characteristics. Leading theories provide insights we would not ordinarily have. When you read a really good theory, you have an "aha" reaction. You realize that this makes sense, yet it is not something you would necessarily have invented or considered on your own. In other words, the theory introduces you to new ideas and helps you see things in new ways.

Leading theories are conceptually interesting; they do not belabor the obvious or repeat what most of us already know from our cultural background. Instead, leading theories can be fascinating precisely because their concepts are intriguing and helpful. At the same time, such theories are constantly evolving. They morph into new forms. The leading theory of today is an evolution of earlier theoretical ideas that have grown, combined, and expanded through research and careful thinking. One of the hallmarks of a leading theory is that it has a history. It started small and was developed over time, and will continue to evolve in the future as other scholars grapple with it and contribute to it.

Leading theories have staying power. They may change, but they stick around for a while. They are so useful, insightful, or interesting that they are not easily abandoned. The best theories of the present are not new to the scene. Certain theories are seen as leaders because they have been known in one form or another for a number of years. Indeed, some theories continue to be taught, not because they are necessarily in vogue today, but because they had an important influence on scholars in earlier times. Such theories are classics.

Leading theories are the product of collaboration, extension, or elaboration. Rarely is a single person responsible for a major theory. Although a theory may be associated with a particular scholar, you will see many contributors in the literature. This is an important sign because it means that the work has attracted a number of curious scholars, that these individuals have introduced their students to the work, and that the original team of researchers are now "grandparents" and sometimes even "great-grandparents" to generations of scholars who continue the line of work and carry on theorizing further and further. With this general introduction to theory, we now turn to the particulars of theory development.

DEVELOPING THEORIES

A Basic Model of Inquiry

At the heart of theory construction is the process of inquiry. Inquiry is the systematic study of experience that leads to understanding, knowledge, and theory. People engage in inquiry when they attempt to find out about something in an orderly way. A process of systematic inquiry can be thought of as involving three stages.[15]

The first stage is asking questions. Gerald Miller and Henry Nicholson believe that inquiry is "nothing more . . . than the process of asking interesting, significant questions . . . and providing disciplined, systematic answers to them."[16] Questions can be of various types. Questions of *definition* call for concepts as answers, seeking to clarify what is observed or inferred: What is it? What will we call it? Questions of *fact* ask about properties and relations in what is observed: What does it consist of? How does it relate to

other things? Questions of *value* probe aesthetic, pragmatic, and ethical qualities of the observed: Is it beautiful? Is it effective? Is it good?

The second stage of inquiry is *observation*. Here, the scholar looks for answers by observing the phenomenon under investigation. Methods of observation vary significantly from one tradition to another. Some scholars observe by examining records and artifacts, others by personal involvement, others by using instruments and controlled experimentation, and others by interviewing people. Whatever method is used, the investigator employs some planned method for answering the questions.

The third stage of inquiry is *constructing answers*. Here, the scholar attempts to define, describe, and explain—to make judgments and interpretations about what was observed. This stage is usually referred to as *theory* and is the focus of this book.

People often think of the stages of inquiry as linear, occurring one step at a time—first questions, then observations, and finally answers. But inquiry does not proceed in this fashion. Each stage affects and is affected by the others. Observations often stimulate new questions, and theories are challenged by both observations and questions. Theories lead to new questions, and observations are determined in part by theories. Inquiry, then, is more like running around a circle and back and forth between different points on it than walking in a straight line. Figure 1.1 illustrates the interaction among the stages of inquiry.

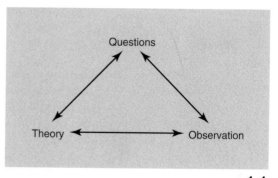

FIGURE **1.1**

The Stages of Inquiry

Types of Scholarship

The preceding section outlines the basic elements of inquiry, but it ignores important differences. Different types of inquiry ask different questions, use different methods of observation, and lead to different kinds of theory. Methods of inquiry can be grouped into three broad forms of scholarship—scientific, humanistic, and social scientific.[17] Although these forms of scholarship share the common elements discussed in the previous section, they also have major differences.[18]

Scientific Scholarship. Science often is associated with objectivity. This means it seeks standardization; the scientist attempts to look at the world in such a way that all other observers, trained the same way and using the same methods, would see the same thing. Replications of a study should yield identical results.

Standardization and replication are important in science because scientists assume that the world has observable form, and they view their task as seeing the world as it is. The world sits in wait of discovery, and the goal of science is to observe and explain the world as accurately as possible. Because there is no divinely revealed way to know how accurate one's observations are, the scientist must rely on agreement among observers. This is why objectivity and replicability are so important to the world of science. If all trained observers using the same method report the same results, the object is presumed to have been accurately observed. Because of the emphasis on discovering a knowable world, scientific methods are especially well suited to problems of nature.

In its focus on standardization and objectivity, science sometimes appears to be value free. Yet, this appearance may belie reality, as science is based on many implicit values. Humanistic scholarship is a tradition that more deliberately acknowledges the place of values in research.

Humanistic Scholarship. Whereas science is associated with objectivity, the humanities are associated with subjectivity. Science aims to standardize observation; the humanities seek creative interpretation. If the aim of science is to reduce human differences in what is observed, the aim of the humanities is to understand individual subjective response.[19] Most humanists are more interested in individual cases than generalized theory.

Whereas science is an "out there" activity, the humanities stress what is "in here." Science focuses on the discovered world; the humanities focus on the discovering person. Science seeks consensus; the humanities seek alternative interpretations. Humanists often are suspicious of the claim that there is an immutable world to be discovered, and they tend not to separate the knower from the known. The classical humanistic position is that what one sees is largely determined by who one is. Because of its emphasis on the subjective response, humanistic scholarship is especially well suited to problems of art, personal experience, and values.

Science and the humanities are not so far apart that they never come together. Almost any program of research and theory building includes some aspects of both scientific and humanistic scholarship. At times the scientist is a humanist, using intuition, creativity, interpretation, and insight to understand the data collected or to lead in entirely new directions. Many of the great scientific discoveries were in fact the result of creative insight. Archimedes discovered in the bathtub how to measure the volume of liquid using displacement; Alexander Fleming used, rather than threw away, the mold in the petri dish—which in fact produced penicillin. Ironically, the scientist must be subjective in creating the methods that will eventually lead to objective observation, making research design a creative process. In turn, at times the humanist must be scientific, seeking facts that enable experience to be understood. As we will see in the next section, the point where science leaves off and the humanities begin is not always clear.

Social-Scientific Scholarship. A third form of scholarship is the social sciences. Although many social scientists see this kind of research as an extension of natural science, using methods borrowed from the sciences, social science is actually a very different kind of inquiry.[20] Paradoxically, it includes elements of both science and the humanities but is different from both.[21]

In seeking to observe and interpret patterns of human behavior, social-science scholars make human beings the object of study. To understand human behavior, scholars must observe it. If behavioral patterns do, in fact, exist, then observation must be as objective as possible. In other words, the social scientist, like the natural scientist, must establish consensus on the basis of what is observed. Once behavioral phenomena are accurately observed, they must be explained or interpreted.

Interpreting may be complicated by the fact that the object of observation—the human subject—is an active, knowing being. Unlike objects in the natural world, the human subject is capable of having knowledge, possessing values, making interpretations, and taking action. Can "scientific" explanation of human behavior take place without consideration of the "humanistic" knowledge of the observed person? This question is the central philosophical issue of social science and has provoked considerable concern and debate akin to a crisis of professional identity in the academy.[22] In the past, the majority of social scientists believed that scientific methods alone would suffice to uncover the mysteries of human experience, but today many realize that a strong humanistic element is also needed.

Communication involves understanding how people behave in creating, exchanging, and interpreting messages. Consequently, communication inquiry makes use of the range of methods, from scientific to humanistic.[23] The theories covered in this book vary significantly in the extent to which they use scientific, social-scientific, or humanistic elements.

Making Communication Theories

Although standards vary from one academic community to another, scholars follow a fairly predictable pattern of theory development. First, a scholar or group of scholars becomes curious about a topic. Sometimes the topic relates to something personal in the scholar's own life. Sometimes it is an extension of what he or she has been reading in the literature. Often a conversation with mentors or colleagues provokes an interest in a particular subject. Also, professors are often challenged by questions that come up in class discussions.

While scholars are motivated to investigate interesting subjects because they genuinely care about communication, their professional advancement may depend on it as well. They must develop their scholarly curiosity into a research topic of their choice for their doctoral dissertations. They often cannot get pay raises, tenure, or promotion without engaging in research and theory building. Many other incentives exist as well, including the ability to get grant money, travel, be recognized as a leader in the field, earn awards, and so forth. Thus, while the theory-making process begins with curiosity about a topic, it does not end there. The results of reading, observing, and thinking—of scholarly investigation—must be shared with others. On the most informal level, scholars share their work with students. They may bring some of their latest work into the classroom as a lecture or basis for discussion, which can be helpful in refining ideas. Graduate students are aware of this, but undergraduates often do not realize that their professors "test" their theoretical ideas in classes. In the process of preparing a lecture on a topic, the weaknesses of the argument become apparent, along with the strengths of the conceptualization as well.

Ultimately, a scholar's work must go out for peer review. One of the first formal theory "tests" a scholar uses is the convention paper. The researcher writes a paper and submits it to a professional association to be presented at a regional or national meeting. Most of these convention submissions are reviewed by a panel of peers. This peer review can help a scholar determine if he or she is on the right track. Universities usually encourage professors to submit papers by agreeing to pay their travel expenses if they have a paper accepted.

Whether a paper is reviewed for acceptance before the convention or not, the presentation permits at least two other forms of peer assessment. Often a designated critic delivers comments about several papers to the audience right after the papers are presented; this is the most formal kind of critique. Less formal feedback consists of the comments that colleagues make after hearing the presentation. This kind of feedback may come during the question-and-answer session following the paper presentation, in the hallway after the session, later that evening in the hotel bar, or at the airport. Colleagues may even enjoy a phone call or e-mail exchange about one another's work after the convention is over.

Conventions are very valuable for scholars as an initial testing ground for ideas. Not only do convention attendees have the opportunity to hear the most recent research, but the presenters can refine their work based on the reactions they receive. Often a group of researchers will present various iterations of their work several times at conventions before they submit the work for publication.

Two forms of publication are most valued in the academic community. The first is a journal article, and the second is a monograph, or book. Literally thousands of academic journals are published around the world, and every field, no matter how small, has at least one (and usually several) journals. A glance through the bibliography of this book will reveal several of the most important journals in the communication field. One of the most important publications in communication theory is a journal by the same name, *Communication Theory*. This journal is an outlet for introducing theories to the field. Indeed, if you scan the notes of each chapter of this book, you will see just how important this journal has become. But many other journals are also highly recognized, including, for example, *Human Communication Research, Critical Studies in Media Communication,* and *Communication Monographs.*

Members of the communication field subscribe to these journals, use their contents as background for their own research, and learn about the latest and best developments in the field. Usually, the articles in a journal are refereed, meaning that they are formally reviewed and judged by a panel of peers for quality. Since only the best articles are published, the majority of papers submitted to journals do not appear in print. This rigorous form of review is the primary force establishing what is taken seriously within an academic community.[24]

Since no universal, objective scale can be found, peers must judge potential publications subjectively. Evaluation is always a matter of judgment, and consensus about the value of a piece of scholarship is rare. Just as a group of students might disagree about whether their professor is a good or bad teacher, scholars also disagree about the merits of particular research and theory. The references and footnotes in essays show the history of research and theory in that area. These notes are an excellent place to start researching in a particular area; they show the work that is valued in that area of the discipline.

Through this process of convention presentation and journal publication, the scholarship considered most interesting, profound, useful, or progressive "bubbles up" and forms the corpus of recognized work within the community of scholars. As this work develops, theorists, along with their colleagues, begin to develop more formal explanations that tie the work together. Initially, these explanations may be mere interpretations of research findings, but as theorists give more convention papers and publish more articles on their work, the explanations offered by the other scholars involved in this line of research become more formal and codified.

Many scholarly projects find their way to another level of publication—the scholarly book. After a group of scholars develops a line of research and theory in some detail (usually by means of a number of convention presentations and journal articles), the scholars may publish a book that provides the theory and its various permutations in one volume. In contrast to textbooks written primarily to help students learn the content of certain courses, scholarly treatises are published for the benefit of other scholars; such volumes serve as a convenient way to make available the results of a major research program. Graduate students and other scholars use these books, and many professors use this material as a basis for their class lectures. And once a theory, or emerging theory, is identified and codified, other scholars may use it to guide additional research, which adds, in turn, to the body of research and theory accepted as standard within the community.

One final level of publication further elaborates a theory. After a group of scholars has established a name for itself, the scholars are often invited to write about and summarize their work in edited volumes, or books of essays around a topic, consisting of the work of a number of theorists. This form of publication is very useful because it helps students and professors see what is the current state of theory in a particular area of the field.

Theories, then, are made. In the academic world, scholars label the concepts in the theory, decide what connections or relationships to feature, determine how to organize the theory, and give the theory a name. They then use the theory to talk about what they experience. The creation and development of a theory is a human social activity: People create it, test it, and evaluate it. As a social activity, theory making is done within scholarly communities that share a way of knowing and a set of common practices. In the end, the community of scholars or practitioners decides what works for them and what theories prevail. Because the communities vary tremendously, they differ in what they consider to be valid and valuable. A theory widely adopted by one community may be rejected entirely by another. So creating a theory is largely a question of persuading some community that the theory fits and has utility for their purposes.

◖ COMMUNICATION THEORY AS A FIELD

For many years, communication scholars have grappled with the problem of how to characterize communication theory as a field. This has been a challenge for theorists, teachers, and students because of the number of theories, and the complexity of their philosophical and practical differences, and the fact that communication as a phenomenon intersects with virtually every other scholarly discipline.[25] In a landmark article, Robert T. Craig proposes a vision for communication theory that takes a huge step toward unifying our otherwise disparate field.[26] Craig argues that our field will never be united by a single theory or group of theories. Theories will always reflect the diversity of practical ideas about communication in ordinary life, so we will always be presented with a multiplicity of approaches. Our goal cannot and should not be to seek a standard model that applies universally to any communication situation. If this impossible state of affairs were to happen, communication would become "a static field, a dead field."[27]

Instead, we must seek a different kind of coherence based on (1) a common understanding of the similarities and differences, or tension points, among theories; and (2) a commitment to manage these tensions through dialogue. Craig writes, "The goal should not be a state in which we have nothing to argue about, but one in which we better understand that we all have something very important to argue about."[28] Here, then, we have two requirements for communication theory as a field.

The first requirement is a common understanding of similarities and differences among theories. More than a list of similarities and differences, we must have a common idea of where and how theories coalesce and clash. We need a *metamodel*. The term *meta* means "above," so a *metamodel* is a "model of models."

The second requirement for coherence in the field is a definition of *theory*. Rather than viewing a theory as an explanation of a process, it should be seen as a statement or argument in favor of a particular approach. In other words, theories are a form of *discourse*. More precisely, theories are a discourse about discourse, or *metadiscourse*.

As a student of communication theory, you will find these twin concepts very important because they will help you sort out what this enterprise is all about. If you can find a useful metamodel, you will be able to make connections among theories, and if you see communication theory as metadiscourse, you will begin to understand the value of multiple perspectives in the field. In other words, communication theories will look less like a bunch of rocks laid out on tables in a geology laboratory and more like a dynamic computer model of the way the earth was formed.

As a basic premise for a metamodel, Craig says that communication is the primary process by which human life is experienced; communication *constitutes* reality. How we communicate about our experience itself forms or makes our experience. The many forms of experience are made in many forms of communication. Our meanings change from one group to another, from one setting to another, and from one time period to another because communication itself is dynamic across situations. Craig describes the importance of this thought to communication as a field:

> Communication . . . is not a secondary phenomenon that can be explained by antecedent psychological, sociological, cultural, or economic factors; rather, communication itself is the primary, constitutive social process that explains all these other factors.[29]

Craig suggests that we move the same principle to another level. Theories are special forms of communication, so theories constitute, or make, an experience of communication. Theories communicate about communication, which is exactly what Craig means by metadiscourse. Different theories are different ways of "talking about" communication, each form having its own powers and limits. For unity in the field, then, we need to acknowledge the constitutive power of theories and find a shared way to understand what various theories are designed to address and how they differ in their forms of address.

Craig writes that all communication theories are ultimately practical because every theory is a response to some aspect of communication encountered in everyday life. Every theory attempts to address communication practice in one form or another. So the dialogue within the field can focus on *what* and *how* various theories address the social world in which people live. Craig describes seven traditional standpoints that enter this dialogue: (1) rhetorical, (2) semiotic, (3) phenomenological, (4) cybernetic, (5) sociopsychological, (6) sociocultural, and (7) critical. These traditions are described in greater detail in Chapter 3 and constitute the frame we use to organize this book.

Levels of Communication

In addition to a schema for organizing theories, we also need to account for various communication contexts. Traditionally, the communication discipline has been divided along the lines of increasing levels of individual involvement. The usual pattern, with some variation, has been interpersonal, group, public, organizational, and mass communication. Handbooks, textbooks, and college curricula often are divided into sections corresponding to these levels. In your communication major, for example, you will be asked to select a track in which to focus from among the various divisions.

Interpersonal communication deals with communication between people, usually in face-to-face, private settings. *Group communication* relates to the interaction of people in small groups, usually in decision-making settings. Group communication necessarily involves interpersonal interaction, and most of the theories of interpersonal communication apply also at the group level. *Public communication,* or rhetoric, traditionally focuses on the public presentation of discourse. *Organizational communication* occurs in large cooperative networks and includes virtually all aspects of both interpersonal and group communication. It encompasses topics such as the structure and function of organizations, human relations, communication and the process of organizing, and organizational culture. Finally, *mass communication* deals with public communication, usually mediated. Many aspects of interpersonal, group, public, and organizational communication are involved in the process of mass communication.

Unfortunately, organizing communication in this way reinforces the tendency to think of these communication levels as types that are different from one another, but the levels are really nothing more than a convenient way of organizing content. The division of the field into these levels—especially the division between mass communication and the others—has been contested, and considerable work has been done to bridge these groups.[30]

The Intellectual Structure of the Communication Field

John Powers has created a model of the intellectual structure of the discipline that accommodates all of the context categories traditionally found in the communication field.[31] Powers imagines the work of the field in four tiers that can be summarized as follows:

Tier 1—The content and form of messages

Tier 2—Communicators as
(a) Individuals
(b) Participants in social relationships
(c) Members of cultural communities

Tier 3—Levels of communication, including
(a) Public
(b) Small group
(c) Interpersonal

Tier 4—Contexts and situations in which communication occurs, such as health care, courts, organizations, religion, and many others.

Using levels of communication, then, becomes another way to view the communication field. Any organizational schema has its limits. Again, the breadth of the communication discipline means we need a variety of ways of viewing it.

DEFINING COMMUNICATION

Now that we have defined theories and offered various schema to organize both theories and communication contexts, there is one more task remaining before we turn to the theories themselves. That is the task of defining *communication*—and communication is not easy to define.[32] Theodore Clevenger has noted that "the continuing problem in defining communication for scholarly or scientific purposes stems from the fact that the verb 'to communicate' is well established in the common lexicon and therefore is not easily captured for scientific use. Indeed, it is one of the most overworked terms in the English language."[33] Scholars have made many attempts to define communication but establishing a single definition has proved impossible and may not be very fruitful.

Frank Dance took a major step toward clarifying this muddy concept by outlining a number of elements used to distinguish communication.[34] He found three points of "critical conceptual differentiation" that form the basic dimensions of communication. The first dimension is *level of observation,* or abstractness. Some definitions are broad and inclusive; others are restrictive. For example, the definition of communication as "the process that links discontinuous parts of the living world to one another" is general.[35] On the other hand, communication as "the means of sending military messages, orders, etc., as by telephone, telegraph, radio, couriers," is restrictive.[36]

The second distinction is *intentionality.* Some definitions include only purposeful message sending and receiving; others do not impose this limitation. The following is an example of a definition that includes intention: "Those situations in which a source transmits a message to a receiver with conscious intent to affect the latter's behaviors."[37] Here is a definition that does not require intent: "It is a process that makes common to two or several what was the monopoly of one or some."[38]

The third dimension is normative *judgment.* Some definitions include a statement of success or accuracy; other definitions do not contain such implicit judgments. The following definition, for example, presumes that communication is successful: "Communication is the verbal interchange of a thought or idea."[39] The assumption in this definition is that a thought or idea is successfully exchanged. Another definition, on the other hand, does not judge whether the outcome is successful or not: "Communication [is] the transmission of information."[40] Here information is *transmitted,* but it is not necessarily *received* or understood.

Clearly, debates over what communication is and the dimensions that characterize it will continue. Dance's conclusion is appropriate: "We are trying to make the concept of 'communication' do too much work for us."[41] He calls for a family of concepts; collectively, that define communication rather than a single theory or idea. These definitional issues are important, as Peter Andersen reminds us: "While there is not a right or wrong perspective, choices regarding [definitions] are not trivial. These perspectives launch scholars down different theoretical trajectories, predispose them to ask distinct questions, and set them up to conduct different kinds of communication studies."[42] Different definitions have different functions and enable the theorist to do different things.

A definition should be evaluated on the basis of how well it helps a scholar to accomplish the purposes of an investigation. Different sorts of investigations often require separate, even contradictory, definitions of communication. Definitions, then, are tools that should be used flexibly. In this book we do not offer a single definition of communication but instead look at a range of theories that defines communication in a variety of ways. We hope this range of definitions will help you determine what communication means to you as you begin to explore the many arenas of communication theory.

● NOTES

1. For the importance of the study of diverse theories, see Robert T. Craig, "Communication Theory as a Field," *Communication Theory* 9 (1999): 119–161.
2. N. R. Hanson, *Patterns of Discovery* (Cambridge: Cambridge University Press, 1961), p. 30.
3. Thomas S. Kuhn, *The Structure of Scientific Revolutions* (Chicago: University of Chicago Press, 1970), p. 111.
4. See, for example, John Stewart, *Language as Articulate Contact: Toward a Post-Semiotic Philosophy of Communication* (Albany: SUNY Press, 1995), pp. 33–101; W. Barnett Pearce and Karen A. Foss, "The Historical Context of Communication as a Science," in *Human Communication: Theory and Research,* ed. G. L. Dahnke and G. W. Clatterbuck (Belmont, CA: Wadsworth, 1990), pp. 1–20; Nancy Harper, *Human Communication Theory: The History of a Paradigm* (Rochelle Park, NJ: Hayden, 1979).
5. W. Barnett Pearce, *Communication and the Human Condition* (Carbondale: Southern Illinois University Press, 1989).
6. This brief history is based on Jesse G. Delia, "Communication Research: A History," in *Handbook of Communication Science,* ed. C. R. Berger and S. H. Chaffee (Newbury Park, CA: Sage, 1987), pp. 20–98. See also Donald G. Ellis, *Crafting Society: Ethnicity, Class, and Communication Theory* (Mahwah, NJ: Lawrence Erlbaum, 1999), pp. 16–19; Gustav W. Friedrich and Don M. Boileau, "The Communication Discipline," in *Teaching Communication,* ed. Anita L. Vangelisti, John A. Daly, and Gustav Friedrich (Mahwah, NJ: Lawrence Erlbaum, 1999), pp. 3–13; John Durham Peters, ed., "Tangled Legacies," *Journal of Communication* 46 (1996): 85–147; and Everett M. Rogers, *A History of Communication Study: A Biographical Approach* (New York: Free Press, 1994).
7. For an exploration of the value of treating communication as an interdisciplinary study, see Thomas Streeter, "Introduction: For the Study of Communication and Against the Discipline of Communication," *Communication Theory* 5 (1995): 117–129; and David Sholle, "Resisting Disciplines: Repositioning Media Studies in the University," *Communication Theory* 5 (1995): 130–143.
8. Dean Barnlund, *Interpersonal Communication: Survey and Studies* (New York: Houghton Mifflin, 1968), p. v.
9. The multidisciplinary nature of the study of communication is examined by Craig, "Communication Theory as a Field"; see also Stephen W. Littlejohn, "An Overview of the Contributions to Human Communication Theory from Other Disciplines," in *Human Communication Theory: Comparative Essays,* ed. F. E. X. Dance (New York: Harper & Row, 1982), pp. 243–285; and W. Barnett Pearce, "Scientific Research Methods in Communication Studies and Their Implications for Theory and Research," in *Speech Communication in the 20th Century,* ed. T. W. Benson (Carbondale: Southern Illinois University Press, 1985), pp. 255–281.
10. For a recent discussion of the status of the communication field, see Tony Atwater, "Communication Theory and Research: The Quest for Credibility in the Social Sciences," in *An Integrated Ap-*

proach to Communication Theory and Research, ed. M. B. Salwen and D. W. Stacks (Mahwah, NJ: Lawrence Erlbaum, 1996), pp. 539–549; and Stanley A. Deetz, "Future of the Discipline: The Challenges, the Research, and the Social Contribution," in *Communication Yearbook 17,* ed. S. A. Deetz (Thousand Oaks, CA: Sage, 1994), pp. 565–600.

11. This distinction is made by Robert Fortner, "Mediated Communication Theory," in *Building Communication Theories: A Socio/Cultural Approach,* ed. Fred L. Casmir (Hillsdale, NJ: Lawrence Erlbaum, 1994), pp. 209–240.

12. See D. Lawrence Kincaid, *Communication Theory: Eastern and Western Perspectives* (San Diego: Academic, 1987); Peter R. Monge, "Communication Theory for a Globalizing World," in *Communication: Views from the Helm for the 21st Century,* ed. Judith S. Trent (Boston: Allyn & Bacon, 1998), pp. 3–7; Wimal Dissanayake, *Communication Theory: The Asian Perspective* (Singapore: Asian Mass Communication Research and Information Center, 1988); Wimal Dissanayake, "The Need for the Study of Asian Approaches to Communication," *Media Asia* 13 (1986): 6–13; G-M Chen, "Toward Transcultural Understanding: A Harmony Theory of Chinese Communication," in *Transcultural Realities: Interdisciplinary Perspectives on Cross-cultural Relations,* ed. V. H. Milhouse, M. K. Asante, and P. O. Nwosu (Thousand Oaks, CA: Sage, 2001), pp. 55–70.

13. For summaries of Asante's work, see Molefi K. Asante, *Afrocentricity: The Theory of Social Change* (Trenton, NJ: Africa World Press, 1988), and Molefi K. Asante, "An Afrocentric Communication Theory," in *Contemporary Rhetorical Theory: A Reader,* ed. John L. Lucaites, Celeste M. Condit, and Sally Caudill (New York: Guilford Press, 1999), pp. 552–562. For Miike's theory of Asiacentricity, see Yoshitaka Miike, "Theorizing Culture and Communication in the Asian Context: An Assumptive Foundation," *Intercultural Communication Studies* 11 (2002): 1–21; and Yoshitaka Miike, "Japanese *Enryo-Sasshi* Communication and the Psychology of *Amae:* Reconsideration and Reconceptualization," *Keio Communication Review* 25 (2003): 3–25.

14. For an excellent case in favor of multiple approaches to communication, see John Waite Bowers and James J. Bradac, "Issues in Communication Theory: A Metatheoretical Analysis," in *Communication Yearbook 5,* ed. M. Burgoon (New Brunswick, NJ: Transaction, 1982), pp. 1–28.

15. The process of inquiry is described in Gerald R. Miller and Henry Nicholson, *Communication Inquiry* (Reading, MA: Addison-Wesley, 1976).

16. Miller and Nicholson, *Communication Inquiry,* p. ix. See also Don W. Stacks and Michael B. Salwen, "Integrating Theory and Research: Starting with Questions," in *An Integrated Approach to Communication Theory and Research,* ed. M. B. Salwen and D. W. Stacks (Mahwah, NJ: Lawrence Erlbaum, 1996), pp. 3–14.

17. An excellent discussion of scholarship can be found in Ernest G. Bormann, *Theory and Research in the Communicative Arts* (New York: Holt, Rinehart & Winston, 1965). See also Nathan Glazer, "The Social Sciences in Liberal Education," in *The Philosophy of the Curriculum,* ed. S. Hook (Buffalo: Prometheus, 1975), pp. 145–158; James L. Jarrett, *The Humanities and Humanistic Education* (Reading, MA: Addison-Wesley, 1973); Gerald Holton, "Science, Science Teaching, and Rationality," in *The Philosophy of the Curriculum,* ed. S. Hook (Buffalo: Prometheus, 1975), pp. 101–108.

18. See, for example, C. P. Snow, *The Two Cultures and a Second Look* (Cambridge: Cambridge University Press, 1964).

19. James A. Diefenbeck, *A Celebration of Subjective Thought* (Carbondale: Southern Illinois University Press, 1984).

20. See, for example, Charles R. Berger and Steven H. Chaffee, "The Study of Communication as a Science," in *Handbook of Communication Science,* ed. Charles R. Berger and Steven H. Chaffee (Newbury Park, CA: Sage, 1987), pp. 15–19. For an interesting discussion of the scientific nature of communication research, see Glenn G. Sparks, W. James Potter, Roger Cooper, and Michel Dupagne, "Is Media Research Prescientific?" *Communication Theory* 5 (1995): 273–289.

21. See, for example, Robert T. Craig, "Why Are There So *Many* Communication Theories?," *Journal of Communication* 43 (1993): 26–33; Hubert M. Blalock, *Basic Dilemmas in the Social Sciences* (Beverly Hills, CA: Sage, 1984), p. 15; Anthony Giddens, *Profiles and Critiques in Social Theory* (Berkeley: University of California Press, 1983), p. 133; Peter Winch, *The Idea of a Social Science and Its Relation to Philosophy* (London: Routledge & Kegan Paul, 1958).

22. See, for example, Klaus Krippendorff, "Conversation or Intellectual Imperialism in Comparing Communication (Theories)," *Communication Theory* 3 (1993): 252–266; Donald W. Fiske and Richard A. Shweder, eds., "Introduction: Uneasy Social Science," in *Metatheory in Social Science: Pluralisms and Subjectivities* (Chicago: University of Chicago Press, 1986), pp. 1–18; Kenneth J. Gergen, *Toward Transformation in Social Knowledge* (New York: Springer-Verlag, 1982).

23. This position is developed in Thomas B. Farrell, "Beyond Science: Humanities Contributions to Communication Theory," in *Handbook of Communication Science,* ed. Charles R. Berger and Steven H. Chaffee (Newbury Park, CA: Sage, 1987), pp. 123–139.

24. Publishing in journals is not an unbiased process. Based on the peer review process, the editor's overall judgment, disciplinary trends and interests, and the like, sometimes very good essays are

overlooked and some of lesser quality are accepted. For an interesting discussion of this process, see Carole Blair, Julie R. Brown, and Leslie A. Baxter, "Disciplining the Feminine," *Quarterly Journal of Speech* 80 (November 1994): 383–409.

25. Many typologies of scholarship have been developed. For a discussion of the problems involved in describing differences, see Stanley Deetz, "Describing Differences in Approaches to Organization Science," *Organization Science* 7 (1996): 191–207. See also Fred R. Dallmayr, *Language and Politics* (Notre Dame, IN: University of Notre Dame Press, 1984); Lawrence Grossberg, "Does Communication Theory Need Intersubjectivity? Toward an Immanent Philosophy of Interpersonal Relations," in *Communication Yearbook 6*, ed. Michael Burgoon (Beverly Hills, CA: Sage, 1984), pp. 171–205; and John Stewart, "Speech and Human Being," *Quarterly Journal of Speech* 72 (1986): 55–73; Gibson Winter, *Elements for a Social Ethic: Scientific and Ethical Perspectives on Social Process* (New York: Macmillan, 1966); and "Gibson Winter's Elements for a Social Ethic: A Review," *Journal of Religion* 49 (1969): 77–84. Winter's scheme was later elaborated by Richard McKeon. See also Ted J. Smith III, "Diversity and Order in Communication Theory: The Uses of Philosophical Analysis," *Communication Quarterly* 36 (1988): 28–40; and G. Burrell and G. Morgan, *Sociological Paradigms and Organizational Analysis* (London: Heinemann, 1979). For an elaboration of the Burrell and Morgan model, see Karl Erik Rosengren, "From Field to Frog Ponds," *Journal of Communication* 43 (1993): 6–17; and Karl Erik Rosengren, "Culture, Media, and Society: Agency and Structure, Continuity and Change," in *Media Effects and Beyond*, ed. Karl Erik Rosengren (London: Routledge, 1994), pp. 3–28.

26. Craig, "Communication Theory as a Field." A similar effort is offered by James A. Anderson, *Communication Theory: Epistemological Foundations* (New York: Guilford, 1996).

27. Craig, "Communication Theory as a Field," p. 123.

28. Craig, "Communication Theory as a Field," p. 124.

29. Craig, "Communication Theory as a Field," p. 126.

30. See, for example, Patrick B. O'Sullivan, "Bridging the Mass-Interpersonal Divide," *Human Communication Research* 25 (1999): 569–588; Everett M. Rogers, "Anatomy of the Two Subdisciplines of Communication Study," *Human Communication Research* 25 (1999): 618–631; Jonathan Cohen and Miriam Metzger, "Social Affiliation and the Achievement of Ontological Security Through Interpersonal and Mass Communication," *Critical Studies in Mass Communication* 15 (1998): 41–60; Kathleen K. Reardon and Emmeline G. dePillis, "Multichannel Leadership: Revisiting the False Dichotomy," in *An Integrated Approach to Communication Theory and Research*, ed. M. B. Salwen and D. W. Stacks (Mahwah, NJ: Lawrence Erlbaum, 1996), pp. 399–407; John Durham Peters, "The Gaps of Which Communication Is Made," *Critical Studies in Mass Communication* 11 (1994): 117–140; Joseph N. Cappella, ed., "Symposium on Mass and Interpersonal Communication," *Human Communication Research* 15 (1988): 236–318; Robert P. Hawkins, John M. Wiemann, and Suzanne Pingree, eds., *Advancing Communication Science* (Newbury Park, CA: Sage, 1988).

31. John H. Powers, "On the Intellectual Structure of the Human Communication Discipline," *Communication Education* 44 (1995): 191–222.

32. There are 126 definitions of communication listed in Frank E. X. Dance and Carl E. Larson, *The Functions of Human Communication: A Theoretical Approach* (New York: Holt, Rinehart & Winston, 1976), Appendix A.

33. Theodore Clevenger, Jr., "Can One Not Communicate? A Conflict of Models," *Communication Studies* 42 (1991): 351.

34. Frank E. X. Dance, "The 'Concept' of Communication," *Journal of Communication* 20 (1970): 201–210.

35. Jürgen Ruesch, "Technology and Social Communication," in *Communication Theory and Research*, ed. L. Thayer (Springfield, IL: Thomas, 1957), p. 462.

36. *The American College Dictionary* (New York: Random House, 1964), p. 244.

37. Gerald R. Miller, "On Defining Communication: Another Stab," *Journal of Communication* 16 (1966): 92.

38. Alex Gode, "What Is Communication?" *Journal of Communication* 9 (1959): 5.

39. John B. Hoben, "English Communication at Colgate Re-examined," *Journal of Communication* 4 (1954): 77.

40. Bernard Berelson and Gary Steiner, *Human Behavior* (New York: Harcourt, Brace, & World, 1964), p. 254.

41. Dance, "The 'Concept' of Communication," p. 210.

42. Peter A. Andersen, "When One Cannot Not Communicate: A Challenge to Motley's Traditional Communication Postulates," *Communication Studies* 42 (1991): 309.

THE IDEA OF THEORY

Almost all college and university communication programs include at least one course in communication theory. Theories are the academic foundation of every discipline; they are important because they are the means by which we codify and organize what we know. They allow us—scholars, teachers, and students—to transform information into knowledge.

We do not see the world as separate bits of data. Rather, we organize, categorize, and synthesize information,[1] seeking patterns and discovering connections among the data in our worlds. Because theories have been developed that arrange and synthesize existing knowledge, we do not need to start over again with each investigation. A starting point, then, to understanding any field is its organized knowledge—or theories—developed by generations of previous scholars.

Besides organizing data, theories also focus our attention on important variables and relationships. A theory is like a map of a city on which you can view the streets, housing devel-

opments, shopping centers, picnic grounds, and rivers because there is a key that helps you interpret what you see. Similarly, theories function as guidebooks that help us understand, explain, interpret, judge, and act into, in this case, the communication happening around us. They help us clarify what we are observing, which helps us understand relationships among various parts and helps us better interpret and evaluate what is going on around us. This makes theories valuable observational aids, indicating not only *what* to observe but *how* to observe, as well as enabling us to make predictions about outcomes and effects in the data.

Theories are indispensable in academic life. Theoretical speculation can serve a heuristic function, guiding a series of studies that fill in gaps in our knowledge about some communication phenomenon. But theories do not simply help us to grow knowledge; they also help us communicate knowledge. They are like knowledge packages. As investigators publish their theoretical observations and speculations, the theories function to encourage discussion, debate, and criticism.[2] Through the communication of numerous explanations of the things we study, comparison and theory improvement become possible.

Theories contribute to evaluation as well. They can address values and enable us to judge the effectiveness and propriety of certain behaviors. Many theorists now believe that all theory is value laden and control oriented, even when the theory is not explicit about it.[3] Theories also provide a way to challenge existing cultural life and to generate new ways of living. Kenneth Gergen calls this "the capacity to challenge the guiding assumptions of the culture, to raise fundamental questions regarding contemporary social life, to foster reconsideration of that which is 'taken for granted,' and thereby to generate fresh alternatives for social action."[4]

◖● BEGINNING TO KNOW THEORY

What is theory? We have been talking around the term without really defining it. Uses of the term range from Farmer Jones's theory about when his chickens will start laying eggs to Einstein's theory of relativity. Even scientists, writers, and philosophers use the term in a variety of ways. The purpose of this book is to represent a wide range of thought—or theories—about the communication process. Therefore, we use the term *theory* in its broadest sense as any organized set of concepts, explanations, and principles of some aspect of human experience.[5]

All theories are abstractions. They always reduce experience to a set of categories and as a result always leave something out. A theory focuses on certain things and ignores others. This truism is important because it reveals the basic inadequacy of any one theory. No single theory will ever reveal the whole "truth" or be able to totally address the subject of investigation.

Theories are also constructions. Theories are created by people, not ordained by God. When

scholars examine something in the world, they make choices—about how to categorize what they are observing, what to name the concepts upon which they have focused, how broad or narrow their focus will be, and so on. Thus, theories represent various ways observers see their environments more than they capture reality itself.[6] They are less a record of reality than a record of scholars' conceptualizations about that reality. Abraham Kaplan writes, "The formation of a theory is not just the discovery of a hidden fact; the theory is a way of looking at the facts, of organizing and representing them."[7] Stanley Deetz adds that "a theory is a way of seeing and thinking about the world. As such it is better seen as the 'lens' one uses in observation than as a 'mirror' of nature."[8]

Two observers using microscopes may see different things in an amoeba, depending on each observer's theoretical point of view. One observer sees a one-celled animal; the other sees an organism without cells. The first viewer stresses the properties of an amoeba that resemble all other cells—the wall, the nucleus, the cytoplasm. The second observer compares the amoeba to other whole animals, which have complex, multicelled systems of ingestion, excretion, reproduction, and mobility contained within them. Neither observer is wrong. Their theoretical frameworks simply stress different aspects of the observed object.[9]

Because theories are constructions, questioning a theory's usefulness is wiser than questioning its truthfulness. Any given truth can be represented in a variety of ways, depending on the theorist's orientation.[10] Here is a simple example:

> The teacher presents four boxes. In each there is a picture—of a tree, cat, dog, and squirrel, respectively. The child is asked which one is different. A child worthy of second grade immediately picks the tree. The child knows not only how to divide plants from animals, but also that the plant/animal distinction is the preferred one to apply . . . [but] the choice is arbitrary and hardly a very interesting way to think about the problem. The squirrel as easily could have been picked if the child had distinguished on the basis of domesticity or things we bought at the

store. Or the dog could have been picked because the cat, squirrel, and tree relate in a playful, interactive way. Or the child could have picked the cat since the other three are in the yard.[11]

Finally, theories are intimately tied to action. How we think—our theories—guide how we act; and how we act—our practices—guide how we think. In the world of scholarship, formal theories and intellectual practices are inseparable.[12] James Anderson says that, "Theory . . . contains a set of instructions for reading the world and acting in it. . . . [It] speaks to the singular, overarching question of 'What do I believe to be true . . .?' "[13]

In terms of theory, then, this book is like an art gallery. Just as when you stroll through a gallery, you find some art to be more personally appealing—you like the subject matter, the colors, the composition, the artistic medium, the artistic genre—so, too, is the case with communication theories. Some theories will naturally resonate with your perspective on the world. You may find yourself questioning others, just as you question certain pieces of art, but you can still appreciate the theory because it offers some understanding of a communication phenomenon. We now turn to the elements that make up a theory.

● BASIC ELEMENTS OF THEORY

In this section, we describe four elements of theory: (1) *philosophical assumptions*, or basic beliefs that underlie the theory; (2) *concepts*, or building blocks; (3) *explanations*, or dynamic connections made by the theory; and (4) *principles*, or guidelines for action. Although some theories, or quasi theories, include only the first two elements, most scholars believe that a theory worthy of the name must have at least the first three elements—assumptions, concepts, and explanations. However, not all theories include the final element, and, in fact, as we will see later, the inclusion of principles is somewhat controversial.

Philosophical Assumptions

The starting point for any theory is the philosophical assumptions that underlie it. The assumptions to which a theorist subscribes determine how a particular theory will play out. Knowing the assumptions behind a theory, then, is the first step to understanding any given theory. Philosophical assumptions are often divided into three major types: assumptions about *epistemology*, or questions of knowledge; assumptions about *ontology*, or questions of existence; and assumptions about *axiology*, or questions of value. Every theory, explicitly or implicitly, includes assumptions about the nature of knowledge and how it is obtained, what constitutes existence, and what is valuable. Looking for these assumptions provides a foundation for understanding how a given theory positions itself in relation to other theories on these basic issues that help construct a theory.

Epistemology.   Epistemology is the branch of philosophy that studies knowledge, or how people know what they claim to know. Any good discussion of inquiry and theory will inevitably come back to epistemological issues. The following questions are among the most common questions of epistemological concern to communication scholars.

To what extent can knowledge exist before experience? Many believe that all knowledge arises from experience. We observe the world and thereby come to know about it. Yet is there something in our basic nature that provides a kind of knowledge even before we experience the world? The capacity to think and to perceive often are cited as evidence for such inherent mechanisms. For example, strong evidence exists that children do not learn language entirely from hearing it spoken. Rather, they may acquire language by using innate models to test what they hear. In other words, a capacity for or structure for language exists in the brain *a priori*, even before a child begins to know the world through experiencing it.

To what extent can knowledge be certain? Does knowledge exist in the world as an absolute, there for the taking by whoever can discover it? Or is knowledge relative and changing? The debate over this issue has persisted for hundreds of years among philosophers, and communication theorists position themselves in various places on this continuum as well. Those who take a universal stance—who believe they are seeking absolute and unchangeable knowledge—will admit to errors in their theories, but they believe that these errors are merely a result of not yet having discovered the complete truth. Relativists believe that knowledge will never be certain because universal reality simply does not exist. Instead, what we can know is filtered through our experiences, perceptions, and theories and is ever changing.

To this point, Anatol Rapoport presents the following amusing anecdote about three baseball umpires:[14]

> The first umpire, who was a "realist," remarked, "Some is strikes and some is balls, and I calls them as they is." Another, with less faith in the infallibility of the professional, countered with, "Some is strikes and some is balls, and I calls them as I sees them." But the wisest umpire said, "Some is strikes and some is balls, but they ain't nothing till I calls them."[14]

The first case represents knowledge as certain or absolute that exists to be discovered. The third umpire suggests the relativist position—nothing is certain until it is labeled; the label plays a large part in determining what something is. The middle umpire represents a kind of middle ground in terms of the nature of knowledge, a position that acknowledges the role of perception and the human element in the discovery of knowledge.

By what process does knowledge arise? This question is at the heart of epistemology because the kind of process selected for discovering knowledge determines the kind of knowledge that can develop from that process. There are at least four positions on the issue. *Rationalism* suggests that knowledge arises out of the sheer power of the human mind to know the truth ("I calls them as they is"). This position places ultimate faith in

human reasoning to ascertain truth. *Empiricism* states that knowledge arises in perception. We experience the world and literally "see" what is going on ("I calls them as I sees them"). *Constructivism* holds that people create knowledge in order to function pragmatically in the world and that they project themselves into what they experience ("They ain't nothing till I calls them"). Constructivists believe that phenomena in the world can be fruitfully understood many different ways and that knowledge is what the person has made of the world. Finally, taking constructivism one step further, *social constructionism* teaches that knowledge is a product of symbolic interaction within social groups. In other words, reality is socially constructed and a product of group and cultural life. In the case of the umpires, the knowledge of what a ball is and what a strike is can only be known within the framework of the game of baseball, and both terms, *ball* and *strike,* have many other meanings in English that are quite different from the meanings they have within the game of baseball.

Is knowledge best conceived in parts or wholes? Those who take a gestalt approach are holistic; they believe that phenomena are highly interrelated and operate as a system. True knowledge, in other words, cannot be divided into parts but consists of general, indivisible understandings. Analysts, on the other hand, believe that knowledge consists of understanding how parts operate separately. They are interested in isolating the various components that together comprise what can be considered knowledge.

To what extent is knowledge explicit? Many philosophers and scholars believe that you cannot know something unless you can state it. Within this view, knowledge is that which can explicitly be articulated. Others claim that much of knowledge is hidden—that people operate on the basis of sensibilities that are not conscious and that they may be unable to express. Such knowledge is said to be tacit.[15]

The way scholars conduct inquiry and construct theories depends largely on their epistemological assumptions because what they think knowledge is and how they think knowledge is obtained determines what they find. The same holds for the next type of philosophical assumptions—assumptions of ontology.

Ontology.   Ontology is the branch of philosophy that deals with the nature of being.[16] Epistemology and ontology, then, go hand in hand because our ideas about knowledge depend in large part on our ideas about being the one known about. In the social sciences, ontology deals largely with the nature of human existence; in communication, ontology centers on the nature of human social interaction because being is intricately intertwined with issues of communication. In other words, the way a theorist conceptualizes interaction depends in large measure on how the communicator is viewed. At least four issues are important.[17]

First, to what extent do humans make real choices? Although all investigators probably would agree that people perceive choice, there is a long-standing philosophical debate on whether real choice is possible. On one side of the issue are the *determinists* who state that behavior is caused by a multitude of prior conditions that largely determine human behavior. Humans, according to this view, are basically reactive and passive. On the other side of the debate are the *pragmatists*, who claim that people plan their behavior to meet future goals. This group sees people as active, decision-making beings who affect their own destinies. Middle positions also exist, suggesting either that people make choices within a restricted range or that some behaviors are determined whereas others are a matter of free will.

A second ontological issue is whether human behavior is best understood in terms of states or traits.[18] This question deals with whether there are fairly stable dimensions—*traits*—or more temporary conditions affecting people, called *states*. The *state view* argues that humans are dynamic and go through numerous states in the course of a day, year, and lifetime. The *trait view* believes that people are mostly predictable because they display more or less consistent characteristics across time. Traits, then, do not change easily, and in this view, humans are seen as basically static. There is, of course, an in-between position, and many theorists believe that both traits and states characterize human behavior.

Is human experience primarily individual or social? This ontological question deals with whether the individual or the group carries the most weight in terms of determining human action. Those scholars who attend to the individual focus on particular behaviors. Although these scholars understand that people are not isolated from one another and that interaction is important, they understand behavior as individualistic, and their unit of analysis is the individual human psyche. Many other social scientists, however, focus on social life as the primary unit of analysis. These scholars believe that humans cannot be understood apart from their relationships with others in groups and cultures. This issue is especially important to communication scholars because of their focus on interaction.[19]

To what extent is communication contextual? The focus of this question is whether behavior is governed by universal principles or whether it depends on situational factors. Some philosophers believe that human life and action are best understood by looking at universal factors; others believe that behavior is richly contextual and cannot be generalized beyond the immediate situation. In communication, the middle ground is a strong stance, with scholars believing that behavior is affected by both general and situational factors.

Axiology.   Axiology is the branch of philosophy concerned with studying values. For the communication scholar, three axiological issues are especially important.[20] Can research be value free, what are the ends for which scholarship is conducted, and to what extent should scholarship aim to effect social change?

Can theory be value free? Classical science answers this first axiological concern in the affirmative—that theories and research are value free, that scholarship is neutral, and that what the scholar attempts to do is to uncover the facts as they are. According to this view, when a scientist's values impinge on his or her work, the result is bad science.[21] But there is a different position on this issue: that science is not value free because the researcher's work is always guided by preferences about what to study, how to conduct inquiry, and the like.[22] Scientists' choices, then, are affected by personal as well as institutional values. Government and private organizational values determine what research is funded; political and economic ideologies both feed and are fed by particular ways of viewing the world embodied by different forms of theory and research.[23] From this position, then, any lens of necessity colors what is seen, making value-free inquiry an impossibility.

A related value issue centers on the question of whether scholars intrude on and thereby affect the process being studied. *In other words, to what extent does the process of inquiry itself affect what is being seen?* To what degree does the researcher become part of the system under examination and thus affect that system? The traditional scientific viewpoint is that scientists must observe carefully without interference so that accuracy can be achieved. Critics doubt this is possible, believing that no method of observation is completely free of distortion. Even when you look at planets through a telescope, you are automatically distorting distance because of the properties of lenses. When the doctor puts a stethoscope on your chest, your nervous system reacts, and sometimes your heart rate is affected. If you bring participants into a laboratory and ask them to talk to one another as part of an experiment—as communication researchers often do—they do not respond exactly the same way they would outside the laboratory.

On the other side, critics maintain that theory and knowledge themselves affect the course of human life.[24] This presents two potential problems. First, the scholar, by virtue of scholarly work, becomes an agent of change. This is a role that he or she must actively understand and take into consideration. At the very least, scholars must consider the ethical issues raised by doing whatever kind of research they do. Second, studying human life changes that life.[25] For example, if you interview a married couple about

their relationship, the interview itself will affect some aspect of that relationship.

A second issue of axiology concerns the ends for which scholarship is conducted. *Should scholarship be designed to achieve change or to reveal knowledge without intervention?* Traditional scientists claim that they are not responsible for the ways scientific knowledge is used—that it can be used for good or ill. The discovery of nuclear fission was in and of itself an important scientific discovery; that it was used to make atomic bombs is not the scientist's concern. Critics object, saying that scientific knowledge by its very nature is instrumentalist and control oriented and necessarily promotes power domination in society. Traditional communication knowledge, in this view, is an administrative tool of the power elite. The critics of science do not themselves claim to be above power, but they see themselves as making a choice in favor of a set of values that challenges domination in society rather than perpetuating it.

Finally, to what extent should scholarship attempt to achieve social change? Should scholars remain objective, or should they make conscious efforts to help society change in positive ways? Many believe that the proper role of the scholar is to produce knowledge: Let the technicians and politicians do what they will with it. Other scholars vociferously disagree, believing that responsible scholarship involves an obligation to promote positive change.[26]

Overall then, two general positions reside in these axiological issues. On the one hand, some scholars seek objectivity and knowledge that they believe is largely *value free*. On the other side is *value-conscious* scholarship in which researchers recognize the importance of values to research and theory, are careful to acknowledge their particular standpoint, and make a concerted effort to direct those values in positive ways.

Concepts

The second element of a theory is its concepts or categories.[27] Things are grouped into conceptual categories according to observed qualities. In our everyday world, some things are considered to be trees, some houses, some cars. Humans are by nature conceptual beings. Thomas Kuhn writes, "Neither scientists nor laymen learn to see the world piecemeal or item by item; . . . both scientists and laymen sort out whole areas together from the flux of experience."[28]

Concepts—terms and definitions—tell us what the theorist is looking at and what is considered important. To determine concepts, the communication theorist observes many variables in human interaction and classifies and labels them according to perceived patterns. The result—and a goal of theory—is to formulate and articulate a set of labeled concepts. The set of conceptual terms identified becomes an integral part of the theory and often, these terms are unique to that theory. What functions as a set of conceptual terms for one theory may not be applicable to another.

Those theories that stop at the conceptual level—theories in which the goal is to provide a list of categories for something without explaining how they relate to one another—are known as *taxonomies*. Because they do not provide an understanding of how things work, many theorists are reluctant to even label them theories. The best theories, then, go beyond taxonomies to provide *explanations*—statements about how the variables relate to one another—to show how concepts are connected.

Explanations

An explanation is the next element of a theory, and here the theorist identifies regularities or patterns in the relationships among variables. In simplest terms, explanation answers the question, Why? An explanation identifies a "logical force" among variables that connect them in some way. A theorist might hypothesize, for example, that if children see a lot of television violence, they will develop violent tendencies. In the social sciences, the connection is rarely taken as absolute. Instead, we can say that one thing is "often" or "usually" associated with another, that there is a probable relationship: If children

see a lot of television violence, they probably will develop violent tendencies.

There are many types of explanations, but two of the most common are causal and practical.[29] In *causal explanation*, events are connected as causal relationships, with one variable seen as an outcome or result of the other. *Practical explanation*, on the other hand, explains actions as goal related, with the action designed to achieve a future state. Causal explanation explains outcomes as responses, whereas practical explanation sees action as controllable and strategic. In causal explanation, the consequent event is determined by some antecedent event. In practical explanation, outcomes are made to happen by actions that are chosen.[30]

To better understand the difference between causal and practical explanation, consider how you might explain to a friend why you failed a test. If you said that you just aren't very good at this subject and had bad teachers in high school, you would be using causal explanation: "My bad grade was caused by things I can't control." On the other hand, if you did well on the test, you would probably use practical explanation: "I needed to increase my grade-point average and so I studied hard."

The distinction between causal and practical explanation is important in the debate about what a theory should do. Many traditional theorists say that theories should stop at the level of explanation. These scholars believe that theories depict things as they are by identifying and explaining the causal mechanisms of events. Other scholars maintain that theories should go beyond depiction and should guide practical action, an approach that makes practical explanation central. For these theorists, practical explanation leads to a third element of theory—the element of principle.

Principles

Principles are the final component of theory we will discuss. A *principle* is a guideline that enables you to interpret an event, make judgments about what is happening, and then decide how to act in the situation. A principle has three parts: (1) It identifies a situation or event; (2) it includes a set of norms or values; and (3) it asserts a connection between a range of actions and possible consequences. Principles enable a researcher to reflect on the quality of actions observed and to provide guidelines for practice as well. For example, you may see grades as an important indicator of success (your principle) and, valuing success, study hard to improve your grade (your action).

There is no consensus, at least in the social sciences, about whether theories should include principles for judgment and action. Some theorists are content to simply offer concepts and explanations without making recommendations on the basis of their theorizing. For other theorists, generating principles that can be used as the basis of action in the world is the whole purpose for engaging the theoretical enterprise.

◖ THEORETICAL IDEALS

The various components of theory just described—assumptions, concepts, explanations, and principles—combine in different ways to construct different kinds of theories. Here we will outline two types—nomothetic theory and practical theory.[31] These types are ideal in the sense that they have evolved into prototypes of certain research modes, each embodies different assumptions and different approaches to concepts, explanations, and principles. They also are ideal in the sense that they represent model endpoints of a theory and research continuum that is not always so tidy in reality. We will describe each of these endpoints in order to differentiate how the different components of theory help construct different research perspectives and approaches.[32]

Nomothetic Theory

Nomothetic theory is defined as that which seeks universal or general laws. This approach, dominant in the experimental natural sciences, has been the model for much of the research in the social sciences as well.[33] The goal of such theory is to depict accurately how social life works. This theory tradition does not make judgments about these states of affairs, and such theories do not give advice. Scientists simply wish to paint a picture and leave it up to others to decide how to use this knowledge. Traditional science is based on four processes: (1) developing questions; (2) forming hypotheses; (3) testing the hypotheses; and (4) formulating theory. This approach is known as the *hypothetico-deductive method*, and it is based on the assumption that we can best understand complex things by analyzing the various parts or elements that comprise it. Thus, this approach is also sometimes called the *variable-analytic tradition*.

The research process in this tradition is well codified. First, the researcher forms an hypothesis, or well-formed guess about a relationship between variables. Ideally, the hypothesis emerges from previous research. The researcher undertakes an inductive process of generalizing from numerous observations. A hypothesis must be testable and framed in such a way that potential rejection is possible—it must be *falsifiable*. If it is not, any test will yield either a positive result or an equivocal one, and it will be impossible to discover whether the hypothesis is wrong. Hypothesis testing, then, is really a process of looking for exceptions.

Hypothesis testing is a painstakingly slow procedure in which theories are fine-tuned by numerous tests. The four steps—questioning, hypothesizing, testing, and theorizing—are repeated in incremental building blocks. Figure 2.1 illustrates the hypothetico-deductive method.[34]

Suppose, for example, that you think that people do things they find personally rewarding, suggesting the following hypothesis: *People are more likely to do what they find rewarding than what they do not find rewarding.* While you could certainly find instances of people doing things because they like to do them, you also could find instances of people doing things they do not like. Some people may even do certain things because, in some perverse way, they find punishment itself rewarding. Because virtually anything

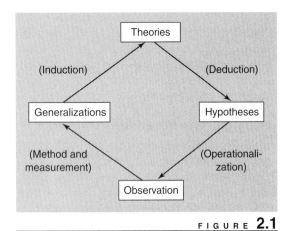

FIGURE **2.1**

The Classical Ideal of Science

Reprinted with permission: Walter L. Wallace (ed.), *Sociological Theory: An Introduction* (New York: Aldine de Gruyter). Copyright © 1969 by Walter L. Wallace.

could be intrinsically rewarding to someone, no action could be ruled out. This hypothesis, then, is poorly stated because you could never disprove it—it is not falsifiable.

Only through research *control* and *manipulation* can causality be tested. If one set of variables is held constant (controlled) and another set systematically varied (manipulated), the researcher can detect the effect of the manipulated variables without worrying about whether other variables had hidden effects. Control and manipulation can be exercised directly, as in experiments, or through certain kinds of statistics.

Let's return to the intrinsic rewards hypothesis. Assume that you have refined your rewards scale and found it valid and reliable. How would you then test your hypothesis? Would you give a list of activities to a group of subjects and have them rate each in terms of intrinsic rewards? That would tell you how rewarding the subjects found each activity, but it would not tell you whether they would actually do the things they say are rewarding. You might consider having the subjects rate each item twice—once on reward value and once on how frequently they actually do it. That would give you an idea of the correlation between reward and activity, but it would not be sufficient to say that one caused the other.

To really test your hypothesis, you would need to set up an experiment in which you actually tested rewarding activities against unrewarding ones, to see if the former are repeated and the latter not. You might do this by having one group of people do a rewarding set of tasks, such as watching a movie, and another an unrewarding one, such as studying for an exam, to see if the first group spends more time at their task than the second.

As we look at this ideal type, then, in terms of scientific theory, we'll focus on philosophical assumptions, concepts, and explanations. Notice that we do not include the fourth aspect— principles—in our discussion of scientific theory. As we will see later in the chapter, possessing principles is one of the important distinguishing characteristics of alternative theories.

Philosophical Assumptions.   Nomothetic theories take a particular position on questions of epistemology, ontology, and axiology. In epistemology, these theories tend to espouse empiricist and rationalist ideas, treating reality as distinct from the human being. Reality, in other words, is something that people discover outside themselves. Researchers in this tradition assume a physical, knowable reality that is self-evident to the trained observer.[35] Discovery is important in this position; the world is waiting for the scientist to find it. Because knowledge is viewed as something acquired from outside oneself, nomothetic theories seek to discover what is called the "received view." Objectivity is all important, with investigators being required to define the exact operations to be used in observing events.

In terms of axiology, such theories take a value-neutral stance, believing that science is aloof from value issues and that values do not play a role in science and should not be of great concern. In terms of ontology, scientific theories tend to assume that behavior is basically determined by and responsive to biology and the environment. These theories, then, aim to make lawful statements about phenomena, developing generalizations that hold true across situations and over time. Scholars in this tradition try to reveal how things appear and work. In so doing, the scholar is highly analytical, attempting to define each part and subpart of the object of interest.

Concepts. Because of the need in scientific research to be precise in observation, concepts are typically operationalized in traditional science. *Operationism* means that all variables in a hypothesis should be stated in ways that explain exactly how to observe them. Operational definitions are the most precise definitions possible because they tell you how the concept is to be observed. One operational definition of *intelligence*, for example, is the Stanford-Binet intelligence test. An operational definition of *dominance* might be a particular set of observer ratings on dominant versus submissive messages.

Return to the example of the intrinsic reward hypothesis described above. You could improve this hypothesis by specifying more precisely what you mean by highly rewarding and what you mean by an intrinsic reward. Thus, you could hypothesize that a person will repeat an action rated as highly rewarding on an intrinsic rewards test. Here, *intrinsic reward* is operationally defined as a rating on an intrinsic rewards scale. Notice that this wording makes the hypothesis falsifiable.

As you can see from this example, operationism relies on measurement, or the use of precise, usually numerical, indications. Measurement enables the detection of differences that might otherwise be hard to specify. For example, you might have individuals rate their activities on a 7-point scale, from highly unrewarding to highly rewarding. With this scale you could measure the difference between an activity that is moderately rewarding and one that is only mildly rewarding. You could also measure the difference between one person who found a particular activity highly rewarding and another who found the same activity unrewarding.

Measurement is evaluated in terms of two criteria—validity and reliability. *Validity* is the degree to which an observation measures what it is supposed to measure. How do we know, for example, that the subject's rating really measures reward? Perhaps the rating is influenced by

some other hidden factor, or perhaps it reflects nothing in particular. Researchers have methods for estimating whether their measures are valid.

Reliability is the degree to which the construct is measured accurately, and it is most often estimated by consistency. If your bathroom scale gives you a different weight each day, even though you have not gained or lost weight, it is unreliable, just as an intelligence test giving a different result on separate occasions is also unreliable. If all items on a test are designed to measure the same thing—intelligence—and they prove to be very inconsistent with one another, the test is said to be unreliable.

Returning to your intrinsic rewards study, you must now determine whether your scale actually measures rewards—whether it is valid. You might do this, for example, by making sure that it is consistent with other known measures of rewards. If you can show this, you can argue that the scale you have devised for measuring reward is valid. But you would still need to establish its reliability. You might do this by administering the test to the same group of people on two occasions to see if the responses were nearly the same.

Explanations. Explanations are almost exclusively *causal* in nomothetic theories. In other words, they posit a linear relationship between cause and effect. Causal explanations—expressed as *covering laws* in ideal theory—are carefully tested in a highly formalized way. The covering law is a theoretical statement of cause and effect relevant to a particular set of variables across situations. The statement, "Rewarded behaviors are repeated," is an example of a covering law. In traditional science, the covering law is believed to be significant because of its power in explaining events. Covering laws also enable researchers to make predictions about future events.

The chief value of a law is that it enables us to predict what will happen when a causal variable is in play. In the theory of gravity, for example, we can predict that an object that is not held in place will fall. Prediction is an important outcome of inquiry because it gives people power over their environment. If, for example, I can predict that certain behaviors will be repeated if they are rewarding, I may be able to control people's behavior by manipulating the reward value of the desired actions.

This traditional idea most closely approximates what Charles Pavitt now calls *scientific realism*, the philosophy that believes in a real world of real things with true characteristics and causal effects.[36] Theories may not completely and accurately reflect the order of things in the world, but well-worked theories can approximate this reality, and the concepts of a theory can and ultimately should accurately represent objects in the world.

Very few social scientists seek covering laws anymore. They realize that absolutely universal statements are unrealistic. Instead, investigators seek statistical relationships among variables, and their "laws" are probabilistic.[37] Instead of saying that reward leads to action, you would say that reward usually leads to action.

According to Pavitt, if communication theorists are to adopt scientific realism, they must commit to the importance of their concepts, reducing these to an essential set of accurate categories. Theorists should avoid adding new and unnecessary concepts. Furthermore, theorists must use causal explanation and attempt to capture the true causal relations among variables in the real world. Finally, communication theorists must commit to the reliability of meaning and trust that readers will understand terms sufficiently for accurate communication to take place. As we will see in the following section, Pavitt's position is controversial.

This approach to research and theory is firmly planted in the scientific tradition of "knowledge as discovery," but scholars in other traditions often reject this method in favor of other approaches to theorizing.[38]

Practical Theory

Practical theory represents the opposite ideal from the nomothetic. Practical theory is designed to capture the rich differences among situations and

to provide a set of understandings that lets you weigh alternative courses of action to achieve goals. Returning to the example of your study of rewards can begin to suggest some of the reasons why some scholars prefer practical theory over nomothetic. We imagined that you were trying to test the relationship between action and rewards. Practical theorists would not appreciate your intrinsic rewards hypothesis very much. They might find your idea interesting and even useful, but they would say that this is just one of many ways to understand a person's behavior. Furthermore, they would find reducing rewards to a check on a scale to be a very limited way to approach this issue. They might also say that your statement that rewards cause behavior is arbitrary and that the link could just as validly be stated in the opposite direction: Action is undertaken purposely to create rewards.

Robyn Penman has outlined five tenets of an alternative paradigm to traditional science.[39] First, action is voluntary. Humans are in large part self-motivating, and you cannot predict behavior based on outside variables. If this is true, it would be hard to predict how people would behave based on rewards. For example, some people like watching movies more than studying, but they would study anyway because of long-term benefits and consequences.

Second, knowledge is created socially. That means that communication theories themselves are created by communication, the very process they are designed to explain. There is no one-to-one relationship between the ideas in a theory and objective reality. So the intrinsic rewards hypothesis is a creation of the theorist; it is one of many ways of understanding behavior, not a mirror of the "real" reason people do things.

Third, theories are historical. They reflect the settings and times in which they are created, and as times change, so too will theories. Our culture in the United States often is considered to be materialistic and individualistic. The entire system is predicated on the idea that people are motivated by rewards and punishments. No wonder, then, that an intrinsic rewards hypothesis would seem logical. In another era or in another culture, such an idea might not even come up. Stanley Deetz writes:

> All current theories will pass in time. It is not as if they are in error, at least little more or less so than those in the past. They were useful in handling different kinds of human problems, problems we might find ill-formed and even silly, as others will ours. What remains is the human attempt to produce theories that are useful in responding to our own issues. We are struggling to find interesting and useful ways of thinking and talking about our current situations and helping us build the future we want.[40]

A fourth element identified as part of the practical theoretical paradigm is that theories affect the reality they are covering. Theorists are not separate from the worlds they create but are part of those worlds. If your intrinsic rewards hypothesis is believed, people will start treating others as reward driven. They will offer rewards when they want something done and withhold them when they do not. Soon, people will be operating in an environment created by the ideas of the theorist, and a kind of self-fulfilling prophecy may result.

Finally, theories are value laden, never neutral. From the standpoint of the practical paradigm, your hypothesis is rife with values that should be acknowledged in your research. You chose to look at rewards because your attention was drawn to this particular variable above all other possible ones—perhaps because of some experience you had with rewards. You chose to look at individual behavior because you value the person over other possible units of analysis such as the group or culture. This priority is not inherently bad, but it does contain values; researchers within the practical paradigm want to see underlying values acknowledged.

Philosophical Assumptions.   In terms of epistemology, practical theories tend to assume that people take an active role in creating knowledge.[41] A world of things may exist outside the person, but observers can conceptualize these things in a variety of useful ways. Knowledge therefore arises not out of discovery but from interaction between knower and known. For this reason the perceptual and interpretive processes

of individuals are important in research methods. Further, these theories attempt not to seek universal or covering laws but to describe the rich context in which individuals operate. They tend to be humanistic in stressing the subjective responses. Knowing is interpreting—an activity in which everybody engages. Indeed, communication itself is a vital vehicle in the social construction of reality.[42]

In terms of ontology, practical theories tend to take an actional approach, assuming that individuals create meanings, have intentions, make real choices, and act in situations in deliberate ways. These theorists are reluctant to seek universal laws because they assume that individual behavior is not governed entirely by prior events. Instead, they assume that people behave differently in different situations because rules and goals change.

Axiologically, most practical theories tend to be value conscious, although here is a dividing point among them. Many of these theories tend to be descriptive, showing *how* people interpret and act on their experience in various social and cultural situations, while others are more evaluative, making strong judgments about common cultural understandings and actions. In general, theories that resist or criticize normal forms of life are called *critical theories*, a tradition we explore in much more detail later in the book.

Concepts.   Concepts in most practical approaches to theory tend not to be represented as universal. Instead, such theories acknowledge that people respond differently in different situations and that the words and actions that people use to express their understandings will change over time. Important concepts, then, cannot be measured operationally. Theoretical concepts, therefore, are used as a kind of organizing framework to classify the dynamic interpretations and actions of people in actual situations.

Explanations.   Practical theories tend to use practical necessity as a basis for explanation. In other words, communicators are guided to achieve future goals by following certain social rules or norms that enable them to think through a situation and select from a range of options. These rules are practical because they empower the communicator to understand what is happening and make choices in the face of problems and dilemmas.

Principles.   We wrote earlier in this chapter that theories consist of four aspects—assumptions, concepts, explanations, and principles—but not all types of theories have all four. Indeed, practical theories differ from nomothetic ones in featuring the fourth dimension of principles. Principles are guidelines for reflection and action. When a theory includes principles, we can say that it is a practical theory.[43]

Robert Craig and Karen Tracy write that practical theories provide a set of principles that enable communicators to "construct a tentative, revisable, but still rationally warranted normative model that is relevant to a broad range of practical situations."[44] Such theories can address any combination of three levels: Level 1 is the technical level where specific strategies or actions are available to communicators; level 2 is the problem level—problems and obstacles that might be encountered are addressed; and level 3 is the philosophical level consisting of ideals, values, and general principles that communicators can use. Practical theory is most powerful when it enables communicators to make their way through a difficult situation (level 2) by using general principles (level 3) to reflect on actual practice (level 1).

Let's return to our example of your emerging reward theory. Within the scientific tradition, your theory would hypothesize a clear, operationalized statement of relationship between reward and action—that rewarded behavior is repeated. As you continue to look at a variety of situations, you begin to conclude that the situation is not so simple. People do seek rewards, but they have many ways of doing so, and they understand rewards very differently. Some think of rewards as personal achievements, some as building relationships, and others as fulfilling traditional roles. You notice that individuals actu-

ally think through what they want and gear their actions to achieve their hopes. Now your theory has started to migrate from a behavior-reward hypothesis to a practical theory of goal seeking.

As you study goal-seeking behavior, you come to realize that achieving goals is often complicated. Sometimes one goal contradicts another goal, and people puzzle over how to communicate in such situations where contradictory goals are present. For example, you find that sometimes a person wants to build a relationship, but doing so would prevent them from achieving a personal goal, and they really have to think through how to do both. Your effort to think through this situation leads you to generate a principle: A meaningful relationship in European-American culture requires the parties to integrate their respective interests and individual desires. Perhaps it would be different in other cultures, so your emerging principle of goal integration will probably specify a cultural context.

Now you have the three parts of a practical theory according to Craig and Tracy. On level 1, you have an idea of the kinds of goals that people can seek and how they might achieve these. On level 2, you recognize at least one kind of dilemma communicators may face in achieving their goals, and on level 3, you have a principle that can be used by communicators to reflect on and make decisions about how to proceed.

This example of a theory of goal-seeking is consistent with Vernon Cronen's idea that practical theory "offers principles informed by engagement in the details of lived experience that facilitate joining with others to produce change."[45] For Cronen, practical theory is a system of connected ideas that allow individuals to reason their way through actual situations and make informed decisions about what to do. A practical theory does not prescribe the action you should take, but enables you to act in a coherent way that leads to understanding how you might improve the situation. A good practical theory enables you to (1) focus on a real situation you are facing; (2) explore what is unique about this situation; (3) consider both the powers and limits of each action you could take; (4) take actions that enhance your life and achieve positive outcomes as well; and (5) learn from experience in the actual situations you face and prepare you to manage new ones.

As you can see, the differences between nomothetic and practical theories are not trivial. Each starts from different philosophical assumptions, makes use of different kinds of concepts and explanations, and has different orientations toward principles. In the case of nomothetic theories, the development of principles lies outside the scientific endeavor, whereas with most practical perspectives, the principles that evolve from the theory are a critical part of that theory. Each school strongly defends its point of view, and each has its place within the communication tradition. In turn, you may find that a certain theoretic ideal is most appealing to you—that it better fits how you view the world. For others of you, both might be intriguing, and you might find yourself drawn to different traditions, based on the subject matter of the theory or other factors. The remainder of the book will give you many opportunities to explore different theories from both traditions, a process that will further clarify your personal stance in regard to theory.

◐ EVALUATING COMMUNICATION THEORY

As you encounter theories of communication, you will need a basis for judging one against another. The following is a list of criteria that can assist you to systematically evaluate theories.[46] All have limitations, so you will not find a theory for which each of these criteria holds "true" with equal weight. Furthermore, certain criteria will be more important to certain kinds of theories. This list, however, does offer a starting point from which you can begin to assess the theories you will encounter in this text.

Theoretical Scope

A theory's scope is its comprehensiveness or inclusiveness. Theoretical scope relies on the principle of generality or the idea that a theory's ex-

planation must be sufficiently general to extend beyond a single observation.[47] When an explanation is a mere speculation about a single event, it is not a theoretical explanation. To be theoretical, an explanation must go beyond a single instance to cover a range of events.

The scope of a theory is critical. Stanley Deetz writes that "Few theories are failures in regard to specific situations, and all theories ultimately fail if applied far enough outside of the specific conditions for which they were developed."[48] A theory, then, can fail for generalizing too narrowly—from a single instance—or too broadly, by attempting to cover all human interactional behavior, for instance.

Two types of generality exist. The first concerns the extent of coverage. A theory that covers a sufficiently broad domain is considered a good theory. A communication theory that meets this test would explain a variety of communication-related behaviors usually confined to a specific context—communication apprehension, relationship initiation, or group consensus making, for example.

A theory need not cover a large number of phenomena to be judged good, however. Indeed, many fine theories are narrow in coverage. Such theories possess the second type of generality: They deal with a narrow range of events, but their explanations of these events apply to a large number of situations. Such theories are said to be powerful. Certain theories of relationship breakups illustrate this type of generality. They only cover one topic, but they are powerful because they explain many instances of relationship dissolution, whether of an intimate partnership, work colleagues, or parents and children.

Appropriateness

Are the theory's epistemological, ontological, and axiological assumptions appropriate for the theoretical questions addressed and the research methods used? In the last section, we discussed the fact that different types of theory allow scholars to do different kinds of things. One criterion by which theories can be evaluated is whether their claims are consistent with or appropriate to their assumptions. If you assume that people make choices and plan actions to accomplish goals, it would be inappropriate to predict behavior on the basis of causal events. If you assume that the most important things affecting behavior are unconscious, it would be inappropriate to report survey data in which subjects were asked why they did certain things. If you believe that theory should be value free, it would be inappropriate to base your definition of communication on some standard of effectiveness or any other value.

In a way, then, appropriateness is a kind of logical consistency between a theory and its assumptions. For example, some writers from the cognitive tradition state that people actively process information and make plans to accomplish personal goals. Yet theories produced by these researchers often make law-like statements about universal behaviors, which, if true, would leave little room for purposeful action. In other words, causal explanation is not appropriate for explaining purposeful action.

Heuristic Value

Will the theory generate new ideas for research and additional theory? Does it have heuristic value? Theories within the nomothetic and practical ideals differ significantly in this regard. Both need to be heuristic—to aid discovery—but they accomplish this value in different ways. Scientific theories are heuristic in generating new research questions, new hypotheses, and new concepts or variables. Practical theories are heuristic to the extent that they produce new ideas by continually exploring new situations.

Validity

Generally speaking, validity is the truth value of a theory. "Truth" is not intended to mean absolute unchanging fact; rather, there may be a variety of "truth values" in an experience. Validity as a criterion of theory has at least three meanings.[49]

One kind of validity is that of *value*, or worth. This kind of validity refers to the importance or utility of a theory—does the theory have value? This is the primary form of validity in practical theories. Stanley Deetz writes: "The problem with most theories is not that they are wrong or lacking in confirming experiences but that they are irrelevant or misdirect observation, that is, they do not help make the observations that are important to meeting critical goals and needs."[50]

The second kind of validity is that of *correspondence*, or fit. Here the question is whether the concepts and relations specified by the theory can actually be observed. Nomothetic theorists assume that one and only one representation will fit, whereas practical theorists believe that a number of theories may fit simultaneously.

The third kind of validity is *generalizability*, which is exactly the same as theoretical scope, discussed above. This is the classical definition of validity and applies almost exclusively to traditional, discovery-oriented, law-like theories.[51]

Parsimony

The test of parsimony involves *logical simplicity*. If two theories are equally valid, the one with the simplest logical explanation is said to be the best. For example, if I can explain your behavior based on one simple variable such as reward, the theory is more parsimonious than if I need three variables such as reward, personality, and difficulty. We need to be careful with parsimony, however, as highly parsimonious explanations may be overly simple and may leave out many important factors that expand our insight into what is happening. Parsimony must always be balanced with the other criteria.

Openness

Finally, theories can be judged according to their *openness*. This criterion is especially important in the practical paradigm. It means that a theory is open to other possibilities.[52] It is tentative, contextual, and qualified. The theorist recognizes that his or her construction is a way of looking rather than a reproduction of reality. It admits to diversity and invites dialogue with other perspectives. It acknowledges its own incompleteness.

◖ LOOKING FORWARD

Theories differ not only because they look at different aspects of reality, but they make drastically different assumptions about reality and assume many different forms. Instead of thinking of theories as presenting little puzzle pieces that can be hooked together to make one unified picture, you should think of them as diverse perspectives on a variety of related pictures.

In this spirit, we move now to a discussion of a series of genres, or traditions, of communication theory, each of which paints a rather different picture of our subject matter. You will see that each tradition has a special combination of philosophical assumptions about being, knowledge, and values; makes use of particular concepts and explanations; and approaches the matter of the generation of principles quite differently.

◖ NOTES

1. This function is discussed in some detail by Charles R. Berger, "Evidence? For What?" *Western Journal of Communication* 58 (1994): 11–19.
2. The communicative function is addressed in Klaus Krippendorff, "Conversation or Intellectual Imperialism in Comparing Communication (Theories)," *Communication Theory* 3 (1993): 252–266.
3. For a good recent exploration of normative theory, see Robert T. Craig and Karen Tracy, "Grounded Practical Theory: The Case of Intellectual Discussion," *Communication Theory* 5 (1995): 248–272.
4. Kenneth Gergen, *Toward Transformation in Social Knowledge* (New York: Springer-Verlag, 1982), p. 109.
5. See Steven H. Chaffee, "Thinking About Theory," in *An Integrated Approach to Communication Theory and Research*, ed. M. B. Salwen and D. W. Stacks (Mahwah, NJ: Lawrence Erlbaum, 1996), pp. 15–32; Stephen W. Littlejohn, "Communication Theory," in *Encyclopedia of Rhetoric and Composition: Communication from Ancient Times to the Information Age*, ed. T. Enos (New York: Garland, 1996), pp. 117–121; Karl Erik Rosengren, "Substantive Theories and Formal Models—Bourdieu Confronted," *European Journal of Communication* 10 (1995): 7–39; Fred L. Casmir, "The Role of Theory and Theory Building," in *Building Communication Theories: A Socio/Cultural Approach*, ed. Fred L. Casmir (Hillsdale, NJ: Lawrence Erlbaum, 1994), pp. 7–45.
6. This idea is explored by Klaus Krippendorff, "Conversations or Intellectual Imperialism"; and W. Barnett Pearce, "On Comparing Theories: Treating Theories as Commensurate or Incommensurate," *Communication Theory* 2 (1991): 159–164.
7. Abraham Kaplan, *The Conduct of Inquiry* (San Francisco: Chandler, 1964), p. 309.
8. Stanley A. Deetz, *Democracy in an Age of Corporate Colonization: Developments in Communication and the Politics of Everyday Life* (Albany: SUNY Press, 1992), p. 66. The mirror analogy is developed and critiqued by Richard Rorty, *Philosophy and the Mirror of Nature* (Princeton, NJ: Princeton University Press, 1979).
9. Examples from N. R. Hanson, *Patterns of Discovery* (Cambridge, MA: Cambridge University Press, 1961), pp. 4–5.
10. This point is also made in Thomas L. Jacobsen, "Theories as Communications," *Communication Theory* 2 (1991): 145–150.
11. Deetz, *Democracy*, pp. 71–72.
12. See James Anderson, *Communication Theory: Epistemological Foundations* (New York: Guilford, 1996), pp. 7–9.
13. Quoted in "Anderson Succeeds Ellis as *Communication Theory* Editor, Invites Papers," *ICA Newsletter* 24 (January 1996): 1.
14. Anatol Rapoport, "Strategy and Conscience," in *The Human Dialogue: Perspectives on Communication*, ed. F. Matson and A. Montagu (New York: Free Press, 1967), p. 95.
15. See Michael Polanyi, *Personal Knowledge* (London: Routledge & Kegan Paul, 1958).
16. For a discussion of ontology, see Alasdair MacIntyre, "Ontology," in *The Encyclopedia of Philosophy*, vol. 5, ed. P. Edwards (New York: Macmillan, 1967), pp. 542–543. For an excellent recent explora-

tion of ontological issues in communication theory, see Anderson, *Communication Theory*, pp. 13–101.

17. For an ontological discussion of communication theory, see John Waite Bowers and James J. Bradac, "Issues in Communication Theory: A Metatheoretical Analysis," in *Communication Yearbook 5,* ed. Michael Burgoon (New Brunswick, NJ: Transaction, 1982), pp. 1–28.

18. This debate is summarized by Peter A. Andersen, "The Trait Debate: A Critical Examination of the Individual Differences Paradigm in the Communication Sciences," in *Progress in Communication Sciences,* ed. Brenda Dervin and M. J. Voigt (Norwood, NJ: Ablex, 1986).

19. See, for example, Peter Berger and Thomas Luckmann, *The Social Construction of Reality: A Treatise in the Sociology of Knowledge* (Garden City, NY: Doubleday, 1966); Kenneth Gergen, "The Social Constructionist Movement in Modern Psychology," *American Psychologist* 40 (March 1985): 266–275.

20. For a good contemporary discussion of axiology, see Anderson, *Communication Theory,* pp. 186–199.

21. See, for example, Kaplan, *Conduct of Inquiry,* p. 372.

22. For a development of this position, see, for example, Joli Jensen, "The Consequences of Vocabularies," *Journal of Communication* 43 (1993): 67–74.

23. See, for example, Brian Fay, *Social Theory and Political Practice* (London: Allen & Unwin, 1975); and Robyn Penman, "Good Theory and Good Practice: An Argument in Progress," *Communication Theory* 3 (1992): 234–250.

24. See, for example, Fay, *Social Theory and Political Practice;* Gergen, *Toward Transformation,* pp. 21–34; Penman, "Good Theory and Good Practice."

25. This issue is explored by Sheila McNamee, "Research as Social Intervention: A Research Methodology for the New Epistemology" (paper delivered at the Fifth International Conference on Culture and Communication, Philadelphia, October 1988).

26. See, for example, Cees J. Hamelink, "Emancipation or Domestication: Toward a Utopian Science of Communication," *Journal of Communication* 33 (1983): 74–79.

27. For an elaboration of this idea, see John R. Taylor, *Linguistic Categorization: Prototypes in Linguistic Theory* (London: Clarendon Press, 1995).

28. Thomas S. Kuhn, *The Structure of Scientific Revolutions,* 2nd ed. (Chicago: University of Chicago Press, 1970), p. 128.

29. Based on P. Achinstein, *Laws and Explanation* (New York: Oxford University Press, 1971); see also Donald P. Cushman and W. Barnett Pearce, "Generality and Necessity in Three Types of Theory About Human Communication, with Special Attention to Rules Theory," *Human Communication Research* 3 (1977): 344–353. For an excellent discussion of explanation in the social sciences, see Paul F. Secord, ed., *Explaining Human Behavior: Consciousness, Human Action, and Social Structure* (Beverly Hills, CA: Sage, 1982).

30. For an excellent recent discussion of this distinction, see Lise VandeVoort, "Functional and Causal Explanations in Group Communication Research," *Communication Theory* 12 (2002): 469–486.

31. This analysis is supported in part by several sources. See, for example, C. Arthur VanLear, "Dialectical Empiricism: Science and Relationship Metaphors," in *Dialectical Approaches to Studying Personal Relationships,* ed. Barbara M. Montgomery and Leslie A. Baxter (Mahwah, NJ: Lawrence Erlbaum, 1998), pp. 109–136; Anderson, *Communication Theory;* Georg H. von Wright, *Explanation and Understanding* (Ithaca, NY: Cornell University Press, 1971); and Joseph Houna, "Two Ideals of Scientific Theorizing," in *Communication Yearbook 5,* ed. Michael Burgoon (New Brunswick, NJ: Transaction, 1982), pp. 29–48. Many other schemes have been devised to classify epistemological approaches. See, for example, Stephen Pepper, *World Hypotheses* (Berkeley: University of California Press, 1942); B. Aubrey Fisher, *Perspectives on Human Communication* (New York: Macmillan, 1978); Kenneth Williams, "Reflections on a Human Science of Communication," *Journal of Communication* 23 (1973): 239–250; Barry Brummett, "Some Implications of 'Process' or 'Intersubjectivity': Postmodern Rhetoric," *Philosophy and Rhetoric* 9 (1976): 21–51; Gerald Miller, "The Current Status of Theory and Research in Interpersonal Communication," *Human Communication Research* 4 (1978): 175.

32. See, for example, the critique of the new paradigm by Robert Bostrom and Lewis Donohew, "The Case for Empiricism: Clarifying Fundamental Issues in Communication Theory," *Communication Monographs* 59 (1992): 109–129.

33. See, for example, Franklin J. Boster, "On Making Progress in Communication Science," *Human Communication Research,* 28 (2002): 473–490; Michael A. Shapiro, "Generalizability in Communication Research," *Human Communication Research,* 28 (2002): 491–500; Michael J. Beatty and James C. McCroskey, *The Biology of Communication: A Communibiological Perspective* (Cresskill, NJ: Hampton Press, 2001), pp. 13–26; Steven H. Chaffee, "Thinking About Theory"; Michael J. Beatty, "Thinking Quantitatively," in *An Integrated Approach to Communication Theory and Research,* ed. M. B. Salwen and D. W. Stacks (Mahwah, NJ: Lawrence Erlbaum, 1996), pp. 33–44; Myron W. Lustig, "Theorizing About Human Communication," *Communication Quarterly* 34 (1986): 451–459.

34. Figure 2.1 is adapted from Walter L. Wallace, *Sociological Theory: An Introduction* (Chicago: Aldine, 1969), p. ix.

35. Bostrom and Donohew, "The Case for Empiricism."

36. Charles Pavitt, "The Third Way: Scientific Realism and Communication Theory," *Communication Theory* 9 (1999): 162–188.

37. Bostrom and Donohew, "The Case for Empiricism."

38. See, for example, Ed McLuskie, "Ambivalence in the 'New Positivism' for the Philosophy of Communication: The Problem of Communication and Communicating Subjects," in *Communication Yearbook* 24, ed. William B. Gudykunst (Thousand Oaks, CA: Sage, 2001), pp. 255–269; Penman, "Good Theory and Good Practice"; and Krippendorff, "Conversation or Intellectual Imperialism"; Rom Harré and Paul F. Secord, *The Explanation of Social Behavior* (Totowa, NJ: Littlefield, Adams, 1979), pp. 19–25.

39. Penman, "Good Theory and Good Practice," based on Gergen, *Toward Transformation*; see also James A. Anderson, "Thinking Qualitatively," in *An Integrated Approach to Communication Theory and Research,* ed. M. B. Salwen and D. W. Stacks (Mahwah, NJ: Lawrence Erlbaum, 1996), pp. 45–59.

40. Deetz, *Democracy*, p. 77.

41. Krippendorff, "Conversation or Intellectual Imperialism"; and Penman, "Good Theory and Good Practice." See also Joanna Macy, *Mutual Causality in Buddhism and General System Theory* (Albany: SUNY Press, 1991), pp. 117–137.

42. See, for example, Berger and Luckmann, *The Social Construction of Reality;* Alfred Schutz, *The Phenomenology of the Social World,* trans. George Walsh and Frederick Lehnert (Evanston, IL: Northwestern University Press, 1967); Gergen, "The Social Constructionist Movement"; Harré and Secord, *Explanation of Social Behavior.*

43. See Robert T. Craig, "Communication as a Practical Discipline," in *Rethinking Communication: Paradigm Issues*, ed. Brenda Dervin, Lawrence Grossberg, Barbara J. O'Keefe, and Ellen Wartella (Newbury Park, CA: Sage, 1989), pp. 97–122.

44. Robert T. Craig and Karen Tracy, "Grounded Practical Theory: The Case of Intellectual Discussion," *Communication Theory* 5 (1995): 252.

45. Vernon E. Cronen, "Practical Theory, Practical Art, and the Pragmatic-Systemic Account of Inquiry," *Communication Theory* 11 (2001): 14.

46. Evaluation is discussed in greater depth in Penman, "Good Theory and Good Practice"; B. J. Bross, *Design for Decision* (New York: Macmillan, 1952), pp. 161–177; Karl W. Deutsch, "On Communication Models in the Social Sciences," *Public Opinion Quarterly* 16 (1952): 362–363; Calvin S. Hall and Gardner Lindzey, *Theories of Personality* (New York: Wiley, 1970), chap. 1; Kaplan, *Conduct of Inquiry,* pp. 312–322; Kuhn, *Structure of Scientific Revolutions,* pp. 100–101, 152–156. For an excellent illustration of how a critic might use these criteria, see the theoretical critiques of interpersonal deception theory: James B. Stiff, "Theoretical Approaches to the Study of Deceptive Communication: Comments on Interpersonal Deception Theory," *Communication Theory* 6 (1996): 289–296; Bella M. DePaulo, Matthew E. Ansfield, and Kathy L. Bell, "Theories About Deception and Paradigms for Studying It: A Critical Appraisal of Buller and Burgoon's Interpersonal Deception Theory and Research," *Communication Theory* 6 (1996): 297–311.

47. Achinstein, *Laws and Explanation;* Cushman and Pearce, "Generality and Necessity." See also Stuart Sigman, "Do Social Approaches to Interpersonal Communication Constitute a Contribution to Communication Theory?" *Communication Theory* 2 (1992): 347–356.

48. Deetz, *Democracy,* p. 69.

49. This analysis is adapted from David Brinberg and Joseph E. McGrath, *Validity and the Research Process* (Beverly Hills, CA: Sage, 1985).

50. Deetz, *Democracy,* p. 67.

51. Shapiro, "Generalizability in Communication Research."

52. This point is developed in some detail by Penman, "Good Theory and Good Practice."

CHAPTER

3

TRADITIONS OF COMMUNICATION THEORY

As we move into an exploration of actual theories, we need to find a way to understand similarities and differences among them. To this end, we offer a framework, adapted from Robert Craig, to use as a guide and tool for looking at the assumptions, perspectives, and focal points of communication theories. In fact, this framework provides a useful method for understanding the field of communication as a whole and the several traditions within which scholars have worked.

FRAMING COMMUNICATION THEORY

Think of the world of communication in which you live. How would you characterize it? What aspects would become immediately intriguing to you? Would you look first at the symbols in your environment and become fascinated with the ways in which these symbols designate impor-

tant things to you and other people? Would you concentrate on your perceptions and feelings about these symbols and what they are doing to your life? Perhaps you would go beyond looking at objects, words, and acts as symbols to notice the complexity of the world around you and how everything seems to influence everything else. Or maybe you wouldn't think so much about all of these outside forces, but be captivated by individual differences and wonder about how your mind works, how to persuade other people and affect their minds, and how the media affect audience members as individuals. Another track that might capture your imagination is the way in which groups and cultures come together; how they develop their own codes and meanings; how your identity in a group is shaped by your gender, culture, family, or social networks. Maybe you would think of these things, but realize that society and its institutions are shaped by social arrangements that marginalize some groups and privilege others. Finally, as a student of communication, you might be most interested in practice, or how to interact with audiences in a way that actually influences society.

A quick read through the above paragraph will bring many important communication issues to mind; you will not normally think of all of these things, nor will you find each of these questions equally compelling or worthy. Some of these considerations will be yawners for you, while others will draw you right in. What you pay attention to and how you study communication will have a certain character based on what you find important, how you think communication should be studied, and what you think theory should accomplish. This is exactly what has happened in the communication field: Different scholars approach the topic in vastly different ways, and your job as a communication theory student is to understand the various approaches that have influenced our knowledge of communication.

Various typologies have been devised for organizing communication theories.[1] Robert Craig developed one such model that facilitates our ability to reflect on the communication field—to communicate about the human process of communication.[2] Craig suggests, as we noted in Chapter 1, that our field will always be characterized by multiple theories and perspectives. Lacking a unifying theory of communication, we need a coherent "metamodel" that can help us define issues and talk about the assumptions that govern our approaches to theory. Craig's metamodel provides a robust system for ordering communication theory, and we use it here to help organize this book.

Craig divides the world of communication theory into seven traditions: (1) the semiotic; (2) the phenomenological; (3) the cybernetic; (4) the sociopsychological; (5) the sociocultural; (6) the critical; and (7) the rhetorical. We like to think of these traditions as scholarly communities drawn together by similar concerns and ideas. Some of these traditions stand in near opposition to one another, while others have a good deal of overlap. As a group, these traditions provide suffi-

cient coherence to allow us to look at theories side by side and to understand their essential commonalities and divisions.

◖ THE SEMIOTIC TRADITION

Look around your room and select four or five objects that are meaningful to you. Why did you choose these things? Why are they important? Chances are that the objects you picked are not just things in themselves, but bring to mind something else—a relationship, a time of your life, an accomplishment, a trip, a place, or any of a number of other experiences. In other words, the objects you selected are symbols.

Now look again and see if any of these selections have words on or in them. If you thought of a T-shirt, for example, it may be the words on the shirt, more than the shirt itself, that have significance to you. Maybe you even selected a book or a CD that is filled with written words or lyrics. Whether words, objects, or actions, the symbols of your life have meaning because of how they relate to other symbols and how you organize these symbols together into larger patterns that help you understand who you are, what is important to you, and how to act in your life.

Semiotics, or the study of signs, forms an important tradition of thought in communication theory. The semiotic tradition includes a host of theories about how signs come to represent objects, ideas, states, situations, feelings, and conditions outside of themselves. The study of signs not only provides a way of looking at communication but also has a powerful impact on almost all perspectives now employed in communication theory.[3]

Key Ideas of the Semiotic Tradition

The basic concept unifying this tradition is the *sign*, defined as a stimulus designating something other than itself. This concept integrates an amazingly broad set of theories dealing with language, discourse, and nonverbal actions. Within semiotics, you will encounter the terms *sign* and *symbol*. Different theories treat these in different ways. Sometimes symbols are considered a kind of sign, and other times signs and symbols are taken as different forms of the same thing. In Chapter 5, we will look at some of the meanings of these terms as we explore this tradition in depth.

Many communication theories explore the importance of signs and symbols to human life and the often-elaborate ways they are used. In general, this work is referred to as *semiotics*—and hence the source of Craig's label for this tradition. Viewing communication as a process of connecting the private worlds of individuals, the semiotic tradition is especially suited to addressing problems of gaps and misunderstandings that can be bridged by a common language.

Most semiotic thinking involves the basic idea of the *triad of meaning*, which asserts that meaning arises from a relationship among three things—the object (or referent), the person (or interpreter), and the sign. Charles Saunders Peirce, the first modern theorist of semiotics, may have been the originator of this idea.[4] Peirce defined *semiosis* as a relationship among a sign, an object, and a meaning.[5] The sign represents the object, or referent, in the mind of an interpreter. For example, the word *dog* is associated in your mind with a certain animal. The word is not the animal but is instead the association or interpretation you make that links the word with the actual object. A person who loves dogs and has one as a pet will experience the sign *dog* differently than the individual who was bitten by a dog as a child.

All three elements form the irreducible triad depicted in a well-known model created by C. K. Ogden and I. A. Richards, shown in Figure 3.1.[6] Here a sign and object (the referent) are connected through the interpretation in the mind of the person.

A study of personal pronouns by Wendy Martyna provides a better idea of how this three-part process actually works.[7] Traditionally in English, the pronoun *he* has been used to designate both male and female when a singular pronoun is required, as in the sentence, "When a teacher

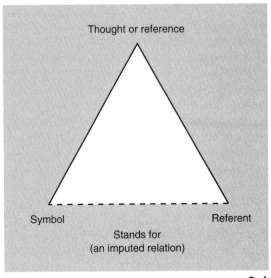

FIGURE 3.1

Ogden and Richards's Meaning Triangle

From *The Meaning of Meaning*, by C. K. Ogden and I. A. Richards. Copyright © 1923. Reprinted by permission of Harcourt Brace Jovanovich and Routledge & Kegan Paul.

returns tests, he usually discusses them with the class." Martyna was interested in finding out what generic pronouns people would actually use in such situations and their meanings for these pronouns. Forty students at Stanford completed a series of sentences requiring the use of a generic pronoun. Some of the sentences referred to people traditionally thought of as male ("Before a judge can give a final ruling, he must weigh the evidence"). Some referred to people traditionally considered female ("After a nurse has completed training, she goes to work"). And some were neutral ("When a person loses money, he is apt to feel bad").

Martyna found that the participants usually used a pronoun that was consistent with sex stereotypes. In the neutral sentences, research subjects most often used the masculine pronoun, although some participants deliberately suggested role reversals by switching the pronouns, and others tried to avoid sexism by using a combination, as in *he or she*. Women were less likely to use the masculine term than men. After the participants completed the sentences, the researcher asked them what image they had when they completed a sentence. Most often, they imagined a man in male-stereotyped sentences and a woman in female-stereotyped ones. In neutral sentences, the image was almost exclusively male.

This study shows that a sign such as a personal pronoun is connected to its referent through the mind, or interpretation, of the user. Meaning thus depends on the image or thought of the person in relation to the sign and the object the sign represents.

Variations in the Semiotic Tradition

Semiotics is often divided into three areas of study—semantics, syntactics, and pragmatics.[8] *Semantics* addresses how signs relate to their referents, or what signs stand for. Semiotics imagines two worlds—a world of things and a world of signs—and brings to light the relationship between these two worlds.[9] Whenever we ask the question, "What does a sign represent?" we are in the realm of semantics. Dictionaries, for example, are semantic reference books; they tell us what words mean, or what they represent. As a basic tenet of semiotics, representation is always mediated by the conscious interpretation of the person, and any interpretation or meaning for a sign will change from situation to situation. A more refined semantic question, then, is, "What meanings does a sign bring to the mind of a person within a situation?" Martyna's study of pronouns described above is firmly planted in the semantic branch of semiotics. Peirce's basic process of semiosis and Ogden and Richards's model of meaning described above are essentially semantic theories, even though semiotics as a tradition goes well beyond this simple connection.

The second area of study is *syntactics*, or the study of relationships among signs. Signs virtually never stand by themselves. They are almost always part of a larger sign system, or group of signs that are organized in particular ways. Such sign systems are often referred to as *codes*. A code is organized by rules, so that different signs designate different things, and signs may be put to-

gether only in certain permissible ways. Semiotics rests on the belief that signs are always understood in relation to other signs. Indeed, a dictionary is nothing more than a catalogue of the relationship of one sign to other signs (one word defined in terms of other words). In general, we think of syntactics as the rules by which people combine signs into complex systems of meaning.[10] When we move from a single word (*dog*) to a sentence (*The cute dog licked my hand.*), we are dealing with syntax or grammar. Gestures are frequently combined with other gestures to form complex systems of nonverbal signs, and nonverbal signs are paired with language to express subtle, complex meanings. Syntactic rules enable human beings to use an infinite combination of signs to express a wealth of meanings.

Pragmatics, the third major semiotic study, looks at how signs make a difference in people's lives, or the practical use and effects of signs. This branch has had the most important impact in communication theory, as signs and sign systems are seen as tools with which people communicate.[11] The pragmatics of signs is important to a number of broad communication concerns but is particularly powerful in looking at understanding and misunderstanding in communication.[12] From a semiotic perspective, we must have some kind of common understanding not just of individual words but of grammar, society, and culture in order for communication to take place. The system of relations among signs must allow communicators to refer to something in common.[13] We must share a sense of coherence in messages, or no amount of understanding will be possible, and we must assume that when we make use of the rules of language, large numbers of people who know those rules will be able to understand the meaning we intend. It is easy to see how pragmatics functions with language: People can communicate if they share meanings.

In contrast, nonlinguistic signs create special pragmatic problems. For example, visual codes are more open in their potential meanings—their interpretation is ultimately subjective and more connected to the internal perceptual and thought processes of the viewer than to conventional restricted representations. This is not to say that a person's meaning for an image is entirely individual; indeed, visual meanings can be and are affected by learning, culture, and other socially shared forms of interaction. But perceiving visual images is not the same as understanding language. Images require pattern recognition, organization, and discrimination, not just representational connections. Thus the meanings of visual images rely heavily on both individualized and social perception and knowledge.[14]

The three-part division—semantics, syntactics, and pragmatics—is used widely to organize the field of semiotics. However, not everyone agrees that this is the most useful way to do so. For example, Donald Ellis asserts that semantics is not a separate branch but is more like the trunk supporting the whole tree.[15] Meaning, for Ellis, is not just a matter of *lexical semantics,* or the meaning of words, but also includes *structural semantics,* or the meanings of grammatical structures. It is fair to say, at the least, that these three dimensions of semiotics are related to one another and that their separation helps us understand the different aspects of meaning, but belies the complexity of semiotic processes.

We learn from semiotics that signs (outside ourselves) come to represent objects, but only through our internal perceptions and feelings. While semiotics tends to focus on the sign and its functions, phenomenology looks much more at the individual as the key component in this process.

◖◗ THE PHENOMENOLOGICAL TRADITION

The phenomenological tradition concentrates on the conscious experience of the person.[16] Theories in this tradition assume that people actively interpret their experience and come to understand the world by personal experience with it.

Did you ever lie on your back at night looking at the stars in a really dark place? Sometime during childhood, nearly everyone begins to ask cosmological questions as they gaze into the sky and contemplate the enormity of the universe. Light, speed, time, matter, energy, movement, and distance come to be known to us by looking at the night sky and consciously contemplating the meaning of it all. We may expand our experience by using telescopes, looking at Hubbell pictures, and comparing astronomical distances and times with those closer to home. The process of knowing through direct experience is the province of phenomenology, our second tradition in the communication discipline.

Key Ideas of the Phenomenological Tradition

The term *phenomenon* refers to the appearance of an object, event, or condition in your perception. *Phenomenology,* then, features direct experiences as the way in which human beings come to understand the world. You come to know an experience or event by consciously examining it and testing your feelings and perceptions about it. Maurice Merleau-Ponty, a theorist in this tradition, wrote that "all my knowledge of the world, even my scientific knowledge, is gained from my own particular point of view, or from some experience of the world."[17] Phenomenology, then, makes actual lived experience the basic data of reality. All you can know is what you experience: "Phenomenology means letting things become manifest as what they are."[18] If you want to know what love is, you would not ask psychologists; you would tap into your own experience of love.

Stanley Deetz summarizes three basic principles of phenomenology.[19] First, knowledge is conscious. Knowledge is not inferred from experience but is found directly in conscious experience. Second, the meaning of a thing consists of the potential of that thing in one's life. In other words, how you relate to an object determines its meaning for you. For example, you will take your communication theory course seriously as an educational experience when you experience it as something that will have positive impact on your life. The third assumption is that language is the vehicle of meaning. We experience the world through the language used to define and express that world. We know *keys* because of their associated labels: "lock," "open," "metal," "weight," and so forth.

The process of *interpretation* is central to most phenomenological thought. Sometimes known by the German term *Verstehen* (understanding), interpretation is the active process of assigning meaning to an experience. In the semiotic tradition, interpretation is considered to be separate from reality, but in phenomenology, interpretation literally forms what is real for the person. You cannot separate reality from interpretation. Interpretation is an active process of the mind, a creative act of clarifying personal experience.

Interpretation emerges from a *hermeneutic circle* in which the interpreters constantly go back and forth between experiencing an event or situation and assigning meaning to it, moving from the specific to the general and back to the specific again. We construct an interpretation of an event or experience and then test that interpretation by looking closely at the specifics of the event once again—a continual process of refining our meaning for what we see and do. An example might be a woman who had a particularly rocky relationship with her father. That experience forms the basis of her understanding of relationships with men. This interpretation will probably undergo continual shifting throughout life as she continues to go back and forth between experiencing relationships and interpreting them.

Variations in the Phenomenological Tradition

Three general schools of thought make up the phenomenological tradition: (1) classical phenomenology; (2) the phenomenology of perception; and (3) hermeneutic phenomenology. *Classical phenomenology* is primarily associated with Edmund Husserl, the founder of modern phenomenology.[20] Husserl, who wrote during the first half of the twentieth century, attempted to develop a method for ascertaining truth through focused consciousness. For Husserl, truth can only be ascertained through direct experience, but we must be disciplined in how we experi-

ence things. In other words, the conscious experience of the individual is the correct route for discovering reality. Only through conscious attention can truth be known. In order to do so, however, we must put aside, or *bracket*, our biases. We must suspend our categories of thinking and habits of seeing in order to experience the thing as it really is. In this way, the objects of the world present themselves to our consciousness. Husserl's approach to phenomenology thus is highly objective; the world can be experienced without the knower bringing his or her own categories to bear on the process.

In contrast to Husserl, most phenomenologists today subscribe to the idea that experience is subjective, not objective, and believe that subjectivity is an important kind of knowledge in its own right. Maurice Merleau-Ponty, a major figure in this second tradition, is associated with what is called the *phenomenology of perception*—a reaction against the narrow objectivist view of Husserl.[21] For Merleau-Ponty, the human being is a unified physical and mental being who creates meaning in the world. We know things only through our own personal relationship to these things. As persons, we are affected by the world, but we also affect the world by how we experience it. For Merleau-Ponty, then, things do not exist in and of themselves apart from how they are known. Rather, people give meaning to the things in the world, and any phenomenological experience is necessarily a subjective one. Thus, the world of things and events exists in a give-and-take, or dialogic relationship, with each affecting the other.

The third branch, *hermeneutic phenomenology*, is quite consistent with the second, but extends the tradition further by applying it more completely to communication. Hermeneutic phenomenology is associated with Martin Heidegger, known primarily for his work in *philosophical hermeneutics* (an alternative name for this movement).[22] His philosophy has also been called the *hermeneutic of Dasein*, which means "interpretation of being." Most important for Heidegger is the natural experience that inevitably occurs by merely existing in the world. For Heidegger, the reality of something is not known by careful analysis or re-duction but by natural experience, which is created by the use of language in everyday life. What is real is what is experienced through the natural use of language in context: "Words and language are not wrappings in which things are packed for the commerce of those who write and speak. It is in words and language that things first come into being and are."[23] Communication is the vehicle by which you assign meaning to experience. Your thoughts result from speech because meaning itself is created by your speech. When you communicate, you work out new ways of seeing the world. Language, thus, is packed with meaning, and the "spoken word," available to us in everyday life, constantly affects our experience of events and situations. Consequently, this tradition of phenomenology—linking experience with language and social interaction—is especially relevant to the communication discipline.[24]

To many scholars the phenomenological tradition is naive. For them, life is shaped by complex, interacting forces, only some of which can ever be known consciously at any one time. You cannot interpret something by consciously looking at it and thinking about it. Real understanding comes from careful analysis of a system of effects. In the following section, we look at the tradition most associated with this form of theory.

◖ THE CYBERNETIC TRADITION

What characterizes your family? Could you adequately describe your family by showing a picture? How about adding a description of each person, including what they are like? Neither of these approaches would be sufficient to really get across an idea of what your family *is*. This is because a family is more than a collection of persons. In order to fully understand family life—as a family therapist might want to do, for example—you would need to look at how the members act toward one another, how they respond to each other, how they influence one another, how they use communication to maintain stability, and how they change over time. In other words, family dynamics can only be adequately explained with a cybernetic perspective.

Cybernetics is the tradition of complex systems in which many interacting elements influence one another. Theories in the cybernetic tradition offer broad perspectives on how a wide variety of physical, biological, social, and behavioral processes work.[25] Communication is understood as a system of parts, or variables, that influence one another, shape and control the character of the overall system, and, like any organism, achieve balance as well as change.

Key Ideas of the Cybernetic Tradition

The idea of a *system* forms the core of cybernetic thinking.[26] Systems are sets of interacting components that together form something more than the sum of the parts. A family is a good example of a communication system.[27] Family members are not isolated from one another, and their relationships must be taken into account to fully understand the family as a system. Like families, all systems are unique wholes characterized by a pattern of relationships.[28] Any part of the system, therefore, is always constrained by its dependence on other parts, and this pattern of interdependence organizes the system itself.[29] But a system cannot remain alive without importing new resources in the form of inputs. Thus, a system takes in inputs from the environment, processes these, and creates outputs back into the environment. Sometimes the inputs and outputs are tangible materials; sometimes they consist of energy and information.

In addition to interdependence, systems are also characterized by self-regulation and control. In other words, systems monitor, regulate, and control their outputs in order to remain stable and achieve goals. A thermostat and heater are a simple example of system control. An airplane is an example of an incredibly complex system that is able to maintain sufficient control through a highly complex system of interactions among

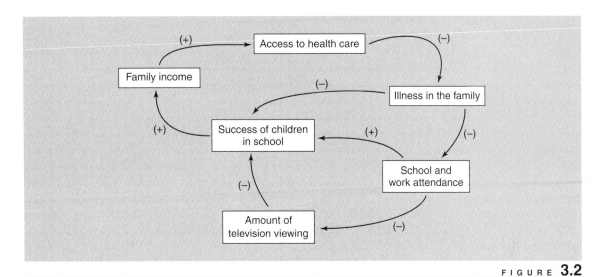

FIGURE **3.2**

Hypothetical Cybernetic Network

parts to get cargo and passengers to their desired destinations.

Because the system exists in a dynamic environment, it must be adaptable and able to change.[30] Systems theorists, then, are not simply interested in the nature of the system and its functions, but in how it manages to sustain and control itself over time. How does a plane manage to fight gravity, wind currents, and other forces and to direct itself along a programmed course? This can only happen because of systems within systems.

In other words, systems are embedded within one another such that one system is part of a larger system, forming a series of levels of increasing complexity.[31] We can take a very broad view by observing a number of systems that interact with one another in a large suprasystem, or we can take a narrower view by observing a smaller subsystem.

In a complex system, a series of feedback loops exist within and among subsystems. These feedback loops are called *networks*.[32] A simple illustration of a cybernetic network is the hypothetical example in Figure 3.2.[33] In this figure the pluses (+) represent positive relationships and the minuses (–) negative ones. In a positive rela-

tionship, variables increase or decrease together. In a negative relationship, they vary inversely, so that as one increases, the other decreases. For example, as family income goes up, access to health care also increases. With increased access to health care comes decreased family illness, which in turn improves school and work attendance. Notice that some of the loops in the network are positive feedback loops, and some are negative.

The key ideas of system theory are amazingly coherent and consistent, and they have had a major impact on many fields, including communication. Although you may think of systems mostly in terms of computers and machines, the human mind and human social life can be understood usefully in system terms as well. As a result, the cybernetic tradition has had an impact not only on information technology and engineering, but also in the social sciences and communication.

Because of its wide applicability in virtual, physical, and social environments, the cybernetic tradition is not monolithic. Here we will make distinctions among four variations of system theory. These include (1) basic system theory; (2) cybernetics; (3) General System Theory; and (4) second-order cybernetics.

Variations in the Cybernetic Tradition

The ideas outlined in the previous section can be thought of as *basic system theory*. In its most elementary form, this approach depicts systems as actual structures that can be analyzed and observed from outside. In other words, you can see the parts of the system and how they interact. You can observe and objectively measure the forces among parts of the system, and you can detect inputs and outputs of the system. Further, you can operate on or manipulate the system by changing its inputs and tinkering with its processing mechanisms. A whole raft of professions, such as systems analysts, management consultants, and system designers, has developed to analyze systems and improve them.

Beyond basic system theory, *cybernetics* has been an important area of study. Norbert Wiener in the 1950s popularized this term, which Craig adopted to name the entire systems tradition.[34] The term can be confusing, because it applies to both the general tradition (as Craig has done) and the more specific field of cybernetics (as Wiener used the term). As a field of study, cybernetics is the branch of system theory that focuses on feedback loops and control processes. Emphasizing circular forces, cybernetics challenges the very idea that one thing causes another in a linear fashion. Instead, this work calls our attention to how things impact one another in a circular way, how systems maintain control, how balance is achieved, and how feedback loops can maintain balance and create change.[35]

The third branch or area of study within system theory is *General System Theory* (GST), originally formulated by Ludwig von Bertalanffy, a biologist. Bertalanffy used GST as a broad, multidisciplinary approach to knowledge.[36] This tradition uses system principles to show how things in many different fields are similar to one another, forming a common vocabulary for communication across disciplines.[37] More than this, however, GST recognizes the universal nature of systems of all types and points out, for example, the commonalities among economic growth, biological development, and social movements.

In recent decades, some theorists have come to reject the idea that systems can be observed objectively. *Second-order cybernetics* developed as an alternative and is the last variation within cybernetics that we will discuss. Second-order cybernetics holds that observers can never see how a system works by standing outside the system itself because the observer is always engaged cybernetically with the system being observed. According to this perspective, whenever you observe a system, you affect and are affected by it. This branch, most associated with Heinz von Foerster, is also called the *cybernetics of knowing* because it shows that knowledge is a product of feedback loops between the knower and the known.[38] What we observe in a system is determined in part by the categories and methods of observation, which in turn are affected by what is seen. This circle is a cybernetic system, and observers cannot escape it.

The cybernetic tradition has been a popular and influential line of work in communication, useful for understanding communication in general as well as instances of communication occurring in everyday life. In general, you will also notice that these theories tend to be consistent and mutually supportive. Because of system influences, a common vocabulary makes these theories coherent and useful as a group.

Although theories of the cybernetic tradition are excellent for understanding relationships, they are less effective in helping us understand individual differences among the parts of the system. In contrast, the following tradition has been powerful in helping us understand individual human beings as communicators.

◖ THE SOCIOPSYCHOLOGICAL TRADITION

Almost certainly, you will think of yourself first as an individual. You have a body, a brain, and a skin that marks a boundary between yourself and the outside world. You have a unique appearance, and, even if you are an identical twin, your face is never exactly the same as anyone else's. If you ever took a personality test, you probably accepted the results without objection, since you assume that you have a certain combination of traits that do make you different from other people. At the same time, you are clearly aware that you are not an island but are part of a community of other people bound together by social interaction. You are, in part, a social being, and you probably notice all kinds of characteristics that you exhibit in communicating with others.

The study of the individual as a social being is the thrust of the *sociopsychological* tradition. Originating in the field of social psychology, this tradition has been a powerful tradition within communication.[39] It has been useful in helping us understand situations in which personality seems important, judgments are biased by beliefs and feelings, and people have obvious influence over one another. The theories of this tradition focus on individual social behavior, psychological variables, individual effects, personalities and traits, perception, and cognition. Although these theories have many differences, they share a common concern for behavior and for the personal traits and cognitive processes that produce behavior.

The individualistic approach is common in the study of communication and in the behavioral and social sciences at large. This is understandable within our cultural milieu.[40] The individual has dominated Western thought since the eighteenth-century Enlightenment, and the autonomous person is the primary unit of analysis in much Western thinking.[41] This psychological view sees persons as entities with characteristics that lead them to behave in independent ways. It views the single human mind as the locus for processing and understanding information and generating messages, but it acknowledges the power that individuals can have over other individuals and the effects of information on the human mind. Hardly surprising, then, is that psychological explanations have been so appealing to many communication scholars, especially in the study of attitude change and interaction effects.[42]

Key Ideas of the Sociopsychological Tradition

In the sociopsychological tradition, psychological explanations are crucial, assuming that the universal mechanisms that govern action can be discovered through careful research.[43] Consequently, this tradition is most often associated with "the science of communication." Most of the current work in this tradition in communication focuses on message processing, with an emphasis on how individuals plan message strategies, how receivers process message information, and the effects of messages on individuals. Given these three interests, it is no mystery that persuasion and attitude theory have dominated this tradition for many years. A still-popular part of the sociopsychological approach is trait theory, which identifies personality variables and communicator tendencies that affect how individuals act and interact.

Most sociopsychological theories of communication today are cognitive in orientation, providing insights into the ways human beings process information.[44] In this area, the sociopsychological and cybernetic traditions come together to explain individual human information-processing systems.[45] Of special interest are the inputs (information) and outputs (plans and behaviors) of the cognitive system. Questions of importance to this line of investigation include how perceptions get represented cognitively and how those representations get processed through mechanisms that serve attention, retention, interference, selection, motivation, planning, and strategizing.

Much of the work in this tradition assumes that mechanisms of human information processing are beyond our awareness. As communicators, we may be made aware of specific aspects of the process such as attention and memory, and we may be very aware of certain outputs like plans and behaviors, but the internal processes themselves are behind the scenes. Communication scientists seek to discover and describe these systems.

Several themes are apparent in the sociopsychological tradition: (1) How can individual communication behavior be predicted? (2) How does an individual take into account and accommodate to different communication situations? (3) How do communicators adapt their behaviors to one another? (4) How is information assimilated, organized, and used in forming message strategies and plans? (5) By what logic do people make decisions about the types of message they wish to use? (6) How is meaning represented in the mind? (7) How do people attribute the causes of behavior? (8) How is information integrated to form beliefs and attitudes? (9) How do attitudes change? (10) How are messages assimilated into the belief/attitude system? (11) How are expectations formed in interactions with others? (12) What happens when expectations are violated? The variations in this tradition answer these questions in different ways.

Variations in the Sociopsychological Tradition

The sociopsychological tradition can be divided into three large branches: (1) the behavioral; (2) the cognitive; and (3) the biological. The first variation is the *behavioral*. Here we see theories that concentrate on *how* people actually behave in communication situations. Such theories typically look at the relationship between communication behavior—what you say and what you do—in relation to such variables as personal traits, situational differences, and learning. Until 1960 or so, the emphasis in psychology was on how we learn behavior by associating stimulus and response. When certain behaviors are rewarded, they tend to be repeated. Psychologists call this "learning." When responses are punished, they tend to be extinguished, or "unlearned." Today theorists of the sociopsychological tradition generally believe that this depiction is an overly simple explanation for human behavior.

The second approach, *cognitive theory*, is much in favor these days. Centering on patterns of thought, this branch concentrates on how individuals acquire, store, and process information in a way that leads to behavioral outputs. In other words, what you actually do in a commu-

nication situation depends not just on stimulus-response patterns, but also on the mental operations used to manage information.

The third general variation is *biological*. As the study of genetics assumed increasing importance, psychologists and other behavioral researchers became interested in the effects of brain function and structure, neurochemistry, and genetic factors in explaining human behavior. The idea is that many of our traits, ways of thinking, and behaviors are wired in biologically and derive not from learning or situational factors, but from inborn neurobiological influences.[46] These theories, which began to gain prominence in the 1990s, are probably best labeled *psychobiology*, which may be an emerging tradition in its own right; at least for the present edition of this book, we will include them with their cousins in social psychology. Already in communication, the term *communibiology* has been employed to capture the study of communication from a biological perspective.[47]

The individual in social interaction with other individuals is a definition of the communicator shared by the theories within this chapter. The sociopsychological tradition focuses on the "individual" part of this definition. In the following section, we shift from an individual to a "social interaction" emphasis.

◖ THE SOCIOCULTURAL TRADITION

Write twenty statements that answer the question, "Who am I?" Look back at your list and see what kinds of descriptions you included. If you wrote words like "artistic," "bashful," "good student," "likes horses," and "kind to others," you are thinking of yourself in terms of qualities, traits, or individual differences—all sociopsychological conditions. On the other hand, if you put down things like "father," "Catholic," "student," "lesbian," and "lives in Missoula," you are defining yourself in terms of your identity as a member of a group, your place within a larger community, your role in regard to others, or your relationships. This latter idea of identity is the focus of the *sociocultural* tradition. This is an informative exercise, but it is also an officially recognized test used in research. We'll have more to say about the Twenty Statements Test in Chapter 4.

Sociocultural approaches to communication theory address the ways our understandings, meanings, norms, roles, and rules are worked out interactively in communication.[48] Such theories explore the interactional worlds in which people live, positing the idea that reality is not an objective set of arrangements outside us but is constructed through a process of interaction in groups, communities, and cultures.

Key Ideas of the Sociocultural Tradition

This tradition focuses on patterns of interaction between people rather than on individual characteristics or mental models. Interaction is the process and site in which meanings, roles, rules, and cultural values are worked out. Although individuals do process information cognitively, this tradition is much less interested in the individual level of communication. Instead, researchers in this tradition want to understand ways in which people *together* create the realities of their social groups, organizations, and cultures. Indeed, the categories used by individuals to process information are socially created in communication.

Clearly, then, this tradition is very interested in the processes of communication that occur in actual situations. Although this tradition has been largely responsible for outlining the aspects of relationships, groups, and cultures created in social interaction, the processes that generate these outcomes are the focus of this tradition.

There is a healthy skepticism within this movement about discovery methods of research. These theories tend to subscribe to the idea that reality is constructed by language, so whatever is "discovered" must be heavily influenced by the interaction patterns of the research protocol itself. Thus, within the sociocultural approach,

knowledge is highly interpretive and constructed.

Furthermore, these theories tend to be interested in how meaning is created in social interaction. The meaning of words within actual social situations assumes high importance. Behavioral patterns in interaction in real time are also interesting to sociocultural researchers, and these researchers are always interested in what is getting made by these patterns of interaction.

Many sociocultural theories also focus on how identities are established through interaction in social groups and cultures. Identity becomes a fusion of our selves as individuals within social roles, as members of communities, and as cultural beings. Sociocultural scholars thus focus on how identity is negotiated from one situation to another. Culture is also seen as a significant part of what gets made in social interaction. In turn, culture forms a context for action and interpretation in communication situations. Because communication is something that happens *between* people, the community assumes tremendous importance to many of these theories.

Context is explicitly identified within this tradition as crucial to the forms of communication and meanings that occur. Symbols, already important in any interaction, assume different meanings, as communicators move from situation to situation. The symbols and meanings important to particular social groups and cultures are fascinating to sociocultural researchers.

Because of the importance of culture and context, then, sociocultural work is generally, though not always, holistic. Researchers in this tradition may focus on a small aspect of the whole situation in a particular study, but they fully recognize the importance of the whole situation to what happens on a microlevel.

Variations in the Sociocultural Tradition

Like all of the traditions, the sociocultural has various contributing lines of work: symbolic interactionism, constructionism, and sociolinguistics.[49] Based on the idea that social structures and meanings are created and maintained in social interaction, *symbolic interactionism* (SI) has been highly influential in this tradition.[50] Symbolic interactionism had its origins in the discipline of sociology with the work of Herbert Blumer and George Herbert Mead, who emphasized the importance of participant observation in the study of communication as a way of exploring social relationships.[51] The basic ideas of symbolic interactionism have been adopted and elaborated by many social scientists and today are incorporated into studies of groups, emotions, self, politics, and social structure.[52]

A second line of work highly influential in the sociocultural approach is *social constructionism.* Originally called *the social construction of reality* after the work of Peter Berger and Thomas Luckmann, this line of work has been an investigation of how human knowledge is constructed through social interaction.[53] The identity of a thing results from how we talk about that object, the language used to capture our concepts, and the way in which social groups orient to their common experience. The nature of the world, then, is less important than the language used to name, discuss, and approach that world.

A third influence in the sociocultural tradition of communication theory is *sociolinguistics*, or the study of language and culture.[54] Important in this tradition is that people use language differently in different social and cultural groups. Not merely a neutral vehicle for connecting individuals, language enters into the formation of who we are as social and cultural beings.

Closely related to sociolinguistics is work from the *philosophy of language*, particularly "ordinary language philosophy." Ludwig Wittgenstein, a German philosopher, began this line of work, suggesting that the meaning of language depends on its actual use.[55] Language, as used in ordinary life, is a *language game* because people follow rules to do things with language. When you give and obey orders, ask and answer questions, and describe events, you are engaged in language games. Like ordinary games such as chess and poker, each language game has a different set of rules. J. L. Austin came to

refer to the practical use of language as *speech acts.*[56] When you speak, you are actually performing an act. The act may be stating, questioning, commanding, promising, or a number of other possibilities.

Another influential perspective within the sociocultural approach is *ethnography,* or the observation of how actual social groups come to build meaning through their linguistic and nonlinguistic behaviors.[57] Ethnography looks at the forms of communication used in specific social groups, the words they use and what these mean to the group, as well as the meanings for a variety of behavioral, visual, and auditory responses.

Finally, the sociocultural tradition has been influenced by *ethnomethodology,* or the careful observation of microbehaviors in real situations.[58] Attributed primarily to sociologist Harold Garfinkel, this approach looks at how, in social interaction, we manage or mesh behaviors at actual moments in time. In communication, ethnomethodology has influenced how we look at conversations, including the ways in which participants manage the back-and-forth flow with language and nonverbal behaviors.

The following tradition follows closely many of the interests and assumptions of the sociocultural, but it adds an important dimension that moves it from the descriptive to the critical.

◖ THE CRITICAL TRADITION

Think for a moment about your privileges. What advantages and resources do you have at this point in your life? How did these come to you? What has happened in society for these particular assets to gain value or to be a resource that enables you to move forward in a healthy, self-fulfilling way, both as an individual and as a member of a community? Now think for a few minutes about what privileges others have that you do not. Why don't you have these? What stands in the way? Now think of a third set of questions: What special assets, abilities, or resources do you possess that have not come to be valued in our society? Why do these things remain unimportant to other groups? What symbols, rules, and meanings have emerged from communication within our society that give power to some groups and take it away from others? How do these power arrangements get reinforced through communication?

The questions of privilege and power have assumed importance in communication theory, and it is the *critical* tradition that carries this banner. If you have privilege, or lack it, because of the color of your skin, your nationality, your language, your religion, your sex, your sexual orientation, your regional affiliation, your income level, or any other aspect of your identity, then you are facing the kind of social difference that assumes great importance to critical scholars. These theories show that power, oppression, and privilege are the products of certain forms of communication throughout society, making the critical tradition significant in the field of communication theory today.

The critical tradition stands in opposition to many of the basic assumptions of the other traditions. Heavily influenced by work in Europe, by U.S. feminism, and by postmodern and postcolonial discourses, this tradition is growing in its popularity and impact on communication theory.

Key Ideas of the Critical Tradition

Although there are several varieties of critical social science, all share three essential features.[59] First, the critical tradition seeks to understand the taken-for-granted systems, power structures, and beliefs—or ideologies—that dominate society, with a particular eye to whose interests are served by those power structures. Questions such as who does and does not get to speak, what does and does not get said, and who stands to benefit from a particular system are typical of those asked by critical theorists.[60] Second, critical theorists are particularly interested in uncovering oppressive social conditions and power arrangements in order to promote emancipation, or a freer and more fulfilling society. Understanding oppression is the first step to dispelling

the illusions of ideology and to taking action to overcome oppressive forces.

Third, critical social science makes a conscious attempt to fuse theory and action. Such theories are clearly normative and act to accomplish change in the conditions that affect society, or as Della Pollock and J. Robert Cox put it, "to *read* the world with an eye towards *shaping* it."[61] Critical research aims to reveal the ways in which competing interests clash and the manner in which conflicts are resolved in favor of particular groups over other ones.[62] Critical theories therefore frequently ally themselves with the interests of marginalized groups.

In the field of communication, critical scholars are particularly interested in how messages reinforce oppression in society. Although critical scholars are interested in social action, they also focus on discourse and the texts that promote particular ideologies, establish and maintain power, and subvert the interests of certain groups and classes. Critical discourse analysis looks at actual features of texts that manifest these oppressive arrangements,[63] without separating communication from other factors in the overall system of oppressive forces.[64]

Because critical theories are so broad and cast such a wide net, they are often hard to place and categorize within the overall body of communication theory. We will describe several of the major branches: Marxism, the Frankfurt School of Critical Theory, postmodernism, cultural studies, poststructuralism, postcolonialism, and feminist studies.

Variations in the Critical Tradition

Although critical theory has come a long way since the work of Karl Marx and Friedrich Engels, *Marxism* is clearly the originating branch of critical theory.[65] Marx taught that the means of production in society determines the nature of society;[66] so the economy is the base of all social structure. In capitalistic systems, profit drives production, therefore oppressing labor or the working class. Only when the working class rises up against dominant groups can the means of production be changed and the liberation of the worker be achieved.[67] Such liberation furthers the natural progress of history in which forces in opposition clash in a dialectic that results in a higher social order. This classical Marxist theory is called the *critique of political economy.*

Today, Marxist critical theory is thriving, although it has become diffused and multitheoretical. Few critical theorists today wholeheartedly adopt Marx's ideas on political economy, although his basic concerns of dialectical conflict, domination, and oppression remain important. For this reason critical theory today is frequently labeled "neomarxist" or "marxist" (with a lowercase *m*). And in contrast to the simple materialist model of Marxism, most contemporary critical theories view social processes as *overdetermined*, or caused by multiple sources. They see social structure as a system in which many things interact and affect one another.

An interest in language remains important to critical theorists. In Marxism, communication practices are seen as an outcome of the tension between individual creativity and the social constraints on that creativity. Only when individuals are truly free to express themselves with clarity and reason will liberation occur. Paradoxically, however, language is also an important constraint on individual expression, for the language of the dominant class makes it difficult for working-class groups to understand their situation and to get out of it. In other words, the dominant language defines and perpetuates the oppression of marginalized groups. It is the job of the critical theorist to create new forms of language that will enable the predominant ideology to be exposed and competing ideologies to be heard.

The *Frankfurt School* is a second branch of critical theory and, in fact, was largely responsible for the emergence of the label "critical" theory; the Frankfurt School is still often described as synonymous with the label. The Frankfurt School refers to a group of German philosophers, sociologists, and economists—Max Horkheimer, Theodor Adorno, and Herbert Marcuse are among its most important members—associated with the Institute for Social Research, established in Frankfurt in 1923.[68] The

members of the school are generally united around the need for an integration of disciplines—philosophy, sociology, economics, and history—in order to promote a broad social philosophy or critical theory capable of offering a comprehensive examination of the contradictions and interconnections central to the reproduction and transformation of society, culture, the economy, and consciousness. The Frankfurt School is clearly Marxist in inspiration; its members saw capitalism as an evolutionary stage in the development, first, of socialism and then of communism. The failure of working-class movements and the rise of Fascism, however, led many members of the Frankfurt School to abandon their belief in the working-class proletariat as the agent of revolutionary change in favor of intellect and reason. As a result, the Frankfurt School has been criticized for its elitism, distaste for popular culture, and dismissal of activism in favor of intellectualism.

With the rise of the National Socialist Party (Nazi) in Germany in the 1930s, the Frankfurt scholars immigrated to the United States, where they established the Institute for Social Research at Columbia University. While in the United States, they became intensely interested in mass communication and the media as structures of oppression in capitalistic societies. Communication continues to be central to critical theory, and the study of mass communication has been especially important.[69] The best-known contemporary Frankfurt scholar is Jürgen Habermas, whose theories continue the valorization of reason and call for a return of rational ideas from the Enlightenment or modern period.[70]

Critical theory clearly falls within a modernist paradigm. Whether intellectual or populist in approach, there is a reliance on reason established through science; the individual as the agent of change; and the discovery of taken-for-granted but knowable facets of a culture. Three additional branches that can be grouped with critical theory break with modernity in various ways: postmodernism, poststructuralism, and postcolonialism. What these philosophical traditions have in common is an insistence on the plurality and instability of meaning, a distrust of the scientific, and a reluctance to grant credence to grand narratives.

Postmodernism, in its most general sense, is characterized by a break with modernity and the Enlightenment project. It coincides in large part with the end of the industrial society and the emergence of an information age, in which the production of commodities has given way to the production and manipulation of knowledge. Mainly originating in the 1970s, the postmodern rejects the "elitism, puritanism and sterility" of the rational in favor of pluralism, relativity, novelty, complexity, and contradiction.[71] Jean-François Lyotard's contribution to postmodernity is the rejection of grand narratives of progress; Jean Baudrillard's contribution is an insistence on the increasing separation of signs from their referents. Both call into question traditional notions of "reality" if the "stories" of culture cannot be believed and artificial constructions of signs often are deemed more real than the signs themselves.[72] Today, the line of work known as "cultural studies" is most often associated with the postmodern variation of the critical tradition. As a loosely knit tradition-within-a-tradition, cultural studies looms large as an important postmodern branch of the critical tradition.

Cultural studies theorists share an interest in the ideologies that dominate a culture but focus on social change from the vantage point of culture itself: "to make intelligible the real movement of culture as it registered in social life, in group and class relations, in politics and institutions, in values and ideas."[73] This interdisciplinary enterprise began at the Centre for Contemporary Cultural Studies in Birmingham, England, in 1964. With its focus on culture as ordinary and worthy of investigation, it has made available for academic study a range of subjects and subcultures traditionally not deemed suitable for academic attention. Cultural studies, then, is decidedly populist in orientation in contrast with the intellectual bias of the Frankfurt School.

The possibility of studying all kinds of subcultures not usually studied in the academy gave rise to cultural studies' most important contributions to contemporary scholarship—studies of previously marginalized concepts such as gen-

der, race, class, age, and most recently, sexuality. This is not to say that these topics were only studied by cultural theorists—in fact, virtually every discipline has seen an emergence of these subject matters from a variety of origins. The value cultural studies placed on the marginalized and the ordinary, however, has been a major impetus behind the continuing scholarly interest in these subjects.

Poststructuralism can be seen as part of the postmodern impulse or its larger impetus, depending on orientation. It is usually said to have begun at about the same time as the postmodernist impulse, with its specific origins dated to a 1966 paper by Jacques Derrida. Both structuralism and poststructuralism center on the study of signs and symbols, thus making them both very applicable to communication theory. Whereas structuralism is very much a modernist project—an effort to unify the various disciplines by developing a theory of signs applicable to all human areas of activity—poststructuralism is a postmodern one. Poststructuralism seeks to deconstruct the study of signs rather than generate a unifying theory. It also rejects the "dream of scientificity,"[74] privileging instead a plurality of methodologies; and it focuses on the instability of meaning in texts instead of trying to link particular signs with particular functions. Jean Baudrillard, Jacques Derrida, Roland Barthes, and Richard Rorty are identified with poststructuralism.

Next, *postcolonial theory* refers to the study of "all the cultures affected by the imperial process from the moment of colonization to the present day."[75] At the core of postcolonial theories is the notion, first put forth by Edward Said, that the colonializing process creates "othering," which is responsible for stereotypic images of nonwhite populations. It is very much a critical project and a postmodern one, seeking not simply to describe processes of colonization and why they came about, but to intervene with an "emancipatory political stance."[76] The postcolonial is also a postmodern project in its questioning of established knowledge structures rooted in modernity, asking that the geographic, national, and historical links and erasures be made explicit in discourses. Postcolonial scholars, then, study many of the same issues as critical and cultural studies do—race, class, gender, sexuality—but always as they are situated "within geopolitical arrangements, and relations of nations and their inter/national histories."[77]

Finally, *feminist studies* has for many years been a highly influential area within the critical tradition. *Feminism* has been defined in many ways, ranging from movements to secure rights for women to efforts at ending all forms of oppression; thus scholars today are more likely to talk about feminisms in the plural rather than the singular. Feminist scholars first began with a focus on gender and sought to distinguish between sex—a biological category—and gender—a social construction. They have examined, critiqued, and challenged the assumptions about and experiences of masculinity and femininity that pervade all aspects of life in an effort to achieve more liberating ways for women and men to exist in the world.[78] But feminist inquiry is much more than a study of gender. It seeks to offer theories that center women's experiences and to articulate the relations between the categories of gender and other social categories including race, ethnicity, class, and sexuality. Feminist scholarship, then, crosses all of the other variations of the critical tradition outlined above.[79]

◖ THE RHETORICAL TRADITION

Do you enjoy learning how to communicate effectively, especially in public situations? Would you enjoy being a speaker—maybe a politician or minister? Does public art as a symbolic statement intrigue you? Do you like to study texts and think about their meaning and impact? If so, you are probably drawn to the rhetorical tradition within communication theory.

The word *rhetoric* often has a pejorative meaning today—empty or ornamental words in contrast to action. In actuality, however, the study of rhetoric has a distinguished history dating back,

in the West, to fifth-century BC Greece. The study of rhetoric is really where the communication discipline began because rhetoric, broadly defined, is human symbol use. Originally concerned with persuasion, rhetoric was the art of constructing arguments and speechmaking. It then evolved to include the process of *"adjusting ideas to people and people to ideas"* [italics in the original] in messages of all kinds.[80] The focus of rhetoric has broadened even more to encompass all of the ways humans use symbols to affect those around them and to construct the worlds in which they live.

Key Ideas of the Rhetorical Tradition

Central to the rhetorical tradition are the five canons of rhetoric—invention, arrangement, style, delivery, and memory. These were the elements involved in preparing a speech; the rhetor is concerned with the discovery of ideas, their organization, choices about how to frame those ideas in language, and finally, issues of delivery and memory. With the evolution of rhetoric, these five canons have undergone a similar expansion. *Invention* now refers to conceptualization—the process through which we assign meaning to data through interpretation, an acknowledgment of the fact that we do not simply discover what exists but create it through the interpretive categories we use. *Arrangement* is the process of organizing symbols—arranging information in light of the relationships among the people, symbols, and context involved. *Style* concerns all of the considerations involved in the presentation of those symbols, from choice of symbol system to the meanings we give those symbols, as well as all symbolic behavior from words and actions to clothing and furniture. *Delivery* has become the embodiment of symbols in some physical form, encompassing the range of options from nonverbals to talk to writing to mediated messages.[81] Finally, *memory* no longer refers to the simple memorization of speeches but to larger reservoirs of cultural memory as well as to processes of perception that affect how we retain and process information.

Regardless of the choice of symbol and medium, rhetoric involves a rhetor, or symbol user, who creates a text or artifact for a particular audience, subject to various situational constraints. Many see *rhetoric* as synonymous with the term *communication*, and the decision of which term to use depends largely on the philosophical tradition with which you most identify. In fact, we will not focus further on rhetoric in this book because it has a lengthy tradition apart from communication theory, and we cannot do justice to both here. Still, it is important to the discipline of communication, so we do include it as a tradition in this chapter.

Variations in the Rhetorical Tradition

Rhetoric has had different meanings in different time periods, which has contributed to confusion over its meaning. We will identify several such periods to indicate the various possibilities of the rhetorical tradition: classical, medieval, Renaissance, Enlightenment, contemporary, and postmodern.

The origins of rhetoric in the *classical* era were dominated by efforts to define and codify the art of rhetoric. Traveling teachers called *Sophists* taught the art of arguing both sides of a case—the earliest rhetorical instruction in Greece. Plato disliked the Sophists' relativistic approach to knowledge, believing instead in the possibility of ideal or absolute truths. That Plato's dialogues on rhetoric have survived is in large part what gave the field of rhetoric a bad name. Plato's student Aristotle took a more pragmatic approach to the art, codifying it in his lecture notes that were compiled into what we now know as the *Rhetoric*. Greek writings on rhetoric were further refined and elaborated by the Romans, including Isocrates, Quintilian, and Cicero.

The *Middle Ages* saw the study of rhetoric focus largely on matters of arrangement and style. Medieval rhetoric was debased to a practical and pagan art and contrasted with Christianity, whose truth alone was seen as enough to persuade. Augustine, a rhetoric teacher who converted to Christianity, revitalized the rhetorical

tradition with his book, *On Christian Doctrine*. In it he argued that preachers needed to be able to teach, to delight, and to move—Cicero's conception of the duties of an orator.

The pragmatic orientation of medieval rhetoric also was evident in another major use of rhetoric in the Middle Ages—for letter writing. Letter writing had become increasingly important as a means of record keeping and because many decisions were made privately in decrees and letters. Matters of style were emphasized in teaching the adaptation of salutation, language, and format to a particular audience.

The *Renaissance* that followed the Middle Ages (about 1400–1600 BC) saw a rebirth of rhetoric as a philosophical art. Humanist scholars, interested in and concerned for all aspects of the human being, rediscovered classical rhetorical texts in an effort to know the human world. They were especially interested in the power of the word and believed language, not philosophy, to be the foundation discipline because of its capacity to disclose the world to humans.

Rationalism was a trend that began during the Renaissance but was especially characteristic of the next rhetorical period—the *Enlightenment* (1600–1800 BC). During this era, thinkers such as René Descartes sought to determine what could be known absolutely and objectively by the human mind. Francis Bacon, seeking to subject sensory perceptions to empirical investigation, argued that the duty of rhetoric was to "apply Reason to Imagination for the better moving of the will."[82] Logic or knowledge thus became separated from language, and rhetoric became only the means to communicate the truth once known. This split—separating content from rhetorical concerns—contributed to the negative definitions of rhetoric that persist today.

The focus on the rational during the Enlightenment also meant that rhetoric once again was limited to matters of style, giving rise to the *belles lettres* movement—literally fine or beautiful letters. *Belles lettres* referred to literature and all fine arts—rhetoric, poetry, drama, music, and even gardening—and all of these could be examined according to the same aesthetic criteria. Given the interest in matters of style, taste, and aesthetics, it is not surprising that an elocution movement teaching pronunciation and a system of gestures and movement to speakers also sprang up. Elocutionists had two main goals: to restore the canon of delivery, largely neglected since classical times, in order to improve the poor delivery styles of speakers of the era; and to contribute scientifically to the understanding of the human being by studying the effects of various aspects of delivery on the minds of audience members.

The twentieth century—and the contemporary rhetorics that accompanied it—exhibited a growing interest in rhetoric as the amount, kinds, and influence of symbols have increased. While the century began with an emphasis on the value of public speaking for the ideal citizen, the invention of mass media brought a new focus on the visual and verbal. Rhetoric shifted from a focus on oratory to every kind of symbol use. During the two world wars, institutes of mass media, established to study propaganda, began studying advertising and mass-mediated messages from rhetorical perspectives. Today, television and movies, billboards and video games, websites and computer graphics are studied by rhetoricians as much as are discursive texts. There is literally no form of symbol use that cannot be investigated by rhetorical scholars.

Most important, the contemporary period has also seen a return to an understanding of rhetoric as epistemic—as a way to know the world, not simply a way to communicate about the world. Most rhetorical theorists today subscribe, to some degree, to the notion that humans create their worlds through symbols—that the world we know is the one offered to us by our language. The strong form of this position suggests that the material conditions around us are less important than the words we use to name that reality and that changing one's labels or symbols can literally produce another world by creating a different perspective or vantage point on that world. The weaker form simply suggests the critical role language plays in how we approach the world.

Another trend emerging in the late twentieth and early twenty-first century stems from the *postmodern* recognition of the fragmented nature of reality, the failure of grand narratives to explain history and culture, and the need to appreciate and value diverse and unique standpoints. Postmodern rhetorical theorists, for example, privilege the standpoints of race, class, gender, and sexuality as they intersect in an individual's unique life experience rather than seek broad theories and explanations about rhetoric. Postmodern rhetorics thus explore alternative frames outside the mainstream rhetorical tradition. Feminist and gendered rhetorical practices often fall within the postmodern purview, as does queer theory, in which rhetorical scholars examine distinctive features of queer public address and other rhetorical forms to understand the nuances offered by a queer rhetor.[83]

Alternative rhetorics of another type also are emerging in response to the postmodern interest in diverse standpoints—non-Western rhetorics. Although they do not always look like Western rhetorical practices, there are indeed rhetorics in virtually every culture in the world. Rhetorical scholars are beginning to map the rhetorical traditions of various cultures to produce Afrocentric and Asiacentric rhetorics,[84] Native American rhetorics, Aboriginal rhetorics, and the like, and to consider how these might inform Western rhetorical practices.[85] These alternatives start from different assumptions, center different values, and therefore produce different rhetorical practices and products.

Rhetoric, then, is far more than meaningless or ornamental talk. It is the basic art and practice of human communication. Where once it was concerned with the practice of oratory according to a singular standard developed in Greece, today we recognize the existence of many "rhetorics," each of which offers a different perspective on symbol use. But because this book focuses on the communication theories in the discipline, we will not include many theories that are considered traditionally "rhetorical." Thus, we will not have a section for the rhetorical tradition per se as we move through the various contexts of communication; those theories that are rhetorical will be encompassed in other traditions as appropriate.

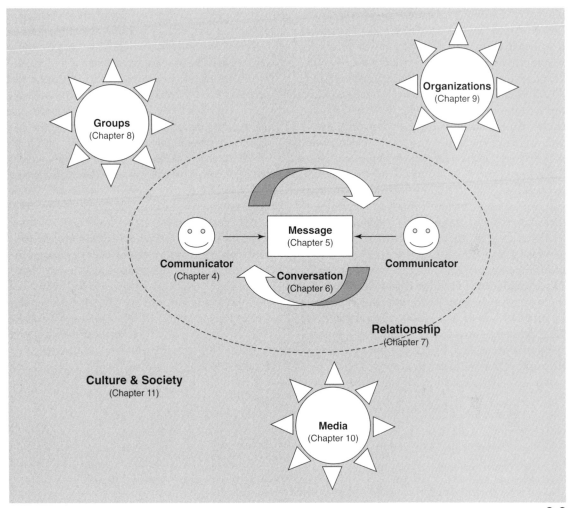

FIGURE **3.3**

Expanding Contexts for Communication Theory

◖ EXPANDING CONTEXTS FOR COMMUNICATION

Theories within the above-mentioned traditions address many aspects of communication. To organize theories, we have decided to look at their primary interests, or focal points. Imagine looking at the process of communication through a zoom lens. We can narrow the area of focus down to individuals and then zoom out slowly to look at increasingly wide views. At each point,

we can pan the lens around a bit to see other features of the scene in focus. As we do this, we realize that each aspect of communication is part of a larger context. We see, too, that each level of communication affects and is affected by these larger contexts.

For purposes of organization, we have arranged theories of communication into eight contexts, illustrated in Figure 3.3. We begin in Chapter 4 with the individual, looking at ways in which the various traditions have explained *com-*

municators as persons engaged in social interaction. Then, in Chapter 5, we look at theories of *messages* and, in Chapter 6, *conversations*. As people use messages in conversations with others, they develop *relationships*, which are explored in Chapter 7. Next, in Chapter 8, we move to the larger context of *groups* and, in Chapter 9, *organizations*. We then discuss theories of *media* (Chapter 10). Finally in Chapter 11, we broaden our lens to the widest level to look at communication in *culture and society*.

The contexts of communication—from the communicator to society—impact one another. For example, our relationships are defined and managed through the exchange of messages in conversations. Communicators make decisions about messages, but messages, organized into conversations, impact communicators. Culture is built up through communication over time, but the kinds of messages we send, how we understand those messages, and the resulting relationships are determined in many ways by the cultures and communities in which we live.

It would be a mistake, then, to treat these contexts as discrete. They are not. As we focus on individual theories within particular contexts, don't lose sight of the telescoping nature of contexts and forget their mutual influence. As we move from one context to the next in the following chapters, we encourage you to broaden or narrow the lens from time to time to keep an eye on these connections.

Within each of the following chapters, we organize theories by tradition, so that you can see how different traditions have contributed to the topic at hand. We have tried to organize individual chapters based on the most logical order of theories, so the traditions are not always presented in the same order in every chapter. Indeed, not all traditions contribute to every chapter, so some chapters include four traditions, some five, and some all six. To help you see the connection between the theories and the traditions, we reflect on each tradition in every chapter and point out interesting and important relationships.

◖ NOTES

1. Many typologies of scholarship have been developed. For a discussion of the problems involved in describing differences, see Stanley Deetz, "Describing Differences in Approaches to Organization Science," *Organization Science* 7 (1996): 191–207. See also Fred R. Dallmayr, *Language and Politics* (Notre Dame, IN: University of Notre Dame Press, 1984); Lawrence Grossberg, "Does Communication Theory Need Intersubjectivity? Toward an Immanent Philosophy of Interpersonal Relations," in *Communication Yearbook 6*, ed. Michael Burgoon (Beverly Hills, CA: Sage, 1984), pp. 171–205; and John Stewart, "Speech and Human Being," *Quarterly Journal of Speech* 72 (1986): 55–73; Gibson Winter, *Elements for a Social Ethic: Scientific and Ethical Perspectives on Social Process* (New York: Macmillan, 1966). Winter's scheme was later elaborated by Richard McKeon, "Gibson Winter's Elements for a Social Ethic: A Review," *Journal of Religion* 49 (1969): 77–84; and by Ted J. Smith III, "Diversity and Order in Communication Theory: The Uses of Philosophical Analysis," *Communication Quarterly* 36 (1988): 28–40. See also G. Burrell and G. Morgan, *Sociological Paradigms and Organizational Analysis* (London: Heinemann, 1979). For an elaboration of the Burrell and Morgan model, see Karl Erik Rosengren, "From Field to Frog Ponds," *Journal of Communication* 43 (1993): 6–17; and Karl Erik Rosengren, "Culture, Media, and Society: Agency and Structure, Continuity and Change," in *Media Effects and Beyond*, ed. Karl Erik Rosengren (London: Routledge, 1994), pp. 3–28.
2. Robert T. Craig, "Communication Theory as a Field," *Communication Theory* 9 (1999): 119–161.
3. For a good overview, see Wendy Leeds-Hurwitz, *Semiotics and Communication: Signs, Codes, Cultures* (Hillsdale, NJ: Lawrence Erlbaum, 1993). See also Kaja Silverman, *The Subject of Semiotics* (New York: Oxford University Press, 1983); Arthur Asa Berger, *Signs in Contemporary Culture: An Introduction to Semiotics* (Salem, WI: Sheffield, 1989); Elizabeth Mertz and Richard J. Parmentier, eds., *Semiotic Mediation: Sociocultural and Psychological Perspectives* (Orlando: Academic, 1985).
4. Charles Saunders Peirce, *Charles S. Peirce: Selected Writings*, ed. P. O. Wiener (New York: Dover, 1958). See also, for example, John Stewart, *Language as Articulate Contact: Toward a Post-Semiotic Philosophy of Communication* (Albany: SUNY Press, 1995), pp. 76–81; Christopher Hookway, *Peirce* (London: Routledge & Kegan Paul, 1985); Max H. Fisch, *Peirce, Semiotic, and Pragmatism* (Bloomington: Indiana University Press, 1986); Thomas A. Goudge, *The Thought of Peirce* (Toronto: University of

Toronto Press, 1950); John R. Lyne, "Rhetoric and Semiotic in C. S. Peirce," *Quarterly Journal of Speech* 66 (1980):155–168.

5. For a good summary of Peirce's theory, see Richard J. Parmentier, "'Signs' Place in *Medias Res*: Peirce's Concept of Semiotic Mediation," in *Semiotic Mediation: Sociocultural and Psychological Perspectives*, ed. Elizabeth Mertz and Richard Parmentier (Orlando: Academic, 1985), pp. 23–48.

6. C. K. Ogden and I. A. Richards, *The Meaning of Meaning* (London: Kegan, Paul, Trench, Trubner, 1923).

7. Wendy Martyna, "What Does 'He' Mean?" *Journal of Communication* 28 (1978): 131–138.

8. This model is attributed to Charles Morris, *Signs, Language, and Behavior* (New York: Braziller, 1946). A shorter version can be found in "Foundations of the Theory of Signs," in *International Encyclopedia of Unified Science*, vol. 1, part 1 (Chicago: University of Chicago Press, 1955), p. 84. A unified theory of signs and values is developed in Charles Morris, *Signification and Significance* (Cambridge, MA: MIT Press, 1964).

9. The two-world assumption is described and critiqued by John Stewart, "The Symbol Model vs. Language as Constitutive Articulate Contact," in *Beyond the Symbol Model: Reflections on the Representational Nature of Language*, ed. John Stewart (Albany: SUNY Press, 1996), pp. 9–63; see also Stewart, *Language as Articulate Contact*. A similar argument is made by Pierre Bourdieu, *Language and Symbol Power* (Cambridge, MA: Harvard University Press, 1991).

10. The tendency in semiotics to atomize and analyze sign systems is described and critiqued by Stewart, "The Symbol Model."

11. The tool assumption is described and critiqued by Stewart, "The Symbol Model."

12. Leeds-Hurwitz, *Semiotics and Communication*, pp. 3–21. See also, Umberto Eco, *A Theory of Semiotics* (Bloomington: Indiana University Press, 1976), p. 9; and Thomas Sebeok, "The Doctrine of Sign," in *Frontiers in Semiotics*, ed. J. Deely, B. Williams, and F. E. Kruse (Bloomington: Indiana University Press, 1986), p. 36.

13. Donald G. Ellis, "Fixing Communicative Meaning: A Coherentist Theory," *Communication Research* 22 (1995): 515–544.

14. Sandra E. Moriarty, "Abduction: A Theory of Visual Interpretation," *Communication Theory* 6 (1996): 167–187.

15. Donald G. Ellis, *From Language to Communication* (Mahwah, NJ: Lawrence Erlbaum, 1999).

16. For a good recent overview of these areas, see James A. Anderson, *Communication Theory: Epistemological Foundations* (New York: Guilford, 1996).

17. Maurice Merleau-Ponty, *The Phenomenology of Perception*, trans. C. Smith (London: Routledge & Kegan Paul, 1974), p. viii. For an excellent general discussion of phenomenology, see also Michael J. Hyde, "Transcendental Philosophy and Human Communication," in *Interpersonal Communication*, ed. J. J. Pilotta (Washington, DC: Center for Advanced Research in Phenomenology, 1982), pp. 15–34.

18. Richard E. Palmer, *Hermeneutics: Interpretation Theory in Schleiermacher, Dilthey, Heidegger, and Gadamer* (Evanston, IL: Northwestern University Press, 1969), p. 128.

19. Stanley Deetz, "Words Without Things: Toward a Social Phenomenology of Language," *Quarterly Journal of Speech* 59 (1973): 40–51.

20. Edmund Husserl, *Ideas: General Introduction to Pure Phenomenology*, trans. W. R. B. Gibson (New York: Collier, 1962); and Edmund Husserl, *Phenomenology and the Crisis of Philosophy*, trans. Q. Lauer (New York: Harper & Row, 1965). For a brief summary of Husserl's ideas, see Zygmunt Bauman, *Hermeneutics and Social Science* (New York: Columbia University Press, 1978).

21. Merleau-Ponty's most important work is *Phenomenology of Perception* (New York: Humanities, 1962), original published in 1945 in Paris. See also Richard L. Lanigan, *Phenomenology of Communication: Merleau-Ponty's Thematics in Communicology and Semiology* (Pittsburgh: Duquesne University Press, 1988); Remy C. Kwant, *The Phenomenological Philosophy of Merleau-Ponty* (Pittsburgh: Duquesne University Press, 1963); Samuel B. Mallin, *Merleau-Ponty's Philosophy* (New Haven, CT: Yale University Press, 1979); Wayne Froman, *Merleau-Ponty: Language and the Act of Speech* (Lewisburg, PA: Bucknell University Press, 1982).

22. Martin Heidegger, *Being and Time*, trans. J. Macquarrie and E. Robinson (New York: Harper & Row, 1962); *On the Way to Language*, trans. P. Hertz (New York: Harper & Row, 1971); *An Introduction to Metaphysics*, trans. R. Manheim (New Haven, CT: Yale University Press, 1959). For secondary treatments, see Bauman, *Hermeneutics and Social Science*, pp. 148–171; Palmer, *Hermeneutics: Interpretation Theory*, pp. 124–161; Deetz, "Words"; John Stewart, "One Philosophical Dimension of Social Approaches to Interpersonal Communication," *Communication Theory* 2 (1992): 337–347.

23. Heidegger, *Introduction*, p. 13.

24. Bauman, *Hermeneutics and Social Science*.

25. For excellent discussions of general system theory and other system approaches, see Chang-Gen Bahg, "Major Systems Theories Throughout the World," *Behavioral Science* 35 (1990): 79–107. For an excellent brief history of system theory, see Armand Mattelart and Michèle Mattelart, *Theories of Communication: A Short Introduction* (London: Sage, 1998), pp. 43–55.

26. A. D. Hall and R. E. Fagen, "Definition of a System," in *Modern Systems Research for the Behavioral Scientist,* ed. W. Buckley (Chicago: Aldine, 1968), pp. 81–92.

27. Considerable research has been done over the years on family communication. See, for example, Arthur P. Bochner and Eric M. Eisenberg, "Family Process: System Perspectives," in *Handbook of Communication Science,* ed. Charles R. Berger and Steven H. Chaffee (Newbury Park, CA: Sage, 1987), pp. 540–563.

28. Rapoport, "Foreword"; Hall and Fagen, "Definition of a System."

29. For a sophisticated discussion of the various ways in which people can think about interdependence in systems, see Magoroh Maruyama's theory of mindscapes, summarized in *Mindscapes: The Epistemology of Magoroh Maruyama,* eds. Michael T. Caley and Daiyo Sawada (Amsterdam: Gordon and Breach, 1994).

30. Hall and Fagen, "Definition of a System"; Buckley, "Adaptive System"; and Arthur Koestler, *The Ghost in the Machine* (New York: Macmillan, 1967).

31. For excellent discussions of hierarchy, see Koestler, *The Ghost in the Machine*; W. Ross Ashby, "Principles of the Self-Organizing System," in *Principles of Self-Organization,* eds. H. von Foerster and G. Zopf (New York: Pergamon, 1962), pp. 255–278.

32. Magoroh Maruyama, "The Second Cybernetics: Deviation-Amplifying Mutual Causal Processes," *American Scientist* 51 (1963): 164–179. See also Caley and Sawada, *Mindscapes,* pp. 99–109.

33. Caley and Sawada, *Mindscapes,* p. 311.

34. Norbert Wiener, *The Human Use of Human Beings: Cybernetics in Society* (Boston: Houghton Mifflin, 1954), pp. 49–50.

35. See, for example, Klaus Krippendorff, "Cybernetics," in *International Encyclopedia of Communications,* vol. 1, ed. Erik Barnouw and others (New York: Oxford University Press, 1989), pp. 443–446.

36. For a biographical sketch of von Bertalanffy, see "Ludwig von Bertalanffy," *General Systems* 17 (1972): 219–228. For a good general summary of GST, see Joanna Macy, *Mutual Causality in Buddhism and General System Theory* (Albany: SUNY Press, 1991), pp. 69–89.

37. For an example of formalized GST, see Masanao Toda and Emir H. Shuford, "Logic of Systems: Introduction to a Formal Theory of Structure," *General Systems* 10 (1965): 3–27.

38. Heinz von Foerster, *Observing Systems: Selected Papers of Heinz von Foerster* (Seaside, CA: Intersystems, 1981).

39. Stephen W. Littlejohn, "An Overview of the Contributions to Human Communication Theory from other Disciplines," in *Human Communication Theory: Comparative Essays,* ed. Frank E. X. Dance (Cambridge, MA: Harper & Row, 1982), pp. 243–285.

40. John W. Lannamann, "Deconstructing the Person and Changing the Subject of Interpersonal Studies," *Communication Theory* 2 (1992): 139–148; "Interpersonal Communication Research as Ideological Practice," *Communication Theory* 1 (1991): 179–203.

41. See, for example, Robert N. Bellah and others, *Habits of the Heart* (Berkeley: University of California Press, 1985); Alistair MacIntyre, *After Virtue* (Notre Dame, IN: University of Notre Dame Press, 1984); Floyd W. Matson, *The Idea of Man* (New York: Delacorte, 1976). A critique of the assumptions of the individual mind is presented in Rom Harré, "Language Games and Texts of Identity," in *Texts of Identity,* ed. John Shotter and Kenneth Gergen (London: Sage, 1989), pp. 20–35.

42. Dean E. Hewes and Sally Planalp, "The Individual's Place in Communication Science," in *Handbook of Communication Science,* ed. Charles R. Berger and Steven H. Chaffee (Newbury Park, CA: Sage, 1987), pp. 146–183.

43. For an example of this point of view, see John O. Greene, "Action Assembly Theory: Metatheoretical Commitments, Theoretical Propositions, and Empirical Applications," in *Rethinking Communication: Paradigm Exemplars,* ed. Brenda Dervin, Lawrence Grossberg, Barbara O'Keefe, and Ella Wartella (Newbury Park, CA: Sage, 1989), pp. 117–128.

44. Sally Planalp and Dean E. Hewes, "A Cognitive Approach to Communication Theory: *Cogito Ergo Dico?*" in *Communication Yearbook 5,* ed. Michael Burgoon (New Brunswick: Transaction Books, 1982), pp. 49–77.

45. Michael A. Shapiro, Mark A. Hamilton, Annie Lang, and Noshir S. Contractor, "Information Systems Division: Intrapersonal Meaning, Attitude, and Social Systems," in *Communication Yearbook 24,* ed. William B. Gudykunst (Thousand Oaks, CA: Sage Publications, 2001), pp. 17–50.

46. Michael J. Beatty and James C. McCroskey, *The Biology of Communication; A Communibiological Perspective* (Cresskill, NJ: Hampton Press, 2001).

47. Beatty and McCroskey, *The Biology of Communication.*

48. For a good general discussion of this school of thought, see Wendy Leeds-Hurwitz, ed., *Social Approaches to Communication* (New York: Guilford, 1995). See also the forum "Social Approaches to Interpersonal Communication," *Communication Theory* 2 (1992): 131–172, 329–359. Much of this tradition is based on the work of American pragmatism, especially the work of John Dewey and George Herbert Mead. For a philosophical discussion, see Vernon Cronen and Peter Lang, "Language and

Action: Wittgenstein and Dewey in the Practice of Therapy and Consultation," *Human Systems: The Journal of Systemic Consultation and Management*, 5 (1994): 4–43. For a discussion of the ideas of Wittgenstein in regard to the social construction of meaning, see John Shotter, "Before Theory and After Representationalism: Understanding Meaning 'From Within' a Dialogue Process," in *Beyond the Symbol Model: Reflections on the Representational Nature of Language*, ed. John Stewart (Albany: SUNY Press, 1996), pp. 103–134.

49. For a good description of the intellectual traditions and various versions of constructionism, see W. Barnett Pearce, "A Sailing Guide for Social Constructionists," in *Social Approaches to Communication*, ed. Wendy Leeds-Hurwitz (New York: Guilford, 1995), pp. 88–113; Klaus Krippendorff, "The Past of Communication's Hoped-For Future," *Journal of Communication* 43 (1993): 34–44; W. Barnett Pearce, "A 'Camper's Guide' to Constructionisms," *Human Systems: The Journal of Systemic Consultation and Management* 3 (1992): 139–161.

50. Barbara Ballis Lal, "Symbolic Interaction Theories," *American Behavioral Scientist* 38 (1995): 421–441. See also Joel M. Charon, *Symbolic Interactionism: An Introduction, an Interpretation, an Integration* (Englewood Cliffs, NJ: Prentice-Hall, 1992); Larry T. Reynolds, *Interactionism: Exposition and Critique* (Dix Hills, NY: General Hall, 1990); Jerome G. Manis and Bernard N. Meltzer, ed., *Symbolic Interaction* (Boston: Allyn & Bacon, 1978). For continuing coverage of SI, see the ongoing editions of the journal *Studies in Symbolic Interaction*.

51. Mead's primary work in symbolic interactionism is *Mind, Self, and Society* (Chicago: University of Chicago Press, 1934). See also Herbert Blumer, *Symbolic Interactionism: Perspective and Method* (Englewood Cliffs: NJ: Prentice-Hall, 1969).

52. Gary Alan Fine, "The Sad Demise, Mysterious Disappearance, and Glorious Triumph of Symbolic Interactionism," *Annual Review of Sociology* 19 (1993): 61–87.

53. Peter L. Berger and Thomas Luckmann, *The Social Construction of Reality: A Treatise in the Sociology of Knowledge* (New York: Doubleday, 1966). See also Alfred Schutz, *The Phenomenology of the Social World*, trans. G. Walsh and F. Lehnert (Evanston, IL: Northwestern University Press, 1967). The name *social constructionism* was later given by Kenneth J. Gergen, "The Social Constructionist Movement in Modern Psychology," *American Psychologist* 40 (1985): 266–275.

54. Gillian Sankoff, *The Social Life of Language* (Philadelphia: University of Pennsylvania Press, 1980), p. xvii.

55. Wittgenstein's best-known early work was *Tractatus Logico-Philosophicus* (London: Routledge & Kegan Paul, 1922); his later work, which forms the foundation for ordinary language philosophy, is *Philosophical Investigations* (Oxford: Basil Blackwell, 1953). See also the excellent summary by David Silverman and Brian Torode, *The Material Word: Some Theories of Language and Its Limits* (London: Routledge & Kegan Paul, 1980); Richard Buttny, "The Ascription of Meaning: A Wittgensteinian Perspective," *Quarterly Journal of Speech* 72 (1986): 261–273; and Allan Janik and Stephen Toulmin, *Wittgenstein's Vienna* (New York: Simon & Schuster, 1973).

56. J. L. Austin, *How to Do Things with Words* (Cambridge, MA: Harvard University Press, 1962). See also Jonathan Potter and Margaret Wetherell, *Discourse and Social Psychology: Beyond Attitudes and Behavior* (London: Sage, 1987), pp. 14–18.

57. See Michael Agar, *Speaking of Ethnography* (Beverly Hills, CA: Sage, 1986); and Paul Atkinson, *Understanding Ethnographic Texts* (Newbury Park, CA: Sage, 1992).

58. Ethnomethodology is most often associated with its originator, sociologist Harold Garfinkel; see his *Studies in Ethnomethodology* (Englewood Cliffs, NJ: Prentice-Hall, 1967). For a brief description of this tradition, see Potter and Wetherell, *Discourse and Social Psychology*, pp. 18–23. See also Graham Button, ed., *Ethnomethodology and the Human Sciences* (Cambridge, UK: Cambridge University Press, 1991).

59. Brian Fay, *Social Theory and Political Practice* (London: Allen & Unwin, 1975), p. 94.

60. See Philip Wander, "Review Essay: Marxism, Post-Colonialism, and Rhetoric of Contextualism," *Quarterly Journal of Speech*, 82 (November 1996): 419.

61. Della Pollock and J. Robert Cox, "Historicizing 'Reason': Critical Theory, Practice, and Postmodernity," *Communication Monographs* 58 (1991): 171.

62. This characteristic of critical theory is discussed by Nancy Fraser, *Unruly Practices: Power, Discourse, and Gender in Contemporary Social Theory* (Minneapolis: University of Minnesota Press, 1989), p. 113.

63. See, for example, Teun van Dijk, "Discourse Semantics and Ideology," *Discourse and Society* 6 (1995): 243–289; Teun van Dijk, "Principles of Critical Discourse Analysis," *Discourse and Society* 4 (1993): 249–283.

64. For a discussion of the problems associated with separating communication as a focus, see Milton Mueller, "Why Communications Policy Is Passing 'Mass Communication' By: Political Economy as the Missing Link," *Critical Studies in Mass Communication* 12 (1995): 455–472.

65. For a brief overview of the movement, see Everett M. Rogers, *A History of Communication Study: A Biographical Approach* (New York: Free Press, 1994), pp. 102–128; Tom Bottomore and Armand

Mattelart, "Marxist Theories of Communication," in *International Encyclopedia of Communications*, vol. 2, ed. Erik Barnouw and others (New York: Oxford University Press, 1989), pp. 476–483. For coverage of a variety of Marxist-based ideas, see Cary Nelson and Lawrence Grossberg, eds., *Marxism and the Interpretation of Culture* (Urbana: University of Illinois Press, 1988).

66. Karl Marx's best-known works are *The Communist Manifesto* (London: Reeves, 1888) and *Capital* (Chicago: Kerr, 1909).

67. For a discussion of capitalist oppression as the basis for critical theory, see Graham Murdock, "Across the Great Divide: Cultural Analysis and the Condition of Democracy," *Critical Studies in Mass Communication* 12 (1995): 89–95.

68. For a brief historical perspective, see Thomas B. Farrell and James A. Aune, "Critical Theory and Communication: A Selective Literature Review," *Quarterly Journal of Speech* 65 (1979): 93–120. See also Andrew Arato and Eike Gebhardt, eds., *The Essential Frankfurt School Reader* (New York: Continuum, 1982).

69. Michael Huspek, "Toward Normative Theories of Communication with Reference to the Frankfurt School: An Introduction," *Communication Theory* 7 (1997): 265–276. See also Douglas Kellner, "Media Communications vs. Cultural Studies: Overcoming the Divide," *Communication Theory* 5 (1995): 162–177.

70. The important works of Habermas include *Postmetaphysical Thinking: Philosophical Essays*, trans. William Mark Hohengarten (Cambridge, MA: MIT Press, 1992); *Knowledge and Human Interests*, trans. J. J. Shapiro (Boston: Beacon, 1971); *Legitimation Crisis*, trans. T. McCarthy (Boston: Beacon, 1975); *Communication and the Evolution of Society*, trans. Thomas McCarthy (Boston: Beacon, 1979); *The Theory of Communicative Action, Volume 1: Reason and the Rationalization of Society*, trans. T. McCarthy (Boston: Beacon, 1984); and *The Theory of Communicative Action, Volume 2: Lifeworld and System*, trans. Thomas McCarthy (Boston: Beacon, 1987). For critical commentary, see the special issue of *Communication Theory* 7 (November 1997). Excellent secondary summaries can be found in Thomas B. Farrell, *Norms of Rhetorical Culture* (New Haven, CT: Yale University Press, 1993); Sonja K. Foss, Karen A. Foss, and Robert Trapp, *Contemporary Perspectives on Rhetoric*, 3rd ed. (Prospect Heights, IL: Waveland, 2002), pp. 233–264; Sue Curry Jansen, "Power and Knowledge: Toward a New Critical Synthesis," *Journal of Communication* 33 (1983): 342–354; Richard L. Lanigan, *Phenomenology of Communication: Merleau-Ponty's Thematics in Communicology and Semiology* (Pittsburgh: Duquesne University Press, 1988), pp. 75–99; and Dennis K. Mumby, *Communication and Power in Organizations: Discourse, Ideology, and Domination* (Norwood, NJ: Ablex, 1988), pp. 23–54.

71. David Macey, *The Penguin Dictionary of Critical Theory* (London: Penguin Books, 2000), p. 306.

72. See, for example, Jean-François Lyotard, *The Postmodern Condition: A Report on Knowledge* (Manchester, UK: Manchester University Press, 1984). For a complete listing and overview of Baudrillard's work, see Foss, Foss, and Trapp, *Contemporary Perspectives on Rhetoric*, 3rd ed., pp. 299–338.

73. Stuart Hall, "Introduction," *Working Papers in Cultural Studies* 1 (1971), cited in Macey, p. 77.

74. Roland Barthes, cited in Macey, p. 309.

75. Bill Ashcroft, Gaareth Griffiths, and Helen Tiffin, eds., *The Post-Colonial Studies Reader* (London: Routledge, 1995), cited in Macey, p. 304.

76. Raka Shome and Radha S. Hegde, "Postcolonial Approaches to Communication: Charting the Terrain, Engaging the Intersections," *Communication Theory* 12 (August 2002): 250. For more on postcolonial theory, see also Raka Shome, "Postcolonial Interventions in the Rhetorical Canon: An 'Other' View," *Communication Theory* 6 (1996): 40–59; Saba Mahmood, "Cultural Studies and Ethnic Absolutism: Comments on Stuart Hall's 'Culture, Community, and Nation,'" *Cultural Studies* 10 (1996): 1–11. See also Anandam P. Kavoori, "Getting Past the Latest 'Post': Assessing the Term 'Post-Colonial,'" *Critical Studies in Mass Communication* 15 (1998): 195–202; Raka Shome, "Caught in the Term 'Post-Colonial': Why the 'Post-Colonial' Still Matters," *Critical Studies in Mass Communication* 15 (1998): 203–212.

77. Shome and Hegde, 252.

78. Feminist theory is discussed in numerous sources. See, for example, Karen A. Foss, Sonja K. Foss, and Cindy L. Griffin, *Feminist Rhetorical Theories* (Thousand Oaks, CA: Sage, 1999); Ramona R. Rush and Autumn Grubb-Swetman, "Feminist Approaches," in *An Integrated Approach to Communication Theory and Research*, ed. Michael B. Salwen and Don W. Stacks (Mahwah, NJ: Erlbaum, 1996), pp. 497–518; Lisa McLaughlin, "Feminist Communication Scholarship and 'The Woman Question' in the Academy," *Communication Theory* 5 (1995): 144–161; Karen A. Foss and Sonja K. Foss, "Personal Experience as Evidence in Feminist Scholarship," *Western Journal of Communication* 58 (1994): 39–43; Lana F. Rakow, ed., *Women Making Meaning: New Feminist Directions in Communication* (New York: Routledge, 1992); Cheris Kramarae, "Feminist Theories of Communication," in *International Encyclopedia of Communications*, vol. 2, eds. Erik Barnouw and others (New York: Oxford University Press, 1989), pp. 157–160; and Brenda Dervin, "The Potential Contribution of Feminist Scholarship to the Field of Communication," *Journal of Communication* 37 (1987): 107–120.

79. Linda Aldoory and Elizabeth L. Toth, "The Complexities of Feminism in Communication Scholarship Today," in *Communication Yearbook 24*, ed. William B. Gudykunst (Thousand Oaks, CA: Sage, 2001): 345–361.
80. Donald C. Bryant, "Rhetoric: Its Functions and Its Scope," *Quarterly Journal of Speech*, 39 (December 1953): 401–424. Reprinted in Douglas Ehninger, *Contemporary Rhetoric: A Reader's Coursebook* (Glenview, IA: Scott, Foresman, 1972), p. 26.
81. For a contemporary updating of the classical canons, see Nancy L. Harper, *Human Communication Theory: The History of a Paradigm* (Rochelle Park, NJ: Hayden, 1979).
82. Hugh C. Dick, ed., *Selected Writings of Francis Bacon* (New York: Modern Library, 1955), p. x.
83. For sources on practical rhetorics, see Cheryl Glenn, *Rhetoric Retold: Regendering the Tradition from Antiquity Through the Renaissance* (Carbondale: Southern Illinois University Press, 1997); and Laura Gray-Rosendale and Sibylle Gruber, *Alternative Rhetorics: Challenges to the Rhetorical Tradition* (Albany: State University of New York Press, 2001).
84. Molefi Asante has been primarily responsible for the development of Afrocentricity in the rhetorical tradition. For a summary of Asiacentricity, see Yoshitaka Miike, "Theorizing Culture and Communication in the Asian Context: An Assumptive Foundation," *Intercultural Communication Studies* 11 (2002): 1–21.
85. For an example of rhetorics from other cultures, see George A. Kennedy, *Comparative Rhetoric: An Historical and Cross-Cultural Introduction* (New York: Oxford University Press, 1998).

CHAPTER

THE COMMUNICATOR

As you move through life communicating in a variety of situations with many people, one constant is always there: You bring yourself to the encounter. Whether you are watching television, talking to a friend, arguing with your boss, working on a radio production, or designing a PR campaign, you most often look at the situation from your own perspective as a communicator. In Western society, the individual assumes tremendous importance as the "key player" in social life. It is natural, then, for us to start with the individual as we begin to think about communication theories. Core questions are these: Who am I as a communicator? What resources enable me to communicate? How am I different from other communicators? How do other people see my behavior? How do I change from one situation to another?

Given the centrality of the individual in communication, it is appropriate to begin our survey of communication theories by looking at the communicator as a person, a topic that has captured the attention of a significant number of researchers and theorists in our field. In this chapter, we look at several traditions of theorizing about the individual communicator. The most prominent of these has been the sociopsychological, but other traditions have provided insights as well, including the cybernetic, sociocultural, and critical traditions.

We notice almost immediately how one person is different from others. In order to do this, we must also notice how a single person's behavior tends to have a certain character, no matter what situation he or she is in. One of the goals of psychology has

Topics Addressed	Sociopsychological Theories	Cybernetic Theories	Sociocultural Theories	Critical Theories
Traits	Conversational narcissism Argumentativeness Social and communicative anxiety Trait-factor models Traits, temperament, and biology			
Cognition and information processing	Attribution theory Social judgment theory Elaboration likelihood theory	Information-integration theory • Expectancy-value theory • Theory of reasoned action Consistency theories • Theory of cognitive dissonance • Beliefs, attitudes, and values Problematic integration theory		
Self			Symbolic interactionism Social construction of self Social construction of emotion Presentational self	
Identity				Standpoint theory Identity as constructed and performed Queer theory

been to identify the traits on which people vary, and many of these have been identified and measured. You probably have taken one or two personality tests over the years. Communication theorists are also interested in individual differences and have developed a number of tests to find out how you might score on communication traits such as conversational narcissism, argumentativeness, and communication anxiety.

How do you think you are as a communicator? What is your style? What kinds of communication do you like, and what do you avoid? What kinds of people are similar to you, and what kinds of people are different? If these kinds of questions intrigue you, you will enjoy communication trait theories.

More interesting for many researchers is what lies behind behavior. In other words, these are questions about what drives our behavior and the mental processes we use to make decisions about what to say and how to react in communication situations. We get information on many subjects every day. Some of this information is factual, some is loaded with values and opinions, some of it urges action, and some of this information provides explanations for various kinds of things. How do you process this information? What do you do with it? How does it fit into your mental maps and the other information you have absorbed over the years? These are theoretical questions, because, according to several theories in this chapter, you really are not conscious of the ways in which information impacts and is organized into your cognitive system. In this chapter, you will have the opportunity to learn theories that can help you explore these themes.

The theories that address traits and information processing are based heavily in psychology and have a psychological orientation, but when you think about yourself, you soon realize that much of who you are is shaped by interaction in social groups and consists of your culture, your history as a person, and the meanings you have created with other people over a lifetime of interaction. Your identity is shaped very much by the groups of which you have been a member. Although many Western societies characterize individuals in terms of traits and differences, this is only part of the story. Indeed, your identity depends just as much on what you share with others. If you ask some people who they are, they will answer with a list of traits; but others will answer by telling you about their families, social groups, racial identification, geographical location, gender, sexual orientation, or any number of socially created identification markers.

This difference—between psychological constructs and social ones—creates a dividing point between sociopsychological and sociocultural theories of the communicator. The chapter map on page 63 outlines the theories we will cover here.

THE SOCIOPSYCHOLOGICAL TRADITION

The sociopsychological tradition in communication theory clearly has had the most powerful effect on how we think of communicators as individuals. This is certainly understandable when we realize that most of this work either comes from or is modeled on research in psychology, which is the study of human behavior. The drive behind the sociopsychological tradition is to understand how and why individual human beings behave the way they do, and in communication, the work of this tradition tries to answer the question, "What predicts how individual communicators will think and act in communication situations?" Here we will look at several theories of communication based in this tradition. Two types of theory within this tradition have been important—trait theory and cognitive theory.

Traits

A trait is a distinguishing quality or characteristic; it is an individual's relatively consistent way of thinking, feeling, and behaving across situations. Traits are often used to predict behavior, so it makes sense organizationally to include trait and behavior theories in the same section in this book. Perhaps the most commonly held belief among psychology researchers today is that your behavior is determined by a combination of traits and situational factors. How you communicate at any given moment depends on your traits as an individual and the situation in which you find yourself.[1]

Numerous traits have been studied in communication research, and we cannot cover them all here.[2] As examples, we feature three interesting and commonly discussed traits from the communication literature—conversational narcissism, argumentativeness, and social and communicative anxiety. We then discuss the trait-factors approach in which groups of traits are considered together and discuss studies that extend trait research to temperament and biology.

Conversational Narcissism. Narcissism—meaning self-love—has been discussed in psychology for many years. Applying this concept to communication, Anita Vangelisti, Mark Knapp, and John Daly have identified a communication trait that they call *conversational narcissism*, or the tendency to be self-absorbed in conversation.[3] Conversational narcissists tend to inflate their self-importance by such behaviors as "one-upping" or boasting. They tend to want to control the flow of conversation, especially to provide opportunities for them to talk about themselves. They are known to use nonverbal, exhibitionist behaviors such as exaggerated gestures in order to maintain conversational control, and they tend to be insensitive or nonresponsive to others. This is a variable, so you could rank high, medium, or low on this trait.

Argumentativeness. Argumentativeness is a second trait that has been studied extensively in communication. It is the tendency to engage in conversations about controversial topics, to support your own point of view, and to refute opposing beliefs.[4] Dominic Infante and his colleagues, who have been primarily responsible for developing this concept, believe that argumentativeness can improve learning, help people see others' points of view, enhance credibility, and build communication skills. Argumentative individuals are by definition assertive, although not all assertive people are argumentative. In other words, you need to be somewhat forward in order to put forth arguments, but it is entirely possible to be assertive without arguing your point. To help sort these concepts out, these authors distinguish between two clusters of variables—argumentativeness, which is a positive trait, and verbal aggressiveness and hostility, which are negative ones. Indeed, knowing how to argue properly may be a solution to otherwise hurtful aggressive tendencies.

As a case in point, Infante and two colleagues studied husbands and wives in violent relationships and discovered that violent marriages are characterized by higher verbal aggressiveness and lower argumentativeness than are non-violent ones.[5] It seems that many nonviolent spouses deal with their problems by arguing constructively, whereas violent spouses may be unable to solve their differences in this way.

Social and Communicative Anxiety. Many people are afraid of communication, and there has been much research about communication anxiety and apprehension. Within the communication field, the best-known work is that of James McCroskey and his colleagues on *communication apprehension*.[6] Although everyone has occasional stage fright, *trait CA* is an enduring tendency to be apprehensive about communication in a variety of settings. Normal apprehension is not a problem, but pathological CA, in which an individual suffers persistent and extreme fear of communication, certainly is. Abnormally high CA creates serious personal problems, including extreme discomfort and avoidance of communication to the point of preventing productive and satisfying participation in society.

Communication apprehension is part of a family of concepts including, for example, social avoidance, social anxiety, interaction anxiety, and shyness. As a group these have been called *social and communicative anxiety*. In a huge survey of literature and analysis of this literature, Miles Patterson and Vicki Ritts outlined several parameters.[7]

In general, Patterson and Ritts have found that social and communicative anxiety has *physiological* aspects such as heart rate and blushing, *behavioral* manifestations such as avoidance and self-protection, and *cognitive* dimensions such as self-focus and negative thoughts. Interestingly, cognitive correlates were found to be the strongest of the three, which may mean that social and communicative anxiety has mostly to do with how we think about ourselves in regard to communication situations. Negative thinking can lead to anxious self-preoccupation that keeps a person from considering all of the information and cues in the environment, disrupts normal information processing, and leads to reinforcing behaviors such as withdrawal.

Trait-Factor Models. In psychology and communication, many traits have been investigated. At some point, researchers began to realize that listing one trait after another is not very helpful and so began to work on a more parsimonious way of understanding traits. In response to this need, psychologists have developed various trait-factor models, sometimes called *super traits*.[8] These models consist of a small set of general traits that can explain many other traits and individual differences. One of the most popular trait-factor models is the commonly known *five-factor model*, described by Digman.[9]

The five factors include (1) *neuroticism*, or the tendency to feel negative emotions and distress; (2) *extraversion*, or the tendency to like groups, be assertive, and think optimistically; (3) *openness*, or the tendency to be reflective, have imagination, pay attention to inner feelings, and be an independent thinker; (4) *agreeableness*, or the tendency to like and be sympathetic toward others, to be eager to help other people, and to avoid antagonism; and (5) *conscientiousness*, or the tendency to be self-disciplined, to resist impulses, be well organized, and see tasks to completion.

The task of the communication-trait theorist is to use models such as this to help explain various communication behaviors. For example, conversational narcissism might be explained as a combination of something like medium neuroticism, high extraversion, low openness, low agreeableness, and high conscientiousness. Argumentativeness might be understood as a combination of low neuroticism, high extraversion, low openness, low agreeableness, and high conscientiousness. Communication anxiety could include high neuroticism, low extraversion, low openness, low agreeableness, and low conscientiousness.

Seeing human differences in terms of a small set of factors has made researchers wonder about the role of biology and heredity in explaining behavior. Indeed, within communication, the trait-factors approach has led to serious investigation of the role of biology in communication.

Traits, Temperament, and Biology.   For a number of years, psychologists have been exploring the biological bases of human behavior, and traits have been increasingly explained in terms of genetic predisposition. Recently, James McCroskey and Michael Beatty have brought this line of work into the communication field.[10] Generally, this work is predicated on the idea that traits are predispositions of temperament rooted in genetically determined neurobiological structures, or brain activity. This is very important because brain functioning lies behind all psychological processes, including how we think, feel, and behave. According to McCroskey and Beatty, how we experience the world is very much a matter of what is happening in our brain, and that in turn is largely genetically determined. The impact of the environment, or learning, is not very large according to this theory, so we can expect that individual differences in how people communicate can be explained biologically. Consistent with the trait-factors approach, McCroskey and Beatty point to work in psychology suggesting that all traits can be reduced to just a few dimensions that are about 80 percent determined by genetics.[11] Using psychologist H. J. Eysenck's "Big Three" model, these theorists posit that communication behavior manifests various combinations of three factors, including (1) extraversion, or outward focus; (2) neuroticism, or anxiety; and (3) psychotocism, or lack of self-control.

McCroskey and Beatty apply the communibiological paradigm to their own work in communication apprehension, calling this trait a form of "neurotic introversion," which is a particular type of temperament. After years of exploring an explanation for this trait, they are now convinced that the cause of high trait CA is biological. This is a retreat from the generally accepted thesis held by many researchers—including McCroskey himself at an earlier time—that fear of communication is learned. From a bio-logical perspective, temperamentally based traits are caused by activity deep in the brain.

The limbic system of the brain controls emotion, and our emotional differences often relate to these brain differences. The more sensitive your limbic system, the more anxiety you may experience. Stimuli in the environment are processed through a part of your brain known as the behavioral inhibition system (BIS). Negative stimuli cause an arousal of the BIS, which in turn activates your limbic system. When your BIS is stimulated, you tend to pay more attention to threats. Thus, people who have an overactive BIS will be more prone to anxiety and fear than individuals with a less active one.

In communication apprehension, something has to happen to cause communication to be viewed as a very aversive stimulus. This involves yet another part of your brain, the behavioral activation system (BAS). Because it is associated with rewards, this system seems to stimulate motivation and bring about action. Even apprehensive persons are at least occasionally motivated to communicate because of perceived rewards. For example, despite high CA, you might go ahead and give a presentation in a speech class because you want a good grade. In this case the BAS would enable you to do something potentially fearful. The problem for highly apprehensive individuals is that they will experience extreme fear in the process of giving the speech, making the overall experience unpleasant. They will remember this and continue to associate the communication experience with negative stimuli.

Along with whatever neurochemical processes may be going on, you also bring cognitive processes—your thoughts—to bear on any given communication situation. In the next section, we look at theories that specifically address this concern.

Cognition and Information Processing

If trait theories give you some labels to describe yourself and other communicators, information processing theories go behind the scenes to explain how you think, how you organize and store information, and how cognition helps shape your behavior. Several cognitive theories are presented here. These include attribution theory, social judgment theory, and elaboration likelihood theory.

Attribution Theory. Attribution theory paints an interesting picture of human beings. Starting with the notion that individuals try to understand their own behavior and that of others, this line of work has focused on how individuals actually behave. As communicators, we seem to need to figure out why we act as we do, and we somehow want to be able to explain why others act in certain ways as well.

Attribution theory, then, deals with the ways people infer the causes of behavior. It explains the processes by which you come to understand your own behavior and that of others. Fritz Heider, founder of attribution theory, outlines several kinds of causal attributions that people commonly make.[12] These include situational causes (being affected by the environment), personal effects (influencing things personally), ability (being able to do something), effort (trying to do something), desire (wanting to do it), sentiment (feeling like it), belonging (going along with something), obligation (feeling you ought to), and permission (being permitted to). How many times have you said something to another person and later asked yourself, "Why did I do that?" Likely, your answer sounded something like this: "I couldn't help it; I had to say that," or "I wanted to," or "I felt like it," or "I wanted to fit in," or "I was obligated to."

Regardless of how you might explain what you said, it would be impossible from outside to find a one-to-one relationship between your statement and your explanation for it. In other words, you might explain why you said a certain thing in any number of ways. A variety of behaviors may be perceived as stemming from a single cause, or, conversely, one behavior may be thought to arise from several causes. When you are communicating, then, you often need to resolve such ambiguities, and attribution theory helps you understand how you do so.

For example, let's say you are the supervisor in a small company. You notice that one of your employees seems particularly industrious all of a sudden. You will probably want to figure out why. You might think that the workload has gone way up, which would be attributing it to the environment. Or you might think that the employee is angling for a raise. Or maybe he is ingratiating himself to you because he hopes to get a managerial slot someday. Or maybe he is bored and needs to keep himself busy. Naturally, you would make use of the context to help you determine the cause of your employee's behavior. So in assessing your employee's hard work, you also can get additional information by observing him at work repeatedly over time: You can observe when he works hard and when he does not.

Causal perception is mediated further by variables in your own psychological makeup. You always assign meaning to what you observe, and this meaning is crucial to what you "see." Meanings help you integrate your perceptions and organize your observations into patterns that help you make sense of the world. Because of a need for consistency, you define things in such a way that helps you make sense of them as a coherent whole. For example, if you think that you have a great company, you may have a tendency to attribute your employee's hard work to loyalty.

The way you resolve ambiguities and establish a consistent pattern may be different from the way other people do so. Heider calls individual patterns of perception *perceptual styles*. He recognizes that any state of affairs may give rise to a number of interpretations, each of which seems true to the person involved, depending upon their style of attribution. For example, maybe you are essentially optimistic and tend to attribute behavior to good intentions. If this were the case, you probably would feel that your employee's behavior came from his or her desire for self-improvement.

When we believe someone is doing something on purpose, a whole other dimension of attribution comes into play. If you think someone did something on purpose, you are recognizing two underlying attributes: ability and motivation. Suppose, for example, that an associate of yours fails to show up for a meeting. You figure that she could not make it or didn't try. If she wasn't able, something might have been wrong with her (such as illness), or something else might have prevented her appearance (for example, a flat tire). If she did not try, she either didn't want to (an attribution of intent) or was too lazy (an attribution of exertion). In perception, then, you infer the causes of your associate's behavior according to your overall experience, your meanings, the situational factors, and your own perceptual style.

Another interesting kind of attribution happens when you think that you "ought" to do something. An obligation is seen as an impersonal, objective demand. It can have a tremendous sense of validity because most people would agree with it. For example, you might say, "I ought to go to the dentist," or "I ought to report the theft." But "oughts" do not necessarily correspond with values. Perhaps you dread going to the dentist even though you think you should. Because people want to be consistent, they will balance their obligations and values so that what they want to do is consistent with what they think they should do.[13]

Heider's theory, though influential as the original theory of attribution, is not the only theory in this movement; it has been extended in many ways.[14] Brant Burleson has done research on how attributes play out in real life. Burleson tape-recorded a conversation between two teaching assistants about a student.[15] In this conversation one teacher, Don, complains to his colleague, Bob, that one of his students failed an exam three times. Don is very concerned and explores the reasons for the student's failure. Don and Bob first explore the possibility that the test was too hard, but Don says that the test was not changed from the previous semester and that no one else failed it. They also establish that the student's behavior was consistent over time. Thus, they were able to rule out test difficulty as a cause. They then conclude that the failure must have something to do with the student herself. Either she did not have the ability or she wasn't trying. She completed all assignments

and took the test three times, so she appeared to be trying. By deduction, then, they conclude that she just did not have the ability to pass the test. In the end Don says that he will ask her to drop the class because he doesn't think she can pass the course.

In this example, it looks like Don and Bob are being very logical and systematic in trying to determine the student's problem, but one of the most common research findings is that people are often illogical and biased in their attributions. People are not always objective when making causal inferences about themselves and other people. Rather than weighing all factors, people seem to make quick judgments based on available cues and emotional factors. Research also shows that people's prior judgments are hard to dislodge, no matter how compelling the evidence. Thus, once you make an attribution, you are apt to stick with it.

Yet there is a persistent assumption in attribution theory that people are logical and systematic. How do we reconcile these research findings? Several researchers have adopted the position that people can process information in both logical and illogical ways, depending on circumstances such as motivation. If motivation to promote the self is high, as when we need to save face, there is probably a tendency to be biased in favor of self-serving, situational attributions. If you were late for a date, for example, you would probably make an excuse. On the other hand, when a person is motivated to control the situation, there will probably be a bias toward attributions of personal responsibility. So if your boss gave you a compliment about your work, you would probably think that you were personally responsible for doing so well.

This example illustrates one of the most persistent findings in attribution research: the *fundamental attribution error.* This is the tendency to attribute the cause of events to personal qualities. It is a feeling that people are personally responsible for what happens to them. In general, we seem to be insensitive to many circumstantial factors that cause events when considering others' behavior but are sensitive to circumstances when considering our own behavior. In other words, we tend to blame other people for what happens to them but blame the situation—things beyond our control—for what happens to us. If your roommate fails a test, you are apt to claim that he did not study hard enough, but if you fail the test, you will probably say that the test was too hard. Clearly, social life is filled with evaluations and attributions of all kinds. Let's take a closer look at the process of social judgment.

Social Judgment Theory.   Attribution theory shows us that interpersonal judgment is an important process. Social judgment theory, a classic in social psychology, focuses on how we make judgments about statements we hear. Suppose, for example, that your best friend "drops a bomb" on you by favoring something you absolutely abhor. How will you handle it? What impact will this statement have on your own beliefs? Social judgment theory, based on the work of Muzafer Sherif and his colleagues, tries to predict how you will judge your friend's message, and how this judgment will affect your own belief system.[16]

Sherif was influenced by early physical judgment research, in which people were tested on their ability to judge such things as the weight of an object or the brightness of a light. Thinking that similar processes might explain the judgment of non-physical stimuli, Sherif investigated the ways individuals judge messages.

Here is how the judgment process works. Suppose that you were asked to judge the relative weight of five objects without a scale. On what would you base this judgment? You would need some reference point. A common way of doing this would be to find something that you know has a certain weight—a 10-pound sack of flour, for instance. You would first lift the sack of flour and then judge the weight of the other objects based on the feeling of the bag. The known weight would act as an "anchor," influencing your perception of the others. We make these kinds of physical judgments all the time. We might judge how long something is without a ruler, how late in the day it is based on the light in the room, or how hot it is based on the feeling in the air.

To demonstrate this power of anchors, try a simple experiment. Take three bowls. Fill the first with hot water, the second with cold water, and the third with tepid water. Put one hand in the hot water and the other in the cold water. After a few moments, place both hands in the third, tepid bowl. Your perceptions of the temperature of this water will be different for each hand (even though both hands are now in the same tepid bowl) because each hand came from a different bowl and had a different anchor or reference.

Sherif reasoned that similar processes operate in judging communication messages. This is called *social perception*. In social life, our anchors are in our heads and are based on experience. Since we don't have a sack of flour we can use to judge a message, we have to rely on an internal anchor, or reference point.

In a social judgment experiment, you would be given a large number of statements about some issue. You then would be asked to sort them into groups according to their similarities, using a process called a Q-sort. You could use as many groups as you wished. Then you would put the piles in order from positive to negative. Next you would indicate which piles of statements are acceptable to you personally, which are not acceptable, and which are neutral.

The first pile forms your *latitude of acceptance*—the statements you can agree with; the second your *latitude of rejection*—those you cannot agree with; and the third your *latitude of noncommitment*. This research procedure is just a systematic way of simulating what happens in everyday life. On any issue, there will usually be a range of statements that you accept, another that you are willing to tolerate, and a range that you reject.

A person's latitudes of acceptance and rejection are influenced by a key variable—ego involvement. *Ego involvement* is your sense of the personal relevance of an issue. For example, you may have read much about the depletion of the ozone layer. If you have not yet experienced any personal difficulties because of this problem, it may be unimportant to you, because your ego involvement is low. On the other hand, if you have already been treated for skin cancer or live in the Southern Hemisphere, where the problem is dangerous, the issue would be considerably more ego involving.

Ego involvement makes a great deal of difference in how you respond to messages related to a topic. Although you probably have a more extreme opinion on those topics with which you are ego involved, this is not always the case. You could have a moderate opinion and still be ego involved. This would be the case, for example, if you prided yourself on being a political independent and like to see the arguments on both sides of political issues.

What does social judgment say about communication? First, we know from Sherif's work that individuals judge the favorability of a message based on their own internal anchors and ego involvement. However, this judgment process can involve distortion. On a given issue, such as the ozone hole, a person may distort the message by contrast or assimilation. The *contrast effect* occurs when individuals judge a message to be farther from their own point of view than it actually is, and the *assimilation effect* occurs when people judge the message to be closer to their own point of view than it actually is.

When a message is relatively close to one's own position, that message will be assimilated, whereas more distant messages will be contrasted. These assimilation and contrast effects are heightened by ego involvement. So, for example, if you believe strongly that industry should be regulated to stop chlorofluorocarbon (CFC) emissions, a moderately favorable statement might seem like a strong positive statement because of the assimilation effect, whereas a slightly unfavorable statement might be perceived to be strongly opposed to regulation because of the contrast effect. If you were highly ego involved in the issue, this effect would be even greater.

Another area in which social judgment theory aids our understanding of communication is attitude change. Social judgment theory predicts that messages falling within the latitude of acceptance facilitate attitude change. An argument in favor of a position within the range of acceptance will be somewhat more persuasive than an

argument outside of this range. If you think that no CFC emissions should be allowed as a way to reduce the ozone threat you might be persuaded by a message advocating that some CFC emissions be permitted, provided this position is within your latitude of acceptance.

Furthermore, if you judge a message to lie within the latitude of rejection, attitude change will be reduced or nonexistent. In fact, a *boomerang effect* may occur in which the discrepant message actually increases your position on the issue. Thus, your positive attitude toward CFC regulation would probably not be changed by a message advocating no regulation, assuming it was in your latitude of rejection. In fact, such a message might even make you more firmly favor regulation.

Third, within the latitude of acceptance and noncommitment, the more discrepant the message from your own stand, the greater the expected attitude change. However, once the message hits the latitude of rejection, change is not likely. A statement farther from your own attitude will probably bring about more change than one that is not very far from your position.

Finally, the greater your ego involvement in the issue, the larger the latitude of rejection, the smaller the latitude of noncommitment, and thus the less the expected attitude change. Highly ego-involved persons are hard to persuade. They tend to reject a wider range of statements than people who are not highly ego involved, so if you were highly ego involved in the ozone-depletion problem, you would have a large latitude of rejection and would be persuaded by very few statements divergent from your own.

To illustrate how social judgment works, consider an interesting experiment done by a group of researchers shortly after Oklahoma passed an alcohol prohibition law in the 1950s.[17] The researchers recruited a number of people who were deeply involved in the issue on one side or the other and several who were moderate and not very involved in the issue. They found that those who were highly ego involved and extreme in their opinions had much wider latitudes of rejection than did moderates, and the moderate subjects had much wider latitudes of noncommitment than did those who held extreme opinions. Interestingly, when presented with the same moderate message, the extreme "drys" judged the message to be much more toward the nonprohibition side than did other subjects, and the "wets" judged it to be much more toward the prohibition side than the other subjects. In other words, both extreme groups had a contrast effect. Generally, the attitude change experienced by the moderates after hearing a message on the issue was about twice as great as the attitude change experienced by those who were highly involved in the issue. Clearly, ego involvement is a central concept of social judgment theory. The following theory continues this line of reasoning.

Elaboration Likelihood Theory. As you read about social judgment in the section above, you might have realized that you do not always make conscious judgments about what you hear. You take some things with a grain of salt, while reflecting on other topics very seriously. Sometimes you go along with something almost unconsciously, and other times, you really resist on a highly conscious level. Sometimes, too, you ponder something for a while and make a rather conscious decision to change your opinion.

Social psychologists Richard Petty and John Cacioppo developed elaboration likelihood theory (ELT) to help us understand these differences.[18] ELT is essentially a persuasion theory because it tries to predict when and how you will and will not be persuaded by messages. Elaboration likelihood theory seeks to explain the different ways in which you evaluate the information you receive. Sometimes you evaluate messages in an elaborate way, using critical thinking, and sometimes you do so in a simpler, less critical manner. Sometimes you are thoughtful about arguments and other times you are not.

Elaboration likelihood, then, is the probability that you will evaluate information critically. Elaboration likelihood is a variable, meaning that it can range from little to great. The likelihood of elaboration depends on the way you process a message. There are two routes for processing information—the central route and a peripheral route. Elaboration, or critical thinking, occurs in the *central route*, while the lack of critical thinking occurs in the *peripheral* one. Thus, when you process information through the central route, you actively think about and weigh it against what you already know. When you process information through the peripheral route, you are much less critical.

When you use the central route, you consider arguments carefully; if your attitude changes, it is apt to be a relatively enduring change that will probably affect how you actually behave. On the other hand, if you use the peripheral route, any resulting change is probably temporary and may have less effect on how you act. Keep in mind, however, that because elaboration likelihood is a variable, you will probably use both routes to some extent, depending on the degree of personal relevance.

The amount of critical thinking that you apply to an argument depends on two general factors—your motivation and your ability. When you are highly motivated, you are likely to use central processing, and when motivation is low, peripheral processing is more likely. For example, if you are a typical college student, you probably pay more attention to the campus newspaper's arguments for and against fee increases than you do to its arguments for and against installing new roofing on the student center (unless your family owns the roofing business!).

Motivation consists of at least three things. The first is involvement, or the personal relevance of the topic. The more important the topic is to you personally, the more likely it is that you will think critically about the issues involved. The second factor in motivation is diversity of argument. You will tend to think more about arguments that come from a variety of sources. The reason for this is that when you hear several people talking about an issue, you cannot make snap judgments very easily. Other things being equal, then, where multiple sources and multiple arguments are involved, receivers tend to process the information centrally.

The third factor in motivation is your personal predisposition to enjoy critical thinking. People who enjoy mulling over arguments will probably use more central processing than those who do not. This would be the case with individuals high in the argumentativeness trait discussed earlier in the chapter.

No matter how motivated you are, however, you cannot use central processing unless you are knowledgeable about the issue. Most students, for example, would be more critical of a speech on fashion trends than one on quarks and electrons.

If you are not motivated and do not have the ability to process the message, you will be monitoring peripheral cues. If you are motivated and can process the message, you will compare the information in the message with what you already know. If that knowledge is insufficient to make these kinds of judgments, you'll go the peripheral route.

When processing information in the central route, you will carefully consider the arguments. The degree to which the message matches your previous attitude will have an effect here. Messages that are more favorable to your view will probably be evaluated more positively than those that are not. On the other hand, the strength of the argument certainly plays a role because in central processing you are thinking critically. You identify good and bad arguments, and you tend to be influenced more by good ones.

In peripheral processing, you do not look closely at the strength of the argument. Indeed, you make judgments quickly about whether to believe what you hear or read on the basis of simple cues. For example, when source credibility is high, the message may be believed regardless of the arguments presented. Also, you tend to believe people you like. Or you may simply rely on the number of arguments to determine whether to accept a message. In most peripheral processing, many types of cues are used.

Richard Petty, John Cacioppo, and Rachel Goldman did an experiment that shows how central and peripheral processing work. One hundred forty-five students were asked to evaluate audio taped arguments in favor of instituting comprehensive examinations for seniors at their college.[19] Two versions were used—one with strong arguments and the other with weak ones. Half of the students were told that the examination could go into effect the following year, but the other half were led to believe that the change would not occur for ten years. Obviously, the first group would find the message more personally relevant than the second group and would therefore be more motivated to scrutinize the arguments carefully. Based on ELT, you would expect that these students in the high-relevance group would be less susceptible to peripheral cues.

To test this hypothesis, the researchers told half of the high-relevance group and half of the low-relevance group that the tape was based on a report from a high school class, and the remaining half of both groups was told that the tape was based on a report of the Carnegie Commission. Thus, the first group was presented with a low source-credibility cue, whereas the other group was presented with a high-credibility cue.

As expected, the students who heard the highly relevant message were motivated to pay careful attention to the quality of the arguments and were more influenced by the arguments than were the students who heard the less relevant message. Those students who heard the less-relevant message were more influenced by credibility as a peripheral cue than were the other students. Petty, Cacioppo, and their colleagues have done a number of similar studies with the same results.

The lesson from this theory might seem to be that you should always be critical in evaluating messages, but, practically speaking, you cannot always attend carefully to every message. Some combination of central and peripheral processing is always to be expected. Even when motivation and ability are low, you might still be influenced somewhat by strong arguments, and even when you are processing in the central route, other less-critical factors can also affect your attitudes.

◖● REFLECTIONS ON

The Sociopsychological Tradition

It comes as no surprise that the sociopsychological tradition has an immense influence on how we think about communicators. The study of social psychology gained prominence in the early part of the twentieth century and popularized the individualistic perspective on social life. The earliest empirical studies of communication in the United States were highly influenced by the methodology of social psychology. The theories in this section all share a focus on the individual, the use of research methods from social psychology, and a goal of prediction.

Within the world of the individual, there is a strong kinship between the sociopsychological and cybernetic traditions of communication theory. It is fair to say that within this realm, cybernetic theories are also sociopsychological in orientation, although the former take a more systemic view of individual cognition.

● ● ●

◖● THE CYBERNETIC TRADITION

Here we will present two genres of cybernetic theory. The first is a group of theories that generally come under the rubric of *information-integration*. The second is a group of theories generally known as *consistency theories*.

Information-Integration Theory

The information-integration approach to the communicator centers on the ways we accumulate and organize information about persons, objects, situations, and ideas to form *attitudes*, or predispositions to act in a positive or negative way toward some object. The information-integration approach is one of the most popular models of the formation of attitudes and of attitude change.[20] Cognition is depicted as a system of interacting forces, in which information has

the potential of affecting an individual's belief system or attitudes. An attitude is considered an accumulation of information about an object, person, situation, or experience. Attitude change occurs because new information adds to the attitude or because it changes one's judgments about the weight or valence of other information. Any one piece of information usually does not have too much influence because the attitude consists of a number of beliefs that could counteract the new information.

Two variables seem especially important in affecting attitude change. The first is valence, or direction. *Valence* refers to whether information supports your beliefs or refutes them. When information supports your beliefs, it has "positive" valence. When it does not, it has "negative" valence. If you favor school vouchers, a statement opposing school vouchers would be negative and one supporting them would be positive.

The second variable that affects the impact of information is the *weight* you assign to the information. Weight is a function of credibility. If you think the information is probably true, you will assign a higher weight to it; if not, you will assign a lower weight. Clearly, the more the weight, the greater the impact of that information on the system of beliefs relevant to the voucher system.

So valence affects *how* information influences your belief system, and weight affects *how much* it does so. Suppose that you have two friends—one who strongly favors legalized euthanasia and another who strongly opposes it. Imagine that you and your friends view a television documentary contending that legalized mercy killing has been badly abused in other countries. How will this documentary affect your friends' attitudes toward the issue?

Let's begin with your friend who favors euthanasia. If he assigns little weight to the television program, it will not affect his attitude much one way or the other because it will not have much impact on his system of beliefs. On the other hand, if he decides that the documentary is true, he will assign a high weight to it, and it will affect his system of beliefs. The combination of a high weight and a negative valence will change his attitude to be less in favor of euthanasia. Now let's look at your friend who opposes legalized euthanasia. Again, if she assigns low weight to the information, it will have little effect, but if she believes this information and assigns high weight to it, it will make her even more opposed to legalization than she originally was because the combination of high weight and positive valence reinforces her opinion.

You would not expect your friends to completely reverse their attitudes because they have other beliefs that enter the picture. Your friend who favors legalized euthanasia does so for a number of reasons, and he may not be very worried about abuse. Even though the television program persuades him that mercy killing has been abused in certain other countries, he might say that abuse can be prevented by good regulations. This is the basic idea of information-integration theory.

One of the best-known and respected information-integration theorists is Martin Fishbein.[21] Fishbein highlights the complex nature of attitudes in what is known as *expectancy-value theory*.

Expectancy-Value Theory. According to Fishbein, there are two kinds of belief. The first is *belief in* a thing. When you believe in something, you would say that this thing exists. The second kind of belief—*belief about*—is your sense of the probability that a particular relationship exists between two things. For example, you might believe in the existence of pain and suffering late in life. You may also have a belief about pain and suffering—that modern medicine makes it possible for people to avoid pain.

According to Fishbein, attitudes differ from beliefs because they are evaluative. Attitudes are correlated with beliefs and lead you to behave a certain way toward the attitude object. So the two beliefs mentioned above would probably lead you to vote against a ballot proposition that would legalize euthanasia. Fishbein sees attitudes as organized, so that general attitudes are predicted from specific ones in a summative fashion. So a general positive attitude toward eu-

thanasia would consist of other attitudes—about life, death, individual rights, and pain and suffering. The relationship between beliefs and attitudes is represented algebraically as follows:[22]

$$A_o = \sum_{i}^{N} B_i a_i$$

where

A_o = attitude toward object o
B_i = strength of belief i about o; that is, the probability or improbability that o is associated with some other concept x
a_i = evaluative aspect of B; that is, the evaluation of x
N = number of beliefs about o

Thus, an attitude toward an object equals the sum of each belief about that object times its evaluation.

The distinctive feature of Fishbein's formula is its proposition that attitudes are a function of a complex combination of beliefs and evaluations. The example in Table 4.1 helps clarify this model. This table describes a hypothetical attitude toward jogging. Here, jogging is associated with beliefs about six concepts—cardiovascular health, disease, obesity, mental health, friendship, and physique. Each of these concepts is associated with a belief, and each belief has either positive or negative valence. In this example, when you add up all the beliefs and multiply them by the evaluations, you end up with a very positive attitude about jogging.

According to expectancy-value theory, attitude change can occur from three sources. First, information can alter the believability, or weight, of particular beliefs. The two friends mentioned above in our euthanasia example might learn, for instance, that the report on the abuse of euthanasia is erroneous. Information can also change the valence of a belief. For instance, your friends might learn that these "abuses" were technical and legal and not self-serving in any way, making the information seem positive rather than negative. Finally, information can add new beliefs to the attitude structure. In our example, this could occur if

TABLE **4.1**

A Simplified Example of an Attitude Hierarchy According to the Fishbein Model

Attitude object (o) → jogging		$N = 6$ (number of beliefs in system)
Associated concepts (x_i)	Probability of association (B_i)	Evaluation (a_i)
x_1 Cardiovascular health	B_1 Jogging promotes cardiovascular vigor.	a_1 Cardiovascular vigor is good.
x_2 Disease	B_2 Jogging reduces the chance of disease.	a_2 Disease is bad.
x_3 Obesity	B_3 Jogging reduces weight.	a_3 Being overweight is bad.
x_4 Mental health	B_4 Jogging promotes peace of mind.	a_4 Letting off mental tensions is good.
x_5 Friendship	B_5 Jogging introduces a person to new friends.	a_5 Friendship is important.
x_6 Physique	B_6 Jogging builds better bodies.	a_6 A beautiful body is appealing.

your friends learn that euthanasia was actually requested in the vast majority of cases.

Theory of Reasoned Action.   Adding to expectancy-value theory, Icek Ajzen and Martin Fishbein argue that behavior results in part from intentions, a complex outcome of attitudes.[23] Specifically, your intention to behave in a certain way is determined by your attitude toward the behavior and a set of beliefs about how other people would like you to behave. Consider your progress in college as an example. Do you plan to continue until you get your degree or drop out for a while? The answer to this question depends on your attitude toward school and what you think other people want you to do. Each factor—your attitude and others' opinions—is weighted according to its importance. Sometimes your attitude is most important, sometimes others' opinions are most important, and sometimes they are more or less equal in weight. The formula is as follows:

$$BI = A_B w_1 + (SN) w_2$$

where

BI = behavioral intention
A_B = attitude toward the behavior
SN = subjective norm (what others think)
w_1 = weight of attitude
w_2 = weight of subjective norm

So your intention to do something equals your attitude toward the behavior multiplied by the strength of that attitude plus what others think times the strength of their opinion.

Let's return to the example of your intention regarding college. If you have developed a poor attitude toward school, and your friends are encouraging you to drop out for a semester to work, that is probably what you will do. On the other hand, if your friends are encouraging you to stick it out, and their opinions are very important to you, you will probably stay despite your negative attitude. If your friends' opinions don't matter that much, your attitude will win out, and your intention will be to leave college and get a job.

The preceding formula predicts your behavioral intention, but it does not necessarily predict the actual behavior. This is because we do not always behave in accordance with our intentions. We know that people are notorious for going against their own best intentions. Sometimes, for example, people cannot do what they want because they are not able to. Smokers may want to stop smoking but cannot because they are addicted. You might want to drop out of school, but your parents' threat to cut off your support might prevent you from doing so.

Before we move on, let's take a moment to reflect on how information-integration theory is cybernetic. Remember that cybernetic theories emphasize the interrelationship among parts of a system. Part of your cognitive, or thinking, system is a cluster of variables including attitudes toward objects, attitudes toward behaviors, belief strength, belief probability, evaluations, behavioral intentions, weight of attitude, subjective norm, and weight of subjective norms. What you think about issues and how you behave will result from a complex interaction among these variables, and the work of Fishbein and Atzen helps us see what those relationships are. Consistency theories, the topic of the following section, show how these factors seek balance, or homeostasis.

Consistency Theories

Undoubtedly, one of the largest bodies of work related to attitude, attitude change, and persuasion falls under the umbrella of consistency theory. All consistency theories begin with the same premise: People are more comfortable with consistency than inconsistency. Consistency, then, is a primary organizing principle in cognitive processing, and attitude change can result from information that disrupts this balance. Although the vocabulary and concepts of these theories differ, the basic assumption of consistency is present in all of them. In cybernetic language, people seek *homeostasis*, or balance, and the cognitive system is a primary tool by which this balance is achieved.

We will summarize two very prominent theories of cognitive consistency here—Leon Festinger's theory of cognitive dissonance and Milton Rokeach's theory of beliefs, attitudes, and values. We chose these theories because of their relatively complete explanations of the process of cognitive consistency.

Theory of Cognitive Dissonance.   Leon Festinger's theory of cognitive dissonance is one of the most important theories in the history of social psychology. As such, the theory is firmly planted in the sociopsychological tradition. At the same time, however, it is so infused with system thinking that it must be included in the cybernetic tradition as well. Over the years the theory of cognitive dissonance has produced a prodigious quantity of research and volumes of criticism, interpretation, and extrapolation.[24]

Festinger imagines that the communicator carries around a rich assortment of *cognitive elements* such as attitudes, perceptions, knowledge, and behaviors. These are not isolated cognitive elements, but relate to one another within a system, and each element of the system will have one of three kinds of relationships with each of the others. The first type of relationship is null, or *irrelevant*: Neither really affects the other. The second is consistent, or *consonant*, with one element reinforcing or bolstering the other. The third type of relationship is inconsistent, or *dissonant*. Dissonance occurs when one element would not be expected to follow from the other. Believing that saturated fats are harmful to your health is inconsistent with eating a lot of red meat. What is consonant or dissonant for one person, however, may not be for another, so the question always is what is consistent or inconsistent within a person's own psychological system. You might think, for example, that meat provides valuable protein that cancels out the harmful effects of the fat in the meat.

Two overriding premises govern dissonance theory. The first is that dissonance produces tension or stress that creates pressure to change. Second, when dissonance is present, the individual will not only attempt to reduce it but will also avoid situations in which additional dissonance might be produced. The greater the dissonance, the greater the need to reduce it. For example, the more inconsistent your diet is with your knowledge about cholesterol, the greater the pressure you will feel to do something about it to reduce the dissonance.

Dissonance itself is a result of two other variables—the importance of the cognitive elements and the number of elements involved in the dissonant relation. In other words, if you have several things that are inconsistent and they are all important to you, you will experience greater dissonance. So in our example, if health is not important to you, knowledge that certain fats are bad for your health is probably not going to affect your actual eating habits.

Festinger imagined a number of methods for dealing with cognitive dissonance. First, you might change one or more of the cognitive elements—a behavior or an attitude, perhaps. For example, you might become a vegetarian, or you might start believing that fats are less important than genetics to resolve the dissonance between eating red meat and fat. Second, new elements might be added to one side of the tension or the other. For instance, you might switch to using olive oil exclusively. Third, you might come to see the dissonant elements as less important than they used to be. For example, you might decide that what you eat isn't as important as state of mind to overall health. Fourth, you might seek consonant information such as evidence for the benefits of meat by reading new studies on the topic. Finally, you might reduce dissonance by distorting or misinterpreting the information involved. This could happen if you decided that although a lot of meat poses a health risk, meat is not as harmful as the loss of important nutritional ingredients like iron and protein. No matter which of these methods you employed, it would reduce your dissonance and make you feel better about your attitudes, beliefs, and actions.

Much of the theory and research on cognitive dissonance has centered around the various situations in which dissonance is likely to occur. These include such situations as decision making, forced compliance, initiation, social support, and effort. Salespeople label the dissonance that occurs after buying something "buyer's remorse." Often, while waiting for delivery of a car, a customer will cancel the purchase because of buyer's remorse or what is technically called *postdecisional dissonance*. In a 1970 study, a group of automobile customers were called twice during the period between signing the contract and actual delivery to reassure them about their purchase. Members of a control group were not called. As expected, about twice as many of those who were not called canceled the order compared to those who were.[25]

The amount of dissonance one experiences as a result of a decision depends on four variables. First is the importance of the decision. Certain decisions such as skipping breakfast may be unimportant and produce little dissonance, while buying a car can result in a great deal of dissonance. The second variable is the attractiveness of the chosen alternative. Other things being equal, the less attractive the chosen alternative, the greater the dissonance. You will probably suffer more dissonance from buying an ugly car than a snazzy one. Third, the greater the perceived attractiveness of the not-chosen alternative, the more dissonance you will feel. If you wish you had saved your money to go to Europe instead of buying a car, you will suffer dissonance. Finally, the greater the degree of similarity or overlap between the alternatives, the less the dissonance. If you are debating between two similar cars, making a decision in favor of one will not result in much dissonance, but if you are deciding between buying a car and going to Europe, you might experience quite a bit of dissonance.

Another situation in which dissonance is apt to result is forced compliance, or being induced to do or say something contrary to your beliefs or values. This situation usually occurs when a reward for complying or a punishment for not complying is involved. This could happen at work, for example, when your boss asks you to do something you would rather not do. Dissonance theory predicts that the less the pressure to conform, the greater the dissonance. If you were asked to do something you didn't like doing but were offered a handsome bonus for doing so, you would feel more justified than if you were offered a company mug.

In one well-known experiment, students were asked to complete a boring task, after which they were "bribed" to tell other students that the task would be fun.[26] Some of these participants were paid $1 to lie, and the others were paid $20. As expected, because they experienced more dissonance, the $1 liars tended to change their opinion of the task to actually believe it was fun, whereas the $20 liars tended to maintain their belief that the task was dull but justi-

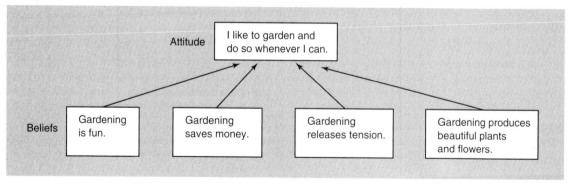

FIGURE **4.1**

A Simple Example of the Belief Structure of an Attitude

fied the lie on the basis that they could pocket a considerable amount of cash.

The less external justification (such as reward or punishment) is involved, the more you must focus on the internal inconsistency within yourself. This is why, according to the dissonance theorist, "soft" social pressures such as suggestions or encouragements can be so powerful by causing a great deal of dissonance. It also explains why you might stay in a high-paying job you dislike. The high pay can be used as a justification for doing so.

Dissonance theory also makes several other predictions. The theory predicts, for example, that the more difficult one's initiation into a group, the greater commitment one will develop. The more social support one receives from friends on an idea or action, the greater the pressure to believe in that idea or action. The greater the amount of effort one puts into a task, the more one will rationalize the value of that task. Have you ever put a lot of work into an assignment you hadn't looked forward to, only to discover after completing it that you liked it after all?

A Theory of Beliefs, Attitudes, and Values. One of the most comprehensive consistency theories is that of Milton Rokeach, who developed an extensive explanation of human behavior based on beliefs, attitudes, and values.[27] His theory builds on earlier work and expands the complexity of the cognitive system.

Rokeach believes that each person has a highly organized system of beliefs, attitudes, and values that guides behavior. *Beliefs* are the hundreds of thousands of statements that we make about the self and the world. Beliefs can be general or specific, and they are arranged within the system in terms of their centrality or importance to the ego. At the center of the belief system are those well-established, relatively unchangeable beliefs that form the core of the belief system. At the periphery of the system lie numerous insignificant beliefs that can change easily. Believing that your parents have a good marriage is probably fairly central, since it impacts many other things you assume to be true. Believing that you need a haircut, on the other hand, is peripheral.

The more central a belief, the more resistant it is to change and the more impact such change will have on the overall system. In other words, if one of your central beliefs changes, expect rather profound changes in how you think about many things. This is why children are often shaken when parents get a divorce.

Attitudes are groups of beliefs that are organized around a focal object and predispose a person to behave in a particular way toward that object. You have hundreds of thousands of beliefs and probably thousands of attitudes, each consisting of a number of beliefs about the attitude object. Figure 4.1 illustrates, in overly simple form, the organization of an attitude.

Rokeach believes attitudes are of two important kinds that must always be viewed together. These are *attitude toward object* and *attitude toward situation*. One's behavior in a particular situation is a function of these two in combination. If you do not behave in a given situation consistently with your attitudes toward certain things, it is probably because your attitude toward the situation prevents it. An example of this kind of inconsistency is eating foods you do not like when they are served to you as a guest. You have a negative attitude toward mushrooms, for example, but a positive attitude toward a situation in which you are a dinner guest in someone's home. The point here is that behavior is a complex function of a variety of sets of attitudes, and the system consists of many beliefs ranging in their centrality.

Rokeach believes that of the three concepts available for explaining human behavior—beliefs, attitudes, and values—values are the most important. *Values* are specific types of beliefs that are central in the system and act as life guides. *Instrumental values*—such as hard work and loyalty—are guidelines for living on which we base our daily behavior. *Terminal values* are the ultimate aims of life toward which we work; examples include wealth and happiness.

Another component in the belief-attitude-value system that assumes great overall importance is your *self-concept*—your beliefs about yourself. It is your answer to the question, Who am I? Self-concept is particularly important to the system because self-regard is a primary motivation supported by all other elements of the cognitive system. Thus, while beliefs, attitudes, and values comprise the components of your system, self-concept provides its guiding goal or purpose.

Rokeach concludes that people are guided by a need for consistency and that inconsistency creates pressure to change. However, his approach to consistency is more systemic and more cognitive than any of the other consistency theories. Taking the total system into consideration, he sees consistency as extremely complex. For this reason, Rokeach calls his work a *comprehensive theory of change*.

Rokeach believes that the most important inconsistencies in a person's psychological system are those involving cognitions about the self. Only when inconsistencies involve the self-conception will there be significant, lasting change. The reason for this is that such contradictions increase self-dissatisfaction. Because maintenance of self-regard is the overall aim of the psychological system, it is natural that this should be so.

As Rokeach and the other consistency theories show us, we do want to behave and think in a coherent way. Often, as we have seen, the lack of consistency creates a problem for us. The following theory adds depth to our understanding of problematic integration.

Problematic Integration Theory

Cybernetic theories of the communicator feature cognitive integration as central to human life. The mind is characterized by a set of attitudes, beliefs, and values that move always in a direction of increasing integration or consistency. Austin Babrow adds to this line of work by explaining the role of communication in helping individuals manage what he calls *problematic integration*, or PI.[28] Babrow's theory rests on three pillars, or propositions: First, you have a natural tendency to align your expectations (what you think will happen) and your evaluations (what you want to happen). Second, integrating expectations and evaluations is not always easy and can be problematic. Third, problematic integration stems from communication and is managed through communication.

The first proposition is that you experience a tension to align your expectations with your values. In other words, as a rule, you are more comfortable when you like the things you think you can have, and you tend to expect the things you like. For example, you are not likely to fall in love with a movie star. More likely, you will be attracted to people around you, with whom you are more likely to establish a relationship.

The second proposition is that the integration of expectations and evaluations is often problematic. Indeed, you may find that you are very attracted to a movie star and know at the same time that it is impossible ever to develop a relationship with this celebrity. Problematic integration can happen under four conditions. The first is *divergence* between an expectation and an evaluation. Here your evaluation and expectation do not match. This might happen, for example, when you are getting very good grades in a class you hate. The second condition of problematic integration is *ambiguity* or lack of clarity about what to expect. For example, you might be very interested in a new sport like tennis, but be quite unclear about whether you can ever succeed in this sport. The third condition is *ambivalence*, or contradictory evaluations. You may, for example, have an acquaintance who is constantly bugging you about becoming your roommate, but you are not sure whether you like this person or not. Finally, problematic integration can occur when the chance of something happening is impossible. This final state of problematic integration is especially interesting, because valuing something we know we can never achieve can be a source of wonder and mystery. Unlike divergence, which can be manipulated to some degree, *impossibility* is certain and cannot be changed.

Often, PI is minor and inconsequential. However, it can become quite a problem when the problematic evaluations and expectations are tied closely to a strong network of beliefs, values, and feelings within the cognitive system. The more central the evaluations and expectations are, the greater the problematic integration. In other words, the more you have at stake, the more you will experience PI.

The third proposition of this theory is that problematic integration entails communication. This is true in part because we come to experience PI through communication. For example, if you were unattached, it would be quite normal for you to be attracted to another student and perhaps want to explore a romantic relationship with this person. However, if a mutual friend told you that your love interest was already engaged to be married, you would indeed have a problem.

Communication is also a way to resolve or manage PI. For example, you may try through communication to change things by persuading others to do what you want them to do. You might reframe what is happening so that something that is about to happen seems less unpleasant. When PI is caused by ambiguity or ambivalence, you might ask questions to clarify. You might seek information to change other parts of your cognitive system so that the expectations and evaluations are easier to integrate.

Problematic integration theory is one of many that helps us understand the ways in which individual communicators think—how they integrate and organize information that affects attitudes, beliefs, values, and behaviors.

◖ REFLECTIONS ON
The Cybernetic Tradition

Cybernetic theories of the communicator share much with the sociopsychological, because both focus on the cognitive system of the individual—a complex, interacting set of beliefs, attitudes, and values that affect and are affected by behavior. Imagine your mind as a system that takes inputs from the environment in the form of information, often in messages sent by others. The mind operates on, or processes, this information and then creates behavioral outputs in the environment.

Within theories of the communicator, the cybernetic and sociopsychological traditions merge, as both come from studies of social psychology, and both use research methods that focus on the prediction of individual behavior. However, cybernetic theories are distinguished by their emphasis on the cognitive system and relationships among various aspects of human information processing. In this regard, these theories are both sociopsychological and systemic in orientation. This connection begins to fade, however, as we move to higher levels of communication analysis. As we will see in upcoming chapters, most cybernetic thinking goes beyond the individual mind to look at social and cultural factors as well.

● ● ●

THE SOCIOCULTURAL TRADITION

As a communicator, do you think of yourself as a separate entity communicating with other autonomous human beings, or do you think of yourself as a member of a social group with bonds that shape your communication experience? Are you first an individual or first a member of the group? This question marks the dividing line between the traditions discussed in this chapter. Sociopsychological and cybernetic theories of the communicator assume that individual differences come before social relationships, while sociocultural theories assume just the opposite—that social relationships prefigure individual differences.

Social and cultural theories show how communicators come to understand themselves as unified beings with individual differences and how such differences are socially constructed rather than determined by fixed psychological or biological mechanisms. Social theories, too, imagine that a history of social interaction gives individuals a set of tools for shifting their ideas about who they are, based on the situations in which they find themselves. In other words, through interaction, we construct a unified, yet flexible sense of self. In this section we look at four lines of work related to the self—symbolic interactionism, social construction of self, social construction of emotion, and presentational self.

Symbolic Interaction and the Development of Self

Symbolic interactionism (SI) is a way of thinking about mind, self, and society that has contributed greatly to the sociocultural tradition of communication theory.[29] With foundations in the field of sociology, SI teaches that as people interact with one another over time, they come to share meanings for certain terms and actions.

George Herbert Mead is normally considered the founder of symbolic interactionism, and he taught that meaning arises from human beings interacting verbally and nonverbally with one another. Through action and response, we come to assign meaning to words and actions and thereby come to understand events in particular ways. Society itself arises from interlinked conversations among individuals. Because of the importance of conversation to the SI movement, we will discuss symbolic interactionism in more detail in Chapter 6. Here we will consider one concept from SI that has special relevance to the communicator—the *self*.

Indeed, an important outcome of interaction is a certain idea of the self—who you are as a person. Manford Kuhn and his students placed the self at the center of social life. According to these interactionists, one's sense of self lies at the heart of communication.[30] Kuhn sees the self as crucial to interactionist thought. The child is socialized through interaction with others in the society in which he or she lives. The person makes sense of and deals with objects in the environment through social interaction. An *object* can be any aspect of the person's reality: a thing, a quality, an event, or a state of affairs. The only requirement for something to become an object is that the person must name it or represent it symbolically. Objects, then, are more than objective things; they are *social objects* and reality is the totality of a person's social objects. To Kuhn, the naming of an object is important, for naming is a way of conveying the object's meaning.

Kuhn reinforces the view that communicators undertake self-conversations as part of the process of interacting. In other words, we talk to ourselves, have conversations in our minds in order to make distinctions among things and persons. When making decisions about how to act toward a social object, we create what Kuhn calls a *plan of action*, guided by *attitudes,* or verbal statements that indicate the values toward which action will be directed. For example, going to college involves a plan of action, actually a host of plans, guided by a set of attitudes about what you want to get out of college. How you relate to college could be influenced, for example, by positive attitudes toward money, career, and personal success.

We do not work out the meaning of social objects, attitudes, and plans of action in isolation. Indeed, the whole premise of SI is that these things arise from interaction with others. Certain other people, *orientational others*, are particularly influential in a person's life. They are people to whom we are emotionally and psychologically committed. Orientational others are people, like parents, who provide us with general vocabulary, central concepts, and categories that come to define our realities. These individuals also help us learn to distinguish between ourselves and other people, continually sustaining our sense of self. Orientational others may be in our present or past; they may be present or absent. The important thing is that at some point in our lives, these individuals were especially important in helping us work out who we are as persons.

The *self*, then, is itself an important social object, defined and understood in terms developed over time in interaction with orientational others. Your self-concept is nothing more than your plans of action toward yourself, your identities, interests, aversions, goals, ideologies, and self-evaluations. The self-concept provides anchoring attitudes, for they act as your most common frame of reference for judging other objects. All subsequent plans of action stem primarily from the self-concept.

Kuhn invented the *Twenty Statements Test* (TST) for measuring various aspects of the self. If you were to take the TST, you would be confronted with twenty blank spaces preceded by the following simple instructions:

> There are twenty numbered blanks on the page below. Please write twenty answers to the simple question, "Who am I?" in the blanks. Just give twenty different answers to this question. Answer as if you were giving the answers to yourself, not to somebody else. Write the answers in the order that they occur to you. Don't worry about logic or "importance." Go along fairly fast, for time is limited.[31]

There are a number of ways to analyze the responses from this test, each tapping a different aspect of the self. The *ordering variable* refers to the relative salience of identifications the individual possesses. It is observable in the order of statements listed on the form. For example, if the person lists "Baptist" a great deal higher than "father," the researcher may conclude that the person identifies more readily with religion than with family affiliation. The *locus variable*—another way to assess the test—is the extent to which the subject in a general way tends to identify with consensual groupings such as "American" rather than idiosyncratic, subjective qualities such as "strong."

In scoring the self-attitude test, you can place statements in one of two categories. A statement is *consensual* if it consists of a discrete group or class identification, such as "student," "woman," "husband," "Baptist," "from Chicago," "premed student," "daughter," "oldest child," and "engineering student." Other statements are not descriptions of commonly agreed-on categories. Examples of *subconsensual* responses are "happy," "bored," "pretty," "good student," "too heavy," "good wife," and "interesting." The number of statements in the consensual group is the individual's locus score.

Other theorists have explored the self as well; we will see it become an even more important concept in social constructionism.

Social Construction of Self

In Chapter 3, we explained that the social construction of reality is a major tenet of the sociocultural tradition. It is the idea that our social worlds are made in human interaction. The way in which we communicate over time creates our very understanding of experience, including our ideas about ourselves as persons and as communicators. These ideas are essentially "personal" theories of life. These theories, developed over time through interaction, are templates that help us define our experience.

Among contemporary social scientists who have made constructionist assumptions central to their work is Rom Harré.[32] Recognizing that human beings are both individual and social, Harré says that like any other experience, the self is structured by a personal "theory." You learn to understand yourself by employing an idea, or theory, of personhood and selfhood. For Harré, the *person* is a publicly visible being that is characterized by certain attributes and characteristics established within a culture or social group. For example, in most European American cultures, people are viewed as autonomous beings who make choices to achieve goals.

The *self,* in contrast to the person, is your private notion of your own unity as a person. Personhood is *public,* whereas the self, though you may share it with others, is ultimately *private.* The nature of personhood is governed by culture; your self is governed by your theory of your own being as one member of the culture.

Personal being is thus two-sided, consisting of a social being (person) and a personal being (self). Many traditional cultures conceptualize the person as the embodiment of a role (such as mother, father, priest, worker), and people in general are seen as manifestations of these roles. Any single person, on the other hand, will assign a particular nature, feeling, and character to the self, as an individual within a role: "I am the father of Zack and a field-worker. I am a good father and worker."

Your self-theory is learned through a history of interaction with other people. All of our thoughts, intentions, and emotions are cast in terms learned through social interaction. The range of possible "selves" is highly variable from one culture to another because the social realities of cultures are different from one to another. For instance, most Western industrialized cultures stress theories of self that emphasize whole, undivided, and independent persons. The Javanese, in contrast, see themselves as being two independent parts—an inside of feelings and an outside of observed behaviors. Moroccans have yet another theory of self—as embodiments of places and situations—and their identities are always tied to these situations.[33]

The self consists of a set of elements that can be viewed spatially along three dimensions. The first dimension is *display*—whether an aspect of the self is displayed publicly or remains private. For example, you might define *emotions* as private and *personality* as public. In other cultures, *emotions* might be defined as quite public.

The second dimension is *realization* or source— the degree to which some feature of the self is believed to come from within the individual or a group. Elements of a self that are believed to come from the person are *individually realized,* whereas those elements believed to derive from the person's relationship to the group are *collectively realized.* For instance, a self-theory might treat "purpose" as individually realized because it seems to be something that individuals have on their own. On the other hand, "cooperation" may be collectively realized because it seems to be something that one can only do as a member of a group.

The third dimension—*agency*—is the degree of active power attributed to the self. *Active* elements ("speaking" or "driving") are contrasted with *passive* elements (like "listening" or "riding"). One person's self may differ from another's because the various aspects of self such as emotion, personality, purpose, and cooperation are defined differently within the three-dimensional scheme. For example, people of Anglo-Saxon descent tend to treat emotions as privately displayed, individually realized, and passive. In other words, they believe that emotions just happen to them and are within them. Many southern Europeans, on the other hand, see emotions as public, collective, and active. In other words, they believe that emotions are something they create as a group and display together.

All self theories have three elements in common. First, they all contain a sense of *self-consciousness.* This means that you think of yourself as an object. When you think about yourself or talk about yourself, you are displaying consciousness of yourself. There are, then, two senses of the word *I*—the self that "knows" and the self that is "known about." Consider the following statement: "I_1 know that I_2 am afraid." I_1 reflects the sense of being aware, and I_2 reflects the sense of being the person who is afraid.

An important part of our conception of self is the consistency with which we define and practice I_1 and I_2. Harré calls this the *double singularity principle.*[34] A group's idea of self must treat each *I* as a consistent unity. You must possess a continual awareness of yourself as a unified being, and if you don't, you will be judged abnormal or mentally ill. In other words, you must always see yourself as "you." You must also have a sense of coherence or consistency among your various self-attributions, making coherent sense out of your experience. The failure to do so will create a problem for you and others. Hypocrisy, for example, is seen as an incoherent and immoral state of saying one thing and doing another.

In addition to self-consciousness, the self consists of *agency* and *autobiography*. The self is always seen as having certain powers to do things. People see themselves as agents, capable of having intentions and actions. *Autobiography* is a sense of having a history and a future. Your agency is evident whenever you plan something, and your autobiography is apparent whenever you tell someone about yourself.

Harré uses the Eskimo as an example of the construction of self.[35] The Eskimo self is viewed in a network of relations with others. An Eskimo may have private feelings, but these are generally considered unimportant. Instead, the self is usually defined in terms of relationships with others. In English we would say, "I hear him." The Eskimo equivalent would be something like, "He is making a sound with reference to me."

Both positive and negative emotions are considered public displays rather than private feelings. Visitors sometimes observe that Eskimos tend to display emotions as a group. For example, they all laugh together or they all cry together. Most Eskimo virtues are social in that they are necessary for the preservation of the community as a whole. Eskimo art illustrates this quality as well. Eskimos do not have a concept for individual creativity but believe they are merely releasing something already present in the material. When they carve a log, for example, the resulting figure is seen as being revealed by the log and not something created by the carver.

The Social Construction of Emotion

While we usually do not think of emotions as "constructed," the Eskimo example above suggests that emotional displays vary according to culture. Harré suggests that emotions are constructed concepts, like any other aspect of human experience, because they are determined by the local language and moral orders of the culture or social group.[36]

One of the scholars best known for work on the social construction of emotions is James Averill.[37] According to Averill, emotions are belief systems that guide one's definition of the situation. As such, emotions consist of internalized social norms and rules governing feelings. These norms and rules tell us how to define and respond to emotions. Emotions do have a physiological component, but identifying and labeling bodily feelings are learned socially within a culture. In other words, the ability to make sense of emotions is socially constructed.

How an emotion is labeled—what it is called—is instrumental in how the emotion is experienced. You may have very different meanings for the same physiological response depending on whether you call it "anger" or "fear." You experience an emotion one way when you call it "jealousy" and quite another when you call it "loneliness." We have rules for what anger, fear, jealousy, and loneliness are, and we have rules for how to respond to these feelings, rules constructed in social interaction throughout a lifetime.

Averill calls emotions *syndromes,* defined as clusters or sets of responses that go together. No single response is sufficient by itself to define an emotion, but all must be viewed together. Emotional syndromes are socially constructed because people learn through interaction what particular clusters of behavior should be taken to mean and how to perform a particular emotion. Emotions are acted out in specific ways, and we learn these roles from communication. What does grief look like? It looks different in various societies. People must learn within their respective cultures how to recognize and carry out the role of the grieving person, or the angry person, or the jealous person.

Each experience of an emotion has an *object*— where the emotion is directed—and each emotion has a limited range of possible objects. When you are angry, you are angry at someone.

When you are envious, you have envy about some achievement or possession. When you grieve, you grieve some loss. As Averill points out, you cannot be proud of the stars because pride is something reserved for accomplishment. You may say that you "love" your new car, but you cannot really be "in love" with it. Nor can you say that someone's angry attack on you makes you feel jealous.

Averill conducted an interesting study in which he isolated over five hundred terms for various emotions, a list that was representative of emotional terms in the English language.[38] His subjects then rated these terms on a number of dimensions, including evaluation (for example, pleasant-unpleasant). He found that far more emotional terms were evaluated as negative (such as *anger, jealousy*) than positive (for instance, *joy, happiness*).

Averill's explanation for the dominant labeling of emotions as negative is that while emotions do not come prepackaged as positive or negative, we define them that way based on our social constructions. In Averill's sample, positive outcomes tend to be action oriented, whereas negative results tend to be seen as beyond one's control. So, for example, courage is the result of one's brave actions, whereas jealousy is the consequence of an unfortunate situation. Further, emotions in general tend to be viewed in our society as beyond control—something that just happens to us. So it is logical that positive outcomes are defined less as emotions and more as actions, whereas negative outcomes are more often seen as emotions, contributing to the idea that emotional terms are more often negative than positive. In other cultures the outcome of Averill's study might be quite different.

For example, the Ifaluk of Micronesia experience several forms of anger, including that which accompanies sickness, that which builds up slowly from several bothersome irritations, that which is experienced when relatives do not live up to expectations, and that which is caused by personal misfortune.[39] Justifiable anger, called *song*, occurs in a highly predictable pattern among the Ifaluk. A rule must be violated, and someone must point out that this occurred.

The person who witnessed the violation must condemn the act, and the one who did it must react to this condemnation with fear, promising not to do it again. Clearly, in the Ifaluk culture, anger is not just anger; the various types are sharply distinguished.

In general, then, four kinds of rules govern emotions, according to Averill. *Rules of appraisal* tell you what an emotion is, where it is directed, and whether it is positive or negative. *Rules of behavior* tell you how to respond to the feeling— whether to hide it, to express it in private, or to vent it publicly. *Rules of prognosis* define the progression and course of the emotion: How long should it last, what are its different stages, how does it begin, and how does it end? *Rules of attribution* dictate how an emotion should be explained or justified. What do you tell others about it? How do you express it publicly?

If you were angry at another person, your rules of appraisal would tell you what you were feeling and who the target of the feeling was. These rules would also define whether that anger was positive (righteous indignation) or negative (rage). Behavior rules would guide your actions, including how to express the anger, whether to lash out or remain quiet, whether to aggress or retreat. Prognosis rules would guide how long the anger episode should last and the different phases through which it might pass. Finally, the rules of attribution would help you explain the anger ("She was acting like a jerk and made me mad").

Thus, emotions are not just things in themselves. They are defined and handled according to what has been learned in social interaction with other people. We learn emotional rules in childhood and throughout life. Averill is clear that people can and do change emotionally. When you enter a new life situation, you are exposed to new ways of understanding emotion, and your feelings, their expression, and the ways you manage those emotions change.

The Presentational Self

Erving Goffman is one of the best-known sociologists of the twentieth century. He is well known for using a theatrical metaphor, in which everyday settings are viewed as a stage and people are actors who use performances to make an impression on an audience. When you come into any situation, you put on a presentation or performance—you must decide how to position yourself, what to say, and how to act.

Goffman begins with the assumption that the person must somehow make sense of events encountered in everyday life.[40] The interpretation of a situation is the *definition* of the situation. When you enter a situation, you tend to ask the mental question, "What is going on here?" Your answer constitutes a definition of the situation. Often the first definition is not adequate and a rereading may be necessary, as in the case of a practical joke, a mistake, a misunderstanding, or even outright deception.

The definition of a situation can be divided into strips and frames. A *strip* is a sequence of activities such as opening the refrigerator door, removing the milk, pouring it into a glass, drinking it, and putting the glass into the dishwasher. A *frame* is a basic organizational pattern used to define the strip. The strip of activities listed above, for example, would probably be framed as "getting a drink."

Frame analysis thus consists of determining how individuals organize or understand their behaviors within a given situation. Frames allow you to identify and understand otherwise meaningless events, giving meaning to the ongoing activities of life. A natural framework is an unguided event of nature with which you must cope, such as a windstorm. A social framework, on the other hand, is seen as controllable and guided by some intelligence—such as planning a meal. These two types of frameworks relate to each other because social beings act on and are in turn influenced by the natural order.

Frameworks, then, are the models we use to understand our experience, the ways we see things as fitting together into some coherent whole. A *primary framework* is a basic organizational unit such as conversing, eating, and dressing, but primary frames can be transformed or altered into *secondary frameworks*. In secondary frameworks, the basic organizational principles of a primary frame are used to meet different ends. A game, for example, is a secondary framework modeled after the primary framework of a fight or competition. Most frameworks are not primary at all, though they are modeled after primary ones. Examples include plays, deceptions, experiments, and other fabrications. Ordinary life is filled with secondary frameworks.

Communication activities, like all activities, are viewed in the context of frame analysis. A *face engagement* or *encounter* occurs when people interact with one another in a focused way.[41] In a face engagement, you have a single focus of attention and a perceived mutual activity. In unfocused interaction in a public place, you acknowledge the presence of another person without paying much attention. This happens, for example, when you are standing in line at a bus stop. In such an unfocused situation, you may be accessible for an encounter that could begin when another passenger strikes up a conversation. Once an engagement begins, a mutual contract exists to continue the engagement to some kind of termination. Face engagements are both verbal and nonverbal, and the cues exhibited are important in signifying the nature of the relationship as well as a mutual definition of the situation.

People in face engagements, then, take turns presenting dramas to one another. Storytelling, or recounting past events, becomes dramatic portrayal in Goffman's scheme:

> I am suggesting that often what talkers undertake to do is not to provide information to a recipient but to present dramas to an audience. Indeed, it seems that we spend most of our time not engaged in giving information but in giving shows. And observe, this theatricality is not based on mere displays of feelings or faked exhibitions of spontaneity or anything else by way of the huffing and puffing we might derogate by calling theatrical. The parallel between stage and conversation is much, much deeper than that. The point is that ordinarily when an individual says something, he is not saying it as a bold statement of fact on his own behalf. He is recounting. He is running through a strip of already determined events for the engagement of his listeners.[42]

In engaging others, you present a particular character to the audience, just as a stage portrays a character in a particular role, and your audience normally accepts the characterization.[43]

Goffman believes that the self is literally determined by these dramatizations. Here is how he explains the self:

> A correctly staged and performed scene leads the audience to impute a self to a performed character, but this imputation—this self—is a product of a scene that comes off, and is not a cause of it. The self, then, as a performed character, is not an organic thing that has a specific location, whose fundamental fate is to be born, to mature, and to die; it is a dramatic effect arising diffusely from a scene that is presented, and the characteristic issue, the crucial concern, is whether it will be credited or discredited.[44]

You have only to think about the many situations in which you project a certain image of yourself. You probably do not behave the same way with your best friend as you do with your parents, and it is unlikely that the self you present to a professor is the same one you present at a party. In most of the situations in which you participate, you decide on a role and enact it.

In attempting to define a situation, you not only give information about yourself; you also get information about the others in the situation. This process of exchanging information enables people to know what is expected of them. Usually, this exchange occurs indirectly through observing the behavior of others and structuring your own behavior to elicit impressions in others. *Self-presentation* is very much a matter of *impression management*.[45] Goffman offers an example of a man intent on impression management: "He may wish them to think highly of him, or to think that he thinks highly of them, or to perceive how in fact he feels toward them or to obtain no clear-cut impression; he may wish to insure sufficient harmony so that the interaction can be sustained, or to defraud, get rid of, confuse, mislead, antagonize, or insult them."[46]

Because all participants in a situation project images, an overall definition of the situation emerges. This general definition is normally unified. Once the definition is set, moral pressure is created to maintain it by suppressing contradic-

tions and doubts. A person may add to the projections but never contradict the image initially set. The very organization of society is based on this principle.

Performance, then, is not trivial, but literally defines who you are as a communicator. The communicator is the presentation of a self, and any one person may have many selves, depending upon the many ways in which they present themselves in the myriad of situations faced in life.

◖ REFLECTIONS ON
The Sociocultural Tradition

You will notice a very different "feel" to the theories in this section. Instead of thinking of individuals as isolated minds, these theories broaden the scope to look at ways in which one's sense of self is a product of social life. This characteristic marks the shift from psychological approaches to social ones. Although the various theories presented in this chapter address somewhat different topics, they share this common commitment. This tradition assumes increasing importance as we move from studies of individual communicators to communication in relationships, groups, organizations, and society as a whole.

• • •

◖ THE CRITICAL TRADITION

In the previous chapter, we looked at several theories that show how our sense of self arises from social interaction. However, many believe that a mere description of self, or even the process by which self arises, is insufficient to give a complete picture of who we are as individuals. In this section, we look at a line of work that centers on the politics of self, or the ways in which we position ourselves socially as empowered or disempowered.

Theories of *identity politics* share a similar critical view of identity with important implications for the communicator. The starting point for theories of identity was the various social movements that emerged in the United States in the 1960s, including the civil rights, black power, women's and gay/lesbian movements. In general, these movements shared some assumptions about identity categories: (1) members of an identity category share a similar analysis of their shared oppression; (2) the shared oppression supersedes all other identity categories; and (3) identity group members are always each other's allies.[47] These assumptions resulted in certain expectations about how individuals involved in these movements behaved on the basis of how they constructed their identities. This analysis assumed, for example, that if you were a woman, you accepted and advocated a feminist analysis of woman's situation, would consider your status as a woman your primary identity category; and count on other women to respond similarly to oppression as you do.

At the core of these assumptions is a conception of identity as a stable, intact, largely self-evident category based on markers such as sex, race, and class—dimensions that exist in the individual. Not only was identity seen as fixed, there was an implicit understanding that one aspect of identity was always most important to an individual—black or female, for example. A third assumption of this identity perspective was that the gaps between identity categories were not only substantial but significant.

The notion of identity as a fixed stable category has pretty much given way to theories that emphasize difference. Scholars began to recognize that there are no essential characteristics that define all women or all men or all Asians or all Latinos. The idea of difference began to be emphasized, and all of the markers of identity that characterized someone were brought into play. Rather than having to identify first, foremost, and only as a woman, you can identify as a Latina lesbian feminist, for example. The term *gay* as a sexual identifier became *gay and lesbian* and then *gay, lesbian, bisexual, and transgendered* to represent a range of identity positions in regard to sexuality. These additive approaches to issues of identity and identity politics also had their limitations and gave rise to theories that recognize that identities are lived as unities and that our theories need to deal with identity as a multilayered, coherent construction. We will discuss three theories here—standpoint theory, identity as constructed and performed, and queer theory—that have been valuable for helping communication scholars think of identity in more complicated and challenging ways.

Standpoint Theory

The first of these theories is standpoint theory. The work of Sandra Harding and Patricia Hill Collins did much to crystallize standpoint theory in the social sciences;[48] Julia Wood and Marsha Stanback Houston[49] have been instrumental in incorporating it into the communication discipline.[50] Standpoint theory focuses on how the circumstances of an individual's life affect how that individual understands and constructs a social world. The starting point for understanding experience, then, is not social conditions, role expectations, or gendered definitions, but the distinctive ways individuals construct those conditions and their experiences within them. Standpoint epistemology thus takes into account the variations within women's communication by understanding the different vantage points that women bring to communication and the many ways they enact those understandings in actual practice. Standpoint theory counters essentialist views of women, to continue with our example, by introducing the importance of the individual's agency in interpreting and implementing a particular understanding of the social world.

Important to standpoint theory, too, is the notion of layered understandings. This means that we have multiple identities that overlap to form our unique standpoints, including intersections of race, class, gender, and sexuality, among many facets of identity. Feminist theorist Gloria Anzaldúa offers an example of her layered identities when she describes herself as a "third world lesbian feminist with Marxist and mystic leanings."[51] She uses the phrase "mestiza consciousness"[52] to signal the perspective or vantage point that is part of her worldview. With this phrase, Anzaldúa not only indicates her multiple identity positions but celebrates the strengths of such a position. Her multiple and interlocking identities enable her to construct a standpoint that offers much more tolerance of ambiguity and awareness of various possibilities than a singular identity could. Rather than forcing an individual to choose an identity construction imposed from without, standpoint epistemology acknowledges the multiplicity of identities as constructed by any given individual.

Standpoint theory also introduces the element of power to the issue of identity. Marginalized or subjugated individuals not only see the world through multiple standpoints—they experience and understand it from their own vantage point—but they also see it from the standpoint of those in power. This survival tactic is not true in reverse. Those in power do not have the need to see from the standpoint of the oppressed; they do not need to learn about others in order to survive. The novel *July's People* by Nadine Gordimer is a good example of this aspect of standpoint theory. Set in South Africa, July is a servant to a white couple. When a revolution occurs, July takes the couple and their three children back to his village, where they learn about who he really is and must depend for the first time on him and his world.[53]

Marsha Houston in particular has developed standpoint epistemology from African American feminist perspectives. She articulates the difficulties of dialogue between white women and black women, given the epistemological differences in terms of lived experience for each. She also describes the culture of resistance as a force that characterizes black women's lives as well as the multiple and interdependent oppressions black women experience. Together these create an angle of vision, or standpoint, that is substantially different from that of communication theorists who do not start from this standpoint.[54]

Identity as Constructed and Performed

In addition to efforts to understand identity as a category that consists of interlocking identities, theories that fall under the label of identity politics today share a concern for construction and performance of identity categories. Following in both the socially constructed and performative traditions, contemporary identity theories suggest that no identity exists outside the social construction of that category by the larger culture. We gain our identities in large part from the constructions offered about that identity from the various social groups of which we are a part—family, community, cultural subgroups, and dominant ideologies. Regardless of the dimension or dimensions of identity—gender, class, race, sexuality—it is also performed according to or against the norms and expectations for that identity.

This means that our identities are always in the process of becoming, as we respond to the contexts and situations around us. Identity politics now is seen as an effort to set identities "in motion."[55] They are moment-by-moment performances that can change. As one example, Barbara Ponse describes steps in the development of lesbian identity as "identity work."[56] Coming out as lesbian or gay is very much a reconfiguration of the self—what Shane Phelan calls a "project rather than an event."[57] Judith Butler's *Gender Trouble* is a strong articulation of identity as both constructed and performed, and her theories have had a major impact on thinking about identity in the communication discipline.[58]

Queer Theory

Judith Butler's work has not only been influential in performative theories of identity but in the field known as *queer theory* as well. Her discussion of queer identity in *Gender Trouble* is often cited as a major impetus to the development of queer theory. Queer theory takes up the challenge of gendered identification by deliberately arguing that not only gender (the masculine/feminine) but also sex (the male/female) are social constructions that can and should be challenged. Gender is always a shifting category, according to Butler: "Gender ought not to be construed as a stable identity or locus of agency from which various acts follow; rather, gender is an identity tenuously constituted in time, instituted in an exterior space through a *stylized repetition of acts*."[59] Queer theory deliberately confronts the binary in all of its forms—male/female, masculine/feminine, gay/lesbian—offering the view that identities always are more than the rigid categories suggested by such dichotomies. The individual who adopts a queer identity, then, refuses both normative heterosexuality and homosexuality. Categorization on the basis of sexual practice is no longer possible: "If gender attributes and acts . . . are performative, then there is no preexisting identity by which an act or attribute might be measured; there would be no true or false, real or distorted acts of gender, and the postulation of a true gender identity would be revealed as a regulatory fiction."[60] Thus, the focus of queer theory is on the voluntarism of identity: "Whatever the source of one's sexual desire and pleasure, one is 'queer' by choice."[61]

Queer theory is interested in all of the ways and combinations of possibilities by which we display gender, more often than not across gender categories. It focuses less on the ways in which any identity category contains the same meanings, expressions, and performances, and more on the different possibilities that are always available. For queer theorists, the most interesting and rich examples are not those in which someone lives up to or fits within an established identity category, but rather all of those times when that person does not. Michael Jackson has been identified as an example of a queer identity, and he is certainly much more visible than many.[62] Ultimately, queerness is about process, focusing "on the lines of movement across ideas, expressions, relationships, spaces, and desires that innovate different ways of being in the world."[63] It is the differences, the intersections and junctures where meanings don't line up perfectly, that are most intriguing.[64]

Queer theorists see strong social implications for adopting the queer model as a framework within which to study issues of gender, sexuality, and identity politics. Queer theory recognizes, along with feminist and gay and lesbian studies that gender has been understood by most societies to be fundamental to the ordering of society, but pushes assumptions of gender and sexuality beyond the rigid categories sanctioned in most societies. Thus many queer theorists and activists see the label *queer* as offering a more profound challenge to traditional identity categories and social norms that other perspectives and labels can do.

Queer theory also has a strong political agenda for social change. The notion of queer "is a point of resistance" that continually problematizes all kinds of issues related to gender and sexuality. As an activist stance, "queer" has become a label that can bring together individuals identified as lesbian, gay, bisexual, transgendered, and straight in political action on issues typically thought of as relevant to one group alone. As an example, ACT UP, a queer political organization, has engaged in activism related to both AIDS and abortion rights issues usually not addressed by a single organization. The "queer" label, then, can transcend identity politics and mobilize action in ways that more specific labels cannot do.

The use of the term *queer* is in fact an example of the very point queer theorists are trying to make. By using a term that contains contradictions—shame, bonding, and now sanction—*queer* extends its own meaning at the same time that it contains it. It has a fluctuating identity and history with multiple meanings and also announces a continuum of possibilities for sexual identities. Queer theory celebrates all of the ways sexuality is expressed with all of its "possibilities, gaps, overlaps, dissonances, and resonances, lapses and excesses of meaning."[65] Queer theory is a particularly good example of postmodernism with its focus on process, flux, and fragmentation of identity. We address post-modernism again in Chapter 11.

REFLECTIONS ON
The Critical Tradition

We see in this section that the sociocultural and critical traditions come together in defining the self as a product of social interaction. What characterizes the critical approaches to identity summarized in this section is the importance of power relations in society in determining where you position yourself vis-à-vis mainstream or marginalized society. This emphasis establishes a critical turn that this tradition brings to the discussion of communicators and communication. This distinction carries forward into many aspects of communication, as we will see in upcoming chapters.

● ● ●

A p p l i c a t i o n s **&** I m p l i c a t i o n s

Many of us begin our thinking about communication with the communicator. Several generalizations characterize the individual as communicator.

1. Each communicator brings a special set of characteristics and resources to any encounter.

As a group, the theories described in this chapter are powerful in helping us understand the nature and genesis of individual differences. They also outline a variety of psychological and social resources that make human communication possible.

Trait theories are appealing because they give us a set of labels to use when we are trying to describe a communicator's characteristics. For example, if you find that someone frequently tends to argue his or her point a lot, it might be useful to think of this person as "highly argumentative." Trait theories can also give you a good sense of your own styles of communication. You can use traits, too, to get a feel for the different styles that might have to be merged in a relationship or group encounter.

Trait theories, however, have strong limitations and must be applied carefully. Communication theories differ on how much control individuals have in their predispositions to respond in certain ways. For example, if you feel that you are low on the argumentativeness scale, how much freedom do you have to change this? If you were to follow the biological approach, you might conclude that you have very little control over your behavior. On the other hand, if you look at many of the sociocultural theories described in this chapter, you would conclude that traits are actually rather malleable.

Cognitive explanations of human behavior, including cybernetic theories of the cognitive system, take us well beyond traits by showing the mental resources that people bring to the communication encounter. These theories can help us understand what people do when they view a television news program, read a novel, attend a play, talk to a friend, or plan a project. These theories also give us a way to understand why equally intelligent, well-meaning, and experienced persons come to different opinions and behave differently within the same situation. Each person brings a set of mental resources to bear, and each person has a different cognitive system that absorbs and reorganizes information. Although you cannot normally control the hidden processes or mechanisms of thought, you can be aware of what information you have and lack, whether you are processing that information critically or peripherally, and the extent to which your ego involvement or existing attitudes affect the information you receive.

Sociocultural theories of the communicator bring an entirely different set of resources to light. They show us that our self-definitions and definitions of situation are critical in shaping our responses. They show that our meanings for words and objects are intimately connected to our actions within situations. Sociocultural explanations give balance to trait theories by introducing choice into the formula. As communicators, we have many socially constructed meanings from which we draw in understanding and responding to events. At the same time, however, we do not have free choice to do whatever we want. Indeed, the social and cultural rules of meaning and action prefigure how we will interpret and act within a situation.

As you think about theories of the communicator, you may find it tempting to ask what makes a person effective as a communicator. In order to answer this question, researchers have conducted many studies of *communicator competence*. Indeed, communicator competence has become an important concept in the communication literature. Ironically, however, we lack coherent theories of competence, which is why competence is not included as a theory in this chapter. Recently, Steven Wilson and Christina Sabee have provided an extremely helpful analysis of this problem.[66] According to these authors, scholars have had a hard time developing theories of competence because it is not a theoretical realm in and of itself, but is related to many other theories. In other words, we must look at *competence* as a theoretical term relevant to other theories, not only of the communicator, but of messages, conversations, and relationships—all subjects of upcoming chapters.

As an application, then, think about translating the theories in this chapter and upcoming ones into questions of competence. For example, we might ask: (1) How can I make constructive attributions of my own and others' behavior—attributions that balance personal responsibility with situational factors? (2) How can I prepare myself to process messages more in a central and critical way? (3) How can I resolve dissonance in ways that achieve optimal balance between stability and change? (4) How can I interact with others in a way that enables me and other people to develop a healthy self-concept? (5) How can I reinterpret my emotions so that they help me grow and guide my actions toward productive, relationship-building ends? (6) How can I learn to consider carefully the self I wish to present in various social situations so that I am both effective in relating to others and building a positive self-image at the same time?

2. A communicator's perspectives are never completely unique, but always shared to some extent with others.

What, exactly, do we share with other communicators? The theories in this chapter outline two types of shared resources. The first are cognitive mechanisms such as social judgment, attribution, information-integration, and cognitive routing. The second kinds of shared resources are social and cultural in nature and include rules, norms, meanings, emotions, and definitions of self. A fascinating quality of shared resources is that they show us how people can be both the same and different.

For example, social judgment theory says that people are the same because they all use mental anchors based on experience to make social judgments, and their ego involvement in an issue determines in large measure how much they will be persuaded by contrary points of view. At the same time, however, each person has a different set of anchors, so their judgments will differ. As ego involvement varies, too, the amount of influence you can have on others varies. People are the same in that everyone wants to control the impression they make on others, but they are different in terms of what impression they want to make.

This idea of similarity and difference can be helpful in understanding communication situations, and the theories in this chapter give you a way to define what is happening, in terms of, say, information-integration or emotions, providing a frame of interpretation when you communicate with others. At the same time, it helps explain why you might be very persuasive with one person, but rejected entirely by another, or why you might bow to the crowd after dropping your tray in the cafeteria, while your sister might run out of the room to hide in the same situation.

How can you be sure what mechanisms are actually operating in persuasion or information processing or social behavior? You can't. As always, realize that each theory is incomplete and continually shift your perspective in order to gain a full appreciation and understanding of what is happening in a communication situation.

3. A communicator's interpretations and actions are always organized according to certain expectations, ways of understanding, and categories of thought. We do not live in an unorganized world of confusion. The human mind is powerful, enabling us to sort out what we see, organize stimuli into categories, apply reasoning to what we experience, and integrate what all of this information means into an existing system of beliefs, attitudes, values, and perceptions. When we act in the world, we are acting on the basis of a highly organized and systematic set of understandings.

The theories detailed in this chapter provide a set of concepts that help us see some of the ways in which we organize our worlds of experience. A very strong theme of these theories is that our perceptions of self lie at the heart of our perceptions of the world. If you want to get a sense of how a person will understand his or her world, develop a sense of how the person understands the self.

Social constructionist ideas of self are especially useful because they draw our attention to the ways in which the self-concept forms through social interaction with significant, or orientational, others. When we interact with important other people in our lives, we are doing more than passing information: We are actually creating, changing, or reinforcing our ideas of self. We will return to the social construction of self in Chapter 6 to explore the ways in which formation of self is an important outcome of conversation.

In this chapter we have encountered a wide variety of constructs, which have been given a host of interesting names: dissonance, elaboration, attitude, expectancy, relevance, attribution, ego involvement, and more. The mere fact that these concepts vie for our attention as competing explanations of thought and action demonstrates the challenge of explaining cognition and action.

We believe that these theories can be very useful if applied judiciously. The cognitive mechanisms outlined by these theories are useful constructs, not universally ordained categories of nature. Use these concepts to gain insight, not to predict truthful outcome. Realize that we do have minds, that we do think, that we do integrate information. There is no need to become overly concerned debating the precise processes that *always* govern our organization of experience. At the same time, we can have a powerful say in the outcome of those processes.

4. A communicator's interpretations and actions change over time through interaction with others.

As we move now from this chapter on the individual communicator to interaction among communications, we will come to realize how important social explanations are for a complete understanding of communication. With the exception of trait theories, all of the theories in this chapter anticipate this move. They all show how the individual's attitudes, beliefs, and values can change when messages are received. They also hint at some of the things that will become important as communicators begin to select, plan, and deliver messages to others.

Most of the theories in this chapter paint a dynamic picture, more like a moving image than a still shot. We know, for example, that ego involvement is an important variable, but ego involvement will change over time. We know that as an individual gains more experience in a certain realm of life, he or she will develop the capacity to process information critically on that subject, and that information will impact the cognitive system differently when this happens. We know from these theories that the self-concept is important as an organizing mechanism of the mind, but the self changes as we live out our lives in increasingly broader communities of interpretation and action.

If you are biologically oriented, you will probably see that some of this change results from natural development and maturation. But in the adult world, and among children too, social experience is vital for natural change within the human being.

A perennially popular application of the theories in this chapter is persuasion or influence. How can we use theories of communication to help us be more persuasive in interaction with other people? This question has been so important in the communication field that most sociopsychological and cybernetic theories of the communicator have been treated as "persuasion" theories. They not only provide insights into why and how people are persuaded, but they provide some guidelines as to what you need to know about people in order to persuade them.[67]

● NOTES

1. For a discussion of situational factors in communication, see Judee K. Burgoon and Norah E. Dunbar, "An Interactionist Perspective on Dominance-Submission: Interpersonal Dominance as a Dynamic, Situationally Contingent Social Skill," *Communication Monographs* 67 (2000): 96–121; and Lynn C. Miller, Michael J. Cody, and Margaret L. McLaughlin, "Situations and Goals as Fundamental Constructs in Interpersonal Communication Research," in *Handbook of Interpersonal Communication*, 2nd ed., ed. Mark L. Knapp and Gerald R. Miller (Thousand Oaks, CA: Sage, 1994), pp. 162–197.
2. For an overview of several traits studied by communication researchers, see Howard Giles and Richard L. Street, Jr., "Communicator Characteristics and Behavior," in *Handbook of Interpersonal Communication*, 2nd ed., ed. Mark L. Knapp and Gerald R. Miller (Thousand Oaks, CA: Sage, 1994), pp. 103–161.
3. Anita L. Vangelisti, Mark L. Knapp, and John A. Daly, "Conversational Narcissism," *Communication Monographs* 57 (1990): 251–274.

4. For a summary of this work, see Dominic A. Infante and Andrew S. Rancer, "Argumentativeness and Verbal Aggressiveness: A Review of Recent Theory and Research," in *Communication Yearbook 19,* ed. Brant R. Burleson (Thousand Oaks, CA: Sage, 1996), pp. 319–352; Dominic A. Infante, Andrew S. Rancer, and Deanna F. Womack, *Building Communication Theory* (Prospect Heights, IL: Waveland, 1993), pp. 162–168.

5. Dominic A. Infante, Teresa A. Chandler, and Jill E. Rudd, "Test of an Argumentative Skill Deficiency Model of Interspousal Violence," *Communication Monographs* 56 (1989): 163–177.

6. This work is summarized in James C. McCroskey, "The Communication Apprehension Perspective," in *Avoiding Communication: Shyness, Reticence, and Communication Apprehension,* ed. J. A. Daly and J. C. McCroskey (Beverly Hills, CA: Sage, 1984), pp. 13–38.

7. Miles L. Patterson and Vicki Ritts, "Social and Communicative Anxiety: A Review and Meta-Analysis," in *Communication Yearbook 20* (Thousand Oaks, CA: Sage, 1997), pp. 263–303.

8. For descriptions and discussions of these models, see Melanie Booth-Butterfield and Steve Booth-Butterfield, "The Role of Affective Orientation in the Five Factor Personality Structure," *Communication Research Reports* 19 (2002): 301–313; James C. McCroskey, Alan D. Heisel, and Virginia Richmond, "Eysenck's BIG THREE and Communication Traits: Three Correlational Studies," *Communication Monographs* 68 (2001): 360–366; and Michael J. Beatty and James C. McCroskey, *The Biology of Communication: A Communibiological Perspective* (Cresskill, NJ: Hampton Press, 2001), pp. 83–92.

9. J. Digman, "Personality Structure: Emergence of the Five-Factor Model," *Annual Review of Psychology* 41 (1990): 417–440. See also Booth-Butterfield and Booth-Butterfield, "The Role of Affective Orientation."

10. Beatty and McCroskey, *The Biology of Communication;* Michael J. Beatty, James C. McCroskey, and Alan D. Heisel, "Communication Apprehension as Temperamental Expression: A Communibiological Paradigm," *Communication Monographs* 65 (1998): 197–219. See also James C. McCroskey, ed., *Personality and Communication: Trait Perspectives* (New York: Hampton Press, 1998).

11. H. J. Eysenck. "Biological Dimensions of Personality," in *Handbook of Personality,* ed. L. A. Pervin (New York: Guilford, 1991), pp. 244–276.

12. Fritz Heider, *The Psychology of Interpersonal Relations* (New York: Wiley, 1958).

13. Heider, *Psychology,* p. 233.

14. For a recent summary, see Eliot R. Smith, "Social Cognition Contributions to Attribution Theory and Research," in *Social Cognition: Impact on Social Psychology,* ed. Patricia G. Devine, David L. Hamilton, and Thomas M. Ostrom (San Diego: Academic, 1994), pp. 77–108. See also David R. Seibold and Brian H. Spitzberg, "Attribution Theory and Research: Formalization, Review, and Implications for Communication," in *Progress in Communication Sciences,* vol. 3, ed. Brenda Dervin and M. J. Voigt (Norwood, NJ: Ablex, 1981), pp. 85–125; Alan L. Sillars, "Attribution and Communication," in *Social Cognition and Communication,* ed. M. E. Roloff and C. R. Berger (Beverly Hills, CA: Sage, 1982), pp. 73–106.

15. Brant R. Burleson, "Attribution Schemes and Causal Inference in Natural Conversations," in *Contemporary Issues in Language and Discourse Processes,* ed. D. G. Ellis and W. A. Donohue (Hillsdale, NJ: Lawrence Erlbaum, 1986), pp. 63–86.

16. The first major work in this area was Muzafer Sherif and Carl I. Hovland, *Social Judgment* (New Haven, CT: Yale University Press, 1961). See also Muzafer Sherif, Carolyn Sherif, and Roger Nebergall, *Attitude and Attitude Change: The Social Judgment-Involvement Approach* (Philadelphia: Saunders, 1965). For a brief overview of the theory, see Muzafer Sherif, *Social Interaction—Process and Products* (Chicago: Aldine, 1967), chaps. 16–18. Several secondary sources are also available; see, for example, James B. Stiff, *Persuasive Communication* (New York: Guilford, 1994), pp. 138–142; Leonard Martin and Abraham Tesser, eds., *The Construction of Social Judgments* (Hillsdale, NJ: Lawrence Erlbaum, 1992); Daniel J. O'Keefe, *Persuasion: Theory and Research* (Newbury Park, CA: Sage, 1990), pp. 29–44.

17. Carl I. Hovland, O. J. Harvey, and Muzafer Sherif, "Assimilation and Contrast Effects in Reaction to Communication and Attitude Change," *Journal of Abnormal and Social Psychology* 55 (1957): 244–252.

18. Richard E. Petty and John T. Cacioppo, *Communication and Persuasion: Central and Peripheral Routes to Attitude Change* (New York: Springer-Verlag, 1986). For brief summaries, see Stiff, *Persuasive Communication,* pp. 179–191; and O'Keefe, *Persuasion,* pp. 95–116. For an additional explanation and refutation of critiques, see Richard E. Petty and others, "Conceptual and Methodological Issues in the Elaboration Likelihood Model of Persuasion: A Reply to the Michigan State Critics," *Communication Theory* 3 (1993): 336–362.

19. Richard E. Petty, John T. Cacioppo, and Rachel Goldman, "Personal Involvement as a Determinant of Argument-Based Persuasion," *Journal of Personality and Social Psychology* 41 (1981): 847–855.

20. Contributors include Norman H. Anderson, "Integration Theory and Attitude Change," *Psychological Review* 78 (1971): 171–206; Martin Fishbein and Icek Ajzen, *Belief, Attitude, Intention, and Behavior*

(Reading, MA: Addison-Wesley, 1975); Robert S. Wyer, *Cognitive Organization and Change* (Hillsdale, NJ: Lawrence Erlbaum, 1974).

21. For an excellent secondary source, see David T. Burhans, "The Attitude-Behavior Discrepancy Problem: Revisited," *Quarterly Journal of Speech* 57 (1971): 418–428. For more recent treatments, see Fishbein and Ajzen, *Belief*; O'Keefe, pp. 45–60.

22. Martin Fishbein, ed., "A Behavior Theory Approach to the Relations Between Beliefs About an Object and the Attitude Toward the Object," in *Readings in Attitude Theory and Measurement* (New York: Wiley, 1967), p. 394.

23. Fishbein and Ajzen, *Belief*; Icek Ajzen and Martin Fishbein, *Understanding Attitudes and Predicting Social Behavior* (Englewood Cliffs, NJ: Prentice-Hall, 1980). See also Stiff, *Persuasive Communication*, pp. 51–57.

24. Leon Festinger, *A Theory of Cognitive Dissonance* (Stanford, CA: Stanford University Press, 1957). Many short reviews of dissonance theory are available. See, for example, Stiff, *Persuasive Communication*, pp. 68–75; O'Keefe, *Persuasion*.

25. J. H. Donnelly and J. M. Ivancevich, "Post-Purchase Reinforcement and Back-Out Behavior," *Journal of Marketing Research* 7 (1970): 399–400.

26. Leon Festinger and James M. Carlsmith, "Cognitive Consequences of Forced Compliance," *Journal of Abnormal and Social Psychology* 58 (1959): 203–210.

27. Milton Rokeach, *Beliefs, Attitudes, and Values: A Theory of Organization and Change* (San Francisco: Jossey-Bass, 1969); *The Nature of Human Values* (New York: Free Press, 1973).

28. Austin S. Babrow, "Communication and Problematic Integration: Understanding Diverging Probability and Value, Ambiguity, Ambivalence, and Impossibility," *Communication Theory* 2 (1992): 95–130; Austin S. Babrow, "Communication and Problematic Integration: Milan Kundera's 'Lost Letters,'" *Communication Monographs* 62 (1995): 283–300; Austin S. Babrow, "Uncertainty, Value, Communication, and Problematic Integration," *Journal of Communication* 51 (2001): 553–573.

29. Barbara Ballis Lal, "Symbolic Interaction Theories," *American Behavioral Scientist* 38 (1995): 421–441. See also Joel M. Charon, *Symbolic Interactionism: An Introduction, an Interpretation, an Integration* (Englewood Cliffs, NJ: Prentice-Hall, 1992); Larry T. Reynolds, *Interactionism: Exposition and Critique* (Dix Hills, NY: General Hall, 1990); Jerome G. Manis and Bernard N. Meltzer, eds., *Symbolic Interaction* (Boston: Allyn & Bacon, 1978). For continuing coverage of SI, see the ongoing editions of the journal *Studies in Symbolic Interaction*.

30. Like many of the interactionists, Kuhn never published a truly unified work. The closest may be C. A. Hickman and Manford Kuhn, *Individuals, Groups, and Economic Behavior* (New York: Holt, Rinehart & Winston, 1956). See also Charles Tucker, "Some Methodological Problems of Kuhn's Self Theory," *Sociological Quarterly* 7 (1966): 345–358.

31. Quoted in Tucker, "Some Methodological Problems," p. 308.

32. Rom Harré, *Social Being: A Theory for Social Behavior* (Totowa, NJ: Littlefield, Adams, 1979); see also *Personal Being: A Theory for Individual Psychology* (Cambridge, MA: Harvard University Press, 1984).

33. Clifford Geertz, *Local Knowledge: Further Essays in Interpretive Anthropology* (New York: Basic, 1983), p. 60.

34. Rom Harré, "Is There Still a Problem About the Self?" in *Communication Yearbook 17*, ed. Stanley Deetz (Thousand Oaks, CA: Sage, 1994), pp. 55–73.

35. Harré, *Personal Being*, p. 87.

36. Rom Harré, ed., "An Outline of the Social Constructionist Viewpoint," in *The Social Construction of Emotions* (New York: Blackwell, 1986), pp. 2–14.

37. Among Averill's most pertinent writings in this line of work are "A Constructivist View of Emotion," in *Theories of Emotion*, ed. K. Plutchik and H. Kellerman (New York: Academic, 1980), pp. 305–339; "On the Paucity of Positive Emotions," in *Assessment and Modification of Emotional Behavior*, ed. K. R. Blankstein, P. Pliner, and J. Polivy (New York: Plenum, 1980), pp. 7–45; *Anger and Aggression: An Essay on Emotion* (New York: Springer-Verlag, 1982); and "The Acquisition of Emotions During Adulthood," in *The Social Construction of Emotions*, ed. Rom Harré (New York: Blackwell, 1986), pp. 98–119.

38. Averill, "On the Paucity of Positive Emotions."

39. Catherine Lutz, "Morality, Domination, and Understandings of 'Justifiable Anger' Among the Ifaluk," in *Everyday Understanding: Social and Scientific Implications*, ed. Gün R. Semin and Kenneth J. Gergen (London: Sage, 1990), pp. 204–226.

40. Erving Goffman, *Frame Analysis: An Essay on the Organization of Experience* (Cambridge, MA: Harvard University Press, 1974). See also Jef Verhoeven, "Goffman's Frame Analysis and Modern Micro-Sociological Paradigms," in *Micro-Sociological Theory: Perspectives on Sociological Theory*, vol. 2, ed. H. J. Helle and S. N. Eisenstadt (Beverly Hills, CA: Sage, 1985), pp. 71–100; Stuart J. Sigman, *A Perspective on Social Communication* (Lexington, MA: Lexington, 1987), pp. 41–56; Spencer Cahill, "Erving Goffman," in *Symbolic Interactionism: An Introduction, an Interpretation, an Integration*, ed. Joel M. Charon (Englewood Cliffs, NJ: Prentice-Hall, 1992), pp. 185–200.

41. On the nature of face-to-face interaction, see Erving Goffman, *Encounters: Two Studies in the Sociology of Interaction* (Indianapolis: Bobbs-Merrill, 1961); *Behavior in Public Places* (New York: Free Press, 1963); *Interaction Ritual: Essays on Face-to-Face Behavior* (Garden City, NY: Doubleday, 1967); and *Relations in Public* (New York: Basic, 1971).

42. Goffman, *Frame Analysis*, p. 508.

43. The best sources on self-presentation are Erving Goffman, *The Presentation of Self in Everyday Life* (Garden City, NY: Doubleday, 1959); and *Relations in Public*.

44. Goffman, *Presentation of Self*, pp. 252–253.

45. There is a large body of literature on impression management. For a summary, see Sandra Metts and Erica Grohskopf, "Impression Management: Goals, Strategies, and Skills," in *Handbook of Communication and Social Interaction Skills*, ed. John O. Greene and Brant R. Burleson (Mahwah, NJ: Lawrence Erlbaum, 2003), pp. 357–399.

46. Goffman, *Presentation of Self*, p. 3.

47. Stacey Young, "Dichotomies and Displacement: Bisexuality in Queer Theory and Politics," in *Playing With Fire: Queer Politics, Queer Theories*, ed. Shane Phelan (New York: Routledge, 1997), pp. 55–56.

48. Sandra Harding, *Whose Science? Whose Knowledge? Thinking from Women's Lives* (Ithaca, NY: Cornell University Press, 1991); and Patricia Hill Collins, *Black Feminist Thought: Knowledge, Consciousness, and the Politics of Empowerment* (Boston: Unwin Hyman, 1990).

49. Julia T. Wood, "Gender and Moral Voice: Moving from Woman's Nature to Standpoint Epistemology," *Women's Studies in Communication* 15 (Spring 1992): 1–24; and Marsha Houston, "The Politics of Difference: Race, Class and Women's Communication," in *Women Making Meaning: New Feminist Directions in Communication*, ed. Lana Rakow (New York: Routledge, 1992): 45–59.

50. For discussions of a variety of other standpoints, including Chinese American, Asian American, Native American, and Mexican American, see Alberto González, Marsha Houston, and Victoria Chen, eds., *Our Voices: Essays in Culture, Ethnicity, and Communication* (Los Angeles: Roxbury, 2004).

51. Gloria Anzaldúa, "La Prieta," in *This Bridge Called My Back: Writings by Radical Women of Color*, 2nd ed., ed. Cherríe Moraga and Gloria Anzaldúa, (New York: Kitchen Table: Women of Color, 1983), p. 205.

52. Gloria Anzaldúa, *Borderlands/La Frontera: The New Mestiza* (San Francisco: Aunt Lute Books, 1987).

53. Nadine Gordimer, *July's People* (New York: Penguin Books, 1981).

54. Marsha Houston, "When Black Women Talk With White Women: Why the Dialogues Are Difficult," in *Our Voices*, pp. 98–104; and Marsha Houston and Olga Idriss Davis, eds., *Centering Ourselves: African American Feminist and Womanist Studies of Discourse* (Cresskill, NJ: Hampton Press, 2002), p. 205.

55. S. Lily Mendoza, Rona T. Halualani, and Jolanta A. Drzewiecka, "Moving the Discourse on Identities in Intercultural Communication: Structure, Culture, and Resignification," *Communication Quarterly* 50 (Summer/Fall 2002): 316.

56. Barbara Ponse, *Identities in the Lesbian World: The Social Construction of Self* (Westport, CT: Greenwood Press, 1978), p. 208.

57. Shane Phelan, *Getting Specific: Postmodern Lesbian Politics* (Minneapolis: University of Minnesota Press, 1994): 52.

58. Judith Butler, *Gender Trouble: Feminism and the Subversion of Identity* (New York: Routledge, 1989). See also David Gauntlett, *Media, Gender, and Identity: An Introduction* (London: Routledge, 2002).

59. Butler, *Gender Trouble*, p. 140.

60. Butler, *Gender Trouble*, p. 141.

61. Leora Auslander, "Do Women's + Feminist + Men's + Lesbian and Gay + Queer Studies = Gender Studies?," *Differences: A Journal of Feminist Cultural Studies* 9.3 (Fall 1997): 11.

62. John Nguyet Erni, "Queer Figurations in the Media: Critical Reflections on the Michael Jackson Sex Scandal," *Critical Studies in Mass Communication* 15 (June 1998): 158–180.

63. Erni, "Queer Figurations," p. 161.

64. Eve Kosofsky Sedgwick, *Tendencies* (Durham, NC: Duke University Press, 1993), pp. 5–9. For overviews of queer theory, see the special issue on queer theory in *Differences: A Journal of Feminist Cultural Studies* 3 (Summer 1991), edited by Teresa de Lauretis. For a discussion of the relationship between feminism and queer theory, see the special issue called "Feminism Meets *Queer* Theory" in *Differences: A Journal of Feminist Cultural Studies* 6 (Summer/Fall 1994).

65. Sedgwick, *Tendencies*.

66. Steven R. Wilson and Christina M. Sabee, "Explicating Communication Competence as a Theoretical Term," in *Handbook of Communication and Social Interaction Skills*, ed. John O. Greene and Brant R. Burleson (Mahway, NJ: Lawrence Erlbaum, 2003), pp. 3–50.

67. This literature is reviewed by James Price Dillard and Linda J. Marshall, "Persuasion as a Social Skill," in *Handbook of Communication and Social Interaction Skill*, ed. John O. Greene and Brant R. Burleson (Mahwah, NJ: Lawrence Erlbaum, 2003), pp. 479–513.

CHAPTER 5

THE MESSAGE

Imagine that you would like to borrow $100 from your roommate to pay for a limousine for a special date. Your reason for needing the money is not all that great, but you think your roommate will go along. How, exactly, will you ask for this loan? You will probably give some thought to the language you use—the words and phrases. You might mention your roommate's experience with special dates, using this as a symbol for something valuable and worth supporting. How will you deliver the message? What nonverbal cues and behaviors will go along with your words? These are interesting questions, but you probably would not actually think of every word and every action that you would use, as these would blend in a seamless message, and much of what happens will be subconscious. Still, you will give the matter some thought.

In asking about the money, you would be doing something with your words, not just transmitting meaning. In other words, your message would have value as an act—a *request* to be exact—and your roommate will recognize this for what it is. There are lots of ways to ask for money, so you will do some strategizing. You will design the message in order to get a result, but what result do you want? Clearly, you want money, but you probably have other goals too. You may want to save your roommate embarrassment, or, better, you might even want this person to feel good about giving you the money. It might be important for you to maintain a good relationship, and your request could help or hurt in this regard, depending upon your strategy. All of these things will need to be integrated into your message so that you can accomplish several goals simultaneously.

Chapter Map / Theories of the Message

Topics Addressed	Semiotic Theories	Sociocultural Theories	Sociopsychological Theories	Phenomenological Theories
Signs and symbols	Symbol theory of Susanne Langer			
Language	Classical foundations			
Nonverbal behavior	Nonverbal codes Kinesics Proxemics			
Speech acts		Speech act theory		
Action assembly			Action assembly theory	
Strategy choice			Compliance gaining strategies Constructivism Politeness strategies	
Message design		Kenneth Burke's theory of identification	Planning theory Message design logics	
Interpreting messages		Cheris Kramarae's theory of feminine style	Semantic meaning theory	Paul Ricoeur Stanley Fish Hans-Georg Gadamer

Once you make the request, your roommate will receive it and must do a bit of interpreting. What will your request mean? Will he or she see it as appropriate? Will he or she appreciate your request? Will your roommate understand that you are acting in friendship and hope to reciprocate sometime? In other words, your roommate will listen to what you say and how you say it and interpret the meaning of the message. Even if you decide to ask for the money indirectly rather than directly, your roommate will probably see right away that this is a request for money, but what else will he or she see in your message?

Notice that all of these questions focus on aspects of the message—How it will be structured, how it will be delivered, what symbols and words it will include, and how it will be interpreted. These are the kinds of questions addressed in this chapter, and a great deal of theory has been created to explain this process. The chapter map on page 100 provides a list of the several traditions and topics addressed.

◖● THE SEMIOTIC TRADITION

Semiotics has been especially important in helping us understand what goes into a message—its parts—and how these are organized structurally. These theories also help us understand how the message comes to have meaning. If you give a speech, for example, the members of your audience tune into the words you select, your grammar, your tone of voice and gestures, your eye contact, and the way you position yourself toward the audience. Semiotic theories would be less concerned with your own characteristics as a communicator, the audience response to your message, or the social and cultural situation in which the speech is delivered, although these theories certainly recognize that the meaning that you and your audience assign to the words and gestures of your speech depend upon all of these things. Here we will include three types of semiotic theories—symbol theory, theories of language, and theories of nonverbal behavior.

Symbol Theory: Susanne Langer

A prominent and useful theory of symbols was created by Susanne Langer, whose *Philosophy in a New Key* has received considerable attention by students of symbolism.[1] Langer's theory is useful because it defines several concepts and terms that are commonly used in the communication field. As such, this theory provides a kind of touchstone for the semiotic tradition in communication studies.

Langer, a philosopher, considers symbolism to be the central concern of philosophy because it underlies all human knowing and understanding. According to Langer, all animal life is dominated by feeling, but human feeling is mediated by conceptions, symbols, and language. Animals respond to signs, but humans go far beyond simple signs by making use of symbols. A *sign* is a stimulus that signals the presence of something else. For example, if you train your dog to roll over when you say, "Roll!" the word is a sign to the dog to turn over. Thus a sign corresponds closely to the actual signified action. Clouds can be a sign of rain, laughter a sign of happiness, and a red light a sign of cross traffic. These simple relationships are called *signification*. Because of signification, you will stop the car when you see a red light.

Symbols, in contrast, operate in a more complex way by allowing a person to think about something apart from its immediate presence. In other words, a *symbol* is "an instrument of thought."[2] Dogs do not have conferences to give papers on the process of rolling over. They don't sit around in the evening pondering the meaning of "Roll." Humans do, however, spend considerable time reflecting on symbol use. Humans even write entire books on the subject of communication. And when you hear someone say, "I love you," your range of meanings and responses to this phrase is rich and complicated. Symbols, then, are central to human life. People have the ability to use symbols, and they have a basic need for symbolization—as important to humans as eating and sleeping. We orient to our physical and social worlds through symbols and their meanings.

Langer sees *meaning* as the complex relation among the symbol, the object, and the person. Thus, meaning consists of both logical and psychological aspects. The logical is the relationship between the symbol and referent, which Langer calls *denotation*; the psychological meaning is the relationship between the symbol and the person, or what Langer calls *connotation*. If you were to say, "An umbrella is an object used to keep the rain off," you would be expressing the logical sense of the symbol *umbrella*. This is the denotation of the term. On the other hand, if you were to say, "I never use an umbrella because it gets all bent up in the wind, and I usually end up leaving it in the car anyway," you are expressing a psychological meaning, the connotation, a more complicated relationship between yourself and the symbol.

Human beings do use one-word symbols, but more often we use words in combination. The real significance of language is in *discourse*, in which we tie words together into sentences and paragraphs. Discourse expresses *propositions*, which are complex symbols that present a picture of something. The word *dog* brings up a conception, but its combination with other words provides a unified picture: *The little brown dog is nestled against my foot*. The potential for combination and organization in language makes language a truly rich and indispensable tool for human beings. In language we think, we feel, and we communicate.

How, then, do symbols work? Any symbol or set of symbols communicates a *concept*, a general idea, pattern, or form. According to Langer, the concept is a meaning shared among communicators, the denotation of the symbol. The personal image, in contrast, is a private *conception*, which is the connotation of the symbol. For example, if you were to look at a painting by Vincent van Gogh, you would assign meaning shared with virtually all other viewers, but you would probably also have a private subjective meaning for the painting as well.[3]

In van Gogh's painting, *Still Life with Open Bible*, for instance, you would see a large Bible sitting next to a candle. Next to the Bible is a small copy of a novel, and if you looked closely, you would see that it is Emile Zola's *The Joy of Living*. The painting, then, denotes a Bible, candle, and book. However, for van Gogh himself, the painting had a much more personal connotation, symbolizing the life and death of his father, a minister. The Bible, therefore, is a symbol of the father. His death is symbolized by the candle, which casts a light on a passage from Isaiah about the suffering servant. The title of the smaller book symbolizes the elder van Gogh's life. Here is what the artist wrote to his brother about his work:

> I want to paint men and women with that something of the eternal which the halo used to symbolize, and which we seek to convey by the actual radiance and vibration of our coloring . . . I am always in the hope of being able to express the love of two lovers by a wedding of two complementary colors, their mingling and their opposition, the mysterious vibration of kindred tones. To express the thought of a brow by the radiance of a light tone against a somber background. To express hope by some star, the eagerness of a soul by a sunset radiance.[4]

Langer notes that humans possess a built-in tendency to abstract. *Abstraction*, a process of forming a general idea from a variety of concrete experiences, builds on the denotations and connotations of symbols. It is a process of leaving out details in conceiving of objects, events, or situations in ever more general terms. For example, the word *dog* may have a specific connotation, but this conception is incomplete; it always leaves something out. The more abstract the symbol, the sketchier the conception: A *dog* is a *mammal,* which is an *animal;* an animal is an *organism,* which is a *thing.* Each successive term in this series leaves out more details and is therefore more abstract than the previous term. Although denotations usually leave out a lot of detail, connotations can include a great deal of detail about what the symbol means to the individual.

So far we have emphasized Langer's ideas about language, which she calls *discursive symbolism.* However, she also admits the importance of nondiscursive, or *presentational,* symbols. Some of the most important human experiences are emotional and are best communicated through forms such as worship, art, and music. Indeed, van Gogh's painting is a presentational symbol. We will now turn to theories that add to Susanne Langer's ideas about both linguistic and nonverbal forms of symbols.

Classical Foundations of Language

The study of language has been heavily influenced by semiotics and vice versa.[5] In this book, we do not have sufficient space to elaborate on linguistic theories, but it is important to know something about the structure of language as it influences messages. The modern founder of structural linguistics was Ferdinand de Saussure, who made substantial contributions to the structural tradition in communication. Saussure teaches that signs, including language, are arbitrary.[6] He notes that different languages use different words for the same thing and that there is usually no physical connection between a word and its referent. Therefore, signs are conventions governed by rules. Not only does this assumption support the idea that language is a structure, but it also reinforces the general idea that language and reality are separate. Saussure, then, sees language as a structured system representing reality. He believes that linguistic researchers must pay attention to language forms, such as speech sounds, words, and grammar. Although language structure is arbitrary, language *use* is not at all arbitrary, because it requires established

conventions. You cannot choose any word you wish, nor can you rearrange grammar at a whim.

Language described in structural terms, then, is strictly a system of formal relations without substance. Only when meanings are attached to the structural features of language does it come to represent something. The key to understanding the structure of the system is *difference.* The elements and relations embedded in language are distinguished by their differences. One sound differs from another (like *p* and *b*); one word differs from another (like *pat* and *bat*); one grammatical form differs from another (like *has run* and *will run*). This system of differences constitutes the structure of the language. Both in spoken and written language, distinctions among signified objects in the world are identified by corresponding distinctions among linguistic signs. No linguistic unit has significance in and of itself; only in contrast with other linguistic units does a particular structure acquire meaning.

Saussure believes that all a person knows of the world is determined by language. Unlike most other semioticians, then, Saussure does not see signs as referential. Signs do not *designate* objects, but rather *constitute* them. There can be no object apart from the signs used to designate it. In this regard, Saussure's work set the stage for much twentieth-century thought about language, interaction, interpretation, and social structure.

Saussure makes an important distinction between formal language, which he calls *langue,* and the actual use of language in communication, which he refers to as *parole.* These two French terms correspond in English to *language* and *speech* respectively. Language (*langue*) is a formal system that can be analyzed apart from its use in everyday life. Speech (*parole*) is the actual use of language to accomplish a purpose. Communicators do not create the rules of language. These rules are worked out over a long period and "given" to us when we are socialized into a language community. In contrast, communicators do create forms of speech all the time.[7] In other words, you don't sit around with your friends and invent new grammatical forms to designate past, present, and future; but you do, through interaction, make use of these forms in quite creative and constantly changing ways. This is the difference between *language* and *speech.*

We cannot, then, have speech without language, but speech is less regular and more variable than the formal system of language from which it derives. In other words, when you speak you are using language, but you are also adapting it—using speech—to enable you to achieve communication goals. Linguistics, to Saussure, is the study of *langue*, not *parole*: "Taken as a whole, speech [*parole*] is many-sided and heterogeneous; straddling several areas simultaneously . . . we cannot put it into any category of human facts, for we cannot discover its unity. Language [*langue*], on the contrary, is a self-contained whole and a principle of classification."[8]

Influenced by the work of Saussure, structural language theorists developed the standard model of sentence structure between 1930 and 1950.[9] Basically, this model breaks down a sentence into components in hierarchical fashion. Sounds and sound groups combine to form word parts, which in turn combine to form words, then phrases. Phrases are put together to make clauses or sentences. Thus, language can be analyzed on various levels, roughly corresponding to sounds, words, and phrases. Structural analysis by itself, however, did not prove powerful in explaining human use of language. Consequently, linguists have moved beyond the structural approach and more commonly today embrace a different approach called *generative grammar.*

Primarily attributed to the work of Noam Chomsky and his colleagues, generative grammar is actually more akin to the sociopsychological tradition than to the semiotic one. As a young linguist in the 1950s, Chomsky parted company with the classical theorists to develop an approach that since has become the mainstay of contemporary linguistics.[10] This branch of linguistics is more concerned with the human cognitive system, how rules of language are embedded in the human mind, and how these mental resources enable us to generate spoken language. Like any theoretical tradition, generative grammar now has several positions within it that go well beyond the scope of this book. Communication scholars have been less interested in the structure of language and mental linguistic rules and more interested in how people actually bring language and behavior together into discourse to accomplish goals. An important aspect of this process is that we integrate verbal, or linguistics, and nonverbal elements.

Theories of Nonverbal Signs

Communication scholars recognize that language and behavior more often than not work together, so theories of nonverbal signs are an important element within the semiotic tradition. Scholars disagree about what nonverbal communication is, as Randall Harrison points out:

> The term "nonverbal communication" has been applied to a bewildering array of events. Everything from the territoriality of animals to the protocol of diplomats. From facial expression to muscle twitches. From inner, but inexpressible, feelings to outdoor public monuments. From the message of massage to the persuasion of a punch. From dance and drama to music and mime. From the flow of affect to the flow of traffic. From extrasensory perception to the economic policies of international power blocks. From fashion and fad to architecture and analog computer. From the smell of roses to the taste of steak. From Freudian symbol to astrological sign. From the rhetoric of violence to the rhetoric of topless dancers.[11]

Making the question of nonverbal communication even more challenging, research on this subject is extensive and comes from many fields.[12] Various topics relevant to nonverbal communication are covered later in the book; here we will concentrate on structural approaches to nonverbal coding, which help us see how nonverbal communication is constructed.

Nonverbal Codes.   Nonverbal codes are clusters of behaviors that are used to convey meaning. Judee Burgoon characterizes nonverbal code systems as possessing several structural properties. First, nonverbal codes tend to be *analogic* rather than digital. Whereas digital signals are discrete, like numbers and letters, analogic signals are continuous, forming a spectrum or range, like sound volume and the brightness of light. Therefore, nonverbal signals such as facial expression and vocal intonation cannot simply be classed into discrete categories but rather are gradations.

A second feature found in some, but not all, nonverbal codes is *iconicity*, or resemblance. Iconic codes resemble the thing being symbolized (as when you depict the shape of something with your hands). Third, certain nonverbal codes seem to elicit *universal meaning.* This is especially the case with such signals as threats and emotional displays, which may be biologically determined. Fourth, nonverbal codes enable the *simultaneous transmission* of several messages. With the face, body, voice, and other signals, several different messages can be sent at once. Fifth, nonverbal signals often evoke an *automatic response* without thinking. An example would be stepping on the brake at a red light. Finally, nonverbal signals are often emitted *spontaneously,* as when you let off nervous energy by playing with your hair or jiggling your foot.

Nonverbal codes have semantic, syntactic, and pragmatic dimensions. *Semantics* refers to the meanings of a sign. For example, two fingers held up behind someone's head is a way of calling him a "devil." *Syntactics* refers to the ways signs are organized into systems with other signs. One might, for example, hold up two fingers behind someone's head, laugh, and say "Joke's on you!" Here a gesture, a vocal sign (laughing), facial expressions, and language combine to create an overall meaning. *Pragmatics* refers to the effects or behaviors elicited by a sign or group of signs, as when the "devil" sign is taken as a joke rather than an insult.

The meanings attached to both verbal and nonverbal forms are context-bound, or determined in part by the situation in which they are produced. Both language and nonverbal forms allow communicators to combine relatively few signs into an almost limitless variety of complex expressions of meaning.

Nonverbal code systems are often classified according to the type of activity used in the code. Burgoon suggests seven types: kinesics (bodily activity); vocalics or paralanguage (voice); physical appearance; haptics (touch); proxemics (space); chronemics (time); and artifacts (objects).[13] Two of the best developed of these are kinesics and proxemics.

Kinesics. Ray Birdwhistell is considered the originator of the field of kinesics.[14] An anthropologist interested in language, Birdwhistell uses linguistics as a model for his kinesics work. So strong is this connection, in fact, that the popular term for kinesics is *body language.* In *Kinesics and Context,* Birdwhistell lists seven assumptions on which he bases his theory of body language.[15]

1. All body movements have potential meaning in communicative contexts. Somebody can always assign meaning to any bodily activity.
2. Behavior can be analyzed because it is organized, and this organization can be subjected to systematic analysis.
3. Although bodily activity has biological limitations, the use of bodily motion in interaction is considered to be a part of the social system. Different groups will therefore use gestures—and any other movement of the body—differently.
4. People are influenced by the visible bodily activity of others.
5. The ways in which bodily activity functions in communication can be investigated.
6. The meanings discovered in research on kinesics result from the behavior being studied as well as the methods used for research.
7. A person's use of bodily activity will have idiosyncratic features but will also be part of a larger social system shared with others.

Building on Birdwhistell's work, Paul Ekman and Wallace Friesen collaborated on research that led to an excellent general model of kinesic behavior, concentrating their work on the face and hands.[16] Their goal was ambitious: "Our aim has been to increase understanding of the individual, his feelings, mood, personality, and attitudes, and to increase understanding of any given interpersonal interaction, the nature of the relationship, the status or quality of communication, what impressions are formed, and what is revealed about interpersonal style or skill."[17]

These authors analyzed nonverbal activity three ways: by origin, by coding, and by usage. *Origin* is the source of an act. A nonverbal behavior may be *innate* (built into the nervous system), *species-constant* (universal behavior required for survival), or *variant* across cultures, groups, and individuals. As examples, one could speculate that eyebrow raising as a sign of surprise is innate, that marking territory is species-constant, and that shaking the head back and forth to indicate *no* is culture-specific.[18]

Coding is the relationship of the act to its meaning. An act may be *arbitrary,* with no meaning inherent in the sign itself. By convention in our culture, for example, we agree that nodding is an indication of yes, but this coding is purely arbitrary. Other nonverbal signs are *iconic* and resemble the thing being signified. For instance, we often draw pictures in the air or position our hands to illustrate what we are talking about. The third category of coding is *intrinsic.* Intrinsically coded cues contain their meaning within them and are themselves part of what is being signified. Crying is an example of intrinsic coding. Crying is a sign of emotion, but it is also part of the emotion itself.

The third way to analyze a behavior is by *usage.* Usage also includes the degree to which a nonverbal behavior is intended to convey information. A *communicative act* is used deliberately to convey meaning. *Interactive acts* actually influence the behavior of the other participants. An act is both communicative and interactive if it is intentional and influential. For example, if you deliberately wave to a friend as a sign of greeting and the friend waves back, your cue is communicative and interactive. Some behaviors are not intended to be communicative but nevertheless provide information for the perceiver. Such acts

are said to be *informative.* On a day when you are feeling less than friendly, you may duck into a hallway to avoid meeting an acquaintance coming your way. If the other person sees the avoidance, your behavior has been informative even though you did not intend to communicate.

According to Ekman and Friesen, all nonverbal behavior can be classified as one of five types, depending on origin, coding, and usage. The first type is the *emblem.* Emblems can be verbally translated into a rather precise meaning. They are normally used in a deliberate fashion to communicate a particular message. The "V" for victory sign and the black power fist are examples. Emblems emerge out of cultures, and emblems may be either arbitrary or iconic.

Illustrators are the second kind of nonverbal cues. Illustrators are used to depict what is being said verbally. They are intentional, though we may not always be directly aware of them, and include such things as pointing or drawing a picture in the air. These types can be combined, since some motions are combinations of types. Illustrators are learned nonverbals that may be informative or communicative in use; occasionally they are interactive as well.

The third type of nonverbal behavior is the *adaptor,* which serves to facilitate release of bodily tension. Examples are hand wringing, head scratching, or foot jiggling. *Self-adaptors* are directed at one's own body. They include scratching, stroking, grooming, and squeezing. *Alter-adaptors,* like slapping someone on the back, are directed to another's body. *Object-adaptors,* such as twisting a paper clip, are directed at things. In any case, adaptors can be iconic or intrinsic. Rarely are they intentional, and one is usually not aware of one's own adaptive behaviors. Although they are rarely communicative, they are sometimes interactive and often informative.

Regulators, the fourth type of behavior, are used to control or coordinate interaction. For example, we use eye contact to signal speaking and listening roles in a conversation. Regulators are primarily interactive. They are coded intrinsically or iconically, and their origin is cultural learning.

TABLE **5.1**

Characteristics of Nonverbal Behavior

Behavior	Origin	Coding	Usage
Emblems	Learned	Arbitrary or iconic	Communicative
Illustrators	Learned	Iconic	Informative Communicative Interactive
Adaptors	Innate Species-constant Variant	Iconic or intrinsic	Informative Interactive
Regulators	Learned	Intrinsic or iconic	Interactive
Affect displays	Innate Species-constant Variant	Intrinsic	Informative Interactive

The final category of behavior is the *affect display*. These behaviors, which may be in part innate, involve the display of feelings and emotions. The face is a particularly rich source for affect display, although other parts of the body may also be involved. Affect displays are intrinsically coded. They are rarely communicative, often interactive, and always informative.[19] These types of nonverbal behaviors are summarized in Table 5.1.

Proxemics. A second category of nonverbals that has been studied extensively in communication is proxemics. Specifically, *proxemics* refers to the use of space in communication. It is the study of how humans unconsciously structure microspace. Edward Hall, the founder of proxemics, describes it as the distances between people in the "conduct of daily transactions, the organization of space in . . . houses and buildings, and ultimately the layout of . . . towns."[20]

According to Hall, the way space is used in interaction is very much a cultural matter. Different senses are important to different cultures. In some countries, such as the United States, sight and hearing predominate; in other places, such as Arab cultures, smell is also important. And some cultures rely on touching more than others.

In general, the predominant senses of a culture partially determine the ways in which space is used within that culture. Cultures also have different definitions of the self, which also affect how space is defined and used. People in most Western cultures learn to identify the self through the skin and clothes. Arabs, however, place the self deeper in the middle of the body.

Hall defines three basic types of space. *Fixed-feature space* consists of unmovable things such as walls and rooms. *Semifixed-feature space* includes movable objects like furniture. *Informal space* is the personal territory around the body that travels with a person, and that determines the interpersonal distance between people. Anglo-American culture, for example, uses four discernible distances: intimate (0 to 18 inches), personal (1 to 4 feet), social (4 to 12 feet), and public (over 12 feet).

When people are engaged in conversation, eight factors may be involved in how they use their space:

- *Posture-sex factors*: These include the sex of the participant and the basic body position (standing, sitting, lying).
- *Sociofugal-sociopetal axis*: The word *sociofugal* means discouragement of interaction, and *sociopetal* implies encouragement. Axis is the

angle of the shoulders relative to the other person. The speakers may be facing each other, may be back to back, or may be positioned toward any other angle in the radius. Thus, some angles, like face to face, encourage interaction, while others, like back to back, discourage it.

- *Kinesthetic factors*: This is the closeness of the individuals in terms of touch. Individuals may be in physical contact or within close distance, they may be outside body contact distance, or they may be positioned anywhere in between these extremes. This factor also includes the positioning of body parts as well as which parts are touching.
- *Touching behavior*: People may be involved in caressing and holding, feeling, prolonged holding, pressing against, spot touching, accidental brushing, or no contact.
- *Visual code*: This category includes the manner of eye contact ranging from direct (eye to eye) to no contact.
- *Thermal code*: This element involves the perceived heat from the other communicator.
- *Olfactory code*: This factor includes the kind and degree of odor perceived in the conversation.
- *Voice loudness*: The loudness of speech can affect interpersonal space.

Notice that all of the theories in this section—theories of symbols, language, and nonverbal communication—share the idea that messages consist of certain parts and features, including verbal (linguistic) and nonverbal (behavioral), to which communicators assign meaning. This idea is the essence of semiotic thinking, but it only makes up a very small part of the large tapestry of communication.

◐ REFLECTIONS ON

The Semiotic Tradition

Language studies can take several directions and can therefore relate to a number of traditions. Studies that look at the relationship of language to power will reflect something of the critical tradition, studies that examine the use of language by various cultural groups would

probably reflect the sociocultural, and studies that look at how we interpret the language of texts will clearly reflect the phenomenological. Yet, the study of the structure of language is inherently semiotic because it treats signs as a bridge between the world of experience and the world of understanding. Language, then, is a place where the traditions can and do come together, as many critical, sociocultural, and phenomenological theories do have a semiotic base.

Studies of nonverbal communication can also be a nexus of traditions. For example, nonverbal behavior is at once semiotic and cultural. When the two are brought together in a single view, the semiotic and sociocultural traditions merge. You can look at nonverbal behavior as a kind of individual behavior as well, which can bring together the semiotic and sociopsychological traditions. In fact, many nonverbal communication theories do take a distinctly psychological approach and are, in other chapters of this book, classified with the latter tradition. To continue our exploration of the message, let us now turn to the Sociocultural tradition.

• • •

◐ THE SOCIOCULTURAL TRADITION

The semiotic tradition in communication theory is helpful for showing us the structural components and organization of a message, but communication is a great deal more than the structure of a message. Important too is the question of what we do with words and nonverbal codes. To answer this question, we move now to the sociocultural tradition. This tradition moves us away from individual differences and cognitive processing to social linkages, groups, and meanings that are worked out through interaction. Here we look at theories of speech acts, identification, and language and gender.

Speech Act Theory

If you make a promise, you are communicating an intention about something you will do in the future, but more important, you are expecting the other communicator to realize from what you have said what your intention is. If you say, "I promise to pay you back," you assume the other person knows the meaning of the words. Knowing the words is not enough. Knowing what you intend to accomplish by using the words is vital. Speech act theory, most notably attributed to John Searle, is designed to help us understand how people accomplish things with their words.[21]

Whenever you make a statement like, "I will pay you back," you are accomplishing several things. First, you are producing a piece of discourse. This is called your *utterance act,* a simple pronunciation of the words in the sentence. Second, you are asserting something about the world, or performing a *propositional act.* In other words, you are saying something either you believe to be true, or you are trying to get others to believe to be true. Third, and most important from a speech-act perspective, you are fulfilling an intention, which we call an *illocutionary act.* The illocutionary act is so central to this theory that we will spend some time with it below. Before we do, however, let's look at the fourth possible accomplishment of a message. This is the *perlocutionary act,* which is designed to have an actual effect on the other person's behavior.

Let's say that your friend sends you an e-mail that says, "I want to go out tonight." Your friend's English sentence is an *utterance act,* not unusual or problematic. Second, she expressed a *proposition* or truth statement that means something about what she wants to do, but again, in this case, it is hardly worth mentioning because it is so obvious. Third, your friend's message is an *illocutionary act* because it makes what you interpret to be an offer or invitation—asking you to go out with her. Fourth, she is trying to get you to actually do something, and if you accept her invitation, she has completed a successful *perlocutionary act.*

These distinctions are more important than they sound. Let's begin with the difference between illocution and perlocution. An illocution is an act in which the speaker's primary concern is that the listener understand the *intention*—to make a promise, an invitation, a request, or whatever. A perlocution is an act in which the speaker expects the listener not only to understand the intention, but to act on it. If you say, "I am thirsty," with the intention of having your brother understand that you need something to drink, you are performing an illocutionary act. If you also want him to bring you a Diet Coke, you are delivering a perlocutionary act. In the speech-act literature, this example is called an indirect request, and it is both illocutionary and perlocutionary.

Now let's look at the distinction between propositional and illocutionary acts. A proposition, as one aspect of the content of a statement, designates some quality or association of an object, situation, or event. "The cake is good," "Salt is harmful to the body," and "Her name is Marta" are all examples of propositions. Propositions can be evaluated in terms of their truth-value, but—here is where speech-act theory has been so important—you almost always want to communicate something more than just the truth of a proposition: You want to do something else with your words.

In speech-act theory, truth is not considered terribly important. Instead, the real question is what a speaker intends to do by uttering a proposition. Hence, for Searle propositions must always be viewed as part of a larger context—the illocution. Searle would be interested in acts such as the following: I *ask* whether the cake is good; I *warn* you that salt is harmful to the body; I *state* that her name is Marta. What the speaker is doing with the proposition is the speech act—in these examples, *asking,* *warning,* and *stating.*

The meaning of a speech act is its *illocutionary force.* For example, the statement, "I'm hungry," could count as a request if the speaker's intent is to have the listener offer food. On the other hand, it could count as an offer, if the speaker means to say that he or she is going to start making dinner; or, it might simply have the illocutionary force of a statement designed just to convey information and nothing more. We know the intention behind a certain message, according to Searle, because we share a common language game, consisting of a set of rules that helps us define the illocutionary force of a message. In this case, we share an understanding of what an insult is.

Searle states fundamentally that "speaking a language is engaging in a rule-governed form of behavior."[22] Two types of rules are important—constitutive and regulative. *Constitutive rules* actually create games; that is, the game is created, or "constituted," by its rules. For example, the game of football exists only by virtue of its rules. The rules make up the game. When you observe people following that set of rules, you know the game of football is being played. These rules therefore tell you what to interpret as football, as opposed to baseball or soccer. In speech acts, constitutive rules tell you what to interpret as a promise, as opposed to a request or a command. One's intention is largely understood by another person because of the constitutive rules; they tell others what to count as a particular kind of speech act.

For example, how do you know a promise when you hear one? Promising involves five basic rules: First, it must include a sentence indicating the speaker will do some future act. Second, the utterance only counts as a promise if the listener prefers that the speaker do the act rather than not do it. In other words, in the context of the interaction, the listener is expecting a promise. Third, a statement is a promise only if done outside the normal course of events. If you do what you normally would do, a promise is not needed. Fourth, the speaker must intend to do the act. Finally, a promise involves the establishment of an obligation for the speaker to do the act. These five rules "constitute" a sufficient set of conditions for a speech act to count as a promise.

Any illocutionary act must have a basic set of constitutive rules. The *propositional content rule* specifies some condition of the referenced object. In a promise, for example, the speaker must state that a future act will be done—to repay a debt perhaps. *Preparatory rules* involve the presumed preconditions in the speaker and hearer necessary for the act to take place. For example, in a promise, the utterance has no meaning unless the hearer would rather the future act be done than not be done. In our illustration, the hearer wants to get repaid. The *sincerity rule* requires the speaker to mean what is said. You must truly intend to repay the debt for the statement to count as a promise. The *essential rule* states that the act is indeed taken by the hearer and speaker to represent what it appears to be on the face. In other words the promise establishes a contractual obligation between speaker and hearer. These constitutive rule types are believed to apply to a wide variety of illocutionary acts, such as requesting, asserting, questioning, thanking, advising, warning, greeting, and congratulating.

The second kind of rule is regulative. *Regulative rules* provide guidelines for acting within a game. The behaviors are known and available before being used in the act, and they tell us how to use speech to accomplish a particular intention. For example, if I want something, I make a request. When I request something of you, you are obligated either to grant the request or to turn it down.

Speech acts are not successful when their illocutionary force is not understood, and they can be evaluated in terms of the degree to which they employ the rules of that speech act. Whereas propositions are evaluated in terms of truth or *validity,* speech acts, then, are evaluated in terms of *felicity,* or the degree to which the conditions of the act are met. The felicity of a promise is whether the essential rules for executing a promise have been met.

Although many speech acts are direct and involve the use of an explicit statement of intent, other speech acts are indirect. To request that his family to come to the table for dinner, a father might say, "Is anybody hungry?" On the face this appears to be a question, but in actuality it is an indirect request and maybe even a command.

Searle outlines five types of illocutionary acts. The first he calls *assertives.* An assertive is a statement that commits the speaker to advocate the truth of a proposition. It includes such acts as stating, affirming, concluding, and believing. The second are *directives*—illocutions that attempt to get the listener to do something. They are commands, requests, pleadings, prayers, entreaties, invitations, and so forth. *Commissives,* the third type, commit the speaker to a future act. They consist of such things as promising, vowing, pledging, contracting, and guaranteeing. The fourth, *expressives*, are acts that communicate some aspect of the speaker's psychological state, such as thanking, congratulating, apologizing, consoling, and welcoming. Finally, a *declaration* is designed to create a proposition that, by its very assertion, makes it so. Examples include appointing, marrying, firing, and resigning. To illustrate, you are not married until an authorized person actually says the words, *I pronounce you husband and wife*.

We include classical speech-act theory in this chapter because it focuses on the elements of a message that constitute particular speech acts. As this line of work has expanded, however, it has moved more into the realm of interaction between speakers. Speech-act theory identifies what it takes to make a successful statement, to have an intention understood. But speech acts are rarely isolated; they are usually part of ongoing conversations. How we organize conversations is a fascinating and important question in communication theory, and we take up this subject in detail in Chapter 6.

Searle's work helps us understand how communicators assign meaning to a speech act, but what do speech acts actually do in bridging communicators? In the following section, we will look at a landmark theory that helps us answer this question.

Kenneth Burke's Theory of Identification

Kenneth Burke is no doubt a giant among symbol theorists.[23] He wrote over a period of fifty years, and his theory is one of the most comprehensive of all symbol theories. One follower wrote, "It may be said without exaggeration that anyone writing today on communication, however 'original' he may be, is echoing something said by Burke."[24] In surveying Burke's communication theory, we will begin with a summary of his concept of action. We then will turn to his central ideas on symbols, language, and communication Burke starts with the distinction between action and motion. *Action* consists of purposeful,

voluntary behaviors; *motions* are non-purposeful, non-meaningful ones. Objects and animals possess motion, but only human beings have action. Burke views the individual as a biological and neurological being, distinguished by symbol-using behavior or the ability to act. People are symbol-creating, symbol-using, and symbol-misusing animals. They create symbols to name things and situations; they use symbols for communication; and they often abuse symbols by misusing them to their disadvantage.

Burke's view of symbols is broad, including an array of linguistic and nonverbal elements as well. People filter reality through a symbolic screen. Reality is mediated through symbols. Burke agrees with Mead that language functions as the vehicle for action. Because of the social need for people to cooperate in their actions, language shapes behavior. Especially intriguing for Burke is the notion that a person can symbolize symbols. One can talk about speech and can write about words. History itself is a process of writing about what people have already spoken and written in the course of events.

Language, as seen by Burke, is always emotionally loaded. No word can be neutral. As a result, your attitudes, judgments, and feelings invariably appear in the language you use. Language is by nature selective and abstract, focusing attention on particular aspects of reality at the expense of other aspects. Language is economical, but it is also ambiguous. Language can bring us together or divide us—and this paradox plays an important role in Burke's theory. When symbols bring people together into a common way of understanding, *identification* is said to occur. The opposite, *division* or separation can also happen; just as language can promote identification, it can also promote separation and division.

When you and a friend are relaxing next to the swimming pool on a warm summer morning, you communicate with each other in a free and easy manner because you share meanings for the language in use. You are, in Burke's terms, experiencing *consubstantiality*. On the other hand, when you ask a question of a harried busboy in a Swiss restaurant, you may feel frustration because of your lack of shared meaning with this individual. Consubstantiality is one way *identification* is created between people. In a spiraling fashion, as identification increases, shared meaning increases, thereby improving understanding. Identification thus can be a means to persuasion and effective communication, or it can be an end in itself. Identification can be conscious or unconscious, planned or unplanned.

Three overlapping sources of identification exist among people. *Material identification* results from goods, possessions, and things, like owning the same kind of car or having similar tastes in clothes. *Idealistic identification* results from shared ideas, attitudes, feelings, and values, such as being a member of the same church or political party. *Formal identification* results from the arrangement, form, or organization of an event in which both parties participate. If two people who are introduced shake hands, the conventional form of handshaking causes some identification to take place.

Identification is not an either/or occurrence but a matter of degree. Some consubstantiality will always be present merely by virtue of the shared humanness of any two people. Identification can be great or small, and it can be increased or decreased by the actions of the communicators. Second, although any two persons will always experience some identification and some division, communication is more successful when identification is greater than division.

People of lower strata in a hierarchy often identify with people at the top of the hierarchy, despite tremendous apparent division. This kind of identification can be seen, for example, in the mass following of a charismatic leader. This can happen because individuals perceive in others an embodiment of the perfection for which they themselves strive. Second, the mystery surrounding the charismatic person simultaneously tends to hide the division that exists. This phenomenon can be called *identification through mystification*.

Burke introduces another term that helps explain identification. This is the concept of *guilt*. This term is Burke's all-purpose word for any feeling of tension within a person—anxiety, embarrassment, self-hatred, disgust, and so forth. For Burke, guilt is a condition caused by symbol use. He identifies three related sources of guilt, the first of which is the *negative*. Through language people moralize. They construct myriad rules and proscriptions. These rules are never entirely consistent, and in following one rule, you necessarily are breaking another, creating guilt. Religions, professions, organizations, families, and communities all have implicit rules about how to behave. We learn these throughout life and therefore judge almost any action as good or bad.

The second reason for guilt is the *principle of perfection*. People are sensitive to their failings. Humans can imagine (through language) a state of perfection. Then, by their very nature, they spend their lives striving for whatever degree of this perfection they set for themselves. Guilt arises as a result of the discrepancy between the real and the ideal. A peace activist might be motivated by this kind of guilt, for example. A speaker at a rally may say that war is a barbaric and inappropriate method of resolving conflict in the twenty-first century. This speaker can imagine a world without war and is motivated to speak out because of the principle of perfection.

A third reason for guilt is the *principle of hierarchy*. In seeking order, people structure society in social pyramids or hierarchies (social ratings, social orderings), a process which is done with symbols. Competitions and divisions result among classes and groups in the hierarchy, and guilt results. Ethnic strife is a perfect example. Burke, then, places strong emphasis on the role of language and symbols in bringing people together or driving them apart.[25] He shows that we can develop strategies for doing either.

Although Burke's theory is hard to place in this book, we see it primarily as a theory of the message because Burke tunes us in to the ways in which messages can be structured to create identification or division. Burke observes that communicators develop *strategies* for identification and division. In preparing a speech, for example, you may want to bring certain audiences into your way of thinking through identification, while distancing yourself from other audiences by creating division. Politicians do this all the time. Message strategies, then, make use of forms of identification that will create commonality with certain listeners. Such strategies will almost certainly involve guilt (in the Burkean sense). Burke's intension was not to provide a list of ready strategies, but to present a set of ideas that speakers can use to determine in a particular case the unique forms of identification (and perhaps division) that might be used in the message.

Burke wrote throughout the middle of the twentieth century, but his ideas anticipated a whole movement in communication research around message strategies, which, ironically, were produced not within Burke's tradition at all, but from a psychological perspective. We present some of these theories that deal with message strategy later in the chapter. For now, let's move to the role of language and gender, an area of investigation that has become immensely attractive to scholars in communication and throughout the social sciences and humanities.

Language and Gender

In the past 30 years, a great deal of work has been produced on communication and gender. In this section we look at two representative theories that relate gender to the sociocultural tradition.

Cheris Kramarae.   Like Burke, Cheris Kramarae believes that a primary feature of the world is its linguistic nature, and the words and syntax within messages structure people's thinking and interaction and have a major impact on how we experience the world.[26] The gendered implications of language are of primary concern to Kramarae, as she explores the ways in which messages treat women and men differently. No human experience is free from the influence of language. Even the categories of *male* and *female* are largely linguistic constructions. In other words, we are "trained to see two sexes. And

then we do a lot of work to continue to see only these two sexes."[27]

Kramarae not only notes the importance of language in interpreting experience; she also addresses the dimension of power. Any language system has power relations embedded in it, and those who are part of the dominant linguistic system tend to have their perceptions, experiences, and modes of expression incorporated into language. In the case of English, Kramarae believes that it is a "man-made language"[28] and thus embodies the perspectives of the masculine more than the feminine. The perceptions of white middle-class males, in particular, are normalized in standard linguistic practice. Men are the standard, for instance, in many occupational terms, and women are the aberrant category: *waiter* versus *waitress*, *poet* versus *poetess*. *Mr.* as a title of address does not contain information about marital status whereas the terms *Miss* and *Mrs.* do provide information that is more useful to men than to women. Not only language itself but the instruments of language—dictionaries—feature white men's viewpoints, as do the societal structures and institutions that derive from language, such as educational institutions, technology, and the like.[29]

In addition to outlining the significance of linguistic constructions to experience—especially as it relates to gender—Kramarae also has described an alternative linguistic reality, based on traditionally feminine experience. She sees this reality as characterized by interconnection, safety, holism, trust, mutuality, adaptability, and equal access to information. This worldview is equally powerful as the traditional masculine vantage point but is not always as recognizable or apparent, simply because of the dominance of the masculine viewpoint.[30]

Feminine Style.   The theory of feminine style, first suggested by Karlyn Kohrs Campbell and elaborated by Bonnie J. Dow and Mari Boor Tonn, elaborates on Kramarae's efforts to understand the gendered aspects of language.[31] Central to the theory is that a feminine style originally is linked to what Campbell calls "craft learning." By this she means not only literally crafts traditionally associated with housewifery and motherhood (the feminine role) such as sewing, needlework, cooking, and gardening, but also emotional crafts such as nurturance, empathy, and concrete reasoning.[32]

Campbell suggests that while this style is not exclusive to women, either as speakers or audience members, it emerged out of the experiences of the home and thus produces a certain kind of message:

> Such discourse is personal in tone (crafts are learned face-to-face from a mentor), relying heavily on personal experience, anecdotes, and other examples. It will tend to be structured inductively (crafts are learned bit by bit, instance by instance, from which generalizations emerge). It will invite audience participation, including the process of testing generalizations or principles against the experiences of the audience. Audience members will be addressed as peers, with recognition of authority based on experience.[33]

One of the strategies of early women orators was to use this style to appear more "womanly" on the public platform, and women continue to be socialized to communicate in ways that correspond to the traditionally private sphere of women.

Bonnie J. Dow and Mari Boor Tonn extend the work on feminine style, suggesting it remains an effective strategy by which contemporary women speakers can gain access to the political system. They use the speeches of former Texas Governor Ann Richards to show the existence of a feminine style in mainstream political discourse and to show how it functions as a strategy for audience empowerment. They found that Richards based her claims on experience, citing letters from constituents, for example, to privilege the concrete over abstract reasoning. She also used a personal, self-disclosive tone in her speeches, and a context of care, connection, and relationship in such a way to empower her audience to trust their own perceptions and judgments. At the same time, the way in which she made her points—with humor, the personal story, and anecdote—made her discourse more

acceptable to audiences unused to a woman in high political office. Dow and Tonn suggest that Richards's feminine style goes beyond simply *"adaptation to obstacles posed by patriarchy . . . to offer alternatives* to patriarchal modes of thought and reasoning." They label this alternative worldview a "feminist counter-public sphere."[34]

Jane Blankenship and Deborah Robson examined women's public policy discourse between 1991 and 1994 to determine whether a feminine style could be said to exist in contemporary political discourse. They concluded that it is evident and is characterized by five overlapping properties: (1) concrete experience as a basis for political judgments; (2) inclusivity and connection; (3) public office conceptualized as a place to "get things done" and empower others; (4) a holistic approach to policy formation; and (5) bringing women's legislation to the forefront.[35] What remains to be seen, according to Blankenship and Robson, is whether the feminine style makes or reflects a difference in the process or outcome of public policy.

REFLECTIONS ON
The Sociocultural Tradition

With the sociocultural tradition, we move from elements of the message to larger concerns about the ways in which messages create connections across individuals in social groups and cultures. Here we see a larger pragmatic concern that addresses how messages achieve social purposes and how they function in creating bonds of various types. Notice how the emphasis shifts in the theories in this section from a relatively concentrated focus on the parts of the message and how they are organized—characteristic of the semiotic tradition—to a focus on the ways in which message elements create and reflect larger social categories and connections—characteristic of the sociocultural.

As we move to the sociopsychological tradition, you will see yet another shift, from the message itself to psychological processes involved in the production and reception of those messages.

● ● ●

◖ THE SOCIOPSYCHOLOGICAL TRADITION

Theories of the sociopsychological tradition focus on how individual communicators manage messages. Consistent with work throughout social psychology, this line of research and theory tends to be cognitive in orientation and explains how people integrate information and plan messages accordingly. These theories look at individual choices and strategies for achieving internally established goals for a message. Several of these theories look at individual differences in how people orient to message planning and design. Here we look at four lines of work—action assembly theory, strategy choice models, message design models, and semantic meaning theory.

Action Assembly Theory

We begin this section with a general cognitive theory that explains what humans actually go through to produce communicative action. Developed by John Greene, action assembly theory examines the ways we organize knowledge within the mind and use it to form messages.[36]

According to this theory, you form messages by using *content knowledge* and *procedural knowledge*. You know *about* things, and you know *how to do* things. In action assembly theory, procedural knowledge takes center stage. To get an idea of what your procedural knowledge looks like, imagine that your memory is full of connected elements. Each element of memory is a *node*, and the nodes are connected to one another, much like the way Web sites are linked in the Internet. Specifically, procedural knowledge consists of associated nodes related to behavior, consequences, and situations. For example, you probably smile when you greet someone and say something like, "Hi, how are you?" Then, the other person smiles back and says, "Fine. How are you?" You hold this in your memory as a set of associated nodes in which links are made be-

tween the situation of greeting someone, smiling, using certain words, and the result of having the greeting returned.

Although the above example is very simple, your actual network of associated nodes is a constantly changing, complex system. However, it is not an unorganized system. At any given time, the associations that have been most frequently or most recently activated are stronger, so that certain nodes tend to cluster together into modules, which Greene calls *procedural records*. The smiling-greeting ritual described above is a simple example of a procedural record. However, procedural records are not distinct with firm boundaries. Because the elements—smiling, greeting, asking about health, and so on—are also associated with other things, procedural records are imprecise.

A procedural record, then, is a set of links among nodes in a network of action. Some of these are just automatic associations. Because you have done certain things together over and over, they have become associated, like removing one foot from the gas and pushing in the clutch with your other foot. Other records actually contain information, or meaning—like knowing that the foot routine with the gas and clutch is a part of changing gears, necessary for driving a car with a stick shift.

Whenever you act, you must "assemble" appropriate procedures, or behaviors. Out of all the actions in your procedural memory, you must select the most appropriate ones within the situation to accomplish the consequences you wish. You do this by selecting an action sequence. The word *selecting*, however, belies the complexity of what is really happening behind the scenes within your mind. According to the theory, whenever you act, you must assemble associated behaviors from appropriate procedural records.

Some sets of assembled action are so strongly entrenched and so frequently used that you often rely on them as preformed or programmed actions. Called *unitized assemblies*, these highly efficient routines require little effort. You don't have to think much about what to do because the whole sequence is already there in your memory.

Greeting rituals are a good example of unitized assemblies.

Often, however, situations require you to do some cognitive work. A number of outcomes may be desired, including achieving an objective with another person, expressing information, managing conversations, producing intelligible speech, and other results. When introducing yourself, for example, you may want to meet the other person, make yourself look good, and have a good time, all in one set of actions. You essentially assemble the procedures necessary to accomplish these objectives, and the result is a mental representation for a coordinated set of actions. This mental model is called *output representation*; it is the "plan" your mind holds about what you will do within the situation you face.

Let's say, for example, that you see a friend walking toward you. You are suddenly filled with dread because you know that your friend's mother has just died, and you will need to say and do something appropriate. How will your mind handle this difficult situation?

First, the situation will trigger, or activate, a host of nodes on such topics as death, friend, greeting, feeling, speaking, gesturing, and so on. Each of these activated nodes is part of a variety of procedural records. These coalesce into what Greene calls a *coalition*. So at the time you see your friend, your mind will pull together a coalition of possible procedural records, but you cannot use them all. From the coalition, your mind will quickly and simultaneously piece together a set of actions ranging from very low level (such as uttering words) to high level (such as accomplishing a goal). This is the *output representation*: everything you need to remember in order to act in an appropriate and coordinated way. All of the actions—from remembering how to pronounce certain words to how to express sympathy—are tightly associated at this moment. At that instance, other associations that are part of less relevant procedural records fade away in a process called *decay*, leaving a coherent output representation for this particular situation.

It is clear, then, that no single action can stand by itself. Every action implicates other actions in

one way or another. To introduce yourself, you have to use a variety of actions from moving your vocal chords to using certain words and gestures. To write a paragraph, you must combine a variety of actions from coordinating knowledge to using language to writing or typing. Actions, then, are integrated into a network of knowledge. Each piece of knowledge in the overall routine is a representation of something that needs to be done. Higher-order goals (such as making an introduction) and lower-level routines (such as smiling) are integrated into an output representation that guides your communication actions.

The action-assembly process requires not only knowledge and motivation but also the ability to retrieve and organize the necessary actions efficiently and quickly. If you make a mistake or have trouble doing something, even when you have the correct knowledge and motivation, it means you are not able to put together the best routine for any number of reasons. For example, you may not be practiced in doing it, you may be unable to pay attention to important aspects of the situation, you may be relying too much on unitized routines, or you may experience other problems in the action-assembly process.

Action assembly takes time and effort. Thinking is work. The more complex the assembly task, the more time and effort it takes. Introducing yourself is usually not as difficult as expressing sympathy in an unexpected situation. Even though communicators seem to respond to a situation immediately without effort, research shows that every response does take time, if only a fraction of a second. Complex tasks take more time than simple ones. You know from your own experience that you think through and struggle with communicating in unfamiliar situations. When people take a long time to say something, pause and stutter, or generally seem confused, they may be having difficulty in integrating procedural knowledge and formulating an action. When people respond quickly and fluently, they are demonstrating that the task is relatively easy for them in this situation.

Action assembly theory is what we might call a microcognitive theory because it deals with very specific cognitive operations. The other theories in this section, by contrast, are macrocognitive theories, as they look at how we put messages together on a higher level. Barbara O'Keefe identifies two approaches to theorizing about message production, which she terms the *strategy choice* and *message design* models.[37] Strategy choice models look at how communicators select from among various message strategies to accomplish a goal, and the message design model concentrates on how communicators actually construct messages to meet their goals.[38] As we continue this section on the sociopsychological tradition, we will first discuss theories that use strategy choice models and then move to those that focus on message design.

Strategy Choice Models

Compliance Gaining.   Gaining the compliance of another person is one of the most common communication goals. It involves trying to get other people to do what you want them to do, or to stop doing something you don't like. Compliance-gaining messages are among the most researched areas in the field.[39] The prolific research program on compliance-gaining strategies in the communication field received its impetus from the groundbreaking studies of Gerald Marwell and David Schmitt.[40] These researchers isolated sixteen strategies commonly used in gaining the compliance of other people, as outlined in Table 5.2.

Marwell and Schmitt use an exchange-theory approach: Compliance is an exchange for something else supplied by the compliance seeker. If you do what I want, I will give you something in return—esteem, approval, money, relief from obligations, and good feelings, among other things. The exchange approach, which is frequently used in social theory, rests on the assumption that people act to gain something from others in exchange for something else. This model is inherently power oriented. In other words, you can gain the compliance of others if you have sufficient resources to provide or withhold something they want.

One of the most important theoretical questions about compliance-gaining tactics has been how to reduce the list of all possible tactics to a manageable set of general strategies or dimensions. A long list of how people persuade others does not tell you much more than you already know. A shorter list would crystallize the tactics into essential qualities, functions, goals, or some other set of dimensions that would help explain

---

TABLE **5.2**

Marwell and Schmitt's Compliance-Gaining Strategies

1. *Promising*   Promising a reward for compliance
2. *Threatening*   Indicating that punishment will be applied for noncompliance
3. *Showing expertise about positive outcomes*   Showing how good things will happen to those who comply
4. *Showing expertise about negative outcomes*   Showing how bad things will happen to those who do not comply
5. *Liking*   Displaying friendliness
6. *Pregiving*   Giving a reward before asking for compliance
7. *Applying aversive stimulation*   Applying punishment until compliance is received
8. *Calling in a debt*   Saying the person owes something for past favors
9. *Making moral appeals*   Describing compliance as the morally right thing to do
10. *Attributing positive feelings*   Telling the other person how good he or she will feel if there is compliance
11. *Attributing negative feelings*   Telling the other person how bad he or she will feel if there is noncompliance
12. *Positive altercasting*   Associating compliance with people with good qualities
13. *Negative altercasting*   Associating noncompliance with people with bad qualities
14. *Seeking altruistic compliance*   Seeking compliance simply as a favor
15. *Showing positive esteem*   Saying that the person will be liked by others more if he or she complies
16. *Showing negative esteem*   Saying that the person will be liked less by others if he or she does not comply

what people are actually accomplishing when they try to persuade other people.

In an attempt to create such a set of principles, Marwell and Schmitt asked subjects to apply the sixteen items in Table 5.2 to various compliance-gaining situations. Five general strategies, or clusters of tactics, emerged. These included *rewarding* (which includes, for example, promising), *punishing* (for instance, threatening), *expertise* (as in displaying knowledge of rewards), *impersonal commitments* (examples would include moral appeals), and *personal commitments* (such as debts).

Although the work of Marwell and Schmitt was foundational, it is limited in its ability to explain compliance-gaining messages, and much work has been done to expand our understanding of this process. One of the most comprehensive analyses of the compliance-gaining literature is that of Lawrence Wheeless, Robert Barraclough, and Robert Stewart, who review and integrate the variety of compliance-gaining schemes.[41] These researchers believe that compliance-gaining messages are best classified according to the kinds of power employed by communicators when attempting to gain the compliance of another individual. Power is access to influential resources. It is a result of interpersonal perception, since people have as much power as others perceive that they have.

The Wheeless group isolated three general types of power. The first is the perceived ability *to manipulate the consequences* of a certain course of action. Parents often use this kind of power when punishing and rewarding their children. If you tell your children that you will buy them a video game if they get good grades, you are using this source of power.

The second kind of power is the perceived ability to determine one's *relational position* with the other person. Here the powerful person can identify certain elements of the relationship that will bring about compliance. For example, if your boyfriend or girlfriend thinks you are not all that committed to the relationship, you may be able to get a lot of cooperation because he or she may be afraid you will want to leave the relationship.

The third type of power involves the perceived ability to *define values*, *obligations*, or both. Here one person has the credibility to tell the other what norms of behavior are accepted or necessary. Returning a favor is a good example of this. Behaving kindly is another. Being sensitive to others' needs is still another example. In each case, one communicator defines what is right and good, and the other person complies by behaving in accordance with this standard.

In a compliance-gaining situation, then, you assess your power and choose tactics that invoke that power. Wheeless lists a number of tactics associated with the three classes of power. For example, the ability to affect another person's expectations and consequences may lead you to use tactics like promises, threats, and warnings. The ability to manipulate the relationship may lead you to choose such tactics as saying you like the other person, attributing positive or negative esteem, making emotional appeals, flattering, and so on. The third category of power—defining values and obligations—may lead you to use moral appeals, debt, guilt, and other similar techniques.

The compliance-gaining literature is dominated by lists of possible strategies that people can use, but most of these studies do little to help us understand the basis for strategy choice. The following theory steps in to fill this void.

Constructivism.   Constructivism, a theory developed by Jesse Delia and his colleagues, has had immense impact on the field of communication.[42] The theory says that individuals interpret and act according to conceptual categories of the mind. Reality does not present itself in raw form but must be filtered through the person's own way of seeing things.

Constructivism is based partially on George Kelly's theory of personal constructs, which proposes that persons understand experience by grouping events according to similarities and distinguishing between things by their differences.[43] Perceived differences are not natural, but determined by sets of opposites within the individual's cognitive system. Opposite pairs like tall-short, hot-cold, and black-white, used to understand events and things, are called personal constructs. Hence the name of Kelly's theory— *personal construct theory.*

An individual's cognitive system consists of numerous such distinctions. By classifying an experience into categories, the individual gives it meaning. So, for example, you might see your mother as tall and your father as short, coffee as hot and milk as cold, your favorite jacket as black and a favorite hat as white.

Constructs are organized into interpretive schemes, which identify something and place the object in a category. With interpretive schemes, we make sense out of an event by placing it in a larger category. Interpretive schemes develop as you mature by moving from relative simplicity and generality to relative complexity and specificity. Thus, very young children have simple construct systems, while most adults have much more sophisticated ones. When you were young, for example, you might have placed all people into two types: big and little. Now, on the other hand, you have an immense number of constructs with which to distinguish among different people.

Constructivism recognizes that constructs have social origins and are learned through interaction with other people. Consequently, culture seems especially significant in determining the meanings of events. Culture can influence the way communication goals are defined, how goals should be achieved, as well as the types of constructs employed in the cognitive schema.[44] Although it acknowledges the impact of social interaction and culture on the cognitive system, constructivism deals primarily with individual differences in construct complexity and strategies used in communication.

Individuals with highly developed interpretive schemes make more discriminations than those who see the world simplistically. Although the construct system develops throughout childhood and adolescence, even adults differ widely in their cognitive complexity. Also, different parts of your construct system differ in complexity, so that you might have elaborate thoughts about music but simple ideas about international relations.

Because cognitive complexity plays an important role in communication, this concept is a mainstay of constructivism.[45] Complexity or simplicity in the system is a function of the relative number of constructs and the degree of distinctions you can make. You do not have a consistent level of cognitive complexity, but think at different levels of sophistication on different topics. The number of constructs you use on a particular topic is called cognitive differentiation. Cognitively sophisticated people can make more distinctions than cognitively uncomplicated people. Many of us go to a tax accountant every year because we do not have sufficient cognitive complexity in this subject.

Delia and his colleagues have shown that messages vary according to complexity. Simple messages address only one goal, complex messages separate goals and deal with each in turn, and the most sophisticated messages actually integrate several goals in one message.[46] We often attempt to accomplish more than one thing by a single action, and our messages vary in the extent to which they can achieve multiple, sometimes conflicting, objectives simultaneously. Cognitive differentiation thus affects how complex messages can be.

Further, the simplest persuasive messages only address your own goals without considering the other person's needs, whereas more adaptive, complex persuasive messages are designed to meet your needs and the needs of the other person. For example, if you want to get a person to change his or her behavior, to stop smoking perhaps, you might want to do it in a way that would help the other person save face. This would require you to achieve at least two objectives in the same message: Deliver a non-smoking message and protect the other person's ego. Simple messages cannot do this, but more complex messages can be employed precisely for this purpose. Constructivists have found that the tendency to help the other person save face is directly related to cognitive complexity.

Interpersonal constructs are especially important because they guide how we understand other people. Individuals differ in the complexity with which they view others. If you are cognitively simple, you will tend to stereotype other people, whereas if you have more cognitive differentiation, you will make subtler and more sensitive distinctions. Generally, cognitive complexity leads to greater understanding of others' perspectives and better ability to frame messages in terms understandable to other people. This ability, called *perspective taking*, seems to lead to more sophisticated arguments and appeals.[47] Adjusting one's communication to others is referred to as *person-centered communication*, and people vary in their use of person-centered messages.

Compliance gaining is one of several types of communication that have been studied from a person-centered perspective.[48] Persuasive messages range from the least to the most person-centered. On the simplest level, for example, one could attempt to achieve the single objective of compliance by commanding or threatening. On a more complex level, one might also try to help a person understand why compliance is necessary by offering reasons for complying. On an even higher level of complexity, a communicator could try to elicit sympathy by building empathy or insight into the situation. As one's messages become more complex, they necessarily involve more goals and are more person-centered.

Comforting messages have also been studied from a constructivist perspective. People try to provide social support to others in a variety of ways, and some of these methods are more sophisticated than others. Research on comforting messages generally supports the view that cognitively complex individuals produce more sophisticated messages than less complex individuals, that sophisticated messages are more person-centered than less sophisticated ones, and that more sophisticated messages are more effective in eliciting comfort than less sophisticated ones.[49]

As an example of person-centered communication, consider the study of Susan Kline and Janet Ceropski on doctor–patient communication.[50] This study involved forty-six medical students who completed a variety of tests, participated in videotaped interviews with patients, and wrote statements on what they thought the purpose of medical interviews to be. The interviews were then carefully examined by the researchers and classified according to how person-centered they were.

The person-centered messages used by the medical students were found to be more complex than messages that were not person-centered. The researchers found that about 40 percent of the medical students were person-centered in persuading patients. These individuals explained why compliance was necessary and considered patients' feelings. About 50 percent of the subjects used person-centered communication in dealing with distress by acknowledging rather than denying patients' feelings, helping patients understand their discomfort, and giving advice on how to relieve the distress. Finally, about 70 percent of those studied used person-centered communication in gathering information. Their questions were more detailed, and they gave patients more leeway in telling their story. This research confirms that those who use person-centered strategies have complex cognitive schemas for understanding other people and are better able to take the perspective of others and to have empathy for others.

As sophisticated as it is, constructivism is still basically a strategy-choice theory. Constructivist research procedures usually ask subjects to select different message types and classify these in terms of strategy categories. The following theory applies this idea of strategy choice to a particularly interesting aspects of social life.

Politeness Strategies. As constructivism shows, we often try to accomplish several things at once, and politeness, or protecting the face of the other person, is often one of the goals we aim to achieve. The best-known sociopsychological treatment of politeness and face is that of Penelope Brown and Stephen Levinson.[51] This theory states that in everyday life we design messages that protect face and achieve other goals as well.

Brown and Levinson believe that politeness is often a goal because it is a culturally universal value. Different cultures have different levels of required politeness and different ways of being polite, but all people have the need to be appreciated and protected, which these researchers call *face needs*. *Positive face* is the desire to be appreciated and approved, to be liked and honored. *Positive politeness* is designed to meet these desires. Showing concern, complimenting, and using respectful forms of address are examples. *Negative face* is the desire to be free from imposition or intrusion, and *negative politeness* is designed to protect the other person when negative face needs are threatened. Acknowledging the imposition when making a request is a common example.

Politeness is especially important whenever we must threaten another person's face, which happens frequently in our relations with others. We commit *face-threatening acts* (FTAs) whenever we behave in a way that could potentially fail to meet positive or negative face needs. Face threatening is normal and not itself a problem, but it must be handled in certain ways to mitigate potential problems that could result. There are a wide range of ways to handle FTAs, and we do not always do it the same way. Whether we deliver an FTA, how we do so, and what forms of politeness are used depend on a variety of things.

When an FTA is possible, there are five approaches we can use. We can (1) deliver the FTA baldly or directly, without polite action; (2) deliver the FTA along with some form of positive politeness; (3) deliver the FTA along with some form of negative politeness; (4) deliver the FTA indirectly, off record; or (5) not deliver the FTA at all. These five choices are arranged in order from the most to the least face threatening.

Suppose that you would like to ask your professor to reconsider an exam grade. This is a face issue for the professor because he or she has already declared what your grade is and could be made to feel inadequate by the request. How would you do it? One approach would be to deliver the bald FTA: "I would like you to reconsider my grade," period. You probably would

not choose this approach because it would not be very polite.

A slightly less threatening method would be to combine the request with positive politeness, something like this: "I would appreciate it if you could look at my grade again. Other students have said you're really nice about that." Here we have a request (FTA) combined with a compliment.

Even less threatening would be to combine the FTA with negative politeness: "I'm really sorry. I know you're very busy, but could I have a moment of your time? If you're not too busy, I would really appreciate it if you could look at my grade again." Notice that this message meets negative face needs by acknowledging and apologizing for the imposition.

Number 4 is particularly interesting and complex. An "off-record" FTA is one that is indirect and ambiguous, which enables you to deny having meant the statement as an FTA. For example, you might ask to borrow your friend's car by saying, "I wonder how I will get to town this afternoon to pick up my laundry?" You hope your friend will get the hint and say, "Oh, why don't you use my car?" But if he says, "Well, you can't use *my* car," you can always reply, "Oh, I wasn't asking for it." In requesting your professor to reconsider your grade, you might say something like, "Gosh, I didn't think I had done this badly on the exam." You hope she will reply, "Well, why don't I read it again?"—but if she looks at you funny, you can always deny that you were requesting a reconsideration.

According to Brown and Levinson, which of these strategies we choose to use depends on a simple formula:

$$W_x = D(S,H) + P(H,S) + R_x$$

This formula means that the amount of work (W) one puts into being polite depends on the social distance (D) between the speaker (S) and the hearer (H), plus the power (P) of the hearer over the speaker, plus the risk (R) of hurting the other person.

Let's consider two examples. Imagine that you want to ask your brother for a simple, nonthreatening favor—to drop you off at the mall, let's say. You and your brother have the same status—he does not have any special power over you, and the request is not threatening. You will probably put little work into being polite.

On the other hand, suppose you want to get a loan from your parents. Assuming that you consider your parents somewhat higher in status than you, that they have considerable power over your finances, and that a request for money is considerably more serious than asking for a candy bar, you will probably be quite polite in your request. Of course, these assumptions may not hold in your particular case, but you can probably think of other examples that would require considerable face-saving work on your part.

There are, of course, a variety of levels of politeness between these two extremes. One variable can counteract another. For example, there may be little social distance, but quite a bit of power disparity. Or perhaps the distance and power don't matter much because the FTA is so minor. Each of the theories in this section looks at message strategies we might select under different conditions. The next group looks at how we actually design messages.

Message Design Models

As we saw in the previous section, message-choice models imagine that communicators select strategies for accomplishing their communication goals. In contrast, theories of message design imagine a more complex scenario in which communicators actually design messages that are in line with their intentions within the situations they face. The difference is the same as that between selecting a home from five different floor plans versus custom designing a house to meet your family's particular needs. Like the specially designed house, the form of the message matches its function. Here we look at three theories within this tradition.

Planning Theory. A well-known theory of planning in the communication field was produced by Charles Berger to explain the process that individuals go through in planning their communication behavior.[52] The study of planning is a centerpiece of cognitive science, and psychologists have given the subject considerable thought and research. Linking cognitive planning with communication behavior, however, has not received as much attention, and Berger hopes to close this gap with his own research and theory.

Berger writes that plans are "hierarchical cognitive representations of goal-directed action sequences."[53] In other words, plans are mental images of the steps one will go through to meet a goal. They are hierarchical because certain actions are necessary to set things up so that other actions will work. Planning, then, is the process of thinking up these action plans.

Because communication is so important in achieving goals, planning messages is a critical concern. If you want to do well in a class, you probably talk to other students, friends, and even the professor to find out what might be done. Your assignments will be carefully crafted to meet requirements, and you will think consciously about what to do and how to do it.

Among the many goals we try to achieve every day, from planning meals to getting where we want to go, *social goals* are especially important. Because we are social creatures, other people are important in our lives, and we aim to influence people in a variety of ways. We can achieve many types of goals by communicating in particular ways, but communication is central to meeting social goals. Understanding something about how we plan to meet such goals, then, is an important research aim.

Studying goal behavior is no easy task. For one thing, goals tend to be complex. Goals seem to be arranged in hierarchies, and achieving certain goals first makes it possible to achieve other ones later. For example, you may find another person attractive and want to get to know this person, but you will probably have to accomplish quite a few subgoals first, such as finding a way to start a conversation with this person.

Many of our goals are actually part of the planning process itself. These *metagoals* guide the plans we make. For example, we usually want to do planning in the easiest way possible, making efficiency an important metagoal. (That's why we don't reinvent the wheel every time we take a drive.) We want to behave in socially appropriate ways, so social appropriateness is another metagoal. Another metagoal is politeness, for whatever else we might want to accomplish in our communication, we often aim to be polite.

Because we want our planning to be efficient, we often rely on *canned plans* we have used before. These are stored in *long-term memory,* and we rely on them whenever possible. Because you have started so many conversations in your life, you know how to do it without thinking, and you rely on the same methods you have used repeatedly.

Often canned plans don't work or are foiled in some way. Or the goal is new and complicated and requires fresh thinking. Let's say you need a substantial loan and think you can get the money from a close relative—say, your aunt. You have never done this before and don't know exactly how to approach it. Here you must put a new plan together in your *working memory.* The working memory is a place where you can use parts of old plans, knowledge, and creative thinking to come up with a way to approach the problem.

The strength of the goal seems to influence how complex our plans tend to be. If you want something very badly, you will probably work hard and come up with an elaborate plan. If you really need the loan, you will probably work out the plan carefully. Of course, the complexity of your plan will also depend on how much knowledge you have about loans and about your aunt as well as your knowledge about persuasion. Berger refers to information about the topic (for example, loans and relatives) as *specific domain knowledge* and information about how to communicate (for example, persuading people) as *general domain knowledge.*

The theory predicts that the more you know (specific and general), the more complex your plan will be. Obviously, then, if you have a lot of motivation and knowledge, you will create more complex plans, and if your motivation and knowledge are low, your plan will probably be underdeveloped. Naturally, however, there are limits on how complicated a plan can be. In interpersonal communication, this is especially so because of the metagoals of efficiency and social appropriateness. You can't do just anything you want because of the effort it would take and because some actions are not socially appropriate. For example, you probably would not make up a 100-point plan to get money from your aunt because that would take too much effort, and you certainly would not include the socially unacceptable strategy of insulting her to secure the loan.

What happens if your attempt to achieve a goal is thwarted? If the goal is important, you will probably persist, but it is unlikely that you will repeat the same strategy. You might consider two things. One course of action is to try different specific actions, which Berger calls *low-level plan hierarchy alterations*, or you could adjust more general actions (*abstract alterations*). People tend to make lower-level adjustments first. For example, say you decide to broach the subject of the loan by just mentioning that your tuition is due. Suppose that your aunt replies, "Boy, I bet you're glad you had such a high-paying job last summer!" You don't get the reaction you expected, so you try a different message, something like, "Right, and that did help, but my books were so expensive and my apartment rent is out of sight." This is an example of a low-level alteration.

Sometimes, though, the situation calls for alteration of a higher level of strategy. For example, if your aunt were to say, "Yes, money can sure be a problem. My assets are all tied up in a big investment deal right now, and I am also having a little cash flow problem myself," you would probably reconsider what you were trying to accomplish. Instead of asking for the loan now, you might change your goal a little and decide to wait a few weeks.

Berger's theory suggests that whether you make low- or high-level adjustments depends largely on how motivated you are to achieve the goal. If the goal is very important, you will tend to make higher-level adjustments, and you will do so sooner than if your motivation is low.

Planning and goal achievement are very much tied into our emotions.[54] If our goals are thwarted, we tend to react negatively. On the other hand, if our plans go well, we often feel uplifted. The negative feelings we experience when we fail to meet a goal depend on how important the goal is. They also are determined in part by how hard we have worked to achieve the goal and how close to the goal we actually got. If you worked really hard to get the loan from your aunt, and she led you on so you were pretty optimistic about getting it, you would be really upset if the final answer was, "Sorry, but no."

Berger has said that social appropriateness is an important metagoal. We normally act in socially appropriate ways, but there are exceptions. Because of the negative emotions we often feel when goals are thwarted, we often act in socially unacceptable ways when this happens. This is especially true if our goals are repeatedly thwarted and if the thwarted goals are important to us. Something else will happen at times like this too: We keep trying to get to the goal, but out of desperation, we tend to use simpler and simpler plans.

Even if we try to maintain a complex plan, we may falter and have trouble invoking it. The ease with which we follow a plan is called *action fluidity*, and people find that they sometimes have great fluidity and sometimes not. The more complex a plan and the more emotional we get, the less fluid our actions become. For example, in an experiment conducted by Berger and his colleagues, subjects were asked to present arguments to another person supporting their position on a controversial campus issue.[55] Some of the subjects were given no time to plan their arguments, others were given some planning time, and others were given planning time and invited to prepare contingency plans as well.

The person to whom the subjects gave their argument was actually a confederate of the experimenter instructed to resist their arguments and thereby frustrate the subjects. The experimenters then counted the number of disruptions in the subjects' speech as a measure of fluidity. The subjects who had to develop alternative plans were less fluid in general than those who were not. This result was probably caused by the fact that this group had to devise plans that were more complex. How we approach a message plan, then, can be a complex set of concerns. It will be affected in part by the logic we employ, as the following theory shows.

Message Design Logic. Barbara O'Keefe began her work as a constructivist, but has expanded the theoretical orientation to incorporate a message-design model. Her thesis is that people think differently about communication and messages, and they employ different logics in deciding what to say to another person in a given situation. She uses the term *message design logic* to describe the thought processes behind messages.[56]

O'Keefe outlines three possible message design logics that range from least person-centered to most person-centered. The *expressive logic* sees communication as a mode of self-expression for communicating feelings and thoughts. Its messages are open and reactive in nature, with little attention given to the needs or desires of others. In this regard, the expressive logic is indeed self-centered, but it is not other-centered, or *person-centered* in the parlance of constructivism. An example of a message resulting from this logic would be an angry response to a friend who forgot to get tickets to a concert.

The *conventional logic* sees communication as a game to be played by following rules. Here communication is a means of self-expression that proceeds according to accepted rules and norms including the rights and responsibilities of each person involved. This logic aims to design messages that are polite, appropriate, and based on rules that everyone is supposed to know. For example, in the ticket situation, you might remind the other person that they had a responsibility and had agreed to get the tickets.[57]

The *rhetorical logic* views communication as a way of changing the rules through negotiation. Messages designed with this logic tend to be flexible, insightful, and person-centered. They tend to reframe the situation so that various goals—including persuasion and politeness—are integrated into a seamless whole. An example would be politely suggesting ways in which your friend could solve the concert ticket problem.

O'Keefe has noticed that in certain situations, messages are pretty much the same, but in other situations, they are different. For example, if you asked ten friends to describe their apartments, they would do so in essentially the same way. On the other hand, if you asked them to evaluate your work on a team project, they probably would do so in rather different ways. This example illustrates *message diversity*. In some situations, there is little diversity, and in others there is a great deal. If the goals of the communication are fairly simple and face is not much of an issue, each design logic will lead to the same message form. On the other hand, if goals are numerous and complex and face is an issue, the different design logics will lead to different message forms. In these more complex situations, you can really see the quality of one's thinking process at work.

So far in this section, we have looked at sociopsychological theories of message production, but what about message reception? We looked at some theories related to this topic in the previous chapter on the communicator, including attribution theory, social judgment theory, and elaboration likelihood theory. We covered these theories in Chapter 4 because they really help us to understand how communicators think. To review, we saw that communicators integrate and evaluate the information they receive into the cognitive system, and that information may have an impact on attitudes, beliefs, and values. How a communicator reacts to a message depends in large measure on how he or she interprets that message. We move now to theories of interpretation.

Semantic Meaning Theory

Interpretation is a term for how we understand our experience. Charles Osgood, a well-known social psychologist of the 1960s, developed one of the most influential theories of meaning. In those days, psychology was dominated by behaviorism, but cognitive approaches were just beginning to become popular, and his theory actually has a foot in both traditions. Osgood's theory, then, deals with the ways in which meanings are learned and how they relate to thinking and behavior.[58] This theory was immensely influential and is now considered a classic. Although it is not as popular today, it is still useful and a good place to begin thinking about the topics of this chapter.

Let's begin with a simple example and see how Osgood would work with it. What associations do you have for the word *flying*? Perhaps you see flying as a fun, efficient way to travel, or maybe you see it as rough, dangerous, and frightening. Whatever your associations, these are your *connotations* for the term. Osgood's theory attempts to explain what these connotations consist of and where they come from. In other words, the theory helps us see how messages are understood.

The learning theory used by Osgood begins with the assumption that individuals respond to stimuli in the environment, forming a stimulus–response relationship. He believes that this basic S–R association is responsible for the establishment of meaning, which is an internal, mental response to a stimulus. When you listen to a speech, for example, an internal association will appear in your mind, and this association constitutes your meanings for the concepts being discussed.

Outwardly, you perceive a physical stimulus (the speech), and you have a behavioral response. This response is mediated by internal representations in your mind, which is your meaning lying between the speech and your response. The outward stimulus leads to an internal meaning, which leads to an outward response.

The internal meaning itself can be broken down into two parts: an internal response and an internal stimulus. The whole chain, then, consists of the following: (1) physical stimulus; (2) internal response; (3) internal stimulus; and (4) outward response. A person who is afraid of flying, for example, has an internal response (fear)

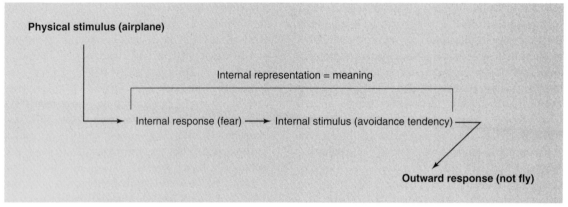

Physical stimulus (airplane)

Internal representation = meaning

Internal response (fear) → Internal stimulus (avoidance tendency)

Outward response (not fly)

FIGURE 5.1

Meaning as Internal Representation

to the airplane, and this fear leads to an avoidance tendency, which is an internal stimulus for the outward response of not boarding the plane. Figure 5.1 illustrates this process.

In addition to physical objects, we also have meanings for the signs of those objects, such as words and gestures. In other words, when the sign is paired with the meaning, that sign comes to elicit the same or a similar response. This is why the mere mention of flying frightens some people. Even if they are not actually scared at the mention of an airplane, they will tell you that they would prefer not to fly because they know what their actual response would be.

Meaning, because it is internal and unique to the person's own experience with the natural stimulus, is said to be *connotative*. If you are afraid of spiders, a spider elicits an escape response. When the word *spider* is associated with the object as it might have been when you were a small child, a portion of your response (fear) becomes associated with the word itself. This internal meaning mediates your response to the word, even when the actual object is not present.[59]

Most meanings are not learned as a result of direct experience with the natural stimulus but are learned by an association between one sign and another, a process that can occur in the abstract, out of physical contact with the original stimulus. Here the meaning of one concept "rubs off" by association with another. To continue our example, imagine that as a child you had already established internal responses to the words *spider, big,* and *hairy*. Let's say you listened to a story about a tarantula, characterized as a "big, hairy spider." Through association you would now have a meaning for the new word *tarantula*, which may also carry some mixture of the connotations earlier attached to the other words because of its association with these words. If you associated *spider* with *fear, big* with *dangerous,* and *hairy* with feeling *creepy,* then you might well react to a real or imagined tarantula by running away. The examples of the fear of flying and the fear of spiders are negative, but all meanings—including positive and neutral ones—are learned the same way.

One of Osgood's major contributions is his work on the measurement of meaning. This method of measuring meaning, the *semantic differential*, assumes that one's meanings can be expressed by the use of adjectives.[60] The method begins by finding a set of adjectives that could be used to express your connotations for any stimulus, including a sign. These adjectives are set against one another as opposites, such as good-bad, high-low, slow-fast. You are given a topic, word, or other sign and are asked to indicate on a 7-point scale how you associate the sign with the adjective pairs. A scale looks like this:

good __:__:__:__:__:__:__ bad

The subject places a check mark on any space between these adjectives to indicate the degree of good or bad associated with the stimulus. The subject may fill out as many as fifty such scales for each stimulus, each with a different set of bipolar adjectives (fast-slow, active-inactive, and so on). You might be presented with a word like *airplane* or *spider* and asked to fill out this set of scales.

Osgood then uses a statistical technique called *factor analysis* to find your basic dimensions of meaning. His findings in this research have led to the theory of *semantic space*.[61] Your meaning for any sign is said to be located in a metaphorical space of three major dimensions: evaluation, activity, and potency. A given sign, perhaps a word or concept, elicits a reaction in the person, consisting of a sense of *evaluation* (good or bad), *activity* (active or inactive), and *potency* (strong or weak). Your connotative meaning will lie somewhere in this hypothetical space, depending on your responses on the three factors. Figure 5.2 illustrates the semantic space.

Airplane, for example, might be viewed as good, active, and strong. Or it might be seen as bad, active, and strong. A *spider* might be perceived as bad, passive, and strong, or perhaps good, active, and weak.

Osgood and others have done semantic differential research on a variety of types of concepts, including words, music, art, and even sonar sounds, as well as across a wide range of cultures.[62] Osgood believes that the three factors of meaning—evaluation, activity, and potency—apply across all people and all concepts.[63] If these dimensions are as universal as Osgood believes they are, he has significantly advanced our understanding of meaning.

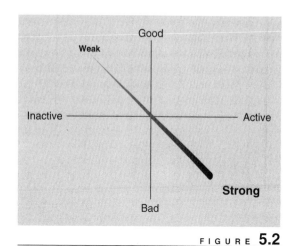

FIGURE **5.2**

Three-Dimensional Semantic Space

REFLECTIONS ON
The Sociopsychological Tradition

All of the theories in this section are clearly psychological in orientation; all are influenced heavily by work in social psychology, relying on individualistic, experimental data. This area has contributed substantially to communication theory, as it bridges the individual and the message. The question of how individuals generate messages has been an important consideration in the communication field for at least four decades. The phenomenological tradition in message theory, which we examine next, is also somewhat individualistic, but it is informed by a different set of assumptions and relies on a very different kind of data.

• • •

THE PHENOMENOLOGICAL TRADITION

The phenomenological tradition emphasizes processes of interpretation, but in a very different sense than did Osgood, as outlined in the previous section. Osgood's theory—clearly based on the sociopsychological tradition—sees interpretation as an intuitive, unconscious, cognitive process. Phenomenological theories, in contrast, see interpretation as a conscious and careful process of understanding.

Hermeneutics, defined as the careful and deliberate interpretation of texts, is the basis for the phenomenological tradition in the study of messages. There are several branches of hermeneutics, including interpretation of scripture (exegesis), interpretation of literary texts (philology), and interpretation of human personal and social actions (social hermeneutics).[64]

Modern hermeneutics began in the early nineteenth century with Friedrich Schleiermacher.[65] Schleiermacher attempted to establish a system for discovering what authors meant in their writings. He used a scientific approach to text analysis, which he believed would be the key to authors' original meanings and feelings. Later in the century, Schleiermacher's biographer, Wilhelm Dilthey, was strongly influenced by these ideas.[66] For Dilthey, however, hermeneutics is the key to all of the humanities and social sciences; he believed that we come to understand all aspects of human life, not by scientific method, but through subjective interpretation. For Dilthey, the human world is social and historical and requires understanding in terms of the community in which human actors live and work. Human works, then, are not fixed and cannot be known objectively. Dilthey therefore promoted a kind of historical relativism common in the social sciences today.

For our purposes, hermeneutic scholars fall into two general groups: those who use hermeneutics to understand texts and those who use hermeneutics as a tool for interpreting actions. The first type is called *text hermeneutics* and the second *social or cultural hermeneutics*.[67] In this chapter, we cover text hermeneutics in this section and cultural hermeneutics in the following one.

Generally speaking, *texts* are any artifacts that can be examined and interpreted.[68] Text hermeneutics, although usually applied to the written word, is not limited to it. Any kind of action can be recorded. A text is essentially a recording, whether written, electronic, photographic, or preserved by some other means. Even actions can be viewed as texts, but more often, the term designates written documents and other records.[69] The problem remains the same: How do we interpret a message that is no longer part of an actual live event?

Although little agreement exists on specific techniques of interpretation, almost all schools of thought rely on a common notion of its general process, called the *hermeneutic circle*. You interpret something by going from general to specific and from specific to general. You look at a specific text in terms of a general idea of what that text may mean, then modify the general idea based on the examination of the specifics of the text. Your interpretation is ongoing, as you move back and forth between specific and general. You can look at the composite meaning of a text and then examine the specific linguistic structures of that text. Then you might return to the overall meaning, only to go back to the specifics again.

Within the circle, you always relate what is seen in the object to what you already know. You then alternate between a familiar set of concepts and the unfamiliar until the two merge in a tentative interpretation. In interpreting the actions of a foreign culture, for example, an anthropologist first tries to understand what is happening with familiar concepts; later the anthropologist discovers how the people themselves understand their experiences in their own way and uses this information to modify the categories initially employed. This back-and-forth process is exactly what is used in textual interpretation as well.

Consider the Bible as an example. The interpreter begins by relating the text to what he or she already understands, looks for strange or unaccounted-for details in the scripture, modifies the original interpretation, reexamines the text, and so on. You can see that this is really a dialogue between the meanings in the text and present-day assumptions and understandings.

The interpretation of texts has long been the central problem of hermeneutics. Hermeneutics arose as a way to understand ancient texts such as the Bible that can no longer be explained by the author. The Supreme Court uses hermeneutics to interpret the U.S. Constitution. Today, virtually any text is open for interpretation, and whether the author is alive to explain what he or she meant is not considered relevant. The text itself speaks to us; it has meanings of its own apart from what any author, speaker, or audience member might mean by it. The challenge of textual hermeneutics, then, is to ascertain the meanings of the text.

There are many prominent writers on text interpretation. Three of the most prominent theories—developed by Paul Ricoeur, Stanley Fish, and Hans-Georg Gadamer—are summarized here.

Paul Ricoeur

Ricoeur is a major interpretive theorist who relies heavily on both the phenomenological and hermeneutic traditions.[70] Although he recognizes the importance of actual speech, most important for Ricoeur is text. Once speech is recorded, it becomes divorced from the actual speaker and situation in which it was produced. Texts cannot be interpreted in the same fashion as live discourse because they exist in a permanent form. Speech is ephemeral, but texts live on. Textual interpretation is especially important when speakers and authors are not available, as is the case with historical documents. However, it need not be limited to these situations. Indeed, the text itself always speaks to us, and the job of the interpreter is to figure out what it is saying.

The separation of text from situation is *distanciation.* The text has meaning irrespective of the author's original intention. In other words, you can read a message and understand it despite the fact that you were not part of the original speech event. Thus, the author's intent does not prescribe what the text can subsequently be taken to mean, nor does any reader's peculiar understanding limit what the text itself says. Once written, the text can be consumed by anybody who can read, providing a multitude of possibilities—and multiple readings (meanings)

are definitely possible. For these reasons the interpretation of textual material is, for Ricoeur, more complex and more interesting than that of spoken discourse.

The problem is like interpreting a musical score.[71] You may not know exactly what mood and feeling Mozart had in composing and conducting the *Jupiter Symphony*. If you are an experienced music lover, you might be able to produce a number of believable interpretations of your own, but those interpretations are not unlimited; they are constrained by the musical notation. A conductor carefully studies the elements of the text to determine what meanings are embedded in it and then proceeds to produce a musical interpretation. Orchestral versions will differ substantially in the interpretation performed, but you will always recognize the piece as the *Jupiter Symphony*.

Like a musical interpretation, the meaning of a text is always a pattern of the whole, never just a composite of individual elements. To account for this, Ricoeur's version of the hermeneutic circle consists of explanation and understanding. *Explanation* is empirical and analytical: It accounts for events in terms of observed patterns among parts. In studying a book of the Bible, for example, you would carefully examine the individual words of each verse and note the ways they form patterns of meaning. In the analysis of a text, an interpreter might look for recurring words and phrases, narrative themes, and theme variations. Ricoeur himself is interested in particular words that have metaphorical value, words that point to meanings hidden below the surface of the writing. None of these structural elements is meaningful in and of itself; they must be put together into a whole pattern in the understanding phase of interpretation.

Understanding is synthetic, accounting for events in terms of overall interpretation. So in continuing your study of the Bible, you would also look for a holistic, or general, meaning of the passage under consideration. In hermeneutics, one goes through both processes, breaking down a text into its parts and looking for patterns, then stepping back and subjectively judging the meaning of the whole. You move from understanding to explaining and back to understanding again in a continuing circle. Explanation and understanding, then, are not separate but are two poles in an interpretive spectrum.

Ricoeur agrees that an intimate interaction exists between text and interpreter. The text can speak to and change the interpreter. Ricoeur refers to the act of being open to the meanings of a text as *appropriation.* If you are open to the message of a text, you appropriate it, or make it your own. Thus, interpretation begins with distanciation but ends with appropriation. To interpret the sections of the Bible, you would remove your own interests from your study of the intrinsic meanings in the text, but then you would apply those meanings to your own situation.

An example of a Ricoeurian interpretation is Barbara Warnick's study of the Gettysburg Address.[72] In a careful examination of the text, Warnick looks at expressions of agent, place, and time. *Agents* include "our fathers," "those who have given their lives," "we," and the people of the future. *Place* references include our nation "upon this continent" and "a great battle-field." *Time* references include the far past ("four score and seven years"), the near past, a frozen present, and a possible future. The text can transcend the immediacy of the present situation by cycling back and forth from the present to other times, from immediate agents to other agents in past and future, and from this place to other places. In so doing, the text tells a story of birth, adversity, recognition of values, rebirth, and perpetuation of treasured values.

In an example of appropriation, Warnick notes that this story parallels that of the Christian narrative, which appeals to people so deeply in our society. Other values of American culture are deeply embedded in the text as well. Warnick shows how the details of the text and the overall understanding of it as a projection of the American ideal go hand in hand. Warnick's overall understanding of the speech, then, is that it expresses values that are part of, but transcend, the immediate situation, and for this reason, the text is relevant to generation after generation of Americans.

Stanley Fish

Fish is a literary critic known mostly in the fields of English, literary studies, and media. With a keen interest in literature, much of his work centers around text interpretation and the question of where meaning resides. Taking a distinctly different turn from Ricoeur, Fish denies that any meaning can be found in text. For him, meaning lies strictly in the reader, which leads to the name most associated with Fish's work—*reader-response theory.*[73] The proper question is not, "What does a text mean?" but "What does a text do?"

Clearly, texts do stimulate active readership, but the readers themselves provide the meaning, not the text. If you have ever taken a nineteenth-century American literature course, you probably spent some time talking about the meaning of *Moby Dick.* You may have discovered that different students saw different things in the text. Perhaps you spent time trying to figure out what the true meaning of the text is, and you probably used hermeneutics to do it. Fish would say that *Moby Dick* as a text means nothing, but readers will take it to mean many things.

Fish is clear, however, that assigning meaning is not an individual matter. You do not arbitrarily decide what meaning to assign to a text, nor is your meaning idiosyncratic. Following a social constructionist approach (Chapter 6), Fish teaches that readers are members of *interpretive communities*—groups that interact with one another, construct common realities and meanings, and employ these in their readings. So meaning really resides in the interpretive community of readers.

In your literature class, then, you may come to share a common reading of *Moby Dick.* This will happen because of your common identity as English students, as well as discussions in class, sharing a common textbook, completing the same assignments, taking the same tests, and having the same professor. It is likely that the class will become an interpretive community with very similar meanings for the novel. Indeed, your class will become linked with other classes, in prior and future semesters, and because your professor reads the same journals as professors in other universities and attends conferences on nineteenth-century literature, it is very possible that you will become a member of a huge interpretive community of the American novel.

Of course, if you subscribe to Fish's theory, you will not search for a single meaning. There is no correct reading of a text. The matter is entirely dependent on the audience's interpretation. Meaning, then, is not objective, so don't look for it in the features of the text. Needless to say, this is a highly controversial idea in literary studies, as much of literary criticism looks at the intention of the author and how the author communicates that in the way the text is written.

On this point, however, Ricoeur and Fish would agree: Don't look to the author for meaning. Where they very much disagree is in the role of the text. Both Ricoeur and Fish use the hermeneutic circle, but they emphasize somewhat different things in doing so. For Ricoeur, the reader is always testing his or her interpretation by looking at features of the text so as to find the meaning that lies there. For Fish, the reader always projects his or her own meaning into features of the text and only comes up with the reader's meaning in the end. For Ricoeur, the text is like a template; for Fish it is like a Rorschach test. Distanciation, the principle that is so important to Ricoeur, is senseless to Fish because readers can never be distanced from the text; they are always embedding their own meanings into it. In contrast to both of these approaches, we turn now to Hans-Georg Gadamer, who gives value to both text and reader.

Hans-Georg Gadamer

Hans-Georg Gadamer, a protégé of Heidegger, teaches that individuals do not stand apart from things in order to analyze and interpret them; in-

stead, we interpret naturally as part of our everyday existence.[74] We cannot be human without interpreting. That means that our experience and the world we interpret are so closely intertwined that they are virtually the same thing.

The central tenet of Gadamer's theory is that one always understands experience from the perspective of presuppositions, or assumptions. Our tradition gives us a way of understanding things, and we cannot divorce ourselves from that tradition. Observation, reason, and understanding are never objectively pure; they are colored by history and our experience with other people.

Further, history is not to be separated from the present. We are always simultaneously part of the past, in the present, and anticipating the future. In other words, the past operates on us now in the present and affects our conceptions of what is yet to come. At the same time, our present notions of reality affect how we view the past.

These ideas do not deny change. Over time we become distanced from the events of the past. Our way of seeing things in the present time creates a temporal distance from an object of the past such that artifacts have both a strangeness and a familiarity. If you find your grandmother's old dress in a dusty trunk in the attic, it will look somewhat familiar, but strange at the same time. We understand an artifact because of what we have learned from history, which is a residue of highly relevant, but essential, meanings. For example, you recognize your grandmother's dress because of its "dressness" learned by viewing old pictures and reading and hearing about old-time fashion. Even though the dress might be very old, you still recognize buttons, lace, and other features that make this a dress.

In some ways, then, interpretation of historical events and objects, including written texts, is enhanced by historical distance. You can understand the Gettysburg Address because the essential meaning of the words lives on. Gadamer would agree that understanding a text involves looking at the enduring meanings of that text within a tradition and apart from the original communicators' intentions. Texts therefore become contemporaneous and speak to us in our own time.

The Gettysburg Address was originally a piece of spoken discourse designed to achieve a certain effect during the Civil War. Once spoken, however, the text lived on as an object of its own, rife with internal meaning. Unessential details—that it was written on the back of an envelope on the train by a tall, lanky president—drop away as the text itself reveals its meanings to us in our own time.

The meaning we get from a text, then, is a result of a dialogue between our own present-day meanings and those embedded in the language of the text. You do recognize and understand an old dress because of its features that still have meaning, but, at the same time, you also apply your own current ideas about the dress—that it is silly, stodgy, inconvenient, heavy, hot, oppressive, or whatever. You understand the terms of the Gettysburg Address because those words live on, but at the same time, your interpretation is influenced by your own background and experience of today.

This interpretive process is paradoxical: We let the text speak to us, yet we cannot understand it apart from our own prejudices and presuppositions. Because change results from the dialogue between the prejudices of the present and the meanings of the text, prejudice is a positive force, to be acknowledged and used productively in our lives. As one observer has noted, "The problem for the study of communication is not the existence of prejudices but the unawareness of their presence and subsequent inability to separate appropriate from inappropriate ones."[75]

Hermeneutics is not only a process of questioning the meaning of the text but also of allowing it to question us. What questions does the text itself suggest, and when we ask those questions, what answers does the text offer? What, for example, can we learn about ourselves from the Gettysburg Address?

Like Heidegger, Gadamer believes that experience is inherently linguistic. We cannot separate our experience from language. The perspectives of tradition, from which we always view the world, are in the words. Note how this conception differs from the structural view of language summarized earlier in this chapter, in which language is seen as an arbitrary tool for expressing and referring to an objective reality. Gadamer's view is also different from the interactionist notion (even Fish's), which suggests that language and meaning are created through social interaction. Gadamer's point is that language itself prefigures all experience. The world is presented to us through language. Thus, in communication, two people are not using language to interact with each other; rather, communication involves a triad of two individuals and a language.[76]

To get this idea across, Gadamer uses the analogy of the game. A game has its own existence apart from individual players. The basic structure of the game will be the same whether it is being played or not and regardless of who is playing. Poker is poker, whether played in 1920 by four old Italian men or in 1994 by a young college student and her roommates. The game lives on, only the players change.

Language and life are like games: We play them, just as we experience life, but they come to us preformed and remain intact after our particular playing is finished. One commentator explains it this way: "The world is already meaningful. That is, the world which comes to us in the only way that the human world can come to us, through language, is an already meaningful world."[77] Gadamer brings phenomenology and hermeneutics together in one process.

◖● REFLECTIONS ON
The Phenomenological Tradition

The phenomenological tradition is unlike any of the other traditions featured in this chapter. Its contribution is special and important in that it provides a perspective and power that the other traditions cannot. How do you come to understand the intent of an ancient text? How do texts and traditions interact with one another?

Where is meaning—in the text, the reader, or the author? These questions can only be answered by phenomenological inquiry.

Interestingly, however, as we move from the confines of a strictly message-oriented focus to broader concerns, as we will in upcoming chapters, phenomenology begins to support and even merge with certain other traditions such as the sociocultural and critical.

We will see later, for example, that understanding culture within the sociocultural tradition is not unlike reading a text. We will see, too, that critical theory relies heavily on hermeneutic data produced in a process very similar to the interpretation of texts.

● ● ●

APPLICATIONS & IMPLICATIONS

When you first thought seriously about communication, you probably focused on the message. You may have been in a course like public speaking or television production, where producing messages was your immediate concern. Actually, throughout life, you will be confronted with the question of how to create effective messages, whether you are disciplining a child, conducting a performance review of a subordinate at work, or persuading a group to support a political initiative. Unfortunately, this overemphasis on message effectiveness belies the complexity of communication and the importance of conversations, relationships, and contexts for the production and reception of messages. Still, a respectable body of research and theory has emerged on the message, and this material is important as a significant part of communication theory.

As we think about the general ideas emerging from this literature, we will concentrate on five points:

1. Symbol use is central to human life.

Messages are important as a means for transmitting information and influence, but they are much more than this. Human beings by nature must communicate. We must have the means for abstracting, capturing what is important to us, and expressing our experience to others and to ourselves. From Langer to Gadamer, the theories in this chapter drive this point home again and again. Semiotic theories address signs and symbols as *the* way in which we represent reality. Language theory, especially, demonstrates how human beings manipulate complex codes to express and understand their experience; and theories of nonverbal communication show that language and behavior go together in the creation of meaning. But words and actions do more than designate things. Human beings accomplish goals by using messages. We strategize on how to achieve our goals, how to create identification and division with the audience, how to appeal to the rationality of the audience, and how to achieve compliance. And audiences themselves must go through a process of interpretation, in which they "read" the meaning of what is spoken, performed, and written.

It is apparent that this process of strategizing, producing the message, and interpreting symbols does function to transfer meaning from one mind to another—the fundamental semiotic notion of symbolic representation. But in applying the theories of this chapter, we must go far beyond this simplistic idea of what communication is.

Responding to what he perceives to be an overly simple view of semiotics, John Stewart writes that language is "constitutive articulate contact," meaning that using language contact with other people constructs the very categories and logics by which we understand the world.[78] In other words, language *constitutes* the world. Critics like Stewart believe that language and communication cannot be separated in the way that Saussure does with his *langue-parole* distinction because communication is the mechanism by which language and signs are created, maintained, and changed.[79] In other words, symbols do more than represent things. They do more than communicate meaning. Symbols make our social worlds.

Although the implications of symbol use run deep, it is hard to deny that messages do convey meaning. Communication relies on this assumption. Donald Ellis agrees that signs are not simple representations of objects, but he writes that in order for communication to occur, we must assume that there is some agreement as to what a sign represents.[80] We must share a sense of coherence in messages, or no amount of understanding will be possible. We must assume that when we make use of the rules of language, large numbers of people who know those rules will be able to understand the meaning we intend.

For example, how can you understand a novel by Charles Dickens if you can't have a dialogue with Dickens to find out what he meant? Even after 200 years, you can still understand the novel quite well. You may enhance your understanding by talking about the book with others or consulting historical documents, but you cannot deny that there was meaning in the text. Textual interpretation is topic of hermeneutics, and we see in this chapter that readers are able to look carefully at the text, compare it with their own experience, and generate an increasingly refined meaning for what the text is saying. Of course, your meaning for a passage in a Dickens novel is never entirely determined by the text itself. Your own experience and era give you an interpretive frame, and your "final" reading of the text is an outcome of the interaction between your contemporary experience and the structure of the message itself, which leads to our next point.

2. The meaning of a message depends upon structural features and interpretive processes.

As a group, the theories of this chapter show that the impact of a message—its meaning and effects—are determined in part by the actual signs, symbols, words, and actions in the message, and in part by the interpretive processes used by the receiver. To understand a message is to understand meaning, and both of these elements are critical when we apply the theories of this chapter.

The key to structural meaning is the *rule*, or guideline about what a certain structure of symbols should be taken to mean. The rules of grammar, for example, tell us whether an action is being done by one person or several (plurality); whether it happens in the past, the present or the future (tense); and whether the subject is acting or being acted on (voice). Further, rules of semantics tell us what the symbols should be taken to represent. All literate speakers of English will know how to interpret the sentence, "I am hungry," because they all share an understanding of the semantic and syntactic rules of the language, but they will know more than the literal meaning of the sentence. From context, they may also know what the speaker intends to accomplish by uttering this sentence. It is not surprising, then, that many listeners would respond to this sentence by saying something like, "Can I get you something to eat?" Here the first sentence counts as a request, and the second as an offer.

Although messages do have certain structural features, you cannot legitimately separate the message from the communicators who send and receive it. Structural features of the message certainly reflect rules of interpretation, but these rules emerge from social interaction within groups and communities, and they are part of the cognitive resources that each person carries around. Also, we will have different connotations for the symbols used in messages. Although we may agree on the literal meaning, even the illocutionary force, of the message, our connotations are bound to differ, at least a little. A contribution of Osgood's semantic meaning theory is that individuals may have rather different reactions to the evaluation, potency, and activity of a concept.

To see the interaction between the structure of the text and the interpretive scheme of the receiver, take a look at the following sentence: *A well regulated Militia, being necessary to the security of a free State, the right of the people to keep and bear Arms, shall not be infringed.* This is the Second Amendment to the U.S. Constitution, and its meaning is very much in dispute. Does this amendment mean that every individual has the right to carry a gun? You could read it that way. Or does the amendment mean that guns may be kept in the armory for use by law enforcement agencies and the National Guard in times of threat? The language of the amendment does give you some clues, but your interpretation will probably depend on your own point of view as well. Some take the term *people* to mean, "citizens as a group," while others take this term to mean "each and every individual." Some people say that the first phrase, referring to the militia, should tell us how to interpret "the right of the people." Others say that the term "well-regulated" casts light on the meaning of *keep and bear.* Still others, say that the meaning of the main clause is self-evident: ". . . the right of the people to keep and bear Arms, shall not be infringed."

As you ponder the meaning of the Second Amendment, you have to rely in part on the structure of the message and in part on the interpretive categories of your culture, community, and the era in which you live. This is exactly why unanimous decisions of the Supreme Court are rare.

Notice that different theories stress different aspects of the interpretive process. Ricoeur, for example, stresses the content of the message, but Fish claims that it is all in the reader. Gadamer balances both of these, claiming that interpretations are an outcome of a dialogue between the text and the interpreter. Charles Osgood takes yet another view, which is that our understandings are colored by universal categories of mind, and that your interpretation of the Second Amendment will be greatly influenced by whether you think that guns are good or bad, strong or weak, active or inactive.

3. We communicate with complex message codes.

Interpreting texts, or written discourse, is hard enough, but in the flux and flow of everyday communication, we are challenged by a complexity of language and behavioral codes. We fuse symbols, each with rich denotations and connotations, into sentences and paragraphs according to the rules of grammar and deliver these simultaneously in a performance, often along with other presentational symbols such as graphics, sound and music, and other contextual features. Where we stand, how we look, what we do with our eyes—a mix of codes—all shape the message.

Typical of much of communication theory, this chapter tends to chop up the topic of messages into types and parts. In communication theory, we face a paradox. To understand communication, we must look at it piece by piece; but doing so distorts the actual process itself. This difficulty is not unlike studying music. Music theory focuses on the parts of the music—tone, scale, tempo, key, etc. Although music can be divided into these parts, a performance is an integration of parts into a whole. The difference between learning to play the piano and being a virtuoso is precisely this: The beginner is stringing together individual finger strokes of varying duration, tempo, etc. The virtuoso does not think of finger strokes, but looks at the musicality of the whole piece. We must think of messages the same way. Verbal and nonverbal components merge seamlessly as a performance.[81]

4. Message production is made possible by micro- and macrocognitive processes.

Given the strong psychological orientation of Western society, it is not surprising that much communication theory has focused on the cognitive processes used by individuals to plan messages to achieve their individual goals. This fascinating literature paints the picture in which an individual makes rational decisions about what he or she wants to accomplish and then actively plans out strategies for doing so. Some of the processes—from macrocognitive theory—appear very conscious, while other behind-the-scenes processes—microcognitive processes—are almost automatic and certainly out of awareness. This is like the difference between a driver and car engine. The driver makes conscious plans and drives the car to get to a particular destination, while the engine is operating simultaneously under the hood to make it possible for the conscious plan to be followed. The driver may decide to make a turn to go to the store on the way and never thinks about the braking, accelerating, and turning systems of the car that "follow his orders" once the decision is made to turn.

A decision that serious students of cognition come to make is this: Am I more interested in the driver, the driver's plans, and the driver's actions, or am I more interested in the engine that lies under the hood? The kind of research and theory you end up producing will depend in part on the answer to this question. If you are interested in the driver, you will probably end up looking at overt, conscious planning processes, but if you like engines, you will be attracted to microprocesses behind message behavior. John Greene's action assembly theory is a theory of the engine, while Charles Berger's theory of planning addresses concerns of the driver.

Both strategy choice and message design models give individual communicators quite a bit of power in preplanning their messages. This is probably not a very good representation of how communication actually takes place, however. Although the cognitive processes that occur before interaction takes place are important, Burgoon and her colleagues have consistently found in their research that the actual behavior encountered in interaction has far more power to influence what a communicator does than any preplanning.[82] Most of the cognitive work of interaction is probably done moment-to-moment as communicators adjust and adapt to one another.

Obviously, the boundary between Chapter 4 (The Communicator) and Chapter 5 (The Message) is fuzzy. To get the most from these chapters, we encourage you to hold them up side-by-side, to look at each in light of the other. An important interface between communicator and message lies in the question, "How can communicators effectively produce and receive messages?" The literature on this question is vast. From what we have seen in this chapter, we can fairly state that effective communication involves creating and tracking goals, looking for connections between your goals and those of the receiver, developing messages that are both efficient and socially appropriate, being adaptable in modifying plans and messages, being sensitive to timing issues, becoming knowledgeable about the topic of conversation, and understanding what others wish to accomplish with their messages and how this affects us.[83]

5. Messages are created to meet multiple goals and designed to achieve several levels of meaning.

Consider the number of accomplishments that a simple message can achieve. It can get across a denotation, or representational meaning; it can express feelings and connotations; it can fulfill an intention; it can elicit a response; it can save face; it can achieve compliance; it can build identification and division; or it can accomplish a plan or goal. In other words, communicators use messages to manage meaning on many levels at the same time. The theories of this chapter, taken together, can unhitch blinders, broaden our view of communication, and help us see the many dimensions of communication reflected in the message.

● NOTES

1. Susanne Langer, *Philosophy in a New Key* (Cambridge, MA: Harvard University Press, 1942). See also *Mind: An Essay on Human Feeling*, 3 vols. (Baltimore: Johns Hopkins University Press, 1967, 1972, 1982). A good secondary source is John Stewart, *Language as Articulate Contact: Toward a Post-Semiotic Philosophy of Communication* (Albany: SUNY Press, 1995), pp. 92–101.
2. Langer, *Philosophy in a New Key*, p. 63.
3. A semiotic analysis of van Gogh's work was done by Mark Roskill, "'Public' and 'Private' Meanings: The Paintings of van Gogh," *Journal of Communication* 29 (1979): 157–169.
4. Quoted in Roskill, "'Public' and 'Private' Meanings," p. 157.
5. Wendy Leeds-Hurwitz, *Semiotics and Communication: Signs, Codes, Cultures* (Hillsdale, NJ: Lawrence Erlbaum, 1993), p. 13. For good brief overviews of the study of language, see Donald G. Ellis, *From Language to Communication* (Mahwah, NJ: Lawrence Erlbaum, 1999); Scott Jacobs, "Language and Interpersonal Communication," in *Handbook of Interpersonal Communication*, ed. Mark L. Knapp and Gerald R. Miller (Thousand Oaks, CA: Sage, 1994), pp. 199–228; Irwin Weiser, "Linguistics," in *Encyclopedia of Rhetoric and Composition*, ed. Theresa Enos (New York: Garland, 1996), pp. 386–391; David Graddol, Jenny Cheshire, and Joan Swann, *Descriptive Language* (Buckingham, UK: Open University Press, 1994), pp. 65–101; Adrian Akmajian, Richard A. Demers, Ann K. Farmer, and Robert M. Harnish, *An Introduction to Language and Communication* (Cambridge, MA: MIT Press, 1994), pp. 123–192.
6. Ferdinand de Saussure's primary work on this subject is *Course in General Linguistics* (London: Peter Owen, 1960). Excellent secondary sources include Stewart, *Language as Articulate Contact*, pp. 81–87; Anthony Giddens, *Central Problems in Social Theory: Action, Structure, and Contradiction in Social Analysis* (Berkeley: University of California Press, 1979); and Fred Dallmayr, *Language and Politics* (Notre Dame, IN: University of Notre Dame Press, 1984).
7. One difference between *langue* and *parole*, according to Saussure, is stability. Language is characterized by *synchrony*, meaning that it changes very little over time. Speech, on the other hand, is characterized by *diachrony*, meaning that it changes constantly from situation to situation.
8. Saussure, *Course in General Linguistics*, p. 9.
9. The major writings of this period include Leonard Bloomfield, *Language* (New York: Holt, Rinehart & Winston, 1933); Charles Fries, *The Structure of English* (New York: Harcourt, Brace & World, 1952);

and Zellig Harris, *Structural Linguistics* (Chicago: University of Chicago Press, 1951). An excellent summary and critique of this period can be found in J. A. Fodor, T. G. Bever, and M. F. Garrett, *The Psychology of Language: An Introduction to Psycholinguistics and Generative Grammar* (New York: McGraw-Hill, 1974).

10. See, for example, Noam Chomsky, *Language and Mind* (New York: Harcourt, Brace, Jovanovich, 1975.

11. Randall Harrison, *Beyond Words: An Introduction to Nonverbal Communication* (Englewood Cliffs, NJ: Prentice-Hall, 1974), pp. 24–25. Conceptual issues are discussed in Judee K. Burgoon, "Nonverbal Signals," in *Handbook of Interpersonal Communication*, ed. Mark L. Knapp and Gerald R. Miller (Thousand Oaks, CA: Sage, 1994), pp. 229–285; see also Mark Knapp and Judith Hall, *Nonverbal Communication in Human Interaction* (New York: Holt, Rinehart & Winston, 1992).

12. For a broad overview of research, see Judee K. Burgoon and Aaron E. Bacue, "Nonverbal Communication Skills," in *Handbook of Communication and Social Interaction Skills*, ed. John O. Green and Brant R. Burleson (Mahwah, NJ: Lawrence Erlbaum, 2003), pp. 179–219.

13. Burgoon, "Nonverbal Signals," p. 232.

14. Birdwhistell's major works include *Introduction to Kinesics* (Louisville, KY: University of Louisville Press, 1952); and *Kinesics and Context* (Philadelphia: University of Pennsylvania Press, 1970).

15. Birdwhistell, *Kinesics and Context*, pp. 183–184.

16. Ekman and Friesen's major works include "Nonverbal Behavior in Psychotherapy Research," in *Research in Psychotherapy*, vol. 3, ed. J. Shlien (Washington, DC: American Psychological Association, 1968), pp. 179–216; "The Repertoire of Nonverbal Behavior: Categories, Origins, Usage, and Coding," *Semiotica* 1 (1969): 49–98; *Emotion in the Human Face: Guidelines for Research and an Integration of Findings* (New York: Pergamon, 1972); *Unmasking the Face* (Englewood Cliffs, NJ: Prentice-Hall, 1975).

17. Paul Ekman and Wallace Friesen, "Hand Movements," *Journal of Communication* 22 (1972): 353.

18. The distinction between biologically determined and socially determined signal systems is explored by Ross Buck and C. Arthur VanLear "Verbal and Nonverbal Communication: Distinguishing Symbolic, Spontaneous, and Pseudo-Spontaneous Nonverbal Behavior," *Journal of Communication* 52 (2002): 522–541.

19. More recent evidence suggests that affect displays are not necessarily as informative as Ekman and Friesen indicated. Interpretation of affect displays in actual interaction has been found not to be very accurate and may serve more as a nonverbal interjection than a display of emotion. See Michael T. Motley, "Facial Affect and Verbal Context in Conversation," *Human Communication Research* 20 (1993): 3–40; Michael T. Motley and Carl T. Camden, "Facial Expression of Emotion: A Comparison of Posed Expressions Versus Spontaneous Expressions in an Interpersonal Communication Setting," *Western Journal of Speech Communication* 52 (1988): 1–22.

20. Edward T. Hall, "A System for the Notation of Proxemic Behavior," *American Anthropologist* 65 (1963): p. 1003. Edward Hall's major works include *The Silent Language* (Greenwich, CT: Fawcett, 1959); and *The Hidden Dimension* (New York: Random House, 1966).

21. John Searle, *Speech Acts: An Essay in the Philosophy of Language* (Cambridge: Cambridge University Press, 1969), p. 22. See also Deborah Cameron, *Working with Spoken Discourse* (London: Sage, 2001), pp. 68–75.

22. Searle, *Speech Acts*, p. 22.

23. See, for example, Bernard L. Brock, "Evolution of Kenneth Burke's Criticism and Philosophy of Language," in *Kenneth Burke and Contemporary European Thought: Rhetoric in Transition*, ed. Bernard L. Brock (Tuscaloosa: University of Alabama Press, 1995), pp. 1–33; Herbert W. Simons and Trevor Melia, eds., *The Legacy of Kenneth Burke* (Madison: University of Wisconsin Press, 1989). Although in the communication field Burke is most often considered a symbol theorist, he is also a major social critic. For a discussion of this aspect of his work, see Omar Swartz, *Conducting Socially Responsible Research* (Thousand Oaks, CA: Sage, 1997), pp. 68–90.

24. Hugh Duncan, "Communication in Society," *Arts in Society* 3 (1964): 105. For a comprehensive overview of Burke's ideas, see William Rueckert, ed., *Critical Responses to Kenneth Burke* (Minneapolis: University of Minnesota Press, 1969. For brief summaries, see Brock, "Evolution"; John F. Cragan and Donald C. Shields, *Symbolic Theories in Applied Communication Research: Bormann, Burke, and Fisher* (Cresskill, NJ: Hampton, 1995), pp. 61–81; Sonja K. Foss, Karen A. Foss, and Robert Trapp, *Contemporary Perspectives on Rhetoric*, 3rd ed. (Prospect Heights, IL: Waveland, 2002).

25. For an excellent and humorous summary of Burke's theory of language, see his "Prologue in Heaven," *The Rhetoric of Religion Studies in Logology* (Berkeley: University of California Press, 1979), pp. 273–316.

26. Kramarae's theory is summarized in "Cheris Kramarae," *Feminist Rhetorical Theories* by Karen A. Foss, Sonja K. Foss, and Cindy L. Griffin (Thousand Oaks, CA: Sage, 1999), pp. 33–68.

27. Cheris Kramarae, "Gender and Dominance." *Communication Yearbook 15*, ed. Stanley A. Deetz (Newbury Park, CA: Sage, 1992), p. 470.

28. Kramarae discusses the male construction and bias of language in *Women and Men Speaking: Frameworks for Analysis* (Rowley, MA: Newbury House, 1981), pp. 33–51.

29. Kramarae addresses the issue of dictionaries specifically in "Words on a Feminist Dictionary," in *A Feminist Dictionary*, ed. Cheris Kramarae, Paula A. Treichler, with Ann Russo (Boston: Pandora, 1985), p. 22.

30. "Cheris Kramarae," in Foss, Foss, and Griffin, pp. 47–52.

31. Karlyn Kohrs Campbell, *Man Cannot Speak For Her: A Critical Study of Early Feminist Rhetoric*, vol. I (Westport, CT: Greenwood, 1989), pp. 12–15; and Bonnie J. Dow and Mari Boor Tonn, " 'Feminine Style' and Political Judgment in the Rhetoric of Ann Richards," *Quarterly Journal of Speech* 79 (August 1993): 286–302.

32. Campbell, *Man Cannot Speak For Her*, p. 13.

33. Campbell, *Man Cannot Speak For Her*, p. 13.

34. Dow and Tonn, " 'Feminine Style' and Political Judgment," p. 299.

35. Jane Blankenship and Deborah C. Robson, "A 'Feminine Style' in Women's Political Discourse: An Exploratory Essay," *Communication Quarterly* 43 (Summer 1995): 359.

36. John O. Greene and Deanna Geddes, "An Action Assembly Perspective on Social Skill," *Communication Theory* 3 (1993): 26–49; John O. Greene, "Action Assembly Theory: Metatheoretical Commitments, Theoretical Propositions, and Empirical Applications," in *Rethinking Communication: Paradigm Exemplars*, ed. Brenda Dervin, Lawrence Grossberg, Barbara J. O'Keefe, and Ellen Wartella (Newbury Park, CA: Sage, 1989), pp. 117–128; "A Cognitive Approach to Human Communication: An Action Assembly Theory," *Communication Monographs* 51 (1984): 289–306.

37. Barbara J. O'Keefe, "Variation, Adaptation, and Functional Explanation in the Study of Message Design," in *Developing Communication Theories*, ed. Gerry Philipsen (Albany: SUNY Press, 1997), pp. 85–118.

38. Steven Wilson uses a similar approach in "Developing Theories of Persuasive Message Production: The Next Generation," in *Message Production: Advances in Communication Theory*, ed. John O. Greene (Mahway, NJ: Lawrence Erlbaum, 1997), pp. 15–46.

39. For some reviews of this work, see James B. Stiff, *Persuasive Communication* (New York: Guilford, 1994), pp. 199–211; David R. Seibold, James G. Cantrill, and Renee A. Meyers, "Communication and Interpersonal Influence," in *Handbook of Interpersonal Communication*, 2nd ed., ed. Mark L. Knapp and Gerald R. Miller (Thousand Oaks, CA: Sage, 1994), pp. 542–588; Michael G. Garko, "Perspectives on and Conceptualizations of Compliance and Compliance-Gaining," *Communication Quarterly* 38 (1990): 138–157; Gerald R. Miller, "Persuasion," in *Handbook of Communication Science*, ed. Charles R. Berger and Steven H. Chaffee (Newbury Park, CA: Sage, 1987), pp. 446–483.

40. Gerald Marwell and David R. Schmitt, "Dimensions of Compliance-Gaining Strategies: A Dimensional Analysis," *Sociometry* 30 (1967): 350–364.

41. Lawrence R. Wheeless, Robert Barraclough, and Robert Stewart, "Compliance-Gaining and Power in Persuasion," in *Communication Yearbook 7*, ed. R. N. Bostrom (Beverly Hills, CA: Sage, 1983), pp. 105–145.

42. For a summary of the theory and its various tributaries and applications, see Anne Maydan Nicotera, "The Constructivist Theory of Delia, Clark, and Associates," in *Watershed Research Traditions in Human Communication Theory*, ed. Donald P. Cushman and Branislav Kovačić (Albany: SUNY Press, 1995), pp. 45–66; John Gastil, "An Appraisal and Revision of the Constructivist Research Program," in *Communication Yearbook 18*, ed. Brant R. Burleson (Thousand Oaks, CA: Sage, 1995), pp. 83–104. See also Brant R. Burleson, "The Constructivist Approach to Person-Centered Communication: Analysis of a Research Exemplar," in *Rethinking Communication: Paradigm Exemplars*, ed. Brenda Dervin, Lawrence Grossberg, Barbara J. O'Keefe, and Ellen Wartella (Newbury Park, CA: Sage, 1989), pp. 29–46; Jesse G. Delia, "Interpersonal Cognition, Message Goals, and Organization of Communication: Recent Constructivist Research," in *Communication Theory: Eastern and Western Perspectives*, ed. D. L. Kincaid (San Diego: Academic, 1987), pp. 255–274; Jesse G. Delia, Barbara J. O'Keefe, and Daniel J. O'Keefe, "The Constructivist Approach to Communication," in *Human Communication Theory: Comparative Essays*, ed. F. E. X. Dance (New York: Harper & Row, 1982), pp. 147–191.

43. George Kelly, *The Psychology of Personal Constructs* (New York: North, 1955).

44. For a discussion of the effects of culture on the cognitive system, see James L. Applegate and Howard E. Sypher, "A Constructivist Theory of Communication and Culture," in *Theories in Intercultural Communication*, ed. Young Yun Kim and William B. Gudykunst (Newbury Park, CA: Sage, 1988), pp. 41–65.

45. The idea of cognitive complexity was originally developed by Walter H. Crockett, "Cognitive Complexity and Impression Formation," in *Progress in Experimental Personality Research*, vol. 2, ed. B. A. Maher (New York: Academic, 1965), pp. 47–90.

46. Multiple goal achievement is developed in detail by Barbara J. O'Keefe and Gregory J. Shepherd, "The Pursuit of Multiple Objectives in Face-to-Face Persuasive Interactions: Effects of Construct Differentiation on Message Organization," *Communication Monographs* 54 (1987): 396–419.

47. This literature is reviewed by Claudia Hale, "Cognitive Complexity-Simplicity as a Determinant of Communication Effectiveness," *Communication Monographs* 47 (1980): 304–311.

48. See, for example, Jesse G. Delia, Susan L. Kline, and Brant R. Burleson, "The Development of Persuasive Communication Strategies in Kindergartners Through Twelfth-Graders," *Communication Monographs* 46 (1979): 241–256; James L. Applegate, "The Impact of Construct System Development on Communication and Impression Formation in Persuasive Messages," *Communication Monographs* 49 (1982): 277–289.

49. Brant R. Burleson, "Comforting Messages: Significance, Approaches, and Effects," in *Communication of Social Support: Messages, Interactions, Relationships, and Community*, ed. Brant R. Burleson, Terrance L. Albrecht, and Irwin G. Sarason (Thousand Oaks, CA: Sage, 1994), pp. 3–28. The study of social and emotional support has expanded well beyond constructivism. For an impressive survey of literature of this area, see Brant R. Burleson, "Emotional Support Skill," in *Handbook of Communication and Social Interaction Skill*, ed. John O. Greene and Brant R. Burleson (Mahwah, NJ: Lawrence Erlbaum, 2003), pp. 551–594.

50. Susan L. Kline and Janet M. Ceropski, "Person-Centered Communication in Medical Practice," in *Emergent Issues in Human Decision Making*, ed. Gerald M. Phillips and Julia T. Wood (Carbondale: Southern Illinois University Press, 1984), pp. 120–141.

51. Penelope Brown and Stephen Levinson, *Politeness: Some Universals in Language Usage* (Cambridge: Cambridge University Press, 1987). See also Roger Brown, "Politeness Theory: Exemplar and Exemplary," in *The Legacy of Solomon Asch: Essays in Cognition and Social Psychology*, ed. Irvin Rock (Hillsdale, NJ: Lawrence Erlbaum, 1990), pp. 23–38. For a discussion of politeness as a factor in social support, see Daena J. Goldsmith, "The Role of Facework in Supportive Communication," in *Communication of Social Support*, ed. Brant R. Burleson, Terrance L. Albrecht, and Irwin G. Sarason (Thousand Oaks, CA: Sage, 1994), pp. 29–49.

52. Charles R. Berger, *Planning Strategic Interaction: Attaining Goals Through Communicative Action* (Mahwah, NJ: Lawrence Erlbaum, 1997).

53. Berger, *Planning Strategic Interaction*, p. 25.

54. The role of emotions in message production has attracted the attention of cognitive researchers in recent years. See, for example, Brant R. Burleson and Sally Planalp, "Producing Emotion(al) Messages," *Communication Theory* 10 (2000): 221–250; Ross Buck, "From DNA to MTV: The Spontaneous Communication of Emotional Messages," in *Message Production: Advances in Communication Theory*, ed. John O. Greene (Mahwah, NJ: Lawrence Erlbaum, 1997), pp. 313–340.

55. Charles R. Berger, Susan H. Karol, and Jerry M. Jordan, "When a Lot of Knowledge Is a Dangerous Thing: The Debilitating Effects of Plan Complexity on Verbal Fluency," *Human Communication Research* 16 (1989): 91–119.

56. Barbara J. O'Keefe, "Variation, Adaptation, and Functional Explanation"; Barbara J. O'Keefe, "The Logic of Message Design: Individual Differences in Reasoning About Communication," *Communication Monographs* 55 (1988): 80–103.

57. O'Keefe, "Logic of Message Design," p. 102.

58. Charles Osgood, "On Understanding and Creating Sentences," *American Psychologist* 18 (1963): 735–751.

59. Charles Osgood, "The Nature of Measurement of Meaning," in *The Semantic Differential Technique*, ed. James Snider and Charles Osgood (Chicago: Aldine, 1969), pp. 9–10.

60. Osgood, "Nature of Measurement of Meaning."

61. Osgood has hypothesized that bipolarity is the basic factor in all language and human thought. See Charles Osgood and Meredith Richards, "From *Yang* and *Yin* to *And* or *But*," *Language* 49 (1973): 380–412.

62. A sampling of studies illustrating the applications can be found in James Snider and Charles Osgood, eds., *The Semantic Differential Technique* (Chicago: Aldine, 1969). This work also includes an atlas of approximately 550 concepts and their semantic profiles.

63. This point of view is expressed in Charles Osgood, "Semantic Differential Technique in the Comparative Study of Cultures," in *The Semantic Differential Technique*, ed. James Snider and Charles Osgood (Chicago: Aldine, 1969), pp. 303–323; and *Cross Cultural Universals of Affective Meaning* (Urbana: University of Illinois Press, 1975).

64. For an analysis of different approaches to hermeneutics, see Zygmunt Bauman, *Hermeneutics and Social Science* (New York: Columbia University Press, 1978). See also David Tracy, "Interpretation (Hermeneutics)," in *International Encyclopedia of Communications*, ed. Erik Barnouw and others (New York: Oxford University Press, 1989), pp. 343–348.

65. Friedrich Schleiermacher, *Hermeneutik*, ed. H. Kimmerle (Heidelberg, Germany: Carl Winter, Universitaetsverlag, 1959).

66. Wilhelm Dilthey, "The Rise of Hermeneutics," trans. F. Jameson, *New Literary History* 3 (1972): 229–244.

67. For an elaboration, see Bauman, *Hermeneutics*.

68. For a good discussion of the various senses of the term *text,* see George Cheney and Phillip K. Tompkins, "On the Facts of the Text as the Basis of Human Communication Research," in *Communication Yearbook 11,* ed. J. A. Anderson (Newbury Park, CA: Sage, 1988), pp. 455–481, and attendant commentaries (pp. 482–501).

69. Actually, the concept of *text* is complex and should not be read simply as an object, action, or writing. For an excellent brief exposition of the concept, see Cheney and Tompkins, "Facts of the Text."

70. Paul Ricoeur, *Interpretation Theory: Discourse and the Surplus of Meaning* (Fort Worth: Texas University Press, 1976); J. B. Thompson, ed. and trans., *Hermeneutics and the Human Sciences: Essays on Language, Action, and Interpretation,* (Cambridge: Cambridge University Press, 1981); Don Ihde, ed., *The Conflict of Interpretations: Essays in Hermeneutics* [by Paul Ricoeur] (Evanston, IL: Northwestern University Press, 1974).

71. The musical analogy of textual hermeneutics can be found in Ricoeur, *Interpretation Theory,* p. 75.

72. Barbara Warnick, "A Ricoeurian Approach to Rhetorical Criticism," *Western Journal of Speech Communication* 51 (1987): 227–244.

73. Stanley Fish, *Is There a Text in This Class?* (Cambridge, MA: Harvard University Press, 1980). For a brief, clear secondary source, see Chris Lang, "A Brief History of Literary Theory III" http://www.xenos.org/essays/litthry4.htm; "A Brief History of Literary Theory VII" http://www.xenos.org/essays/litthry8.htm

74. Gadamer's major work is *Truth and Method* (New York: Seabury, 1975). An excellent secondary treatment can be found in Richard J. Bernstein, *Beyond Objectivism and Relativism: Science, Hermeneutics, and Praxis* (Philadelphia: University of Pennsylvania Press, 1983), pp. 107–169. See also Palmer, *Hermeneutics,* pp. 162–222; Tracy, "Interpretation."

75. Stanley Deetz, "Conceptualizing Human Understanding: Gadamer's Hermeneutics and American Communication Studies," *Communication Quarterly* 26 (1978): 14.

76. John Angus Campbell, "Hans-Georg Gadamer's Truth and Method," *Quarterly Journal of Speech* 64 (1978): 101–122.

77. Campbell, "Hans-Georg Gadamer's Truth and Method," p. 107.

78. John Stewart, "The Symbol Model vs. Language as Constitutive Articulate Contact," in *Beyond the Symbol Model: Reflections on the Representational Nature of Language,* ed. John Stewart (Albany: SUNY Press, 1996), pp. 9–63; Stewart, *Language as Articulate Contact.*

79. Robert Hodge and Gunther Kress, *Social Semiotics* (Ithaca, NY: Cornell University Press, 1988).

80. Donald G. Ellis, "Fixing Communicative Meaning: A Coherentist Theory," *Communication Research* 22 (1995): 515–544.

81. The importance of integrating verbal and nonverbal communication is explored in a special issue of the *Journal of Communication* 52 (September, 2002). For an overview, see Stanley E. Jones and Curtis D. LeBaron, "Research on the Relationship Between Verbal and Nonverbal Communication: Emerging Integrations," *Journal of Communication* 52 (2002): 499–521.

82. This work is summarized by Judee K. Burgoon and Cindy H. White, "Researching Nonverbal Message Production: A View From Interaction Adaptation Theory," in *Message Production: Advances in Communication Theory,* ed. John O. Greene (Mahwah, NJ: Lawrence Erlbaum, 1997), pp. 279–312.

83. These issues are explored in depth by Charles R. Berger, "Message Production Skill in Social Interaction," in *Handbook of Communication and Social Interaction Skill,* ed. John O. Greene and Brant R. Burleson (Mahwah, NJ: Lawrence Erlbaum, 2003), pp. 257–290; Robert S. Wyer, Jr. and Rashmi Adaval, "Message Reception Skills in Social Communication," in *Handbook of Communication and Social Interaction Skill,* ed. John O. Greene and Brant R. Burleson (Mahwah, NJ: Lawrence Erlbaum, 2003), pp. 291–355.

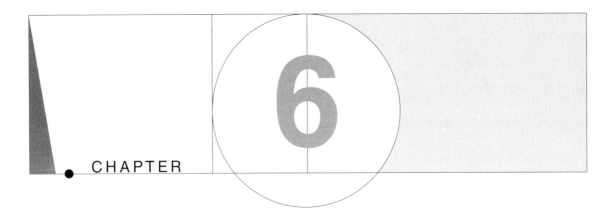

THE CONVERSATION

You probably associate the word *conversation* with social niceties. For most people, conversations are informal, everyday interactions, but in communication theory, the term has a special meaning. A conversation is an interaction sequence with a defined beginning and end, turn taking, and some sort of purpose or a set of goals.[1] Conversations are also governed by rules; they have structure and display coherence and sense. Conversations include all types of interaction, including social talk as well as debates and arguments, problem solving efforts, conflict episodes, romantic exchanges, and any other type of discourse in which communicators use language and nonverbal communication to interact with one another. Examples include family talks, dinner with a friend, business meetings, telephone conversations, Internet chats and e-mail exchanges, and any other well defined periods of interaction. When you think about it, conversations are really the heart of communication, and for this reason conversations are an important subject of communication theory.

Whenever you enter a new situation or encounter people with whom you may need to interact, you begin to think about conversation. If you are on your way to a party that will have many guests you don't know, you will probably think about how to begin conversations and integrate into the party. If you have scheduled a business meeting with someone you haven't met before, you will be thinking about what you want to accomplish with this person, what they are like, and how you will get started in the meeting. Each of these situations creates uncertainty for you, and part of what you do, as

Topics Addressed	Sociopsychological Theories	Sociocultural Theories	Cybernetic Theories	Critical Theories
Uncertainty management	Uncertainty reduction theory Anxiety-uncertainty management theory			
Adaptation	Accommodation theory Interaction adaptation theory Expectation violations theory Interpersonal deception theory			
Meaning in interaction		Symbolic interactionism Symbolic convergence theory Conversation analysis • Conversational maxims • Sequencing approaches • Rational approaches • Conversational argument	Coordinated management of meaning	Language-centered perspective Invitational rhetoric
Culture		Face negotiation theory		

you prepare for an interaction, is to try to reduce this uncertainty in some way. It turns out that this process of uncertainty reduction, which also reduces anxiety, is theoretically interesting, as we will see a bit later.

It is fascinating to watch people once they actually start talking. Sometime soon in a social situation, stand back for a few minutes and watch people interact. You will see a curious dance going on, in which behaviors are mimicked, eye contact moves in and out, and people gracefully (and sometimes not so gracefully) move their bodies forward, backward, and from side to side. What you will see is a dynamic and complex process of interpersonal adaptation, and this topic has not escaped the attention of communication theorists.

But what gets made in all of this dancing and uncertainty reduction? Why does it matter? As the chapter moves on, you will gain insight into these questions, as a significant body of theory tells us some of the larger outcomes of social interaction in terms of meaning, social institutions, relationships, and goal accomplishment. We see, too, how people operate from socially negotiated rules to determine how to "read" social situations and actions and how to respond to others in conversations. Larger institutions as well as power arrangements are constructed in a history of conversations within society over time.

Conversations matter, and in this chapter, we will have a chance to look at this topic from many angles. The chapter map on the previous page shows the landscape we will traverse here.

◖ THE SOCIOPSYCHOLOGICAL TRADITION

Sociopsychological theories have concentrated on identifying variables that affect our behavior in interaction. Two major themes have emerged in this literature. First, the literature has focused on the conditions in which individuals manage uncertainty about other people, including how they go about getting information about others, how uncertainty and anxiety are related to one another, and how uncertainty-reduction processes are related to culture. The second theme prevalent in the sociopsychological work on conversation involves the organization, coordination, and meshing of behavior in interactional episodes. These theories tells us a great deal about how we match our behaviors to that of others, how and when our behaviors diverge,

what happens when our expectations are violated, and how we come to detect deception based on the behavior of others.

Managing Uncertainty and Anxiety

The first theme in the conversation literature—managing uncertainty—emerged in large part from the work of Charles Berger, William Gudykunst, and their colleagues. This line of theory deals with the ways we gather information about other people, why we do so, and what results we obtain when we do.[2] In other words, the focus is on the ways individuals monitor their social environments and come to know more about themselves and others through interaction. Berger's theory is referred to as *uncertainty reduction theory* (URT) and Gudykunst's extension of Berger's work is called *anxiety-uncertainty management* (AUM).[3]

Uncertainty Reduction Theory.   This theory addresses the basic process of how we gain knowledge about other people.[4] When we encounter a stranger, we may have a strong desire to reduce uncertainty about this person. In such a situation, we tend to be uncertain about the other's ability to communicate his or her goals and plans, feelings at the moment, and the like. Berger proposes that people have a difficult time with uncertainty, that they want to be able to predict behavior, and that they are therefore motivated to seek information about others. Indeed, this kind of uncertainty reduction is one of the primary dimensions of a developing relationship.

As we communicate, according to Berger, we are making plans to accomplish our goals. We formulate plans for our communications with others based on our goals as well as the information we have about the others involved. The more uncertain we are, the more vigilant we must become, and the more we must rely on data available to us in the situation. At highly uncertain moments, we will become more conscious or mindful of the planning we are doing. When we are very uncertain about another person, we will tend to be less confident in our plans and make more contingency plans, or alternative ways of responding.

Attraction or affiliation seems to correlate positively with uncertainty reduction. For example, nonverbal expressiveness seems to reduce uncertainty, and reduction in uncertainty seems to increase nonverbal expressiveness. Higher levels of uncertainty seem to create distance, but reduced uncertainty tends to bring people together. As communicators discover similarities between them, their attraction to one another goes up, and their apparent need for more information goes down.

Often, the behavior of the other person immediately leads to a reduction in your uncertainty, and you do not feel the need to get additional information. This is especially true when your involvement with the other person is limited to a particular situation and you have all the information you need to understand their behavior in this situation. However, under other circumstances, you have a heightened need to know. Such circumstances include abnormal behavior on the part of the other person, the expectation that you will be communicating with the other person in the future, or the prospect that the encounter will be especially rewarding or costly. Under these conditions, you will probably take action to get more information about the other person.

For example, if you hired a plumber to fix a leak in your house, you would probably not have a very great need to learn more about this contractor, assuming you would not see her or him again. On the other hand, if the plumber noticed that you had a "Room for Rent" sign in your window and expressed an interest in finding a new place to live, you would suddenly be motivated to get more information about this person. In particular, you would be interested in reducing *predictive uncertainty* about this individual so that you would have a better idea of *what* to expect in his or her behavior, and you would want to reduce *explanatory uncertainty*, so that you could better *understand* your possible tenant's behavior. In initial interactions, then, people tend to talk more in order to get information; as uncertainty is eliminated, questioning and other information-seeking strategies decline.

Berger suggests a variety of ways we go about getting information from others. *Passive strategies* are observational, whereas *active* ones require the observer to do something to get the information. *Interactive strategies* rely directly on communication with the other person.

The first passive strategy is *reactivity searching.* Here the individual is observed actually doing something—reacting in some situation. For example, if you were interested in getting to know a classmate, you might observe this person discreetly for a period of time. You might watch the way he or she reacts to events in the class—questions from the instructor, class discussions, and so forth. Observers generally prefer to see how a person reacts when communicating with another person, so you might listen in on conversations this person is having with other people in class. *Disinhibition searching* is another passive strategy in which people are observed in informal situations where they are less likely to be self-monitoring and are behaving in a more natural way. You might therefore be especially interested in observing your classmate outside of class in settings such as the cafeteria or residence hall.

Active strategies of information involve asking others about the target person and manipulating the environment in ways that set up the target person for observation. You might, for example, try to get assigned to a project group with this classmate.

Interactive strategies include interrogation and self-disclosure. Self-disclosure, which is discussed in more detail in Chapter 7, is a significant strategy for actively obtaining information because if you disclose something about yourself, the other person is likely to disclose in return. Once in the project group, for instance, you could talk to this other person, where you might ask questions and make disclosures in order to encourage him or her to disclose information as well.

To discover the ways strangers get information about one another, Charles Berger and Katherine Kellermann videotaped about fifty conversations in their laboratory.[5] The pairs in the study were told to get varying amounts of information from their conversational partners. Some participants were told to get as much information about the other person as possible, others were told to get as little as possible, and a third group was not given any instructions along these lines. Also, the dyads themselves were mixed, so that some consisted of pairs in which both had been asked to get a great deal of information, some consisted of pairs in which both had been asked to get little information, and some included one person from each category.

The videotaped conversations were coded by judges in a variety of ways. The researchers were interested chiefly in finding out what the communicators actually did to get or to resist getting information. Predictably, the most common strategy for getting information was to ask questions, but some other strategies were also used, such as putting the other person at ease and using self-

disclosure. Even the low-information seekers used questions, but their questions tended to be innocuous inquiries into the weather and other non-informative topics.

Individuals who were trying to get a great deal of information asked significantly more questions than the low-information subjects. Those who were not given any instructions asked about the same number of questions as those who were told to get a great deal of information, which suggests that we normally tend to ask many questions when talking with strangers. This hypothesis was supported because the low-information seekers in this experiment had a harder time trying to keep from getting a lot of information than did the high-information seekers and normal subjects. As expected, high-information seekers asked more open-ended questions, requiring explanation, than did low-information seekers.

Anxiety-Uncertainty Management.   William Gudykunst and his colleagues have extended Berger's work in important ways, especially by looking at uncertainty and anxiety in intercultural situations. They have found that all cultures seek to reduce uncertainty in the initial stages of a relationship, but they do so in different ways.[6] The difference can be explained by whether one is a member of a high-context culture or a low-context culture.[7] *High-context cultures* rely heavily on the overall situation to interpret events, and *low-context cultures* rely more on the explicit verbal content of messages. Members of high-context cultures, such as the Japanese, rely on nonverbal cues and information about a person's background to reduce uncertainty, but members of low-context cultures, such as the British, ask direct questions related to experience, attitudes, and beliefs.

The process of uncertainty reduction between people from different cultures is affected by additional variables as well. When you strongly identify with your own cultural group and you think the other person is typical of a different group, you will probably feel a certain amount of anxiety, and your uncertainty will be great. On the other hand, your confidence in getting to know the other person will be higher and your anxiety about doing so will be lower if you expect the results to be positive. Experience and friendships with other people from different cultures may also increase your confidence when meeting a stranger from another cultural group. In addition, knowing the other person's language will help, as will a certain amount of tolerance for ambiguity. Also, when you are more confident and less anxious about meeting someone from a different group, you will probably do a better job of getting information and reducing uncertainty.

Uncertainty and anxiety in intercultural situations seem to be underlying causes of ineffectiveness and lack of adaptation. The less you know and the more anxious you are, the less effective you will probably be in intercultural situations. This makes the reduction or management of uncertainty anxiety especially important.

There is no clear line that marks the point at which difficult or problematic communication will result. Instead, different individuals have different thresholds for uncertainty and anxiety. If your level of uncertainty exceeds your upper threshold, you will not feel very confident, and if the level of anxiety is too high for you, you might avoid communication altogether. There are also low-end thresholds, below which your motivations to communicate would disappear. If you met a stranger from another culture and you were too uncertain about this person, you might avoid communicating with her because you felt that you didn't know how to manage the interaction. At the same time, if you did not feel enough uncertainty, you would not be motivated to communicate because you might feel you already knew enough. If you are too anxious, you will be nervous and avoid communicating, but if you are not anxious enough, you will not care enough to try. The ideal in intergroup situations, then, is for uncertainty and anxiety to be between your upper and lower thresholds, which would lead to motivation to communicate and the adoption of uncertainty reduction strategies.

In recent years, Gudykunst has elaborated this theory in detail, to the point that it now in-cludes about fifty propositions related to self-concept, motivation, reactions to strangers, social categorization, situational processes, connection with strangers, and a host of other concerns dealing with anxiety and effectiveness.[8] Clearly, anxiety and uncertainty correlate with a whole host of communication traits, behaviors, and patterns.

Accommodation and Adaptation

If you observe interaction closely, you will notice that speakers frequently adjust their behaviors to one another. For example, two speakers may adjust their accents to sound more alike, may begin to speak at the same speed, or may use mirror-like gestures. Sometimes speakers do just the opposite and actually exaggerate their differences. Researchers have also noticed these behaviors and have studied them in a variety of ways. Here we look at two landmark projects that address this issue.

Accommodation Theory.   This theory is one of the most influential behavioral theories of communication. Formulated by Howard Giles and his colleagues, accommodation theory explains how and why we adjust our communication behaviors to the actions of others.[9] Have you ever noticed, for example, that two people in a conversation will both have their arms crossed? Giles and his colleagues have confirmed the common observation that communicators often seem to mimic one another's behavior. They call this *convergence,* or coming together. The opposite— *divergence*—or moving apart, happens when speakers begin to exaggerate their differences.

Accommodation in both of these forms has been seen in almost all imaginable communication behaviors, including accent, rate, loudness, vocabulary, grammar, voice, gestures, and other features. Convergence or divergence can be *mutual,* in which case both communicators come together or go apart, or it can be *nonmutual,* in which one person converges and the other diverges. Convergence can also be *partial* or *complete.* For example, you might speak somewhat faster so that you are a little closer to another person's speech rate, or you might go all the way and speak just as fast as this person does.

Although accommodation is sometimes done consciously, the speaker is usually unaware of doing so. The use of accommodation is similar to any number of other functional but subconscious processes that are scripted or enacted without having to attend to all the details of each behavior. You are probably more aware of divergence than convergence because differences become more noticeable in the process.

Accommodation researchers have found that accommodation can be important in communication. It can lead to social identity and bonding or disapproval and distancing. For instance, convergence often happens in situations in which you seek the approval of others. This can occur in groups that are already alike in certain ways because such groups consist of similar individuals who can coordinate their actions. The result of convergence can be increased attractiveness, predictability, intelligibility, and mutual involvement.

Typically, some convergence is appreciated. You tend to respond favorably to someone who makes an attempt to speak in your style, but you will probably dislike too much convergence, especially if you think it is inappropriate. For example, people sometimes converge not with the other person's actual speech but with a stereotype, such as when a nurse speaks to an elderly patient using baby talk or when someone speaks loudly and slowly to a blind person. People tend to appreciate convergence from others that is accurate, well intended, and appropriate in the situation, and tend to be irritated by the convergence effort if it is not.

How you evaluate convergence depends in part on motivation—why you think others are copying you. Studies have shown that when listeners perceive that the speaker is intentionally speaking in a style close to the listeners' own, they will tend to like it. But listeners will evaluate negatively any convergence move that is seen as inappropriate in the situation or done out of ill will. This includes, for example, mocking, teasing, insensitivity to social norms, or inflexibility.

Of course, you do not always match the behavior of others in order to seek their approval. Often higher-status speakers will slow their speech or use simpler vocabulary when talking with a person who has lower status to increase understanding. In contrast, lower-status communicators will sometimes upgrade their speech to match the higher-status person because they want that person's approval.

Although the rewards of speech convergence can be substantial, so are the costs. Convergence requires effort, and it may mean the loss of personal identity. Sometimes it is even viewed as abnormal and may be frowned on. Instead of converging, you sometimes maintain your own style or actually move in the opposite direction of your conversational partner's style. You may work to maintain your own style when you want to reinforce your identity. This would be the case, for example, among members of an ethnic group with a strong accent, who work to perpetuate the accent in the face of homogenizing influences of a dominant culture. Divergence often functions to accentuate in-group identity vis-à-vis members of an out-group.

Sometimes members of a group will accentuate their speech characteristics in a strange community to elicit sympathy from the host group. This is a kind of self-handicapping method that frees speakers from responsibility for violation of certain social norms with which they may not be familiar. Sometimes, too, speakers will diverge from the style of other speakers in order to affect the others' behavior in some way. Teachers may deliberately talk over the heads of students in order to challenge the students to learn. You might speak extra slowly when talking with a very fast speaker in order to get him or her to slow down. To learn more about these processes, we turn to the work of Judee Burgoon and her colleagues.

Interaction Adaptation Theory. Accommodation theory lays the basic groundwork for identifying various types of accommodation and their correlates, but this phenomenon is actually part of a much more complex process of adaptation in interaction—the topic of the interaction adaptation theory of Judee Burgoon and her associates.[10] These researchers noticed that communicators have a kind of *interactional synchrony*, a coordinated back-and-forth pattern. If you were to videotape a conversation with a friend, you would probably notice this effect. At some moments you might see the two of you behaving in a similar way, mirroring or converging in a *reciprocal* pattern. At other moments, you might see yourselves sort of backing away or diverging in a pattern of *compensation*. Using the lens of interaction adaptation theory, you would begin to notice your behaviors are influencing each other, creating the pattern, rather like a dance.

According to Burgoon and her associates, when you begin communicating with another person, you have a rough idea about what will happen. This is your *interaction position*, the place where you will begin. It is determined by a combination of factors that the theorists cleverly named *RED*, which stands for *requirements*, *expectations*, and *desires*. Your *requirements* are the things you really need in the interaction. These may be biological as in a request for food, or they may be social in terms of needed affiliation, continued friendship, or even managing a smooth interaction. Your *expectations* are the patterns you predict will happen. If you are not that familiar with the other person, you will rely on social norms of politeness and aspects of the situation such as the purpose of the meeting. If you know the other person well, your expectations will probably be based largely on past experience. Your *desires* are what you want to accomplish, what you hope will happen.

Your initial behaviors in the interaction consist of a combination of verbal and nonverbal behaviors that reflect your interaction position, environmental factors, and skill level. However, in most interactions, your behavior will change— and so will that of your partner—as you experience mutual influence. Mutual influence can be considerable and, in most situations, probably far greater than any preplanning you have done. Normally, you will *reciprocate* your partner's behavior as a kind of default response. A hug, for example, will probably be reciprocated. Humans seem to need organized patterning, which reciprocation can help achieve. This tendency to reciprocate may be caused by a combination of biological and socially conditioned factors. This does not mean that we always reciprocate, however. Sometimes the reciprocal pattern is disrupted or disabled, leading to a second kind of response—*compensation.*

If you like your partner's behavior more than you thought you would, you will probably reciprocate, or converge, making your behavior more like that of your partner. If it turns out that your partner's behavior is more negative than you thought it would be, you will probably engage in a pattern of compensation, maintaining your own style and maybe even exaggerating what you would have initially done. Let's say, for example, that you feel very close to your friend and would like to get a hug, but you don't really expect to. Surprisingly, however, he comes up and puts his hand on your shoulder, so you reciprocate by putting your arm around his waist. That's an example of positive evaluation and reciprocation.

On the other hand, assume that you hope to get a hug but are disappointed when your partner fails to touch you. In this situation, you would probably compensate by walking over and giving him a hug. On the other hand, if you expected a hug but didn't want one, his failure to touch you would be a good thing, and you would reciprocate that by backing off or maintaining some distance. Human interaction is complex and involves a mix of motives and patterns. You can actually reciprocate some behaviors and compensate others at the same time.

Burgoon and her colleagues have discovered that the ways in which we adapt to other people depend in large measure on the extent to which other people violate our expectations for behavior. They explore this hypothesis in greater detail in expectancy violations theory.

Expectancy Violations Theory. As a natural extension of their work on interaction adaptation, Burgoon and her colleagues, among others, have explored the ways in which people react when their expectations are violated.[11] According to Burgoon's theory, we have expectations about the behavior of another person based on social norms as well as our previous experience with the other person and the situation in which the behavior occurs. These expectations can involve virtually any nonverbal behavior, including, for example, eye contact, distance, and body angle.[12]

The common assumption is that when expectancies are met, the other person's behaviors are judged as positive, and when they are violated, the behaviors are judged as negative. Burgoon has found, however, that this is not always the case. Violations are often judged favorably. This may be the case because violations sometimes draw our attention to the other person's behavior, and we learn something positive we might not otherwise have noticed.

Whether judged as good or bad, violations cause the perceiver to be aroused. If someone stands too close to you or too far away, if another person's eye contact is abnormal, or if an individual violates some other set of expectations, you will feel differently. This arousal is not necessarily negative. In fact, in some cases it might feel pleasant, especially when the other person seems to like you. Sometimes, however, violations can make you feel uncomfortable. Apparently, we learn to have expectations and to detect violations early in life, even in infancy.

What seems to happen is that your attention is drawn to behavior that would otherwise go unnoticed. When your expectations are met, you don't notice the behavior, but when they are violated, you become distracted by it. This distraction can certainly get your attention and lead you to evaluate the other person's behavior.

Imagine, for example, that you have just been introduced to an attractive person. In getting to know each other, you talk about everything from the weather to family. Suddenly you become aware that this person is standing unusually close to you. You try to back off, but the other person continues to move in. Your first tendency will be to interpret this behavior and then to evaluate it. You might interpret the behavior as a "come on." If you like this person, this will be good, but if you don't, it will be bad.

As this example shows, an important variable in the evaluation process is *reward valence,* or the degree to which you find the interaction rewarding. A conversation might be rewarding, for example, because it will lead to a positive outcome. On the other hand, valence might be negative because it entails more costs than benefits. One of the reasons sexual harassment can be such a problem is that it is a negative behavior in what may be an otherwise rewarding setting, such as a job situation.

Figure 6.1 illustrates the violation–evaluation process. The figure shows that expectations arise from one's perception of the communicator's characteristics, the state of the relationship, and the context in which the behavior occurs.

Violations accentuate the judgments made in this process. Here the reward valence of the other communicator is especially strong: Violations cause arousal, which in turn accentuate evaluation of communication with the other person and the meaning of the message. If the exchange is valued and the behavior has a positive meaning, a positive outcome will result.

Figure 6.1 includes other possibilities as well. The meaning of the behavior may be ambiguous, and one is not sure what to make of it. This theory predicts that ambiguous behavior by a valued communicator will be taken as positive, but such behavior by an unrewarding communicator will be taken as negative. Again, this effect will be accentuated in cases of a violation.

An interesting study of eye gaze shows how violations can affect judgments of behavior and communication outcomes.[13] The researchers trained four confederates to manipulate their eye behavior to effect seemingly natural violations in an interview. About 150 students in an organizational communication course volunteered to participate in the study as part of an interviewing assignment. They took the role of an employment interviewer, and each interviewed one of the confederates. In preparation for half of the interviews, the subjects were given a high-status résumé, and the other half

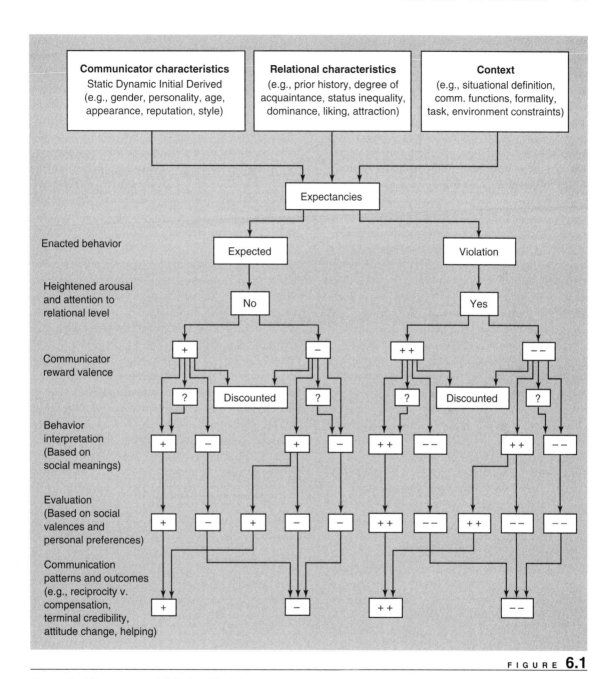

FIGURE **6.1**

Nonverbal Expectancy Violation Model

NOTE: For simplicity, communicator reward valence, behavior interpretation, and behavior evaluation valence have been dichotomized into positive and negative but should be understood to represent continua. Double pluses and minuses denote greater magnitude of effect.

From Judee K. Burgoon and Jerold L. Hale, "Nonverbal Expectancy Violations: Model Elaboration and Application," *Communication Monographs* 55 (1988): 64. Reprinted by permission of Speech Communication Association and the authors.

were given a low-status one. The first group was set up to find the interview rewarding, whereas the other would obviously find it less so. Some interviewers got a confederate who gave them normal eye contact, some got a person who gave them no eye contact, and some got a confederate who gave above-normal eye contact. After the interview, each subject completed a set of scales related to the credibility of the applicant, how likely they would be to hire this individual, how attracted they were to this person, and other aspects of the relationship that developed between them in the interview.

The results of this experiment showed that the failure to have eye contact with the interviewer definitely hurt the applicants' images whether they were high or low status. A higher-than-normal level of eye gaze was also found to be a violation, but it was interpreted somewhat differently between the two conditions. High-status applicants with nearly constant eye contact were judged more favorably than were low-status applicants with constant eye contact.

One of the most interesting judgments we make about the behavior of others is in terms of their honesty. Over the past twenty years or so, there has been a great deal of research on deception and deception detection. As a natural extension of their work on expectancy violations, David Buller and Judee Burgoon have pulled much of this work together in a developing theory of interpersonal deception.

Interpersonal Deception Theory.   Buller and Burgoon see deception and its detection as part of an ongoing interaction between communicators involving a back-and-forth process.[14] Deception involves the deliberate manipulation of information, behavior, and image in order to lead another person to a false belief or conclusion. Typically, when a speaker deceives, that person engages in strategic behavior that distorts the truthfulness of the information or is incomplete, irrelevant, unclear, or indirect. Speakers may even disassociate themselves from the deceptive information. Listeners often detect the use of

these strategies and can become suspicious that they are being deceived.

The deceiver may experience a certain amount of apprehension about being detected, and the receiver may experience a certain amount of suspicion about being deceived. These "internal" thoughts can often be seen in "outward" behavior. This being so, receivers look for signs of lying, and liars look for signs of suspicion. Over time, in this back-and-forth process, the sender may come to perceive that the deception was successful or not, and the receiver may come to see that the suspicion was warranted or not.

Deception apprehension and suspicion can come out in strategically controlled behaviors, but they are more apt to show up in nonstrategic behaviors, or behaviors that are not being manipulated. This is a process called *leakage*. You might be suspicious that you are being lied to because of behaviors that the other person is not aware of, and if you are trying to deceive another person, you may experience apprehension based on the fact that the receiver could detect it through some behavior you are not controlling. For example, you might have perfect control of your voice and face, but movements of your feet or hands give you away.

As we learned above, communicators' expectations are significant anchors with which to judge behavior. So expectations play a definite role in deception situations. When receivers' expectations are violated, their suspicions may be aroused. Likewise, when senders' expectations are violated, their deception apprehension may also be aroused.

Many factors affect this ongoing process—for example, the degree to which the communicators can actually interact fully. This variable is called *interactivity*. Talking face to face is more interactive than talking on the telephone, which in turn is more interactive than communicating by e-mail or letter. Interactivity can increase *immediacy*, or the degree of psychological closeness between the communicators. When we have high immediacy, we pay close attention to a variety of live cues. We may stand closer, look more attentively at what is going on, and generally avail ourselves of a richer set of actions. You might predict that the more access communicators have to one another's behavior, the more cognitive data they have to assess one another's intentions or suspicions. Research seems to indicate, however, that the opposite can also happen. Immediacy and relational closeness can cause you to feel more engaged with others and less suspicious.

When we are relationally close, we also have a degree of familiarity between us. In a close relationship, we have certain biases or expectations about what we are going to see. A *truth bias* makes us less inclined to see deception. Most married couples, for example, don't expect and thus don't see deception. This may explain why learning about an extra-marital affair or other deception is especially devastating. In a positive relationship, communicators more or less assume that they are telling one another the truth. Under these conditions, we will not be very suspicious about lying and may not pay close attention to behavioral deception cues. On the other hand, a *lie bias* may accentuate our suspicions and lead us to think people are lying when they may not be. If someone repeatedly lies to you, you are likely to take everything they say with a grain of salt.

Our ability to deceive or detect deception is also affected by *conversational demand,* or the amount of demands made on us while we are communicating. If several things are going on at once or if the communication is complex and involves numerous goals, we cannot pay as close attention to everything as we would if the situational demands were light.

Two other factors that affect the deception-detection process are the level of motivation to lie or to detect lying and the skill in deception and deception detection. Where motivation is high, our desire to deceive may override our apprehension about being caught. At the same time, if the receiver knows that our motivation is high, his or her suspicions will be increased. Some people are more skilled at deceiving than others because they have a larger range of behaviors they can perform. This could be counteracted, however, by the other person's ability to detect deception.

Remember, however, that communicators engage in both strategic and nonstrategic behaviors. When we lie, we typically exert a great deal of control over how we manage information, behavior, and image (all strategic behaviors); at the same time, some of our behavior that is not being controlled (nonstrategic) is sometimes detected by others, depending on their motivation and skill. In highly interactive situations—those in which we are fully engaged with one another—we often dampen our use of nonstrategic behaviors, which in some situations could make it harder to detect the deception.

The purpose of deception also seems to enter the formula. Senders deceiving for personal gain may have a harder time hiding it than senders who deceive for more altruistic purposes. Of course, the results of deceptive behavior depend in part on how motivated the receiver is to detect it. If the receiver is suspicious and the lying matters, he or she will probably put considerable effort into detecting the lie. The sociopsychological dimensions that we bring to bear on a conversation are not the only ones affecting our interactions with each other. Sociocultural factors also come into play.

REFLECTIONS ON
The Sociopsychological Tradition

Traditionally, there have been two strong trends in this tradition—the behavioral and the cognitive. Understanding individual communicators and how they process messages has been most usefully informed by the latter, as information processing lies at the center of the individual's involvement with messages. However, as we move to the larger concern of interaction, behavioral patterns start to get interesting.

It is no wonder, then, that the theories in this section feature the careful examination of human behavior in social situations. Even though interpersonal behavior is carefully considered by these theories, they still say more about what individuals do than what is created or made in the process of interaction between individuals. In the following section, we see a shift from the individual to the social in how conversations are framed.

• • •

THE SOCIOCULTURAL TRADITION

Sociocultural theories of the conversation take us in a very different direction from the work summarized in the previous section. Here we encounter explanations of what gets made or constructed in conversations, how meaning arises in conversation, and how symbols come to be defined through interaction. These theories tell us about what themes of conversation bring people together and how participants come to share meaning, and they focus, too, on how communicators work together in a structured way to organize their talk. Four areas are covered—symbolic interactionism, symbolic convergence theory, conversation analysis, and face negotiation theory.

Symbolic Interactionism

We introduced symbolic interactionism in Chapter 4 in describing the process by which the self is developed. Symbolic interactionism, a movement within sociology, focuses on the ways in which people form meaning and structure in society through conversation. Barbara Ballis Lal summarizes the premises of this movement:

- People make decisions and act in accordance with their subjective understandings of the situations in which they find themselves.
- Social life consists of interaction processes rather than structures and is therefore constantly changing.
- People understand their experience through the meanings found in the symbols of their primary groups, and language is an essential part of social life.

- The world is made up of social objects that are named and have socially determined meanings.
- People's actions are based on their interpretations, in which the relevant objects and actions in the situation are taken into account and defined.
- One's self is a significant object and, like all social objects, is defined through social interaction with others.

In this chapter we concentrate on classical symbolic interactionism, the basic ideas of the movement, and the theoretical extensions most recognized in the communication field.

George Herbert Mead is usually viewed as the founder of the movement, and his work certainly forms the core of the Chicago School.[15] Herbert Blumer, Mead's foremost apostle, invented the term *symbolic interactionism*, an expression Mead himself never used. Blumer refers to this label as "a somewhat barbaric neologism that I coined in an offhand way. . . . The term somehow caught on."[16]

The three cardinal concepts in Mead's theory, captured in the title of his best-known work, are society, self, and mind. These categories are different aspects of the same general process, the *social act*—a complete unit of conduct that cannot be analyzed into specific subparts. An act may be short and simple, such as tying a shoe, or it may be long and complicated, like the fulfillment of a life plan. Acts relate to one another and are built up throughout a lifetime. Acts begin with an impulse; they involve perception and assignment of meaning, mental rehearsal, weighing of alternatives, and consummation.

In its most basic form, a social act involves a three-part relationship: an initial gesture from one individual, a response to that gesture by another, and a result. The result is what the act means for the communicator. Meaning does not reside solely in any one of these things but in the triadic relationship of all three.[17] In a holdup, for example, the robber indicates to the victim what is intended. The victim responds by giving money or belongings, and in the initial gesture and response, the defined result (a holdup) has occurred.

Even individual acts, such as a solitary walk, are interactional because they are based on gestures and responses that occurred many times in the past and continue in the mind of the individual. One never takes a walk by oneself without relying on meanings and actions learned in social interaction with others.

The *joint action* of a group of people, such as marriage, trade, war, or church worship, consists of an *interlinkage* of smaller interactions. Blumer notes that in an advanced society the largest portion of group action consists of highly recurrent, stable patterns that possess common and established meanings for their participants. Because of the frequency of such patterns and the stability of their meanings, scholars have tended to treat them as structures, forgetting their origins in interaction. Blumer warns us not to forget that new situations present problems requiring adjustment and redefinition. In a recent treatment, Donald Ellis writes, "that macrotopics of sociology (e.g., ethnicity) are never actually seen but exist in and through the activities of individuals in microsituations."[18]

Even in highly repetitious group patterns, nothing is permanent. Each case must begin anew with individual action. No matter how solid a group action appears to be, it is still rooted in individual human choices: "It is the social process in group life that creates and upholds the rules, not the rules that create and uphold group life."[19]

Interlinkages may be pervasive, extended, and connected through complicated networks: "a network or an institution does not function automatically because of some inner dynamics or system requirements: it functions because people at different points do something, and what they do is a result of how they define the situation in which they are called on to act."[20] With this idea of social acts in mind, then, let us look more closely at the first facet of Meadian analysis—society.

Society, or group life, consists of the cooperative behaviors of society's members. Human cooperation requires that we understand others' in-

tentions, which also entails figuring out what we will do in the future. Thus, cooperation consists of "reading" other people's actions and intentions and responding in an appropriate way.

Meaning is an important outcome of communication. Your meanings are the result of interaction with others. So, for example, although you may never have heard of a "toilet telephone," prison inmates know it well; they have learned that they can communicate by listening to voices traveling through the sewer pipes in the prison. We use meanings to interpret the happenings around us. Interpretation is like an internal conversation: "The actor selects, checks, suspends, regroups, and transforms the meanings in light of the situation in which he is placed and the direction of his actions."[21] Clearly, we could not communicate without sharing the meaning of the symbols we use.

Mead calls a gesture with shared meaning a *significant symbol.* Society is made possible by significant symbols. Because of the ability to vocalize symbols, we literally can hear ourselves and thus can respond to the self as others respond to us. We can imagine what it is like to receive our own messages, and we can empathize with the listener and take the listener's role, mentally completing the other's response. Society, then, consists of a network of social interactions in which participants assign meaning to their own and others' actions by the use of symbols.[22] Even the various institutions of society are built up by the interactions of people involved in those institutions.

Consider the court system in the United States as an example. The courts are nothing more than the interactions among judges, juries, attorneys, witnesses, clerks, reporters, and others who use language to interact with one another. *Court* has no meaning apart from the interpretations of the actions of those involved in it. The same can be said for school, church, government, industry, and any other segment of society. This interplay between responding to others and responding to self is an important concept in Mead's theory, and it provides a good transition to his second concept—the *self.*[23]

You have a self because you can respond to yourself as an object. You sometimes react favorably to yourself and feel pride, happiness, and encouragement. You sometimes become angry or disgusted with yourself. The primary way you come to see yourself as others see you is through *role taking* or assuming the perspective of others, and this is what leads you to have a self-concept. Another term for self-concept is *generalized other,* a kind of composite perspective from which you see yourself. The generalized other is your overall perception of the way others see you. You have learned this self-picture from years of symbolic interaction with other people in your life. *Significant others,* the people closest to you, are especially important because their reactions have been very influential in your life.

Consider, for example, the self-image of adolescents. As a result of their interactions with significant others such as parents, siblings, and peers, teenagers come to view themselves as they think others view them. They come to take on the persona that has been reflected to them in their many interactions with other people. As they behave in ways that affirm this image, it is strengthened, and others respond accordingly in a cyclical fashion. So, for example, if a young person feels socially inept, he or she may withdraw, further reinforcing the image of being inadequate.

The self has two facets, each serving an essential function. The *I* is the impulsive, unorganized, undirected, unpredictable part of you. The *me* is the generalized other, made up of the organized and consistent patterns shared with others. Every act begins with an impulse from the *I* and quickly becomes controlled by the *me.* The *I* is the driving force in action, whereas the *me* provides direction and guidance. Mead used the concept of *me* to explain socially acceptable and adaptive behavior and the *I* to explain creative, unpredictable impulses.

For example, many people will deliberately change their life situations in order to alter their self-concepts. Here, the *I* moves the person to change in ways that the *me* would not permit. Such a change might have occurred, for example, when you went to college. Many high school students decide that they will use college to establish a new *me* by associating with a new group of significant others and by establishing a new generalized other.

Your ability to use significant symbols to respond to yourself makes thinking possible. Thinking is Mead's third concept, which he calls *mind.* The mind is not a thing, but a process. It is nothing more than interacting with yourself. This ability, which develops along with the self, is crucial to human life, for it is part of every act. *Minding* involves hesitating (postponing overt action) while you interpret the situation. Here you think through the situation and plan future actions. You imagine various outcomes and select and test possible alternatives.

People possess significant symbols that allow them to name objects. You always define something in terms of how you might act toward it. You might have a friend, for instance, for whom you are starting to have romantic feelings. You will act differently toward this person depending on whether you see that person as a friend or as a romantic partner. Objects become the objects they are through our symbolic minding process; when we envision new or different actions toward an object, the object itself is changed because we see it through a different lens.

For Blumer, objects are of three types—physical (things), social (people), and abstract (ideas). People define objects differently, depending on how they act toward those objects. A police officer may mean one thing to the residents of an inner-city ghetto and something else to the inhabitants of a posh residential area; the different interactions among the residents of these two vastly different communities will determine different meanings.

A fascinating study of marijuana use by Howard Becker illustrates the concept of social object very well.[24] Becker found that marijuana users learn at least three things through interaction with other users. The first is to smoke the drug properly. Virtually everyone Becker talked to said that they had trouble getting high at first until others showed them how to do it. Second, smokers must learn to define the sensation produced by the drug as a "high." In other words, the individual learns to discriminate the effects of marijuana and to associate these with smoking. Becker claims that this association does not happen automatically and must be learned through social interaction with other users. In fact, some experienced users reported that novices were absolutely stoned and didn't know it until they were taught to identify the feeling. Finally, users must learn to define the effects as pleasant and desirable. Again, this is not automatic; many beginners do not find the effects pleasant at all until they are told that they should consider them so.

Here, we see that marijuana is a social object. Its meanings are created in the process of interaction. How people think about the drug (mind) is determined by those meanings, and the assumptions of the group (society) are also a product of interaction. Although Becker does not report information about self-concept specifically, it is easy to see that part of the self may also be defined in terms of interactions in the marijuana-smoking community.

Symbolic interactionism as a movement is devoted to studying the ways in which people come together, or converge, on meaning. In the following section, we look at a popular theory from the communication literature that centers on one significant way in which this convergence happens.

Symbolic Convergence Theory

Symbolic convergence theory, often known as *fantasy-theme analysis,* is a well-developed theory by Ernest Bormann, John Cragan, and Donald Shields dealing with the use of narrative in communication.[25] The theory imagines that individuals' images of reality are guided by stories reflecting how things are believed to be. These stories are created in symbolic interaction within small groups, and they chain out from person to person and group to group.

Fantasy themes are part of larger dramas that are longer, more complicated stories called rhetorical visions. A *rhetorical vision* is a view of how

things have been, are, or will be. In large measure, these visions form the assumptions on which a group's knowledge is based, structuring a sense of reality. Fantasy themes, and even the larger rhetorical visions, consist of characters, plot line, scenes, and sanctioning agent. The *characters* can be heroes, villains, and other supporting players. The *plot line* is the action or development of the story. The *scene* is the setting, including location, properties, and sociocultural milieu. Finally, the *sanctioning agent* is a source that legitimizes the story. This source may be an authority who lends credibility to the story or authorizes its telling, a common belief in God or another sanctioning ideal like justice or democracy, or a situation or event that makes telling the story seem appropriate.

Imagine a group of executives gathering for a high-level meeting. Just before the meeting starts, at the beginning, and at various points during the meeting, members will share experiences and stories—fantasy themes—that bring the group together. Some of these will be stories heard again and again. Each will have a cast of characters, a plot, a scene, and sanctioning agents. In many cases the sanctioning agent will be the company itself.

Rhetorical visions are never told in their entirety but are built up piecemeal by sharing associated fantasy themes. To grasp the entire vision, one must attend to the fantasy themes because these comprise the content of conversation in groups of people when the vision is being created and chained out. You can recognize a fantasy theme because it is repeated again and again. In fact, some themes are so frequently discussed and so well known within a particular group or community that the members no longer tell the whole episode, but abbreviate it by presenting just a "trigger" or *symbolic cue.* This is precisely what happens with an inside joke. An executive might say, for example, "Yeah, that's just like the *Frasier* episode!" and everyone will laugh, knowing just what she is referring to. Fantasy themes that develop to this point of familiarity are known as *fantasy types*—stock situations told over and over within a group. Often these retold stories relate to personal, group, or community achievements and take on the form of a *saga*. You probably have sagas within your family and your work organization, and you have certainly heard many national and societal sagas such as George Washington and the cherry tree, about the writing and signing of the Declaration of Independence, and even the story of the rise of Bill Gates.

As people come to share fantasy themes, the resulting rhetorical vision pulls them together and gives them a sense of identification with a shared reality. In this process, people converge or come to hold a common image as they share their fantasy themes. In fact, shared rhetorical visions—and especially the use of fantasy types—can be taken as evidence that convergence has occurred.

As rhetorical visions get established through the sharing of fantasy themes within a limited group, they fulfill a consciousness-creating function. They make people more aware of a certain way of seeing things. This happens because the elements of rhetorical visions at this stage are novel and have explanatory power. Yet they can also attract attention and build consciousness because they imitate former ways of seeing things that look familiar. In other words, they build or maintain a group or community's *shared consciousness*.

Once consciousness is created among early adherents to a rhetorical vision, the consciousness can be disseminated, as more and more people are converted through *consciousness-raising* communication. There seems to be a critical mass of adherence at which widespread dissemination of the rhetorical vision takes place. After this happens, the rhetorical vision begins to fulfill a *consciousness-sustaining* function. Here the fantasy themes serve to maintain commitment.

Rhetorical visions are not just narrative stories but have a deep structure that reflects and influences our sense of reality. The Bill Gates story, for example—depending upon which version you hear—has a deep structure of individual ingenuity, hard work, and success. The underlying stories are master analogues that compete for our

attention and vie for truth. *Righteous analogues* attempt to tell us how to live our lives morally, what is right and good. *Social analogues* tell us how we should relate to other people. And *pragmatic analogues* tell us how to do things, offering practical, efficient solutions.

Clearly, fantasy themes are an important ingredient in persuasion. Public communicators—in speeches, articles, books, films, and other media—often tap into the audience's predominant fantasy themes. Public communication can also add to or modify the rhetorical vision by amplifying, changing, or adding fantasy themes. One way to evaluate the use of fantasy themes, then, is to look at their effectiveness. If you listened to a speaker draw in an audience effectively with the use of shared fantasy themes, you might say that the speech was effective.

But use of fantasy themes goes well beyond the world of persuasion. It is a social bonding agent, a way in which we create narrative structures that give meaning to our lives and a sense of community. Perhaps a better way to evaluate fantasy themes, then, is in their *artistry*—the creativity, novelty, and wisdom with which they are used, combined, and formed into visions. If you look beyond the surface of a highly rated movie, for example, you may notice that it taps into an underlying current of reality in the culture, and it does so in a very artistic way.

Fantasy themes are one of the many things that are created and reproduced within conversations. When you listen to a conversation, you will be able to hear fantasy themes in action; but if you listen even more carefully, you will also hear other micro-actions taking place. Many communication researchers are very interested in these finite, coordinated actions that bring a conversation together. Let's take a look at conversation analysis as a way of examining coordinated stories.

Conversation Analysis

One of the most interesting and popular lines of work in communication is conversation analysis.[26] This is part of a branch of sociology called *ethnomethodology,* which is the detailed study of how people organize their everyday lives.[27] It involves a set of methods for looking carefully at the ways people work together to create social organization.[28]

A conversation is viewed as a social achievement because it requires that we get certain things done cooperatively through talk.[29] Conversation analysis (CA) attempts to discover in detail exactly what those achievements are by carefully examining transcriptions of conversations. CA, therefore, is characterized by the careful examination of actual sequences of talk. The analyst looks at a segment of conversation for the kinds of actions that are accomplished within the talk, examining what the speakers seem to be doing as they communicate. They are probably doing many things at once—possibly asking and answering questions, managing turn taking, and protecting face. Most important is *how* these things are done *in language.* What devices and forms are used in the interaction between the parties to accomplish action?

Unlike cognitive theory, featured in the sociopsychological tradition, conversation analysis (firmly within the sociocultural tradition) deals not with individual differences or hidden mental processes, but with what is going on in the language, in the text, or the discourse. CA focuses on interaction in discourse—the back and forth, turn-taking moves that communicators make—and how they manage to organize their sequences of talk, as it is evident in actual behavior.[30]

Of utmost importance in conversation analysis are the ways in which communicators create stability and organization in their talk. Even when conversations look sloppy on the surface, there is an underlying organization and coherence to talk, and the participants themselves actually create it as they go along. The analyst works inductively by first examining the details of actual conversations—many conversations—and then generalizing possible principles by which the participants themselves structure their talk.

As an example, consider the simple task of telling a story. When you tell a story, it may appear that you just say it, but your story is really a joint achievement accomplished by you and your listeners. Although you probably take an extended turn, your story is made possible by the cooperation of others in carefully organized turns. First, you have to get the floor by offering to tell a story, and others acknowledge and permit you to do so. During the story itself, listeners may take various types of turns to recognize and reinforce the story, indicate understanding, give you further permission to continue talking, direct or affect the story in some way, or correct or repair something you said. All of this requires work and organization on the part of everyone.[31]

Conversation analysis is concerned with a variety of issues.[32] First, it deals with what speakers need to know to have a conversation—knowing the rules of conversation. The features of a conversation such as turn taking, silences and gaps, and overlaps have been of special interest. Conversation analysis is also concerned with rule violations and the ways people prevent and repair errors in talk.

Certainly the most popular, and perhaps the most significant, aspect of conversation analysis is *conversational coherence.*[33] Simply defined, coherence is connectedness and meaningfulness in conversation. A coherent conversation seems well structured and sensible to the participants. Coherence is normally taken for granted, yet the production of coherence is complex and not altogether understood. A good place to begin the topic of coherence is the theory of H. Paul Grice.

Conversational Maxims. Grice proposed a set of very general assumptions to which all conversationalists must subscribe in order to have a coherent conversation.[34] The first and most general is the *cooperative principle*: One's contribution must be appropriate. Cooperation here does not necessarily mean expression of agreement, but it does mean that one is willing to contribute something in line with the purpose of the conversation. For example, if someone asks you a question, you should answer it or respond in some other way that at least acknowledges the question. Otherwise you will be considered rude. We are bothered when others fail to complete the speech act appropriately because it leads to confusion and the lack of coherence. According to Grice, cooperation is achieved by following four maxims.

Grice's first is the *quantity maxim*: A contribution to a conversation should provide sufficient, but not too much, information. You violate the quantity maxim when your comments don't say enough or say too much. The second is the *quality maxim*: A contribution should be truthful. You violate the quality maxim when you deliberately lie or communicate in a way that does not reflect an honest intention. The third is the *relevancy maxim*: Comments must be pertinent. You violate this maxim when you make an irrelevant comment. The fourth maxim is the *manner maxim*: Do not be obscure, ambiguous, or disorganized in how you express what you want to say.

You are probably thinking by now that these maxims seem absurdly simple and obvious, but the associated question of how speakers actually use them and how they handle apparent violations is far more complicated and interesting. The cooperative principle and maxims are often violated, sometimes on purpose, but what makes them so important is that they are never violated without disrupting the flow of conversation or affecting the perceptions of others in the conversation. In other words, violations are a problem communicators must deal with cooperatively.

One of the most common types of violation is to say something indirectly. Indirect communication is important for a variety of social and personal reasons such as politeness. If, for example, someone asks you how much your car cost, you might say, "Oh, quite a bit." Now, on the surface, that violates the maxim of quantity and appears uncooperative, but competent conversationalists will realize that this is really an indirect statement meaning, "It's none of your business."

We manage violations by making certain interpretations, called *conversational implicatures,* to help us understand what is implied or implicated by the apparent violation.[35] To assume that the violator is living up to the cooperative principle, the listener must attribute some additional meaning that will make the speaker's contribution seem to conform to the principle. In fact,

when you deliberately violate a maxim, you assume that your listener will understand that you really do intend to be cooperative. If, for example, you say, "It is raining cats and dogs," you are technically violating the quality maxim, but others know that you are speaking metaphorically. This is an example of conversational implicature. Conversational implicature allows you to use all kinds of interesting, indirect statements to achieve your purposes, without being judged incompetent.

The study of conversational implicature is really the study of the rules people use to justify violations of other rules, and these implicatures are very important for the overall management of conversations. In fact, competence itself requires the effective use of implicature. Without it our conversations would be dull, predictable, and lifeless.

Another way that you manage the cooperative principle is to give clues that you are violating a maxim while still intending to be cooperative. Such clues are called *licenses for violations* because they enable you to violate a maxim without objection. For example, you could say, "I might be exaggerating a little, but . . . ." Or you might end a statement by prompting, ". . . if you know what I mean." Using phrases and qualifications such as these is a way of asking for a license to violate one or more of the maxims. Here's a portion of a typical conversation:

Kay: How did you and your husband meet?

Betty: Well, that's a long story.

Kay: Okay, I'm not going anywhere, let's hear it.

When Betty says, "That's a long story," Kay takes this as a request to violate the quantity maxim.[36] There is another possible interpretation, Betty's reply may be a polite way of saying that she does not want to talk about that subject, but Kay—deliberately or not—misinterprets that request.

Traditional views assume that competent communicators at least intend to cooperate. In an interesting line of work, Steven McCornack and his colleagues question this view. In their *infor-

mation manipulation theory, they assert that people often intentionally deceive by violating the maxims.[37] For example, if you wanted to lie, you would violate the quality maxim. If you wanted to obscure, you would violate the quantity maxim. If you wanted to distract, you would violate the relevancy maxim. Scott Jacobs and his colleagues acknowledge that deception may involve either blatant or covert violation of the quality maxim, but these authors point out that covert violations of the other maxims are deceptive only when they also include false implicatures. In other words, the deceiving communicator violates the maxim while implying that it is a normal, not deceptive, violation.[38] For example, if a co-worker asked if you had finished a certain report, you might reply, "Uh, just running to lunch. Catch you later." This is a clear violation of the relevancy maxim. By getting up and going to the door, you imply that this is a normal violation, when you really are trying to get out of admitting that you did not in fact complete the report. Of course, conversations are more than simple replies, as the following section shows.

Sequencing Approaches.   How do you know what is appropriate or inappropriate for keeping a conversation well organized? A variety of sequencing theories have been proposed.[39] The idea behind the sequencing approach is that a conversation consists of a series of rule-governed speech acts, and coherence is achieved by making sure that each act is an appropriate response to the previous act. For example, the question, "Hi, how are you?" is normally followed by, "Fine. How are you?" Recall from speech-act theory in Chapter 5 that when we speak, we are actually doing something with our words like promising, requesting, demanding, or greeting. A coherent conversation is one in which the communicators' speech acts follow logically from those of the other communicators in the conversation.

Sequencing approaches focus on the *adjacency pair,* or two speech acts tied together. The *first-pair part* (FPP) is the first utterance, and the *second-pair part* (SPP) is the second one. The SPP completes the speech act. If I intend to promise something to you and say I will do such and

such, you complete my promise by accepting or turning it down. By this approach, a conversation is coherent if proper rules of sequencing are consistently used between the FPP and the SPP. If I say, "Hi, how are you?" and you answer, "Trees are green," I might think you are crazy because I cannot see how your speech act in any way logically completes mine.

Perhaps the most influential sequencing model is that of Harvey Sacks, Emanuel Schegloff, and Gail Jefferson.[40] This is basically a turn-taking theory that stipulates that the next turn in a conversation must be a proper response to complete a particular adjacency-pair type. For instance, a question is to be followed by an answer, a greeting by another greeting, an offer by an acceptance, a request by an acceptance or a rejection. A number of adjacency-pair types have been discussed in the literature: assertion-assent/ dissent, question-answer, summons-answer, greeting-greeting, closing-closing, request-grant/ denial, insult-response, apology-acceptance/ refusal, compliment-acceptance/rejection, threat-response, challenge-response, accusation-denial/ confession, and boast-appreciation/derision.

The completion of one speech act signals a turn for another speaker, who is obligated to respond according to appropriate rules. The speaker may designate who the next speaker is to be, or another speaker can appropriately take a turn, as long as a proper response is given. Failing a response, the speaker may continue talking.

Further, adjacency pairs include a *preference for agreement.* In other words, the SPP is normally expected to agree with the FPP. For example, a statement is normally followed by an agreement ("Don't you just love the sun?" "Sure do.") and a request is followed by an acceptance ("Can I borrow your sunscreen?" "Sure."). This does not mean that people always agree, but disagreement calls for special action in the form of an account, excuse, or argument.

Conversation analysts recognize that people do not communicate mechanically in a series of adjacency pairs. In fact, most conversation looks untidy in this regard, so the real challenge of this line of work is to show how conversation partners are able to make sense out of a series of utterances that appear on the surface to be unorganized. In examining actual tape-recorded texts, these researchers are able to show the rules that the communicators are using to assure coherence. Presequence, insertion, and expansion are examples.

A *presequence* is an adjacency pair whose meaning depends on another series of acts that has not yet been uttered. Here, the initial FPP is an invitation for a subsequent one:

FPP: Have you washed your hands? (*presequence*)

SPP: No, why?

FPP: 'Cause dinner's ready.

SPP: Okay, I'll do it.

The speaker here intends to make a request, but it cannot be understood as such without including the presequence question.

An *insertion* is an adjacency pair that is between the two parts of another pair and is subordinate to the main pair. Such insertions are necessary to clarify the intention of the initial FPP. Here is an example:

FPP_1: Would you like to go out sometime?

FPP_2: With you? (*insertion*)

SPP_2: Yeah, me.

SPP_1: Oh, okay.

Such a move is also an example of an *expansion,* which means that a subsequent speaker expands the sequence to include additional or subsidiary intentions. An expansion is involved whenever a segment of talk that could theoretically be accomplished in one turn, like a greeting, compliment, or request, is played out over several turns. This system enables us to parse, or separate, a conversation into parts. Table 6.1 shows an example.

The adjacency-pair idea has been useful and applies to many conversations, but conversation analysts now generally agree that coherence can-

TABLE **6.1**

A Conversational Sequence

Greeting-greeting		FPP	Hi.
	FPP	SPP	Hi. Great dress.
Compliment-acceptance			
	SPP	FPP	Thanks. My mom bought it for me this weekend.
Assertion-assent			
	FPP	SPP	Yeah, it looks great on you.
Compliment-rejection			
	SPP		Well, not that great really.
		FPP	How's Terry?
Question-answer			
		SPP	He's okay, getting better and better.
		FPP	Will he be out of the hospital soon?
Question-answer			
	FPP	SPP	In about three days, I think.
Assertion-assent			
	SPP		Great.
		FPP	Well, I gotta go.
Closing-closing			
		SPP	Yeah, me too. See ya.

not be explained strictly by local rules such as these. It is easy to identify sequences that are obviously clear to the communicators but have adjacent statements that do not make sense out of context. We turn now to how these more complicated situations are handled—by means of global rules.

Rational Approach.   The second approach to conversational coherence assumes that conversations are practical acts that achieve goals. For this reason, such approaches are called *rational*. Achieving the goal of a conversation requires that the participants reason their way through it. "If I want such and such, I have to do thus and so." Thus the coherence of a conversation depends on the reasoning process of the communicators. They make decisions about what to say and how to achieve their intentions, and coherence is really judged in accordance with this overall reasoning. If the sequence of acts appears rational in relation to agreed-on goals, it is judged coherent.

The sequencing approach described above uses *local rules*, meaning that turns are organized one after another. In contrast, the rational approach relies on *global rules* that govern the conversation as a whole. The rational approach, most often associated with Sally Jackson and Scott Jacobs, definitely uses a global approach.[41] These scholars use the game analogy to explain how conversation works. The game itself is controlled by a set of rules, which players must know. The players have objectives in the game, and they use the rules of the game to achieve those objectives. The game is coherent because the appropriate use of rules accomplishes rational objectives. So players must have two kinds of knowledge: They must know the rules of the game and what constitutes rational play within the parameters of the rules.

For example, in playing Monopoly you are expected to accumulate properties and cash by purchasing property, houses, and hotels, and you must do this according to rules. In Monopoly your moves are not judged rational or coherent based on whether they are consistent with the moves that came before or after, as in a local approach, but on whether they are consistent with the overall objectives of the game, which is a global approach.

Conversations can be complicated because, like a game, they are played with other people. One person's moves must mesh with those of other players, and this requires agreement on purpose and some reciprocity of perspective. Utterances have a force that obliges a hearer to understand the speaker's intent, and the speaker must meet certain felicity conditions in order for understanding to occur. Communicators respond not to each individual speech act but to the overall intentions of others. The coherence of a conversation is not judged by adjacency pairs but by the unfolding plan of the game.

Jackson and Jacobs stipulate two kinds of rules necessary for global coherence. *Validity rules* establish the conditions necessary for an act to be judged as a sincere move in a plan to achieve a goal. *Reason rules*—Jackson and Jacob's second type—require the speaker to adjust statements to the beliefs and perspectives of the other participants. This does not mean that speakers say only what listeners want to hear but that they frame their statements in a way that makes logical sense within the perspective of what the other person thinks is going on. For example, you would probably find a request to borrow money odd in a conversation about politics. You would question the person's *sincerity* and you would take his or her request as *invalid*.

Basically, then, these rules help communicators set up a logical system so that a conversation will feel coherent. Remember that these rules may be violated, and coherence is not always achieved. Communicators may also disagree about whether a sequence meets the required conditions of validity and reason, and such disagreement is often the basis for conflict. Ultimately, because conversations are practical, goal-oriented acts, communicators must constantly judge whether the interaction is leading toward the desired goal and, if it is not, whether and what kinds of adjustments must be made in the conversational moves. This fact makes conversation a dynamic process of back-and-forth practical reasoning.

Donald Ellis proposes a *coherentist theory of meaning* to explain this process further.[42] Understanding discourse is a pragmatic act in which communicators use shared meanings to achieve coherence. Communication is possible only because communicators possess shared meanings. Three characteristics of discourse make understanding possible.

The first characteristic is *intelligibility*. Discourse is intelligible if it contains or points to evidence that enables communicators to make inferences about its meaning. A father may ask his son, "Is that your coat on the floor?" The son correctly reasons that this is a request or command for him to pick up the coat. Both father and son have experience in similar situations that make it possible for them to share this meaning. The coat on the floor, the timing of the father's question, and the use of similar questions in the past are evidence that the boy can use to draw this conclusion.

The second characteristic is *organization*. Statements are part of larger organized systems of linguistic structures. You cannot assign any meaning you want to a sentence; a statement's meaning is limited, and competent communicators know what the possible range of meanings is. This quality of discourse makes rational talk possible.

Jackson and Jacobs's analogy of the game is useful here. The rules of the game tell us what moves mean and how to respond rationally within the system of permissible moves. In the game of making requests, communicators know that questions can be taken as a form of request, so the father's question may be understood as a statement about what his son should do. Indeed, within this situation, it probably should be understood in this way.

And this fact leads to Ellis's third characteristic of discourse—*verification*. In the stream of a conversation, one's statements can verify, or confirm, the meaning of other statements. When the son in our example replies, "Yeah, I'll pick it up." He is verifying the command issued by the fa-

ther. Thus, participants use the give-and-take of their conversation to test meaning and reason their way to an agreed-upon conclusion.

Using global principles does not negate the value of local principles. Indeed, adjacency-pair coherence is a special case of a rational action. The FPP invites the listener to join into a kind of microplan for achieving a goal, and the SPP is coherent if it joins into that plan. A greeting invites the listener to make contact, and a returned greeting fulfills a kind of greeting contract. Responses to an FPP may simply and directly cooperate; indirectly cooperate; approximate agreement; or attempt to extend, change, or refuse the goal set up by the first utterance. Over a sequence of utterances, communicators actually negotiate a goal-achievement plan. Jackson and Jacobs call this the *transformation of belief/want contexts*. Communicators ask themselves mentally, What do we want to accomplish here, and what logical moves are required by each of us to accomplish this? The conversation will be coherent if agreement is achieved and the actions seem appropriate for achieving the goals.

To see more concretely how these ideas can be applied, let's look at Jackson and Jacobs's applications of their theory to requests.[43] Actually, requests are among the most studied of all speech acts, and their theory provides an excellent extension and modification of a whole line of research.

You can handle requests in a variety of ways. Your actions can range from very direct to indirect to irrelevant. The clearer and more direct a request and the clearer and more direct the response, the more coherent the request sequence. This is because directness supports clarity and relevance. Therefore, if I say, "Please pass the butter," my goal is clear and your response, "Sure," is obviously relevant. On the other hand, if I say, "My toast is dry," my goal of getting you to pass the butter is less clear, and your response, "You should turn the toaster down a little," just frustrates me.

Jackson and Jacobs provide a list of utterance types that may be taken as a request, ranging from direct to irrelevant. "Please pass the butter" is an absolutely direct request. An indirect request would be less clear: "My toast is dry." A hint is even less direct: "Some people at this table have something I sure would like."

There are also utterances commonly found in conversations that function as prerequests. These set up the listener for a request in the future. An example is, "Could I interrupt to ask for something?" Once a request or prerequest is made, a listener can respond in a variety of direct or indirect ways. If the communicator recognizes the intent of a request, he or she can clarify things by responding directly. An example would be an *anticipatory move,* in which the listener recognizes the hidden or indirect request and grants it immediately. ("My toast is sure dry." "Here, have some butter.") Such moves provide coherence because they are oriented to the apparent goals of the other communicator. Responses that misinterpret the speaker's statement are less coherent, as in the case of someone who takes an innocent statement to be a request that was never intended as such.

A fruitful line of theory that illustrates the inferential-strategic approach is conversational argument, the topic of the following section.

Conversational Argument. The study of conversational argument is another major application of the rational-pragmatic model explained above, and it illustrates that model very well.[44] This area of study treats arguments as conversations, showing how they follow rational coherence rules. Specifically, conversational argument allows people to manage disagreement. Managing disagreement, like any of the structural features of talk, is a rule-governed, cooperative achievement.

There can be a number of levels of disagreement in conversation. In the typical case, both parties openly disagree and state reasons for their positions. More typically, however, the disagreement is less open. Because of the preference for agreement, the goal of conversational argument is to achieve agreement. Each turn must be a rational move toward bringing agreement about, and the coherence of an argument is largely judged in terms of the rationality of moves in achieving this objective. Thus, conversational argument is a method of managing disagreement so that it is minimized and agreement is achieved as quickly as possible.

There are basically two kinds of arguments. *Argument$_1$* involves *making* an argument, or stating a case. One makes an argument by giving reasons, as in "Mary is arguing that smoking is bad for her son's health." *Argument$_2$* is *having* an argument, or exchanging objections, as in "Mary and her son are arguing about smoking." People can make an argument without having one, but they cannot easily have an argument without making one.[45] Here is an example of a typical argument:

George: Well, I better get this grass cut.

Harry: Yeah, me too.

George: Can I borrow your mower?

Harry: Well, I really need it myself.

George: I'll return it right away.

Harry: Last time you kept it two weeks.

George: No, I'll return it.

Harry: Last spring you kept it a month.

George: Gosh, Harry, I really will get it back to you today.

Here, George makes a request and a promise. The argument (argument$_2$) ensues because Harry does not grant the request as would normally be expected, and he challenges George's promise. In objecting, Harry makes an argument (argument$_1$) by saying that George has not been reliable in the past, and George comes back by supporting his intent to return the item.

Like all conversations, arguments have a certain order and rationality that may or may not be apparent on the surface. For the participants, the argument will probably seem coherent because of the cooperative principle, which, in the case of arguments, requires the communicators to cooperate in creating a dispute-resolving episode.

This is ironic because arguments do not sound very cooperative, but you cannot have an argument unless both parties cooperate in doing so. Notice that the following somewhat comical conversation is not a very coherent argument because one party refuses to cooperate:

Katie: You never turn your reports in on time, Sara.

Sara: I know, I really like taking my time on things.

Katie: But this infuriates me!

Sara: Just what I really like, a good emotional reaction.

Katie: Stop it. I want to know why you are falling down on the job.

Sara: I sure do enjoy being the center of attention. This is great!

Arguers are essentially agreeing to use certain kinds of speech acts and to meet certain goals, and in the above conversation, Sara refuses to participate in the game.

Just as promises and requests have their own requirements, so do arguments. To have an argument, you must put forth an opinion that you do not expect the other person to initially accept. In conversational argument theory this is called a *standpoint.* You have to support the standpoint with certain assertions that you expect will not be immediately apparent to the other person. And, of course, you are not cooperating in "having an argument" if you do not at least initially believe your own standpoints and assertions.

There are many forms an argument can take, but there is one idealized form that most arguments approximate. This consists of four stages necessary for a complete argument to occur: confrontation, opening, argumentation, and concluding. The *confrontation stage* identifies the disagreement. The *opening stage* establishes agreement on how the dispute will be handled. The *argumentation stage* includes an exchange of competing positions. The *concluding stage* establishes resolution or continued disagreement.

These should not be considered the "steps" of an argument because they rarely occur in this order. Instead, you should think of these as aspects or parts of an argument. When they are all pres-

	T A B L E **6.2**

Distribution of Speech-Act Types Across Functional Stages in Discussion

Stage in Discussion	Speech-Act Type
Confrontation	
1.1	expressing standpoint (assertive)
1.2	accepting or not accepting standpoint (commissive)
Opening	
2.1	challenging to defend standpoint (directive)
2.2	accepting challenge to defend standpoint (commissive)
2.3	deciding to start discussion; agreeing on discussion rules (commissive)
Argumentation	
3.1	advancing argumentation (assertive)
3.2	accepting or not accepting argumentation (commissive)
3.3	requesting further argumentation (directive)
3.4	advancing further argumentation (assertive)
Concluding	
4.1	establishing the result (assertive)
4.2	accepting or withholding acceptance of standpoint (commissive)
4.3	upholding or retracting standpoint (assertive)
(Any stage)	
5.1	requesting usage declarative (directive)
5.2	defining, precizating [*sic*], amplifying, and so on (usage declarative)

ent, the communicators are said to be participating in a *critical discussion.*

These stages are characterized by certain kinds of speech acts, as outlined in Table 6.2.[46] In general the idealized model is like a code of conduct for having an argument. People will come as close to it as they can within the constraints of the situation. The idealized model is a measuring stick by which actual arguments can be compared and evaluated.

One of the problems arguers must manage is face. We look at this fascinating topic in the following section.

Face Negotiation Theory

Developed by Stella Ting-Toomey and her colleagues, face negotiation theory provides a basis for predicting how people will accomplish facework in different cultures.[47] Thus it is a natural extension of argument theories. *Face* refers to one's self-image in the presence of others. It involves feelings of respect, honor, status, connection, loyalty, and other similar values. In other words, face means feeling good about yourself in whatever ways your culture prescribes. For some, it means being a good member of the family; for others, it may mean being an effective professional practitioner. *Facework* is the communication behaviors people use to build and protect their own face and to protect, build, or threaten the face of another person.

When you observe facework in action, you can see various things going on. For example, you might notice the *locus of facework*, or whether it is directed at self or others. You might notice people bragging about an accomplishment or praising another person for a job well done. As you observe people communicating, you might also notice *face valence*, or whether a person's actions are positive (as in the case of defending, maintaining, or honoring one's face) or negative (as in attacking). Next, you might notice *temporality*, or whether the communication is designed to prevent loss of face in the future or restore loss of face that has already happened.

Face is a universal concern, but how face is defined and the ways in which facework is accomplished vary significantly from person to person and culture to culture. All cultures have ways to accomplish both preventive and restorative facework. *Preventive facework* involves communication designed to protect a person from feelings of threat to personal or group face. If

you needed to discuss a problem with your boss, for example, you begin by saying, "I know you are very busy, and I'm sorry to intrude, but . . ." *Restorative facework* is designed to rebuild one's face after loss has already occurred. If you made an insulting comment to a friend in a moment of anger, you might later apologize and say, "You are really a great friend, and I'm sorry I said that, 'cause I didn't really mean it."

Two primary cultural variables seem to affect facework. The first is *individualism-collectivism*. Many cultures honor the individual above the community or group. These cultures promote autonomy, individual responsibility, and individual achievement. Governed by an "I-identity," these cultures are considered *individualist*. Other cultures, in contrast, tend to honor the community or collective above the individual person. Important for these cultures is the connection among people, and promoting the interests of any one person would feel odd or inappropriate. These cultures, defined as *collectivist*, are governed by a "we-identity."

Cultures are never purely one or the other. Most people have feelings of both individuality and collectivism, but within a given culture, one of these will usually predominate. Northern and western European and North American cultures tend to be individualist, while collectivism is common in Asia, Africa, the Middle East, and Latin America.

The second cultural variable affecting facework is *power distance*. In many cultures of the world, there is a strong hierarchy, or sense of status, in which certain members or groups exert great influence and control over others. Members of these cultures accept the unequal distribution of power as normal. In different cultures, however, the felt distance among groups and individuals is less. Again, power distance is a variable, with some cultures having a great deal and other cultures having less. High power-distance cultures can be found in such regions as Malaysia, certain Latin American cultures, the Philippines, and Arab countries. Lower power-distance cultures can be found in such places as New Zealand and Scandinavia.

Because honor means different things in different cultures, facework will vary significantly across cultures. We would expect that members of individualist cultures would do more work to honor people as autonomous individuals. They would see themselves as important apart from others and work to build their own esteem as well as that of other individuals. When a person in an individualist culture is attacked or threatened in some way, it would be considered appropriate to help build that individual's face, to repair the damage or honor the person to compensate for the face threat. In collectivist cultures, by contrast, honor is defined in terms of how one defers to the values of the group, and facework is not normally self-oriented. Instead, one acknowledges the group or community. Members of collectivist cultures tend to be somewhat self-effacing and deferential. They accept face loss and rebuild it by acknowledging the need to work harder on behalf of the group.

In an individualist culture, you might be expected to make excuses for yourself, explaining why you were unable to live up to someone's expectations. You would probably compliment other people for a job well done, or restore their face by reminding them of something they were good at. In a collectivist culture, on the other hand, you would accept criticism, talk about the effectiveness of others, and promise to do a better job of living up to the group's standards in the future. In restoring another person's face in such cultures, you would compliment a group with which the person affiliates or perhaps tell the person what a good member of the group he or she is.

Face is usually an issue in conflict situations. When you are having a conflict with another person, respect and honor are often compromised. Face threats can happen because of a competition or desire to win; as a result of anger or feeling disconfirmed in some way; or due to conflicting values, opinions, or attitudes. In any case, face threats are common in conflict, so that facework is a regular part of conflict communication. Often the facework is negative and takes the form of an attack on the other person. Other times, we try hard to work through the conflict using positive facework to accomplish our own goals while helping the other person feel good about him or herself in the process.

Because of culture, people have different styles in conflict. Individualists, for example, tend to use more direct personal attack and may try to protect or rebuild face—theirs and that of others—by showing personal respect. Collectivists, on the other hand, will use less personal attack and be more indirect in conflicts. They may avoid the issue at hand, talk around it, discuss side issues, take more time to get to the point, and generally talk in ways that build the group over themselves. Individualists in a conflict tend to want to get through it by solving the problem or settling the dispute. Collectivists, in contrast, are more interested in affirming the relationship. Collaboration and compromise mean different things in these different cultures. For individualists, collaboration and compromise are ways of solving the problem, but for collectivists, they are a means for building a relationship.

Of course, facework and conflict management become even more complex when we factor in power distance. In low power-distance situations, consultation and participation are key. Everyone wants to be involved. As a result, people communicate more directly and personally. In high power-distance settings, decisions will tend to be made by higher-status individuals, which is accepted by everyone. People behave differently depending upon their status, so that their facework varies. High-status members already have the power, so they do not need to be very direct. They can communicate indirectly, avoid threatening the face of lower-status members, and still get their way. Lower-status individuals, on the other hand, will be more self-effacing and deferential. They will acknowledge the high-status person's right to make the decision. In these situations, the aims of the communication are to maintain the power distance by using more formality. Conflict is often resolved by a mediator in such cultures—someone who is respected by both high-power and low-power individuals.

According to Ting-Toomey, culture largely determines how facework and conflict are enacted, but culture is not the only factor. There are important individual differences that must be factored into the equation. The individual characteristic that seems to matter most is *self-construal,* or one's sense of independence or interdependence with other people. This variable is simply how you see yourself in relation to others. "Independents" tend to use more direct, problem-solving communication, while "interdependents" are more relationally oriented in their conflicts. People who see themselves as both independent and interdependent tend to have a larger repertoire of strategies for facework and conflict than the other types. People who are ambivalent may use more third-party (mediator) interventions.

Clearly, intercultural communication presents many challenges.[48] It is hard enough with friends and colleagues who share our cultural views, but in an increasingly intercultural and international world, conflict can be even more difficult. We must be vigilant and develop the ability to communicate with members of other cultures by learning more about them; observing carefully; and developing skills in listening, facework, and dialogue. In short, we must negotiate face as we encounter other people from various cultures.

◉ REFLECTIONS ON
The Sociocultural Tradition

While the sociopsychological tradition defines ways in which individuals respond to each other's behavior, the sociocultural goes beyond behavioral patterns to look at what is achieved or accomplished—what gets done—in this back-and-forth interaction. Again, the sociocultural tradition is interested not in the individual per se, but in what lies beyond the individual in terms of what it means to be social, to create meaning, and to work collaboratively in constructing meaning.

Notice also that the move from the psychological to the sociocultural is a shift in what kind of data is considered important. In the former tradition, individual behavior is taken as data, but in the latter, the discourse is what gets examined. We could say—and some do—that discourse is actually a kind of behavior. When you make a statement, you are producing language, which is behavioral. In the sociocultural tradition, however, discourse is considered more than individual behavior; instead, it is a jointly produced text, in which meaning must also emerge in the collaboration, never in the individual statement.

Face negotiation theory departs to some degree from this generalization. Although cultural in orientation, this theory makes heavy use of psychological assumptions and methods. This line of work is sociocultural to the extent that it characterizes cultural communities and looks at facework as a manifestation and construction of culture, but the research methods and general theoretical approach has a somewhat psychological feel. Face negotiation theory really does take the cultural down to the individual level by trying to predict how you would manage face based on your culture, personal traits, and situational factors. This is interesting, because sociopsychological and sociocultural theories rarely resonate with one another, but this theory does show that there may be more possibilities for the two to come together than we would normally think.

Once again, then, we see that the presence of insights from various traditions deepens our understanding of communication, in this case conversations, so that all of the facets of the process come to light in a way that no one tradition could accomplish. Let's add yet another perspective to this common, everyday occurrence called conversation.

● ● ●

◉ THE CYBERNETIC TRADITION

What is the systemic connection among meaning, action, and coordinated behavior? How do various contexts for understanding conversations impact and inform one another? These questions are addressed by the theory summarized in this section.

The Coordinated Management of Meaning

The theory of the coordinated management of meaning (CMM), developed by W. Barnett Pearce, Vernon Cronen, and their colleagues, is a comprehensive theory of social interaction that addresses the ways in which people's varying meanings are coordinated in conversations.[49] Although conversations seem to be the focus of CMM, this theory is powerful in showing how conversations come to have meaning in relationship and culture as well. As a result, CMM is an integrative theory that could have been placed in a number of this book's chapters.

As a rule theory, CMM states that people interpret and act on the basis of rules. Individuals within any social situation first want to understand what is going on and apply rules to figure things out. They then act on the basis of their understandings, employing rules to decide what kind of action is appropriate.

There are two types of rules. *Constitutive rules* are essentially *rules of meaning,* used by communicators to interpret or understand an event or message. *Regulative rules* are essentially *rules of action,* used to determine how to respond or behave. For example, if a friend says something to you, you decipher the meaning of the message: You interpret it; you figure out what it means. Usually this is a simple and almost unconscious experience because your interpretation rules are immediately available and simple. Sometimes, however, interpretation is more difficult, and you may have to dig for appropriate rules of understanding. Once you feel you know what was said, action rules help you decide how to respond.

Rules of meaning and action always operate within a *context* or frame of reference for interpreting and acting. One context is always embedded within another so that each context is itself part of a bigger one. Figure 6.2 illustrates this idea. Here, four typical contexts are depicted. The *relationship context* includes mutual expectations among members of a group. The *episode context* is an event. The *self-concept context* is one's sense of

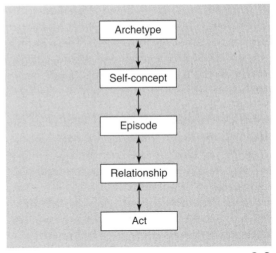

FIGURE **6.2**

Hierarchy of Contexts

Adapted from *Communication, Action, and Meaning* by W. Barnett Pearce and Vernon Cronen. Copyright © 1980 by Praeger Publishers. Reprinted by permission of the authors.

personal definition. Finally, the *archetype context* is an image of general truth. As an example, you might interpret your daughter's snippy remark as an insult within the context of your negative relationship. The relationship, in turn, might be judged as negative in terms of the episode of an argument, which you view as typical given your self-concept as a headstrong person.

The order of contexts shown in Figure 6.2 is not universal and often shifts. Sometimes, for example, self is understood within the context of the relationship, but on other occasions the relationship is understood in reference to the self. Also, although the contexts listed in Figure 6.2 are representative and common, they by no means exhaust the possible contexts within which interpretations and actions are made. Humans have the ability to create numerous contexts for interpretation and action.

Any event or action being interpreted is known as a *text.* In the example above, the snippy comment is the "text," and your relationship is the "context." Often text and context form a loop (Figure 6.3), such that each is used from time to time to interpret the other.[50] This situa-

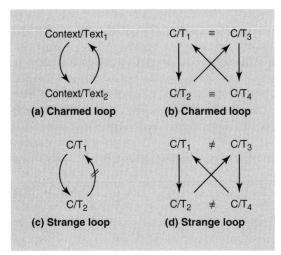

FIGURE **6.3**

Text-Context Loop Patterns

Adapted from "Between Text and Context: Toward a Rhetoric of Contextual Reconstruction" by Robert J. Branham and W. Barnett Pearce, in *Quarterly Journal of Speech* 71 (1985): 23, 25. Reprinted by permission of the authors and publisher.

tion is called *reflexivity* because each context reflects the other. Reflexivity always enters the context hierarchy at some point because the hierarchy cannot keep going up forever. At some point the ladder of contexts must come to an end and start coming down again. In other words, at some point, the context must become the text.

When the rules of meaning are consistent throughout the loop, the loop is said to be *charmed*, or self-confirming. The example of the link between your daughter's insult and relationship is a charmed loop; each confirms the other. Often, however, the rules of interpretation change from one point in the loop to another, causing a paradox, or *strange loop*, in which each context disconfirms the other. This would happen, for example, if you felt that you had a good relationship, but it included lots of insulting comments. Here the relationship would not confirm the insults, and the insults would not confirm the relationship. The result would be confusion.

The strange loop of the alcoholic is illustrated in Figure 6.4. Notice here the alcoholic is confused about control. Within the context of the self as a controlled drinker, drinking is accepted as okay, but within the context of the episode of drinking, the self is defined as out of control, making drinking not okay. If you follow the loop in Figure 6.4, you see what many alcoholics go through. First, they drink and come to see themselves as out of control. Then they stop drinking, now believing they are in control, so that they can begin drinking again. Pearce and Cronen developed a set of symbols to demonstrate how rules operate within contexts. Figure 6.5 shows how to depict rules graphically.

Rules give us a sense of what is logical or appropriate in a given situation. This is called *logical force*. Because people behave in a manner consistent with their rules, rules provide a logical force for acting in certain ways. Four types of logical force operate in communication.

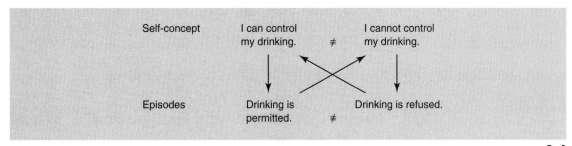

FIGURE **6.4**

The Alcoholic's Paradox

Adapted from "Between Text and Context: Toward a Rhetoric of Contextual Reconstruction" by Robert J. Branham and W. Barnett Pearce, in *Quarterly Journal of Speech* 71 (1985): 26. Reprinted by permission of the authors and publisher.

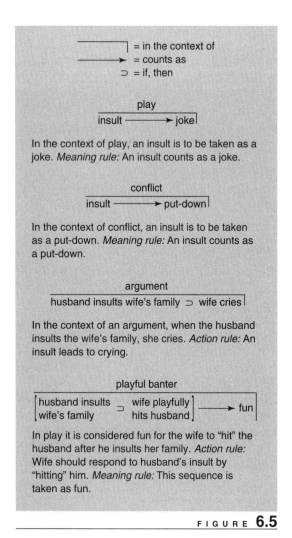

= in the context of
= counts as
⊃ = if, then

play
insult ⟶ joke

In the context of play, an insult is to be taken as a joke. *Meaning rule:* An insult counts as a joke.

conflict
insult ⟶ put-down

In the context of conflict, an insult is to be taken as a put-down. *Meaning rule:* An insult counts as a put-down.

argument
husband insults wife's family ⊃ wife cries

In the context of an argument, when the husband insults the wife's family, she cries. *Action rule:* An insult leads to crying.

playful banter
husband insults wife's family ⊃ wife playfully hits husband ⟶ fun

In play it is considered fun for the wife to "hit" the husband after he insults her family. *Action rule:* Wife should respond to husband's insult by "hitting" him. *Meaning rule:* This sequence is taken as fun.

FIGURE **6.5**

Logical Rules

The first type of logical force is *prefigurative,* or *causal force,* an antecedent-to-act linkage in which you perceive that you are being pressured to behave in certain ways because of prior conditions. If you think that you are being caused to do something, prefigurative force is at play. For example, you might tell someone that you are in school because your parents made you go. *Practical force* is an act-to-consequent linkage in which you behave in a certain way to achieve a future condition. So, for example, you might believe you are in college because you want to get

a better job than you could get with only a high school education.

The third type of logical force is contextual. *Contextual force* is a pressure from the context. Here, you believe that the action or interpretation is a natural part of the context. Within the context of your self-concept, for example, you might feel that going to college is just necessary, just part of who you are. Finally, *implicative force* is a pressure to transform or change the context in some way. Here, you act to create a new context or to change an existing one. Implicative force might come into play, for example, if your family did not value college and never encouraged its children to go on to school. You might take it on yourself to change this situation, to create a new family definition, to make the family proud of one of its members for getting a degree. In this kind of situation, you would actually be trying to change the context of family expectations.

In modern society a person is part of many systems, each with its own set of meaning and action rules. The rules are learned through interaction in social groups. Over time, individuals internalize many of these rules and draw on them to guide their actions. The basic problem of communication is that when an individual enters an interaction, that person has no way of knowing precisely what rules the other participants will be using. The primary task in all communication, then, is to achieve and then sustain some form of coordination.

Coordination involves meshing one's actions with those of another to the point of feeling that the sequence of actions is logical or appropriate. The communicators in an exchange need not interpret the events the same way, but each must feel, from within his or her own system of rules, that what is happening makes sense.

Figure 6.6 shows how coordination operates.[51] Person A acts in a certain way, and person B takes this as a message. Person B uses meaning rules to interpret the message. Person A's act thus becomes an antecedent event to which person B responds, based on B's action rules. B's act is in turn interpreted by A as a message from the standpoint of A's meaning rules, and B's act be-

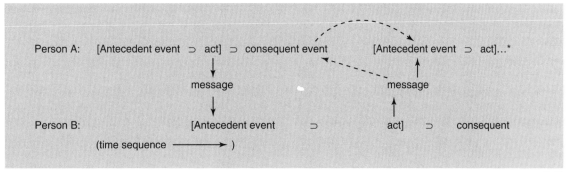

FIGURE **6.6**

Coordination Process

*Solid arrows denote constitutive rules. Broken arrows denote the coorientational state of comparing the subsequent message to the anticipated consequent event in anticipation of the next act. From *Communication, Action, and Meaning* by W. Barnett Pearce and Vernon Cronen. Copyright © 1980 by Praeger Publishers. Reprinted by permission of the authors.

comes the consequent to A's initial move. If A and B are operating with substantially different rule structures, they will quickly discover that one person's behavior does not represent the consequent intended, and they will readjust their rules until some level of coordination is achieved.

Consider the simple example of a child trying to get a ball back after accidentally throwing it through a neighbor's window.[52] The adult essentially begins with the following rule structure:

- *Meaning rule:* Saying, "Is this ball yours?" in a stern fashion, will result in this act being taken as anger, a demand for a confession, and a threat.
- *Action rule:* My act, taken as anger, will elicit crying and apologies. I, in turn, will become less angry and will give the ball back.

The child, on the other hand, has a different set of rules:

- *Meaning rule:* When the neighbor says, "Is this your ball?" he is asking for information. My statement, "Give it back," will be taken as a request.
- *Action rule:* When the neighbor requests information, I will respond with a factual answer, "Yes, it is." I will say, "Give it back," and he will give it back.

Now observe the actual conversation:

Neighbor: Is this your ball?

Child: Yes, it is. Give it back.

Obviously, the neighbor did not get the expected response and will interpret the child's remark as impudence rather than the simple request intended by the child. At this point the interaction is not coordinated. Now the neighbor must adjust the action rule by trying a different approach:

Neighbor: Give it back? This ball went through my window. Do you know that?

If the child has a sufficiently complex rule structure to provide options, he may adjust so that a successful outcome can be achieved. If not, coordination may not be achieved. Consider:

Unsatisfactory outcome:

Child: Give my ball back. I'll tell Daddy if you don't give it back.

Neighbor: Get out of my yard, kid!

Successful outcome (coordination achieved):

Child: I'm sorry. I didn't mean to do it, and I will be careful in the future.

Neighbor: Okay. Here's your ball.

An important contribution of CMM is the idea that people can have perfectly satisfactory coordination without understanding one another. In other words, communicators can organize their actions in ways that seem logical to all parties, yet they understand what is going on in a variety of different ways. For example, a speaker and audience may coordinate very well. The speaker is dynamic and effusive, and the audience responds enthusiastically. The speaker thinks she is educating and persuading the audience, but the audience is merely entertained and forgets the point of the message within hours. Here, both sides are satisfied, and each thinks what happened was appropriate, even though their meanings were different.

REFLECTIONS ON
The Cybernetic Tradition

CMM, the sole theory in this section, combines the sociocultural and cybernetic traditions. Although it could be included justifiably in the sociocultural section of this chapter, its strong reliance on system theory singles this theory out as a strong reflection of the cybernetic tradition. CMM shows the power of the loop as a cybernetic device. Eschewing linear explanations, Pearce, Cronen, and their colleagues see meaning and action as inextricably linked, creating logics that drive action in various situations.

So far in this chapter, we have discussed how conversations are organized behaviorally, how language structures conversations, and how people use socially established rules and forms to understand and participate in conversations. Social institutions are made in conversations, and these large social arrangements are not incidental, but critical to human life. As a result, struggle and conflict are an important part of social interaction, as the theories in the following section illustrate.

• • •

THE CRITICAL TRADITION

Although conversations are a natural part of human life—we cannot avoid having conversations—they are not inconsequential. Indeed, our conversations shape who and how we are as individuals and as a society. Critical theories show us how the use of language in conversations creates social division and holds out a vision for egalitarian forms of communication that empower all groups.

Language-Centered Perspective on Culture

Fern Johnson's language-centered perspective brings cultural linguistics to bear on issues of cultural diversity in the United States.[53] Johnson posits six assumptions or axioms of a language-centered perspective: (1) all communication occurs within cultural frameworks; (2) all individuals possess tacit cultural knowledge through which they communicate; (3) in multicultural societies, there is a dominant linguistic ideology that in turn displaces or marginalizes other cultural groups; (4) members of marginalized cultural groups possess knowledge about both their own culture and the dominant culture; (5) cultural knowledge is both preserved and passed down and constantly changing; and (6) when cultures coexist, each influences and affects the other.

This theory is designed to promote an understanding of the particular linguistic and cultural variables of any particular cultural group as well as how the discourses of that group emerge, develop, and play out against dominant linguistic ideologies of the United States. In terms of our focus on conversation, Johnson would assert the need for any conversation to be nuanced by an understanding of the various cultural factors each participant brings to it. Also important to the conversation, however, is the matter of English hegemony, or the power of one language group over others in the United States, and the belief that there must be a single dominant language in a country.

Johnson examines four cultural discourses in the United States—gender, African American, Hispanic, and Asian American—each with different implications for communication practice and social policy in the United States in four primary institutions—health care, legal setting, education, and the workplace. While any non-dominant group is to some degree invisible across these institutional contexts, the historical and cultural factors inherent to each group are positioned differently within these institutions. As examples of discursive consequences of linguistic dominance in the United States, Johnson cites a reticence on the part of Asian Americans to seek treatment for physical or mental ailments because of a greater cultural reserve; the difficulties of using black vernacular and "broken" English in schools where teachers insist on "correct" English; and the use of "English only" workplaces where non-native speakers of English are at a decided disadvantage. In offering a theory that takes into account the cultural particulars of the various language groups that co-exist in U.S. society, Johnson seeks to promote a greater understanding of the various factors that contribute to multiculturalism and to promote linguistic policy that is appropriately complicated, thoughtful, and respectful of the cultural nuances that comprise contemporary America.

Invitational Rhetoric

Continuing the analysis of the relationship of conversation and culture is the theory of invitational rhetoric. The phrase was coined by Sonja K. Foss and Cindy L. Griffin in their essay, "Beyond Persuasion,"[54] in which the authors argue for a different interactional mode than that of persuasion—than trying to change the other. They base their theory on the work of Sally Miller Gearhart, who sees persuasion as a kind of "violence" because it implicitly, if not explicitly, says to another, "my perspective is right and yours is wrong." For Gearhart, persuasion is

problematic because it denies the authenticity and integrity of the other's perspective—a perspective that has developed, as anyone's perspective does, from various life experiences. Seeking a way to converse without persuasion as a central demand, Foss and Griffin propose a perspective based in feminist values of equality, immanent value, and self-determination. An attitude of equality places each perspective on an equal plane and engenders relationships of respect and non-domination. An attitude of immanent value acknowledges the worth and dignity of all life—reputation or earned credibility are not privileged over inherent value. Finally, an attitude of self-determination affords everyone the right to decide for him or herself what to do and how to live.

Invitational rhetoric uses the idea of an invitation both literally and metaphorically as a conversational mode. When you issue an invitation for others to consider your perspective, you invite audience members to see the world as you do and to take your perspective seriously. It is up to them, however, to decide whether to adopt that perspective or not, and the primary goal is the clarification of ideas among all people involved—not persuasion.

When an interaction is approached from this perspective, the desired outcome is not to change others but to invite the understanding of different perspectives on the part of all involved in the interaction. Unlike traditional efforts at persuasion, then, where audience members are expected to change in the direction advocated by the speaker, here the speaker can choose to change too as a result of the interaction. Any changes that result as part of the interaction are the result of insight, not influence, because all change is self-chosen. Rather than having to get others to agree that your perspective is "right," diverse perspectives are seen as resources for better understanding an issue. When we deliberately expose ourselves to ideas that are different from ours, we have more opportunities for understanding.[55]

Sonja Foss and Karen Foss refined and elaborated on the notion of invitational rhetoric in their presentational speaking book, *Inviting Transformation*.[56] They contrast what they call different modes of rhetoric (which, for our purposes, can be thought of as different conversational patterns) in our culture. *Conquest rhetoric* is an interaction in which winning is the goal; you want to establish your "idea, claim, or argument as the best one from among competing positions."[57] It is perhaps the most prevalent form in U.S. culture and includes the legislative, judicial, and political systems. *Conversion rhetoric*, on the other hand, is designed to change others' perspectives or behaviors based on the superiority or rightness of a position. Religious groups, social movement groups, and advertising campaigns exemplify conversion rhetoric; each seeks to convert others to its perspective or point of view. A third rhetorical mode is *benevolent rhetoric*, which is designed to help others improve their lives. In the benevolent rhetoric mode, one typically provides information to the other with the aim of benefiting them in some way. Health campaigns are an example of benevolent rhetoric. Finally, there is a kind of rhetoric called *advisory*, in which you provide requested information to another. Counseling and education are two cases of advisory rhetoric; in both situations, you expose yourself to new and different perspectives in the hopes of improving your life.

Foss and Foss suggest that conquest and conversion modes function as default modes in our culture—they are the forms of interaction or conversation most privileged and, as a result, the world they create is an adversarial one. Deborah Tannen uses the phrase *argument culture* to describe this world; this is a world in which we approach almost everything as if it were a fight.[58] By exploring other modes, such as the invitational, different realities can be created.

Foss and Foss suggest that a necessary first step in moving to an invitational mode is creating an appropriate environment in which the assumptions of invitational rhetoric are realized and upheld. An environment conducive to all parties reaching greater understanding consists of four factors: freedom, safety, value, and openness. Freedom is the power to choose or decide and means allowing those with whom you are communicating more than one option, not insisting that the others adopt your perspective, and not doing things that will restrict others' participation. You probably have found yourself in a situation where you have felt that you would be humiliated if you spoke up. Freedom is not present in that situation.

The condition of safety refers to feeling emotionally, physically, and intellectually secure in the interaction. Of course, what makes a situation "safe" for one person—the ability to speak freely and setting up systems that allow for each person to speak—might mean extreme lack of safety to someone who is very shy and does not wish to speak up. Nonetheless, determining what is safe in a speaking situation is critical if an invitational approach is to be realized.

Value, the third element of an invitational environment, refers to the intrinsic worth of each individual and their perspective. Each perspective is valued and respected, in other words, and value is communicated by listening well, acknowledging, and taking seriously the perspectives offered by others.

The fourth and final condition is openness, a desire for, willingness to consider, and genuine curiosity about a variety of perspectives. Unless a feeling of openness exists in the interaction, participants will not feel free to share their perspectives fully, to consider different perspectives, and to utilize fully all the diverse perspectives that are available.[59] The theory of invitational rhetoric, then, suggests an alternative conversational approach to the default modes traditionally privileged in our culture. Rather than accepting the dominance of those default modes, Foss and Griffin and Foss and Foss urge exploration and consideration of more invitational approaches that create an understanding rather than adversarial culture.

REFLECTIONS ON

The Critical Tradition

The theories in this chapter imagine new kinds of conversation designed both to honor the contributions of all groups as well as to promote freedom and choice. Because they react to the customary power relations embedded in conversations, these theories are distinctly critical in tone. These theories do not merely react to domination in society, but go a step further in suggesting ways of conducting conversations that empower all cultural groups.

We will return to the critical tradition in several chapters of this book to see how ideas of power, struggle, conflict, and inclusion play out in various communication contexts.

● ● ●

A P P L I C A T I O N S I M P L I C A T I O N S

In many respects, human life can be characterized by conversation. Our species is distinguished by the fact that we have ongoing, complex, conversations; we define our realities in talk; and that our relationships to one another and to the world are structured through a history of symbolic interaction from birth to death. It is no wonder, then, that conversation has been an important topic of communication theory.

From the sampling of theories presented in this chapter, we see that conversation can be understood in a diverse set of ways. Yet, five themes seem to cut across the many variables that are explored in these theories.

1. Everyday talk matters.

Many students and scholars get most excited about "big splash" communications like popular television and movies, media news, public demonstrations, communication technology, and historic speeches. Increasingly, however, we have come to realize that everyday conversation is more than a sidelight to human life. Indeed, our constant social interactions with others structure our individual lives, provide ways of understanding experience, create interpersonal relationships, and build social institutions. How could you have a romantic relationship, a friendship, or a family without conversation? How could organizations exist without conversations? Indeed, even the "big splash" would never happen without conversations behind the scenes.[60] In other words, we need to understand the importance of and pay attention to ordinary conversations. Even the most mundane talk is significant in defining who we are and producing the cultures in which we live.

2. Conversations require coordinated interaction.

We must have tremendous intuitive knowledge about culture, language, and nonverbal behavior in order to have a conversation. We also need the skill to be able to mesh our behaviors with those of others. The theories in this chapter say volumes about the knowledge and skill necessary to do what often feels and looks effortless. Of course, conversation is not always easy, and problematic moments make us realize that interaction taxes our cultural and social knowledge and skills.

Especially in problematic situations, we treat information as a valuable resource in interaction. We are sometimes compelled to go out of our way to get information by watching other people's behavior and by seeing how they respond to us. We use this information to reduce uncertainty and make decisions about how to react to certain other people, as uncertainty-reduction theory demonstrates. Michael Sunnafrank suggests that we seek information not just to reduce uncertainty but also to assess the potential outcome of the communication. One reason for doing this is to figure out whether continued communication will be positive or negative and to adjust our actions accordingly.[61]

While we are seeking certain kinds of information on a conscious level, we also take note subconsciously of interactional behaviors and adjust and adapt our behaviors as part of the flow of the conversation. Verbal and nonverbal behavior is adapted to what we see going on around us. Accommodation theory, for example, shows how people match or distinguish their behavior from that of others: We compare the way people behave to how we think they should behave, and we respond to others based on the ways and extent to which our expectations are violated. This kind of comparison is a key factor in deception and deception detection, for example. Face negotiation is another example of this principle in action.

Theories of the conversation show that it is difficult, and probably not very useful, to separate verbal and nonverbal communication in the ongoing stream of talk. The theories in this chapter show that interaction involves both and that the two are tied together. Some of the theorists featured in this chapter tend to focus more on one or the other, but all freely acknowledge that this is more a research convenience than a reflection of reality.[62]

3. Conversations achieve meaning through convergence.

Although the information we seek is important, conversations are much more than information exchanges. Conversations are also instances of what Hartmut Mokros and Mark Aakhus call "meaning engagement practice."[63] In conversation, partners come to share, and often to create, jointly understood meaning. Conversations are more than scripts. They are the creative form in which we make our social worlds. Although we may hold concepts and ideas in our individual brains, our mental constructs are created, sustained, and changed through conversation. Curtis LeBaron, Jenny Mandelbaum, and Phillip Glenn remind us, "Human minds extend beyond the skin as people depend upon social and material worlds to acquire knowledge and display intellectual ability."[64]

By going back and forth in an interaction, communicators come to make something that is logical, sensible, or coherent to them. They organize their talk together, drawing on certain social conventions. Much can be learned about how coherence is achieved through discourse analysis.[65] In communication, the term *discourse* usually denotes segments of talk. Discourse is always understood as part of an ongoing stream of communication that has some sense of coherence. In other words, our discourse at any moment responds to and anticipates interaction with others in an exchange of messages. When a professor asks a discussion question in class and students respond with answers, you are seeing discourse in action. If the discussion is very good, students will begin to respond to one another and the professor will join the conversation. We can look at any one speech that a participant makes as discourse, or we can look at the entire discussion as discourse, but always the question is how the messages gain meaning from the whole conversational context.[66]

Scott Jacobs outlines three things we can learn by examining conversations carefully in what is known as *discourse analysis*.[67] The first thing we can learn is how people understand messages. What information is embedded in the structure of a statement that enables another person to know what it means? How do you know, for example, that "Is Sybil there?" means that someone wants to talk to her on the telephone? How do you know that, "You sure are hot," means someone thinks you are on a winning streak and not that you are sexy? We acquire this information by learning conventions of discourse that enable us to converge or come together on the meaning of what is being said.

The second thing we can learn from discourse analysis is how to get something done through talk. What kinds of choices do we have when we want to do something like make a request or greet someone? How does a person decide how to say something, and how can he or she know the difference between an appropriate and an inappropriate way of putting something into words? Again, over time within a social group, certain patterns of interaction become resources that we can rely on to accomplish our goals. Others understand what we are doing because of the shared meanings for these patterns of interaction. For example, if you wanted to ask a friend to go out without feeling pressured about it, you might say, "I would love to figure out how to get out of this pile of work I have tonight." Your friend knows you are "fishing" for an invitation, but also realizes that you have provided an "out," which gives him a perfectly good excuse to turn you down without hurting your feelings. He could say, "Hey, why don't you blow off your work and let's get a pizza," or he might say, "Sounds like you are boxed in tonight. Me too."

Finally, we can figure out how to make patterns of talk sensible and logical. In a conversation, for example, there is a back-and-forth flow among participants. How do they string words together rationally? What principles are used to connect one statement with another in a way that everyone understands? If you look at a transcript of a conversation carefully, you often find that it seems disjointed; yet, the communicators made sense of what they were saying as they went along. How did they do this? Next time you get together with a group of friends, pay close attention to the turns in the conversation. Notice how people respond to one another and how the topic changes from time to time. Notice, too, how people exchange turns, and how, despite all of these unpredictable bends, the talk still makes sense. It hangs together.

Conversations are cooperative events. People must play the game by the same rules or they would never know what was going on. For cooperation to occur, participants make certain assumptions about the other person—an assumption that everyone is conversing in good faith with the intent to speak in accordance with the rules. Even blatant violations of conversational rules are interpreted through implicature as being cooperative. Indeed, the combination of basic rules of cooperation—such as appropriate quantity of talk, truthfulness, relevance, and organization with the flexibility permitted by conversational implicature—makes it possible for humans to enact an infinite number of often creative expansions of talk to meet a whole array of intentions.

Coherence, then, is achieved through convergence of many types. Symbolic interactionism addresses the ways in which certain words and gestures come to have a shared meaning within a social group. Objects are more than things—they have meaning because of the symbols we use to talk about them. Even the self, as we saw in Chapter 4, is a social object, as we come to see ourselves in certain ways because of how we are symbolized and talked about in ordinary conversation.

Narrative is especially powerful in bringing people together in the construction of common understandings of experience. Over time, little stories combine to form large narratives, or rhetorical visions, that structure our sense of reality and value. A conversation with old friends or colleagues "clicks" because communicators rely again and again on the fantasy themes that form these larger visions emerging from a common history.

4. Conversations are organized.

Conversations are structured, but they are not pre-organized in the same way that a play is pre-scripted. A conversation is more like an improvisation, in which the participants rely on conventions of several types to organize as they go. Theories about conversation help us see how communicators create order as they interact.

Conventions of conversation can be thought of as rules, as Susan Shimanoff points out in the following passage:

> In order for communication to exist, or continue, two or more interacting individuals must share rules for using symbols. Not only must they have rules for individual symbols, but they must also agree on such matters as how to take turns at speaking, how to be polite or how to insult, to greet, and so forth. If every symbol user manipulated symbols at random, the result would be chaos rather than communication.[68]

A rather large body of literature has been created to explain the place of rules in discourse.[69] These theories teach that rules govern how discourse can be organized and understood. Rules affect the options available in a given situation, yet because they are situational, rules allow communicators to behave differently at various times and places.

Many of the theories in this chapter rely on the rules concept to some extent. The rules concept has been popular in communication studies because it acknowledges that people can make choices while still behaving somewhat predictably. Whether we are talking about maxims and implicature (from Grice), adjacency pairs (from conversation analysis), or logical force (from CMM), some sense of rule is at play. Many rules of conversational interaction are universal within a culture and have staying power over time. Other rules are limited to small social groups like families and have a limited life span. In either case, the rules function to provide organization and structure to the conversation.

5. Conversations derive their meaning from the contexts in which they occur.

The ongoing flow of communication within our lives at all levels creates a set of contexts that give meaning to particular conversations. No conversation stands by itself, but always follows a history and leads to a future. As an observer, you can focus on a particular aspect of the conversation, which scholars call the text. At the same time, however, you cannot forget that the meaning of the text is always influenced by some context. One of the most important contexts for meaning is the culture, or set of cultures, within which the conversation occurs. As CMM teaches us, however, culture is but one context. Others can include the self, the relationship, or any other arrangement that can provide guidelines for interpretation and action. A powerful example is face negotiation, in which we build, maintain, and sometimes threaten the personal dignity of self and others within a cultural frame.

◖ Notes

1. Rom Harré and Paul Secord, *The Explanation of Social Behavior* (Totowa, NJ: Rowman & Littlefield, 1972).
2. For reflections and applications on this subject, see Austin Babrow, ed., "Special Issue: Uncertainty, Evaluation, and Communication," *Journal of Communication* 51 (2001); and Walid A. Affifi, ed., "Colloquy on Information Seeking," *Human Communication Research* 28 (2002): 207–312.
3. For an excellent summary of the two theories together, see William Gudykunst, "The Uncertainty Reduction and Anxiety-Uncertainty Reduction Theories of Berger, Gudykunst, and Associates," in *Watershed Research Traditions in Human Communication Theory*, ed. Donald P. Cushman and Branislav Kovačić (Albany: SUNY Press, 1995), pp. 67–100.
4. Uncertainty reduction theory is summarized in various versions in Charles R. Berger, "Producing Messages Under Uncertainty," in *Message Production: Advances in Communication Theory*, ed. John O. Greene (Mahwah, NJ: Lawrence Erlbaum, 1997), pp. 221–244; Charles R. Berger and James J. Bradac, *Language and Social Knowledge: Uncertainty in Interpersonal Relations* (London: Arnold, 1982). See also Charles R. Berger and R. J. Calabrese, "Some Explorations in Initial Interaction and Beyond: Toward a Developmental Theory of Interpersonal Communication," *Human Communication Research* 1 (1975): 99–112; Charles R. Berger, R. R. Gardner, M. R. Parks, L. Schulman, and Gerald R. Miller, "Interpersonal Epistemology and Interpersonal Communication," in *Explorations in Interpersonal Communication*, ed. Gerald R. Miller (Beverly Hills, CA: Sage, 1976), pp. 149–171; and Charles R. Berger and William Douglas, "Thought and Talk: 'Excuse Me, But Have I Been Talking to Myself?'" in *Human Communication Theory*, ed. F. E. X. Dance (New York: Harper & Row, 1982), pp. 42–60. For a good, comprehensive secondary treatment, see John F. Cragan and Donald C. Shields, *Understanding Communication Theory: The Communicative Forces for Human Action* (Boston: Allyn & Bacon, 1998), pp. 122–148.
5. Charles R. Berger and Katherine Ann Kellermann, "To Ask or Not to Ask: Is That a Question?," in *Communication Yearbook 7*, ed. R. Bostrom (Beverly Hills, CA: Sage, 1983), pp. 342–368.
6. This work is summarized in Gudykunst, "The Uncertainty Reduction and Anxiety-Uncertainty Reduction Theories"; William B. Gudykunst, "Uncertainty and Anxiety," in *Theories in Intercultural Communication*, ed. Young Yun Kim and William B. Gudykunst (Newbury Park, CA: Sage, 1988), pp. 123–156; and "Culture and the Development of Interpersonal Relationships," in *Communication Yearbook 12*, ed. J. A. Anderson (Newbury Park, CA: Sage, 1989), pp. 315–354.
7. This concept is developed by Edward T. Hall, *Beyond Culture* (New York: Doubleday, 1976).
8. Gudykunst, "The Uncertainty Reduction and Anxiety-Uncertainty Reduction Theories."
9. See Howard Giles, Justine Coupland, and Nikolas Coupland, "Accommodation Theory: Communication, Context, and Consequence," in *Contexts of Accommodation: Developments in Applied Sociolinguistics*, ed. Howard Giles, Justine Coupland, and Nikolas Coupland (Cambridge: Cambridge University Press, 1991), pp. 1–68. See also Howard Giles, Anthony Mulac, James J. Bradac, and Patricia Johnson, "Speech Accommodation Theory: The First Decade and Beyond," in *Communication Yearbook 10*, ed. M. L. McLaughlin (Newbury Park, CA: Sage, 1987), pp. 13–48.
10. Judee K. Burgoon, "It Takes Two to Tango: Interpersonal Adaptation and Implications for Relational Communication," in *Communication: Views from the Helm for the 21st Century*, ed. Judith S. Trent (Boston: Allyn & Bacon, 1998), pp. 53–59; Judee K. Burgoon and Cindy H. White, "Researching Nonverbal Message Production: A View from Interaction Adaptation Theory," in *Message Production: Advances in Communication Theory*, ed. John O. Greene (Mahwah, NJ: Lawrence Erlbaum, 1997), pp. 279–312; Judee K. Burgoon, Lesa A. Stern, and Leesa Dillman, *Interpersonal Adaptation: Dyadic Interaction Patterns* (New York: Cambridge University Press, 1995); Judee K. Burgoon, Leesa Dillman, and Lesa A. Stern, "Adaptation in Dyadic Interaction: Defining and Operationalizing Patterns of Reciprocity and Compensation," *Communication Theory* 3 (1993): 295–316.
11. Judee K. Burgoon and Jerold L. Hale, "Nonverbal Expectancy Violations: Model Elaboration and Application," *Communication Monographs* 55 (1988): 58–79. For brief summaries see also Beth A. LePoire, "Two Contrasting Explanations of Involvement Violations: Expectancy Violations Theory Versus Discrepancy Arousal Theory," *Human Communication Research* 20 (1994): 560–591; Judee K. Burgoon, "Nonverbal Signals," in *Handbook of Interpersonal Communication*, ed. Mark L. Knapp and

Gerald R. Miller (Thousand Oaks, CA: Sage, 1994), pp. 253–255. For other approaches to expectancy violations, see Joseph N. Cappella, "The Management of Conversational Interaction in Adults and Infants," in *Handbook of Interpersonal Communication*, ed. Mark L. Knapp and Gerald R. Miller (Thousand Oaks, CA: Sage, 1994), pp. 406–407; Peter A. Andersen, "Nonverbal Immediacy in Interpersonal Communication," in *Multichannel Integrations of Nonverbal Behavior*, ed. A. W. Siegman and S. Feldstein (Hillsdale, NJ: Lawrence Erlbaum, 1985), pp. 1–36; Joseph N. Cappella and John O. Greene, "A Discrepancy-Arousal Explanation of Mutual Influence in Expressive Behavior for Adult-Adult and Infant-Adult Interaction," *Communication Monographs* 49 (1982): 89–114; M. L. Patterson, *Nonverbal Behavior: A Functional Perspective* (New York: Springer-Verlag, 1983).

12. We probably have expectations for verbal behavior as well, but this theory does not address this subject.

13. Judee K. Burgoon, "Communicative Effects of Gaze Behavior: A Test of Two Contrasting Explanations," *Human Communication Research* 12 (1986): 495–524.

14. David B. Buller and Judee K. Burgoon, "Interpersonal Deception Theory," *Communication Theory* 6 (1996): 203–242; Judee K. Burgoon et al., "Interpersonal Deception: XII. Information Management Dimensions Underlying Deceptive and Truthful Messages," *Communication Monographs* 63 (1996): 50–69.

15. Mead's primary work in symbolic interactionism is *Mind, Self, and Society* (Chicago: University of Chicago Press, 1934). For a general discussion of the history, influence, and methods of the Chicago School, see Jesse G. Delia, "Communication Research: A History," in *Handbook of Communication Science*, ed. Charles R. Berger and Steven H. Chaffee (Newbury Park, CA: Sage, 1987), pp. 30–37. For outstanding secondary sources on Mead and the Chicago School, see Everett M. Rogers, *A History of Communication Study: A Biographical Approach* (New York: Free Press, 1994), pp. 137–202; Bernard N. Meltzer, "Mead's Social Psychology," in *Symbolic Interaction*, ed. J. G. Manis and B. N. Meltzer (Boston: Allyn & Bacon, 1972), pp. 4–22; Charles Morris, "George H. Mead as Social Psychologist and Social Philosopher" (Introduction), in *Mind, Self, and Society* (Chicago: University of Chicago Press, 1934), pp. ix–xxxv; and C. David Johnson and J. Stephen Picou, "The Foundations of Symbolic Interactionism Reconsidered," in *Micro-Sociological Theory: Perspectives on Sociological Theory*, vol. 2, ed. H. J. Helle and S. N. Eisenstadt (Beverly Hills, CA: Sage, 1985), pp. 54–70.

16. Herbert Blumer, *Symbolic Interactionism: Perspective and Method* (Englewood Cliffs: NJ: Prentice-Hall, 1969), p. 1.

17. Wayne Woodward, "Triadic Communication as Transactional Participation," *Critical Studies in Mass Communication* 13 (1996): 155–174.

18. Donald G. Ellis, *Crafting Society: Ethnicity, Class, and Communication Theory* (Mahwah, NJ: Lawrence Erlbaum, 1999), p. xii.

19. Blumer, *Symbolic Interactionism*, p. 19.

20. Blumer, *Symbolic Interactionism*, p. 19.

21. Blumer, *Symbolic Interactionism*, p. 5.

22. For a thoughtful discussion of the social nature of symbols, see Wendy Leeds-Hurwitz, "A Social Account of Symbols," in *Beyond the Symbol Model: Reflections on the Representational Nature of Language*, ed. John Stewart (Albany: SUNY Press, 1996), pp. 257–278.

23. For a probing discussion of self within this tradition, see Norbert Wiley, *The Semiotic Self* (Chicago: University of Chicago Press, 1994).

24. Howard Becker, "Becoming a Marihuana User," *American Journal of Sociology* 59 (1953): 235–242.

25. See, for example, Ernest G. Bormann, John F. Cragan, and Donald C. Shields, "Three Decades of Developing, Grounding, and Using Symbolic Convergence Theory (SCT), in *Communication Yearbook 25*, ed. William B. Gudykunst (Mahwah, NJ: Lawrence Erlbaum, 2001), pp. 271–313; and John F. Cragan and Donald Shields, *Understanding Communication Theory: The Communicative Forces for Human Action* (Boston: Allyn & Bacon, 1998), pp. 93–121; Bormann's major works on fantasy-theme analysis are *Communication Theory* (New York: Holt, Rinehart & Winston, 1980), pp. 184–190; *The Force of Fantasy: Restoring the American Dream* (Carbondale: Southern Illinois University Press, 1985); "Fantasy and Rhetorical Vision: The Rhetorical Criticism of Social Reality," *Quarterly Journal of Speech* 58 (1972): 396–407; "Fantasy and Rhetorical Vision: Ten Years Later," *Quarterly Journal of Speech* 68 (1982): 288–305; Ernest G. Bormann, John F. Cragan, and Donald C. Shields, "An Expansion of the Rhetorical Vision Component of the Symbolic Convergence Theory: The Cold War Paradigm Case," *Communication Monographs* 63 (1996): 1–28. See also John F. Cragan and Donald C. Shields, *Applied Communication Research: A Dramatistic Approach* (Prospect Heights, IL: Waveland, 1981); John F. Cragan and Donald C. Shields, *Symbolic Theories in Applied Communication Research: Bormann, Burke, and Fisher* (Cresskill, NJ: Hampton, 1995), pp. 29–48.

26. This section deals with conversation in the discourse analysis tradition, emphasizing the verbal structure of conversational texts. There is also a tradition that studies the management of conversations in a broader sense, including its nonverbal elements. See Joseph N. Cappella, "The Manage-

ment of Conversations," in *Handbook of Interpersonal Communication,* ed. Mark L. Knapp and Gerald R. Miller (Beverly Hills, CA: Sage, 1985), pp. 393–439.

27. Ethnomethodology is most often associated with its originator, sociologist Harold Garfinkel; see his *Studies in Ethnomethodology* (Englewood Cliffs, NJ: Prentice-Hall, 1967). For a brief description of this tradition, see Jonathan Potter and Margaret Wetherell, *Discourse and Social Psychology: Beyond Attitudes and Behavior* (London: Sage, 1987), pp. 18–23. See also Graham Button, ed., *Ethnomethodology and the Human Sciences* (Cambridge: Cambridge University Press, 1991).

28. For an excellent overview of this entire tradition of work, see Karen Tracy, *Everyday Talk: Building and Reflecting Identities* (New York: Guildford Press, 2002).

29. For detailed discussions of conversation analysis, see Deborah Cameron, *Working with Spoken Discourse* (London: Sage Publications, 2001), pp. 87–105; Jonathan Potter, *Representing Reality: Discourse, Rhetoric and Social Construction* (London: Sage Publications, 1996), pp. 42–67; George Psathas, *Conversation Analysis: The Study of Talk-in-Interaction* (Thousand Oaks, CA: Sage, 1995); Anna-Brita Stenstrøm, *An Introduction to Spoken Interaction* (London: Longman, 1994); Robert Nofsinger, *Everyday Conversation* (Newbury Park, CA: Sage, 1991).

30. For a good discussion of how the conversation analyst works, see Anita Pomerantz and B. J. Fehr, "Conversation Analysis: An Approach to the Study of Social Action as Sense Making Practices," in *Discourse as Social Interaction,* ed. T. A. van Dijk (Thousand Oaks: Sage, 1997), pp. 64–91. See also Donald G. Ellis, *From Language to Communication* (Mahwah, NJ: Lawrence Erlbaum, 1999), pp. 85–89.

31. Jenny Mandelbaum, "Interpersonal Activities in Conversational Storytelling," *Western Journal of Speech Communication* 53 (1989): 114–126.

32. These issues are outlined in Margaret L. McLaughlin, *Conversation: How Talk Is Organized* (Beverly Hills, CA: Sage, 1984).

33. See Robert T. Craig and Karen Tracy, eds., *Conversational Coherence: Form, Structure, and Strategy,* 3rd ed. (Beverly Hills, CA: Sage, 1983).

34. H. Paul Grice, "Logic and Conversation," in *Syntax and Semantics,* vol. 3, ed. P. Cole and J. Morgan (New York: Academic, 1975), pp. 41–58.

35. This subject is explored and expanded by Thomas Holtgraves, "Comprehending Speaker Meaning," in *Communication Yearbook 26,* ed. William B. Gudykunst (Mahwah, NJ: Lawrence Erlbaum, 2002), pp. 2–35.

36. Examples of violations are from Susan Swan Mura, "Licensing Violations: Legitimate Violations of Grice's Conversational Principle," in *Conversational Coherence: Form, Structure, and Strategy,* ed. R. T. Craig and K. Tracy (Beverly Hills, CA: Sage, 1983), pp. 101–115.

37. Steven A. McCornack, "Information Manipulation Theory," *Communication Monographs* 59 (1992): 1–17; Steven A. McCornack et al., "When the Alteration of Information Is Viewed as Deception: An Empirical Test of Information Manipulation Theory," *Communication Monographs* 59 (1992): 17–29.

38. Scott Jacobs, Edwin J. Dawson, and Dale Brashers, "Information Manipulation Theory: A Replication and Assessment," *Communication Monographs* 63 (1996): 70–82. See also Steven A. McCornack, Timothy R. Levine, Kelly Morrison, and Maria Lapinski, "Speaking of Information Manipulation: A Critical Rejoinder," *Communication Monographs* 63 (1996): 83–92; David B. Buller and Judee K. Burgoon, "Another Look at Information Management: A Rejoinder to McCornack, Levine, Morrison, and Lapinski," *Communication Monographs* 63 (1996): 92–98; Scott Jacobs, Dale Brashers, and Edwin J. Dawson, "Truth and Deception," *Communication Monographs* 63 (1996): 98–103.

39. For a summary of some of the approaches, see Craig and Tracy, *Conversational Coherence.*

40. Harvey Sacks, Emanuel Schegloff, and Gail Jefferson, "A Simplest Systematics for the Organization of Turn Taking for Conversation," *Language* 50 (1974): 696–735.

41. Scott Jacobs, "Language," in *Handbook of Interpersonal Communication,* ed. Mark L. Knapp and Gerald R. Miller (Beverly Hills, CA: Sage, 1985), pp. 330–335; also see Scott Jacobs and Sally Jackson, "Speech Act Structure in Conversation: Rational Aspects of Pragmatic Coherence," in *Conversational Coherence: Form, Structure, and Strategy,* 3rd ed., ed. Robert T. Craig and Karen Tracy (Beverly Hills, CA: Sage, 1983), pp. 47–66.

42. Donald G. Ellis, "Fixing Communicative Meaning: A Coherentist Theory," *Communication Research* 22 (1995): 515–544.

43. Scott Jacobs and Sally Jackson, "Strategy and Structure in Conversational Influence Attempts," *Communication Monographs* 50 (1983): 285–304; Sally Jackson and Scott Jacobs, "Conversational Relevance: Three Experiments on Pragmatic Connectedness in Conversation," in *Communication Yearbook 10,* ed. M. McLaughlin (Newbury Park, CA: Sage, 1987), pp. 323–347.

44. The best recent statement of the theory of conversational argument is Frans H. van Eemeren, Rob Grootendorst, Sally Jackson, and Scott Jacobs, *Reconstructing Argumentative Discourse* (Tuscaloosa: University of Alabama Press, 1993). See also Frans H. van Eemeren and Rob Grootendorst, *Argumentation, Communication, and Fallacies: A Pragma-Dialectical Perspective* (Hillsdale, NJ: Lawrence

Erlbaum, 1992); Douglas N. Walton, *Plausible Argument in Everyday Conversation* (Albany: SUNY Press, 1992); Scott Jacobs and Sally Jackson, "Building a Model of Conversational Argument," in *Rethinking Communication: Paradigm Exemplars,* vol. 2, ed. Brenda Dervin, Lawrence Grossberg, Barbara J. O'Keefe, and Ellen Wartella (Newbury Park, CA: Sage, 1989), pp. 153–171.

45. This distinction was originally made by Daniel J. O'Keefe, "Two Concepts of Argument," *Journal of the American Forensic Association* 13 (1977): 121–128.

46. Van Eemeren, Grootendorst, Jackson, and Jacobs, *Reconstructing Argumentative Discourse,* p. 31.

47. Stella Ting-Toomey, "Toward a Theory of Conflict and Culture," in *Communication, Culture, and Organizational Processes,* ed. William B. Gudykunst, Lea Stewart, and Stella Ting-Toomey (Beverly Hills, CA: Sage, 1985), pp. 71–86; Stella Ting-Toomey, "Intercultural Conflict Styles: Face-Negotiation Theory," in *Theories in Intercultural Communication,* ed. Young Yun Kim and William Gudykunst (Newbury Park, CA: Sage, 1988), pp. 213–235; Stella Ting-Toomey and Atsuko Kurogi, "Facework Competence in Intercultural Conflict: An Updated Face-Negotiation Theory," *International Journal of Intercultural Relations* 22 (1998): 187–225.

48. For a summary of work in intercultural communication generally, see Young Yun Kim, "Mapping the Domain of Intercultural Communication: An Overview," in *Communication Yearbook 24,* ed. William B. Gudykunst (Thousand Oaks, CA: Sage, 2001), pp. 139–157.

49. For a recent summary of the theory, see Gerry Philipsen, "The Coordinated Management of Meaning Theory of Pearce, Cronen, and Associates," in *Watershed Research Traditions in Human Communication Theory,* ed. Donald P. Cushman and Branislav Kovačić (Albany: SUNY Press, 1995), pp. 13–43. For some primary sources, see W. Barnett Pearce and Vernon Cronen, *Communication, Action, and Meaning* (New York: Praeger, 1980); W. Barnett Pearce and Kimberly A. Pearce, "Extending the Theory of the Coordinated Management of Meaning (CMM) Through a Community Dialogue Process," *Communication Theory* 10 (2000): 405–423; Vernon Cronen, Victoria Chen, and W. Barnett Pearce, "Coordinated Management of Meaning: A Critical Theory," in *Theories in Intercultural Communication,* ed. Young Yun Kim and William B. Gudykunst (Newbury Park, CA: Sage, 1988), pp. 66–98; Vernon Cronen, W. Barnett Pearce, and Linda Harris, "The Coordinated Management of Meaning," in *Comparative Human Communication Theory,* ed. F. E. X. Dance (New York: Harper & Row, 1982); W. Barnett Pearce, "The Coordinated Management of Meaning: A Rules Based Theory of Interpersonal Communication," in *Explorations in Interpersonal Communication,* ed. Gerald R. Miller (Beverly Hills, CA: Sage, 1976), pp. 17–36; Vernon Cronen, W. Barnett Pearce, and Linda Harris, "The Logic of the Coordinated Management of Meaning," *Communication Education* 28 (1979): 22–38.

50. Loops are discussed in Vernon E. Cronen, Kenneth M. Johnson, and John W. Lannamann, "Paradoxes, Double Binds, and Reflexive Loops: An Alternative Theoretical Perspective," *Family Process* 20 (1982): 91–112; and Robert J. Branham and W. Barnett Pearce, "Between Text and Context: Toward a Rhetoric of Contextual Reconstruction," *Quarterly Journal of Speech* 71 (1985): 19–36. For an interesting recent extrapolation and extension of this idea, see James R. Taylor, Francois Cooren, Nicole Giroux, and Daniel Robichaud, "The Communicational Basis of Organization: Between the Conversation and the Text," *Communication Theory* 6 (1996): 1–39.

51. Pearce and Cronen, *Communication, Action, and Meaning,* p. 174.

52. This example is adapted from Pearce and Cronen, *Communication, Action, and Meaning,* pp. 162–164. Originally, the example was developed in K. T. Alvy, "The Development of Listener-Adapted Communication in Grade-School Children from Different Social Class Backgrounds," *Genetic Psychology Monographs* 87 (1973): 33–104.

53. This theory is detailed in her book. See Fern L. Johnson, *Speaking Culturally: Language Diversity in the United States* (Thousand Oaks, CA: Sage, 2000).

54. Sonja K. Foss and Cindy L. Griffin, "Beyond Persuasion: A Proposal for an Invitational Rhetoric," *Communication Monographs* 62 (March 1995): 2–18.

55. These ideas are elaborated in Foss and Foss, *Inviting Transformation: Presentational Speaking for a Changing World,* 2nd ed. (Prospect Heights, IL: Waveland, 2003), pp. 10–14.

56. Foss and Foss, *Inviting Transformation.*

57. Foss and Foss, *Inviting Transformation,* p. 5.

58. Deborah Tannen, *The Argument Culture: Stopping America's War of Words* (New York: Ballantine, 1998), p. 3.

59. For an explanation of these conditions, see Foss and Foss, *Inviting Transformation,* pp. 36–39.

60. For an elaboration of this point, see Curtis D. LeBaron, Jenny Mandelbaum, and Phillip J. Glenn, "An Overview of Language and Social Interaction Research," in *Studies in Language and Social Interaction in Honor of Robert Hopper,* ed. P. J. Glenn, C. D. LeBaron, and J. Mandelbaum (Mahwah, NJ: Lawrence Erlbaum, 2003), pp. 1–44.

61. Michael Sunnafrank, "Predicted Outcome Value During Initial Interactions," *Human Communication Research* 13 (1986): 3–33; and Michael Sunnafrank, "Predicted Outcome Value and Uncertainty Re-

duction Theories: A Test of Competing Perspectives," *Human Communication Research* 17 (1990): 76–103.

62. LeBaron, Mandelbaum, and Glenn, "An Overview of Language," p. 9.

63. Hartmut B. Mokros and Mark Aakhus, "From Information-Seeking Behavior to Meaning Engagement Practice: Implications for Communication Theory and Research," *Human Communication Research* 28 (2002): 298–312.

64. LeBaron, Mandelbaum and Glenn, "An Overview of Language," p. 8.

65. Karen Tracy identifies several strands of discourse analysis in the communication field in "Discourse Analysis in Communication," in *Handbook of Discourse Analysis,* ed. Deborah Schiffrin, Deborah Tannen, and Heidi Hamilton (Oxford, UK: Blackwell, 2001). For other approaches, see Glenn F. Stillar, *Analyzing Everyday Texts: Discourse, Rhetoric, and Social Processes* (Thousand Oaks, CA: Sage, 1998); Moira Chimombo, and Robert L. Roseberry, *The Power of Discourse: An Introduction to Discourse Analysis* (Mahwah, NJ: Lawrence Erlbaum, 1998); Potter and Wetherell, *Discourse and Social Psychology*, pp. 6–7.

66. For overviews of this subject, see Ellis, *From Language to Communication;* Scott Jacobs, "Language and Interpersonal Communication," in *Handbook of Interpersonal Communication,* ed. Mark L. Knapp and Gerald R. Miller (Thousand Oaks, CA: Sage, 1994), pp. 199–228; Donald G. Ellis and William A. Donohue, eds., *Contemporary Issues in Language and Discourse Processes* (Hillsdale, NJ: Lawrence Erlbaum, 1986).

67. Jacobs, "Language and Interpersonal Communication."

68. Susan B. Shimanoff, *Communication Rules: Theory and Research* (Beverly Hills, CA: Sage, 1980), pp. 31–32.

69. Shimanoff, in *Communication Rules,* pp. 31–88, lists some of the major scholars who have studied rules as well as a variety of definitions and explanations of rules. See also Donald P. Cushman, "The Rules Perspective as a Theoretical Basis for the Study of Human Communication," *Communication Quarterly* 25 (1977): 30–45; W. Barnett Pearce, "Rules Theories of Communication: Varieties, Limitations, and Potentials" (paper delivered at the meeting of the Speech Communication Association, New York, 1980); Stuart J. Sigman, "On Communication Rules from a Social Perspective," *Human Communication Research* 7 (1980): 37–51; and Donald Cushman, "The Rules Approach to Communication Theory: A Philosophical and Operational Perspective," in *Communication Theory: Eastern and Western Perspectives,* ed. D. L. Kincaid (San Diego: Academic, 1987), pp. 223–234.

THE RELATIONSHIP

Conversations are rarely isolated. Instead, they are connected to one another over time and create communication contexts much larger than any one conversation. In the following chapters of this book, we explore these larger contexts, including relationships, groups, organizations, media, culture, and society. These contexts are more than containers in which conversations happen. Instead, they are the patterns, connections, and institutions that "get made" in conversations. In a circular way, these contexts then affect and shape the conversations that are part of them.

We have taught communication courses for over thirty years. Of all the topics we have covered in our classes, relationships immediately capture the interest of students. People are fascinated with relationships because they differ greatly—some relationships are easy and comfortable and others are hard and seemingly contorted. We are fascinated, too, because relationships change and evolve, often dramatically, and such changes have the ability to affect families, friends, and romantic relationships in significant ways. Finally, relationships can be problematic, and studying about them can be a way of trying to find answers to their problematic aspects. The topic of relationships, then, is highly relevant to all of us, and it is not surprising that it has occupied a great deal of time and attention from communication scholars.

The communication field has been powerful in helping us to understand relational differences and relational change. With a communication lens, we see that relationships are comprised of *interactional patterns*—a back-and-forth set of responsive

Topics Addressed	Cybernetic Theories	Sociopsychosocial Theories	Sociocultural Theories	Phenomenological Theories
Interaction patterns	Relational patterns of interaction			
Schemas and types		Relational schemas in the family		
Disclosure and privacy		Social penetration theory		
Managing difference			Bakhtin's theory of dialogics Dialectical theory Communication privacy theory	
Dialogue				Carl Rogers Martin Buber

behaviors that are extremely dynamic. In long-term relationships, the patterns can become relatively stable over time, but events can also project the flux and flow of a relationship into new and sometimes unexpected directions. The theories in this chapter help us understand this dynamic process.

How would you characterize some of the significant relationships you have had in your life? Which have been intimate? Which have been casual? In which relationships have you been a dominant influence, and when have others taken a more dominant role with you? Which relationships have been more egalitarian? Several researchers have been interested in looking at the different *qualities* of relationships, and such qualities are often tied to particular ways of thinking about relationships, or *schemas*, that seem to govern stabilized patterns of relationships over time.

We must constantly decide how much information about ourselves to share with others. Sometimes you really feel like sharing something private with a friend and other times you feel more guarded. In some relationships, you share a lot of information about yourself, and in others, you do not. Even more interesting is the fact that over time within a single relationship, you negotiate what topics you can talk about and what levels of information can be revealed, not only between yourselves, but also with others outside the relationship. The topics of *disclosure* and *privacy* have been extremely interesting to theorists in communication.

But disclosure and privacy are really a manifestation of something larger. A constant challenge within any relationship is *managing difference*. The tension between disclosure and privacy is only one example of a difference we have to manage effectively in relationships. Many opposing forces impact our relationships, and it is no small task to deal with these. We often feel confused about whether we should be dependent or independent, whether we should keep things the way they are or change them, and whether we should be an individual or be part of a couple. How do you present yourself authentically in a relationship so that others are authentic with you? How can we allow for both difference and unity? An important body of theory is developing within the field to explain (1) how relationships are defined through the management of contradictions like these; and (2) ways in which communicators within a relationship actually manage these kinds of tensions.

Relationships have been an important subject related to interpersonal communication since the 1960s.[1] In this chapter, we include significant theories from four traditions—the cybernetic, the sociopsychological, the sociocultural, and the phenomenological. In combination, these theories help us understand relationships from many perspectives. The chapter map on the previous page outlines the theories in this chapter and helps to clarify the traditions from which they emerge and the topics they address.

◖● THE CYBERNETIC TRADITION

The cybernetic tradition has had a vital impact on how communication scholars think about relationships. Relationships are not static entities that never change. Instead, they consist of cybernetic patterns of interaction in which individuals' words and actions affect how others respond. We keep adapting what we do and say to the reactions of others, and over time the relationship develops a kind of character. Another way of thinking about this—using strictly cybernetic terms—is that we continually adapt our behaviors to the feedback from others, and in a relationships, both parties are doing this simultaneously.

Relational Patterns of Interaction

This idea about relationship was greatly influenced by the work of Gregory Bateson, Paul Watzlawick, and their colleagues in the early years of the study of interpersonal communication. Known as the Palo Alto Group, these theorists founded the Mental Research Institute based in Palo Alto, California. Their ideas are most clearly laid out in the now-classic *Pragmatics of Human Communication*.[2] In this book, Paul Watzlawick, Janet Beavin, and Don Jackson present an analysis of communication from a cybernetic perspective. We do not summarize their entire theory here, but present the basic idea of relational interaction, which illustrates the importance of the cybernetic tradition in much of the work in relationships over the past thirty-five years.

We learned from the Palo Alto Group that when two people communicate with each other—in addition to whatever else they may be doing—they are defining their relationship by the way in which they interact.[3] As you talk with a friend, a co-worker, a professor, or a family member, you are always creating a set of expectations for your own and the other person's behavior. Sometimes you reinforce old expectations and at other times, you engage in new patterns of interaction that may establish new expectations for future interactions.

In a marriage, for example, a dominant-submissive relationship might come into being over time. Communication between co-workers might result in a status hierarchy, in which one person is more highly esteemed than the other. The interaction between neighbors might turn out to be an equal-and-polite relationship. Implicit rules are numerous in any ongoing relationship, be it a friendship, business partnership, love affair, family, or any other type, and these can change as interaction patterns change.

Patterns get established, in part because any behavior is potentially communicative.[4] In other words, when you are in the presence of other people, you are always expressing something about your relationship with the other person, whether you are conscious of it or not.[5] This axiom holds, even if you don't want to interact with the other person, because, at least potentially, the other individual may "read" your avoidance as a statement.

For example, when your professor announces an upcoming test, many possible relationship messages might be inferred at the same time. She could be saying, "I am the authority in this classroom"; "I teach, you learn—what I have lectured about is important"; "I need feedback on your progress"; "I have a need to judge you"; or "I want you to think I am fulfilling my role as professor." Of course, students' responses also include a relationship dimension, which might express compliance, defiance, respect, fear, equality, or other messages. In communicating about tests and all other topics, the teacher and student constantly define and redefine the nature of their relationship.

Suppose a father at a playground sees his daughter fall and scrape her knee. Immediately, he says, "Don't cry. Daddy is coming." The content meaning is clear, but what is the relationship message? It depends on how the message is delivered. The father might communicate his own fear, worry, anger, boredom, or dominance. At the same time, he might communicate a number of possible perceptions, including, "You are careless," "You are an attention getter," "It was just an accident," and so on. When it comes to relationships, then, actions can speak louder than words. The basic unit of relationship is not the person nor two individuals but interaction—behaviors responding to other behaviors. Over time, the nature of the relationship is formed, or made, through a series of interactions—responses to responses to responses.

Two kinds of patterns important to the Palo Alto Group illustrate this idea. If two people keep responding to one another the same way, they are said to be involved in a *symmetrical relationship.* Power struggles are exactly this: One partner asserts control, the other responds by asserting control back. The first responds again in kind, and a struggle ensues. Symmetrical relationships are not always power struggles, however. Both partners might respond passively, both could respond in a questioning way, or both might behave in ways that seem nurturing.

The second type of relationship is *complementary.* In these relationships, communicators respond in opposing ways. When one is domineering, the other is submissive; when one is argumentative, the other is quiet; when one is nurturing, the other is rejecting. Since the Palo Alto Group took a mental-health perspective, these practitioners were especially interested in distinguishing pathological patterns from healthy ones.

To further elaborate the general idea of relational patterns of interaction and the more specific concepts of symmetrical and complementary relationships, we turn now to a study of *relational control.* The investigations of L. Edna Rogers and Frank Millar demonstrate how control in a relationship is a cybernetic process.[6] They found that control could not be defined by one person's behavior. In other words, the control within a relationship does not depend upon any one person's actions or even the individuals' personalities.

Instead, you have to look at the pattern of behavior between partners over time—how they respond to one another cybernetically. When one person makes an assertion, the other person can respond in one of three ways. He or she can accept the assertion, which is a *one-down* move. He or she can make a counter assertion, or reject the first person's move—a *one-up* response. The third kind of response is a *one-across* move, which neither accepts nor rejects the first person's bid for control.

A *complementary exchange* occurs when one partner asserts a one-up message and the other responds one-down. When this kind of interaction predominates in a relationship, we can say that the relationship itself is complementary. The individual whose one-up message predominates at a given time is said to be *dominant.* Notice the difference here between "dominance" and "domineeringness." A one-up move is domineering, but it is not dominant unless the other person accepts it by behaving in a one-down fashion. A *symmetrical exchange* involves both partners responding the same way—either one-up/one-up, one-down/one-down, one-across/one-across.

Table 7.1 illustrates nine control states generated by combinations of these types of control messages.[7] Although control is only one of the aspects of a relationship, it does show clearly how relationships come to be defined over time cybernetically through patterns of interaction.

◖ REFLECTIONS ON
The Cybernetic Tradition

The cybernetic tradition has been very important in the field of relational communication. Indeed, the idea that relationships are formed systemically by interaction patterns across time has been the mainstay of our ideas about what relationships are, how they form, how they are maintained, and how they change. Significant in this foundational work is that relationships are defined as a system of interactions that over time create something larger than any one person or institution.

To get more insight into what gets "worked out" in these patterns of interaction, we summarize two examples of this type of theory in the following section. Notice the difference in emphasis from cybernetic patterns to types and to individual actions as we move now into the sociopsychological tradition.

• • •

TABLE **7.1**

Control Configurations

Control direction of speaker A's message	Control direction of speaker B's message		
	One-up (↑)	One-down (↓)	One-across (→)
One-up (↑)	1.(↑↑) Competitive symmetry	4. (↑↓) Complementarity	7. (↑→) Transition
One-down (↓)	2. (↓↑) Complementarity	5. (↓↓) Submissive symmetry	8. (↓→) Transition
One-across (→)	3. (→↑) Transition	6. (→↓) Transition	9. (→→) Neutralized symmetry

Control Pattern Examples

1. Competitive symmetry (one-up/one-up):
   A: You know I want you to keep the house picked up during the day.
   B: I want you to help sometimes.

2. Complementarity (one-down/one-up):
   A: Please help. I need you.
   B: Sure, I know how.

3. Transition (one-across/one-up):
   A: Let's compromise.
   B: No, my way is best.

4. Complementarity (one-up/one-down):
   A: Let's get out of town this weekend.
   B: Okay.

5. Submissive symmetry (one-down/one-down):
   A: I'm so tired. What should we do?
   B: I can't decide. You decide.

6. Transition (one-across/one-down):
   A: My Dad was pretty talkative tonight.
   B: You're right; he sure was.

7. Transition (one-up/one-across):
   A: I definitely think we should have more kids.
   B: Lots of people seem to be having kids these days.

8. Transition (one-down/one-across):
   A: Please help me. What can I do?
   B: I don't know.

9. Neutralized symmetry (one-across/one-across):
   A: The neighbor's house needs paint.
   B: The windows are dirty too.

◖ THE SOCIOPSYCHOLOGICAL TRADITION

Interpersonal behavior has been a mainstay within the field of social psychology, and a great deal of research in the field of communication is influenced by this tradition. The work in the sociopsychological tradition relies heavily on typing and characterizing individuals and relationships. It relies on measurement and analysis of variables as a way of assessing what people are like within a relationship as well as what the relationship itself is like. Here we look at two lines of work—family schemas and social penetration.

Relational Schemas in the Family

For many years, Mary Anne Fitzpatrick and her colleagues have been developing a line of research and theory on family relationships.[8] More recently, Ascan Koerner and Mary Anne Fitzpatrick have expanded this work to encompass the entire family.[9] The resulting theory provides a set of terms that describe different family types and explain the differences among them.

As a sociopsychological theory, this work bases family types on the ways in which family members as individuals think about families. Following the lead of psychological theory in this area, Koerner and Fitzpatrick refer to these ways of thinking as *schemas,* or more specifically, *relational schemas.*[10] Your relational schemas consist of your knowledge about yourself, others, and relationships you have known, along with knowledge about how to interact in relationships. This knowledge provides an image of relationships based on your own experience and guides your behavior within relationships. A schema is an organized set of memories that you make use of whenever you interact with other people. Since everyone has different experiences, his or her schemas will be somewhat different.

Your relational schemas are organized into levels from general to specific, including knowledge about social relationships in general, knowledge of types of relationships, and knowledge of specific relationships. Your family schema, therefore, includes (1) what you know about relationships in general; (2) what you know about family relationships as a type; and (3) what you know about your relationship with other members of your own family.

Your interaction with other members of your family at any given time will be directed first by your specific schema, then by your family schema and then by your general schema. In other words, when you and your brother interact, you will rely first on your knowledge of this particular relationship. If, for some reason, that doesn't work you will fall back on your general knowledge of how family members should behave. If that fails, you will rely as a last resort on your knowledge of relationships in general.

Suppose, for example, that during childhood your brother was your close companion, and your behavior together relied on this specific schema of companionship, a schema that consists of a lot of shared experiences between you and your brother. Imagine, however, that your brother goes off to college comes back for the summer a changed person. You fully expect to hang out with him all the time, but he actually pays little attention to you. In other words, your previous schema does not work any more, and you must think of new ways of interacting. You are most likely to make decisions about how to respond based on your schema for families in general, so you may decide to take on more of a "distant sibling" relationship similar to what you have seen in other families.

Continuing the example above, perhaps your brother gets married and moves overseas, and you have little opportunity to interact. Years later, he comes to town for a family reunion but you really don't know how to respond to him since you feel that you hardly know him any more. You may just follow general rules of social etiquette such as hospitality and politeness—at least until a new relationship is negotiated.

According to these theorists, family communication, then, is not random, but highly patterned based on particular schemas that determine how the family members communicate with one another. These schemas consist of knowledge about (1) how intimate the family is; (2) the degree of individuality within the family; and (3) factors external to the family, such as friends, geographical distance, work, and other concerns outside the family unit.

In addition to this kind of content knowledge, a family's schema will include a certain kind of orientation to communication. Two kinds predominate: The first is *conversation orientation,* and the second, *conformity orientation.* These are variables, so families differ in how much conversation and conformity orientations the family schema includes. Families that have a high-conversation schema like to talk; in contrast, families with a low-conversation schema do not spend much time talking. Families with a high-conformity schema, tend to go along with family authorities such as the parents, while families low in this variable, expect more individuality. Your family's communication pattern will depend on where your schema fits within these two types of orientation.

Various schema create different family types. Fitzpatrick and her colleagues have identified four types: (1) consensual; (2) pluralistic; (3) protective; and (4) laissez-faire. Each of these families has certain types of parents, determined by the ways in which they use their space, time, and energy and the degree to which they express their feelings, exert power, and share a common philosophy of marriage.[11] The marriage types are (1) traditional; (2) independent; and (3) separate, each of which function in very different ways.

The first type of family is *consensual.* Such families are high in both conversation and conformity. Consensual families have a lot of talk, but the family authority—usually a parent—makes decisions. These families experience the tension of valuing open communication while also wanting clear parental authority. Parents typically listen well to their children, but make the decisions and then explain these to the children in an effort to help the children understand the reasoning behind the decisions.

Parents in consensual families tend to be *traditional* in marital orientation. This means that they will tend to be conventional in their views of marriage and place more value on stability and certainty in role relations than on variety and spontaneity. They have strong interdependence and share much companionship. Although they are not assertive about disagreements, they do not avoid conflict. According to Fitzpatrick and her colleagues, a traditional wife would take her husband's name, both members of the couple would have strong feelings about infidelity in the relationship, and they would share much time and space. They would try to work out a standard time schedule and spend as much time together as possible, and they probably would not have separate rooms for their own activities.

The research data suggest that there is not too much conflict in a traditional marriage because power and decision making are distributed according to customary norms. Husbands, for example, may be in charge of certain kinds of decisions and wives in charge of others. Consequently, there is little need to negotiate and resolve conflict in these marriages. At the same time, there is little impetus for change and growth in the relationship. A traditional couple can be assertive with each other when necessary, but each person tends to support his or her requests with appeals to the relationship rather than by refuting each other's arguments. Traditional couples are highly expressive and disclose both joy and frustration, which probably explains why they value open communication and produce consensual families.

Now to the second family type: If your family is high in conversation, but low in conformity, it will display characteristics of the *pluralistic* type. Here you will have lots of unrestrained conversation, but everyone will decide for themselves in the end what actions to take on the basis of that talk. Parents do not feel the need to control the children; instead, opinions are evaluated on the basis of merit, and everyone participates in family decision-making.

The parents of pluralistic families tend to be typed in this theory as *independent*, as they usually are unconventional in their views of marriage. As independents, the husband and wife do not rely on each other very much and tend to produce independent-thinking children. Although these types of parents may spend time together and share a great deal, they value their own autonomy and often have separate rooms in the house for their own activities—they both might have studies of their own, or one might have a woodworking shop and the other a sewing room. They may also have separate interests and friends outside the family.

Because they do not rely on conventional roles, independent marriages are constantly renegotiated. There is much conflict in a typical independent marriage, and partners often vie for power, use a variety of persuasive techniques, and are not reluctant to refute each other's arguments. Like the traditionals, the independents are also expressive. They respond to each other's nonverbal cues, and they usually understand each other well, which explains why they value open communication.

The third type of family is *protective*. If your family tends to be low in conversation, but high in conformity, there is a lot of obedience but little communication. Parents in these types of families do not see why they should spend a lot of time talking things through, nor do they owe the children an explanation for what they decide. For this reason, such parents tend to be typed as *separates*. These individuals seem to be ambivalent about their roles and relationship. They may have a conventional view of marriage, but they are not very interdependent and do not share much. Fitzpatrick refers to separates as "emotionally divorced." They have their opinions and can be contentious, but conflicts never last long because separates are quick to retreat from conflict. Actually, they do not seem able to coordinate their actions long enough to sustain a conflict. Their attempts to gain compliance rarely use relationship appeals and often mention the bad things that will happen if the spouse does not comply. Couples of this type have a watchful attitude. They ask many questions but offer little advice. Predictably, then, they are not very expressive, and they do not understand their partners' emotions very well.

Finally, if you are low in both conversation and conformity, then your family is *laissez-faire*—hands-off and low involvement. Members of this family type really don't care much what other members of the family do, and they certainly don't want to waste time talking about it. The parents in such families tend to be mixed in orientation, meaning that they do not have the same schema from which they are operating. They may be a combination of separate and independent or some other combination. Actually, mixed marital types are quite common. About 40 percent of the couples Fitzpatrick tested display some combination of types—separate-traditional, traditional-independent, or independent-separate. The characterization of mixed types is naturally more complex.

Are all of these forms of communication and marriage types equally positive? Fitzpatrick now believes that they are not. Although different family patterns work well for different people, mixed and laissez-faire families probably tend to be dysfunctional. A strong implication of this theory is that families differ in terms of togetherness and separateness. The following theory was instrumental in helping communication theorists think about how relationships move from distant to close; thus it extends our understanding of families and relationships.

Social Penetration Theory

Self-disclosure was an important theme in communication theory in the 1960s and 1970s.[12] *Social penetration* came to identify the process of increasing disclosure and intimacy within a relationship and represents a formative theory in the intellectual history of relationship theory. Spurred by the work of Irwin Altman and Dalmas Taylor, social penetration theory set in motion a long tradition of investigation into relational development.[13] Most of the early investigators of social penetration focused on individual behavior and motivation, planting this work firmly within the sociopsychological tradition. Today, we realize that relationship development is governed by a complex set of forces that participants must manage over time. For the most part, these more sophisticated ways of looking at relationship development arose from within the sociocultural and phenomenological traditions, as we will see later in the chapter.

To begin to explain social penetration, imagine yourself as a sphere. Within this ball is contained everything that might be known about you—your experiences, knowledge, attitudes, ideas, thoughts, and deeds. The information that is contained in this sphere, however, is not a jumble, but is highly organized around a core. Those things that are close to your center are farthest from the outside, farthest from what others can see or detect. These are the most private aspects of your self. As you move toward the outside of the sphere, this information is closer to what other people can see and less central to your inner core. The "skin" of the sphere is what people can easily detect—how you dress, your outward behavior, what you carry around for anyone to see.

This metaphor is not far from the image of the individual espoused in early social penetration theory. According to the theory, you get to know another person by "penetrating" his or her sphere. The sphere contains both breadth and depth. You could learn many different kinds of things about another person (breadth), or you could learn increasingly detailed information about one or two things (depth). As the relationship between two individuals develops, the partners share more aspects of the self, adding both depth and breadth to what they know about one another.

Altman and Taylor's original theory was based on one of the most popular ideas in the sociopsychological tradition—the economic proposition that human beings make decisions based on costs and rewards. In other words, if something will be very costly, you will think twice before you do it. If the results could be very rewarding, you may go ahead, despite the costs. Every decision is a balance between costs and rewards. When we apply this principle to human interaction, we are looking at a process known as *social exchange.*[14]

Within social exchange theory, human interaction is like an economic transaction: You seek to maximize rewards and minimize costs. Applied to social penetration, you will reveal information about yourself when the cost-rewards ratio is acceptable to you. According to Altman and Taylor, then, relational partners not only assess the rewards and costs of the relationship at a given moment but also use the information they have gathered to predict the rewards and costs in the future. Slowly, as long as rewards continue to outweigh costs, a couple will become increasingly intimate by sharing more and more personal information.

Altman and Taylor suggested four stages of relational development: (1) orientation; (2) exploratory affective exchange; (3) affective exchange; and (4) stable exchange. *Orientation* consists of impersonal communication, in which one discloses only very public information. If this stage is rewarding to the participants, they will move to the next stage, the *exploratory affective exchange,* in which movement to a deeper level of disclosure takes place. The third stage, *affective exchange,* centers on evaluative and critical feelings at a deeper level. This stage will not be en-

tered unless the partners perceive substantial rewards relative to costs in earlier stages. Finally, *stable exchange* is highly intimate and allows the partners to predict each other's actions and responses very well. Using romantic couples as one example, early dating would illustrate the orientation stage, later dating would probably be exploratory exchange, full affective exchange would happen once the couple becomes exclusive and begins to plan a future together, and marriage is like stable exchange.

Original social penetration theory was important in focusing our attention on relationship development as a communication process; however, it did not hold up very well to the actual experience of relationships in daily life. The idea that you move increasingly from public to private in a linear fashion now seems naive. We know from experience that relationships develop in a variety of ways, often moving back and forth from sharing to privacy. Today's theory is more consistent with the experience that social penetration is a cyclical, dialectical process.[15] It is cyclical because it proceeds in back-and-forth cycles, and it is dialectical because it involves the management of the never-ending tension between the public and the private.

In their later writings, Altman and his colleagues recognized this limitation and revised social penetration theory to provide a more complex notion of relational development.[16] More than a linear progression from privacy to openness, relationship development came to be seen as involving cycles of stability and change as a couple manages its contradictory needs for predictability and flexibility.

A couple's cycle of openness and closedness possesses a certain regularity or predictable rhythm. In more developed relationships, the cycle is longer than in less developed relationships. This is because, consistent with the basic tenet of social penetration theory, developed relationships have on average more disclosure than do less developed ones. In addition, as relationships develop, partners become more able to coordinate the cycle of disclosure. Their timing and extent of disclosure are more likely to be synchronized.

To test this idea, C. Arthur VanLear paired students into dyads.[17] Each couple met to talk for one-half hour per week for five weeks, and their conversations were tape recorded. These tapes were then examined statistically for cyclical patterns. The analysis indicated that cycles of openness did occur in these conversations as well as some synchronization, suggesting that such cycles can be established even in very new relationships.

To compare these results with real, ongoing relationships, another group of students was asked to monitor their conversations with another person with whom they were having a relationship (such as a spouse, friend, or romantic partner) for ten weeks. After each conversation of at least fifteen minutes, they filled out a "conversation monitoring form" that asked about satisfaction and perceived openness/closedness. The results of this study mirrored those of the first study. Both studies indicated that cycles do occur, that these are complex, that the partners recognize their cycles, and that matching and synchronization often occur. Important to note, however, is the finding that the amount of synchrony is not the same for each couple, which means that there are differences between couples in their ability to coordinate self-disclosure cycles.

In contrast to the sociopsychological theories in the current section, sociocultural theories, presented in the following section, have explored and expanded the idea of managing tensions in relationships, bringing cultural factors to bear. We begin the following section by looking at a current theory that elaborates on the role of communication in managing the tension between the need for sharing and the need for privacy.

REFLECTIONS ON
The Sociopsychological Tradition

As psychologists, Altman and Taylor used a common frame from their field for understanding interpersonal behavior, noticing that individuals weigh costs and re-

wards in deciding how to act. Increasing intimacy, then, is a process of judging whether increasingly personal communication will be worth it or not. Intriguing as this hypothesis has been, Altman and Taylor themselves came to see its limitations and developed a much more cybernetic view of social penetration. As a result, their theory really cuts across the sociopsychological and the cybernetic.

We have also included the work on family schemas and types as part of the sociopsychological tradition. We do so for two reasons. One is the tendency, easily learned in psychology, of defining traits or types. Additionally, Fitzpatrick and her colleagues explain typing in terms of individual cognitive schemas, or ways of thinking about relationships. Notice now, as we move to the sociocultural tradition, that there is much more of an emphasis on how meanings are constructed and how relationships actually are managed in interactional processes.

• • •

THE SOCIOCULTURAL TRADITION

As we move from sociopsychological theories to sociocultural ones, we see a dramatic shift from an emphasis on individuals to an emphasis on interaction and from a focus on typology to process explanations. First we will look at a general theory that shows how relationships integrate a mix of diverse "voices" that pull and push the relationship over time. This is called *dialogical theory*. Next, we look more specifically at how the tensions created by these voices are managed through communication in what is called *dialectical theory*. Finally, continuing the analysis of the previous section, we show how the flow of relationships actually affects the management of disclosure and privacy.

Bakhtin's Theory of Dialogics

Mikhail Bakhtin was a Russian philosopher and teacher whose work was discovered by scholars in the 1960s. Much of his work is now republished and translated, making it available to the larger academic community. Bakhtin's work actually constitutes a cross-over theory, since it contributes to both the sociocultural and critical traditions. We decided to include it in the sociocultural because it offers a useful foundation to the other sociocultural theories detailed here.

Bakhtin's notion of dialogue is very much a theory about relationships with strong cultural implications as well. Bakhtin begins with the notion of everyday reality—what he calls the *prosaic*—which simply refers to the ordinary, taken-for-granted, familiar world—eating, sleeping, walking, talking. Bakhtin sees the everyday sphere as one of constant activity and creativity and the starting point for change of any kind. These changes occur very slowly, so slowly they often cannot be observed until after the fact, but nonetheless, this is the realm where critical decisions are made.[18] Accumulated decisions about what to wear, where to go, what to eat, and how to organize your work on a given day end up having enormous impact on your life. The big issues—social norms, values, standards, and systems—are actually built up over time from these small microbehaviors. In everyday mundane life—the prosaic—we face all kinds of competing influences that push and pull us in many directions, and these forces are not trivial.

Bakhtin identifies two general kinds of forces that impact everyday life—centripetal and centrifugal.[19] *Centripetal forces* seek to impose order on the apparent chaos of life, while *centrifugal forces* disrupt that order. You can see the analogy from physics, as centripetal forces such as gravity pull objects together into a center, while centrifugal forces like rotation pull objects away from each other. When a rocket takes off into space, gravity wants to pull it back to earth, but at a certain point, the force of the trajectory of the rocket starts to pull it away from the earth.

Social life is like this. Just when you think you have something, it gets pulled away. Just when you think things are nicely organized, something happens to remind you that life is not tidy. Some forces, then, support the existing order, while others, by chance or design, work in ways that ultimately produce changes in the fabric of daily life by giving events new meanings.

The constant presence of disorder in the form of centrifugal forces is what intrigues Bakhtin; he is interested in how individuals, cultures, and even language itself construct an integrated whole when there are so many things operating that work against a sense of order. Language illustrates this dance very well. In the United States, we learned that it was not politically correct to call African Americans *colored people*—the label used until the 1960s, but in recent years, the term *people of color* has come into fashion. Many members of earlier generations have difficulty understanding the differences between these two sets of labels. Similarly, earlier generations learned to avoid the use of the term *queer* to refer to gay men and lesbians because of its derogatory meanings but now are confronted with a scholarly body of work in the academy known as *queer theory*. Language becomes a medium for both centripetal and centrifugal forces. We are thrown off when meanings migrate, but we use language itself to help us re-establish order.

Questions of identity are especially central to social life. Who am I? Who are we? What is the nature of our relationship? Centripetal and centrifugal forces embedded in everyday situations require that we answer these questions differently, almost from moment to moment. It is fascinating to see how people use communication to form order in the face of change.

If you realize that everyday life requires a constant effort to reintegrate diverse forces, you are assuming a certain kind of responsibility by fully engaging the obligations of each situation that presents itself. Many people refuse to do this. What Bakhtin calls *pretenders*, these people avoid the effort of defining their identity by living according to abstract norms; they live "representatively" and "ritualistically" by a set of standards that ignore the need for constant reintegration. Instead, Bakhtin calls for a way of life that confronts the particulars of everyday life and forces the development of an appropriate individual ethic based on who you are within the situation at any given moment. In Bakhtin's words, "There is no alibi for being."[20]

Bakhtin's focus on the prosaic leads to a second important aspect of his theory—*unfinalizability*.

Bakhtin believes that the world is not only messy and chaotic but genuinely open and free—nothing is yet decided. In the process of interacting in the world, we influence the future and emerge "along with the world."[21] There is not, then, a static world that we enter; rather, we help construct all of the events and contexts that make the world a complex one of multiple voices or a *heteroglossia*, meaning "many voices." This idea helps us to understand why identity is constantly evolving. In the 1950s, black people referred to themselves as *Negroes*, in the 1960s and 1970s it was *black*, and in the 1980s *African American*. Today, some Americans of African descent object to all of these terms, preferring some entirely different identity that better characterizes who they are as individuals.[22]

Against the context of everydayness, unfinalizability, and heteroglossia is Bakhtin's notion of *dialogue*. Bakhtin used this word in several ways throughout his writing, but scholars generally agree that it refers to a particular kind of interaction.[23] Just as Bakhtin prefers to engage the world in its specificity rather than its abstraction, so dialogue is about how we interact in specific interactions. There is no "general language," spoken by a general voice, divorced from what that voice is saying. There is always somebody talking to somebody else, even when you are talking to yourself. Dialogue, then, is something that happens within a specific situation among specific participants, like a discussion in your communication theory class.

At the heart of his conception of dialogue is the *utterance*—a unit of exchange, spoken or written, between two people. Unlike a sentence taken out of context, an utterance refers to language spoken in context. An utterance contains a theme—the content of the conversation, the communicator's attitude toward that subject, and some degree of responsiveness on the part of the person being addressed. The communicator, then, expresses an idea and makes an evaluation about it, anticipating some kind of response from the person addressed. The speaker not only anticipates the viewpoint of the other and adapts his or her communication on the basis of that an-

ticipation; the addressee also participates literally by responding, evaluating, and initiating utterances of their own. Dialogue, then, is a complex web of interrelations with others. What you say as part of a class discussion must always be understood as part of an ongoing conversation with the other students in the class, both within and outside of the classroom. Those interactions can only be understood as part of something even larger. Bakhtin explains:

> The living utterance, having taken meaning and shape at a particular historical moment in a socially specific environment cannot fail to brush up against thousands of living dialogic threads, woven by socio-ideological consciousness around the given object of an utterance; it cannot fail to become an active participant in social dialogue.[24]

Dialogue represents a contextualized, ongoing, and evolving subject matter that contributes to the constant redefinition of the participants in the dialogue as well. The products and potentials of dialogue are endless; "the final word has not yet been spoken and never will be spoken."[25] The process of dialogue, then, is multiply enriching; it is a process in which each side learns about self and the other. Dialogue, then, "not only discovers but activates potentials."[26] Each participant in dialogue is open to the possibilities that may be suggested by the other, each is enriched by the dialogue, and each is a cocreator of the future that is being created in the interaction, a future that is ever changing as the interaction changes.

Bakhtin contrasts dialogue with *monologue* (he sometimes uses the term *finalization* as another word for monologue). This occurs when an interaction becomes static, closed, dead. The potential implicit in everyday engagement with particulars is lost in abstraction, generalization, and a failure to engage the moment because the multiple voices are lost, the themes become dogmatic, and there is no mutual enrichment between the parties.[27] Habitual ways of thinking and acting can produce such monologues, devoid of reference to context, but these, too, can be transcended. Bakhtin essentially envisioned all life as an ongoing, unfinalizable dialogue, possible at every moment of existence: "To live means to participate in dialogue: to ask questions, to heed, to respond, to agree, and so forth. In this dialogue a person participates wholly and throughout his whole life: with his eyes, lips, hands, soul, spirit, with his whole body and deeds. He invests his entire self in discourse, and this discourse enters into the dialogic fabric of human life, into the world symposium."[28]

Dialogue also shapes cultures, because every dialogic interaction is a viewing of each culture from the standpoint of the other. We negotiate our understanding in interaction with another, testing our views, our understandings, our standpoints against those of others we encounter. Culturally, your grandparents may have negotiated their identity in terms of the language of the white culture and called themselves *Negroes*. Your parents may have negotiated an identity based on pride of community color and called themselves *black*. Later, they may have evolved their sense of self to a pan-world identity and changed their label to *African American*. Who am I? Who are we? What is the nature of our relationship? All of these issues are continually negotiated in the dialogues of everyday life.

Bakhtin's ideas have received considerable attention from critical and cultural theorists, interested in understanding processes of negotiation from marginalized places in a culture. Bakhtin is important, then, not only for providing a view of relationship between two individuals as an opening to potentials that may never be realized, but between cultures as well. In the following section, we look at a theory that shows the relevance of Bakhtin's work to our everyday relationships.

A Dialectical Theory of Relationships

For a number of years, Leslie Baxter and her colleagues have been exploring the complex ways in which persons-in-relationship use communication to manage the naturally opposing forces that impinge on their relationship at any given time.[29] Over the years, Baxter has come to see

Bakhtin's dialogics as a way to better understand the flux and flow of relationships. Incorporating many of Bakhtin's concepts, Baxter refers to her theory as a *dialogical* theory of relationships. In other words, relationships are defined through a dialogue among many voices. At the same time, Baxter also characterizes her theory as *dialectical*, meaning that relationships are a place where contradictions are managed.

Before we see how Baxter uses them, let's look more closely at these two terms—*dialogue* and *dialectic*. *Dialectic* refers to a tension between opposing forces within a system. In our lives, we often experience equally compelling "voices" that impinge upon our decision making. For example, you may want to achieve material success, but your humanitarian and environmental values make you question this goal. This contradiction is serious because you realize that in order to achieve humanitarian and environmental goals, you must achieve material success to provide the resources to allow you to have an impact. You may go back and forth about this tension, confused about how to proceed. Perhaps you decide to take a job that allows you to work on environmental issues, or perhaps you have a job that allows you summers off to do the humanitarian work you most value. In the end, you will probably not resolve it, but manage it in any number of creative ways.

Dialectical tensions are seen very easily in larger societal institutions. For example, corporations are sustained by profit, which often exists in tension with the income and job security of workers; yet, the profits that corporations generate enable them to develop and expand, creating jobs and income for the workforce. This is a classic dialectic involving the natural tension between inevitable opposing forces. Baxter and other dialectical communication theorists apply this concept to human relationships.

How does dialogue enter the picture? In general, a *dialogue* is a coming together of diverse voices in a conversation. Instead of saying, "We had a conversation," you might say, "We had a dialogue." In fact, the term is a metaphor from literature and theatre, referring to an interaction between characters. Following from Bakhtin, Baxter sees dialogues as conversations that define and redefine relationships as they emerge in actual situations over time. (Later in this chapter we look at a somewhat different view of dialogue.) When Baxter writes that relationships are both dialogical and dialectical, she means that the natural tensions of relationships are managed through coordinated talk. Let's unpack this idea.

Relationships are dynamic, and communication manages both similarity and difference. Indeed, it draws us together through similarity, while creating, maintaining, and managing areas of difference as well. Using Bakhtin's terminology, relational communication creates centripetal forces that give a sense of order while managing the centrifugal forces that lead to change. This idea of relationships is multidimensional, and in order to really see it, you have to move around and take several perspectives, as you would when looking at a sculpture in a gallery. Baxter provides five vantage points for viewing this process of relational dialogue.

Relationships are made in dialogue. In this first vantage point of Baxter's theory, it is in dialogue that you define your relationships with others. Your ideas about your *self*, the *other*, and the *relationship* are constructed in talk, which happens in several ways. You create moments, often turning points, that you later remember as important. You even retell old stories from the relationship that bring a sense of similarity or shared experience over time. Baxter calls this *chronotopic similarity.* At the same time, you identify differences between yourself and the other person within a relationship, which enables you to set yourself apart and to develop as a person, a concept she calls *self-becoming.* In other words, both similarity and difference are made in the conversations of a relationship over time. This happens in conversations within the relationship and with people outside of it.

Imagine for a moment that you joined your department's tutoring program and are matched up with a freshman looking for help in her basic communication courses. You meet with her a couple times a week for a year to help her organize speeches, prepare for exams, and plan projects—a job you very much enjoy. By talking together about courses and assignments as well as things going on within your personal lives, you create shared moments that you will look back on in the future. She might call you excitedly after the fall semester to let you know that she got an A on a final exam that the two of you worked to prepare for.

At the same time, many differences are accentuated in the tutoring relationship. You are older, more experienced in the major, and more knowledgeable than your new friend. In the tutoring relationship, you come to see what you have accomplished and the directions in which you are going. Even though you and your tutee feel quite close to one another and enjoy the shared moments you create together, each of you also acknowledges and appreciates your different trajectories of life. These points are made even clearer when you talk with your friends about the relationship you have with your tutee. From the first angle, then, you literally make your relationship within dialogue.

Baxter's second vantage point is that *dialogue affords an opportunity to achieve a unity within diversity.* Through dialogue, we manage the dynamic interplay between centrifugal and centripetal forces—those that push us apart and those that pull us together, those that create a sense of chaos and those that provide a feeling of coherence. These opposing forces are dialectical in that they involve a tension between two or more contradictory elements of a system, and relationships provide a context in which we manage *contradictions.*[30]

You can see the influence of cybernetics in this idea. Remember that the cybernetic tradition leads us to see the ways in which counteracting forces in a system create balance and change. Baxter, however, distances her work from the cybernetic, because she does not want to leave the impression that a relationship is a kind of balancing system of forces. Instead, her work more accurately reflects the ideas of social constructionism (Chapter 6)—that we both make and manage the many forces that define or shape a relationship in its development over time. The key here is contradiction.

Although frequently discussed as bipolar opposites such as dependence-independence or stability-change, Baxter and Montgomery feel that bipolar opposites oversimplify the much more complex process of contradiction in which various forces tug at one another. At any moment, certain dominant, or *centripetal*, forces work in opposition to countervailing, or *centrifugal*, ones. Baxter and Montgomery see these as a cluster of forces or a "knot of contradiction."[31]

Each cluster consists of a variety of related contradictions that can occur in relationships.[32] One cluster, for example, is *integration and separation*, or the tension between feeling close and feeling more distant. Whenever you struggle with decisions about whether to support another person or strike out on your own, you are facing this contradiction. A second cluster is *expression-nonexpression*. This is the tension between whether to reveal information or keep it secret. When you are trying to decide whether to tell your partner something and feel reluctant to do so, you are probably experiencing this tension.

A third cluster is *stability-change*, or the tension between being predictable and consistent versus being spontaneous and different. Often couples experience a quandary about whether to keep doing the same old thing or to try new things, and when this happens, they are feeling this particular contradiction. Baxter has put special emphasis here because of the impact of this pair on relationship development. How do you interact in a way that keeps things somewhat predictable and stable while allowing the relationship to change and grow?

Carol Werner and Leslie Baxter write about five qualities that change as relationships develop.[33] These are amplitude, salience, scale, sequence, and pace/rhythm.

1. *Amplitude*—the strength of feelings, behaviors, or both. For example, at certain points in a relationship, you may be very active and have strong feelings about what is going on.

At other times, you may be more laid back or calm.

2. *Salience*—focus on past, present, or future. At some moments in a relationship, you may find yourself concentrating a lot on what happened between you in the past. At other times you may be very centered on what is going on right now; and at other times, you may think mostly about the future, or where the relationship seems to be headed, or where you would like it to be going.

3. *Scale*—how long patterns last. You and your partner may have some rituals that stick for a very long time, or perhaps you find yourselves doing things a certain way for a much shorter period of time.

4. *Sequence*—the order of events in the relationship. As a relationship changes, a variety of things may be undertaken, but they are not always organized the same way for the entire length of the relationship. It is interesting to reflect back on the history of your relationship. Look at how the two of you have organized your time and the actions you do around and with each other. You will probably find that these sequences are different from one moment to another. Some sequences are rather stable and last a long time, while others are short-lived and easily replaced by new patterns of behavior in the relationship.

5. *Pace/Rhythm*—the rapidity of events in the relationship and the interval between events. During certain periods in a relationship, events may occur in a rapid-fire way, with everything seeming to happen quickly. At other times, the pace may be much slower.

At a given time, a relationship will be characterized by some combination of these variables. Tracking the development of a relationship means watching the ways in which the profile changes over time.

To recap, then, dialogue is a process in which centripetal and centrifugal forces are managed over time, thus bringing order and coherence to the relationship, while also allowing for development and change. Now let's view the process from yet another angle.

Dialogue is aesthetic. This is Baxter's third vantage point. Aesthetics involve a sense of balance, of coherence, of form, and of wholeness. The mere fact that you can say that you are having a relationship means that there is some pattern there that, like a portrait, gives the picture identity, uniqueness, and wholeness. You are not only able to name the relationships in which you take part, but you can describe them, characterize them, and tell stories that show what the relationship is like. The character of a relationship is a reflection of its aesthetic, which is created in dialogue.

Thus, although social life is "messy" in many respects, we are able to provide a sense of order through dialogue. Communicators in a relationship can construct a feeling of wholeness and unity, a momentary feeling of completion, an aesthetic through dialogue. This can happen in several ways. You can, for example, create a feeling of temporal continuity, or a sense that what is happening now is logically connected to what happened before. You can also create a feeling of a unified relationship, so that despite your differences, you are able to get a sense of "being together" as one. This can happen, for example, when conversation feels like an effortless flow or when you easily participate in a common ritual within the relationship.

Dialogue is discourse. Baxter's fourth vantage point refers to the idea that the practical and aesthetic outcomes are not things-in-themselves but are made, or created, in communication. Baxter reminds us, with Bakhtin, that dialogue is conversation. Hailing back to the early work in relational theory, summarized earlier in the chapter, Baxter notes that relationships are never a series of single-person statements, but consist of an ongoing back-and-forth process over time. Important, then, are the actual behaviors or practices in which communicators engage along the trajectory of a relationship. In relationship theory, this idea is very important because it means that some sort of relational pattern and definition arises in the give-and-take of material action. Re-

lationships are not something you work out cognitively in your head, but are the product of discourse.

By definition, every interaction occurs within a larger context; it is always understood in part by what came before, and it sets the stage for new turns to happen in the future. Discourse, then, is ongoing—an unending conversation—which makes relationships *unfinalizable* in the Bakhtinian sense of the word. As a final part of this section on the sociocultural tradition, we move now to a theory that shows one of the fascinating manifestations of relational dialogue—the management of privacy.

Communication Privacy Management

A recent theory that further elaborates the dialectical process within a relationship is Sandra Petronio's communication privacy management theory (CPM).[34] The central concern of this theory is the management of the tension between openness and privacy, between being "public" and being "private." Thus it provides a good example of a specific theory with dialectic at its core.

According to Petronio, individuals involved in relationships are constantly managing boundaries between the public and private, between those feelings and thoughts they are willing to share with others and those they are not. Sometimes the boundary is permeable, meaning that certain information can be revealed; other times, it is impermeable, and information is never shared. Of course, the permeability of a boundary will change, and situations may lead to opening or closing the boundaries. Maintaining a closed boundary can lead to greater autonomy and safety, whereas opening the boundary can promote greater intimacy and sharing but also greater personal vulnerability.

This play between the need to share and the need to protect oneself is present in every relationship and requires persons to negotiate and coordinate their boundaries. When do you disclose and when do you not? And when your partner discloses personal information, how do you respond? We all have a sense of ownership of information about ourselves, and we feel we have the right to control that information. We are constantly making decisions about what to reveal, who should have this information, and when and how to reveal it. Petronio sees this decision-making process as a dialectic—an interplay between pressures to reveal and to conceal.

Notice the difference between this explanation and that of Altman and Taylor discussed earlier in the chapter. Couples do not make a simple "disclose/not disclose" decision based on *individual costs and rewards*. Instead, they must together figure out how to manage a "tension" between revelation and concealment when there are good reasons to do both.

Further, disclosure is never simply an individual decision, but is governed by a relational contract that includes consensus on *shared costs and rewards*. Once we reveal private information to another person, that person becomes a co-owner of the information, and *co-ownership* has its own set of negotiated rights and responsibilities. For example, your family may have an implicit rule that certain things are not to be discussed with others outside the family. Thus, coordination between the persons in a relationship is key. When a person discloses something, he or she must negotiate this disclosure in terms of when, how, and to whom this information may later be disclosed. Part of what happens in defining a relationship, then, is establishing rules that govern how persons will manage and use the information they share with one another.

Petronio therefore sees boundary management as a rule-based process. It is not merely an individual decision—"Do I tell or not?" Rather, it is a negotiation of the rules by which the information will be kept and managed. When a married woman thinks she might be pregnant, she will usually consider when and how to reveal it. Some women will tell their husbands immediately. Others will wait a while to make sure about the pregnancy and to make sure all goes well. Eventually, when the woman tells her husband, the information becomes co-owned and the couple will need to discuss when and how to

make it known to others. Do they tell other family members first? Do they announce it to all of their friends and family at the same time? When and how do they reveal that they are expecting? Some couples wait until "it shows." Others may rush to tell everyone as soon as the test shows positive.

The rules for boundary management are developed, in part, with a kind of risk-benefit ratio. What do you have to gain from disclosing private information, and what risks come into play? *Risk assessment* means thinking about the costs and rewards of revealing the information. For example, if you have had a series of miscarriages, you may find that revealing a new pregnancy is very risky. On the other hand, if you have been trying to get pregnant and this is your first one, you may want to share your joy with your friends and family immediately and receive their congratulations and support in return.

Other *criteria* are also used to make these rule decisions, including, for example, cultural expectations, gender differences, personal motivations, and situational demands. When you become pregnant, you will probably decide whom and when to tell based on your sense of privacy as a woman, how pregnancy has been traditionally handled in your family, how you are personally feeling about it, and even how many children you already have.

Boundary rules do change as circumstances change. Some rules are persistent, routine, and dependable. There may be a long-standing rule among family members, for example, not to discuss family finances with others. This rule could last for years and years, and yet at some point, maybe in retirement, it changes as the benefits of discussing money with friends become productive.

Negotiating the rules for co-ownership of information can be tricky. The various parties who share private information must coordinate and synchronize their behavior. Explicit and implicit agreements must be forged about how to manage shared information. Partners must negotiate rules about *boundary permeability*, or how open or closed the boundary is supposed to be. This is why a married couple will discuss how and when to reveal that they are expecting a baby. Partners also need to negotiate rules about *boundary linkage*, which involves an agreement about who is in and who is out. In other words, who is included within our boundary, and who is not. So, for example, the couple may agree that their parents can be told about the pregnancy, but no one else. Third, partners must negotiate *boundary ownership*, or the rights and responsibilities of the co-owners. This is a clear concern when you tell someone something and then swear him to secrecy. Permeability, linkage, and ownership, then, are all part of boundary coordination.

Boundary rules are sometimes ambiguous. Sometimes, too, persons in a relationship deliberately violate the rules. Gossiping about something you know is private is a good example of this type of violation. When this occurs, sanctions may be invoked. For example, you may be reluctant to reveal future private information to a person who violated your rules of privacy. Petronio refers to these moments of fuzzy, unshared, or violated boundary rules as *boundary turbulence*. Such turbulence is frequently the source of conflict and presents the need for stronger or more careful action in establishing or changing the rules.

◖ REFLECTIONS ON
The Sociopsychological Tradition

The theories in this section look at the "work" that partners in a relationship must do in order to manage the challenges they face. These theories share the idea that the work of a relationship is not individual work, but conjoint effort, negotiated in communication. These theories have a strong cybernetic base, as they see how things get worked out through a back-and-forth movement, or interaction, across time. In many ways, then, these theories are systemic and create a bridge between the cybernetic and sociocultural traditions in communication theory.

• • •

◖ THE PHENOMENOLOGICAL TRADITION

Phenomenology as a tradition focuses on the internal, conscious experience of the person. It looks at the ways in which people understand and give meaning to the events of their lives as well as their own sense of self. In this section, we continue the discussion of dialogue started in the previous section and look at two important figures in dialogue theory—Carl Rogers and Martin Buber—whose work stems from the phenomenological tradition.

Carl Rogers

Carl Rogers was a giant of twentieth-century approaches to human relationships.[35] Although Rogers was a psychologist, his work, in contrast to the mainstream of his own field, was not of the sociopsychological tradition, but very much phenomenological. Rogers, a therapist, devoted his career to listening to how patients expressed their experience of the self, leading him to theorize about communication and provide guidelines on how to communicate more effectively within relationships. In this sense, Rogers's approach was normative or prescriptive. Often called a "self theory," Rogers's approach was much more a relationship theory because, according to Rogers, the self cannot be separated from relationships.

Your overall experience as a person constitutes your *phenomenal field*, all that you know and feel. It is the totality of your experience. Although no one can really know your experience as you do, we can and do infer the experience of others based on what they say and do. In fact, your ideas about how another person is feeling become part of your own phenomenal field, leading to *empathy*.

As you mature in childhood, your phenomenal field grows, and a certain portion becomes identified as the *self*. The self is an organized set of perceptions of who you are and what distinguishes you from other persons and from other aspects of your environment, so that you know exactly what you mean when you use the terms *I* and *me*. As the self develops, you want autonomy and growth, a sense of self-development. You want your life to change in ways that work well for you. At the same time, however, you also want to feel part of a consistent pattern that fits into your overall experience of life in general.

A healthy person is able to achieve both of these aims. When you are feeling strong and clear, you experience *congruence*, or a consistency between who you are, what you do, and how you fit into the world. During times when you feel confused about yourself, you experience *incongruence*, or a loss of consistency in your life. In other words, how you feel, what you do, and what you experience are not lined up. For Rogers, congruence leads to growth, while incongruence leads to frustration. This is what Rogers found in his patients. Clients who came to him for help were out of balance, incongruent, and required a new kind of relationship to allow realignment.

The degree to which you experience congruence is very much affected by your relationships with others. Relationships characterized by negative, critical communication tend to breed incongruence, precisely because they create inconsistency between your sense of self and other aspects of your experience. This would be the case, for example, if someone criticized your behavior. Let's say you like to eat, but others are telling you that you eat too much.

In contrast, congruence is a product of affirming, supportive relationships. In other words, a supportive relationship is characterized by *unconditional positive regard*, which creates a threat-free environment in which we can be self-actualizing. In healthy relationships, partners have a high regard both for self and other. In such relationships, partners are free to explore new avenues of development, try out new things, and move in directions that work well for each without the threat of criticism from the other.

Sometimes we find ourselves in relationships in which we play a supportive role, seeking to facilitate growth and change on the part of the other person. Whenever someone comes to get support—whether you are a professional therapist or not—you have the opportunity to engage in what Rogers calls a *helping relationship*. Such relationships—along with all healthy relationships—are characterized by ten qualities:

1. The communicators are perceived by one another as trustworthy, or consistently dependable.
2. They express themselves unambiguously.
3. They possess positive attitudes of warmth and caring for the other.
4. A partner in a helping relationship keeps his or her own separate identity.
5. A partner permits the other to do the same.
6. The helping relationship is marked by empathy, in which each attempts to understand the feelings of the other.
7. The helper accepts the various facets of the others' experience as they are communicated by the other person.
8. The partners respond with sufficient sensitivity to create a safe environment for personal change.
9. Communicators are able to free themselves from the threat of evaluation from the other.
10. Each communicator recognizes that the other is changing and is flexible enough to permit the other to change.

Rogers developed a style of therapy that embodies these ten elements, which he called *client-centered therapy*. They are also qualities of an *authentic relationship*, or *person-centered approach*, which Rogers believed we can and should have in everyday life.

Consistent with several of the other theories presented in this chapter, Rogers concentrated not on psychological variables, but on actual communication patterns. In an authentic relationship, we can acknowledge and allow our differences, while moving toward mutuality, which is a feeling of satisfaction with the communication we experience within the relationship. Further, one's self is a product of relationship, not the other way around. That is, who you are as a person is made or constructed within relationships with others. This fact makes communication central to human development. In dialogue, then, we come to relate to others by (1) being present and connected to what the other person is saying; (2) being congruent; (3) showing positive regard; and (4) having empathy, or perceiving where the other person is coming from.

Although Carl Rogers was discovered and embraced by communication scholars and teachers in the 1960s and 1970s, his work fell out of favor in the communication field for several years. We came to think of Rogers's ideas as naive and simplistic. However, his theory has undergone something of a renaissance in the last decade or so, and has been reinterpreted by Kenneth Cissna, Rob Anderson, Ronald Arnett, and others, who see Rogers's work as a foundation for understanding dialogue.[36] Cissna and Anderson call dialogue from a Rogerian perspective "an interplay . . . between two partners . . . such that when one partner is able to listen more sensitively to the other, to respond with greater caring and respect, or to be more careful in identifying and expressing his or her own feelings and needs, both parties and the relationship benefit."[37]

The work of Carl Rogers is frequently associated with that of Martin Buber, and together these theorists provide a relatively unified view of the dialogic relationship. Indeed, Rogers acknowledged the influence of Buber on his own work, and the two actually met and had a public dialogue about their respective ideas—a dialogue on dialogue.[38]

Martin Buber

Martin Buber was an important figure in twentieth-century religious thought.[39] Writing about many subjects, Buber provided a coherent view of what it means to be a human being in modern times.[40] For Buber, God can only be known by means of personal relationships with God, with other human beings, and with all aspects of the natural world. There is, then, no unified, objective definition of God, as God is always intensely personal and defined in a special type of relationship that Buber referred to as *dialogue*.[41]

Dialogue embodies a special kind of communication that Buber labeled the *I-Thou* relationship. When you have such a relationship, you see yourself and others as whole persons who cannot be reduced to any simple characterization. Each person has important life experiences that warrant positive regard, even when the experience of others is different from your own.

Communication in Buberian dialogue, or in an I-Thou relationship, is tricky. Because you are a whole person worthy of your own experiences, opinions, ideas, and feelings, you must stand by what is important to you. At the same time, however, you must also acknowledge the full life experience of others and allow them to express what is important to them. This is what Buber calls *the narrow ridge*. In the genuine dialogue of interpersonal relationships, we walk the narrow ridge between self and other. In a good dialogue, you stay on the ridge of honoring yourself and the other, even though substantial differences may be present. This means clearly expressing your own ideas, but listening well and honoring the ideas of others. We also walk the narrow ridge whenever we manage opposites like freedom and discipline, and individualism and community. Because all human beings are complex, the I-Thou relationship always means staying in the dialectical tension of managing opposing forces, much as Baxter describes, and being willing to go back again and again to face our own complexity and that of others in a continual resistance of any generalizations or universals.

Much of the time, however, we do not treat others as worthy individuals. In an *I-It* relationship, you think of the other person as an object to be labeled, manipulated, changed, and maneuvered to your own benefit. In an I-It relationship, you privilege yourself over others.

Buber identified three types of interaction within an I-It frame, where one's own voice is privileged over that of others: monologue, technical dialogue, and monologue disguised as dialogue. *Monologue* exists when you simply monopolize the conversational show, privileging your ideas and interests over those of the others present. *Technical dialogue* is an exchange that is mostly about information rather than about participants' experiences. There is nothing inherently wrong with monologue and technical dialogue; each can be useful. The point is to recognize what kind of communication is going on, to make sure it is appropriate for the relationship, and to be honest about which form is being used. *Disguised monologue*, on the other hand, is communication in which participants talk around the issues without honestly and directly engaging the self and other in their complexity, and it is neither appropriate nor honest.

REFLECTIONS ON
The Phenomenological Tradition

Dialogue theories, as represented by the work of Rogers and Buber, are based in personal experience. They acknowledge that individuals come to know the world through their experience. Communication, then, is a process by which we acknowledge and express the self. These theories share the value of honoring personal experience as the chief way in which we come to understand self and other. Communication is a process of sharing that enables diverse experience, making these theories intensely phenomenological in orientation.

• • •

APPLICATIONS IMPLICATIONS

In this chapter, we have taken a brief look at some of the most significant theorizing in relational communication, a set of theories that have been immensely popular and influential. As we look back over the landscape we have just surveyed, five generalizations seem warranted.

1. Relationships are formed, maintained, and changed through communication.

In the back-and-forth interaction of a conversation, many things get made. You can work out the meaning of gestures, define objects, create new connotations for words, accomplish goals, and change your self-image. But if you talk very often with another person over time, you will create something else as well—a relationship. It might be a friendship, a co-worker relationship, a marriage, a parent-child relationship, a customer relationship, a relationship between neighbors, or any number of other types. Clear to students of communication—and this is not always obvious to people who do not study communication—is that every relationship is made by the participants in their conversations. Relationships don't just happen; they are created.

We also know that no relationship will remain the same indefinitely. Indeed, many relationships are highly dynamic. Whether constantly changing or relatively stable, the relationship is always characterized by certain patterns of interaction. This is easiest to see in your simplest relationships. For example, you can quite accurately predict the pattern of conversation that will take place between you and your hair stylist. Unless your hairdresser is a relative or very good friend, the conversation will follow the same pattern repeatedly. In more complex relationships, such as in the family, certain forms of interaction may last a long time, while other forms—even with the same person—change almost daily.

How you communicate with others, then, really does matter. Beyond achieving whatever immediate goals you may have for a conversation, the implications are always bigger. For example, when someone tells you what to do, you have a choice among accepting, demurring, or resisting. Over time, the way in which partners react to one another establishes a pattern that could be complementary or symmetrical, comfortable or uncomfortable, coordinated or uncoordinated, and positive or negative for the parties and the relationship. Such patterns may determine who controls the relationship, what direction the relationship will take, how privacy is managed, and who is included or excluded.

The practical implication of this insight is that we can have a say in what a relationship is like, not by dictating it, but by being conscious of how we act in the situations we face. Of course, once a pattern is broken, a period of discomfort may result as we "renegotiate" the definition of the relationship. A divorce is hard, because it involves severe, often traumatic, redefinitions of relationships, both with spouse and children.

Sandra Petronio's theory of privacy management is especially useful in helping us identify moments of interaction that may be important in maintaining existing patterns or initiating new ones. Because private information is so important, we really do make conscious decisions about what to reveal to others, and once revealed, how to manage the information that is shared between the two people involved. Here is a spot in ongoing interaction where you really do stop to think consciously about how to act into a situation.

Carl Rogers taught that deliberate interaction is very important in creating positive relationships. In his career as a therapist and theorist, Rogers found that certain patterns of relationship inhibit personal growth. He devoted his life to finding ways for human beings to establish healthy relationships that enhance personal congruence.

If the way in which we communicate determines the kind of relationship we have, then interaction must somehow organize the relationship in a way that gives it certain characteristics. This leads to our next generalization about relationships.

2. Relationships are coordinated.

In modern life, most of us must contend with periods of stability and periods of change within our relationships. Following Bakhtin, we might call these centripetal periods and centrifugal ones. Yet there is always a tendency to find a way to organize, or coordinate, the interaction within the relationship. Even the management of dynamic tension between opposing forces is organized, or structured, in some way.

Koerner and Fitzpatrick have shown that families eventually tend to settle into types. Some of these types (like protective families) are very stable and complementary in interactional pattern, while others (like pluralistic families) will be quite dynamic. The mere fact that you can tell one family type from another shows that patterns of interaction are palpable.

Two fundamental organizational patterns commonly found in relationships are symmetry and complementarity. Either form can be functional and comfortable or destructive and uncomfortable, but how the partners in a relationship respond to one another will always organize the interaction. Even a power struggle—uncomfortable as it might be—is a way of structuring a relationship. Although a relationship always has structure, it is not always organized the same way, and the structure will inevitably change over time.

Fitzpatrick and colleagues look more at stable structures of relationships while Baxter and her colleagues look at the dynamic and process-oriented nature of relationships. Each is focusing on different aspects of relationships, so we understand from these theories that both elements exist in relationships. It is not that we have to see relationships as stable or see them in flux; indeed, every relationship is both, and the characteristic you choose to focus on serves as the lens through which you examine and understand that relationship.

3. Relationships are dynamic.

Bakhtin reminds us that we live in a multivoiced world, a world of heteroglossia. The metaphor of voice is valuable because it reminds us that conversations do consist of voices that somehow have to be structured or organized together into discourse beyond any one message. Unlike talking to yourself, a conversation (let alone a relationship) requires that you blend or mesh your voice with that of others. Sometimes this is very easy because everyone shares a common view of how to interact and relate. Here the rules are largely shared and the conversation is coherent, not unlike a choir. Other times, organizing talk is tough business because very different cultural traditions clash, differing political views compete to be heard, and voices do not blend very well—like to trying to listen to Hip Hop and Big Band music at the same time. Although we have moments in which organization and coherence are high, nothing is ever fixed because there is an eventual intrusion of someone else's voice into the stream of conversation.

In a single week, for example, you may have a talk with your pastor about Christian love, a discussion with a coworker to plan the office holiday party, an office visit with a professor to clarify a point about political theory, a difficult interaction with your teenage daughter, and an orientation meeting for new international students in your department. At moments during this week, you will experience centripetal forces that tend to pull things together into meaningful patterns and centrifugal forces that remind you that nothing is complete and final. This is the challenge of coordination in the ongoing organization of talk.

Relationships are both a haven from this clamor of many voices and a place in which such turbulence can actually be intensified. The relatively straightforward idea from Millar and Rogers that relational patterns can be complementary or symmetrical illustrates both of these features of a relationship. For example, if you have a complementary relationship with your spouse around control issues, one of you will call the shots. This predictable pattern could be quite comforting because you will not have to re-negotiate decision making every time. After a week like the one we described above, it might be nice to come home on Friday evening and have your partner tell you exactly what your plans are for the weekend. The long-term implications of this type of relationship, however, could be stifling for some people, and most individuals would not put up with it very long—especially in our postmodern world. So the weekend could turn into a symmetrical power struggle, even worse than the storms you experienced during the week.

The process of social penetration itself is dynamic, and we go back and forth between disclosing and withdrawing. Privacy management involves constant negotiation; and staying in the tension of the "narrow ridge" between self and other can make you feel a little dizzy as well. The dynamism of a relationship is driven in many ways by dialectical tension.

4. Partners in a relationship actively manage tension.

Virtually all of the theories in this chapter address this point in one way or another. Whether in terms of when and how to manage relational information, when to disclose and when to keep information private, how to stay in the tension between self and other, how to coordinate varying relational schemas, how to manage conversation and conformity, and how to negotiate managing similarity and difference, all suggest that contradictory forces need to be actively managed in relationships.

Dialectical theory suggests that relationships inherently involve the management of natural tensions. Friendships illustrate this very point; the challenges of friendship arise chiefly from the need to manage a variety of dialectical contradictions, such as being dependent versus being independent, using friends for affection versus help, judging versus accepting friends, and being honest versus being protective toward friends.[42] The practical point for everyday life is that we cannot escape contradiction. When we get confused about whether to do A or B, it does not mean there is something wrong with our logic, only that opposites can and do exist side by side. We should not ask whether there is something wrong with contradiction, but how to use communication to manage it well.

Relational communication theory is an immensely interesting, important, and challenging field of study. We see in the theories established to date noble efforts to advance our understanding of one of the most difficult aspects of human life, and although any single theory leaves many questions unanswered, as a group they provide a great deal of insight.

◐ NOTES

1. For an overview of interpersonal communication, see Mark L. Knapp and Gerald R. Miller, eds., *Handbook of Interpersonal Communication* (Thousand Oaks, CA: Sage, 1994). For a brief history, see Charles R. Berger, "Interpersonal Communication," in *An Integrated Approach to Communication Theory and Research,* ed. Michael B. Salwen and Don W. Stacks (Mahwah, NJ: Lawrence Erlbaum, 1996), pp. 277–296; Mark L. Knapp, Gerald R. Miller, and Kelly Fudge, "Background and Current Trends in the Study of Interpersonal Communication," in *Handbook of Interpersonal Communication,* ed. Mark L. Knapp and Gerald R. Miller (Thousand Oaks, CA: Sage, 1994), pp. 3–20.
2. Paul Watzlawick, Janet Beavin, and Don Jackson, *Pragmatics of Human Communication: A Study of Interactional Patterns, Pathologies, and Paradoxes* (New York: Norton, 1967).
3. Watzlawick, Beavin, and Jackson, *Pragmatics of Human Communication,* pp. 120–121.
4. This axiom has been challenged by Michael Motley, "On Whether One Can(not) Not Communicate: An Examination via Traditional Communication Postulates," *Western Journal of Speech Communication* 54 (1990): 1–20. See also "Forum: Can One Not Communicate?," *Western Journal of Speech Communication* 54 (1990): 593–623; Peter A. Andersen, "When One Cannot Not Communicate: A Challenge to Motley's Traditional Communication Postulates," *Communication Studies* 42 (1991): 309–325; Michael T. Motley, "How One May Not Communicate: A Reply to Andersen," *Communication Studies* 42 (1991): 326–339; Theodore Clevenger, Jr., "Can One Not Communicate? A Conflict of Models," *Communication Studies* 42 (1991): 351.
5. Janet Beavin Bavelas, "Behaving and Communicating: A Reply to Motley," *Western Journal of Speech Communication* 54 (1990): 593–602.
6. Although this work is explained in several sources, perhaps the most complete theoretical treatment is Frank E. Millar and L. Edna Rogers, "A Relational Approach to Interpersonal Communication," in *Explorations in Interpersonal Communication,* ed. G. R. Miller (Beverly Hills, CA: Sage, 1976), pp. 87–105. See also Millar and Rogers, "Power Dynamics in Marital Relationships," in *Perspectives on Marital Interaction,* ed. P. Noller and M. Fitzpatrick (Clevedon, England: Multilingual Matters, 1988), pp. 78–97; "Relational Dimensions of Interpersonal Dynamics," in *Interpersonal Processes: New*

Directions in Communication Research, ed. Michael E. Roloff and Gerald R. Miller (Newbury Park, CA: Sage, 1987), pp. 117–139.

7. Millar and Rogers, "A Relational Approach," p. 97.

8. Mary Anne Fitzpatrick, *Between Husbands and Wives: Communication in Marriage* (Newbury Park, CA: Sage, 1988). For updates on the theory, see Mary Anne Fitzpatrick, "Interpersonal Communication on the Starship Enterprise: Resilience, Stability, and Change in Relationships in the Twenty-First Century," in *Communication: Views from the Helm in the 21st Century,* ed. Judith S. Trent (Boston: Allyn & Bacon, 1998), pp. 41–46.

9. Ascan F. Koerner and Mary Anne Fitzpatrick, "Understanding Family Communication Patterns and Family Functioning: The Roles of Conversation Orientation and Conformity Orientation," in *Communication Yearbook 26,* ed. William B. Gudykunst (Mahwah, NJ: 2002), pp. 36–68; Ascan F. Koerner and Mary Anne Fitzpatrick, "Toward a Theory of Family Communication," *Communication Theory* 12 (2002): 70–91.

10. M. W. Baldwin, "Relational Schemas and the Processing of Social Information," *Psychological Bulletin* 112 (1992): 461–484; G. J. O. Fletcher, "Cognition in Close Relationships," *New Zealand Journal of Psychology* 22 (1993): 69–81; A. P. Fiske and S. E. Taylor, *Social Cognition* (New York: McGraw-Hill, 1991).

11. David Kantor and William Lehr, *Inside the Family* (New York: Harper & Row, 1975).

12. For a review of early research on self-disclosure, see Shirley J. Gilbert, "Empirical and Theoretical Extensions of Self-Disclosure," in *Explorations in Interpersonal Communication,* ed. Gerald. R. Miller (Beverly Hills, CA: Sage, 1976), pp. 197–216. A leader in this movement was Sidney Jourard. See Sidney Jourard, *Disclosing Man to Himself* (New York: Van Nostrand, 1968); *Self-Disclosure: An Experimental Analysis of the Transparent Self* (New York: Wiley, 1971); *The Transparent Self* (New York: Van Nostrand Reinhold, 1971). See also P. W. Cozby, "Self-Disclosure: A Literature Review," *Psychological Bulletin* 79 (1973): 73–91. For a good summary of self-disclosure theories, see the second edition of this book, *Theories of Human Communication* (Belmont, CA: Wadsworth, 1983), pp. 193–199.

13. Irwin Altman and Dalmas Taylor, *Social Penetration: The Development of Interpersonal Relationships* (New York: Holt, Rinehart & Winston, 1973). For an update and summary, see Dalmas A. Taylor and Irwin Altman, "Communication in Interpersonal Relationships: Social Penetration Theory," in *Interpersonal Processes: New Directions in Communication Research,* ed. Michael E. Roloff and Gerald R. Miller (Newbury Park, CA: Sage, 1987), pp. 257–277.

14. An excellent summary of this entire line of work is Michael E. Roloff, *Interpersonal Communication: The Social Exchange Approach* (Beverly Hills, CA: Sage, 1981). The best-known social exchange theory is that of John W. Thibaut and Harold H. Kelley, *The Social Psychology of Groups* (New York: Wiley, 1959); see also Harold H. Kelley and John W. Thibaut, *Interpersonal Relations: A Theory of Interdependence* (New York: Wiley, 1978). For a brief summary of the theory, see the third edition of this book, *Theories of Human Communication,* 1989, pp. 185–186.

15. This work is briefly summarized by C. Arthur VanLear, "Testing a Cyclical Model of Communicative Openness in Relationship Development: Two Longitudinal Studies," *Communication Monographs* 58 (1991): 337–361.

16. Irwin Altman, "Dialectics, Physical Environments, and Personal Relationships," *Communication Monographs* 60 (1993): 26–34; Irwin Altman, A. Vinsel, and B. Brown, "Dialectic Conceptions in Social Psychology: An Application to Social Penetration and Privacy Regulation," in *Advances in Experimental Social Psychology,* vol. 14, ed. L. Berkowitz (New York: Academic, 1981), pp. 76–100.

17. VanLear, "Testing a Cyclical Model."

18. Gary Saul Morson and Caryl Emerson, *Mikhail Bakhtin: Creation of a Prosaics* (Stanford, CA: Stanford University Press, 1990), p. 23. For a brief overview, see also J. Kevin Barge and Martin Little, "Dialogical Wisdom, Communicative Practice, and Organizational Life," *Communication Theory* 12 (2002): 375–397.

19. Morson and Emerson, p. 30.

20. Morson and Emerson, p. 31.

21. Morson and Emerson, p. 48.

22. The first recorded use of the term *Negro* was in 1442; it gained popularity in the 1920s when its use was promoted by black community leaders such as Marcus Garvey and W. E. B. DuBois who saw it as a stronger and more versatile term than *colored*. The term *black* replaced *negro* during the civil rights movement of the 1950s and 1960s as an antonym for *White* and the best way to promote pride within the black community. *African American* was introduced by Jesse Jackson in December 1988 as a way of providing blacks with a connection both to their cultural as well as their ancestral homeland. For a summary and analysis of these terms, see Vitania M. Quinones, "The Paradox as Expressed Through Ethnic Labels," paper prepared for Rhetorical Criticism, Department of Communication & Journalism, University of New Mexico, Fall 2003.

23. Mikhail M. Bakhtin, *The Dialogic Imagination: Four Essays*, ed. Michael Holquist, trans. Caryl Emerson and Michael Holquist (Austin: University of Texas Press, 1981), p. xxi.

24. Mikhail M. Bakhtin, "Discourse in the Novel," in *The Dialogic Imagination: Four Essays*, ed. Michael Holquist, trans. Caryl Emerson and Michael Holquist (Austin: University of Texas Press, 1981), p. 276.

25. Morson and Emerson, p. 52.

26. Morson and Emerson, p. 55.

27. Mikhail M. Bakhtin, "Toward a Methodology for the Human Sciences," in Mikhail M. Bakhtin, *Speech Genres and Other Late Essays*, ed. Caryl Emerson and Michael Holquist, trans. Vern W. McGee (Austin: University of Texas Press, 1986), p. 162.

28. M. M. Bakhtin, "Toward a Reworking of the Dostoevsky Book," in *Problems of Dostoevsky's Poetics*, ed. and trans. Caryl Emerson (Minneapolis: University of Minnesota Press, 1984), p. 293.

29. Leslie A. Baxter, "Relationships as Dialogues," *Personal Relationships*, in press; Rob Anderson, Leslie A. Baxter, and Kenneth N. Cissna, eds., *Dialogic Approaches to Communication* (Thousand Oaks, CA: Sage, 2004); Leslie A. Baxter and Dawn O. Braithwaite, "Social Dialectics: The Contradictions of Relating," in *Contemporary Communication Theories and Exemplars*, ed. Bryan Whaley and Wendy Samter (Mahwah, NJ: Lawrence Erlbaum, in press).

30. Leslie A. Baxter and Barbara M. Montgomery, "A Guide to Dialectical Approaches to Studying Personal Relationships," in *Dialectical Approaches to Studying Personal Relationships*, ed. Barbara Montgomery and Leslie Baxter (Mahwah, NJ: Lawrence Erlbaum, 1998), pp. 1–15.

31. Barbara M. Montgomery and Leslie A. Baxter, "Dialogism and Relational Dialectics," in *Dialectical Approaches to Studying Personal Relationships*, ed. Barbara Montgomery and Leslie Baxter (Mahwah, NJ: Erlbaum, 1998), p. 160.

32. Leslie Baxter, "The Social Side of Personal Relationships: A Dialectical Perspective," in *Social Context and Relationships: Understanding Relationship Processes,* vol. 3, ed. Steve Duck (Newbury Park, CA: Sage, 1993), pp. 139–169; Carol M. Werner and Leslie A. Baxter, "Temporal Qualities of Relationships: Organismic, Transactional, and Dialectical Views," in *Handbook of Interpersonal Communication*, ed. Mark L. Knapp and Gerald R. Miller (Thousand Oaks, CA: Sage, 1994), 323–379.

33. Werner and Baxter, "Temporal Qualities."

34. Sandra Petronio, *Boundaries of Privacy: Dialectics of Disclosure* (Albany: State University of New York Press, 2002); Sandra Petronio, *Balancing the Secrets of Private Disclosures* (Mahwah, NJ: Lawrence Erlbaum, 2000). We thank Sandra Petronio for her guidance in writing this section.

35. Among Carl Rogers's many works are *Client-Centered Therapy* (Boston: Houghton-Mifflin, 1951); "A Theory of Therapy, Personality, and Interpersonal Relationships, as Developed in the Client-Centered Framework," in *Psychology: A Study of Science*, S. Koch, ed., vol. 3 (New York: McGraw-Hill, 1959), pp. 184–256; *On Becoming a Person* (Boston: Houghton-Mifflin, 1961); and *A Way of Being* (Boston: Houghton Mifflin, 1980).

36. Kenneth N. Cissna and Rob Anderson, "The Contributions of Carl R. Rogers to a Philosophical Praxis of Dialogue," *Western Journal of Speech Communication* 54 (1990): 125–147; Ronald C. Arnett and Pat Arneson, *Dialogic Civility in a Cynical Age* (Albany: State University of New York Press, 1999).

37. Cissna and Anderson, "Contributions of Carl R. Rogers," p. 141.

38. Ronald C. Arnett, "Rogers and Buber: Similarities, yet Fundamental Differences," *Western Journal of Speech Communication* 45 (1981): 358–372; Maurice Friedman, "Reflections on the Buber-Rogers Dialogue: Thirty-Five Years After," in *Martin Buber and the Human Sciences*, ed. Maurice Friedman (Albany: State University of New York Press, 1996), pp. 357–370; Rob Anderson and Kenneth N. Cissna, *The Martin Buber-Carl Rogers Dialogue: A New Transcript With Commentary* (Albany: State University of New York Press, 1997).

39. Among his many works, Martin Buber's most recognized treatise on human relationships is *I and Thou*, trans. Walter Kaufmann (New York: Charles Scribner, 1958).

40. See Maurice Friedman, ed. *Martin Buber and the Human Sciences* (Albany: State University of New York Press, 1996).

41. For elaborations on Buber's theory of dialogue, see Arnett and Arneson, *Dialogic Civility*, pp. 127–148; and Ronald C. Arnett, *Communication and Community: Implications of Martin Buber's Dialogue* (Carbondale: Southern Illinois University Press, 1986).

42. From William Rawlins, *Friendship Matters: Communication, Dialectics, and the Life Course* (Hawthorne, NY: Aldine, 1992).

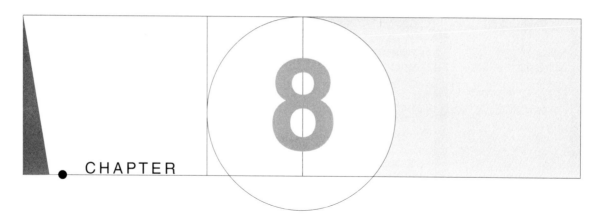

CHAPTER

THE GROUP

If you were to count the number of times in a week that you are involved in group communication, you might be surprised. Meetings alone would number quite a few, and if you expanded the count to include social groups, the number would balloon. Of course, the number of hours per week that we spend communicating in groups tells only part of the story. Groups take up time, but they also help to structure time. They sap our energy, but they also energize. They can be deadly boring, but provide much enjoyment as well. They create constraints on what we can do, but they can also shape future directions that open opportunities in our lives.[1]

Have you ever had the experience of worrying that a group was getting off track when someone made a joke or members talked about sports instead of getting right to work? If so, you were struggling with balancing relationship building and task effort—a tension common to all groups. Some humor and drama can help with the tension inherent to a group and actually increase members' effectiveness. Too much joking around will distract from the work and hurt effectiveness as well. This fact illustrates an aspect of group communication; namely, everything you say in a group helps to make the group what it is and helps to shape the work that the group is doing.

For example, how often do you ask a question in a group? How does this compare to the number of times that you share an opinion? Research has shown that giving opinions far exceeds asking questions in most groups,[2] but how would a group change if the opposite were true? What may be even more important is not so much

Topics Addressed	Sociopsychological Theories	Cybernetic Theories	Sociocultural Theories
Messages, roles and personalities	Interaction process analysis		
Environment/system/ context		Bona fide group theory Input-process-output model	
Interaction		Interactional analysis	
Diversity		Effective intercultural work group theory	
Group structure			Structurational perspective
Group task			Functional theory Groupthink theory

the kinds of things that individuals say, but how they respond to one another. If, for example, one person asks a question, to what extent do others (1) answer it; (2) use it as an opportunity to launch into a new topic; (3) ignore the question entirely; (4) or remain silent? Each of these kinds of responses creates a different relationship among members. From a theoretical perspective, then, communication interaction is very important in shaping both relationships and task accomplishment.

We know that groups really cannot be legitimately examined in isolation. They are always part of some larger system. Group members come and go, people belong to several overlapping groups, the environment changes, and groups must adapt to these developments. In a group, then, your affiliations with other groups affect what you do and say, and roles change as members leave or new members come into a group.

Actually, roles constitute just part of the structure of a group. Groups do have form, and you can see this form in the interactional patterns over time. Something gets created through interaction within the group, including roles and norms, but also relationships and task accomplishments. Power structures are also formed within these interactional patterns. So when old members leave and new ones arrive, these structures can change, sometimes dramatically.

Because you spend so much time in groups, it is natural to question their effectiveness. Is it better to do things by yourself or work with a group? The answer, of course, depends upon how well the group works together, how focused it is, and how much creative and critical thinking the group allows. How well does the group weigh information, how effectively does it create options, and how critically does the group evaluate ideas?

Groups do vary in their ability to do these things well, and the theories in the chapter help us to see what works and what does not. Contemporary research and theory in group communication stems from a variety of early twentieth-century sources.[3] One such source was the work of Mary Parker Follett on integrative thinking.[4] Follett wrote in 1924 that group, organizational, and community problem solving is a creative threefold process of (1) gathering information from experts; (2) testing that information in everyday experience; and (3) developing integrative solutions that meet a variety of interests rather than competing among interests. Groups further deal with problems and conflicts through discussion. These are the topics pursued in this chapter. They are outlined in the chapter map on the facing page.

◖ THE SOCIOPSYCHOLOGICAL TRADITION

Much of the original work in small group communication occurred in social psychology. In fact, the group dynamics movement was an important step in the evolution of what we know about groups today. We do not devote any space here to group dynamics theory per se, but we do include one classic theory—interaction process analysis—that had a great influence on group communication theory. This theory addresses the kinds of messages that people express in groups and how these affect group roles and personalities.

Interaction Process Analysis

Robert Bales's *interaction process analysis* is a classic in the field.[5] Using his many years of research as a foundation, Bales created a unified and well-developed theory of small-group communication, aiming to explain the types of messages that people exchange in groups, the ways in which these shape the roles and personalities of group members, and thereby the ways they affect the overall character of the group.

Figure 8.1 illustrates the types of messages you often hear in groups.[6] These twelve categories are grouped into four broader sets, as outlined at the left of the figure. In addition, the behavior types are paired, and each pair implies a particular problem area for groups, as labeled in the figure. *Gives information* is paired with *asks for information, gives opinion* is paired with *asks for opinion,* and *gives suggestion* is paired with *asks for suggestion.*

If people do not adequately share information, they will have what Bales calls "problems of communication"; if they do not share opinions, they will experience "problems of evaluation"; if they fail to ask for and give suggestions, the group will suffer from "problems of control"; if the group cannot come to agreement, they will have "problems of decision"; and if there is insufficient dramatizing, there will be "problems of tension." Finally, if the group is unfriendly, it will have "problems of reintegration," by which Bales means that the group is unable to successfully rebuild a "we feeling," or cohesiveness, within the group.

You can easily see the logic of Bales's scheme. Suppose, for example, that you are a member of a project team in a class. The job of this team is to decide upon a project, execute it, and write up a report. If group members keep withholding information from one another, they will not be able to communicate very well and will have little idea of what each person can contribute. If they fail to share opinions, they will not evaluate ideas very much, and the group may end up doing a terrible job. Let's say that group members give very few suggestions. In this case, the group will lack the element of control, since no one wants to tell the group what to do. If the members of your project group agree too much, ideas will not be tested, and you will make poor decisions. On the other hand, if you all disagree too much, there will be too much conflict, and you won't be able to make decisions at all. If people do not relax to some degree, tension will build up, creating a poor and unproductive group and interpersonal atmosphere.

The category of *dramatizing* assumed special importance in Bales's theory. Dramatizing means relieving tension by telling stories and sharing experiences that may not always relate directly to the task of the group. In Chapter 6, we looked at Ernest Bormann's use of the concept of dramatizing in symbolic convergence theory. Bormann, who got the idea originally from Bales, believes that this form of communication is crucial not only in reducing tension but also in affecting the quality of group discussion in general.[7] Stories are often told and retold within a group. They consist of fantasy themes, or shared knowledge, that build a common identity in the group. Fantasy themes constitute the mechanism by which cohesiveness, or a sense of community, is developed in a group.

Bales's theory includes two general classes of communication behavior, a division that has had immense impact in the small group literature. The first includes *socioemotional* behaviors, represented in Figure 8.1 by actions like *seeming*

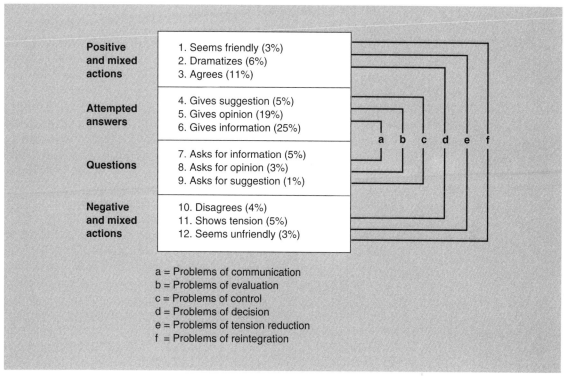

Positive and mixed actions	1. Seems friendly (3%) 2. Dramatizes (6%) 3. Agrees (11%)	
Attempted answers	4. Gives suggestion (5%) 5. Gives opinion (19%) 6. Gives information (25%)	a b c d e f
Questions	7. Asks for information (5%) 8. Asks for opinion (3%) 9. Asks for suggestion (1%)	
Negative and mixed actions	10. Disagrees (4%) 11. Shows tension (5%) 12. Seems unfriendly (3%)	

a = Problems of communication
b = Problems of evaluation
c = Problems of control
d = Problems of decision
e = Problems of tension reduction
f = Problems of reintegration

FIGURE **8.1**

Categories for Interaction Process Analysis

friendly, showing tension, and *dramatizing.* The second category is *task behavior,* represented by *suggestions, opinions,* and *information.* In investigating leadership, Bales found that the same group will have two different kinds of leaders. The *task leader* facilitates and coordinates the task-related comments and directs energy toward getting the job done. Equally important is the *socioemotional leader,* who works for improved relations in the group, concentrating on interactions in the positive and negative sectors.

Usually the task and socioemotional leaders are different people. In a group that is working on a class project together, for example, you may have one member who calls meetings, makes sure everyone gets there, prepares the agenda, makes follow-up calls, and shows great concern for the quality of the project. This would be your task leader. There may also be someone who attends to the relationships in the group—a socio-

emotional leader. This is the individual who encourages others, smoothes over conflict, praises people for good work, and generally facilitates positive relationships.

Bales has shown how the perception of an individual's position in a group is a function of three dimensions. These include (1) dominant versus submissive; (2) friendly versus unfriendly; and (3) instrumental versus emotional. Within a particular group, any member's behavior can be placed in this three-dimensional space. An individual's position depends on the quadrant in which that individual appears (for instance, dominant, friendly, instrumental).

The way you appear to other members of a group is very much determined by how you combine these three dimensions in your communication. If your talk tends to be dominant, unfriendly, and emotional, you will be probably be perceived as a hostile, abrasive person. On the other hand, if you are dominant, friendly, and instrumental, you will probably be appreciated for your helpful task leadership. If you tend to be submissive, unfriendly, and emotional, you will probably be perceived as sulky and a negative influence. Since these factors are variables, you can score high, medium, or low on any of them, so that the types are not absolute categories but a blend. When all group members' behavior types are plotted on this graph, their relationships and networks can be seen. The larger the group, the greater the tendency for subgroups of individuals with similar values to develop.

REFLECTIONS ON
The Sociopsychological Tradition

In this chapter, we present only a single example of the sociopsychological tradition. In the group communication field, the cybernetic and sociocultural traditions predominate. Bales's work is no longer in the mainstream of group communication theory, but it had tremendous influence on how we think about groups. As a research psychologist, Bales was mostly interested in the individual behavior of group members. Although he named his theory, "interaction process analysis," it really had little to do with "interaction" or "process," as we understand these terms today. We now realize that Bales's focus on individual behavior limited the theory's ability to take into account larger systemic concerns, and current thinking in the communication field is that these broader issues should take center stage. To gain this larger perspective, we must turn to the cybernetic tradition.

• • •

THE CYBERNETIC TRADITION

The cybernetic tradition has been especially powerful in helping us see the systemic nature of groups. Although the theories of this tradition vary considerably, as a whole they remind us of the fact that groups are part of larger systems of interacting forces. A group gets fresh input from outside, processes this input in some way, and creates outputs or effects that influence the larger system as well as the group itself. Here we look at four theories that develop this idea. They are bona fide group theory, input-process-output theory, interaction analysis, and effective intercultural work group theory.

Bona Fide Group Theory

Bales's theory, presented in the previous section, is one example of a theory that uses a "container" metaphor, likening groups to a bottle separated off from the environment. In fact, groups are not separate from the larger environment, and Linda Putnam and Cynthia Stohl started a line of thinking called *bona fide groups* as a response to this critique.[8] A *bona fide group* is a naturally occurring group. In this sense, all groups, unless they are artificially created in a laboratory, are bona fide, because all groups are part of a larger system. Instead of thinking of bona fide groups as a type of group, then, think of it as a perspective or way of looking at all groups.

Bona fide groups have two characteristics: They have permeable boundaries, and they are interdependent with the environment. The group's boundaries are permeable, meaning that what is defined as "in" the group or "out" of the group is sometimes vague, always fluid, and frequently changing. At the same time, you cannot have a group without some sense of boundary, meaning that the group does have a notion of itself in relation to an environment, but the boundary is always being negotiated.

The permeability of a group's boundaries is obvious when you consider that members are always part of other groups as well. They will bring into a group roles and characteristics established in other groups. Actually, you cannot separate a group member from the other groups to which he or she may belong. Sometimes, group roles actually conflict, and members must resolve differences between what they are supposed to do in one group versus what is expected of them in others.

Further, as a group member you rarely represent only yourself. Instead, you have other people's interests at stake. Outside interests will influence what you do and say within the group. Also, group members change, so that someone who was outside the group at one time becomes a member at another time, and vice versa. Because of multiple group membership, you may not be equally committed to every group, and not all members of a group show the same amount of loyalty or sense of belonging to a group.

From a bona fide group perspective, the group is always interdependent with its environment. In other words, the environment influences it, and the group, in turn, affects the relevant contexts in which it works. From a systems perspective, a group's environment really consists of other groups, interacting together. Groups communicate with one another, they coordinate their actions, they negotiate which group is responsible for what, and they must interpret the meaning of inter-group relationships. The point of contact or overlap between two or more groups is a *nexus*. If you look at the nexus, you will see interdependence in action.

Among its many functions—such as accomplishing tasks and resolving internal conflicts—a group must also adjust and adapt its work coherently with the situation in which it is working. It must relate its work to an ongoing history of accomplishment within the larger system and to larger institutional opportunities and constraints. There are moments, however, when the group feels that it is "in transition," when it is not clear just how it does relate to history or institutions. These moments, referred to as *liminality*, create feelings of being in a suspended state. At these moments, groups work to define themselves vis-à-vis the larger context.

Gaming methodology offers an opportunity to easily see the interdependence of bona fide groups. Gaming methodology is a planning tool in which "players" from stakeholder groups are brought together for several days to simulate an environment in which they must work with other groups to plan a future of mutual concern.[9] After players—usually 50 to 150 professionals—are assigned to stakeholder groups, they begin strategic planning around an issue like health care, homeland security, technology, or water quality.

Although they begin their planning in isolated stakeholder groups, they quickly learn that they cannot go very far without thinking about the larger system of groups of which they are a part. This realization occurs in a moment of liminality, in which they must think about their role in the larger system, talk about how they want to relate to this larger context, the specific other groups with which they want to interact, and what they hope to accomplish by doing so. After a short team-planning period, players leave their team areas and begin to interact with individuals from other stakeholder teams, forging agreements, sharing information, establishing partnerships and alliances, and creating plans larger than any one stakeholder group could do by itself. Sometimes teams compete with one another, sometimes they collaborate, and at other times they complement one another. Each of these points of contact in the game is a nexus of opportunity, and it is always fascinating to watch the play unfold in these ways.

In a game, as in real life, group work is influenced by inputs and creates outputs that affect the group as well as the system as a whole. The input-process-output model of group functioning has been a mainstay in group studies, and we take a closer look at this approach now.

Input-Process-Output Model

Groups are often viewed as cybernetic systems in which information and influence come into the group (input), the group processes this information, and the results circulate back out to affect others (output). Collectively, this idea is known as the *input-process-output model*.[10] A simple example is a study group in which the members bring information about the course along with certain attitudes, the group talks about this material and provides mutual assistance, and the

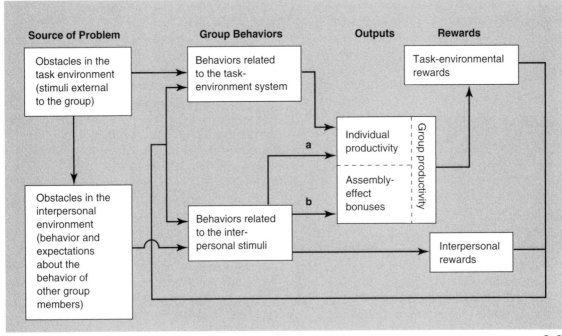

FIGURE **8.2**

A Simple Working Model of Decision-Making Groups

From *A Social Psychology of Group Processes for Decision-Making* by Barry Collins and Harold Guetzkow; John Wiley & Sons, publisher. Used by permission.

result is higher—or lower—grades in the course as a result. The results of the study group provide feedback that affects future content as well as feelings about the group in its future work.

This basic idea about groups has influenced how we look at them, and most of the research over the years has followed this model. Researchers look at the factors that affect the group (input), the happenings within the group (process), and the results (output). For example, a study might examine the effects of heterogeneity of group members (input variable) on the amount of talking in a group and the effect of interaction patterns (process variables) on member satisfaction (output variable).[11] Barry Collins and Harold Guetzkow elaborated this basic idea in an early model, shown in Figure 8.2.[12]

Resonating with Bales, this model shows that a task group is confronted with two types of problems—task and interpersonal obstacles. *Task*

obstacles are the difficulties encountered by the group in tackling its assignment, such as planning an event or approving a policy. Group members deal directly with the problem by analyzing the situation, suggesting possible solutions, and weighing alternatives.

If a group member makes a decision, that member not only must weigh the decision itself, but must work effectively with other members of the group. Whenever two or more people come together to handle a problem, *interpersonal obstacles* arise. Such obstacles include the need to make ideas clear to others, handle conflict, manage differences, and so forth. Thus, in any group discussion, members will be dealing simultaneously with task and interpersonal obstacles.

The basic distinction between task work and interpersonal relations has been an overriding concern in the research and theory on small group communication. Both types of behavior are important to productivity, and any analysis of group problem solving must deal with both.[13] When task and interpersonal work is integrated effectively, an *assembly effect* occurs in which the group solution or product is superior to the individual work of even the best member. So, for example, if a club meets to plan a picnic and handles its interpersonal relations and task work well, the event should turn out to be better than if just one person planned it.

Group rewards can be positive or negative, and this holds true for both task and interpersonal work. A successful class project, for instance, is a task reward, and the fun involved in planning it is an interpersonal reward. If the job is well done and enjoyed by the members, their future work together will be affected in a positive way. If the task was not well done or the members did not handle their differences well, negative feedback may make it more difficult next time.

Think of group effort as a kind of energy. Some of this energy goes into solving task obstacles, and some goes into dealing with interpersonal ones. Raymond Cattell uses the term *synergy* for this group effort. The amount of energy devoted to interpersonal hassles is called *intrinsic synergy,* and the remaining energy available for the task is *effective synergy.* If effective synergy is high, the task will be accomplished effectively; if not, it will be done poorly.[14] The level of synergy in a group results from the attitudes of the members toward one another. Conflict requires that a great deal of energy be devoted to group maintenance, leaving little for task accomplishment. On the other hand, if individuals possess similar attitudes, there is less need for an interpersonal investment, and the effective synergy will be greater.

Think again about your class project group. Imagine that you discover that the members of your group have different attitudes toward the subject matter, different levels of motivation on the project, and different styles of working. One member, for example, is gung ho, plans ahead, likes to get things done in advance, and has little tolerance for the competing demands experienced by other group members. Another member, by contrast, is laid back, not terribly interested in the class, and procrastinates. In your meetings, you may end up wasting a lot of time arguing about how to organize your efforts and learn the material. You will be frustrated by the fact that not everyone is contributing equally to the group effort. All of the hassles around these interpersonal issues constitute its intrinsic synergy. After getting your grade, you sense that the group failed to achieve the goal of mutual benefit, and you decide to suggest to the professor that the next project be done individually rather than in a group. In this case the effective synergy of the group was so low that it did not accomplish more than you could have done by yourself.

Now imagine a different scenario. Suppose that your group agrees immediately on how to proceed and gets down to work. Because the interpersonal barriers are few, the group is cohesive. The effective synergy is high, and group members do better on the project than they would have done by themselves. Experience in these two groups shows the importance of interpersonal energy (intrinsic synergy) and its relationship to outcome (effective synergy).

Now let's look more closely at what actually happens in the "process" part of the input-process-output model. Staying within the cybernetic tradition, we turn now to the work of B. Aubrey Fisher and interaction analysis.

Fisher's Interaction Analysis

Because Bales's theory looks at individual acts, B. Aubrey Fisher and Leonard Hawes refer to his approach as a *human system model*, by which they mean a model that looks at individual human behaviors. More appropriate for the communication field is the *interact system model*, which focuses not on acts, but on "interacts."[15] An *interact* is the act of one person followed by the act of another—for example, question-answer, statement-statement, and greeting-greeting. Here, the unit for analysis is not an individual message, like making a suggestion, but a contiguous pair of acts, like making a suggestion and responding to it.

Interacts can be classified along the *content dimension* and the *relationship dimension.* For example, if someone were to ask you a question, you would probably answer it, but the manner in which you stated the answer might tip off the group that you thought it was a dumb question. In such a case, your answer is the content dimension and your nonverbal manner the relationship dimension.

Despite the potential utility of analyzing the relational dimension in a group discussion, Fisher concentrates on the content dimension. Because almost all comments in a task group are related in one way or another to a decision proposal—to coming up with an action or outcome on which all can agree—Fisher classifies statements in terms of how they respond to a decision proposal.[16] Statements might agree or disagree with a proposal, for example.

In his theory of *decision emergence,* Fisher outlines four phases through which task groups tend to proceed: orientation, conflict, emergence, and reinforcement.[17] In observing the distribution of interacts across these phases, Fisher notes the ways interaction changes as the group decision formulates and solidifies.

The *orientation phase* involves getting acquainted, clarifying, and beginning to express points of view. A high level of agreement characterizes this stage, and comments are often designed to test the group. Thus, positions are both qualified and tentative. In this phase people grope for direction and understanding. The *conflict phase* includes a great deal of dissent. People in this second phase begin to solidify their attitudes, and much polarization results. Here the interacts include more disagreement and unfavorable evaluation. Members argue and attempt to persuade, and they may form coalitions.

These coalitions tend to disappear in the third phase, which Fisher labeled *emergence.* Here the first inklings of cooperation begin to show. People are less tenacious in defending their viewpoints. As they soften their positions and undergo attitude change, their comments become more ambiguous. The number of favorable comments increases until a group decision begins to emerge.

In the final phase, *reinforcement,* the group decision solidifies and receives reinforcement from group members. The group unifies and stands behind its solution. Comments are almost uniformly positive and favorable. The ambiguity that marked the third phase tends to disappear.

To illustrate the phases of group development, Fisher presents an analysis of a mock jury deliberation in a lawsuit over an automobile-pedestrian accident.[18] In the first phase, the jury explores its responsibility. What is it supposed to do, and how is it supposed to do it? What are the possible verdicts? Much uncertainty is expressed until clarification emerges. Considerable disagreement arises in the conflict phase as the jury argues over whether the defendant is negligent and the criteria by which the jury should decide. Here, the interaction tends to be somewhat emotional and heated.

In the emergence phase, the jury begins to agree that the defendant is not negligent and that the pedestrian could have avoided the accident. This agreement is somewhat tentative, and the jurors go back and forth on the issue, but the emotionality and debate definitely subside during this period. In the final reinforcement phase, the jury is convinced, and all of its members affirm their agreement with this verdict.

The phases of group decision making characterize the interaction as it changes over time. An important related topic is that of *decision modification.*[19] Fisher finds that groups typically do not introduce only one idea at a time, nor do they introduce a single proposal and continue to modify it until consensus is reached. Instead, decision modification is cyclical. Several proposals are made, each is discussed briefly, and some of them are reintroduced at a later time. Discussion of proposals seems to proceed in spurts of energy. Proposal A will be introduced and discussed. The group will suddenly drop this idea and move to proposal B. After discussion of this, the group may introduce and discuss other proposals. Then someone will revive proposal A, perhaps in modified form. The group finally will settle on a modified plan that was introduced earlier in the discussion in a different form.

Why does discussion typically proceed in such an erratic fashion? According to Fisher, it is because the interpersonal demands of discussion require "breaks" from task work. In effect, the group attention span is short because of the intense nature of group work, and "flight" behavior helps manage tension and conflict.

Fisher finds that in modifying proposals, groups tend to follow one of two patterns. If conflict is low, the group will reintroduce proposals in less abstract, more specific language. For example, in a discussion of a public health nursing conference, an original idea to begin the conference program "with a nonthreatening something" was modified to "begin with a history of the contributions which public health has made to the field of nursing."[20] A group, as it successively returns to a proposal, seems to follow the pattern of stating the problem, discussing criteria for solution, introducing an abstract solution, and moving finally to a concrete solution. Keep in mind, however, that the group most likely will not move through these four steps smoothly, but will probably do so sporadically as members depart from and return to the proposal in a stop-and-start fashion. When conflict is higher, the group does not attempt to make a proposal more specific. Because disagreement exists on the basic idea, the group introduces substitute proposals of the same level of abstraction as the original.

Fisher's theory tunes us in to the importance of interaction as the basic process of communication that transforms inputs into outputs. It also shows us how you can better understand a group's decisions by analyzing interaction, but it does not go very far in examining the variables that may affect group outcomes. An example of a theory that looks more closely at variability in groups is John Oetzel's intercultural work group theory.

Effective Intercultural Work Group Theory

John Oetzel employs the input-process-output model in establishing important variables that affect group functioning.[21] Interested in diversity as well as group effectiveness, Oetzel creates a model in which a culturally diverse group, facing certain inputs, creates outcomes through communication that feed back to affect the situation in which the group is working. This is a perfect cybernetic loop: inputs-process-outcomes-situation.

The groups with which Oetzel is concerned are culturally diverse, meaning that the cultural differences among members—nationality, ethnicity, language, gender, job position, age, disability, and others—are important in some way to the functioning of the group. The most important cultural differences cluster in three areas: (1) individualism-collectivism; (2) self-construal; and (3) face concerns.

The first area of difference is *individualism-collectivism*. Many cultures tend to be individualistic in orientation. Members of individualistic cultures tend to think of themselves as independent and give priority to their own goals over group goals. In contrast, collectivist cultures tend to think of themselves as part of a community and give priority to collective goals rather than personal ones. For example, one group member with an individualistic cultural background may assume that everyone is speaking just for themselves and will weigh what each person says individually. Another member from an collectivist society, however, might "beat around the bush" in terms of what he or she thinks, preferring to defer to the group as a whole.

The second cluster of differences is in terms of *self-construal*, or how members think about themselves. There are two general types—independent and interdependent. If you think of yourself in *independent* ways, you will see yourself as a unique person, separate from the thoughts and feelings of others. On the other hand, if you think of yourself in *interdependent* ways, you will focus more on how you are connected to others. Clearly, independent self-construals are common in individualistic cultures, while interdependent construals are more common in collectivist ones. You can imagine the problems that might occur when some group members evaluate success in terms of how well they achieve their personal goals, while other members of the group evaluate success in terms of the achievement of overall group goals.

The third cluster of difference is *face concerns*, or differences in how members manage personal image. *Self-face* is one's own image, *other-face* involves the image of other people, and *mutual-face* involves concerns about the relationship between self and other. Cultures differ in terms of how they manage these three types of face. Some, for example, are somewhat self-effacing, preferring to build the face of the other. Other cultures tend to focus on self-face, sometimes at the expense of others. A culturally mixed group could have some members who constantly try to make themselves look good, other members who work to make others look good, and still others who want the group as a whole to look good.

These kinds of cultural differences necessitate effective communication, but also make it difficult. In other words, the very thing that diverse groups need—effective communication—is also very difficult for them to accomplish. The more heterogeneous the group, the harder it will be to communicate effectively in terms of (1) equal participation; (2) consensus-based decision making; (3) non-dominating conflict management; and (4) respectful communication. Of course, you have to be careful, because an intercultural group is not necessarily a heterogeneous group; it just depends upon how important the cultural differences turn out to be. It is also true that the cultures represented in a diverse group may share the same orientation in terms of individualism/collectivism, self-construal, and/or face.

The degree to which a group is able to manage intercultural diversity is determined by several situational factors, including (1) a history of unresolved conflict among the cultural groups in society at large; (2) in-group–out-group balance, determined by the number of group members representing the different cultures; (3) the extent to which the group's task is cooperative or competitive; and (4) status differences. If the cultures represented in the group have a history of good conflict resolution, the representation among cultures is fairly well balanced, the task is cooperative in nature, and members have more or less equal status, then they will tend to communicate effectively.

Suppose, for example, that you attend a multiracial university and are accustomed to working in classes with individuals from various cultural backgrounds. At least in recent years, there has been little ethnic conflict on campus, and people have learned to work pretty effectively with one another in student government, activities, sports, and academics. A class-project group under these circumstances would probably work well, if everyone were committed to the project. On the other hand, if recent racial tensions had broken out on campus, making it uncomfortable for, say, Jews and Muslims to interact equally and productively, then the group could fail. This situation could be exacerbated if one group felt superior to the other, if the two groups were not equally represented in the class-project group, or if the task itself were competitive in nature (such as seeing who can get the best grade on an exam).

The blend of cultures within a diverse group will affect its communication processes in several ways: First, if a group is individualistic or independent in orientation, it will tend to use dominating conflict strategies, but if it is collectivist or interdependent in orientation, it will tend to use collaborating conflict strategies. Group members who are more culturally individualistic or independent will tend to speak more frequently, or take more turns while collectivist or interdependent groups will tend to have more equal participation among members. Finally, when group members are mostly concerned with other-face or mutual-face, they will tend to use collaboration and be more satisfied with the group's communication.

Using an input-process-output model, Oetzel shows that the quality of communication affects both task and relational effectiveness. In general, he believes that if a culturally diverse group has good communication, the effectiveness of the task and relationships among group members will increase. In one study, for example, Oetzel found that if a group has equal participation, cooperation, and respectful communication, members will be more satisfied and will be more likely to participate fully in the group effort.[22]

■ REFLECTIONS ON

The Cybernetic Tradition

Because groups are part of larger systems—they take input from the system and produce outputs—the cybernetic tradition has been important in understanding this relationship. Indeed, bona fide group theory clearly shows how groups are constantly in flux and have steady give-and-take with larger systems, while the other theories in this section stress more of the internal workings (cybernetic nonetheless) of individual groups. Two ideas from the cybernetic tradition predominate here. One is that group action is more than a sum of individual action, that it is a product of interaction. The second major idea is that group outputs always provide feedback that affects group performance.

The cybernetic tradition has had a clear impact on our thinking about communication in groups. For the most part, these theories tend to be descriptive in approach, showing how, in different ways, groups act as systems of interacting forces. There is actually a fine line between cybernetic and sociocultural theories of groups. All of the theories in this section on the cybernetic tradition have some sociocultural elements. However, we decided to place them in the cybernetic section because each of these theories uses system terminology and/or makes explicit use of the input-process-output model.

We move now to a set of theories that are somewhat more sociocultural in focus, although they still deal with some of the features we saw in cybernetic theories.

• • •

■ THE SOCIOCULTURAL TRADITION

This section deals with two general topics—group structure and group task. As a group works on its task, it actually creates a structure, which in turn affects how it manages its task. In other words, these two topics are closely related, as the theories in this section show.

Specifically, we will summarize three theories here, moving from the most general to the most specific. The first theory in the series, structuration theory, describes the general process by which groups create structure, with special attention to task. The second functional theory looks at a variety of factors that affect task effectiveness. Finally, we conclude with groupthink theory, which focuses specifically on one of the most common problems encountered by task groups.

The Structurational Perspective

Structuration theory, the brainchild of sociologist Anthony Giddens and his followers, is a general theory of social action.[23] This theory states that human action is a process of producing and reproducing various social systems. In other words, when we communicate with one another, we create structures that range from large social and cultural institutions to smaller individual relationships.

As communicators act strategically according to rules to achieve their goals, they do not realize that they are simultaneously creating forces that return to affect future actions. Structures like relational expectations, group roles and norms, communication networks, and societal institutions both affect and are affected by social action. These structures provide individuals with rules that guide their actions, but their actions in turn create new rules and reproduce old ones. Interaction and structure are so closely related that Donald Ellis calls them "braided entities."[24] In other words, we do act deliberately to accomplish our intentions but at the same time, our actions have the *unintended consequences* of establishing structures that affect our future actions.

Let's say that you join a Habitat for Humanity group in your church that builds homes for low-income families. The group has some land, but needs to get materials donated so that construction can begin. Let's say that your aunt owns a building supply store, and you suggest to the group that you might "at least check to see if she would be willing to donate some lumber." Everyone happily agrees, and you call your aunt that evening. As it turns out, she is delighted to make the contribution, and your group is thrilled. Because of your action, the group solved an immediate problem. A little later, the group needs some roofing materials, so they naturally turn to you. You are hesitant to ask your aunt a second time, but you agree to visit various supply stores to see what you can do. Over time, the group comes to rely on you as the person who can get them materials, and a role is created. You never intended to create this role for yourself, but it happened because of expectations created in the process of taking local action. This is the process of structuration.

Giddens believes that this kind of structuration saturates all social life, in ways far more profound than can be seen in simple group roles. As an example, Donald Ellis shows how ethnicity is entailed in structuration.[25] We create ethnic difference by interactional patterns within and between groups. Ethnicity is a structural arrangement created over history through many local practices throughout the world. Yet once created, ethnicity has a life of its own, so that it becomes almost impossible not to see and act in accordance with ethnic experience in some way or another. Well-intentioned people acting normally in their everyday lives to solve problems and achieve goals create unintended categories of social structure, which limit what they can do in future interactions. These structures are not necessarily bad, but they do include power arrangements by which one group may dominate another.

Giddens believes that structuration always involves three major modalities or dimensions. These are (1) an interpretation or understanding; (2) a sense of morality or proper conduct; and (3) a sense of power in action. The rules we use to guide our actions, in other words, tell us how something should be understood (interpretation), what should be done (morality), and how to get things accomplished (power). In turn, our actions reinforce those very structures of interpretation, morality, and power.

Imagine a group that has created an atmosphere in which everybody is expected to speak up on every topic. Like all structuration, this was not planned but emerged as an unintended consequence of the actions of group members over time. In this scenario, a norm of *interpreting* emerges, in which the group is understood as egalitarian. It is considered proper for everyone to address every issue and not remain quiet on any subject. And *power* is granted to speech, as individuals use language to persuade one another.

In actual practice, your behavior is rarely affected by a single structure such as the "materials acquisition role" role or "speaking-up" norm used as examples above. Rather, your acts are affected by and affect several different structural elements at the same time. Two things can happen. First, one structure can *mediate* another. In other words, the production of one structure is accomplished by producing another. For example, the group may produce a communication network that governs who can talk to whom, but it does so by establishing individual roles. (This is why the custodian may not feel free to file a complaint directly with the CEO.) Here, the role structure mediates the communication network.

The second way structures relate to one another is through *contradiction*. Here, the production of a structure requires the establishment of another structure that undermines the first one. This is the stuff of classical paradox. Contradictions lead to conflict, and through a dialectic or tension between the contradictory elements, system change results. The old problem of task and relationship work in groups is a good example of contradictory structure. To accomplish a task, the group has to work on its interpersonal relationships, but working on relationships detracts from accomplishing the task. Concentrating too much on task does not leave enough time to mend fences and work on relationships, which must be done for high-quality task accomplishment.

The theory of structuration is a general social theory that can be applied to any number of situations. It has had most impact in the communication field in the areas of group and organizational communication. Here we show how it has been used in group communication theory, and in the following chapter (Chapter 9), we apply it to organizations.

Marshall Scott Poole and his colleagues have been working for several years on a structurational theory of group decision making.[26] This theory teaches that group decision making is a process in which group members attempt to achieve *convergence* or agreement on a final decision and, in so doing, structure their social system. In other words, in the process of trying to come to consensus, the group produces unintended consequences that shape the future work of the group. By expressing their opinions and preferences, group members actually produce and reproduce certain rules by which convergence can be achieved or blocked. This structuration process occurs within the three realms outlined by Giddens—interpretation, morality, and power.

Suppose, for example, that you are interested in persuading other members of a group to endorse a particular plan. You might share an *interpretation* of the plan by using the terms that, because of the previous history of the group, are commonly employed and understood by group members. Some of these words might even be rather specialized and specific to the group. By employing a particular style of speaking, then, you would be acting in a manner that is condoned by the group according to its norms, or sense of what is right or wrong (morality). To be effective as a speaker, you would also make use of a variety of sources of *power*, like leadership ability or status. What is powerful within the group is determined by a history of interaction within the group, and you will use these sources of power to persuade the group to endorse the plan.

Outside factors always influence the group's actions. However, these outside factors can only have meaning insofar as they are understood and interpreted by the group, and these interpretations are negotiated through interaction within the group. One of the most important outside factors is task type—what the group has been given to do—for the task makes certain rules appropriate and others inappropriate. For example, a study group will behave in one way when preparing for an exam and in an entirely different way when researching a group report, but the group itself will need to work through what each of these means in practical terms.

Further, we act toward others in ways that reflect our views of their place in the group, and in time, a "group" definition of each person and of the group as a whole emerges. This group definition subsequently affects the interaction among the members of the group and is thereby reproduced again and again. Some members, for example, might become task leaders, others socioemotional leaders, others information providers, and still others conflict managers.

The process of structuration usually leads to contradictions, and task groups are often confronted with these. Group actions both cause and resolve these inherent tensions. For example, the group must make a good decision before a deadline, but the time pressure of the deadline is inconsistent with the need for adequate time to do a good job. A group must attend to the requirements of the task, but in so doing they must also take care of their socioemotional needs. The problem, as we saw earlier in the chapter, is that meeting socioemotional needs can detract from the quality of task work. Further, members join a group to meet individual objectives, but they can only do so by paying attention to group objectives, which may undercut their own individual needs. Convergence can only come about through agreement, yet the group is told it must disagree in order to test ideas.

One of the most interesting contributions of this theory is its version of the processes followed by groups as they make decisions. Poole and his colleagues propose that groups can follow a variety of paths in the development of a decision, depending on the *contingencies* with which they are faced. Groups sometimes follow a standard agenda, but on other occasions, they are unsystematic, and sometimes even develop their own pathway in response to unique needs.

How a group operates depends on three sets of variables. The first is *objective task characteristics,* which are the standard attributes of the task such as the degree to which the problem comes with pre-established solutions, the clarity of the problem, the kind of expertise it requires, the extent of the impact of the problem, the number and nature of values implicit in the problem, and whether the solution is a one-shot action or will have broader policy implications.

For example, you might be involved in a club that has to decide whether and how to participate in a town festival, a difficult decision involving many possible options. The potential number of values entering into the decision is fairly high, and what you decide to do this year may affect what you can do in other years. This decision may take some time, and the decision path may be complex. On the other hand, if your group merely has to decide whether to have a taco booth, the decision is simple. The range of options is limited, the values involved in the decision are few, and the decision will have little impact outside the club. This decision will probably be made quickly and simply.

The second set of variables that affects the group's decision path is *group task characteristics,* and these will vary from group to group. They include the extent to which the group has previous experience with the problem, the extent to which an innovative solution is required as opposed to adoption of a standard course of action, and the urgency of the decision.

The third group of factors affecting the path of a group is *group structural characteristics,* including cohesiveness, power distribution, history of conflict, and group size. If your club has many members, gives the officers most of the power, and has a history of conflict, one kind of process will be used, but if it is small, cohesive, and has shared power, quite another would be predicted. These three sets of factors will operate to influence the process adopted by the group, including whether it uses a standard or a unique path, the complexity of the decision path, the amount of organization or disorganization with which the task is handled, and the amount of time devoted to various activities.

To discover various decision paths adopted by different groups, Poole and Jonelle Roth studied forty-seven decisions made by twenty-nine different groups.[27] The groups differed in their size, task complexity, urgency, cohesiveness, and conflict history. They included a medical school teaching team, an energy conservation-planning group, student term-project groups, and a dormitory management committee. Each discussion was tape recorded and analyzed. Each task statement in a discussion was classified by judges according to type, and these were combined into interacts similar to those Fisher discussed earlier. In addition, every 30-second segment was classified according to a set of relationship categories. With a sophisticated method of analysis, the researchers could see the various decision paths that emerged in these interactions on both the task and relationship tracks.

Three general types of paths were discovered. Some groups followed a *standard unitary sequence* (like a regular agenda), although not always in exactly the same way. Several groups followed what Poole and Roth call a *complex cyclic sequence.* Most of these were problem-solution cycles, in which the group would go back and forth in concentrated work between defining the problem and generating solution ideas, much as Fisher imagined. The third type of sequence was *solution-oriented,* in which almost no problem analysis occurred.

The decision paths taken by a group consist of three interwoven *activity tracks,* or courses along which the group develops or moves. A group may develop in different ways on each track, and the course of action taken on each track is affected in part by the three contingency variables discussed above—objective task characteristics, group task characteristics, and group structural characteristics.

There are probably many possible tracks, but three are elaborated in this theory—the task-process track, the relational track, and the topic-focus track. The *task-process track* consists of activities that deal directly with the problem or task, including, for example, analyzing the problem, designing solutions, evaluating solutions, and getting off on tangents. The *relational track* involves activities that affect interpersonal relationships in the group, such as disagreeing and making accommodations. These two correspond

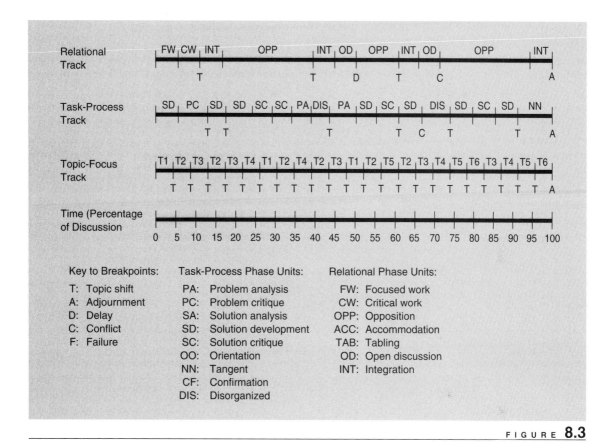

FIGURE **8.3**

Sample Discussion with Activity Tracks

neatly with the task-maintenance duality encountered in several other theories presented in this chapter. The third track, the *topic-focus track,* is a series of issues, topics, or concerns of the group over time. Figure 8.3 illustrates the activity tracks and how they work together.[28]

The multiple-sequence model imagines that the group moves along the various tracks over time, as illustrated by the time scale at the bottom of the graph. At a given moment, the group may be at a particular spot in the development of each track. The figure shows the three tracks divided into various activity segments. Code letters above the line identifies the activity segments. (The letters below the line are breakpoints, which will be explained later.)

In the discussion depicted in Figure 8.3 the group begins with topic 1 (T1). In discussing this

topic, the group is involved in focused work (FW) in the relational track and solution development (SD) in the task-process track. As they move to another topic, the group enters problem critique (PC) on the task-process track while they are engaged in critical work (CW) on the relational track. The discussion goes on for some time through a number of phases until the end, when they go off on a tangent (NN) on the task-process track but accomplish integration (INT) on the relational track. Notice that the activity segments or phases on the different tracks in the discussion depicted in this graph do not necessarily correspond to one another, which adds to the complexity of the path.

During the discussion, points of transition occur from time to time. These are *breakpoint,* or interruptions, designated by a code letter below the lines in Figure 8.3. Sometimes a breakpoint will mark a change in a single track, but often it will mark changes in several tracks. Breakpoints are important because they signal key points in the development of the group's decision-making activity.

Three types of breakpoints are apparent. *Normal breakpoints* are the expected, natural points of termination or transition. They include such things as adjournment, caucusing, or topic shifts. *Delays* are unexpected problems that cause a pause in normal group functioning. Delays often consist of rediscussion of issues necessary for the group to resolve conflicts or establish understanding. Delays may be a sign of impending difficulty, or they may be a more positive sign of careful thought or creative activity. *Disruptions* are more serious. These consist of major disagreements and group failures.

Although this is a somewhat complex and sophisticated theory, it expresses the structurational character of group decision making very well. It shows that groups do adopt particular courses of action to meet their needs but that in so doing they create constraints that limit future action. This idea is clear enough, but it begs the question of what kinds of structures are most effective or productive, and which are least. Functional theory steps in at this juncture to fill the void.

Functional Theory

Functional theories of group communication view the process as an instrument by which groups make decisions, emphasizing the connection between the quality of communication and the quality of the group's output.[29] Communication does a number of things—or *functions* in a number of ways—to determine group outcome: It is a means of sharing information, it is the way group members explore and identify errors in thinking, and it is a tool of persuasion.

The functional approach has been strongly influenced by the pragmatics of teaching small-group discussion. It is based in large measure on the work of philosopher John Dewey, which, since the publication of *How We Think* in 1910,

has greatly influenced twentieth-century pragmatic thought.[30] Although the research methods used to study group functions resemble those commonly seen in the sociopsychological tradition, we have placed it here, in the sociocultural, because of a strong kinship with this larger socio-cultural tradition that has looked at how groups work.

Dewey's version of the problem-solving process has six steps: (1) expressing a difficulty; (2) defining the problem; (3) analyzing the problem; (4) suggesting solutions; (5) comparing alternatives and testing them against a set of objectives or criteria; and (6) implementing the best solution. The theories of the functional tradition address the ways communication affects each of these elements.

Randy Hirokawa and his colleagues have been leaders in the functional tradition, and their description of the group decision-making process mirrors that of Dewey. Their work looks at a variety of mistakes that groups can make, aiming to identify the kinds of things groups need to take into consideration to become more effective.[31]

Groups normally begin by *identifying and assessing a problem,* and here they deal with a variety of questions: What happened? Why? Who was involved? What harm resulted? Who was hurt? Next, the group *gathers and evaluates information* about the problem. As the group discusses possible solutions, information continues to be gathered.

Next, the group generates a variety of *alternative proposals* for handling the problem and discusses the *objectives* it wishes to accomplish in solving it. These objectives and alternative proposals are *evaluated,* with the ultimate goal of reaching consensus on a course of action. This general sequence of problem solving is depicted in Figure 8.4.[32]

The factors contributing to faulty decisions are easily inferred from this decision-making process. The first is *improper assessment* of the problem, which stems from inadequate or inaccurate analysis of the situation. The group may fail to see the problem, or it may not accurately identify the causes of the problem. The second

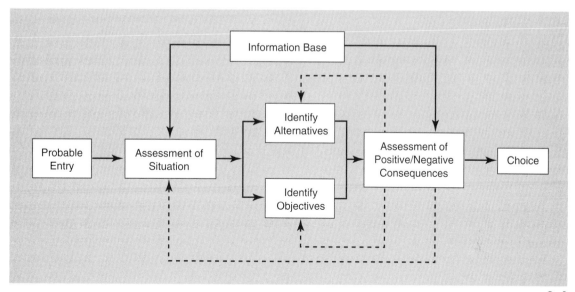

FIGURE **8.4**

General Model of the Group Decision-Making Process

source of error in decision making is *inappropriate goals and objectives.* The group may neglect important objectives that ought to be achieved, or it may work toward unnecessary ones. The third problem is *improper assessment of positive and negative qualities,* ignoring certain advantages, disadvantages, or both of various proposals. Or it may overestimate the positive or negative outcomes expected. Fourth, the group may develop an *inadequate information base,* which can happen in several ways. Valid information may be rejected, or invalid information may be accepted. Too little information may be collected, or too much information may cause overload and confusion. Finally, the group may be guilty of *faulty reasoning* from the information base.

Why do groups fall into these traps? Hirokawa believes that the errors most often arise from the communication in the group. The group is swayed by certain members who unwittingly mislead the group in some way, an outcome that requires someone to counteract it by exerting a positive influence on the group. As part of his investigations, Hirokawa conducted a study of four aspects of decision quality: appropriate understanding of the problem, appro-

priate understanding of the objectives and standards of a good decision, appropriate assessment of the positive qualities of alternatives, and appropriate assessment of the negative qualities of alternatives.[33]

In a laboratory setting, Hirokawa formed about forty three-person groups and had them discuss what to do about a certain plagiarism case at the university. The discussions ranged from 17 to 47 minutes in length, and each was videotaped. Two professors experienced in student ethics cases judged the groups' decisions in terms of overall quality, and a panel of judges rated the extent to which each of the four critical elements listed above was fulfilled. Statistical analysis showed that the quality of a group's decision is definitely related to these four elements, and when the very best groups were compared to the very worst, there was a significant difference in the extent to which each function was accomplished by the group. Clearly, groups that were more effective in meeting the four functions made better decisions. As an example of the kind of trap that groups can encounter, groupthink theory looks at a set of errors that can be devastating.

Groupthink Theory

The work of Irving Janis and his colleagues has been immensely influential within the functional tradition.[34] Here we will look at one of his theories, most often referred to as the *groupthink hypothesis*.[35] Like Hirokawa, Janis examines in some detail the effectiveness of group decisions. Emphasizing critical thinking, he shows how certain conditions can lead to high group satisfaction but ineffective output.

Groupthink is a direct result of cohesiveness in groups, which was first discussed in some depth by Kurt Lewin in the 1930s and has since come to be seen as a crucial variable in group effectiveness.[36] *Cohesiveness* is the degree of mutual interest among members. In a highly cohesive group, a strong mutual identification keeps a group together. Cohesiveness is a result of the degree to which all members perceive that their goals can be met within the group. This does not require that the members have similar attitudes but that members are interdependent and rely on one another to achieve certain mutually desired goals. The more cohesive a group, the more pressure it exerts on the members.

Cohesiveness can be a good thing because it brings the members together and enhances the group's interpersonal relationships. Although Janis does not deny the potential value of cohesiveness, he also recognizes its dangers. For one, highly cohesive groups may invest too much energy in maintaining goodwill in the group to the detriment of decision making. Members invest much intrinsic energy in groups because of the potential rewards for doing so: friendship, prestige, and confirmation of one's self-worth. Because our self-esteem needs are high, we will sometimes devote too much energy to establishing positive bonds, and this can lead to groupthink. Janis found in his research that groupthink can have six negative outcomes:

1. The group limits its discussion to only a few alternatives without considering a full range of creative possibilities. The solution may seem obvious and simple to the group, and there is little exploration of other ideas.

2. The position initially favored by most members is never restudied to seek out less obvious pitfalls. In other words, the group is not very critical in examining the ramifications of the preferred solution.

3. The group fails to reexamine those alternatives originally disfavored by the majority. Minority opinions are quickly dismissed and ignored, not only by the majority but also by those who originally favored them.

4. Expert opinion is not sought. The group is satisfied with itself and may feel threatened by outsiders.

5. The group is highly selective in gathering and attending to available information. The members tend to concentrate only on the information that supports the favored plan.

6. The group is so confident in its ideas that it does not consider contingency plans. It does not foresee the possibility of failure and does not plan for failure.

All these things result from a lack of critical thinking and overconfidence in the group. Janis maintains that groupthink is marked by a number of symptoms. The first symptom is an *illusion of invulnerability,* which creates an undue air of optimism. There is a strong sense that, "We know what we are doing, so don't rock the boat." Second, the group creates collective efforts to *rationalize* the course of action decided on. It creates a story that makes its decision seem absolutely right and literally talks itself into thinking it did the right thing. Third, the group maintains an unquestioned belief in its inherent *morality,* seeing itself as being well motivated and working for the best outcome. That leads the group to soft-pedal ethical and moral consequences.

A fourth symptom is that out-group leaders are *stereotyped* as evil, weak, or stupid. Fifth, *direct pressure* is exerted on members not to express counter opinions. Dissent is quickly squelched, which leads to the sixth symptom—the *self-censorship* of disagreement. Individual members are reluctant to state opposing opinions and silently suppress their reservations. Thus, seventh, there is a shared *illusion of unanimity* within the group. Even if the decision is not unanimous, the group rallies outwardly around a position of solidarity. Finally, groupthink involves the emergence of self-appointed *mindguards* to protect the group and its leader from adverse opinions and unwanted information. The mindguard typically suppresses negative information by counseling participants not to make things difficult.

Janis believes that the answer to the problem of groupthink is to take the following steps in group decision making:

1. Encourage everyone to be a critical evaluator and express reservations whenever they come up.
2. Do not have the leader state a preference up front.
3. Set up several independent and separate policymaking groups.
4. Divide into subgroups.
5. Discuss what is happening with others outside the group.
6. Invite outsiders into the group to bring fresh ideas.
7. Assign an individual at each meeting to be devil's advocate.
8. Spend considerable time surveying warning signals.
9. Hold a second-chance meeting to reconsider decisions before making them final.

Janis uses historical data to support his theory by analyzing six national political decision-making episodes in which outcomes were either good or bad, depending on the extent of groupthink. The negative examples include the Bay of Pigs invasion, the Korean War, Pearl Harbor, and the escalation of the Vietnam War. Positive examples include the Cuban missile crisis and the Marshall Plan.[37]

One of Janis's cases of successful decision making is the Kennedy administration's response to the Cuban missile crisis. In October 1962, Cuba was caught building offensive nuclear weapon stations and arming them with Soviet missiles. President Kennedy had already suffered through one instance of groupthink in the Bay of Pigs invasion the year before, and he seemed to have learned what not to do in these kinds of international crises. In the missile crisis, Kennedy constantly encouraged his advisors to challenge and debate one another. He refrained from leading the group too early with his own opinion, and he set up subgroups to discuss the problem independently so as not to reinforce members' opinions. Various members, including Kennedy, talked with outsiders and experts about the problem to make sure that fresh opinions were heard. In the end, Kennedy successfully invoked a military blockade and stopped the Cuban-Soviet development.

REFLECTIONS ON
The Sociocultural Tradition

Without abandoning the essential assumptions of cybernetics, the theories classified here as sociocultural focus on group work. In other words, these theories emphasize the social construction of groups—what they do and how this action results in something larger than individuals or even groups. Structuration theory is a clear example of the unintended consequences of group action. You will see in this theory a strong cybernetic base as well, as the consequences of action within a group create constraints or structures that further limit group action. Groupthink is a specific example of this kind of effect.

• • •

A P P L I C A T I O N S   &   I M P L I C A T I O N S

Groups are important to individuals and society. As a person moves about in the world, cooperation becomes essential in achieving individual goals. People use communication to share resources to solve problems, and group communication thereby becomes not only an instrument for accomplishing tasks but also a means of building relationships.

Theories of small group communication form a distinct tradition. Their common threads and lines of influence are clear and provide a kind of coherence that binds this work. As we survey the theories summarized in this chapter, several generalizations are apparent.

1. Groups cannot be separated from the context in which they work.
Group communication can be viewed as a system of inputs, internal processes, and outputs. Inputs include information, group resources, and task characteristics. The process includes group interaction and decision development, and the outputs include completed tasks as well as interpersonal relationships. Pervasive in this field, the input-process-output model alerts us to the fact that groups exist within larger systems. When we communicate in groups, we need to pay attention to the nature and quality of inputs and become more aware of the ways in which our actions within a group create effects that influence the larger environment in some way, not to mention the group itself.

Traditionally, we think of groups as a setting for live, face-to-face interaction. This common understanding of groups is changing rapidly, as the Internet allows groups to form and work together without being in the same room and without interacting directly and simultaneously. The rise of communication technology expands the ability of groups, but, whether live or computer-assisted, groups still are part of a large environment and can be characterized with the basic input-process-output model.[38]

Although commonly used, this simple input-process-output model belies the complexity of real groups in context. Even though it acknowledges a larger system, this model relies on the idea that groups are like a container. You may pour things into it and pour things out of it, but the boundary of the container is still impermeable. In an extended critique of traditional group studies, Putnam and Stohl wrote that a bona fide group could not be separated from its context. In the fifteen years or so since they originally presented the idea of bona fide groups, research has become more contextual. As one example, Lawrence Frey has recently published a volume of case studies of bona fide groups illustrating the expanding focus of this work.[39]

The studies in Frey's volume show that a complete analysis of the functioning of a group requires careful attention to interfaces among groups. When you are working within a group, think about the constraints and opportunities that overlapping groups provide. What resources flow into the group because of its fluid membership? What special challenges does the group face in managing the bona fide, systemic nature of groups? Can you anticipate what effect the group will have on other groups and how this may later open opportunities or cause constraints for the groups involved.

We once worked in a university department that had a rotating department chair. Every three years, another member of the department would become chair, so that eventually, most faculty had rotated into that position at one time or another. This system was a terrific resource for the department because it recognized that department chairs encounter several administrative groups that ordinary faculty do not, and in doing so, develop perspectives that can be extremely valuable to the department. As more and more faculty developed this experience, the overall human resources of the department expanded, making the group increasingly effective. The rotating-chair system simply built upon the bona fide group process, so that a cybernetic loop was created, always maintaining a fresh input of perspectives.

All groups—from families to community clubs—are bona fide, but the significance of context is nowhere as obvious as in organizations. David Seibold believes that organizational and group researchers have conducted their work in ways that tend to separate these contexts, when in fact they are so closely associated that they should not be divided.[40] In the following chapter (Chapter 9), we present a number of theories of organizational communication. Since organizations are built through networks of groups, the line between the organization and group is fine, and the distinction between organizational communication and group communication is fuzzy, indeed.

2. Effective group work accomplishes tasks and builds interpersonal relationships.

This idea appears in almost all of the theories discussed in this chapter. Task energy is directed at problem solving, and interpersonal energy is directed at group maintenance and relationships. Group effectiveness seems to depend on the balance between these two aspects of communication, and inadequate attention to either can lead to dissatisfaction and poor decision making. Task and relational functions are thoroughly mixed. You often fulfill both task and social functions in a single statement, and in classifying group behavior, validly separating these functions is difficult.

This powerful lesson from group communication theory teaches the need for balance. You simply cannot do a good job as a group without paying attention to relationships as well as task, in a way that acknowledges the connection between the two. We work on relationships, not just to make us feel good, but because relational bonds allow us to work effectively on the task. The opposite is also true: Successful completion of a task can help build strong relationships. Think about the best groups you have known. These groups were probably good for different reasons, but one common element was surely an appropriate mix of strong working relationships combined with successful task accomplishment.

3. Process and structure are intimately tied together.

The idea of structuration is actually quite simple: The practices of the group create structures that affect future practice. In other words, actions have consequences for future action. Because we are most concerned about the content of our discussion at any given moment, it is hard to keep an eye on this larger issue; yet, the process used by a group does create a certain kind of social world that presents both opportunities and constraints on the group in the future. For this reason, groups need to pay attention to process.

Group members most frequently ask "what" questions: What do we need to talk about? What do we want to accomplish? What are we trying to do? To these, groups should add "how" questions: How shall we address this issue? How shall we work as a group? How should we structure our time? How should we divide our energy? No matter what you do, structuration will occur, but if you are not conscious of it, the results may be unwanted and unproductive. "How" questions are critical because process matters.

Structuration can have several kinds of effects. It will determine, for example, what individuals can and do say in a group. Even Bales's research in the early 1950s showed that group comments are not evenly distributed. Bales showed how certain types of statements shape the group's interaction and the roles assigned to individuals.

As another example, interactional patterns in groups define the structure of decision development. Interaction combines into activity segments, which, in turn, combine into phases. Several theories in this chapter address this concern, and it seems clear that careful, critical consideration is an important ingredient.

4. Effective group work requires careful attention to the quality of communication, creative thinking, and critical thinking.

The fourth trend in small group theory is its *interest in effectiveness,* as the functionalist tradition so well illustrates. For example, Janis's and Hirokawa's theories provide guidelines for improved group functioning. They suggest ways of guarding against various hazards in groups. Consistent with the everyday experience of groups in our society, such theories have practical potential in helping groups become more effective.

Dennis Gouran, a leader in functional group theory, outlines several areas in which skill can matter in the effectiveness of a group.[41] Consistent with the task-relationship distinction, Gouran outlines a number of skills in these areas. To these, he adds the third category of procedural skills. *Task skills* include (1) problem recognition and framing; (2) inference drawing; (3) idea generation; and (4) argument. *Relational skills* include (1) leadership, (2) climate building, and (3) conflict management. *Procedural skills* include (1) planning, and (2) process enactment.

Within the field of group communication, then, pragmatics has been important. Much of this work has been powerful in helping us teach group participants how to be more effective in their work. The same is true within organizational communication, as we will see in the following chapter.

◖ NOTES

1. A number of sources on small groups reflect the breadth of work in this area. See, for example, Lawrence R. Frey, ed., *The Handbook of Group Communication Theory and Research* (Thousand Oaks, CA: Sage, 1999); Randy Hirokawa, Abran J. Salazar, Larry Erbert, and Richard J. Ice, "Small Group Communication," in *An Integrated Approach to Communication Theory and Research,* ed. Michael B. Salwen and Don W. Stacks (Mahwah, NJ: Lawrence Erlbaum, 1996), pp. 359–382; John F. Cragan and David W. Wright, "Small Group Communication Research of the 1980s: A Synthesis and Critique," *Communication Studies* 41 (1990): 212–236; Marshall Scott Poole, "Do We Have Any Theories of Group Communication?," *Communication Studies* 41 (1990): 237–247.
2. See, for example, Robert F. Bales, *Personality and Interpersonal Behavior* (New York: Holt, Rinehart & Winston, 1970), p. 92.
3. For historical overviews of theory development, see Dennis S. Gouran, "Communication in Groups: The Emergence and Evolution of a Field of Study," in *The Handbook of Group Communication Theory and Research,* ed. Lawrence R. Frey (Thousand Oaks, CA: Sage, 1999), pp. 3–36; and Dennis S. Gouran, Randy Y. Hirokawa, Michael Calvin McGee, and Laurie L. Miller, "Communication in Groups: Research Trends and Theoretical Perspectives," in *Building Communication Theories: A Socio/Cultural Approach,* ed. Fred L. Casmir (Hillsdale, NJ: Lawrence Erlbaum, 1994), pp. 241–268.
4. Mary Parker Follett, *Creative Experience* (New York: Longmans, Green, 1924).
5. Robert F. Bales, *Interaction Process Analysis: A Method for the Study of Small Groups* (Reading, MA: Addison-Wesley, 1950); *Personality and Interpersonal Behavior;* Robert F. Bales, Stephen P. Cohen, and

Stephen A. Williamson, *SYMLOG: A System for the Multiple Level Observation of Groups* (London: Collier, 1979).

6. Adapted from Bales, *Personality and Interpersonal Behavior,* p. 92.

7. Ernest Bormann, "Symbolic Convergence and Communication in Group Decision Making," in *Communication and Group Decision-Making,* ed. Randy Y. Hirokawa and Marshall Scott Poole (Beverly Hills, CA: Sage, 1986), pp. 219–236.

8. Cynthia Stohl and Linda L. Putnam, "Communication in Bona Fide Groups: A Retrospective and Prospective Account," in *Group Communication in Context: Studies of Bona Fide Groups,* ed. Lawrence R. Frey (Mahwah, NJ: Lawrence Erlbaum, 2003), pp. 399–414; Linda L. Putnam and Cynthia Stohl, "Bona Fide Groups: An Alternative Perspective for Communication and Small Group Decision Making," in *Communication and Group Decision Making,* ed. Randy Y. Hirokawa and Marshall Scott Poole (Thousand Oaks, CA: Sage, 1996), pp. 147–178; Cynthia Stohl and Linda L. Putnam, "Group Communication in Context: Implications for the Study of Bona Fide Groups," in *Group Communication in Context: Studies of Natural Groups,* pp. 284–292; Linda L. Putnam, "Revitalizing Small Group Communication: Lessons Learned from a Bona Fide Group Perspective," *Communication Studies* 45 (1994): 97–102; Cynthia Stohl and Michael E. Holms, "A Functional Perspective for Bona Fide Groups," in *Communication Yearbook 16,* ed. Stanley Deetz (Newbury Park, CA: Sage, 1993), pp. 601–614; Linda L. Putnam and Cynthia Stohl, "Bona Fide Groups: A Reconceptualization of Groups in Context," *Communication Studies* 41 (1990): 248–265.

9. Stephen W. Littlejohn and Kathy Domenici, *Engaging Communication in Conflict: Systemic Practice* (Thousand Oaks, CA: Sage, 2001), pp. 147–167.

10. This model is discussed by Marshall Scott Poole, David R. Seibold, and Robert D. McPhee, "A Structurational Approach to Theory-Building in Group Decision-Making Research," in *Communication and Group Decision-Making,* ed. Randy Y. Hirokawa and Marshall Scott Poole (Beverly Hills, CA: Sage, 1986), pp. 238–240. See also Susan Jarboe, "A Comparison of Input-Output, Process-Output, and Input-Process-Output Models of Small Group Problem-Solving Effectiveness," *Communication Monographs* 55 (1988): 121–142.

11. See, for example, John G. Oetzel, Trudy E. Burtis, Martha I. Chew Sanchez, and Frank G. Pérez, "Investigating the Role of Communication in Culturally Diverse Work Groups: A Review and Synthesis," *Communication Yearbook 25,* ed. William B. Gudykunst (Mahwah, NJ: Lawrence Erlbaum, 2001), pp. 237–270.

12. Barry Collins and Harold Guetzkow, *A Social Psychology of Group Processes for Decision-Making* (New York: Wiley, 1964), p. 81.

13. One proposed theory that explains leadership competence in terms of task and interpersonal variables is published in J. Kevin Barge and Randy Y. Hirokawa, "Toward a Communication Competency Model of Group Leadership," *Small Group Behavior* 20 (1989): 167–189.

14. Raymond Cattell, "Concepts and Methods in the Measurement of Group Syntality," *Psychological Review* 55 (1948): 48–63.

15. B. Aubrey Fisher and Leonard Hawes, "An Interact System Model: Generating a Grounded Theory of Small Groups," *Quarterly Journal of Speech* 57 (1971): 444–453.

16. B. Aubrey Fisher, *Small Group Decision Making: Communication and the Group Process* (New York: McGraw-Hill, 1980), p. 117.

17. B. Aubrey Fisher, "Decision Emergence: Phases in Group Decision Making," *Speech Monographs* 37 (1970): 53–60; Fisher, *Small Group Decision Making.*

18. Fisher, *Small Group Decision Making,* pp. 298–306.

19. Fisher, *Small Group Decision Making;* also B. Aubrey Fisher, "The Process of Decision Modification in Small Discussion Groups," *Journal of Communication* 20 (1970): 51–64.

20. Fisher, *Small Group Decision Making,* p. 155.

21. John G. Oetzel, "Effective Intercultural Work Group Communication Theory," in *Theorizing about Communication and Culture,* ed. William B. Gudykunst (Thousand Oaks, CA: Sage, in press); John G. Oetzel, "Self-Construals, Communication Processes, and Group Outcomes in Homogeneous and Heterogeneous Groups," *Small Group Research* 32 (2001): 19–54; John G. Oetzel, "Explaining Individual Communication Processes in Homogeneous and Heterogeneous Groups through Individualism-Collectivism and Self-Construal," *Human Communication Research* 25 (1998): 202–224; John G. Oetzel, "Culturally Homogeneous and Heterogeneous Groups: Explaining Communication Processes through Individualism-Collectivism and Self-Construal," *International Journal of Intercultural Relations* 22 (1998): 135–161; John G. Oetzel, "Intercultural Small Groups: An Effective Decision-Making Theory," in *Intercultural Communication Theories,* ed. R. L. Wiseman (Thousand Oaks, CA: Sage, 1995), pp. 247–270.

22. Oetzel, "Self-Construals, Communication Processes, and Group Outcomes."

23. See, for example, Anthony Giddens, *New Rules of Sociological Method* (New York: Basic, 1976); and Anthony Giddens, *Studies in Social and Political Theory* (New York: Basic, 1977). For a brief summary

of the theory, see Anthony Giddens, *Profiles and Critiques in Social Theory* (Berkeley: University of California Press, 1982), pp. 8–11. See also Stephen P. Banks and Patricia Riley, "Structuration Theory as an Ontology for Communication Research," *Communication Yearbook 16,* ed. Stanley Deetz (Newbury Park, CA: Sage, 1993), pp. 167–196.

24. Donald G. Ellis, *Crafting Society: Ethnicity, Class, and Communication Theory* (Mahwah, NJ: Lawrence Erlbaum, 1999), p. 123.

25. Ellis, *Crafting Society.*

26. Marshall Scott Poole, David R. Seibold, and Robert D. McPhee, "Group Decision-Making as a Structurational Process," *Quarterly Journal of Speech* 71 (1985): 74; and Poole, Seibold, and McPhee, "Structurational Approach." See also Julie M. Billingsley, "An Evaluation of the Functional Perspective in Small Group Communication," in *Communication Yearbook 16,* ed. Stanley Deetz (Newbury Park, CA: Sage, 1993), pp. 615–622.

27. Marshall Scott Poole and Jonelle Roth, "Decision Development in Small Groups IV: A Typology of Group Decision Paths," *Human Communication Research* 15 (1989): 323–356; "Decision Development in Small Groups V: Test of a Contingency Model," *Human Communication Research* 15 (1989): 549–589.

28. Adapted from Poole, "Decision Development III," pp. 327, 329; Poole and Roth, "Decision Development IV," pp. 334–335.

29. This tradition is discussed by Lise VanderVoort, "Functional and Causal Explanations in Group Communication Research," *Communication Theory* 12 (2002): 469–486. See also Dennis S. Gouran, Randy Y. Hirokawa, Kelly M. Julian, and Geoff B. Leatham, "The Evolution and Current Status of the Functional Perspective on Communication in Decision-Making and Problem-Solving Groups," in *Communication Yearbook 16,* ed. Stanley A. Deetz (Newbury Park, CA: Sage, 1993), pp. 573–600.

30. John Dewey, *How We Think* (Boston: Heath, 1910).

31. Randy Y. Hirokawa and Dirk R. Scheerhorn, "Communication in Faulty Group Decision-Making," in *Communication and Group Decision-Making,* ed. Randy Y. Hirokawa and Marshall S. Poole (Beverly Hills, CA: Sage, 1986), pp. 63–80; Dennis S. Gouran and Randy Y. Hirokawa, "Counteractive Functions of Communication in Effective Group Decision-Making," in *Communication and Group Decision-Making,* ed. Randy Y. Hirokawa and Marshall Scott Poole (Beverly Hills, CA: Sage, 1986), pp. 81–92; Randy Y. Hirokawa, "Group Communication and Problem-Solving Effectiveness I: A Critical Review of Inconsistent Findings," *Communication Quarterly* 30 (1982): 134–141; Randy Y. Hirokawa, "Group Communication and Problem-Solving Effectiveness II," *Western Journal of Speech Communication* 47 (1983): 59–74; Randy Y. Hirokawa, "Group Communication and Problem-Solving Effectiveness: An Investigation of Group Phases," *Human Communication Research* 9 (1983): 291–305.

32. Hirokawa and Scheerhorn, "Communication in Faulty Group Decision-Making," p. 66.

33. Randy Y. Hirokawa, "Group Communication and Decision Making Performance: A Continued Test of the Functional Perspective," *Human Communication Research* 14 (1988): 487–515.

34. See, for example, Irving Janis and Leon Mann, *Decision Making: A Psychological Analysis of Conflict, Choice, and Commitment* (New York: Free Press, 1977); and Irving Janis, *Crucial Decisions: Leadership in Policy Making and Crisis Management* (New York: Free Press, 1989).

35. Irving Janis, *Groupthink: Psychological Studies of Policy Decisions and Fiascoes* (Boston: Houghton Mifflin, 1982).

36. Kurt Lewin, *Resolving Social Conflicts: Selected Papers on Group Dynamics* (New York: Harper & Row, 1948). For information on Lewin's theory of group dynamics, see Everett M. Rogers, *A History of Communication Study: A Biographical Approach* (New York: Free Press, 1994), pp. 316–355.

37. For a laboratory test of the groupthink hypothesis, see John A. Courtright, "A Laboratory Investigation of Groupthink," *Communication Monographs* 45 (1978): 229–246.

38. For an application of the input-process-output model in group communication technology (GCT), see Craig R. Scott, "Communication Technology and Group Communication," in *The Handbook of Group Communication Theory and Research,* ed. Lawrence R. Frey (Thousand Oaks, CA: Sage, 1999), pp. 432–474.

39. Lawrence R. Frey, ed., *Group Communication in Context: Studies of Bona Fide Groups* (Mahwah, NJ: Lawrence Erlbaum, 2003).

40. David R. Seibold, "Groups and Organizations: Premises and Perspectives," in *Communication: Views from the Helm for the 21st Century,* ed. Judith S. Trent (Boston: Allyn & Bacon, 1998), pp. 162–168.

41. Dennis S. Gouran, "Communication Skills for Group Decision Making," in *Handbook of Communication and Social Interaction Skills,* ed. John O. Greene and Brant R. Burleson (Mahwah, NJ: Lawrence Erlbaum, 2003), pp. 834–870.

CHAPTER

THE ORGANIZATION

> Our society is an organizational society. We are born in organizations, educated
> in organizations, and most of us spend much of our lives working for organiza-
> tions. We spend much of our leisure time playing and praying in organizations.
> Most of us will die in an organization, and when the time comes for burial, the
> largest organization of all—the state—must grant official permission.[1]

In this quotation, Amatai Etzioni's captures the significance of this area of study. Organizational communication can be thought of as "that field that conceptualizes organization as symbolically achieved cooperation."[2] Individuals connect to others in some
kind of structure, which provides organizational form. But form is more than lines of
connection, it also implies directions of influence within a complex system, so that
certain individuals exert influence over others, certain groups exert influence over
other groups, and certain systems exert forces that control or manage other systems.

Hierarchies of forces and connections still do not do justice to organizations. Organizations do consist of human beings, after all, and every organization has a certain feel to it. What do you feel free to do within an organization? What are you constrained from doing? What do people like and appreciate within an organization? How
do people communicate? Is there a sense of formality or informality?

As we think of organizations in these ways, then, three general defining dimensions emerge: (1) organizational structure, form, and function; (2) management, control, and power; and (3) organizational culture. A large body of literature has emerged
in organizational communication within each of these three areas.[3] Gareth Morgan

Topics Addressed	Sociopsychological Theories	Cybernetic Theories	Sociocultural Theories	Critical Theories
Organizational structure, form, and function	Weber's theory of bureaucracy	The process of organizing Network theory	Conversation text Structuration	
Management, control, and power	Likert's four systems		Organizational control theory	Hermeneutics of suspicion Managerialism and democracy Gender and race in organizational communication
Culture			Organizational culture	

outlines a number of metaphors capturing various aspects of this literature.[4] Let's take a closer look at how these relate to the three defining dimensions of organizational communication.

Organizational structure, form, and function can be captured by several metaphors. First, organizations are like *machines.* Like machines, they have parts that produce products and services. You can take a machine apart, lay its parts along a bench, and, if you are skilled enough, put them back together again. The parts of the machine articulate with one another in ways that allow it to do something, just like an organization. Of course, in this information age, this metaphor may be less and less useful since machines now have parts such as electronic impulses that you could not really lay out on a bench. And such parts actually reorganize themselves to adapt to the environment much like any open, living system. Even virtual machines have structure and function.

A second metaphor that captures the structural aspect of organizations is the *organism.* Like a plant or animal, the organization is born, grows, functions, and adapts to changes in the environment, and eventually dies. Organizational structures never remain static, but must grow, change, or die. The whole idea of the learning organization is one in which organizations structure themselves to adapt constantly to a changing environment.[5] For this reason, organizations also embody a sense of *flux and transformation*—another metaphor—because they adjust, change, and grow on the basis of information, feedback, and logical force.

Four metaphors are useful in helping us understand the second dimension (management, control, and power) of the organization. The first of these is the *brain:* Organizations process information, they have intelligence, they conceptualize, and they make plans. The brain is the control system of the body—a centralized organ that has neurological connection to every other aspect of the body. Organizations also have control centers that might be likened to the "brain" of the organization.

But control is never a one-way flow of influence from a single brain to other organs. Instead, it is accomplished by patterns of influence, or control systems, that make organizations like a *political system* in which power is distributed, influence is exerted, and decisions are made. You often hear about the "politics" of an organization, which is nothing more than a useful reference to this metaphor.

Because people are constrained by systems of management, control, and power, organizations are sometimes like *psychic prisons,* because they can shape and limit the lives of their members. Related to this, the element of management, control, and power can make organizations feel like *instruments of domination,* for they possess competing interests, some of which dominate others.

The third defining dimension of organizations is culture, and Morgan actually treats culture itself as a metaphor. Think of the cultures with which you identify. These might be ethnic, national, racial, or some other cultural forms. A culture has an identity as a culture because of shared values, norms, beliefs, and practices. When you think about it, organizations have all of these things. If you say that you work for Boeing, you have a strong sense of what that means culturally, precisely because of the values, norms, beliefs, and practices that predominate in this organization.

Each of these metaphors offers different insights into organizational life. And each of the traditions that have studied organizations interprets these metaphors in different ways.

◖ THE SOCIOPSYCHOLOGICAL TRADITION

Sociopsychological theories of organizations tend to focus on individual and group attributes, or characteristics, rather than communication patterns. As a result, this tradition is not very influential in the communication literature today. This is not to suggest, however, that this tradition has been unimportant, since both sociology and psychology have had considerable impact on organization studies. Because of its previous influence on organizational thought, we do think it necessary to provide a sense of the sociopsychological tradition in this chapter.

In this section, we summarize two theories that are important for their foundational influence. The first is Max Weber's classical theory of bureaucracy. Weber, who was most concerned about how human beings act rationally to achieve their goals, aimed to explain social processes in a way that links individual human motivation to social outcomes. Because of his emphasis on the individual as the driver of action and his interest in causal and rational explanation, his work does manifest a certain quality of the sociopsychological tradition. Also, Weber's theory provides a framework for the traditional view of organizational structure as hierarchical and rule driven. As you read through Weber's principles in this section of the chapter, you will recognize immediately that these principles are alive and well in organizations today, a full century after they were written.[6] You will also notice that they do not say much about communication

per se, but Weber's principles did lay down a base of powerful assumptions that affected the image of communication in organizations.

The second theory presented in this section is an example from the Human Relations Movement, which had an important early influence on how we think about and treat people in organizations. Specifically, we include the theory of Rensis Likert, whose work is still quoted occasionally today. Likert built his theory on ideas about human motivation and action. Although quite different from Weber's thinking, it still follows the basic approach of the sociopsychological tradition. Likert's theory says much more about communication than does Weber's, though it does not explain organizational communication in the sophisticated ways encountered in mainstream organizational communication theory.

Weber's Theory of Bureaucracy

In his lifetime (1864–1920), Max Weber produced a great quantity of work on human institutions, among which is his theory of bureaucracy.[7] Weber's ideas, developed at the beginning of the century, are part of what we now refer to as "classical organizational theory."[8] We all have a common idea of what a bureaucracy is like—hierarchical and layered, rule-driven, and insensitive to individual differences and needs. Although our reaction to bureaucracies is often negative, the principles that govern most complex organizations still have these qualities, which were anticipated and, indeed, advocated as an organizational ideal by Max Weber. Weber attempted to identify the best way for organizations to manage the complexity of work of individuals with a common aim, and his principles have been durable over the years. Weber defines an organization as a system of purposeful, interpersonal activity designed to coordinate individual tasks.[9] This cannot be done without authority, specialization, and regulation.

Authority comes with power, but in organizations, authority must be "legitimate" or authorized formally by the organization. Organizational effectiveness depends upon the extent to which management is granted *legitimate power* by the organization. You tend to do what your boss says because the organization grants your boss the legitimate authority to give orders. In other words, managers do not necessarily have power because of birth, intelligence, persuasiveness, or physical strength, as might be the case in other settings, but because the organization gives them authority. When you become a member of the organization, you "agree," at least tacitly, to follow the rules that grant this authority. The organization is established as a rational system by force of rule, making it a kind of *rational-legal authority*. When you "report to" someone, you understand that this individual has the authority to tell you what to do. At the same time, however, administrators must be able to back up their authority by allocating resources within their respective domains. Although we all know managers who are ineffective, a principle of bureaucracy is that administrators must be appointed and always on the basis of qualifications.

The best way to organize rational-legal authority, according to Weber, is by hierarchy. In other words, bosses have bosses, who themselves have higher bosses. This hierarchy is carefully defined by regulation within the organization. Each layer of management has its own legitimate authority, and only the head of the organization has authority overall. Although Weber said that managers should be appointed on the basis of qualifications, the absolute head is rarely appointed on this basis. More likely, the head is elected or even inherits the position.

In the executive branch of U.S. government, for example, the head is the President, who is elected by the people, while directors and secretaries are appointed to administer various departments. In corporations, the owners elect the Board of Directors, which in turn elects the chairperson of the board. The CEO is appointed, and so is every manager below the CEO. In family businesses, the chairperson of the board can be an inherited position, but managers will be appointed.

A related principle of bureaucratic authority, according to Weber, is that employees of the organization do not share in ownership of the organization, as this would disrupt the flow of legitimate authority. This is one aspect of organizations that has changed since Weber's time; employees often have stock plans, which means they do own part of the company. Even more direct forms of ownership exist as well, such as when the employees of United Airlines literally purchased the company by buying up the majority of shares.

The first large principle of bureaucracy, then, is authority. The second principle is *specialization*. Individuals are divided up according to division of labor, and each person knows his or her job within the organization. The proliferation of titles and job descriptions is a perfect example. Notice the difference between a bureaucracy and other types of organization in this sense. In a small hardware store, employees may do everything from meeting customers to cleaning the toilet. Once the store reaches a certain size, however, it begins to take on bureaucratic characteristics so that a person may be hired just to keep stock and sweep the floor, someone else is hired to be a cashier, and others are salespersons. In very large organizations, division of labor is often extensive, resulting in employees having little or no idea of what their task contributes to the overall organization.

A third aspect of bureaucracy is the necessity of *rules*. What makes organizational coordination possible is the implementation of a common set of regulations that govern everyone's behavior. Organizational rules should be rational, meaning that they are designed to achieve the goals of the organization. In order to track everything that happens, careful records must be kept of all organizational operations.

Weber's bureaucratic model nicely illustrates the machine metaphor of organizations. It follows a top-down, mechanistic view of how large groups should coordinate their activities to achieve common goals. Although still prevalent in management theory today, a counterpoint has been the human relations movement, which advocates vesting much more power in ordinary employees.

Likert's Four Systems

Rensis Likert, a theorist in the human relations school, reacted to classical theories such as Weber's by focusing on the workers—their feelings and needs. This movement was an especially popular from the 1940s through the 1960s. Likert's approach, like most human relations theories, looks at human relations as a management tool.[10] The basic idea is that if you care for and nurture workers, employees will be more highly motivated and productive.[11]

According to Likert, an organization can function at any point along a continuum of four systems. Under system 1, the *exploitative-authoritative system,* the executive manages with an iron hand. The boss makes all the decisions with no feedback from employees. One step away is system 2, *benevolent-authoritative leadership.* Here, the manager is sensitive to the needs of the worker. Moving farther along the continuum, we come to system 3, the *consultative system,* in which authority figures still maintain control but seek consultation from below. At the far extreme of the spectrum, system 4, or *participative management,* allows the worker to participate fully in decision making.

In Likert's scheme, then, the system of management is a *causal* variable because the system selected will cause certain kinds of results. However, certain intervening variables make the link between management system and outcome possible.[12]

For Likert, system 4 is clearly the best alternative because it leads to high performance and an increased sense of responsibility and motivation. If management is authoritative, there is less group loyalty, more conflict, less mutual support, and not much motivation to produce. The predictable result is lower sales, higher costs, and lower earnings. Consultative and participative management, on the other hand, leads to greater loyalty, higher performance goals, more mutual support, and attitudes that are more positive. The motivation to produce is higher, so that sales are greater, costs are less, and earnings are increased.

How does communication figure in all of this? Likert treats communication as one of several intervening variables. Exploitative management does not think about communication very much except to express its desires clearly and forcefully to the workers. There is little upward communication, and what information does go up the line tends to be distorted. Supervisors and subordinates are not very close to one another, and there is little accurate understanding between them. On the other hand, participative management includes strong upward and downward communication. This communication tends to be accurate and clear. Managers and workers tend to be close and to understand one another well. Although Likert's theory and the human relations movement have been criticized for being simplistic and mechanistic, there does seem to be some truth to Likert's notion that in some organizations exploitative systems have negative results, whereas participative ones have positive outcomes.

Virginia Richmond and James McCroskey conducted a study of employee satisfaction among 183 teachers in 39 school districts.[13] The teachers were given a battery of tests related to, among other things, management style, manager's tolerance for disagreement, and satisfaction. Four styles—called "tells," "sells," "consults," and "joins"—were measured in the study. These are essentially identical to Likert's systems 1, 2, 3, and 4, respectively.

The data showed a clear relationship between the perceived style of the manager and employee satisfaction. Employees who thought that their manager used a consulting or joining style were more satisfied than those who thought that a telling or selling style was used. The same relationship held for tolerance for disagreement. Employees who thought that their managers had less tolerance for disagreement were less satisfied than those who thought their managers had a higher level of disagreement tolerance.

REFLECTIONS ON
The Sociopsychological Tradition

Because organizations are systems well beyond the level of the individual, it is not surprising that the sociopsychological tradition should be somewhat downplayed, especially on the question of communication. Notice that the two representative theories in this section have a different flavor than the psychologically oriented theories from previous chapters. You could argue that they do not represent this tradition very well because they deal with social arrangements rather than individual behavior. At the same time, these theories are not very sociocultural either because they do not really examine community constructions beyond how managers can control employees, nor do they distinguish among actual, situated groups. For this reason, we feel that both Weber and Likert fit best into the sociopsychological tradition. Another way of saying this is that they are rather structural without being very cultural.

Notice that both Weber and Likert's theories are highly formal and linear. Each posits that the existence of certain kinds of structures will result in certain kinds of outcomes. This is typical of the sociopsychological tradition in general. Today, we think of organizations much more in cybernetic terms, as we will see in the following section.

• • •

THE CYBERNETIC TRADITION

Weber's theory, summarized in the previous section, defines the structure of an organization in terms of where people are placed in a hierarchy and the kinds of authority and roles given to the organizational members. This is a rather individualistic view of structure. In clear contrast to this approach, cybernetic theories see structure as emerging from patterns of interaction within the organization. You may be able to specify a formal organizational structure that forces certain interaction patterns, but—more interesting from a communication perspective—many forms and structures "get made" by how people interact with one another in various ways. Cybernetic theories have been powerful in showing how this is the case. They also place communication in the foreground as the key process by which organizational structure is accomplished. Here we look at two representative theories of this tradition.

The Process of Organizing

One of the most influential theories of the cybernetic tradition is that of Karl Weick.[14] Weick's theory of organizing is significant in the communication field because it uses communication as a basis for human organizing and provides a rationale for understanding how people organize. According to this theory, organizations are not structures made of positions and roles, but communication activities. It is more proper to speak of "organizing" than of "organization" because organizations are something that people accomplish through a continuing process of communication. When people go through their daily interactions, their activities *create* organization. Behaviors are interlocked, since one person's behavior is contingent on another's.

Specifically, the interaction that forms an organization consists of an *act*, or a statement or behavior of an individual. By itself, the act has no significance. What matters is how others respond to it. An *interact* involves an act followed by a response, and a *double interact* consists of an act followed by a response and then an adjustment or follow-up by the original person. Weick believes that all organizing activities are double interacts.

Consider an executive and an administrative assistant as an example. The executive asks the assistant to undertake an activity (act); the assistant then asks for clarification (interact); and the executive explains (double interact). Or the executive asks a favor of the administrative assistant (act), and the administrative assistant follows through (interact), after which the executive responds with a thank you (double interact). Simple? Yes, but these simple activities are the building blocks with which organizations are made. Interaction serves to achieve common meanings among group members, and the meanings that individuals together assign to information provide the mechanism by which equivocality is reduced. In other words, as we interact we come to some amount of common understanding, which reduces uncertainty.

Organizing activities fulfill the function of reducing the uncertainty of information. Weick's key theoretical term is *equivocality*, meaning uncertainty, complication, ambiguity, and lack of predictability. All information from the environment, according to Weick, is equivocal or ambiguous to some degree, and organizing activities are designed to reduce this lack of certainty. Not all interaction is equally important in reducing uncertainty, but everything does count. The degree of equivocality experienced will vary from situation to situation, but often it is quite large, and reducing it will have major organizational implications. Let's turn to an example that is a bit more profound than the simple example above.

Suppose that you get an e-mail from your boss at work indicating that there is a safety problem in the plant. As you read the e-mail, you see that your boss is asking you to take leadership in solving this problem. You are faced with a situation that is full of equivocation. What is the nature of this safety problem, and how should you go about solving it? The answers to these questions are not clear, inasmuch as the problem can be defined and solved in a number of ways. You will reduce the confusion by communicating with other people. Over time, through interaction, you will move from high equivocality to lower equivocality.

Organizing is an evolutionary process with three parts—enactment, selection, and retention. *Enactment* is the definition of the situation, or registering equivocal information from outside. In enactment, we pay attention to stimuli, and we acknowledge that equivocality exists. When you accepted the task of dealing with safety problems, you focused on one problem, which already removed some uncertainty from the field of all possible problems that you could have addressed. For you, then, saying, "Okay, I'll concentrate on this safety problem," was a form of enactment, because it helped you focus.

The second process is *selection*, in which organizational members accept some information as relevant and reject other information. It narrows the field, eliminating alternatives with which the participants do not wish to deal right now. This process therefore removes even more equivocality from the initial information. For example, in dealing with the safety problem, you may decide to consider only the aspects of safety that present serious hazards and delay work on situations that are only minor. Notice that you have moved already from a fuzzy, highly equivocal situation to a much clearer one.

The third process of organizing is *retention*, in which certain things will be saved for future use. Retained information is integrated into the existing body of information on which the organization operates. Your group may decide to deal with safety problems that are caused strictly by machinery, rejecting all other kinds of problems. As you can see, the problem has become much less ambiguous; it has moved from equivocality toward even greater clarity.

After retention occurs, organization members face a *choice point*. They must decide first whether to reenact the environment in some way. Here, they address the question, "Should we (or I) attend to some aspect of the environment that was rejected before?" You may decide, for example, to have your safety group review the rate of accidents that are not related to machinery.

So far this summary may lead you to believe that organizations move from one process of organizing to another in lockstep fashion: enactment, selection, retention, choice. Such is not the case. Individual subgroups in the organization are continually working on activities in all these processes for different aspects of the environment. Although certain segments of the organization may specialize in one or more of the organizing processes, nearly everybody engages in each part at one time or another. While one group is concentrating on one of the factors, another group may be working on a second one.

As people communicate to reduce uncertainty, they go through a series of *behavior cycles*, or routines, that enable the group to come to an understanding that clarifies things for them. Thus, for example, you might set up a series of safety meetings to discuss the safety problem and decide how to proceed. Behavior cycles such as your safety meetings are a natural part of each of the four aspects of organizing.

Within a behavior cycle, members' actions are governed by *assembly rules* that guide the choice of routines used to accomplish the process being conducted (enactment, selection, or retention). Rules are sets of criteria on which organizers decide what to do to reduce equivocality. The question answered by assembly rules is this: Out of all possible behavior cycles in this organization, which will we use now? For example, in the selection process you might invoke the assembly rule that "two heads are better than one" and on this basis call a meeting of plant engineers.

The basic elements of Weick's model—environment, equivocality, enactment, selection, retention, choice points, behavior cycles, and assembly rules—all contribute to the reduction of equivocality. Weick envisions these elements working together in a system, each element related to the others.

As we move through this theory, we begin to see an expansion from single acts, to interacts, to double interacts, to cycles. If you study these interactions carefully, you begin to notice that they fall into predictable patterns that define the structure of the organization. Interactional patterns bring individuals together into groups and

tie groups together into larger networks. We turn now to a theory that describes this process in greater detail.

Network Theory

You can easily see from Weick's theory that patterns of communication will develop over time within an organization. One way of looking at organizational structure is to examine these patterns of interaction to see who communicates with whom. Since no one communicates equally with all other members of the organization, you can see clusters of communication relationships that link together to establish overall organizational networks.

Networks are social structures created by communication among individuals and groups.[15] As people communicate with others, links are created. These are the lines of communication within an organization. Some of these are prescribed by organizational rules (such at the bureaucratic structure advocated by Weber) and constitute the *formal network*, but these channels reveal only part of the structure of an organization. In contrast, *emergent networks* are the informal channels that are built, not by the formal regulations of an organization, but by regular, daily contact among members.

We used to participate in creating emergent networks by putting memos in inter-office envelopes, picking up the phone, or walking down the hall to talk other employees. Today, our capability of generating links beyond the physical office has exploded, as any reasonably active professional person can verify by a glance at his or her e-mail address directory. Relationships are constantly formed through ongoing communication, and there is no way to capture this ephemeral and dynamic state of affairs in an organization chart. Researchers, however, do take snapshots of organizational networks and have been able to delve into complex, emergent networks.[16] Network research tools enable researchers to conduct *synchronous* analyses, which look at the networks in effect at a given time, and *diachronic* analyses, that show how networks change over time. Here, we only have space to summarize some basic ideas from the vast theoretical literature on networks.[17]

The basic structural idea of network theory is *connectedness*—the idea that there are relatively stable pathways of communication among individuals. Individuals who communicate together are linked together into groups that are in turn linked together into the overall network. Every person has a unique set of connections with others in the organization. These are *personal networks*. Your personal network is the connections you have among the many others with whom you communicate within an organization.

Because individuals tend to communicate more frequently with certain other organizational members, people cluster together into groups. The links among members of a group constitutes the *group network*. Organizations typically consist of many smaller groups, but these groups are not isolated. Since their members communicate with others outside the group, they are linked—again, connected—in such a way that *organizational networks* can be seen. Figure 9.1 is a simple drawing of a network. Notice that individuals are linked into groups, and groups are linked into a larger organization.

If you were to analyze a network, you would be able to look at several things. For example, you could look at the ways in which any two persons are linked together. This would be an analysis of *dyads*. You could look at how three individuals are linked, focusing on the *triad*. Beyond this, you might look at *groups* and how these are divided into *subgroups*. Finally, you could look at the ways in which groups link to one another in a *global network*. Analyzing a network into its parts is helpful, but network analysis can do much more. For example, beyond identifying parts, it can look at the qualities of those parts, or, beyond that, actually describe the multiple functions that the same links within a network can fulfill, such as friendship, information sharing, and influence. This aspect of networks is called *multiplexity*.

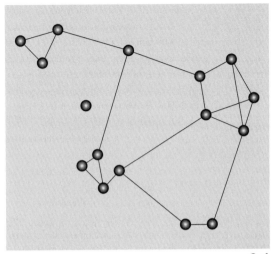

FIGURE **9.1**

A Simple Network

The basic unit of organization, then, is the *link* between two persons, and the organizational system consists of innumerable links that cluster people into groups and connect them to the organization. A link can be defined by its purpose or purposes, how much it is shared, and its functions within the organization. Most links have more than one purpose. You might, for example, use a link for both information sharing and friendship. Occasionally, a link may be exclusive, but usually it is shared with many others.

Links can also define a particular *network role*, meaning that it serves to connect groups in particular ways. As the members of an organization communicate with one another, they fulfill a variety of roles vis-à-vis the network. For example, a *bridge* is a member of a group who is also a member of another group. A *liaison* connects two groups, but is a member of neither. An *isolate* is an individual who is not linked to anyone else. You can also look at the *degree* to which one is linked to others. *In-degree* reflects the number of contacts other people make with you, while *out-degree* involves the number of links you initiate with others. *Centrality* is the extent to which you are connected to everyone else. Network researchers have looked at many variables related to individuals' connectedness within the network.

Researchers also analyze certain qualities of the links among persons. For example, links can be *direct*, involving a straight link between two people, or *indirect*, in which case two people are connected through a third person. The number of links between you and any other person is called *degrees of separation.* Links also vary in terms of *frequency* and *stability*. Again, several types of measurements can be taken to describe the characteristics of links within a network.

An organization never consists of a single network but is shaped by numerous overlapping ones. Although most networks are multifunctional, or *multiplex*, they may concentrate more on one function than another. For example, you may find networks that exert power or influence, often called *authority or instrumental networks*. Others include friendship or affiliation, information, production, and innovation.

A network can be characterized by a number of qualities. One is *size*, or the sheer number of people. Another is *connectedness*, the ratio of actual links to possible links. A highly connected network is strong and close, and such networks can exert much influence by establishing norms for thought and behavior. You will feel closer and be more influenced by a group of students you see and interact with every day in the residence hall than students you only see occasionally in various classes.

Another characteristic of a network is its *centrality*, or the degree to which individuals and groups are connected to just a few go-betweens. A highly centralized organization has lines going from groups into a small number of hubs. A *decentralized* system has more connectedness among members overall, with no one group controlling those links. If you have to go through the same small group of individuals every time you need something, you will not be very connected to other members of the organization. On the other hand, if you have freedom to contact just about anyone, you will be more connected generally throughout the organization.

There is a great deal of theoretical work addressing the ways in which networks function in organizations.[18] For example, networks can (1) control information flow; (2) bring people with common interests together; (3) build common interpretations; (4) enhance social influence; and (5) allow for an exchange of resources. Network theory paints a picture of an organization, or, perhaps more accurately, a variety of pictures, each capturing an aspect of organizational functioning.

◖ REFLECTIONS ON
The Cybernetic Tradition

The theories in this section help us see a system in action. Weick provides a micro-view, in which interaction—back-and-forth responses—create clarity and define the system for its members. At the same time, interaction organizes itself into lines of communication and influence that span out through the organization, as network theory so nicely illustrates.

You can clearly see the effects of the cybernetic tradition on this line of work. Interaction creates mutual influence, and the resultant networks form the overall system itself. As we move in the next section from the structure of connections into the meanings and understandings that are established within these connections, we start to feel the influence of the sociocultural tradition.

● ● ●

◖ THE SOCIOCULTURAL TRADITION

Sociocultural theories are less concerned with the network of connections among individuals and more focused on the shared meanings and interpretations that are constructed within the network and the implications of these constructions for organizational life. Part of what gets made is a sense of what the organization is—its structure and form. In other words, our conversations create maps for understanding the structure of the organization, but these guides or common understandings are made possible by deeper structures of meaning that emerge in talk.

Organizational talk creates a certain amount of control within the organization and thereby may exert power as well. Talk is not just about information, but establishes patterns of influence that affect who we are and what we do within the organization.

Conversations over time give the organization a feel or character that will differ from other organizations. The character of an organization is often called its culture, which consists of shared rules, norms, values, and practices that are commonly used and accepted within the organization. In this section, we present four representative theories of the sociocultural tradition—conversation and text, structuration theory, organizational control theory, and organizational culture.

Conversation and Text in the Process of Organizing

Following many other theorists, James Taylor and his colleagues see organizing as a process of interaction.[19] In a wide-ranging theory drawn from many literatures in linguistics, discourse, and organizational theory, Taylor and associates create a picture of how organizations are constructed in conversations.[20] According to Taylor, organizing is a circular process, with interaction and interpretation affecting one another. In other words, interaction leads to shared meaning, which in turn shapes our interactions. This will be easier to understand if we can make a distinction between two theoretical terms—*conversation* and *text*.

Conversation is the interaction, or how participants behave toward one another—what words they use, their demeanor, their gestures. *Text* is what is said—the content and ideas embedded in the language used. Think of it this way: When you are talking to another person, the two of you behave in a variety of ways, back and forth. But these behaviors mean something—they have content, purpose, and effect. When you are concentrating on what is happening, you are focusing on the conversation; when you are concentrating on what is being said or accomplished, you are focusing on text. The language of the text—whether an employee manual or a joke someone tells—provides a structure of words and grammar that allows you to interpret the meaning of what was written or said.

But these two processes—conversation and text—cannot really be separated. The conversation is understood in terms of the text, and the text is understood in terms of the conversation. This is a process Taylor and associates call *double translation*. To begin, the language and gestures used determine what is being said. This is the first translation—from text to conversation—or from how something should be said to the actual saying of it. At the same time, however, you assign meaning to the behavior, you bracket it, or you focus on connections and make decisions about what the behavior should stand for. This is the second translation—from conversation to text. These two translations are happening simultaneously and are closely tied to each other.

Although we do have freedom to communicate in a variety of ways, we are more or less constrained in how to say things because of the conventions of the language and the forms of communication already established in the organization. The same is true of interpretation. We do interpret texts differently, but within a range of possibilities determined largely by the structure of the language and pre-established forms of discourse. Let's say, for example, that a manager wants to tell employees about a new policy. The manager has lots of ways in which to communicate this information, but the organization has established certain acceptable types of discourse for this sort of communication, and the discourse form selected has certain embedded meanings. So, for example, the manager might send out a memo with the subject line, "Change of policy," which will carry a certain force of authority.

When we communicate, we follow a model or idea of what communication is. For example, the idea that communication involves "transfer" from one person to another seems to be a critical component of the frame for understanding communication. Who is transferring, what is being transferred, and who is receiving the transfer will vary from moment to moment. However, the idea of transfer from one person to another is never sufficient for conversation to take place. To be complete, communication must include *interaction* in which the ultimate meaning of the interaction is determined not only by the act initiated but also by the response to that act.

Taylor and his associates call this process *co-orientation*. This is the idea that two people both orient to a common object (a topic, issue, concern, situation, idea, goal, person, group, and so on), and the communicators work at negotiating a coherent meaning toward that object. Sometimes they are successful in doing so, and sometimes they are not, and it can take considerable interaction to achieve some sort of common meaning. The manager, for example, may feel that a policy change is vital, while a certain employee feels that it would be harmful. Here their co-orientation toward the policy is unbalanced, and there may be many interactions designed to establish a coherent, or workable, co-orientation. Taylor uses the analogy of interlinked tiles to get across this idea of organization. Each tile is like an interaction, and each interaction in turn is connected to others, just as one tile is connected to others in tile work.

This idea of an organization as being built up through a series of connected tiles is what Taylor calls a "flatland" view. It contrasts with the more traditional, top-down view, which suggests that the organization is "made" by those in command who direct the activities below. Although there is some truth to the management model, in fact the actual structure of the organization is constantly reproduced or reinvented by interactions at every level. Managerial interactions are just one type among many, and all interactions contribute to the organization. The macro (overall large view of the organization) and micro (minute daily interactions) entail one another, each affecting the other so that you cannot really separate overall structure from daily interaction.

Our constant interpretations of conversations give form and life to the organization. Organizations are made in this process of interaction in co-orientational triads. Each interaction is always linked to others, so that they become an intertwined net of interactions that bring the organization into being, sustain it, and change it over time.

Let's say that you are a firefighter and work about 40 hours a week for the city fire department. What do you do every day? You talk, give and take directions, maintain the station and equipment, give fire permits, visit schools, respond to emergency calls, and engage in many other often mundane activities. Each of these activities is done in a series of conversations, but the fire department as an organization is more than just a bunch of actions. Something results from all of this that defines and structures the organization itself. Something bigger is happening.

How do you know, then, exactly what characterizes the fire department as an organization? This question shows why text is so important. It is the texts—written and spoken—that represent symbolically how members are defining the organization. Theoretically, you could "listen in" to what people are saying to get a sense of the way they understand their structures and functions—which is what some researchers actually do.

Certain individuals will take the role of *agent* for the organization and codify aspects of the organization in a more or less formal text that is taken as a sort of *map* of some aspect of the organization. For example, Human Resources may write an employee manual, the executive committee may draft an organizational chart, the CEO might give a speech to a community group, a department might write an annual report, a hiring committee might write up a description as part of a job announcement, a work group might keep a log of what they do, or an outside researcher may write a book about the organization. These texts are especially important as maps because they provide a generally accepted picture of the organization's boundaries, activities, and the roles of members.

If you observe people actually communicating and see their patterns of interaction and their relationships, you are noticing the *surface structure* of the organization—the daily activities of the members. But these are not random or unconnected interactions. Rather, they are generated from the *deep structure* of the organization. The deep structure is like a grammar or structural arrangement that gives the organization its character and guides its actions—a complex network of rules about the patterns of interaction that are permissible in the organization, obligations of members, and expected duties and responsibilities. It is a moral order or a sense of how things should be done. A map as an organizational text will provide some clues as to the deep structure of the organization.

There is a recursive relationship between the deep structure and the actual conversations of an organization. The deep structure is made by people communicating with one another, and that deep structure in turn guides the communication itself. This is a circle of influence, a reciprocal back and forth between the deep structure and the surface structure. At times this relationship is highly stable, which makes organizational life very predictable. Other times it is less stable, as the texts and conversations of the organization undergo changes.

Of course, some master designer does not rationally plan all of this. Indeed, it happens incrementally and over time as real people interact with one another in their daily organizational lives. The structures that are created in the process are largely unintended, and we look more closely at how this happens in the following section. In Taylor's work, you see the influence of structuration theory; indeed, Taylor's theory could be considered a theory of structuration, and we turn now to an additional discussion of structuration.

Structuration Theory

In Chapter 8, we presented the ideas of Anthony Giddens on structuration. You will recall that structuration is a process in which the unintended consequences of action create norms, rules, roles, and other social structures that constrain or affect future action. For example, the actions of a problem-solving group may create a variety of tacit understandings, power arrangements, and guidelines for moral action that will determine to some extent what the group can do in the future. Structuration occurs constantly in all social systems. Marshall Scott Poole and Robert McPhee have applied this idea further to organizational communication.[21] For Poole and McPhee, structure is both a manifestation and a product of communication in the organization.

The formal structure of an organization, as announced in employee manuals, organizational charts, and policies, enables two types of communication. First, it is an indirect way of telling employees about the organization—its values, procedures, and methods. Second, it is a way in which members can talk about the communication within their organization. Organizational structure is created when individuals communicate with others in three metaphorical "sites" or *centers of structuration*.[22] The first includes all those episodes of organizational life in which people make decisions and choices that limit what can happen within the organization. This is the site of *conception.* A university's decision to establish a new college of creative arts, for example, will affect the lines of communication within the organization.

The second site of organizational structuration is the formal codification and announcement of decisions and choices—the site of *implementation.* Once the decision is made to establish the new college, the provost may send out a formal memorandum to the faculty and staff announcing the change. That formal announcement itself will be instrumental in shaping the structure of the organization in the future.

Finally, structuration occurs as organizational members act in accordance with the organizational decisions, which is the site of *reception.* To continue the example, after the decision is made to establish a college of arts, a dean will be recruited, certain department heads will meet with the new dean, and faculty lines of communication will change.

Although anyone in an organization may from time to time participate in communication at any or all three sites, structuration tends to be specialized. Top management usually is involved in conceptual communication, various staff personnel perform the job of implementation, and the general workforce itself participates in reception.

The communication activities at these three sites are often difficult and conflict laden. Indeed, rarely is a new college established at a university without considerable disagreement and resistance at all three stages, which is the case with major changes in any kind of organization. The communication patterns at the three sites may be complex and time-consuming, and the outcome is very much affected by the skill of the people involved.

In addition to organizational structure, the climate also emerges from structuration.[23] Traditionally, climate has been viewed as one of the key variables affecting communication and the subsequent productivity and satisfaction of employees. For Poole and McPhee, *climate* is the general collective description of the organization that shapes members' expectations and feelings and therefore the organization's performance. The members of the organization enact climates as they go through their daily activities, and any organization may actually have a variety of climates for different groups of people.

Poole and McPhee define climate structurationally as "a collective attitude, continually produced and reproduced by members' interaction."[24] In other words, a climate is not an objective "variable" that affects the organization, nor is it an individual's perception of the organization. Rather, climate arises out of the interaction among those who affiliate with the organization. Climate is a product of structuration: It is both a medium and an outcome of interaction.[25]

Poole sees climate as a hierarchy of three strata. The first is a set of terms that members use to define and describe the organization: the *concept pool*. The second is a basic, highly abstract shared conception of the atmosphere of the organization: the *kernel climate*. Finally, the groups' translations of the kernel climate into more con-

crete terms affecting their particular part of an organization constitute the third element: the *particular climate.* The kernel climate permeates the entire organization, but particular climates may vary from one segment of the organization to another.

The three layers in the hierarchy are related in a linear way: (1) The concepts create an understanding of what is going on in the organization; (2) from these basic understandings, the kernel climate arises; then (3) subgroups translate these general principles into specific elements of climate that in turn affect the thinking, feeling, and behavior of the individuals.

An example of this process is found in a study of a consulting firm.[26] The firm consisted of two generations of employees—a group that had been with the firm a relatively long time and a group of more recent employees. Though the two groups shared a common set of concepts, they seemed to experience different climates. From these core concepts, four key elements of a kernel climate emerged in this organization:

1. "The firm has a rigid formal structure that is often constraining."
2. "Contribution to profits is very important."
3. "Creative work is valued over routine work."
4. "Commitment of employees is important."

These four elements of the kernel climate were translated differently into the particular climates of the two groups. The first-generation employees believed that "pressure is manageable," and that "there is room for growth." The second-generation employees, however, believed that "pressure hinders performance" and that "there is little room for growth." Figure 9.2 illustrates this example.[27]

How do the elements of climate develop in an organization? We know already from a structurational perspective that the climate is produced by the practices of organizational members; and, in turn, climate affects and constrains those practices. Thus, climate is not static but is constantly in the process of development. Three interacting factors enter into this developmental process.

The first is the *structure of the organization* itself. Because structure limits the kinds of interactions

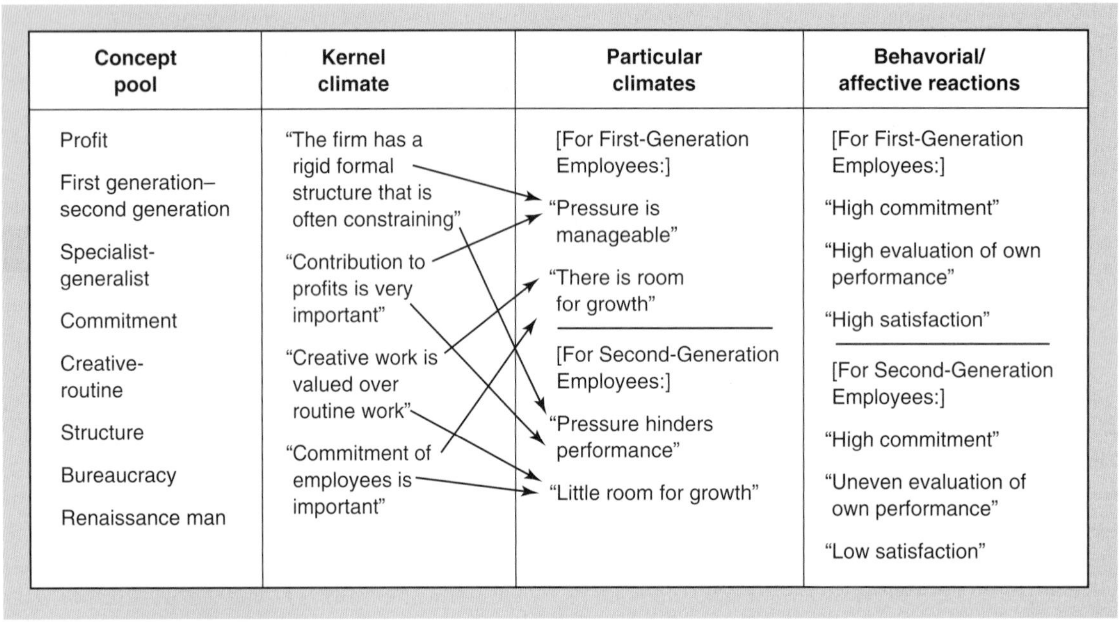

Concept pool	Kernel climate	Particular climates	Behavorial/ affective reactions
Profit	"The firm has a rigid formal structure that is often constraining"	[For First-Generation Employees:]	[For First-Generation Employees:]
First generation–second generation		"Pressure is manageable"	"High commitment"
Specialist-generalist	"Contribution to profits is very important"	"There is room for growth"	"High evaluation of own performance"
Commitment			"High satisfaction"
Creative-routine	"Creative work is valued over routine work"	[For Second-Generation Employees:]	[For Second-Generation Employees:]
Structure		"Pressure hinders performance"	"High commitment"
Bureaucracy	"Commitment of employees is important"	"Little room for growth"	"Uneven evaluation of own performance"
Renaissance man			"Low satisfaction"

FIGURE **9.2**

Schematic of Climate Structure

and practices that can be engaged in, it limits the kind of climate that can result from these interactions and practices. For example, if the organization is highly segmented with strong differentiation among employees and departments, individuals will have a limited pool of co-workers with whom they can communicate, which increases the chance of a "restrained" climate.

The second factor that affects climate is various *climate-producing apparatuses,* or mechanisms designed to affect employee perceptions and performance, such as newsletters, training programs, and the like. The third factor is *member characteristics,* their skills and knowledge. For example, if employees are sufficiently intelligent and reflective, they may challenge existing authority and "see through" apparatuses. Member characteristics also include the degree of agreement or coordination within work groups.

It is interesting to reflect on the ways in which structuration achieves control in the organization. You cannot do anything you want in an or-

ganization because of the structure and climate that is produced in everyday communication. In other words, structuration creates control. The theory discussed in the following section expands in more detail on this idea.

Organizational Control Theory

Phillip Tompkins, George Cheney, and their colleagues have developed a useful and fresh approach to organizational communication.[28] These theorists are interested in the ways in which ordinary communication establishes a certain amount of control over employees. Actually, control is exerted in organizations in four ways.[29] The first is *simple control,* or use of direct, open power. This is much like Likert's system of management, in which supervisors simply force workers to comply.

The second is *technical control,* or use of machinery. For example, if employees are given a computer and told to use it for their work, the computer itself limits what they can do and how they can do it. Internet communications of all kinds, including e-mail, do control how people interact within the organization. The third form of control is *bureaucratic,* which involves the use of organizational procedures and formal rules, much as Weber envisioned. Employees may be given a manual that includes policies to be followed, and memos and reports are used to communicate additional expectations.

The fourth, and most interesting to Cheney and Tompkins, is *concertive control*—the use of interpersonal relationships and teamwork. This is the subtlest form of control because it relies on a shared reality and shared values: "In the concertive organization, the explicitly written rules and regulations are largely replaced by the common understanding of values, objectives, and means of achievement, along with a deep appreciation for the organization's 'mission.' This we call . . . the 'soul of the new organization.' "[30]

Although the four types of control are normally found in various combinations, there is a trend away from simple, direct control toward this more subtle, complex, concertive forms. Concertive control is a kind of "discipline," or force, that maintains order and consistency through power.[31] Power can never be avoided and is always in the system, but power is not an external force. Instead, it is always created by various forms of interaction within the organization. Power, then, accomplishes control, but by submitting to control, the workers themselves reinforce the same sources of power.

In concertive control, discipline is accomplished by "normalizing" behaviors, making certain ways of operating normal and natural, something organizational members want to do. Many things become normalized in organizations, including power relations. So again, we see that discipline reinforces the very power relations that makes discipline possible. In contemporary organizations, disciplinary control is best accomplished in four ways.

First, it involves unobtrusive methods. Discipline is not necessarily obvious or conscious but is part of the ongoing daily activity of the organization. For example, something as simple as

work hours is a form of control, and to the extent that employees accept these hours, they are participating in their own control.

Second, discipline is collaboratively produced. Organizational members work together to make a set of practices normal, to establish a set of standards, a discipline. Meetings are a good example. In many organizations, meetings tend to start on the hour and end on the hour. Whether one, two, or three hours in length, this pattern is common. People collaborate in making this a normal state of affairs. They come on time and when the hour is up, they follow their expectations by packing up and heading for the door.

Third, discipline is a part of social relations. What people say and do to one another is both governed by and produces normalized practices. The unacknowledged rules in an organization tell you what topics you can and cannot talk about on the job, when and where interaction can take place, what nonverbal behaviors are appropriate or inappropriate, and who can initiate conversations.

Finally, the most effective means of control are based on the values that motivate organizational members—the very things for which they strive. This may include money, time, accomplishment, sense of teamwork, and so forth.

Following the classical work of Herbert Simon, Tompkins and Cheney show how control is accomplished by shaping the decisions made by organizational members.[32] Simon believes that organizational decision-making follows a syllogistic pattern, in which participants reason deductively from general premises and in which choices are based on those premises. Control is exerted when workers, who accept certain general premises, reason to the conclusions desired by management.

The premises are accepted because of incentives like wages and the authority of people with legitimate power—very much in line with Weber's notion of bureaucracy. This acceptance does not come automatically, however, because conflict often results from differences between employees' personal beliefs and the premises of the organization. Indeed, a substantial amount of industrial strife results from such differences. How, then, do organizations achieve concertive control in the face of potential conflict? The answer lies in the process of constructing personal identity.[33]

Among many things created through interaction in organizations is identity. Naturally, we have complex personal identities, and much of who we are is based in the relationships we establish with others within groups and organizations. One's identity is tightly connected to identification. *Identification* is a process of linking oneself with others. You might identify with a relative or friend, with a group, or with an entire organization.

In organizational life, we identify, or link ourselves, with many different sources. Here, theorists rely largely on the work of Kenneth Burke (Chapter 5). *Identification* occurs when individuals become aware of their common ground. We identify with individuals with whom we share something in common; and the more we share with one another, the more the potential identification between us. When employees identify with the organization, they are more likely to accept the organization's premises and make decisions consistent with organizational objectives.

Who we are in the organization, our identities, determine to a certain extent the identifications we forge. At the same time, our identifications shape who we are, our identities. This two-way street is referred to in the theory as the *identity-identification duality*. Tompkins and Cheney believe that the identity-identification process is structurational. In other words, in the process of actively seeking affiliations with others, we unwittingly create structures that in turn affect our identities. Many a professor has been made this way. A student finds a professor he or she really likes, identifies with that person, establishes a relationship with the professor, starts to take on academic values, and becomes the professor's research assistant. The effect of all of this is a set of expectations between the student, the professor, and perhaps others that lead to the student's development of an academic identity, which leads the student to the decision to go to graduate school to become a professor and teach in a university, where the pattern is continued.

What will begin to happen within an organization over time is that members create a mutual identification with the organization. Because their personal identity is shaped in part by this identification, they begin to take on the values, ideas, and ideals of the organization. This identification shapes members' assumptions and behaviors, and this is the essence of concertive control, in which members come to "reason" jointly with shared premises. The acceptance of organizational premises is part of a process of organizational identification.[34]

Once a certain amount of identification is achieved, organizational enthymemes make concertive control possible. Described by Aristotle over two thousand years ago, the *enthymeme* is a rhetorical device used to involve audiences in the advocate's reasoning process.[35] In an enthymeme, one or more premises in a reasoning chain are left out and supplied by the audience. In organizations, members are a kind of audience that reaches particular conclusions based on shared implicit premises. Sometimes the suppressed premises are widely accepted cultural values; other times they are inculcated through persuasion.

For example, a speaker advocating the prohibition of offshore drilling might reason that (1) offshore drilling endangers the fragile coastal ecology; (2) coastal ecology is valuable and should be protected; (3) therefore, offshore drilling should be prohibited. In addressing fellow members of an environmental organization, this speaker would not need to be explicit about this argument and could rely on members' acceptance of these premises, leading to an almost automatic acceptance of the claim. They would readily work against offshore drilling because of their identification with the environmental organization.

Tompkins and Cheney are especially interested in how enthymemes are used in organizations for unobtrusive control of decision making. These authors point out that when members display loyalty and behave "organizationally," they are essentially accepting key organizational premises. Often organizations directly sell their premises to employees through company newsletters, training programs, and the like. Other times, organizations employ a variety of incentives to induce employees to become loyal.

In any case, once employees accept certain premises, their conclusions and decisions are controlled. For example, one premise of many industrial firms is that obsolescence is positive because it maintains progress, sustains the market, and protects jobs. Once engineers buy this idea, they opt automatically for designs that include planned obsolescence because they accept the basic organizational premise.

To explore organizational identification, Michael Papa, Mohammad Auwal, and Arvind Singhal studied the Grameen Bank in Bangladesh.[36] Grameen (meaning *rural bank*) was founded in 1976 as an experiment in rural development and empowerment. It was designed to extend banking services to the poor; eliminate exploitation; create an employment base; and establish small, local banking institutions run by the people themselves.

From the beginning, participants, including loan applicants, were recruited to support the mission of the bank. Through such means as inspirational talks, new employees were induced to establish identification and buy into the values and goals of the organization. They were invited to buy into a team concept, in which all employees, and even clients, were to be working together to achieve the permanent elimination of poverty. The bank has been very successful and has received international acclaim, an honor that is shared with employees at every level. The workers are the strongest advocates for the mission and values of the organization, and they enforce very high standards (not mandated by management) on themselves and other employees.

The organization represents the epitome of concertive control through identification. Members work hard to ensure that loan recipients make their payments. Because employees' identities are so wrapped up in the bank, they exert tremendous peer pressure to work hard on behalf of the organization.

Employees identify both with the bank mission of uplifting the poor and with other employees at their local branch office. This very strong level of concertive control is paradoxical. It seems to empower employees to establish their own standards, but in the process, their procedures and work ethic have become institutionalized, which ironically disempowers employees, who might otherwise want to establish new ways of working. Employees are emancipated from oppression, but they are oppressed anew by the very forms they themselves have created.

Concertive control is one of several mechanisms used by organizations to manage multiple identities. The complex organization today does not have a single image with a single set of consistent interests. Rather, it is a complex system of interacting, sometimes contradictory, identities, and organizational communication must manage this multiple state of affairs. George Cheney explains the difficulty:

> To speak of collective identity is to speak of collective or shared interests—or at least of how the interests of a collective are represented and understood. This is a fundamental concern of contemporary organizations. Large bureaucratic organizations are in the business of identity management; their controlling members must be concerned about how to (re)present the organization as a whole *and* how to connect the individual identities of many members to that embracing collective identity.[37]

Thus the organization must have a way of inducing individuals, with all their variable interests, into a common identification with the organization. A diversity of identities, even conflicting ones, can be handled if there is at least some level of overall identification with the organization as a whole. Sometimes organizations must change, which means altering an identity, but to survive, the organization must create a new identity based in part on the interests of a substantial portion of its membership.

For these reasons, unbridled pluralism and diversity cannot be tolerated by an organization, and concertive control through identification is therefore essential. One of the unifying factors of an organization can be its culture.

Organizational Culture

Theories of organizational culture emphasize the ways people construct an organizational reality. As the study of an organization's way of life, this approach looks at the meanings and values of the members. It examines the way individuals use stories, rituals, symbols, and other types of activity to produce and reproduce a set of understandings.[38] The organizational culture movement has become incredibly broad, touching upon almost all aspects of organizational life.[39]

John Van Maanen and Stephen Barley outline four "domains" of organizational culture.[40] The first domain, the *ecological context,* is the physical world, including the location, the time and history, and the social context within which the organization operates. The second domain of culture consists of networks, or *differential interaction.* Then there are the common ways of interpreting events, or *collective understanding.* This is the "content" of the culture—its ideas, ideals, values, and practices. Finally, there are the practices or actions of individuals, which constitutes the *individual domain.* Few large organizations comprise a single culture. In most cases, subcultures identified with particular groups will emerge. You can imagine an organization as a set of Venn diagrams or overlapping cultural circles.

Work on organizational culture marks an important shift in this field from functionalism to interpretation—from the assumption that the organization has preexisting elements that act on one another in predictable ways to the assumption that it is a constantly changing set of meanings constructed through communication. Organizational culture theory has been greatly influenced by the sociocultural tradition within communication. Within this tradition, organizations present opportunities for cultural interpretation;[41] they create a shared reality that distinguishes it from other cultures. Gareth Morgan explains:

> Shared meaning, shared understanding, and shared sense making are all different ways of describing culture. In talking about culture we are really talking about a process of reality construction that allows people to see and understand particular events, actions, objects, utterances, or situations in distinctive ways. These patterns of understanding also provide a basis for making one's own behavior sensible and meaningful.[42]

Organizational culture is something that is made through everyday interaction within the organization—not just task work, but all kinds of communication. As one example, Michael Pacanowsky and Nick O'Donnell-Trujillo in their work on culture ask particular kinds of questions designed to uncover cultural patterns in an organization. Following the lead of Victor Turner (Chapter 11), these authors note that "performances are those very actions by which members constitute and reveal their culture to themselves and others."[43] These scholars explain the difference between this approach and traditional methods in these terms:

> We believe that an intriguing thing about communication is the way in which it creates and constitutes the taken-for-granted reality of the world. Social activity, as we see it, is primarily the communicative accomplishment of interrelated actions. So whereas the underlying motive of traditional research is coming to an understanding of how to make organizations work better, the underlying motive of the organizational culture approach is coming to understand how organizational life is accomplished communicatively. To understand how organizational life is brought into being, we cannot let ourselves be limited to asking questions that require some implicit or explicit link to organizational productivity for their legitimacy.[44]

What do organizational members use to create and display their understanding of events within the organization? According to these theorists, there are many indicators, including relevant constructs and related vocabulary, perceived facts, practices or activities, metaphors, stories, and rites and rituals. All these are performances because they display the lived experience of the group. However, performances, like stage plays, are also accomplishments. They bring about the reality of the culture: "performance brings the significance or meaning of some structural form—be it symbol, story, metaphor, ideology, or saga—into being."[45]

Pacanowsky and O'Donnell-Trujillo outline four characteristics of communication performances. First, they are interactional, more like dialogues than soliloquies. In other words, they are social actions, not solitary ones. Organizational performances are something people participate in together. Second, performances are contextual. They cannot be viewed as independent acts but are always embedded in a larger frame of activity; the performance, in other words, both reflects and produces its context. Third, performances are episodes. They are events with a beginning and an end, and the performers can identify the episode and distinguish it from others. Finally, performances are improvised. There is flexibility in how a communication episode is played out, and although the same performances may be given again and again, they are never repeated in exactly the same way.

The authors present a suggestive list of organizational communication performances. The first is *ritual*—something that is repeated regularly. It is familiar and routine, such as staff meetings or company picnics. Rituals are especially important because they constantly renew our understandings of our common experience, and they lend legitimacy to what we are thinking, feeling, and doing. Here is an example "Each and every day, Lou Polito, owner and general manager of Lou Polito Dodge, opens all the company mail. On those occasions when he is 'free,' he personally delivers this mail to the appropriate divisions in the company. This is just his way of letting his people know that he is keeping in touch with what they are doing."[46] This is an example of a *personal ritual*.

Another type is a *task ritual*, which is a repeated activity that helps members do their jobs. The following example from Pacanowsky and O'Donnell-Trujillo shows a task ritual operating among members of police department:

When a Valley View patrolman stops a driver for some traffic violation, he launches into a conversational routine that involves a question-answer sequence. "May I see your driver's license please?" "Is this your correct address?" "May I see your registration please?" "Do you know why I stopped you?" "Do you know what the speed limit is on this street?" "Do you know how fast you were going?" "Do you want to see the reading on the radar gun?" Although the officer has been taught this routine at the Police Academy as a way of being polite and professional, the Valley View police use it in order to see how the driver responds, to "size him up," and decide whether or not to give him any "breaks" in issuing a citation or warning.[47]

Social rituals are not task-related, yet they are important performances within organizations. The after-work drink is a good example: "Every Friday afternoon, the foremen from Steele Manufacturing go to the 'Pub,' one of the few places in their part of town that serves beer. The conversations are often filled with 'shop talk' but can range from sports . . . to politics."[48]

Finally, *organizational rituals* are those in which an entire work group participates with some regularity: "Each year, the department of communication has its annual picnic, highlighted by the traditional softball game which pits the graduate students against the faculty. Competition is typically fierce; but alas for the graduate nine, they have had but one win in the last five years."[49]

The second category of performances is what the authors call *passion*. Here, workers put on performances that make otherwise dull and routine duties interesting or passionate. Perhaps the most common way this is done is by *storytelling*. Almost everybody tells stories about their work, and the telling is often lively and dramatic. Further, these stories are told over and over, and people often enjoy telling one another the same stories again and again. We tell stories about ourselves (personal stories), about other people (collegial stories), or about the organization (corporate stories).

Another way drama is created on the job is by means of *passionate repartee*, which consists of dramatic interactions and the use of lively language: "The Valley View police, for example, do not deal with 'civilians,' but rather with 'ass-holes,' 'dirtbags,' 'creeps,' and 'maggots'—labels which serve as reminders that the 'negative element' is so much a part of the everyday experience of being a police officer."[50]

A third category of performance involves *sociality*, which reinforces a common sense of propriety and makes use of social rules within the organization. Courtesies and pleasantries are examples. *Sociabilities* are performances that create a group sense of identification and include things like joking, "bitching," and "talking shop." *Privacies* are sociality performances that communicate sensitivity and privacy. They include such things as confessing, consoling, and criticizing.

A fourth category of performance involves *organizational politics*. These performances, which create and reinforce notions of power and influence, may include showing personal strength, cementing allies, and bargaining.

A fifth category is *enculturation,* or processes of "teaching" the culture to organizational members. Enculturation is ongoing, but certain performances are especially vital to this process. Orientation of newcomers is an example. On a less formal scale, "learning the ropes" consists of a series of performances in which individuals teach others how things are done. Although this can be accomplished by direct instruction ("That's how we do it here"), most often this kind of learning occurs when people talk about things that happened in a way that helps other individuals learn how to interpret events.

In a police department, for example, officer Davis tells rookie Benson how to handle a rowdy drunk. Benson says he heard that Davis almost got in a fight with a drunk, and Davis replies, "Not really. I didn't give the guy a chance to get mad at me." Pacanowsky and O'Donnell-Trujillo present the following interpretation of this exchange:

> We take Davis' interaction with Benson as a unique enculturation performance, a meta-communicative commentary that instructs Benson in how he should interpret the prior performance. This metacommunication informs

the rookie that the prior exchange was not an endorsement of fighting but was backstage "play." And, as the rookie observes more instances of this backstage "tough" talk, he comes to understand it as "not real," but serious nonetheless.[51]

Coming to understand the cultural meanings of organizational performances such as this exchange between the officers proceeds like any ethnography (Chapter 11). The researcher first describes the actions of the organizational members and then constructs an interpretation of them in terms that are not only faithful from the native's point of view but are also understandable by people outside the organization. This is in every way a hermeneutic process, which illustrates the crossover between the sociocultural and phenomenological traditions within the organizational culture literature.

◉ REFLECTIONS ON
The Sociocultural Tradition

All of the theories in this section focus on the outcomes of social interaction in organizations. Something is constructed when people interact, and these theories outline a variety of meanings that are worked out in daily organizational communication. The topic of each theory is somewhat different. Some are broader in describing the overall process of social interaction and its outcomes, while others are more narrow in identifying the specific forms that interaction takes as well as what gets made in the process. Notice how consistent these theories are with the tenets of the cybernetic tradition. Indeed, all, except possibly organizational culture, combine both the sociocultural and cybernetic traditions.

Because sociocultural theories rely mostly on an interpretive approach, they are influenced by the tradition of phenomenology. At some level, these theories must rely on data gathered by participants or observers' experiences, which allows them to cross over into the phenomenological. This overlap with phenomenology is not trivial, as the interpretive approach has had a major impact on organization studies. Dennis Mumby believes that this shift has brought forth a series of challenges to mainstream organization theory. One outcome is the emergence of what Mumby calls a "hermeneutic of suspicion," which challenges existing interests and power arrangements in organizations.[52] With this challenge, we move from the sociocultural to the critical tradition.

• • •

◖◗ THE CRITICAL TRADITION

The critical tradition in organizational communication also is concerned with culture, but more specifically with the power relations and ideologies that arise in organizational interaction. Recognizing that mainstream organizational research dealing with organizational structures and functions privileged largely managerial interests such as productivity and effectiveness, critical/cultural scholars of organizations began to take such interests into account. Dennis Mumby states: "One of the principal tenets of the critical studies approach is that organizations are not simply neutral sites of meaning formation; rather, they are produced and reproduced in the context of struggles between competing interest groups and systems of representation."[53] Critical communication scholars have addressed social realities less as physical sites and more as environments in which competing voices and interests vie for dominance.[54]

To suggest the directions of critical organizational communication theory, we describe Dennis Mumby's concern more specifically in terms of how power functions ideologically in organizations. We then move to Stanley Deetz's theory of organizational democracy. Feminist perspectives on organizational power have been particularly prominent in the last decade and provide an example of the particular links between theory and practice that critical theories of organizations advocate, and we conclude this section with a look at feminist approaches.

Dennis Mumby's Hermeneutic of Suspicion

Dennis Mumby's work in organizational communication embodies a shift from approaches that attempt merely to describe the organizational world to one that highlights the ways in which it creates patterns of domination. Mumby calls for a "hermeneutic of suspicion," or an attitude of questioning about and an examination of the deep structure of ideology, power, and control within the organization. Recall from Chapter 3 that hermeneutics involves the process of interpretation, so when Mumby refers to a hermeneutic of suspicion, he is saying that we should look for interpretations that are suspicious of the normal order within organizations.

It is one thing to describe an organization as having a certain structure, function, and culture; it is another thing to question the moral correctness of that structure, function, and culture. For example, you might question the highly valued Weberian bureaucracy as antithetical to the interests of workers, you might challenge a process of concertive control because it subverts what employees most want and need, or you might criticize the culture of an organization as promoting the power of one group over another. All of these are examples of a hermeneutic of suspicion.

Mumby himself undertakes such a critical examination using the concept of hegemony from classical critical theory (see Chapter 11). *Hegemony* in organizational communication involves "relations of domination in which subordinated groups actively consent to and support belief systems and structures of power relations that do not necessarily serve—indeed may work against—those interests."[55] For example, in traditional capitalism, companies work to reduce costs and increase profits. Within this scheme, employees are a "cost," and one way of increasing profitability is to downsize, or lay off employees. Notice that this practice is not value neutral but reflects a particular way of thinking about human beings. The interests of the corporation are clearly higher in priority than those of its employees. How is this justified? Profits are not just profits, but they are thought of as a resource for future expansion and development of the organization, supporting the belief that expanded profits means more jobs in the future, which actually helps personnel in the long run. This is a classic example of hegemony, a "story" or set of understandings that promote the interests of one group over those of another.

Hegemony is rarely a brute power move, but is instead a "worked out" set of arrangements in which stakeholder buy-in actually contributes to domination. Power is established within an organization by the domination of one ideology over others. This occurs through rituals, stories, and the like, and Mumby shows how the culture of an organization involves an inherently political process. Through storytelling, for example, narratives form certain kinds of texts that create and perpetuate ideologies.

For example, there is a story that has been repeatedly retold at IBM. As the story goes, a 22-year-old female security guard stopped the chairman of the board because he did not have the appropriate badge to enter the area she was guarding. Although you might think that the boss would pull rank, he quietly secured the proper badge and gained entry.[56] One reading of this story is that the chairman was a nice guy who wanted to follow the rules. But the story would not be noteworthy at all if power relations were not important. Consequently, the story reinforces the idea of power relations in this company.

Hegemony is normally considered a negative influence in the critical tradition, but Mumby suggests that we have forgotten that resistance and transformation are also involved. Viewed in this way, hegemony can provide a more nuanced way to understand conflicting interests as they play out in organizations. The introduction of the notion of resistance shifts attention away from structures of domination that control to the productive ways organizational members resist and thus reconfigure the terrain of struggle.

More recently, Mumby has made clear his interpretation of hegemony as a pragmatic, interactive, and dialectical process of assertion and resistance. Hegemony is not so much a question of an active and powerful group dominating a passive and less powerful one, but a process of power arrangements emerging as an active process of multigroup social construction. Hegemony is a necessary result—neither always bad, nor always good—of struggle among stakeholder groups in everyday situated action.[57]

It would be a mistake, however, to think of organizations as a huge field of play between two teams, each trying to "beat" the other. Resistance is not simply opposition to domination—such as the case with labor unions. More accurately, hegemony involves a continuum between a single, all-encompassing ideology at one end and widespread resistance on the other; it is a process of struggle rather than a state of domination and ultimately offers scholars a more adequate way to discuss this dynamic. Critical communication scholars are more concerned with the everyday hegemony and resistance that happens in ordinary organizational life than with the more obvious forms of resistance.

For example, a manager may tell his employees, "If you have too much to do, just come to me, and I'll give you a set of priorities." For many employees, this is a solution to the workload problem: Let management decide. This is a minor example of hegemony in operation. However, if you talk to employees, they may tell you that they want more control over prioritizing their own work and may resist asking the manager for help. This is a small act of resistance. To provide a picture of the ideal way in which empowerment should occur, we turn to Stanley Deetz's theory of democracy in organizations.

Deetz on Managerialism and Organizational Democracy

Calling for a democracy of everyday action, Stanley Deetz shows that contemporary organizations privilege managerial interests over the interests of identity, community, or democracy.[58] Small examples such as the daily setting of work priorities are part of a larger picture in which the interests of management dominate those of the workers. Deetz imagines democracy as an alternative, an "ongoing accomplishment" in which stakeholders can reclaim responsibility and agency in the corporation.[59] Democracy, in other words, should occur in the daily practice of communication, and it is here that change in organizational cultures begins. For example, a manager could invite employees to set workplace goals and negotiate priorities. Deetz believes, however, that this kind of effort is not normal in today's organization.

In contrast to a democratic value, the normal discourse of organizations tends to be one of domination. Normal discourse in organizations embodies four dimensions of domination—naturalization, neutralization, legitimation, and socialization. *Naturalization* is the assumption of truth on the part of powerful stakeholders. Players assume that what they believe about organizations, the goals of organizations, and the structure of organizations is natural, normal, and accepted by all. The organizational ethic that management sets priorities is a clear example. *Neutralization* is the idea that information is neutral, or value free. For example, when the Human Resources Department sends out an e-mail describing a new health insurance program, the assumption is that this is just "neutral" information that in no way asserts power. *Legitimation* is the attempt of the organization to privilege one form of discourse as the voice of authority within the organization. Weber's idea of legitimate authority, defined earlier in the chapter, is exactly this: The management perspective is considered authoritative over other perspectives. Finally, *socialization* is the ongoing process of "training" employees to accept and follow the moral order of the organization. Cheney and Tompkins's idea of concertive control is one example of this. Explicit indoctrination and training programs are also examples.

These processes—naturalization, neutralization, legitimation, and socialization—constitute a *systematically distorted communication* that serves the interests of managerial capitalism. *Managerial capitalism*, permeating the modern organization, aims to reproduce the organization for the ulti-

mate survival of management itself. Notice the difference between managerial capitalism and traditional production capitalism. The goal of traditional capitalism was to expand production and make money. While this interest is still alive and well, Deetz is concerned with a different set of interests that serve to preserve management as a stakeholder group. More than a conspiracy of self-aggrandizement, this managerialism is infused throughout the organization in its forms, rules, codes, and policies as an overlay of arrangements that prevents conflict and inhibits democracy.

The effect of managerialism is to inhibit emancipatory democracy, discouraging autonomy and choice. The solution to this state of affairs is a constant, everyday effort to create an "ideal speech situation" within the organization. The *ideal speech situation*, originally proposed by critical theorist Jürgen Habermas, is an ideal for communication in society in which all discourses are legitimized in open dialogue.[60] Real democracy as manifest in the ideal speech situation is a "balanced responsiveness"; it does not involve trying to create any kind of permanent structure, but rather enactment is the attitude of constant critique and empowerment in everyday life. Unlike such processes as collective bargaining, then, organizational democracy happens every day in small ways. For example, a manager may invite employees to collaborate on goal setting and negotiate work priorities.

Gender and Race in Organizational Communication

Mumby's and Deetz's efforts to understand the domination-resistance continuum have been enhanced by feminist scholarship in organizational communication. The notion of organizations as gendered sites dominated by hegemonic masculinity has been one line of research. Angela Trethewey's work on organizations as gendered in ways that marginalize feminine discourse provides one example. She looks at how women perceive their professional bodies and the strategies they use to manage those bodies.[61] Through interviews with professional women, she discovered shared themes of what it is for a professional woman to project an image of success, verbally and nonverbally.

The expectations for the female body are constantly complicated, however, by what Trethewey calls "a tendency to overflow." In other words, "women never know when their bodies may display messages and meanings that were not intended,"[62] and the majority of these unintended messages have to do with femininity—whether expressing emotions, sexuality, pregnancy, or menstruation. For these women, not being in control of bodily presentations of self was really about revealing a feminine body because it exposed gendered differences and could destroy a woman's credibility. To succeed professionally, then, is a paradox of embodied experiences for women.

Karen Ashcroft and her colleague Brenda Allen extend the work on organizations, suggesting that not only are organizations fundamentally gendered but they are also "fundamentally raced."[63] Examining organizational communication textbooks because they disseminate the canons of the field, Ashcroft and Allen found they offer several implicit messages about race: (1) race is a separate, singular concept, of interest only to people of color; thus issues of race often are segregated in textbooks, confined to a chapter at the end; (2) race is relevant when it serves organizational interests such as creativity or productivity; (3) cultural/racial differences are seen as synonymous with international differences; (4) racial discrimination stems from personal bias and the lack of racial minorities in the workplace (as numbers increase, discrimination will naturally diminish); and (5) white workplaces and workers are the norm.

Introducing gender and race into the study of organizational communication has been an important avenue pursued by critical communication scholars. For example, Patricia S. Parker interviewed women African American senior executives, thus taking the issue of race directly into the organization, where she found that these personnel do indeed have challenges related to their identity vis-à-vis white male colleagues and African American co-workers and clients.[64]

In addition to exploring the ways in which organizations are gendered and raced, feminist organizational communication scholars have taken seriously Mumby's definition of hegemony as a site both of domination and resistance. Many scholars have studied the ways resistance emerges in organizations and can lead to alternative organizational structures. Elizabeth Bell and Linda Forbes, for instance, examined the folklore among women support staff at their university, collecting examples that were posted behind desks and hidden away in file cabinets.[65] Ranging from "Are We Having Fun Yet?" to "I Have PMS and a Handgun. Any Questions?," these collections of folklore showed how women resist—with humor, with traditional evidences of femininity ranging from sexuality to hysteria, and with rage. But because the resistance is "safely ensconced in an 8½ by 11" format, it articulates a point of view without expressly disrupting the hierarchy.

Trethewey has been instrumental in theorizing organizational resistance as well. In one study, she looked at client resistance to a social services organization designed to assist low-income single parents in obtaining the education and work necessary to support their families without the assistance of welfare.[66] Positioned as passive and deficient by the organization, the clients in fact found a variety of ways to resist this construction of themselves. Among many different forms of resistance, they made fun of the organizational mandate that they participate in counseling, suggesting that the organization simply make a cardboard cutout of Freud to whom they could talk; they "bitched" about their social workers and the organization; and they transformed client-client relationships into mentoring ones, not sanctioned by the organization. Trethewey suggests that these forms of resistance enabled the women to feel empowered about themselves and to envision alternatives to the conditions of their everyday lives. This study shows the many forms resistance can take and reminds researchers not to privilege any particular form, and to examine each for its ways it can affect personal and community identity.

Trethewey adds to her work on resistance by explicitly articulating a theory of contradiction for organizational life. Using the same social-services organization described above as her case study, Trethewey describes the paradoxes present in the organization.[67] For instance, designed to empower its clients to be self-sufficient, the organization only selected as clients individuals who already demonstrated a considerable degree of self-sufficiency. The client must have goals and the motivation to pursue those goals—capabilities that point to self-sufficiency already. This leads to yet another paradox: Selected on the basis of self-sufficiency, clients accepted into the program are defined as incapable of determining appropriate plans of action or monitoring their own progress toward goals. Instead, a social worker is considered necessary in order for the clients to realize these goals. In complex organizations, understanding the role irony plays in allowing different discourses to remain present at the same time is a way to capture and analyze the complexities, ambiguities, and diversities of contemporary organizational life.

A final example of the work on resistance as a new trend in organizational communication literature comes from the work of Robin Clair. Beginning with the silence-voice binary, she uses narratives of the Cherokee nation to show how narratives are embedded in one another—there are always layers of potential contradiction to be addressed.[68] So, for instance, in one of these narratives, a British philanthropist attempts to save the Cherokee by providing one Cherokee boy with an education. Paradoxically, of course, the education meant to save the Cherokees from destruction forced the boy to silence his Cherokee heritage. Silence and voice exist in a complex tension, and there can be voice in silence and silence in voice: "interests, issues, and identities of marginalized people are silenced and . . . those silenced voices can be organized in ways to be heard."[69]

Clair continues her work on the paradoxes of the voice-silence tension with the issue of sexual harassment. In her analysis, she found that resistance and oppression are a particular kind of voice and silence—complicated communication phenomena that simultaneously contain and oppose the organization in which they occur. In an account of a male nurse's experience with sexual harassment, for example, Clair found that "Oppression becomes resistance when the female nurses *oppress* Michael through sexual harassment in order to *resist* being infiltrated by a male. Resistance becomes oppression when the nurses accept sexual harassment from the patients in order to dominate them. Furthermore, the female nurses contribute to their own oppression through their reliance on and use of sexual orientation as well as racism to taunt Michael."[70] There is not just oppression and just resistance, in other words, and scholars of organizational culture are finding ways to study the shifting terrains of organizational life.

Critical perspectives on organizational communication are a rich area for investigation. Feminist scholarship has led the way in investigating the pitfalls and possibilities of organizational life—its gendered and raced dimensions and the interlocking ways communication functions to preserve and oppose dominant organizational ideologies.

REFLECTIONS ON
The Critical Tradition

Don't be surprised by the close affinity of sociocultural and critical theories of organizational communication. The sociocultural tradition is what Mumby calls the *hermeneutic of description*, while the critical tradition exemplifies his *hermeneutic of suspicion*; both promote the idea that various social arrangements, including culture itself, are created jointly in ongoing everyday communication. Both see that these social structures and arrangements are significant in the lives of organizational members, but critical theories go farther in pointing out that such arrangements are hegemonic and far from democratic in most situations.

Structuration theory is harder to classify than other theories in this chapter. It is clearly sociocultural in orientation, but it also has elements of cybernetics too. Structuration theory is sometimes considered critical as well because it shows how patterns of power and morality are worked out, and how these constrain free-dom in social life. Once again, as with most of the areas covered in this book, the traditions of theory are not discrete and mutually exclusive, but interface with one another in ways that help to broaden our understanding of the communication process.

●   ●   ●

APPLICATIONS IMPLICATIONS

We learn from the theories in this chapter that organizations are created through communication as people interact to accomplish individual and joint goals. The process of communication also results in a variety of outcomes such as authority relations, roles, communication networks, and climates. The outcomes of organizing are results of the interaction among individuals and groups within the organization, and all in turn affect future interactions within the organization. As we review the theories that elaborate this idea, several points emerge:

1. Organizations are made through communication.

All mainstream organizational communication theory today acknowledges that organizations arise through interaction among members over time. In other words, communication, which is considered an instrumental tool by organizational members, is actually the medium that makes organizations possible. Weick had it right: Communication is a process of organizing, and because communication is dynamic, an "organization" is just a snapshot of an evolving process over time.

Always remember, then, that your communication in an organization is a vital part of an ongoing organizing process. The way in which you respond to your boss, for example, makes a link and has a certain quality that contributes to the nature of the organization itself. You can actually get a feel for your place in the organization by thinking about the individuals with whom you have the most contact, the nature of those contacts, what gets accomplished by interaction in your personal network, and the role that you and others take in this network.

If you stop to think about these questions for a few minutes, you will see that individual interactions among people create micro- and macrostructures that define the organization. Network theory shows us that an organization is never just one structure, but many, all overlaid on one another, accomplishing a variety of functions. It also helps us see that these forms are never permanent. Though they are patterned, they do change as interactions evolve.

A formal network reflects one way in which the organization is built, but for the communication scholar, the formal network omits a great deal. Classical theories such as those of Weber and Likert contributed to a powerful cultural norm about how organizing should occur, but they do not provide a sense of how the interaction among members can result in the rich tapestries that define modern organizations. The theories in this chapter describe many of the threads and patterns in these tapestries.

2. Organizational activities function to accomplish individual and joint goals.
Organizing activities have purpose, as organizational life is infused with goals and tasks. Working in an organization is an eminently practical experience. We participate in organizations precisely because they enable us to accomplish something personally important. The most obvious example is income, but we have lots of other goals as well, and many organizations that have nothing to do with income—churches, civic clubs, community associations, educational institutions, and professional organizations—allow us to pursue many other values. Two goals that might not come immediately to mind are social life and structuring time. Many retirees go through a hard period of adjustment precisely because they lose these valued commodities when they leave the organization. Organizations bring you in touch with other people, allow you to make friends, and structure a very large part of your week.

Much of your communication in organizations, then, helps you to meet your personal goals. Much of your communication, as well, is directed at accomplishing organizational goals. Organizations do have their own goals, and these can support, contradict, or ignore individual goals. Often these days, the goals of the organization are written out in mission and vision statements, but these rarely do justice to the richness of an organization's actual goals. Long-range plans are more precise about what the organization thinks it is up to at any given time. Weber's theory of bureaucracy was aimed to help organizations learn how to accomplish their goals in spite of any individual goals workers may have. The human relations movement, which acknowledged the personal goals of individuals, helped us understand that people have needs and values related to organizational functioning and that communication is an important aspect of organizational life.

How can organizational and individual goals be integrated? Likert's theory puts morale in the service of management. In other words, he taught that you could achieve the organization's goals more effectively if you include and acknowledge individual needs. Organizational control theory makes a similar move, but it is more subtle than Likert's approach. While Likert called for explicit and linear use of participative management, Cheney and Tompkins look at natural processes of concertive control that develop when communication creates organizational identity to bring individual goals into line with organizational ones. In other words, there is something seductive about the daily work in an organization that brings personal goals into alignment with organizational goals. Mumby would be suspicious of this state of affairs as a possible site of hegemony, and Deetz would question whether integration of goals is done in a way that creates domination or democracy.

3. In addition to achieving goals, communication activities create patterns that affect organizational life.
A strong theme of the theories in this chapter is that communication is double-faced. The first face of organizational communication is its role in allowing us to accomplish goals. The second face is its role in creating structures and arrangements that organize, constrain, and focus our activities. Structuration theory teaches that the unintended consequences of action come back to bite us. In other words, communication acts are purposeful, but they contribute to outcomes that influence future interaction in ways that are often outside of our awareness.

One of the outcomes of interaction is structure in the sense of lines of communication, as network analysis reveals. However, lines of communication are only one of many structuring elements of an organization. You can look at an organization in terms of behavior cycles, identity and control, culture, climate, power relations, and many others. On the dark side, structuration can create forms of oppression based on race, gender, and other factors.

The lesson we can learn from this theme is that communication matters. It is more than an instrument for achieving personal and organizational goals. Whenever you communicate, something is made, and it behooves us to pay attention to what we are creating by *how* we interact with others in organizations.

4. Communication processes create an organizational character and culture.

The organizational culture movement recognizes the humanizing aspect of the organization. Indeed, apart from work structure, organizations are also human cultures, rich with tradition, shared meaning, and ritual. People's actions create and reflect the underlying culture of the organization.

The cultural approach to organizational theory is a major advance. Traditionally, management was seen as a rational process of manipulating "things" for the benefit of the organization. The culture approach shows us that this is only partly true. The cultural approach refutes the ideas that managers can somehow manipulate "objects" (like materials and machines) that are independent from the organization itself. The objects are only known through the meanings of the organizational culture, and those meanings will change from one organization, or even suborganization, to another. More than adapt to environments, organizations create their own environments based on shared conceptions and interpretations.

The character and feel of an organization is determined by its culture. Culture gives life to daily activities, and when you think about it, you will enjoy, or deplore, your involvement with an organization primarily because of its "feel," or the kind of life it makes possible. Perhaps some organizations are production "machines," but they are also a place where human beings spend most of their time out of the home, making the quality of life within an organization very important to most workers.

The culture of an organization is reflected in both work processes and collateral communication. In other words, the way in which an organization structures its work (the constraints, control processes, and values it promotes) and the informal contacts and styles of communication present in encounters not directly related to the work (coffee breaks, parties, car pools, chats at the water cooler, and other informal moments) reflect and produce the organization's culture.

5. The patterns of power and control that emerge in organizational communication open possibilities and create constraints.

The empirically minded manager may think of culture as just another variable to be manipulated and managed.[71] After all, managers are primarily responsible for ensuring the accomplishment of organizational goals, so why not bring culture into the service of goals? All forms of management exert some kind of ideological control. Even if not manipulated consciously by management, an organization's culture will include power relations. This is unavoidable.

Power, then, is an inevitable outcome of organizational interaction. Power is necessary to get things done. It provides structure, reduces confusion, and lessens uncertainty. Empowerment allows people to use their most valuable personal and community resources to accomplish goals. The question, then, is not how to avoid power and influence, but who is in and who is out. What interests get privileged, and which are marginalized?

Once you acknowledge that all interactions contribute to a cascading construction of culture within the organization, it is a small step to begin wondering about how the network of associations within an organization might be made more humane and inclusive. This question has led to the workplace democracy movement, in which the voices of multiple stakeholder groups, including all employees and important groups "outside" the organization, are recognized as important in organizational decision making.[72] The various theories of organizational democracy constitute a deep critique of structural and positional approaches to the organization. Instead of a top-down, managerial approach to control in which conflict is suppressed, democratic theories call for dialogue, participation, and valuing conflict as a way of enhancing the organizational life of everyone involved.

There is a kinship between much of the work in workplace democracy and that of critical theory. Mumby alerts us to the need to address three issues in critical studies.[73] First, because the act of research is itself political, the researcher must become more aware of his or her own power over those studied and the ways research studies shape organizational relations. Second, organizational communication scholars must look at how the field has constructed a view of organizations that promotes certain interests over others. Finally, organizational communication has been seemingly oblivious to developments in feminist theory and should incorporate feminist insights into the critique of organization.[74]

Communication theory has made a tremendous contribution to our understanding of organizations. By showing the importance of communication patterns in the construction of network connections, power structures, and culture, this work has greatly enhanced the field of organizational studies.

NOTES

1. Amatai Etzioni, *Modern Organizations* (Englewood Cliffs, NJ: Prentice-Hall, 1964), p. 1.
2. David Carlone and Bryan Taylor, "Organizational Communication and Cultural Studies: A Review Essay," *Communication Theory* 8 (August 1998), p. 339.
3. See, for example, Fredric M. Jablin and Linda L. Putnam, eds., *The New Handbook of Organizational Communication: Advances in Theory, Research, and Methods* (Thousand Oaks, CA: Sage, 2001); James R. Taylor, Andrew J. Flanagin, George Cheney, and David R. Seibold, "Organizational Communication Research: Key Moments, Central Concerns, and Future Challenges," in *Communication Yearbook 24*, ed. William B. Gudykunst (Thousand Oaks, CA: Sage, 2001), pp. 99–138.
4. Gareth Morgan, *Images of Organization* (Beverly Hills, CA: Sage, 1986). See also Linda L. Putnam, "Metaphors of Communication and Organization," in *Communication: Views from the Helm for the 21st Century*, ed. Judith S. Trent (Boston: Allyn & Bacon, 1998), pp. 145–152.
5. Peter Senge, *The Fifth Discipline: The Art and Practice of the Learning Organization* (New York: Currency-Doubleday, 1994).
6. For a review of various theories of organizational structure, see Robert D. McPhee and Marshall Scott Poole, "Organizational Structures and Configurations," in *The New Handbook of Organizational Communication: Advances in Theory, Research, and Methods*, ed. Fredric M. Jablin and Linda L. Putnam (Thousand Oaks, CA: Sage, 2001), pp. 503–543.
7. Max Weber, *The Theory of Social and Economic Organizations*, trans. A. M. Henderson and T. Parsons (New York: Oxford University Press, 1947). A lengthy interpretation and discussion of Weber's theory can be found in Parsons's introduction to the above book. For a more complete bibliography

of primary and secondary sources on Weber, see S. N. Eisenstadt, *Max Weber on Charisma and Institution Building* (Chicago: University of Chicago Press, 1968).

8. The most important classical theories are those of Henri Fayol and Frederick Taylor. See Henri Fayol, *General and Industrial Management* (New York: Pitman, 1949), originally published in 1925; and Frederick W. Taylor, *Principles of Scientific Management* (New York: Harper Brothers, 1947), originally published in 1912.

9. Weber, *Theory of Social and Economic Organizations,* p. 151.

10. Rensis Likert, *New Patterns of Management* (New York: McGraw-Hill, 1961); and Rensis Likert, *The Human Organization* (New York: McGraw-Hill, 1967).

11. For a more detailed discussion and critique of the human relations movement, see Charles Perrow, *Complex Organizations: A Critical Essay* (Glenview, IL: Scott, Foresman, 1972).

12. Rensis Likert, "New Patterns in Sales Management," in *Changing Perspectives in Marketing Management,* ed. Martin Warshaw (Ann Arbor: Bureau of Business Research, University of Michigan, 1972), p. 24.

13. Virginia P. Richmond and James C. McCroskey, "Management Communication Style, Tolerance for Disagreement, and Innovativeness as Predictors of Employee Satisfaction: A Comparison of Single-Factor, Two-Factor, and Multiple-Factor Approaches," in *Communication Yearbook 3,* ed. D. Nimmo (New Brunswick, NJ: Transaction, 1979), pp. 359–373.

14. Karl Weick, *The Social Psychology of Organizing,* 2nd ed. (Reading, MA: Addison-Wesley, 1979). For a more recent secondary source, see James L. Everett, "Communication and Sociocultural Evolution in Organizations and Organizational Populations," *Communication Theory* 4 (1994): 93–110. See also the special section in *Communication Studies* 40 (Winter 1989): 231–265.

15. This metaphor is suggested by Cynthia Stohl, *Organizational Communication: Connectedness in Action* (Thousand Oaks, CA: Sage, 1995). See also Peter R. Monge, "The Network Level of Analysis," in *Handbook of Communication Science,* ed. Charles R. Berger and Steven H. Chaffee (Newbury Park, CA: Sage, 1987), pp. 239–270.

16. Peter R. Monge and Noshir S. Contractor, *Theories of Communication Networks* (Oxford: Oxford University Press, 2003).

17. These are summarized by Monge and Contractor, *Theories of Communication Networks.* The material in this section of the chapter relies primarily on this source along with Peter R. Monge and Noshir S. Contractor, "Emergent Communication Networks," *The New Handbook of Organizational Communication: Advances in Theory, Research, and Methods,* ed. Fredric M. Jablin and Linda L. Putnam (Thousand Oaks, CA: Sage, 2001), pp. 440–502.

18. We do not have space in this book to include all of these. For a detailed account, see Monge and Contractor, *Theories of Communication Networks.*

19. James R. Taylor, Francois Cooren, Nicole Giroux, and Daniel Robichaud, "The Communicational Basis of Organization: Between the Conversation and the Text," *Communication Theory* 6 (1996): 1–39. See also James R. Taylor, "Shifting from a Heteronomous to an Autonomous Worldview of Organizational Communication: Communication Theory on the Cusp," *Communication Theory* 5 (1995): 1–35; James R. Taylor, *Rethinking the Theory of Organizational Communication: How to Read an Organization* (Norwood, NJ: Ablex, 1993).

20. For a thorough discussion of the details of this theory and its antecedents, see James R. Taylor and Elizabeth J. Van Every, *The Emergent Organization: Communication as its Site and Surface* (Mahwah, NJ: Lawrence Erlbaum, 2000).

21. Marshall Scott Poole and Robert D. McPhee, "A Structurational Analysis of Organizational Climate," in *Communication and Organizations: An Interpretive Approach,* ed. L. L. Putnam and M. E. Pacanowsky (Beverly Hills, CA: Sage, 1983), pp. 195–220; Marshall Scott Poole, "Communication and Organizational Climates: Review, Critique, and a New Perspective," in *Organizational Communication: Traditional Themes and New Directions,* ed. Robert D. McPhee and Phillip K. Tompkins (Beverly Hills, CA: Sage, 1985), pp. 79–108; Robert D. McPhee, "Formal Structure and Organizational Communication," in *Organizational Communication: Traditional Themes and New Directions,* ed. Robert D. McPhee and Phillip K. Tompkins (Beverly Hills, CA: Sage, 1985), pp. 149–178. For additional commentary on structuration theory, see Stephen P. Banks and Patricia Riley, "Structuration Theory as an Ontology for Communication Research," *Communication Yearbook 16,* ed. Stanley A. Deetz (Newbury Park, CA: Sage, 1993), pp. 167–196.

22. Robert D. McPhee, "Organizational Communication: A Structurational Exemplar," in *Rethinking Communication: Paradigm Exemplars,* ed. Brenda Dervin, Lawrence Grossberg, Barbara J. O'Keefe, and Ellen Wartella (Beverly Hills, CA: Sage, 1989), pp. 199–212.

23. Poole, "Communication and Organizational Climates"; Poole and McPhee, "Structurational Analysis."

24. Poole and McPhee, "Structurational Analysis," p. 213.

25. For a contrast of the structurational approach to climate with traditional approaches, see Poole and McPhee, "Structurational Analysis."

26. This model of climate is based on a reinterpretation of a case study by H. Johnson in "A New Conceptualization of Source of Organizational Climate," *Administrative Science Quarterly* 3 (1976): 275–292.

27. Poole, "Communication and Organizational Climates," p. 98.

28. George Cheney and Phillip K. Tompkins, "Coming to Terms with Organizational Identification and Commitment," *Central States Speech Journal* 38 (1987): 1–15; Phillip K. Tompkins and George Cheney, "Account Analysis of Organizations: Decision Making and Identification," in *Communication and Organizations: An Interpretive Approach,* ed. Linda L. Putnam and Michael E. Pacanowsky (Beverly Hills, CA: Sage, 1983), pp. 123–146; Phillip K. Tompkins and George Cheney, "Communication and Unobtrusive Control in Contemporary Organizations," in *Organizational Communication: Traditional Themes and New Directions,* ed. Robert D. McPhee and Phillip K. Tompkins (Beverly Hills, CA: Sage, 1985), pp. 179–210. For a summary and extension see James S. Sass and Daniel J. Canary, "Organizational Commitment and Identification: An Examination of Conceptual and Operational Convergence," *Western Journal of Speech Communication* 55 (1991): 275–293.

29. Tompkins and Cheney base this conceptualization on the work of R. Edwards, "The Social Relations of Production at the Point of Production," in *Complex Organizations: Critical Perspectives,* ed. M. Zey-Ferrell and M. Aiken (Glenview, IL: Scott, Foresman, 1981).

30. Tompkins and Cheney, "Communication and Unobtrusive Control," p. 184.

31. James R. Barker and George Cheney, "The Concept and the Practices of Discipline in Contemporary Organizational Life," *Communication Monographs* 61 (1994): 19–43.

32. Herbert Simon, *Administrative Behavior* (New York: Free Press, 1976). See also Perrow, *Complex Organizations.*

33. This process is detailed in Scott, Corman, and Cheney, "Development of a Structurational Model." For a broad discussion of organizational identity, see George Cheney and Lars Thøger Christensen, "Organizational Identity: Linkages Between Internal and External Communication," in *The New Handbook of Organizational Communication: Advances in Theory, Research, and Methods,* ed. Fredric M. Jablin and Linda L. Putnam (Thousand Oaks, CA: Sage, 2001), pp. 231–269.

34. George Cheney, "The Rhetoric of Identification and the Study of Organizational Communication," *Quarterly Journal of Speech* 69 (1983): 143–158.

35. Lane Cooper, *The Rhetoric of Aristotle* (New York: Meredith, 1932). See also Lloyd Bitzer, "Aristotle's Enthymeme Revisited," *Quarterly Journal of Speech* 45 (1959): 399–408; Jesse Delia, "The Logic Fallacy, Cognitive Theory, and the Enthymeme: A Search for the Foundations of Reasoned Discourse," *Quarterly Journal of Speech* 56 (1970): 140–148.

36. Michael J. Papa, Mohammad A. Auwal, and Arvind Singhal, "Organizing for Social Change Within Concertive Control Systems: Member Identification, Empowerment, and the Masking of Discipline," *Communication Monographs* 64 (1997): 219–249.

37. George Cheney and others, *Rhetoric in an Organizational Society: Managing Multiple Identities* (Columbia: University of South Carolina Press, 1991), p. 14.

38. See James A. Anderson, ed., *Communication Yearbook 11* (Newbury Park, CA: Sage, 1988), pp. 310–405; Michael E. Pacanowsky, "Creating and Narrating Organizational Realities," in *Rethinking Communication: Paradigm Exemplars,* ed. Brenda Dervin, Lawrence Grossberg, Barbara J. O'Keefe, and Ellen Wartella (Newbury Park, CA: Sage, 1989), pp. 250–257.

39. For an excellent discussion of the breadth of this field, see Eric M. Eisenberg and Patricia Riley, "Organizational Culture," in *The New Handbook of Organizational Communication: Advances in Theory, Research, and Methods,* ed. Fredric M. Jablin and Linda L. Putnam (Thousand Oaks, CA: Sage, 2001), pp. 291–322.

40. John Van Maanen and Stephen R. Barley, "Cultural Organization: Fragments of a Theory," in *Organizational Culture,* ed. P. J. Frost and others (Beverly Hills, CA: Sage, 1985), pp. 31–54.

41. For a brief description of this approach, see Michael Pacanowsky, "Creating and Narrating Organizational Realities," in *Rethinking Communication: Paradigm Exemplars,* ed. Brenda Dervin, Lawrence Grossberg, Barbara J. O'Keefe, and Ellen Wartella (Newbury Park, CA: Sage, 1989), pp. 250–257.

42. Gareth Morgan, *Images of Organization* (Beverly Hills, CA: Sage, 1986), p. 128.

43. Michael E. Pacanowsky and Nick O'Donnell-Trujillo, "Organizational Communication as Cultural Performance," *Communication Monographs* 50 (1983): 131. See also Victor Turner, *Dramas, Fields, and Metaphors* (Ithaca, NY: Cornell University Press, 1974).

44. Michael E. Pacanowsky and Nick O'Donnell-Trujillo, "Communication and Organizational Cultures," *Western Journal of Speech Communication* 46 (1982): 121.

45. Pacanowsky and O'Donnell-Trujillo, "Organizational Communication," p. 129.

46. Pacanowsky and O'Donnell-Trujillo, "Organizational Communication," p. 135.

47. Pacanowsky and O'Donnell-Trujillo, "Organizational Communication," p. 136.

48. Pacanowsky and O'Donnell-Trujillo, "Organizational Communication," p. 137.

49. Pacanowsky and O'Donnell-Trujillo, "Organizational Communication," p. 137.

50. Pacanowsky and O'Donnell-Trujillo, "Organizational Communication," p. 139.

51. Pacanowsky and O'Donnell-Trujillo, "Organizational Communication," p. 145.
52. Dennis K. Mumby, "Critical Organizational Communication Studies: The Next 10 Years," *Communication Monographs* 60 (March 1993): 18–25.
53. Mumby, "Critical Organizational Communication Studies," p. 21.
54. Carlone and Taylor, "Organizational Communication and Cultural Studies," p. 339.
55. Dennis K. Mumby, "The Problem of Hegemony: Rereading Gramsci for Organizational Communication Studies," *Western Journal of Communication* 61 (Fall 1997): 344.
56. Dennis K. Mumby, "The Political Function of Narrative in Organizations," *Communication Monographs* 54 (1987): 120–125; and Dennis K. Mumby, *Communication and Power in Organizations: Discourse, Ideology, and Domination* (Norwood, NJ: Ablex, 1988), pp. 115–124.
57. Mumby, "The Problem of Hegemony."
58. Stanley A. Deetz, *Democracy in an Age of Corporate Colonization: Developments in Communication and the Politics of Everyday Life* (Albany: State University of New York, 1992), p. 333.
59. Deetz, *Democracy in an Age of Corporate Colonization*, p. 338. Deetz's ideas are further developed in Stanley Deetz, "Disciplinary Power in the Modern Corporation," in M. Alvesson and H. Willmott, eds., *Critical Management Studies* (Newbury Park, CA: Sage), pp. 21–45; Stanley Deetz, "The New Politics of the Workplace: Ideology and Other Unobtrusive Controls," in H. W. Simons and M. Billig, eds., *After Postmodernism: Reconstructing Ideology Critique* (Thousand Oaks, CA: Sage, 1994), pp. 172–199); and Stanley Deetz, *Transforming Communication, Transforming Business: Building Responsive and Responsible Workplaces* (Cresskill, NJ: Hampton, 1995).
60. Among Habermas's chief works are Jürgen Habermas, *Knowledge and Human Interests*, trans. J. Shapiro (Boston: Beacon Press, 1971); *Theory and Practice*, trans. T. McCarthy (Boston: Beacon Press, 1973); *Legitimation Crisis*, trans. T. McCarthy (Boston: Beacon Press, 1975); *The Theory of Communicative Action, Volume 1: Reason and the Rationalization of Society*, trans. T. McCarthy (Boston: Beacon Press, 1984); *The Theory of Communicative Action, Volume 2: Lifeworld and System*, Trans. T. McCarthy (Boston: Beacon Press, 1987).
61. Angela Trethewey, "Disciplined Bodies: Women's Embodied Identities at Work," *Organizational Studies* 20 (1999): 423–450.
62. Trethewey, "Disciplined Bodies."
63. Karen Lee Ashcroft and Brenda J. Allen, "The Racial Foundation of Organizational Communication," *Communication Theory* 13 (February 2003): 6.
64. Patricia S. Parker, "Negotiating Identity in Raced and Gendered Workplace Interactions: The Use of Strategic Communication by African American Women Senior Executives Within Dominant Cultural Organizations," *Communication Quarterly* 50 (Summer/Fall, 2002): 251–268.
65. Elizabeth Bell and Linda C. Forbes, "Office Folklore in the Academic Paperwork Empire: The Interstitial Space of Gendered (Con)Texts," *Text and Performance Quarterly* 14 (July 1994): 181–196.
66. Angela Trethewey, "Resistance, Identity, and Empowerment: A Postmodern Feminist Analysis of Clients in a Human Service Organization," *Communication Monographs* 64 (1997): 281–301.
67. Angela Trethewey, "Isn't It Ironic: Using Irony to Explore the Contradictions of Organizational Life," *Western Journal of Communication* 63 (Spring 1999): 140–167.
68. Robin Patric Clair, "Organizing Silence: Silence as Voice and Voice as Silence in the Narrative Exploration of the Treaty of New Echota," *Western Journal of Communication* 61 (Summer 1997): 315–337.
69. Clair, "Organizing Silence," p. 323.
70. Robin Patric Clair, *Organizing Silence: A World of Possibilities* (Albany: State University of New York Press, 1998).
71. A discussion of this possibility is presented by Sonja A. Sackmann, "Managing Organizational Culture: Dreams and Possibilities," in *Communication Yearbook 13*, ed. James Anderson (Newbury Park, CA: Sage, 1990), pp. 114–148.
72. George Cheney and others, "Democracy, Participation, and Communication at Work: A Multidisciplinary Review," in *Communication Yearbook 21*, ed. Michael E. Roloff (Thousand Oaks, CA: Sage, 1998), pp. 35–91.
73. Mumby, "Critical Organizational Communication Studies."
74. See, for example, Judi Marshall, "Viewing Organizational Communication from a Feminist Perspective: A Critique and Some Offerings," in *Communication Yearbook 16*, ed. Stanley A. Deetz (Newbury Park, CA: Sage, 1993), pp. 122–143.

THE MEDIA

With the remote control, you can move through, maybe, fifty television channels within a few minutes and get impressions very quickly about what is on. Even if you pause at various stations for just a few moments, you will be brought in touch with a huge world—not only in terms of geography, but a world of subjects from surgery to animals, from wars to cooking, and from science to art. We are living in what Marshall McLuhan calls the "global village"; modern communication media make it possible for millions of people throughout the world to be in touch with nearly any place on the globe. Mass media not only transmit information around the world, they also construct agendas, telling us what is important to attend to. George Gerbner describes this function of mass media and its importance: "This broad 'public-making' significance of mass media of communications—the ability to create publics, define issues, provide common terms of reference, and thus to allocate attention and power—has evoked a large number of theoretical contributions."[1]

Mass communication is the process whereby media organizations produce and transmit messages to large publics and the process by which those messages are sought, used, understood, and influenced by audiences. Central to any study of mass communication are the media.[2] Media organizations distribute messages that affect and reflect the cultures of society, and they provide information simultaneously to large heterogeneous audiences, making media part of society's institutional forces.

Topics Addressed	Semiotic Theories	Sociocultural Theories	Sociopsychological Theories	Cybernetic Theories	Critical Theories
Media content and structure	Semiotics of media	Medium theory			
Society and culture		Agenda-setting function	Cultivation theory	Spiral of silence	Critical media theories
Audience		Social action media theory	Media effects Uses, gratifications, and dependency		

"Media," of course, imply "mediation" because they come between the audience and the world. Denis McQuail suggests several metaphors to capture this idea: Media are *windows* that enable us to see beyond our immediate surroundings, *interpreters* that help us make sense of experience, *platforms* or *carriers* that convey information, *interactive communication* that includes audience feedback, *signposts* that provide us with instructions and directions, *filters* that screen out parts of experience and focus on others, *mirrors* that reflect ourselves back to us, and *barriers* that block the truth.[3] Joshua Meyrowitz adds three additional metaphors—media as *conduits,* media as *languages,* and media as *environments.*[4] There is no single or simple definition to describe media.

Media scholars recognize two faces of mass communication.[5] One face looks from the media to the larger society and its institutions. Theorists interested in the media-society link are concerned with the ways media are embedded in society and the mutual influence between larger social structures and the media. This is the *macro* side of mass communication theory.

The second face looks toward people, as groups and individuals. This face reflects the link between the media and audiences. Theorists interested in the media-audience link focus on group and individual effects and outcomes of the media transaction. This is the *micro* side of mass communication theory.[6]

In a landscape, then, media theory addresses three large thematic areas—media content and structure, society and culture, and audience. *Media content and structure* includes insights on the effects of the medium of communication as well as content issues with special attention to the role of signs and symbols in media messages. *Society and culture* issues include the functions of mass communication in society, the dissemination of information and influence, public opinion, and power. Finally, the topical theme of *audience* looks at individual effects, audience communities, and audience uses of media.

As always, we organize this chapter in terms of the traditions of communication theory. Five traditions have had an impact on theories of mass communication, including the semiotic, sociocultural, sociopsychological, cybernetic, and critical. These are outlined in the chapter map on the facing page.[7]

◖● THE SEMIOTIC TRADITION

Recall from Chapter 3 that semiotics deals with the relationship among the sign, the referent, and the human mind. This tradition has been especially influential in helping us see how signs and symbols are used, what they mean, and how they are organized. Any study that looks at the organization of symbols within a message is reflecting semiotic thinking.

Media messages are especially intriguing from a semiotic perspective because they usually consist of a fascinating blend of symbols that are organized spatially and chronologically to create an impression, transmit an idea, or elicit a meaning in an audience.[8] If you have had a class in media analysis, you probably did spend time looking at magazine articles, television programs, and commercials to examine the various forms, compositions, texts, and other symbolic forms embedded in these messages. Semiotics has provided a powerful tool for examining the impact of mass media. For the semiotician, content is important, but content is a product of the use of signs. This approach focuses on the ways producers create signs and the ways audiences understand them.

Semiotics has a long history of development in the twentieth century (see Chapter 4).[9] This field helps us see how signs are used to interpret events and can be an especially good tool for analyzing the content of media messages.[10] Most would agree that signs take on special significance in the media, and the media shape in many ways how signs function for us. As an example of a semiotic theory of media, we look to the work of Jean Baudrillard, who wrote that media have forced increasing distance between symbols and the actual world of experience.

Jean Baudrillard and the Semiotics of Media

Jean Baudrillard, a French scholar, believes that signs have become increasingly separated from the objects they represent and that the media have propelled this process to the point where nothing is real.[11] The media are not solely responsible for this effect; sign use has gone through an evolution in society. At first, a sign was a simple representation of an object or condition. The sign had a clear connection with what it signified. This Baudrillard calls the stage of the *symbolic order*, common in feudal society. In the second stage, that of *counterfeits* (common from the Renaissance to the Industrial Revolution), signs assumed a less direct relationship to the things of life. Signs actually produced new meanings that were not necessarily a natural part of the experience of that which was signified. For example, status, wealth, and prestige were connected to things because of how they

were signified. The next stage, that of the Industrial Revolution, is *production*, in which machines were invented to take the place of humans, making objects independent of any human use of signifiers. In the era of production, once you push the right button, the metal press presses the metal, no matter what you might think about it.

Today we are in an era of *simulation*, in which signs no longer represent—but create—our reality. Simulation determines who we are and what we do. We no longer use tools to represent our experience: Signs establish it. The metal press may continue to shape metal parts, but what we program the machine to make is very much determined by the predominant signs in our culture today.

Disneyland epitomizes the era of simulation. Theme parks are fantasies constructed from signs. The real things—pirates, the frontier, and so on—can be reproduced any time anywhere. Rather than have genuine communication involving interaction among people, the media dominate our lives with information that forms what we perceive to be genuine experience, but is far removed from the natural order of things. This leads us to obscenely exaggerated forms of life. We begin to treat the pirates at Disneyland as real experiences, but in fact they are experiences within the simulations created by the media. We think Baudrillard would especially appreciate the fact that movies are now being based on the rides at Disneyland. We are used to movies based on books—something that had a real existence. With the making of *The Pirates of the Caribbean*, starring Johnny Depp, however, a movie was made about the sign of a sign.

Our commodity culture is one aspect of the simulation in which we live. The simulated environment tells us what we want—it forms our tastes, choices, preferences, and needs. Consumption takes on value in and of itself. Most important is that we are consuming, not that we desire real things that have actual functions. Most people's values and behaviors, then, are highly constrained by the "reality" simulated in the media. We think that our individual needs are being met, but these are actually homogenized needs shaped by the use of signs in the media.

Because objects are separated from their original natural state, they take on bizarre meanings for us. Possession is more important than use. Where once we needed farm animals to do work for us, we now value pets as a matter of ownership. Our lives are full of gizmos that have no real use, but sit on shelves for us to possess and look at and make a life of pure "symbolicity." We buy a watch, not really to tell time, but to wear as a form of apparel.

Because of this process of simulation, we make fewer and fewer distinctions. Meanings collapse, or implode, into a huge mass, which Baudrillard refers to as *hypertelia*. In this process of exaggeration, we thrive on hype. Rather than distinguish between good and bad, beautiful and ugly, we mash everything together into the hyperreal, leading to a life of excess in which nuance is unimportant.

◖ REFLECTIONS ON
The Semiotic Tradition

Media messages are filled with carefully designed symbolic images formulated to influence individuals and society. Baudrillard's theory, which concentrates on the role of signs in shaping culture, is firmly planted in this tradition. It also has a sharply critical edge and is part of a line of work sometimes called "the critique of mass society," which reacts to the large, complex, bureaucratic nature of the modern state. This line of work envisions a malleable mass of people in which society-wide depersonalized relations replace small groupings, community life, and ethnic identity.[12] This conception of society has led to criticisms of modern life and of the media.

With its critical emphasis, then, we were tempted to place Baudrillard's theory within the critical tradition. However, the critique of mass society is somewhat different from most of the theories commonly thought of as part of the critical tradition. The former is a general critique of the loss of individuality and community in modern life, while the latter focuses more on power arrangements and oppression. And Baudrillard's specific concern with the sign clearly puts his theory within the semiotic tradition.

• • •

◖ THE SOCIOCULTURAL TRADITION

The media constitute a powerful force in society. Without question, media productions respond to social and cultural developments and in turn influence those very developments. The mere existence of certain kinds of media like television affects how we think about and respond to the world.

Media fulfill a variety of important functions in society, including framing information, influencing opinion, providing entertainment, setting an agenda of issues, and others. At the same time different segments of society—different audiences, if you will—are not uniformly affected, but interact in unique ways with the media. In this section, we summarize three bodies of work. The first of these, medium theory, examines the sociocultural effects of media apart from content. The second, agenda-setting, explores the effect of media on social agenda. Finally, we include here social action media studies, which probe media communities.

Medium Theory

Perhaps Marshall McLuhan is best known for calling our attention to the importance of media as media. He is a well-known figure in the study of popular culture, receiving attention because of his unusual writing style and his startling and thought-provoking ideas.[13] Although the specifics of McLuhan's theory are often rejected today, his general thesis has received widespread acceptance: Media, apart from whatever content is transmitted, impact individuals and society. This idea in its various forms is what we mean by "medium theory."

McLuhan was not the first to write about this idea. Indeed, his ideas were profoundly affected by the work of his mentor Harold Adams Innis, who taught that communication media are the essence of civilization and that history is directed by the predominant media of each age.[14] For McLuhan and Innis, media are extensions of the human mind, so the predominant media in use biases any historical period. Heavy media such as parchment, clay, or stone are durable and therefore *time binding* because they last over time. Something written on stone, for example, will last a long time, is durable, and unchanging. Because they facilitate communication from one generation to another and don't change much, time-biased media are biased toward tradition. In contrast, *space-binding* media such as paper are light and easy to transport, so they facilitate communication from one location to another, fostering empire building, large bureaucracies, and the military.

Speech as a medium, because it is produced one sound at a time, encourages people to organize their experience chronologically. Speech also requires knowledge and tradition and therefore supports community and relationship. Written media, which are spatially arranged, produce a different kind of culture. The space-binding effect of writing produces interests in political authority and the growth of empires across the land.

McLuhan's thesis is that people adapt to their environment through a certain balance or ratio of the senses, and the primary medium of the age brings out a particular sense ratio, thereby affecting perception.[15] McLuhan sees every medium as an extension of some human faculty, exaggerating that sense. "The wheel . . . is an extension of the foot. The book is an extension of the eye. . . . Clothing, an extension of the skin. . . . Electric circuitry, an extension of the central nervous system."[16]

Donald Ellis presents a set of propositions representing a contemporary perspective on this subject.[17] Following Innis and McLuhan, Ellis notes that the predominant media at any given time will shape behavior and thought. As media change, so do the ways in which we think, manage information, and relate to one another. There

are sharp differences among oral, written, and electronic media, each with different effects on how we interact with each medium.

Oral communication is highly malleable and organic. Oral messages are immediate and ephemeral, so that individuals and groups must keep information in their minds and pass it on through speech. Because everyday experience cannot really be separated from the oral medium of transmission, life and knowledge cannot be separated. The telling and retelling of stories over time privilege narrative as a form of communication and require group memory as the "holder" of society's knowledge. This can lead to a collective consciousness in which little distinction is made between self and group. Group identification and cohesiveness are high when oral media predominate.

Writing, and especially the advent of printing, led to profound changes in society. When you can write something down, you can separate it from the moment. You can manipulate it, change it, edit it, and recast it. In other words, you can "act on" information and knowledge in a way that is not possible in the oral tradition. This leads to a separation of knowledge (what is known) from the knower (who knows it). Those who can read and write have special status, so that formal education takes on an important role. Knowledge, then, becomes objectified and can assume the status of truth, and individuals and groups can be divided among those who "have" the truth and those who do not. Further, information can be stored, or saved, which makes literacy a tool of conservation. Importance is assigned to that which is "stored" in written language.

The third major shift occurs when electronic media come to the fore. Electronic media are something like orality in that they can be immediate and ephemeral, but they are not tied down to a particular place because they can be broadcast. Electronic media extend your perception beyond where you are at any given moment, creating the "global village." At the same time, like print, electronic media allow information to be stored. Because they are more readily available than print, electronic media create an information explosion, and a great competition occurs among various media to be heard and seen. Information in electronic media is sold like a commodity, which creates pressure for information to be attractive. Knowledge in the electronic age changes rapidly, and we become aware of different versions of truth. The constant change created by electronic media can make us feel confused and perhaps unsettled.

If orality creates a culture of community and literacy creates a culture of class, then electronic communication creates a culture of "cells," or groups pitted against one another to promote their special interests. A new kind of public not bound to place comes into being. The politics of interest prevails, and democracy, along with its attendant value of civility, assumes importance as a way to manage differences. Yet, ironically the competition and commodity-based economy that accompany electronic media fight against the very values most needed in this environment—civility and collegiality. So, electronic communication creates the paradox of separation through difference and the importance of participatory democracy.

If you were a member of a primarily oral culture, differences would be minimal, and decisions would be made collectively based on the wisdom of tradition as it has been passed down generation to generation. If you were a member of a primarily print-oriented culture, decisions would rely on "truth" stored in documents, and those who had access to information would have great influence as a class in society's decision making. But today, you are likely a member of a primarily electronic culture in which you identify with interest groups that vie against one another. You hear many voices at once, and your challenge is to integrate these in some way.

Although McLuhan taught that content has little influence on society, most theorists today believe that, in addition to the effects of media, content is vitally important. Media content fulfills a variety of functions in society.[18] One of the earliest and best-known theorists in this tradition was Harold Lasswell. In his classic 1948 article,

he presented the simple and often quoted model of communication:[19]

Who

Says what

In which channel

To whom

With what effect

Using this model, Lasswell listed the parts of the mass communication system. He went on to identify three functions of the media of communication, including *surveillance*, which provides information about the environment; presenting options for solving problems, or *correlation;* and socializing and education, referred to as *transmission*.[20]

Since this early work, many other functions have been explored. We will look at several in this chapter, beginning with one of the most studied of all media functions.

The Agenda-Setting Function

Scholars have long known that media have the potential for structuring issues for the public.[21] One of the first writers to formalize this idea was Walter Lippmann, a prominent American journalist.[22] Lippmann took the view that the public responds not to actual events in the environment but to "the pictures in our heads," which he calls the *pseudoenvironment*: "For the real environment is altogether too big, too complex, and too fleeting for direct acquaintance. We are not equipped to deal with so much subtlety, so much variety, so many permutations and combinations. And altogether we have to act in that environment, we have to reconstruct it on a simpler model before we can manage with it."[23]

The agenda-setting function has been further described by Donald Shaw, Maxwell McCombs, and their colleagues, who wrote:

Considerable evidence has accumulated that editors and broadcasters play an important part in shaping our social reality as they go about their day-to-day task of choosing and displaying news. . . . This impact of the mass media—the ability to effect cognitive change among individuals, to structure their thinking—has been labeled the agenda-setting function of mass communication. Here may lie the most important effect of mass communication, its ability to mentally order and organize our world for us. In short, the mass media may not be successful in telling us what to think, but they are stunningly successful in telling us what to think about.[24]

In other words, agenda setting establishes the salient issues or images in the minds of the public.

Agenda setting occurs because the press must be selective in reporting the news. News outlets, as gatekeepers of information, make choices about what to report and how to report it. What the public knows about the state of affairs at any given time is largely a product of media gatekeeping.[25] Further, we know that how a person votes is determined mainly by what issues the individual believes to be important. For this reason some researchers have come to believe that the issues reported during a candidate's term in office may have more effect on the election than the campaign itself.

There are two levels of agenda setting. The first establishes the general issues that are important, and the second determines the parts or aspects of those issues that are important. In many ways the second level is as important as the first, because it gives us a way to frame the issues that constitute the public and media agendas. For example, the media may tell us that deregulation of the electric industry is an important issue (first level), but they may also focus on differences between the states, framing this issue as a question of *how* deregulation is accomplished (second level).[26]

The agenda-setting function is a three-part linear process.[27] First, the priority of issues to be discussed in the media, *or media agenda*, must be set. Second, the media agenda in some way affects or interacts with what the public thinks, creating the *public agenda*. Finally, the public agenda affects or interacts in some way with what policymakers consider important, called the

policy agenda. In the theory's simplest and most direct version, then, the media agenda affects the public agenda, and the public agenda affects the policy agenda.

Although a number of studies show that the media can be powerful in affecting the public agenda, it is still not clear whether the public agenda also affects the media agenda. The relationship may be one of mutual rather than linear causation. Further, it appears that actual events have some impact on both the media agenda and the public agenda.

The prevailing opinion among media researchers seems to be that the media can but does not always have a powerful effect on the public agenda. The power of media depends on such factors as media credibility on particular issues at particular times, the extent of conflicting evidence as perceived by individual members of the public, the extent to which individuals share media values at certain times, and the public's need for guidance. Media will most often be powerful when media credibility is high, conflicting evidence is low, individuals share media values, and the audience has a high need for guidance.

Karen Siune and Ole Borre studied some of the complexities of agenda setting in a Danish election.[28] Three kinds of political broadcasts on radio and television were aired in this election. These included programs made by the political parties, programs in which the candidates were asked questions by a panel of journalists and citizens, and debates. All of these programs were recorded and analyzed by counting the number of statements made about each issue in the campaign. In addition, about 1,300 voters were interviewed at various points in the campaign to establish the public agenda. Because in Denmark the election campaigns last only three weeks and the number of political broadcasts are more limited than in the United States, the researchers had an excellent opportunity to study the agenda-setting process.

Siune and Borre found three kinds of agenda-setting effects. The first is the degree to which the media reflect the public agenda, called *representa-*

tion. In a representational agenda, the public influences the media. The second is the maintenance of the same agenda by the public the entire time, which is called *persistence.* In a persistent public agenda, the media may have little effect. The third occurs when the media agenda influences the public agenda, referred to as *persuasion.* This third kind of effect—media influencing the public—is exactly what classic agenda-setting theory predicts.

If you determine agendas at three points in a campaign—at the beginning (time 1), at the middle (time 2), and at the end (time 3)—you can get a sense of these three effects. A correlation between the public agenda at time 1 and the media agenda at time 2 suggests representation, or audience-influencing media. A correlation between the public agenda at time 1 and time 3 suggests persistence, or stability of the public agenda. Finally, a correlation between the media agenda at time 2 and the public agenda at time 3 suggests persuasion, or media influencing the public agenda. It is possible for any combination of these three to occur at the same time.

In their study, Siune and Borre found much persistence in the public agenda, but there was also some persuasion in the sense that the broadcasts seemed to affect the public agenda somewhat. The most persuasive effects seemed to come from programs in which citizens set the media agenda. There was also a fair agenda-setting effect from the reporters and from the politicians themselves. The researchers did not find a representation effect in which the public affected the media.

A natural question is who affects the media agenda in the first place? This is a complex and difficult question. It appears that media agendas result from pressures both within media organizations and from outside sources.[29] In other words, the media agenda is established by some combination of internal programming, editorial and managerial decisions, and external influences from nonmedia sources such as socially influential individuals, government officials, commercial sponsors, and the like.

The power of media in establishing a public agenda depends in part on their relations with power centers. If the media have close relationships with the elite class in society, that class will probably affect the media agenda and the public agenda in turn. Many critical theorists believe that media can be and usually are an instrument of the dominant ideology in society, and when this happens, that dominant ideology will permeate the public agenda.

Four types of power relations between the media and outside sources can be found. The first is a high-power source and high-power media. In this kind of arrangement, if the two see eye to eye, a positive symbiotic relationship will exert great power over the public agenda. This would be the case, for example, with a powerful public official who has especially good relations with the press. On the other hand, if the powerful media and the powerful sources do not agree, a struggle may take place between them.

The second kind of arrangement is a high-power source and low-power media. Here, the external source will probably co-opt the media and use them to accomplish its own ends. This is what happens, for example, when politicians buy airtime or when a popular President gives the press the "privilege" of interviewing him. In the third type of relation, a lower-power source and high-power media, the media organizations themselves will be largely responsible for their own agenda. This happens when the media marginalize certain news sources such as the student radicals in the 1960s. The fourth type of relation is where both media and external sources are low in power, and the public agenda will probably be established by the events themselves rather than the media or the leaders.

As the agenda-setting function shows, there is an interaction between the public and the media, each influencing the other. But what is the "public"? We can measure average opinions and call this "public opinion," but this oversimplifies the process at best. Instead, of thinking of the public in monolithic terms, we can look at small media audiences, as the following theory shows.

Social Action Media Studies

Many media scholars believe that the audience cannot be characterized as an amorphous mass, that it consists of numerous highly differentiated communities, each with its own values, ideas, and interests. Media content is interpreted within the community according to meanings that are worked out socially within the group, and individuals are influenced more by their peers than by the media.[30]

Gerard Schoening and James Anderson call the community-based approach *social action media studies,* and they outline six premises of this work.[31] First, meaning is not in the message itself but is produced by an interpretive process in the audience. Different audiences will interpret or understand what they read and view in different ways. For example, talk radio programs may be taken to mean many things, depending on who is listening.

The second premise is that the meaning of media messages and programs is not determined passively, but produced actively by audiences. This means that audiences actually do something with what they view and read. They act as they view. Some listeners, for example, may turn on talk radio to combat boredom while driving, others may turn it on late in the evening as a sleep aid, and still others may listen to it actively during the day as a means of getting information about current events. What a particular talk radio program means, therefore, is a product of how listeners treat it, what they do with it.

The third premise is that the meanings of media shift constantly as the members approach the media in different ways. Sometimes the talk radio program may be strictly entertainment, sometimes serious information, and sometimes just background noise, depending on when and how it is listened to.

The fourth, the meaning of a program or message is never individually established, but communal. It is part of the tradition of a group, community, or culture. The implication of this is that when you join a community (by birth or membership),

you accept the ongoing activities and meanings of that community or group. Your own behavior may influence the group or change the activities and meanings in some way, but the outcome at any given time is always sitting in the community or group.

Fifth, the actions that determine a group's meanings for media content are done in interaction among members of the group. In other words, how we act toward the media and what meanings emerge from those actions are social interactions. This does not mean that you never watch TV by yourself, but it does mean that how you watch TV and what you do with the television set are part of an ongoing interaction between yourself and others. If you listen to talk radio in the car while you commute to work, this pattern is part of a larger web of interactions with people at home and at work. It is a routine that is made possible by a huge network of factors involving work, home, radio, boredom, cars, highways, and so on.

Finally, the sixth premise of social action media studies is that researchers join the communities they study, if only temporarily, and therefore have an ethical obligation to be open about what they are studying and share what they learn with those studied. Consistent with social action media studies, an increasingly popular way of approaching media is to think of the audience as numerous *interpretive communities*, each with its own meanings for what is read, viewed, or heard.[32]

In Chapter 5, we presented the theory of Stanley Fish, who discussed the ways in which readers assign meaning to texts. Because of the fact that many texts come through the media, Fish has had a significant impact on interpretive media studies.[33] For Fish, interpretive communities come into being around specific media and content. A community develops around a shared pattern of consumption: common understandings of the content of what is read, heard, or viewed, and shared outcomes. For example, a television audience consists of a number of "cultures," or communities of viewers, who use and perceive the medium—even individual programs—differently. Thus, if you want to discover how television affects the audience, you have to understand the cultures of these various communities.

Because the outcomes of media consumption depend on the cultural constructions of the community, this approach requires cultural interpretation.[34] James Lull refers to this type of work as the "ethnography of mass communication."[35] For example, a program like *Sesame Street* appeals to a variety of interpretive communities. One such community might be middle-class children whose parents encourage them to watch and discuss it with them. Another community might be children who view the program on their own to kill time before dinner every evening.

Another example of an interpretive community would be people who get their news by listening to National Public Radio's *All Things Considered* in the car on the way home from work. Still another might consist of people who watch a lot of weekend football for relaxation, entertainment, and social life. And yet another might be the followers of the soap opera *As the World Turns.*

Any person may be a member of a variety of interpretive communities, and particular social groups, such as the family, may be a crossing point for a number of such communities. For example, various members of a family may enjoy television news, top-40 radio programming, sitcoms, children's programs, biographies, and sports and are therefore members of a variety of communities.

Thomas Lindlof outlines three dimensions of an interpretive community.[36] Because interpretive communities define their own meanings for media, Lindlof refers to these elements as *genres,* or general types of media outcomes created by interaction within the interpretive community. This idea is consistent with social constructionism discussed in Chapter 6.

The first genre that characterizes an interpretive community is *content,* which consists of the types of programs and other media consumed by the community. One group shares an interest in televised football, another in mystery novels, and still another in music videos. It is not enough that a community share an interest in one type of medium content; it must also share some common meanings for that content. A mother who thinks *Sesame Street* is a cute and harmless pastime for her children, the children who become intimately involved with the characters day after day, the teenage son who thinks it is silly, and the grandfather who loves the Muppets do not constitute an interpretive community because they see very different things in the content of that program.

Genres of *interpretation,* then, revolve around shared meaning. Members of a community interpret the content of programs and other media in similar ways. The impact on their behavior, especially what they say about the media and the language used to describe it, is similar. The Tuesday morning quarterback is a good example. Members of the Monday night football club spend a good deal of time on Tuesday morning analyzing the game.

Finally, genres of *social action* are shared sets of behaviors toward the media in question, including not only how the media content is consumed (when and where it is viewed or read) but also the ways it affects the conduct of the members of the community. How are members' relationships among themselves affected by the media? Does a particular type of content facilitate the relationship in some way? Do people talk to one another about what they have seen or heard? Do they use relationships viewed on television as models for their own relationships?

An example of a cultural analysis of media is Linda Steiner's investigation of the "No Comment" section of *Ms.* magazine.[37] *Ms.* has regularly published a page titled "No Comment," featuring quotations and entries from other sources, sent in by readers, to illustrate the oppression of women in media. The title of the section implies that the quotation stands by itself without comment.

Items from other magazines (especially print ads), journals, newspapers, and even textbooks and manuals have found their way onto the "No Comment" page. All items were originally published with a particular meaning in mind, but the readers of *Ms.* interpret them differently. The fact that readers choose similar items again and again to make a point at odds with the original publisher's intent makes these readers an interpretive community, sharing attitudes and perceptions about the media's treatment of women.

In her analysis, Steiner isolates a number of meanings for various items. For example, many depict women as the property of men. Some mock feminism as offensive. Others make use of women's bodies in ways that are exploitative. Still others promote sexual abuse and violence against women. In each case, the deliberate reading opposes that intended by the originator of the quoted item. Steiner shows how contributing to and reading the "No Comment" section solidifies a set of values and views shared by the interpretive community of *Ms.* readers.

REFLECTIONS ON

The Sociocultural Tradition

Sociocultural theories of media are diverse in orientation. The three sample theories presented in this chapter take rather different approaches—looking at the structure, functions, and audiences of the mass media. What these theories share is a concern for larger social and cultural forces. They do not agree on what these forces are, but they do see the need to look beyond media content and individual effects. The primary contribution of the sociocultural tradition, then, is to capture large social and cultural outcomes of society-media interactions.

• • •

THE SOCIOPSYCHOLOGICAL TRADITION

In contrast with the sociocultural approach covered in the last section, much media theory has concentrated on individual effects of media. We turn now to look at how individuals are believed to be impacted, as depicted in the sociopsychological tradition.

Parents wonder how television is affecting their children. Educators want to know if children will learn from films, videos, magazines, and television programs. In other words, we wonder how media affect us as persons. There is a vast literature on this subject, and we can only take an aerial shot of it here by providing an overview of three large theoretical programs within this tradition. The first looks at the effects tradition in general, the second focuses on how individuals use media, and the third points to one cultural outcome of media effects.

The Effects Tradition

The theory of mass communication effects has undergone a curious evolution in this century.[38] Early on, researchers believed in the "magic bullet" theory of communication effects. Individuals were believed to be directly and heavily influenced by media messages, since media were considered to be extremely powerful in shaping public opinion.[39] According to this model, if you heard on the radio that you should try Pepsodent toothpaste, you would.

Then, during the 1950s when the "two-step flow hypothesis" was becoming popular, media effects were considered minimal. The two-step flow hypothesis is the idea that the media inform opinion leaders, who influence others through interpersonal communication. You might try Pepsodent because a friend uses it, but not because of any direct influence from the media. Later, in the 1960s, we came to believe that media effects are mediated by other variables and are therefore only moderate in strength. A Pepsodent commercial might or might not influence you, depending on other variables. Now, after research in the 1970s and the 1980s, many scholars have returned to the powerful-effects model, in which the public is considered to be heavily influenced by media. This later research centers on television as a particularly powerful medium.

Perhaps the best-known early work on limited effects was the reinforcement approach most notably articulated by Joseph Klapper.[40] Klapper, in surveying the literature on mass communication effects, developed the thesis that mass communication is not a necessary and sufficient cause of audience effects but that it is mediated by other variables. Thus, media are only a contributing cause.

Raymond Bauer observes that audiences are difficult to persuade, and he calls them obstinate.[41] Bauer denies the idea that a direct hypodermic-needle effect operates between communicator and audience. Instead, many variables involved in the audience interact to shape effects in various ways.[42] Audience effects are mediated by group and interpersonal factors and by selectivity, among others. Studies have shown that audience members are selective in their exposure to information.[43] In its simplest form, the hypothesis of selective exposure predicts that people in most circumstances will select information consistent with their attitudes.

The reinforcement approach was a definite step in the right direction at the time it was in vogue. Compared with the bullet theory, the reinforcement approach viewed mass communication as more complicated than had previously been imagined. It envisioned situations rife with mediating variables that would inhibit media effects. The research in this tradition did identify some important mediating variables, completing a more elaborate puzzle than had previously been constructed.

The problem of the limited-effects model is that it maintained a linear, cause-to-effect pattern.[44] It failed to take into account the social forces on the media or the ways that individuals might affect the media. In addition, the limited-effects model concentrated almost exclusively on attitude and opinion effects, ignoring other kinds of effects and functions such as cultivation or diffusion. Finally, true to tradition, such research focused on short-term effects of mass communication without questioning whether repeated exposure or time might affect the audience.

The work of Klapper and others on limited effects resulted in two general types of response. The first was a rejection of limited effects in favor of powerful ones, and the second was an attempt to explain limited effects in terms of the powers of audience members rather than media.

Perhaps the most vocal contemporary spokesperson in favor of powerful effects is Elisabeth Noelle-Neumann.[45] She believes that limited-effects theory has "distorted the interpretation of research findings over the years," and "that the 'dogma of media powerlessness' is no longer tenable."[46] Noelle-Neumann claims that the pendulum, which began swinging in the other direction after Klapper's famous work, has now reached its full extension and that most researchers believe that the media indeed have powerful effects.

Noelle-Neumann says that most limited-effects researchers were either academic journalists or people who held the media in a free society in high regard. They were interested in painting a picture of the media as disseminators of information, but not of influence. If viewed as important but not controlling, the media would continue to have the freedom to investigate and report whatever they felt to be important at a particular time—and journalists liked that. This interest led to the tendency to "see" limited rather than powerful effects in media-research results, which Noelle-Neumann calls "the media's effect on media research." Still, the media-effects literature remains complex.

In summarizing the research literature on the effects of media violence, James Potter reports several clear effects.[47] For example, viewing violent portrayals can lead to increased aggressiveness, fear, and desensitization in the short term. Long-term exposure to violence can create increased aggression, which in turn can lead to more viewing of violence. It can also lead to an increased feeling of being potentially victimized and to the greater acceptance of violence. Potter is careful to point out, however, that these results do not necessarily support a powerful-effects model because effects are mediated by individual, situational, institutional, and message variables, all of which complicate the effects picture. Indeed, Potter himself says that the powerful-effects model has been discredited for fifty years![48] He calls for a systemic approach that looks at a host of factors along with methods that admit to more complete definitions of violence and effects.

It is clear, then, that neither the limited-effects nor powerful-effects models have a great deal of credibility at this time. In fact, it may not make sense to polarize the positions in this way. Especially, if we expand the perspectives on the question of effects beyond the sociopsychological tradition to include sociocultural and critical theories, the answer is even more complicated. In a recent survey of the entire theoretical literature, Paul Power, Robert Kubey, and Spiro Kiousis conclude: "Instead of maintaining the usual polarization between different 'camps' or, as disturbing, the complete neglect by one group of the other's work—the near complete talking past one another—we advocate drawing from the strengths and relevant theorizing and observations of various approaches."[49] In the following section, we review theories that paint a more moderate and complex picture than either the limited- or powerful-effects models portray.

Uses, Gratifications, and Dependency

One of the most popular theories of mass communication is the uses-and-gratifications approach.[50] Here, we examine the original idea of uses and gratifications and then look at some interesting extensions. The uses-and-gratifications approach focuses on the consumer—the audience member—rather than the message.[51] Unlike the powerful-effects tradition, this approach imagines the audience member to be a discriminating user of media. The basic stance is summarized as follows:

> Compared with classical effects studies, the uses and gratifications approach takes the media consumer rather than the media message as its starting point, and explores his communication behavior in terms of his direct experience with the media. It views the members of the audience as actively utilizing media contents, rather than being passively acted upon by the media. Thus, it does not assume a direct relationship between messages and effects, but postulates instead that members of the audience put messages to use, and that such usages act as intervening variables in the process of effect.[52]

Here the audience is assumed to be active and goal-directed. The audience member is largely responsible for choosing media to meet needs and knows his or her own needs and how to meet them. In this view, media are considered to be only one way of meeting personal needs. In other words, out of the options that media present, the individual chooses ways to gratify needs.

Expectancy-Value Theory. Acknowledging the lack of theoretical coherence in early uses-and-gratifications work, Philip Palmgreen created a theory based on his own work, that of Karl Rosengren, and others.[53] The theory is based on *expectancy-value theory*, which you read about in Chapter 4. According to this theory, you orient yourself by your own attitudes. An attitude consists of a cluster of beliefs and evaluations. Your attitude toward some segment of the media is determined by your beliefs about and evaluations of it.

The gratifications you seek from media are determined by your attitudes toward the media—your beliefs about what a medium can give you and your evaluations of this material. For example, if you believe that sitcoms provide entertainment and you like to be entertained, you will seek gratification of your entertainment needs by watching sitcoms. If, on the other hand, you believe that sitcoms provide an unrealistic view of life and you don't like this kind of thing, you will avoid viewing them.

Of course, your opinion of sitcoms consists of several beliefs and evaluations, and whether you actually watch them will be determined by several things. Your entire cluster of beliefs and evaluations will determine your orientation to any type of program. Palmgreen's formula for this, which mirrors the general expectancy-value formula presented in Chapter 4, is as follows:

$$GS_i = \sum_i^n b_i e_i$$

where

GS = gratification sought
b_i = belief
e_i = evaluation

The extent to which you seek gratifications in any segment of the media (a program, a program type, a particular kind of content, or an entire medium) would be determined by the same formula. As you gain experience with a part of the media, the gratifications you obtain will in turn affect your beliefs, reinforcing the viewing pattern.

To test the connection between expectancy values and media gratifications, David Swanson and Austin Babrow conducted a study of the television news-viewing habits of students.[54] About 300 students at the University of Illinois were asked to fill out a questionnaire on their news viewing. To find out whether they watched the news and how they felt about it, the students were asked how many times a week they viewed network and local news, how likely they were to view news in an average week, and whether other people thought they should watch the news. The questionnaire also tested the students' attitudes toward the news.

To find out the extent to which the news gratified various media needs, the questionnaire asked whether each of a number of gratifications was met by watching the news. These included such items as keeping up on current events, getting entertained, and giving them things to talk about. In all, fourteen possible gratifications were included. The researchers found that the students' expectancy values (their attitudes) toward the news did relate to how much they used the news to gratify certain media needs.

Dependency Theory.   The uses-and-gratifications approach is a limited-effects theory. In other words, it grants individuals much control over how they employ media in their lives. Although media scholars are divided on just how powerful the media are, some scholars have argued that the limited-effects and powerful-effects models are not necessarily incompatible. Dependency theory takes a step toward showing how both may explain media effects.

Sandra Ball-Rokeach and Melvin DeFleur originally proposed dependency theory.[55] Like uses-and-gratifications theory, this approach also rejects the causal assumptions of the early reinforcement hypothesis. To overcome this weakness, these authors take a broad system approach. In their model, they propose an integral relationship among audiences, media, and the larger social system.

Consistent with uses-and-gratifications theory, dependency theory predicts that you depend on media information to meet certain needs and achieve certain goals. But you do not depend on all media equally.

Two factors determine how dependent you will become on media, according to Ball-Rokeach and DeFleur. First, you will become more dependent on media that meet a number of your needs than on media that satisfy just a few. Media can serve a number of functions such as monitoring government activities, reporting news, and providing entertainment. For any given group of people, some of these functions are more important than others, and your dependence on information from a medium increases when it supplies information that is more central to you. If you follow sports carefully, you will probably become dependent on ESPN or *Sports Illustrated.* A person who is not interested in sports will probably not even know where ESPN is on the dial, may never have looked at *Sports Illustrated,* and typically skips the entire sports section of the newspaper.

The second source of dependency is social stability. When social change and conflict are high, established institutions, beliefs, and practices are challenged, forcing a reevaluation and perhaps new choices in terms of media consumption. At such times your reliance on the media for information will increase. At other, more stable times your dependency on media may go way down. During times of war, for example, people become incredibly dependent on news programming.

This model shows that social institutions and media systems interact with audiences so as to create needs, interests, and motives. These in turn influence the audience to select various media and non-media sources that can subsequently lead to various dependencies. Individuals who grow dependent on a particular segment of the media will be affected cognitively, affectively, and behaviorally by that segment. Consequently, people are affected in different ways and to different degrees by the media.

Of course, one's needs are not always strictly personal but may be shaped by the culture or by various social conditions. In other words, individuals' needs, motives, and uses of media are contingent on outside factors that may not be within the individuals' control. These outside factors act as constraints on what and how media can be used and on the availability of other non-media alternatives.

For example, an elderly person who does not drive and has few friends may come to depend on television in a way that other individuals, whose life situations are different, will not. A commuter may come to rely on radio for information and news. A teenager may become dependent on music videos because of certain norms in the social group. In general, "the more readily available, the greater the perceived instrumentality, and the more socially and culturally acceptable the use of a medium is, the more probable that media use will be regarded as the most appropriate functional alternative."[56]

Furthermore, the more alternatives an individual has for gratifying needs, the less dependent he or she will become on any single medium. The number of functional alternatives, however, is not just a matter of individual choice or even of psychological traits but is limited also by factors such as availability of certain media.

Cultivation Theory

The work of George Gerbner and his colleagues, cultivation theory, states that television brings about a shared way of viewing the world:[57]

Television is a centralized system of storytelling. It is part and parcel of our daily lives. Its dramas, commercials, news, and other programs bring a relatively coherent world of common images and messages into every home. Television cultivates from infancy the very predispositions and preferences that used to be acquired from other primary sources. Transcending historic barriers of literacy and mobility, television has become the primary common source of socialization and everyday information (mostly in the form of entertainment) of an otherwise heterogeneous population. The repetitive pattern of television's mass-produced messages and images forms the mainstream of a common symbolic environment.[58]

Gerbner calls this effect *cultivation,* since television is believed to be a homogenizing agent in culture. Cultivation analysis is concerned with the totality of the pattern communicated cumulatively by television over a long period of exposure rather than by any particular content or specific effect. In other words, this is not a theory of individual media "effects" but instead makes a statement about the culture as a whole. It is not concerned with what any strategy or campaign can do but with the total impact of numerous strategies and campaigns over time. Total immersion in television, not selective viewing, is important in the cultivation of ways of knowing and images of reality. Indeed, subcultures may retain their separate values, but general overriding images depicted on television will cut across individual social groups and subcultures, affecting them all.

As you might imagine, the theory predicts a difference in the social reality of heavy television viewers as opposed to light viewers. Heavy viewers will believe in a reality that is consistent with that shown on television, even though television does not necessarily reflect the actual world. Gerbner's research on prime-time television, for example, has shown that there are three men to every woman on television; there are few Hispanics—and those shown are typically minor characters; there are almost entirely middle-class characters; and there are three times as many law enforcement officers as blue-collar workers.

One of the most interesting aspects of cultivation is the "mean-world syndrome." Although less than 1 percent of the population are victims of violent crimes in any one-year period, heavy exposure can lead to the belief that no one can be trusted in what appears to be a violent world.

Nancy Signorielli reports a study of the mean-world syndrome, in which violent acts in children's television programming were analyzed.[59] Over 2,000 programs, including 6,000 main characters, during prime time and weekends from 1967 to 1985 were analyzed with interesting results. About 71 percent of prime-time and 94 percent of weekend programs included acts of violence. Prime-time programs averaged almost five acts of violence each, and weekend programs averaged six. That amounts to over five acts per hour during prime time and about twenty per hour on weekends.

As part of this study, people were surveyed on five occasions between 1980 and 1986 regarding their views on the state of the world. To measure feelings of alienation and gloom, they were asked whether they agreed with three statements: (1) "Despite what some people say, the lot of the average man is getting worse, not better"; (2) "It's hardly fair to bring a child into the world with the way things look for the future"; and (3) "Most public officials are not interested in the problems of the average man."

In addition, they were asked three questions to measure feelings about a mean world: (1) "Would you say that most of the time people try to be helpful, or are they mostly just looking out for themselves?"; (2) "Do you think that most people would try to take advantage of you if they got a chance, or would they try to be fair?"; or (3) "Generally speaking, would you say that most people can be trusted, or you can't be too careful in dealing with people?" The findings indicate that heavy viewers tend to see the world as gloomier and meaner than do light viewers, and heavy viewers tend to mistrust people more than light viewers do.

Cultivation analysis has also found that there is a general fallout effect from television to the entire culture so that culture becomes homogenized, or *mainstreamed,* through TV. Television is not a force for change as much as it is a force for stability.

Mainstreaming can be seen in the mean-world data reviewed above. Even though heavy viewers scored higher on the mean-world index than did light viewers, a substantial number of light viewers also scored high. In fact, if you remove people with a college education from the sample, heavy and light viewers scored about the same.

Although cultivation is a general outcome of television viewing, it is not a universal phenomenon, despite the mainstreaming effect. In fact, different groups are affected differently by cultivation. Your interaction with others affects your tendency to accept TV reality. For example, adolescents who interact with their parents about television viewing are less likely to be affected by television images than are adolescents who do not talk with their parents about television. Interestingly, people who watch more cable television tend to manifest more mainstreaming than do people who watch less.

REFLECTIONS ON
The Sociopsychological Tradition

You can see a difference between the theories classified as sociocultural and those dubbed sociopsychological. Each of the theories in the sociopsychological section more or less focuses on the individual and psychological processes involved in media effects and uses. Cultivation theory does have some cross-over to the sociocultural, though the cultural effects of television in this theory are clearly mediated by individual behavior. In other words, the amount and type of viewing that an individual does affects his or her ways of thinking about the world, which in turn spreads across society as similar viewing habits are shared with others. For this reason, cultivation theory shows a strong affinity with the sociopsychological tradition.

• • •

◖ THE CYBERNETIC TRADITION

The interplay of public opinion and media content is an interesting phenomenon. How do you come to hold your opinions about public issues? Are you more influenced by other people, by the media, or by both? The theory of the spiral of silence provides insights that may help you answer this question.

Public Opinion and the Spiral of Silence

The topic of public opinion has been of great concern in political science. It is defined as opinions publicly expressed, opinions regarding public affairs, and opinions of the public as a group rather than of smaller groups of individuals. Elisabeth Noelle-Neumann's theory of the "spiral of silence" continues this analysis by demonstrating how interpersonal communication and media operate together in the development of public opinion.[60]

As a political researcher in Germany, Noelle-Neumann observed that in elections, certain views seem to get more play than others. Sometimes people mute their opinions rather than talk about them. Noelle-Neumann calls this the *spiral of silence*. The spiral of silence occurs when individuals who perceive that their opinion is popular express it, whereas those who do not think their opinion is popular remain quiet. This process occurs in a spiral, so that one side of an issue ends up with much publicity and the other side with little.

In everyday life, we express our opinions in a variety of ways: We talk about them, we wear buttons, and we put bumper stickers on our cars. According to this theory, people are more apt to do these kinds of things when they perceive that others share their opinion and less apt to do so when they do not.

This thesis rests on two premises. The first is that people know which opinions are prevalent and which are not. In other words, people are not reluctant to make educated guesses about public opinion and have a sense of the percentages of the population for and against certain positions. This is called the *quasi-statistical sense* because while it is not scientific, there is a sense that is the prevailing viewpoint. The second assumption is that people adjust their expressions of opinion to these perceptions.

Noelle-Neumann presents considerable evidence to support these assumptions. In political elections, for example, people usually perceive quite accurately the prevailing opinion about the candidates and issues, and they are likely to express their preferences when others share them.

An interesting test of the tendency to remain silent on unpopular positions, devised by Noelle-Neumann is the "train test."[61] Here, respondents are asked to imagine that they were in a train compartment with a stranger for five hours and to decide whether they would be willing to discuss certain topics with this person. Respondents were told that they were to imagine that the other person mentioned his or her opinion on the subject and were then asked whether they would prefer to talk to the other person about this topic or not. Topics ranged from spanking children to the government of Germany. Interviewers presented this problem to 3,500 respondents covering numerous topics over several years. The overwhelming tendency was to freely discuss the topic when one agrees with the majority but to let it slide when one does not. People seem not to want to "make waves."

Of course, other factors enter into the decision to express one's opinion: Young people are more expressive than older people; educated individuals will speak up more than uneducated ones; and men are generally more willing to disclose their opinions than women. However, the spiral of silence is also a factor, and according to this research, a powerful one.

The spiral of silence seems to be caused by the fear of isolation. The spiral of silence is not just a matter of wanting to be on the winning side but is an attempt to avoid being isolated from one's social group. Threats of criticism from others were found to be powerful forces in silencing individuals. For example, smokers who are repeatedly criticized for advocating smokers' rights were found to remain silent rather than state their views on this subject in the presence of vocal nonsmokers.

In some cases the threat of expressing an opinion is extreme: "Slashed tires, defaced or torn posters, help refused to a lost stranger—questions of this kind demonstrate that people can be on uncomfortable or even dangerous ground when the climate of opinion runs counter to their views. When people attempt to avoid isolation, they are not responding hypersensitively to trivialities; these are existential issues that can involve real hazards."[62]

One can easily see how this process affects public opinion. There are, of course, exceptions to the spiral of silence. There are groups and individuals who do not fear isolation and who will express their opinions no matter what the consequences—a characteristic of innovators, change agents, and the avant-garde.

The media themselves also contribute to the spiral of silence. When polled, individuals usually state that they feel powerless in the face of media. Two kinds of experience accentuate this feeling of helplessness. The first is the difficulty of getting publicity for a cause or point of view. The second is being scapegoated by the media in what Noelle-Neumann calls the *pillory function* of media. In each case the individual feels powerless against the media, making the media an important part of the spiral of silence. The media publicize which opinions are prevalent and which are not.

Individuals often cannot tell where their opinions come from. They confuse what is learned through the media with what is learned through interpersonal channels. This tendency is especially true for television, with which so many people have a personal relationship:

> The longer one has studied the question, the clearer it becomes that fathoming the effects of the mass media is very hard. These effects do not come into being as a result of a single stimulus; they are as a rule cumulative, following the principle that "water dripping constantly wears

away stone." Further discussions among people spread the media's messages further, and before long no difference can be perceived between the point of media reception and points far removed from it. The media's effects are predominantly unconscious; people cannot provide an account of what has happened. Rather, they mix their own direct perceptions and the perceptions filtered through the eyes of the media into an indivisible whole that seems to derive from their own thoughts and experiences.[63]

Media effects on public opinion, then are cumulative and not always apparent.

It sometimes happens that journalists' opinions differ from those of the general public, so that media depictions contradict the prevailing expressions of individuals. When this occurs, a dual climate of opinion results. Here, two versions of reality operate—that of the media and that of the public. Noelle-Neumann likens this event to an unusual weather situation—interesting and seemingly bizarre.

The spiral of silence, then, is a phenomenon involving personal and media channels of communication. The media publicize public opinion, making evident which opinions predominate. Individuals express their opinions or not, depending on dominant points of view; the media, in turn, attend to the expressed opinion, and the spiral continues.

REFLECTIONS ON
The Cybernetic Tradition

The theory of the spiral of silence could be considered part of the sociopsychological tradition because of its emphasis on what individuals do in response to the conditions they face, but we think that this theory actually demonstrates cybernetic thinking quite well, as larger systemic interactions are at stake. An attraction of Noelle-Neumann's work is the complex interaction among individual statements, media depictions, and public opinion.

Media studies have generally embraced the cybernetic approach. One of the most influential ideas in media theory is that media affect opinion leaders, who in turn disseminate information and influence through interpersonal communication networks, which leads to the adoption of ideas throughout society, which in turn influences the media. In other words, a large cybernetic circle includes media, opinion leaders, and interpersonal networks. We think that the role of interpersonal networks in the dissemination of information and influence goes well beyond the media, so we elaborate this idea in Chapter 11.

• • •

◖ THE CRITICAL TRADITION

The media are more than simple mechanisms for disseminating information: They are complex organizations that comprise an important social institution of society. Clearly, the media are a major player in ideological struggle. Most critical communication theories are concerned with mass media primarily because of the media's potential for disseminating dominant ideologies and their potential for expressing alternative and oppositional ones. For some critical theorists, media are part of a culture industry that literally creates symbols and images that can oppress marginalized groups.

Branches of Critical Media Theory

According to McQuail there are five major branches of critical media theory.[64] The first is *classical Marxism*. Here, the media are seen as instruments of the dominant class and a means by which capitalists promote their profit-making interests. Media disseminate the ideology of the ruling classes in society and thereby oppress certain classes.

The second is *political-economic media theory*, which, like classical Marxism, blames media ownership for society's ills. In this school of thought, media content is a commodity to be sold in the marketplace, and the information disseminated is controlled by what the market will bear. This system leads to a conservative, nonrisk-taking operation, making certain kinds of programming and certain media outlets dominant and others marginalized.

The third line of theory is the *Frankfurt School*. This school of thought, which sees media as a means of constructing culture, places more emphasis on ideas than on material goods. In this way of thinking, media lead to the domination of the ideology of the elite. This outcome is accomplished by media manipulation of images and symbols to benefit the interests of the dominant class.

The fourth school is *hegemonic theory*. Hegemony is the domination of a false ideology or way of thinking over true conditions. Ideology is not caused by the economic system alone but is deeply embedded in all activities of society. Thus, ideology is not forced by one group on another but is pervasive and unconscious. The dominant ideology perpetuates the interests of certain classes over others, and the media obviously play a major role in this process.

The first four schools—classical Marxism, political economy, Frankfurt, and hegemonic—are different approaches within the critical theory tradition. The critical tradition takes a somewhat different direction with the fifth of McQuail's approaches—the *sociocultural approach*—usually called simply "cultural studies." Relying largely on semiotics, this group of scholars is interested in the cultural meanings of media products; they look at the ways media content is interpreted, including both dominant and oppositional interpretations. Cultural studies sees society as a field of competing ideas in a struggle among meanings. What, for example, is the meaning of a music video? In cultural studies, various competing meanings are viewed as cultural productions.

Cultural studies is becoming an increasingly popular and useful approach, and it can be used to integrate insights from a variety of schools of thought.[65] Actually, *hegemony theory* crosses over from critical theory to cultural studies, but refers to somewhat different forms of domination in each. In critical theory, hegemony refers to the domination of one class or group over others; in cultural studies, it designates the domination of a set of ideas over other ideas.

Studies of media and identity are a good case of how hegemony is observed from a cultural frame. For example, the whole idea of gender as a source of identity has been brought into question in queer theory.[66] The idea here is not that gender is unimportant, but that customary ways of thinking about gender are not always healthy and not always necessary. We can perform gender identity in a variety of ways, and how we do so is usually influenced by media portrayals. Other identities can and should be explored. Especially interesting in media depictions of gender and sexuality are ways in which media "normalize" certain forms gender and sexual orientation, which may co-opt or appropriate the interests of particular groups in ways that create a subtle hegemony. For example, positive media depictions of gay men and lesbians may actually serve to reproduce stereotypes.[67] As another example, feminism may be used in the media to "sell" a certain picture of women that restricts the whole range of what it can mean to be a woman in society.[68]

Although critical communication theories have gained presence in North America, their real development and strength occurred in Europe and Latin America. European critical theory is perhaps more widely known, because of the larger number of sources translated into English and the greater attention paid to European traditions. In contrast, Latin American communication theory, which remains largely untranslated, has received relatively little attention in the United States. Robert Huesca and Brenda Dervin have written a good summary of this work.[69]

According to Huesca and Dervin, Latin American communication scholarship challenges the predominant North American approach on many fronts. In general, this work honors horizontal, artistic, democratic, and participatory communication over vertical, industrial, authoritarian, and elite forms. It tends to look more at grass-roots efforts rather than top-down ones, and at self-managed communication systems rather than centralized systems. Latin American communication research also concentrates on human liberation rather than information transfer, consciousness building rather than domination, unity rather than fragmentation, and antiauthoritarian rather than authoritarian content.

Although these trends tend to be dualistic—as is most North American scholarship—pitting one point against another, many Latin American scholars have attempted to overcome dualism altogether. They have done this in a number of ways. For example, they have refused to dichotomize the communication source from the audience and have shown that the audience itself participates in the creation of meaning. These scholars have also emphasized global over national trends and have called for coalitions, networks, and dialogue among groups and ideas.

REFLECTIONS ON
The Critical Tradition

The critical tradition in media studies has been greatly influenced by three other traditions—the cybernetic, the sociocultural, and the semiotic. The influence of cybernetics is clear from the generally held belief in critical studies that domination is reproduced, or "articulated," by many interacting forces. No one force, such as the media, creates all of society's power structures; instead, these are a product of society-wide interaction of many institutions. At the same time, critical theory does tend to reject old-style system theory because it takes an "objective" and descriptive approach and fails to account for the social realities that are actually created through system interactions.

The sociocultural tradition has influenced critical approaches because of its emphasis on interpretation and social interaction as processes in which various structures and meanings get made. Sociocultural theories also emphasize discourse, an important element of most critical work on media. Most critical theory, except classical Marxism, readily adopts the ideas of social meaning and discourse, but rejects mainstream sociocultural work because it fails to make value judgments about the outcomes of social interaction.

Finally, the critical tradition has been influenced by the semiotic tradition. Although most critical theorists would reject early semiotic theories (Chapter 3), they freely acknowledge that symbols are powerful in producing cultural forms, including oppressive arrangements. Indeed, much critical theory research is semiotic in nature, as it focuses on signification within the media.

● ● ●

APPLICATIONS IMPLICATIONS

Because of the diversity of thought about media, theoretical generalizations are difficult. Still, as you peruse the theories in this chapter, three themes emerge.

1. The medium in which communication occurs contributes to the shape of society.

McLuhan's theory is not much in favor anymore, but few would deny the legitimacy of his basic idea—that media forms in and of themselves do have an impact on culture. McLuhan's ideas are useful for stimulating a fresh look at the subject matter, but they provide little guidance on how to understand the process of mass communication. They are valuable in that they point to the importance of media forms in society, but they do not give a realistic picture of the variables involved in the effects of media forms. In sum, Kenneth Boulding points out, "It is perhaps typical of very creative minds that they hit very large nails not quite on the head."[70]

The line of work called medium theory, nicely summarized by Ellis, does call our attention to the impacts of media on society. How did things change as we went from being an oral society to a literate one? What is the difference between hearing news by word of mouth and sitting down to read a book? And how do things change again when we can simply switch on an electronic box to see images from around the world? If you read a novel, you will encounter many semiotic images created by words but if you read a magazine, you will encounter a complex set of visual and textual signs that affect our minds in entirely different ways. Once those images begin to move, as in movies and television, then the complexity of the semiotic representation skyrockets.

Apart from content, then, it behooves us to think critically and creatively about the media we consume, how these affect us as individuals, and how they shape our cultures and society.

2. Media institutions have a major role in the production of culture.

This generalization says a great deal, but it also says very little. The fact that media have an impact is a truism. Clearly, mass communication involves the dissemination of information and influence in society through media and interpersonal channels. It is an integral part of culture and is inseparable from other large-scale social institutions. Media forms like television, film, and print—as well as media content—affect our ways of thinking and seeing the world. Indeed, media participate in the very creation of culture itself, and many believe that media are instrumental in disseminating power and domination in society and are thereby instruments of ideology and hegemony.

The literature on media reflects a persistent conflict in the study of mass communication. How powerful are media in the control of culture? Some argue that media are powerful forces in determining the character of culture and individual life. Other theorists claim that individuals have much control over the outcomes of media transactions in their lives. Yet a third group believes that mass media are important but that they are only part of a complex of factors involved in social domination, and that individuals are influenced by the entire system of dominating forces.

The media-influence process is complex. In the final analysis, the outcome of mass communication may be a product of the interaction among various societal structures and individual needs, desires, and dependencies, and it seems unlikely that this system will ever be reduced to an identifiable calculus. The theories in this chapter emphasize different aspects of this complex relationship.

One of the most important lines of research on the cultural impact of media is critical theory, which maintains that media are powerful forces for dominant interests in society. The so-called media hegemony thesis maintains that media are instruments of the dominant ideology, and by representing the interests of those already in power, media subvert the interests of marginalized groups. This thesis is hotly debated, as Kevin Carragee points out in a review.[71] Scholars opposing media hegemony claim that the media actually represent a diversity of values and often speak out in opposition to the ideology of the powerful in society.

The uses-and-gratifications approach was like a breath of fresh air in media research. For the first time scholars in this tradition focused on receivers as active participants in the communication process, rather than the traditional viewpoint of the passive, unthinking audience. This approach is certainly one of the most popular frameworks for the study of mass communication, but a good deal of criticism has been leveled against it.[72]

Dependency theory attempts to reconcile some of the problems of uses and gratifications with other powerful-effects models. This theory accounts for both individual differences in responses to media and general media effects. As a system theory, it shows the complexity of the interactions among the various aspects of the media transaction. The fusion of uses-and-gratifications and dependency theories provides an even more complete integration.

3. Audience members and communities participate in constructing the meaning of media messages.

No area in media theory has presented such quandaries and debates as studies of the audience. Media theorists are far from reaching consensus on how to conceptualize the audience and audience effects. Disputes on the nature of the audience seem to involve two related dialectics. The first is a tension between the idea that the audience is a mass public versus the idea that it is a small community. The second is a tension between the idea that the audience is passive versus the belief that it is active. Let us consider each of these debates in turn.

Some see the audience as an undifferentiated mass, and some see it as a variegated set of small groups or communities. In the case of the former, audiences are viewed as a large population that can be molded by the media. In the case of the latter, audiences are viewed as discriminating members of small groups who are influenced mostly by their peers.

Many media scholars believe that the mass community and active-passive dichotomies are too simple—that they do not capture the true complexity of audiences. It may be that audiences have some elements of mass society and other elements of local communities. Audiences may be active in some ways and passive in others or active at some times and passive at other times. Rather than ask whether audiences are easily influenced by the media, it might be better to ask when and under what conditions they are influenced and when they are not. This view changes the debate from one about what the audience really is to what the audience means for people at different times and in different places.[73]

○ NOTES

1. George Gerbner, "Mass Media and Human Communication Theory," in *Human Communication Theory*, ed. F. E. X. Dance (New York: Holt, Rinehart & Winston, 1967), p. 45.
2. For recent overviews and histories of mass communication theory, see Bradley S. Greenberg and Michael B. Salwen, "Mass Communication Theory and Research: Concepts and Models," in *An Integrated Approach to Communication Theory and Research*, ed. Michael B. Salwen and Don W. Stacks (Mahwah, NJ: Lawrence Erlbaum, 1996), pp. 63–78; and Robert S. Fortner, "Mediated Communication Theory," in *Building Communication Theories: A Socio/Cultural Approach*, ed. Fred L. Casmir (Hillsdale, NJ: Erlbaum, 1994), pp. 209–240. Definitions of *mass communication* are discussed in Sandra J. Ball-Rokeach and Muriel G. Cantor, eds., *Media, Audience, and Social Structure* (Beverly Hills, CA: Sage, 1986), pp. 10–11; and Denis McQuail, *Mass Communication Theory: An Introduction* (London: Sage, 1987), pp. 29–47.
3. McQuail, *Mass Communication*, pp. 52–53.
4. Joshua Meyrowitz, "Images of Media: Hidden Ferment—and Harmony—in the Field," *Journal of Communication* 43 (1993): 55–67.
5. For an excellent exploration of the links between the media and larger sociocultural structures and smaller personal and individual effects, see Karl Erik Rosengren, "Culture, Media, and Society: Agency and Structure, Continuity and Change," in *Media Effects and Beyond: Culture, Socializations, and Lifestyles*, ed. Karl Erik Rosengren (London: Routledge, 1994), pp. 3–28. See also Veikko Pietilä, "Perspectives on Our Past: Charting the Histories of Mass Communication Studies," *Critical Studies in Mass Communication* 11 (1994): 346–361.
6. This conceptualization is adapted from a discussion of mass communication theory by McQuail, *Mass Communication*, pp. 53–57.
7. For an excellent brief review of theory and research in mass communication, see Alan M. Rubin and Paul M. Haridakis, "Mass Communication Research at the Dawn of the 21st Century," in *Communication Yearbook 24*, ed. William B. Gudykunst (Thousand Oaks, CA: Sage, 2001), pp. 73–99.
8. For a more complete discussion of the semiotic tradition, see Donald L. Fry and Virginia H. Fry, "A Semiotic Model for the Study of Mass Communication," in *Communication Yearbook 9*, ed. M. L. McLaughlin (Beverly Hills, CA: Sage, 1986), pp. 443–462; Klaus Bruhn Jensen, "When Is Meaning? Communication Theory, Pragmatism, and Mass Media Reception," *Communication Yearbook 14*, ed. James A. Anderson (Newbury Park, CA: Sage, 1991), pp. 3–32.
9. See, for example, Wendy Leeds-Hurwitz, *Semiotics and Communication: Signs, Codes, Cultures* (Hillsdale, NJ: Erlbaum, 1993).
10. Especially good summaries of this field are provided by Donald L. Fry and Virginia H. Fry, "A Semiotic Model for the Study of Mass Communication," in *Communication Yearbook 9*, ed. M. L. McLaughlin (Beverly Hills, CA: Sage, 1986), pp. 443–462; and Jensen, "When Is Meaning?," pp. 3–32.
11. Among Baudrillard's many works are *Simulations*, trans. Paul Foss, Paul Patton, and Philip Beitchman (New York: Semiotext(e), 1983); *The Illusion of the End*, trans. Chris Turner (Cambridge: Polity, 1994); *Symbolic Exchange and Death*, trans. Iain Hamilton Grant (Thousand Oaks, CA: Sage, 1993). For a good summary of his work, see Sonja K. Foss, Karen A. Foss, and Robert Trapp, *Contemporary Perspectives on Rhetoric*, 3rd ed. (Prospect Heights, IL: Waveland, 2002).
12. The most prominent critics of mass society are Ortega y Gasset, Karl Mannheim, Karl Jaspers, Paul Tillich, Gabriel Marcel, and Emil Lederer. Syntheses can be found in a variety of sources. See, for example, Patrick Brantlinger, *Bread and Circuses: Theories of Mass Culture as Social Decay* (Ithaca, NY: Cornell University Press, 1983).

13. McLuhan's best-known works are *The Gutenberg Galaxy: The Making of Typographic Man* (Toronto: University of Toronto Press, 1962); *The Mechanical Bride* (New York: Vanguard, 1951); *Understanding Media* (New York: McGraw-Hill, 1964); Marshall McLuhan and Quentin Fiore, *The Medium Is the Massage* (New York: Bantam, 1967). I have relied on the synthesis of Bruce Gronbeck, "McLuhan as Rhetorical Theorist," *Journal of Communication* 31 (1981): 117–128.

14. J. W. Carey, "Harold Adams Innis and Marshall McLuhan," *Antioch Review* 27 (1967): 5–39. Innis's works include *The Bias of Communication* (Toronto: University of Toronto Press, 1951); and *Empire and Communications*, 2nd ed. (Toronto: University of Toronto Press, 1972).

15. Good brief summaries of McLuhan's theory can be found in the following: Kenneth Boulding, "The Medium Is the Massage," in *McLuhan: Hot and Cool*, ed. G. E. Stearn (New York: Dial, 1967), pp. 56–64; Tom Wolfe, "The New Life Out There," in *McLuhan: Hot and Cool*, ed. G. E. Stearn (New York: Dial, 1967), pp. 34–56; Carey, "Innis and McLuhan."

16. McLuhan and Fiore, *Medium Is the Massage.*

17. Donald G. Ellis, *Crafting Society: Ethnicity, Class, and Communication Theory* (Mahwah, NJ: Lawrence Erlbaum, 1999).

18. For a brief history of this tradition, see Carl Patrick Burrowes, "From Functionalism to Cultural Studies: Manifest Ruptures and Latent Continuities," *Communication Theory* 6 (1996): 88–103.

19. Harold Lasswell, "The Structure and Function of Communication in Society," in *The Communication of Ideas,* ed. L. Bryson (New York: Institute for Religious and Social Studies, 1948), p. 37. For information regarding Lasswell's contribution to communication, see Everett M. Rogers, *A History of Communication Study: A Biographical Approach* (New York: Free Press, 1994), pp. 203–243.

20. Lasswell, "Structure and Function."

21. For an overview, see Maxwell McCombs and Tamara Bell, "The Agenda Setting Role of Mass Communication," in *An Integrated Approach to Communication Theory and Research,* ed. Michael B. Salwen and Don W. Stacks (Mahwah, NJ: Lawrence Erlbaum, 1996), pp. 93–110.

22. See, for example, M. Childs and J. Reston, eds., *Walter Lippmann and His Times* (New York: Harcourt Brace, 1959).

23. Walter Lippmann, *Public Opinion* (New York: Macmillan, 1921), p. 16.

24. Donald L. Shaw and Maxwell E. McCombs, *The Emergence of American Political Issues* (St. Paul, MN: West, 1977), p. 5. For a very good summary of this whole line of work, see Jian-Hua Zhu and Deborah Blood, "Media Agenda-Setting Theory: Telling the Public What to Think About," in *Emerging Theories of Human Communication,* ed. Branislav Kovačić (Albany: SUNY Press, 1997): pp. 88–114. See also Maxwell McCombs, "New Frontiers in Agenda Setting: Agendas of Attributes and Frames," *Mass Communication Review* 24 (1997): 4–24; Everett M. Rogers and James W. Dearing, "Agenda-Setting Research: Where Has It Been, Where Is It Going?" in *Communication Yearbook 11,* ed. James A. Anderson (Newbury Park, CA: Sage, 1988), pp. 555–593; Stephen D. Reese, "Setting the Media's Agenda: A Power Balance Perspective," in *Communication Yearbook 14,* ed. James A. Anderson (Newbury Park, CA: Sage, 1991), pp. 309–340. See also David Protess and Maxwell McCombs, *Agenda Setting: Readings on Media, Public Opinion, and Policymaking* (Hillsdale, NJ: Lawrence Erlbaum, 1991).

25. Pamela J. Shoemaker, "Media Gatekeeping," in *An Integrated Approach to Communication Theory and Research,* ed. Michael B. Salwen and Don W. Stacks (Mahwah, NJ: Erlbaum, 1996), pp. 79–91.

26. The idea of framing as a media effect is explored by Dietram A. Scheufele, "Framing as a Theory of Media Effects," *Journal of Communication* 49 (1999): 103–122. See also McCombs, "New Frontiers."

27. This idea is developed by Rogers and Dearing, "Agenda-Setting Research."

28. Karen Siune and Ole Borre, "Setting the Agenda for a Danish Election," *Journal of Communication* 25 (1975): 65–73.

29. Reese, "Setting the Media's Agenda."

30. For an excellent statement of this position, see Thomas R. Lindlof, "Media Audiences as Interpretive Communities," in *Communication Yearbook 11,* ed. James A. Anderson (Newbury Park, CA: Sage, 1988), pp. 81–107. Supportive of this position, too, is reader reception theory, which is most notably developed by John Fiske, *Introduction to Communication Studies* (New York: Methuen, 1982); *Television Culture* (New York: Methuen, 1987); *Reading the Popular* (Winchester, MA: Unwin Hyman, 1989); and *Understanding Popular Culture* (Winchester, MA: Unwin Hyman, 1989).

31. Gerard T. Schoening and James A. Anderson, "Social Action Media Studies: Foundational Arguments and Common Premises," *Communication Theory* 5 (1995): 93–116.

32. This work is part of social action media studies. See Gerard T. Schoening and James A. Anderson, "Social Action Media Studies: Foundational Arguments and Common Premises," *Communication Theory* 5 (1995): 93–116.

33. Stanley Fish, *Is There a Text in This Class?* (Cambridge, MA: Harvard University Press, 1980).

34. See, for example, Thomas R. Lindlof and Timothy P. Meyer, "Mediated Communication as Ways of Seeing, Acting, and Constructing Culture: The Tools and Foundations of Qualitative Research," in *Natural Audiences: Qualitative Research of Media Uses and Effects,* ed. T. R. Lindlof (Norwood, NJ:

Ablex, 1987), pp. 1–32; Thomas R. Lindlof, "Media Audiences as Interpretive Communities," in *Communication Yearbook 11*, ed. James A. Anderson (Newbury Park, CA: Sage, 1988), pp. 81–107; Kevin M. Carragee, "Interpretive Media Study and Interpretive Social Science," *Critical Studies in Mass Communication* 7 (1990): 81–96; Klaus Bruhn Jensen, "When Is Meaning?," pp. 3–32.

35. James Lull, "The Social Uses of Television," *Human Communication Research* 6 (1980): 197–209; see also Shaun Moores, *Interpreting Audiences: The Ethnography of Media Consumption* (London: Sage, 1993).

36. Lindlof, "Media Audiences."

37. Linda Steiner, "Oppositional Decoding as an Act of Resistance," *Critical Studies in Mass Communication* 5 (1988): 1–15.

38. For a recent survey of a portion of this literature, see Tara M. Emmers-Sommer and Mike Allen, "Surveying the Effect of Media Effects: A Meta-Analytic Summary of the Media Effects Research," *Human Communication Research* 25 (1999): 478–497. For an especially good overview of theories of media violence, see W. James Potter, *On Media Violence* (Thousand Oaks, CA: Sage, 1999), pp. 11–24. See also the colloquy summarized by John E. Newhagen, "Colloquy: Information Processing: A More Inclusive Paradigm for the Study of Mass Media Effects," *Human Communication Research* 26 (2000): 99–103.

39. For explorations of the history of the magic bullet or hypodermic needle theory, see J. Michael Sproule, "Progressive Propaganda Critics and the Magic Bullet Myth," *Critical Studies in Mass Communication* 6 (1989): 225–246; Jeffery L. Bineham, "A Historical Account of the Hypodermic Model in Mass Communication," *Communication Monographs* 55 (1988): 230–246.

40. Joseph T. Klapper, *The Effects of Mass Communication* (Glencoe, IL: Free Press, 1960).

41. Raymond Bauer, "The Obstinate Audience: The Influence Process from the Point of View of Social Communication," *American Psychologist* 19 (1964): 319–328.

42. Raymond Bauer, "The Audience," in *Handbook of Communication*, ed. I. de sola Pool and others (Chicago: Rand McNally, 1973), pp. 141–152.

43. Studies on selectivity are well summarized in David O. Sears and Jonathan I. Freedman, "Selective Exposure to Information: A Critical Review," in *The Process and Effects of Mass Communication*, ed. W. Schramm and D. F. Roberts (Urbana: University of Illinois Press, 1971), pp. 209–234.

44. Criticism of the limited-effects approach can be found in Werner J. Severin and James W. Tankard, *Communication Theories: Origins, Methods, Uses* (New York: Hastings House, 1979), p. 249.

45. Elisabeth Noelle-Neumann, "Return to the Concept of Powerful Mass Media," in *Studies of Broadcasting*, ed. H. Eguchi and K. Sata (Tokyo: Nippon Hoso Kyokii, 1973), pp. 67–112; and "The Effect of Media on Media Effects Research," *Journal of Communication* 33 (1983): 157–165.

46. Noelle-Neumann, "Effect of Media," p. 157.

47. Potter, *On Media Violence*, pp. 25–42.

48. Potter, *On Media Violence*, p. 211.

49. Paulo Power, Robert Kubey, and Spiro Kiousis, "Audience Activity and Passivity: An Historical Taxonomy," *Communication Yearbook 26*, ed. William B. Gudykunst (Mahwah, NJ: Lawrence Erlbaum, 2002), p. 152.

50. For historical overviews, see J. D. Rayburn, II, "Uses and Gratifications," in *An Integrated Approach to Communication Theory and Research*, ed. Michael B. Salwen and Don W. Stacks (Mahwah, NJ: Lawrence Erlbaum, 1996), pp. 145–163; Alan M. Rubin, "Audience Activity and Media Use," *Communication Monographs* 60 (1993): 98–105.

51. Elihu Katz, Jay Blumler, and Michael Gurevitch, "Uses of Mass Communication by the Individual," in *Mass Communication Research: Major Issues and Future Directions*, ed. W. P. Davidson and F. Yu (New York: Praeger, 1974), pp. 11–35. See also Jay Blumler and Elihu Katz, eds., *The Uses of Mass Communication* (Beverly Hills, CA: Sage, 1974). See also the entire issue of *Communication Research* 6 (January 1979).

52. Katz, Blumler, and Gurevitch, "Uses of Mass Communication by the Individual," p. 12.

53. Philip Palmgreen, "Uses and Gratifications: A Theoretical Perspective," in *Communication Yearbook 8*, ed. R. N. Bostrom (Beverly Hills, CA: Sage, 1984), pp. 20–55. See also K. Rosengren, L. Wenner, and P. Palmgreen, eds., *Media Gratifications Research: Current Perspectives* (Beverly Hills, CA: Sage, 1985).

54. David L. Swanson and Austin S. Babrow, "Uses and Gratifications: The Influence of Gratification-Seeking and Expectancy-Value Judgments on the Viewing of Television News," in *Rethinking Communication: Paradigm Exemplars*, ed. Brenda Dervin, Lawrence Grossberg, Barbara J. O'Keefe, and Ellen Wartella (Newbury Park, CA: Sage, 1989), pp. 361–375.

55. Sandra J. Ball-Rokeach and Melvin L. DeFleur, "A Dependency Model of Mass-Media Effects," *Communication Research* 3 (1976): 3–21. See also Melvin L. DeFleur and Sandra J. Ball-Rokeach, *Theories of Mass Communication* (New York: Longman, 1982), pp. 240–251.

56. Alan M. Rubin and Sven Windahl, "The Uses and Dependency Model of Mass Communication," *Critical Studies in Mass Communication* 3 (1986): 193.

57. George Gerbner, "Living with Television: The Dynamics of the Cultivation Process," in *Perspectives on Media Effects,* ed. Jennings Bryant and Dolf Zillmann (Hillsdale, NJ: Lawrence Erlbaum, 1986), pp. 17–40; Michael Morgan and James Shanahan, "Two Decades of Cultivation Research: An Appraisal and Meta-Analysis," *Communication Yearbook 20,* ed. Brant R. Burleson (Thousand Oaks, CA: Sage, 1997), pp. 1–45; Nancy Signorielli and Michael Morgan, "Cultivation Analysis: Research and Practice," in *An Integrated Approach to Communication Theory and Research,* ed. Michael B. Salwen and Don W. Stacks (Mahwah, NJ: Erlbaum, 1996), pp. 111–126; Nancy Signorielli and Michael Morgan, eds., *Cultivation Analysis: New Directions in Media Effects Research* (Newbury Park, CA: Sage, 1990).

58. George Gerbner, Larry Gross, Michael Morgan, and Nancy Signorielli, "Living with Television," in *Perspectives on Media Effects,* ed. Jennings Bryant and Dolf Zillmann (Hillsdale, NJ: Lawrence Erlbaum, 1986), p. 18.

59. Nancy Signorielli, "Television's Mean and Dangerous World: A Continuation of the Cultural Indicators Perspective," in *Cultivation Analysis: New Directions in Media Effects Research,* ed. N. Signorielli and M. Morgan (Newbury Park, CA: Sage, 1990), pp. 85–106.

60. Elisabeth Noelle-Neumann, *The Spiral of Silence: Public Opinion—Our Social Skin* (Chicago: University of Chicago Press, 1984). See also "The Theory of Public Opinion: The Concept of the Spiral of Silence," in *Communication Yearbook 14,* ed. J. A. Anderson (Newbury Park, CA: Sage, 1991), pp. 256–287. For a brief summary, see Charles T. Salmon and Carroll J. Glynn, "Spiral of Silence: Communication and Public Opinion as Social Control," in *An Integrated Approach to Communication Theory and Research,* ed. Michael B. Salwen and Don W. Stacks (Mahwah, NJ: Lawrence Erlbaum, 1996), pp. 165–180.

61. Noelle-Neumann, *Spiral,* pp. 16–22.

62. Noelle-Neumann, *Spiral,* p. 56.

63. Noelle-Neumann, *Spiral,* p. 169.

64. McQuail, *Mass Communication,* pp. 63–68.

65. Dennis K. Davis and Thomas F. N. Puckett, "Mass Entertainment and Community: Toward a Culture-Centered Paradigm for Mass Communication Research," in *Communication Yearbook 15,* ed. Stanley Deetz (Newbury Park, CA: Sage, 1992), pp. 3–34.

66. See, for example, David Gauntlett, *Media, Gender, and Identity* (London: Routledge, 2002).

67. See, for example, Robert Alan Brookey and Robert Westerfelhaus, "Pistols and Petticoats, Piety and Purity: *To Wong Foo,* the Queering of the American Monomyth, and the Marginalizing Discourse of Deification," in *Critical Studies in Media Communication,* 18 (2001): 141–155; Helene A. Shugart, "Reinventing Privilege: The New (Gay) Man in Contemporary Popular Media," *Critical Studies in Media Communication* 20 (2003): 67–91.

68. Helene A. Shugart, Catherine Egley Waggoner, and D. Lynn O'Brien Hallstein, "Mediating Third-Wave Feminism: Appropriation as Postmodern Media Practice," *Critical Studies in Media Communication* 18 (2001): 194–210.

69. Robert Huesca and Brenda Dervin, "Theory and Practice in Latin American Alternative Communication Research," *Journal of Communication* 44 (1994): 53–73.

70. Boulding, "The Medium Is the Massage," p. 68.

71. Kevin Carragee, "A Critical Evaluation of Debates Examining the Media Hegemony Thesis," *Western Journal of Communication* 57 (summer 1993): 330–348.

72. See especially Philip Elliott, "Uses and Gratifications Research: A Critique and Sociological Alternative," in *The Uses of Mass Communication,* ed. J. Blumler and E. Katz (Beverly Hills, CA: Sage, 1974), pp. 249–268; and David L. Swanson, "Political Communication Research and the Uses and Gratifications Model: A Critique," *Communication Research* 6 (1979): 36–53.

73. This view is espoused by Martin Allor, "Relocating the Site of the Audience," *Critical Studies in Mass Communication* 5 (1988): 217–233.

CHAPTER

CULTURE AND SOCIETY

We started our survey of communication theories in this book by looking quite narrowly at the individual communicator and expanded our scope of concern from messages, conversations, and relationships to groups and organizations. In the previous chapter, we looked at the media as a broad social institution. In this chapter, we take the broadest perspective to look at communication within the context of society and culture. Every act of communication—whether personal or mediated—is affected by and contributes to large social forms and patterns. Because the social and cultural context of communication is so huge, we often don't see it. To risk a cliché, we lose our view of the forest when we concentrate too much on individual trees.

We forget, for example, that what we perceive, how we understand, and how we act are very much shaped by the language of our culture. Language is not an inert medium for transmitting information but affects and is affected by daily interaction. Patterns of interaction among friends, in communities, and throughout society determine lines of influence, which in turn, shape our values, opinions, and behavior.

If you have traveled to other countries, you have been able to see dramatic changes in human culture, obvious in dress, food, and behavior. In most parts of the world today, you have to travel only to the closest street corner to experience diversity because most of us do not live in homogenous communities. Cultural difference is palpable, but we may not be used to thinking of ourselves as cultural beings whose

Chapter Map / Theories of Society and Culture

Topics Addressed	Semiotic Theories	Cybernetic Theories	Phenomeno-logical Theories	Sociocultural Theories	Critical Theories
Language	Linguistic relativity Elaborated and restricted codes				
Social influence		Dynamic social impact theory Diffusion of information and influence			
Culture			Cultural interpretation	Ethnography of communication Performance ethnography	
Power and domination					Modernism • Marxism • Frankfurt School • Feminism Postmodernism • Cultural studies • Feminist cultural studies • Critical race theory Poststructuralism Postcolonialism

sense of identity and how we relate to others is a product of some combination of cultures that impact our lives.

In this chapter, we will look at several theories from a variety of traditions that help us understand the context of society and culture.

◖ THE SEMIOTIC TRADITION

What does your language enable you to see? If your language is gendered—that is, if it includes masculine and feminine nouns—you probably have a tendency to divide the world into male and female realms. Some languages have no tense, so past, present, and future must be inferred from context. Is the future "ahead of you"? Not all languages have that conceptual construction; in some languages, "the future is behind you," because you can't see it. Recall from Chapter 3 that semiotics is the study of how signs, including language, bridge the world of experience and the human mind. Since there is rarely a natural relationship between language and reality, language indeed shapes reality. One of the key differences among cultures is how language is used, as the two theories in this section show.

Linguistic Relativity

The *Sapir-Whorf hypothesis,* otherwise known as the theory of linguistic relativity, is based on the work of Edward Sapir and his protégé Benjamin Lee Whorf.[1] Known for his fieldwork in linguistics, Whorf discovered that fundamental syntactic differences are present among language groups. The Whorfian hypothesis of linguistic relativity simply states that the structure of a culture's language determines the behavior and habits of thinking in that culture. In the words of Sapir:

> Human beings do not live in the objective world alone, nor alone in the world of social activity as ordinarily understood, but are very much at the mercy of the particular language which has become the medium of expression for their society. . . . The fact of the matter is that the "real world" is to a large extent unconsciously built up on the language habits of the group. . . . We see and hear and otherwise experience very largely as we do because the language habits of our community predispose certain choices of interpretation.[2]

This hypothesis suggests that our thought processes and the way we see the world are shaped by the grammatical structure of the language. As one writer reacted, "All one's life one has been tricked . . . by the structure of language into a certain way of perceiving reality."[3]

Whorf spent much of his life investigating the relationship of language and behavior. His work with the Hopi and their view of time illustrates the relativity hypothesis. Whereas many cultures refer to points in time (such as seasons) as nouns, the Hopi conceive of time as a passage or process. Thus, the Hopi language never objectifies time. The Hopi would not refer to summer as "in the summer." Instead, the Hopi would refer to the passing or coming of a phase that is never here and now but always moving, always accumulating. By contrast, in Standard Average European (SAE) languages, including English, we visualize time as a line. We use three tenses—past, present, and future—to indicate locations or places in a spatial analogy. Hopi verbs, however, have no tense in the same sense. Instead, their verb forms relate to duration and order.

Suppose, for example, a speaker reports that a man is running: "He is running." The Hopi would use the word *wari,* which is a statement of *running as a fact.* The same word would be used for a report of past running: "He ran." For the Hopi, the statement of fact is what is important, not whether the event is presently occurring or happened in the past. If, however, the Hopi speaker wishes to report *running from memory* (the hearer did not actually see it), a different form—*era wari*—would be used. The English sentence "He will run" would translate *warikni,* which communicates *running as expectation.* Another English form, "He runs [on the track team]," would translate *warikngwe.* This latter Hopi form refers to *running as a condition.*[4] Again, it is not the location in past, present, or future that is important to the Hopi but whether it is observed fact, recalled fact, or expectation.

As a result of these linguistic differences, members of Hopi and SAE cultures will think about, perceive, and behave toward time differently. For example, the Hopi tend to engage in lengthy preparing activities. Experiences (getting prepared) tend to accumulate as time "gets later." The emphasis is on the accumulated experience during the course of time, not on time as a point or location. In SAE cultures, with their spatial treatment of time, experiences are not accumulated in the same sense. The custom in SAE cultures is to record events such that what happened in the past is objectified. Whorf summarizes this view: "Concepts of 'time' and 'matter' are not given in substantially the same form by experience to all men but depend upon the nature of the language or languages through the use of which they have been developed."[5]

Notice that the theory of linguistic relativity is different from the social constructionist theories discussed earlier in the book. In social constructionism, people are believed to create their realities in the process of interaction, whereas Whorf and Sapir teach that reality is already embedded in the language and therefore comes preformed. Both theories deal with cultural reality, but they approach the topic in opposite ways.

To illustrate one way in which language difference prefigures cultural difference, Basil Bernstein, in a series of classic studies in the sociology of language, discovered important differences in language use between classes.

Elaborated and Restricted Codes

A classic theory of society and language is that of Basil Bernstein on elaborated and restricted codes.[6] This theory shows how the structure of the language employed in everyday talk reflects and shapes the assumptions of a social group. Bernstein is especially interested in social class and the ways the class system creates different types of language and is maintained by language.

The basic assumption of this theory is that the relationships established in a social group affect the type of speech used by the group. At the same time, the structure of the speech used by a group makes different things relevant or significant. This happens because different groups have different priorities, and language emerges from what is required to maintain relationships within the group. In other words, people learn their place in the world by virtue of the language codes they employ.

For example, in one family where a strict authoritarian control system is used, children learn that they must respond to simple commands. In this kind of family, persuasive appeals would not only be irrelevant but counterproductive. For Bernstein, role and language go hand in hand. The kinds of roles that children learn are reinforced by the kind of language employed in the community, especially the family. The term *code* refers to a set of organizing principles behind the language employed by members of a social group. Two children who both speak English might employ very different codes because their talk is different.

Bernstein's theory centers on two codes—elaborated and restricted. *Elaborated codes* provide a wide range of different ways to say something. These allow speakers to make their ideas and intentions explicit. Because they are more complex, elaborated codes require more planning, explaining why speakers may pause more and appear to be thinking as they talk. *Restricted codes* have a narrower range of options, and it is easier to predict what form they will take. These codes do not allow speakers to expand on or elaborate very much on what they mean.

Restricted codes are appropriate in groups in which there is a strongly shared set of assumptions and little need to elaborate on what is meant. Elaborated codes are appropriate in groups in which perspectives are not shared. Here, people are required to expand on what they mean. Restricted codes are oriented toward social categories for which everybody has the same meaning, whereas elaborated codes are oriented toward individualized categories that others might not share.

For example, in some groups everybody knows the difference between masculine and feminine, and people are clearly identified in a male or female role. Everybody knows the place of a woman and a man, a girl and a boy. You can assume what people think and feel based on their gender identification, and there is little need to explore individual differences. In other groups, however, gender as a category is not as useful because there is not a common understanding of what masculine and feminine mean. You can see that it would take more words to explore what is appropriate behavior for the individual child than it would to tell a girl to go to the kitchen and help her mother.

Thus, elaborated codes are used by speakers who value individuality above group identification. Because the intent of the speakers cannot be inferred from their role, they have to be able to express themselves individually in some detail. Bernstein offers the example of a couple who has just come out of a movie and stops by to visit with friends. There, they discuss the film at some length. The other couple has not seen it but can understand their friends' ideas about the film anyway:

> An hour is spent in the complex moral, political, aesthetic subtleties of the film and its place in the contemporary scene. . . . The meanings now have to be made public to others who have not seen the film. The speech shows careful editing, at both the grammatical and lexical levels. It is no longer contextualized. The meanings are explicit, elaborated and individualized. . . . The experience of the listeners cannot be taken for granted. Thus each member of the group is on his own as he offers his interpretation.[7]

A primary difference between the types of groups that use these two codes is their degree of openness. A *closed-role system* is one that reduces the number of alternatives for the participants. Roles are set, and people are viewed in terms of

those roles. This understanding of who people are and how they should behave forms the basis of a common knowledge within the group. Because of this shared meaning in the group, an elaborated language is not necessary and therefore not cultured or learned.

An *open-role system* is one that expands the number of alternatives for individuals in the group. Roles are not categorical and simple; rather, they are individualized, negotiated, fluid, and changing. Thus, there may be little shared understanding of a person's identity within an open system, and an elaborated code is necessary for communication to take place in this system.

Two major factors contribute to the development of an elaborated or restricted code within a system. The first is the nature of the major socializing agencies within the system, including the family, peer group, school, and work. Where the structure of these groups is well defined in terms of fixed roles, a restricted code is likely to develop. Where the structure of these groups is less well defined and has fluid roles, an elaborated code is more likely to be created. The second major factor is values. Pluralistic societies that value individuality promote elaborated codes, whereas narrower societies promote restricted ones.

Apparent, then, is how codes are so strongly associated with social class. Bernstein says that members of the middle class use both types of systems. They may, for example, be exposed to rather open roles at home but somewhat closed ones in the workplace. Or peer groups may use closed roles, whereas a school employs open ones. Members of the working class, however, are less likely to use elaborated codes. For working-class individuals, both the values and the role systems reinforce restricted codes, which leads Bernstein to write:

> Without a shadow of a doubt the most formative influence upon the procedures of socialization, from a sociological viewpoint, is social class. The class structure influences work and educational roles and brings families into a special relationship with each other and deeply penetrates the structure of life experiences within the family. . . . I shall go on to argue that

the deep structure of communication itself is affected, but not in any final or irrevocable way.[8]

In a well-known study, Bernstein tape-recorded young men from the working class and the middle class in England talking about capital punishment.[9] He analyzed samples of their speech and found interesting class differences. Even when the data were controlled for intelligence, the working-class speakers used longer phrases, shorter words, and less pausing than middle-class speakers. With an elaborated code, the middle-class boys needed more planning time, which explains their shorter phrases and longer pauses.

Many other differences found in this study illustrate elaborated and restricted codes. For example, middle-class speakers used "I think" significantly more than did working-class speakers. Working-class speakers made greater use of short phrases at the end of sentences to confirm the other person's common understanding; these included expressions like "isn't it?" "you know," and "wouldn't he?" Middle-class speakers had longer, more complex verb phrases, more passive verbs, more uncommon adverbs and adjectives. And middle-class speakers made more use of the personal pronoun *I*.

Elaborated codes are empowering because they enable speakers to adapt to a wide range of audiences and appeal to widely different types of people. On the other hand, elaborated codes can be alienating because, as Bernstein writes, they separate "feeling from thought, self from other, private belief from role obligation."[10]

Although he acknowledges the limitations of restricted talk, Bernstein does not devalue it: "Let it be said immediately that a restricted code gives access to a vast potential of meanings, of delicacy, subtlety and diversity of cultural forms, to a unique aesthetic the basis of which in condensed symbols may influence the form of the imagining."[11] However, Bernstein also notes that those in power in society often devalue this type of speech, which further perpetuates the class system.

The family is especially important in the development of code. Two types of families correspond to the two types of codes. *Position families* have a clear and formally determined role structure. They often have a closed communication system and use restricted codes. Such families tend to have sharp boundaries in their use of space and define objects and people in terms of their position.

Person-centered families determine roles on the basis of individuals' personal orientations rather than formally defined divisions. They tend to use open communication and elaborated codes. Roles and relations within these families tend to be unstable and constantly in negotiation. These families do not maintain sharp boundaries in their use of space or in their ideas about people and things.

Although a family may have a variety of means of exerting control and regulating behavior, there seems to be a predominant or preferred method employed, depending on the type of family. Some families prefer an *imperative mode* of regulation, which is based on command and authority. In this type of family, when Dad says, "Shut up," you do. This is preferred in hierarchical families in which certain members are defined as in control according to the role structure. This kind of control is delivered with a restricted code.

Other families prefer *positional appeals,* based on role-related norms. Here, control is exerted by relying on commonly understood norms associated with each role. Examples of this kind of appeal are "You are old enough to know better," or "Boys don't play with dolls." This kind of control can be expressed with restricted or elaborated codes, depending on the degree of differentiation in the system.

Finally, *personal appeals* are based on individualized characteristics and individualized rules, and these appeals often consist of giving reasons for why a person should or should not do something. Again, the code employed can be restricted or elaborated, depending on the degree of shared understanding in the family.

REFLECTIONS ON

The Semiotic Tradition

Because these theories focus precisely on the relationship of signs to culture, they are clearly influenced by the semiotic tradition. Linguistic relativity imagines a more direct relationship between the sign—words and grammar—and the thought processes within a culture. In other words, the semantics and syntactics of language have a direct effect on thought and culture. The theory of elaborated and restricted codes imagines more of a two-way influence. In other words, the social structures of the culture necessitate certain language forms, but those language forms support the culture as well.

As is the case with most of the theories in this chapter—because they do focus on cultural matters—there is a kinship among the traditions represented here. Although we can argue that these two theories are semiotic, we could just as easily say that they are sociocultural. In the study of culture, these two traditions support one another—an overlap we will see again as we move through the different theories summarized here.

• • •

THE CYBERNETIC TRADITION

It should come as no surprise that systems thinking, thoroughly embedded in the cybernetic tradition, would influence how we treat communication in society and culture because society itself can easily be seen as a large system. You do not communicate the same amount with all others, but establish pathways, clusters, or nodes that define large social networks of communication. One way to think about this is to consider all of the members of your family and their friends. Each family member has a unique friendship network that is connected through the nexus of your family. The theories in this section elaborate this idea in terms of social influence.

Dynamic Social Impact Theory

Dynamic social impact theory (DSIT) was developed by Bibb Latané and his colleagues.[12] The theory imagines society as a giant communication system consisting of numerous cultural subsystems, each of which includes individuals interacting with one another. Because the most basic elements of the system are individuals, we'll begin there.

DSIT adopts the widely held axiom that individuals are different in many ways: They have different ideas, beliefs, attitudes, and behaviors. But individuals also share many characteristics with others, and they tend to group together into clusters of like-minded people. Indeed, cultures are large groupings of individuals who share common ideologies and practices. DSIT attempts to explain, in system terms, how these commonalities develop and how cultures form.

Individuals are not isolated. They interact with one another in *social spaces*, or "areas" where people meet, communicate, and influence one another. Latané has found that social space is largely a physical space, constrained by actual physical distance among individuals. Other things being equal, on average you will be more influenced by people close to you than by individuals far away. Physical distance, however, is not the only aspect of social space. For many reasons, we do not interact equally with everyone in proximity. Various social arrangements, such as race and class, keep people from interacting even though they may live and work close to one another. Various media of communication also influence social space, including the telephone, e-mail, and mass media, all of which enable communication across distance.

To help understand how dynamic social impact works, imagine your university as a social world. Let's say you are a graduate student in the communication department. With whom are you most likely to communicate? You probably talk most frequently with other members of the communication department and especially your professors, your peers in the program, and the students you teach—the people with whom you have regular contact. You are less likely to communicate with medical students or staff members in the grounds-maintenance department of the university. You could therefore predict that you will share more attributes with other members of the communication department than with people from other, more distant groups.

In time, as you interact more and more with communication department members, you will begin to influence one another and think alike in certain ways. You will share knowledge, and attitudes will begin to converge. After a while, you might even begin to identify a communication department culture—a way of thinking and doing things common to the department. And even within the department, there will be certain subgroups. For example, a small group of graduate students may get together socially, going out for drinks every Friday afternoon. Another subgroup will only interact at school, stopping for coffee when they see each other between classes. This group-clustering phenomenon is caused by mutual influence among individuals who share a common social space. The shared characteristics of a group change dynamically with new contacts and interactions.

Clearly, this grouping phenomenon is not random. Influence among individuals varies along three dimensions. The first is the *strength* of influence of various individuals in the social space. The second is *immediacy,* or attraction between two persons. The third is the *number* of people in the social space. If you have many people, a large number of whom are influential in the same social space, the grouping tendency will be very high. If there are fewer people, few influential people, and little opportunity to talk, grouping will be less likely.

One thing is clear: Individuals in contact with one another will not remain random, unconnected nodes but will organize themselves cybernetically into a dynamic structure of groups with common characteristics. You can see how the organization of the system perpetuates itself: Groups form by proximity in the social space, but those groups in turn give additional structure to the social space, which in a circular way affects the possible patterns of influence within the space itself.

This self-organizing tendency explains the formation of minority groups. Over time, the influence of the majority is considerable because of sheer numbers, leading to a preponderance of beliefs being shared by most of the people within the social space. Yet, ironically, continued communication within a minority group bolsters its shared beliefs and practices, shielding it from the majority view. This is a cybernetic mechanism that ensures diversity within the larger system.

As another example of the self-organizing tendency, imagine that upon entering the graduate program, you find that the students and faculty differ in their attitudes toward qualitative and quantitative research methods. At first there is no real grouping of individuals into two camps, but over time groups begin to develop. Because of the strong influence of certain members of the department and relatively close relations among some, a majority view favoring quantitative research develops. More and more students come to affiliate with the quantitative group. At the same time, however, a minority qualitative group emerges and reinforces its own view by continual communication among themselves.

An interesting thing happens when groupings like this occur. Once a group is formed, its interaction brings about additional influence and even more convergence on issues that are not logically related to the topics that brought the group together in the first place. For example, suppose that certain members of the quantitative group smoke, and because of their frequent interaction with one another, others start to smoke, too. Perhaps the unique interaction patterns in the qualitative group do not lead to this outcome. You would observe, then, that the members of the quantitative group tend to be smokers, whereas those in the qualitative group are not. Quantitative methods and smoking become correlated, even though there is no logical connection between these variables. Such correlations, in turn, give further structure to the system.

If the individuals within a social space have equal contact with one another, you would expect that divergent views would slowly converge to the center, making everyone in the social space the same and not extreme in any way. Eventually, you might predict, everyone in the department would come to favor quantitative methods. We know, of course, that this is rarely the case, for the system tends to maintain diversity. This is because interaction is never entirely random, and influence is never entirely linear. Nonlinearity in the system is therefore very important for maintaining system change and diversity.

Especially on important issues, people do not just keep changing incrementally over time. They cling to their ideas and practices for a while until a tipping point is reached and a shift occurs—the straw that breaks the camel's back. Once the pressure to change outweighs the pressure to stay the same, a major shift may occur. The more important the issue and the more involved the individual is with the issue, the less linear change seems to be. In fact, in the face of increasing social pressure, you can actually become more extreme in the views you hold. From our example above, the quantitative and qualitative groups may become polarized, creating even more diversity than before.

You can see positive and negative feedback loops at work here. Negative feedback loops tend to cancel out diversity and lead to convergence, whereas positive feedback loops tend to create diversity and lead to divergence. Imagine society as a huge system of interacting individuals in which many such loops continually bring about both social order and diversity.

There are many consequences of the feedback loops at work in dynamic social networks. The following line of work, now a classic in the communication field, offers one explanation of how influence and information is disseminated in social systems.

The Diffusion of Information and Influence

The importance of interpersonal networks was brought to light by an early voting study in 1940 conducted by Paul Lazarsfeld and his colleagues in Elmira, New York.[13] The researchers unexpectedly found that the effect of media was influenced by interpersonal communication. This effect, which came to be known as the *two-step flow hypothesis,* was startling, and it had a major impact on our understanding of the role of mass media.

This study was the beginning of a line of research on how information and influence are distributed in society. Lazarsfeld hypothesized that information flows from the mass media to certain opinion leaders in the community, who pass information on by talking to peers. He found that voters seem to be more influenced by their friends during a campaign than by the media. Since the original Elmira study, much additional data have come in, and this hypothesis has received substantial support.[14]

The two-step flow theory is best summarized in Elihu Katz and Paul Lazarsfeld's classic work *Personal Influence.*[15] These authors confirm that certain individuals known as *opinion leaders* receive information from the media and pass it on to their peers.[16] Every group has opinion leaders but these individuals are difficult to distinguish from other group members because opinion leadership is not a trait but a role taken by some individuals in certain circumstances. Opinion leadership changes from time to time and from issue to issue. In addition, opinion leaders may be of two kinds: those influential on one topic, called *monomorphic,* and those influential on a variety of topics, or *polymorphic.* Monomorphism becomes more predominant as systems become more modern.

Recent research on two-step flow has shown that the dissemination of ideas is not a simple two-step process. A *multiple-step model* is now more generally accepted as more accurate in terms of the actual process.[17] Research has shown that the ultimate number of relays between the media and final receivers is variable. In the adoption of an innovation, for example, certain individuals will hear about it directly from media sources, whereas others will be many steps removed.

The diffusion of information and innovations is now part of the interactional and network tradition. We know that interaction in networks plays an important role in relationships, small groups, and organizations. Here, we see that it plays an important role in mass communication as well. The diffusion of information is one of the most significant outcomes of communication. The diffusion of an innovation occurs when the adoption of an idea, practice, or object spreads by communication through a social system. Several prominent U.S. and foreign researchers in fields such as agriculture and rural studies, national development, and organizational communication have been responsible for this line of research.

The broadest and most communication-oriented theory of diffusion is that of Everett Rogers and his colleagues.[18] Rogers relates dissemination to the process of social change, which consists of invention, diffusion (or communication), and consequences. Such change can occur internally from within a group or externally through contact with outside change agents. Contact may occur spontaneously or accidentally, or it may result from planning on the part of outside agencies.

In the diffusion of innovations, many years may be required for an idea to spread. Rogers states, in fact, that one purpose of diffusion research is to discover the means to shorten this lag. Once established, an innovation will have consequences—be they functional or dysfunctional, direct or indirect, manifest or latent. Change agents normally expect their impact to be functional, direct, and manifest, although this positive result does not always occur.

The diffusion of innovations is well illustrated by the family-planning program instituted in South Korea in 1968. Mothers' clubs were established in about 12,000 villages throughout Korea for the purpose of disseminating information about family planning. Overall, the program was successful, and Korea saw a major decline in birthrate during this period. This program was built on the idea that interpersonal channels of communication would be crucial to the adoption of birth control methods. In 1973 Rogers and his colleagues studied the Korean case by interview-

ing about a thousand women in twenty-four villages to gather information about the networks the women used for family planning.[19]

They found that the village leaders initially received their information about family planning from the mass media and family-planning worker visits, but interpersonal networks turned out to be most important in the dissemination-adoption process. Two network variables were especially important. The first was the degree to which the mothers' club leader was connected with others in the village network. The second variable was the amount of overlap between the family-planning network and the general village network. Birth-control adoption was greatest in the villages in which the leader talked to many people personally, and the village women talked about it among themselves.

When innovations such as the cell phone, DSL lines, a new HIV therapy, or Internet shopping are introduced, it takes a while for them to catch on. Some innovations never catch on, but others spread rapidly. Indeed, the use of the Internet has been perhaps the fastest spreading innovation in the history of technology.[20] Interpersonal influence is very important in this process. People raise awareness of the innovation as they talk with one another about it. They share opinions, discuss their experience with the innovation, sometimes advocate its use, and sometimes resist it.

The rate of adoption is determined by perceptions of the innovation's relative advantage and its compatibility with existing values and experiences. The complexity of the innovation matters, and potential adopters will more readily accept an innovation that they can experiment with, or try out, without making a huge commitment. They may also want to observe others' adoption before taking the plunge.

People vary in their levels of resistance and the social support needed to adopt the new idea, practice, or object. There are always individuals who will adopt an innovation early, before most others consider doing so. These early adopters will set the stage, and they usually have an influence on others. As more and more people adopt, a critical mass of adoption occurs that gives rise to a rapid increase in general adoption.[21] A few people may be very slow to adopt and must see the innovation all around them before they will consider it. These are the late adopters. Of course, some may never adopt the new practice. In general, Rogers and his colleagues have found that adoption approximates an S-curve. On a time scale, the rise of adoption is slow at first, then it hits a critical mass after which a sudden rise in adoption occurs, and then it levels out.

◖● REFLECTIONS ON
The Cybernetic Tradition

Both of the theories in this section are essentially network theories; they depict systems of communication, consisting of lines of communication that cluster people together in cybernetic loops. But they are more than simple connections or contacts because they build consensus and commonality through repeated communication. Although cybernetic theories do not "feel" much like the other traditions in this context, they do provide a way of understanding how cultures and social structures get established and spread.

● ● ●

◖● THE PHENOMENOLOGICAL TRADITION

If you had a friend who had just returned from visiting Mongolia, would you prefer to learn about the trip by sending this person an e-mail questionnaire or listening to stories about the trip? Could you learn more about the culture of a group of Vietnam War veterans by having each one fill out a series of scales or by observing several of their meetings and interviewing them? In these situations, most of us would rely on personal contact and observation as a way of learning more about culture. Many researchers feel the same way and prefer to learn about cul-

ture through personal interpretation rather than from tests, experiments, and questionnaires. This kind of knowledge is what characterizes phenomenology as a tradition. You may recall that the process of interpretation is *hermeneutics*. Cultural interpretation is commonly referred to as *ethnography*.

We look at cultural interpretation in two sections of this chapter. In this section, we focus on cultural interpretation as the core of ethnography—and thus the ways in which it is a phenomenological endeavor. In the following section, we show how ethnography is equally a part of the sociocultural tradition.

Cultural Hermeneutics

Cultural interpretation involves trying to understand the actions of a group or culture such as the Zulu, residents of the Castro in San Francisco, or New York City high-school students.[22] This kind of hermeneutics requires observing and describing the actions of a group, just as one might examine a written text, and trying to figure out what they mean.[23]

A leading cultural interpreter, or ethnographer, is Clifford Geertz.[24] Geertz describes cultural interpretation as *thick description*, in which interpreters describe cultural practices "from the native's point of view." This level of interpretation is contrasted with *thin description*, in which people merely describe the behavioral pattern with little sense of what it means to the participants themselves.

Like all hermeneutics, cultural interpretation uses a hermeneutic circle. As described in Chapter 3, the hermeneutic circle is a process of moving back and forth between specific observations and general interpretations. The circle, vital to all hermeneutics, is a deliberate shifting of perspectives from something that feels familiar to something that may stretch our understanding. In cultural interpretation, this hermeneutic circle involves a movement from experience-near concepts to experience-distant ones. *Experience-near concepts* are those that have meaning to the members of the culture, and *experience-distant concepts* have meaning to outsiders. The cultural interpreter essentially translates between the two, so that observers outside can have an understanding of the insider's feelings and meanings in a situation. The interpretation process, then, is one of going back and forth in a circle between what appears to be happening from outside to what insiders define as happening. Slowly, a suitable vocabulary can be developed to explain the insiders' point of view to outsiders without forsaking participants' own experience-near concepts.[25]

For example, an ethnographer might wonder about the meaning of wearing baggy pants. From an experience-distant perspective, it might appear to be a form of group conformity. If you ask several young people what it means, they would answer in a more experience-near way with something like, "Oh, it's cool, dude." The ethnographer would need to investigate what it means for something to be "cool" and perhaps relate this response to statements made by others. Eventually, a vocabulary acceptable to informants and understandable to those who are not members of this group would be created.

Ethnographic problems arise when an interpreter has a lack of adequate understanding. The researcher witnesses something that cannot be understood from his or her concepts, such as wearing pants so large that you can hardly walk, and seeks to resolve the difficulty by creating an explanation. Ethnography attempts to understand things that are otherwise foreign. How would you make sense of a ceremony involving the fondling of rattlesnakes? Most of us have no frame for understanding such actions, but the ethnographer would—through careful observation, interviews, and inference—create an explanation that would make such behavior understandable to outsiders and still feel "right" to those who actually practice snake handling.

The interpreter, of course, does not begin ethnography empty-handed. Previous experience always provides some kind of schema for understanding an event, but ethnography is a process in which one's understandings become increasingly more refined and accurate. As a hermeneutic activity, then, ethnography is a very personal process, a process in which the researcher experiences a culture and interprets its various forms. Although ethnographers take different approaches to this process, many believe that the best approach is to live the culture firsthand. On this point, Lyall Crawford writes: "As an ethnographer, I am an expert about what only I verify— a state of affairs subject to emotional vulnerabilities, intellectual instabilities, and academic suspicion. Thought of in these terms, taking the ethnographic turn, living and writing the ethnographic life, is essentially a self-report of personal experiences."[26]

Donal Carbaugh and Sally Hastings describe ethnographic theorizing as a four-part process.[27] The first is to develop a basic orientation to the subject. Here the ethnographer assesses his or her own assumptions about culture and its manifestations. Communication ethnographers, for instance, define communication as central to culture and worthy of ethnographic study and decide to focus on various aspects of communication. They may assume further that clothing is an important expression of meaning and a form of communication.

The second phase of ethnographic theorizing defines the classes or kinds of activity that will be observed. A communication ethnographer, for example, might decide to look at the ways clothing is worn.

Next, the ethnographer theorizes about the specific culture under investigation. Here certain activities will be interpreted within the context of the culture itself. So, for example, when young people wear baggy pants, this could be taken as a sign of group conformity and acceptance.

Finally, in the fourth phase, the ethnographer moves back out to look again at the general theory of culture he or she is operating with and tests it with the specific case. The ethnographer might, for example, conclude that baggy pants are yet another instance of how clothing is used by members of a culture to establish communal bonds.

◖● REFLECTIONS ON

The Phenomenological Tradition

Because it relies on the personal experience of the ethnographer, cultural interpretation is thoroughly phenomenological. At the same time, it relies on assumptions common in the sociocultural tradition that capture the situational and emergent nature of meaning and action within cultural groups. We continue now to develop this line of thinking as we move to the following section.

● ● ●

◖● THE SOCIOCULTURAL TRADITION

In this chapter, the sociocultural tradition provides a continuation of the phenomenological because cultural interpretation is both hermeneutic and sociocultural in orientation. Each of the following theories concentrates on the ways in which cultural groups create meaning, values, and practices through communication.

An important assumption of theories in this tradition is that society itself is a product of social interaction, in which small and large social structures—relationships, groups, organizations, and institutions—are constructed in everyday interaction. Symbolic interactionism, particularly the work of George Herbert Mead and Herbert Blumer, previously addressed in Chapters 4 and 6, was very important in establishing the connection between interaction and society.[28]

Sociocultural theories assume that social structure influences interaction. Various social arrangements affect and constrain the very talk that produced them, as structuration theory (Chapters 8 and 9) shows.[29] Recognizing that even the largest social institutions consist of interlinked conversations, we concentrate in this section on two theories relying on cultural interpretation—ethnography of communication and performance ethnography.

Ethnography of Communication

The ethnography of communication is simply the application of ethnographic methods to the communication patterns of a group.[30] Here, the interpreter attempts to make sense of the forms of communication employed by the members of a community or culture.

The originator of this research tradition is anthropologist Dell Hymes.[31] Hymes suggests that formal linguistics is not sufficient by itself to uncover a complete understanding of language because it ignores the highly variable ways in which language is used in everyday communication. According to Hymes, cultures communicate in different ways, but all forms of communication require a shared code, communicators who know and use the code, a channel, a setting, a message form, a topic, and an event created by transmission of the message. Anything may qualify as communication as long as it is construed as such by those who use that code. Is snake handling communication? How about baggy pants? Perhaps these are shared codes for expressing something among the members of the group. We cannot know until further ethnographic study is undertaken.

In short, culture is a powerful influence on human life in general and human lives in particular. Recognizing that cultures are richly different from one another makes generalization difficult. To meet this challenge, comparative ethnography creates categories with which one can compare cultures. Within the ethnography of communication, Hymes suggests a set of nine categories that can be used to compare different cultures:[32]

1. *Ways of speaking,* or patterns of communication familiar to the members of the group
2. *Ideal of the fluent speaker,* or what constitutes an exemplary communicator
3. *Speech community,* or the group itself and its boundaries
4. *Speech situation,* or those times when communication is considered appropriate in the community

5. *Speech event,* or what episodes are considered to be communication for the members of the group
6. *Speech act,* or a specific set of behaviors taken as an instance of communication within a speech event
7. *Components of speech acts,* or what the group considers to be the elements of a communicative act
8. *The rules of speaking in the community,* or the guidelines or standards by which communicative behavior is judged
9. *The functions of speech in the community,* or what communication is believed to accomplish

This set of concepts is nothing more than a list of categories by which various cultures can be compared. Two cultures—the Apache and the Ilongot, for example—would have many different events that count as communication, varying behaviors that would be considered appropriate within those speaking events, and perhaps some distinct rules for how to communicate. On the other hand, they might have some similar types and functions of communication as well.

Gerry Philipsen extends Hymes's work by isolating four assumptions of the ethnography of communication.[33] The first is that participants in a local cultural community create shared meaning by using codes that have some degree of common understanding. Philipsen has written extensively about such codes;[34] he defines a *speech code* as a distinctive set of understandings within a culture about what counts as communication, the significance of communication forms within the culture, how those forms are to be understood, and how they are to be performed. The speech code is a culture's unwritten and often subconscious "guidebook" for how to communicate within the culture. How does a teenager in the United States know how to communicate at school—what to say, how to understand what others say, and how to talk? The group's speech code enables the teenager to do this. Philipsen makes several claims about speech codes.

First, such codes are distinctive. They vary from one culture to another. The manner and meaning of "griping" in Israel are entirely different from communication found in other cultures.

Second, speech codes constitute a culture's distinctive sense of how to be a person, how to connect with other people, and how to act or communicate within the social group. The code is more than a list of semantic meanings; it establishes the actual forms of communication in which competent members of the culture must act.

Third, the code guides what communicators actually experience when they interact with one another. It tells them what certain actions should count as. It defines the meaning of speech acts (Chapter 5). When people engage in a particular communication act such as "griping," they know what they are doing. They have meaning for the act itself.

Fourth, speech codes are not separate entities, but are embedded in daily speech. You can "see" the code in the patterns of communication commonly used, the terms communicators use to describe what they are doing when they speak, and how they explain, justify, or evaluate the communication being used. You can detect speech codes also in how members of the culture change their behavior and vocabulary in different forms of communication.

Fifth, speech codes are powerful. They form the basis on which the culture will evaluate and conduct its communication. The skill or quality of performance in communication is noticed and evaluated based on the requirements of the speech code. Moral judgments are made about whether individuals and groups communicate properly and make appropriate use of cultural communication forms.

Visit any American high school and you will see speech codes at work. Listen to how students talk to one another, notice when they do so, and observe the different forms of communication they use. Notice that they know what they are doing and that their communication patterns have meaning to them. Our communication is always constrained by the codes in use. We are able to switch codes as we move from one cultural setting to another, but we are never free from them.

Philipsen's second assumption is that communicators in any cultural group coordinate their actions. There must be some order or system to what is done in communication. Third, meanings and actions are particular to individual groups. In other words, they differ from culture to culture. Fourth, not only are patterns of behavior and codes different from group to group, but each group also has its own ways of understanding certain codes and actions.

Donal Carbaugh, suggests that ethnography addresses at least three types of problems.[35] The first is to discover the type of *shared identity* created by communication in the cultural community, be it African Americans, cheerleaders, Rotarians, Japanese businessmen, or John's Auto Body Bowlers. This identity is the members' sense of who they are as a group. It is a common set of qualities with which most members of the community would identify.

The second problem is to uncover the *shared meanings of public performances* seen in the group. What constitutes communication within the culture, and what meanings do the various displays evoke? What does "playing the dozens" mean in the black youth culture? What is communicated by cheerleaders at a high school basketball game? What meaning is assigned to the "fines" at a Rotary meeting?

The third is to explore *contradictions*, or paradoxes, of the group. How are these handled through communication? How, for example, might a culture treat its members as individuals while also providing a sense of community? How might autonomy be granted while maintaining authority? How might roles be taught while instilling ideals of freedom?

In addressing these ethnographic problems, three types of questions are pursued. *Questions of norms* look for the ways communication is used to establish a set of standards and the ways notions of right and wrong affect communication patterns. *Questions of forms* look at the types of

communication used within the society. What behaviors count as communication, and how are they organized? *Questions of cultural codes* draw attention to the meanings of the symbols and behaviors used as communication in the cultural community.

Although ethnography highlights aspects of group life, it can also reveal how persons see themselves as persons. In other words, our group identities give rise to our individual identities. Who you are, your identity as a person, is determined in large measure by how you communicate, with whom, and in what settings. From his own studies—of a college basketball audience, workers in a television station, married person's names, a television talk show, and a community land-use controversy—Carbaugh concludes:

> I could not understand very well what people were saying, or communicating to me, until I explored the deeper particulars of their "sayings" in their specific social scenes. . . . I could not hear (or know) the individuals I met along the way very well until I listened within (or understood) their particular social and cultural scenes. . . . Individuals, social identities (or social classes), and cultural agents are not isolates. They are thought of and acted together in the specific scenes of particular communities.[36]

As an example of an ethnography of communication, consider Tamar Katriel's study on Israeli "griping."[37] Based on her own experience as a "native griper" and about fifty interviews with middle-class Israelis, Katriel explains the common communication form *kiturim*. This form of communication takes place throughout adult Israeli society, but it is most often seen among the middle class and commonly takes place at Friday-night social gatherings called *mesibot kiturim*, or griping parties.

This communication form is so common that it is widely recognized by Israelis as part of their national character. Griping does not deal with personal problems but national (and sometimes local), public ones. It seems to affirm the Israeli identity as having important common national concerns. These are concerns that society at large theoretically could address but that the individual has little power to change. Thus, griping is a kind of shared venting. It is more than this, however, since Katriel's informants told her that it provides a sense of solidarity and is fun. In fact, griping and joke telling are often viewed together as the primary means of establishing cohesiveness in a social group.

Griping is ritualistic, and the content of the communication does not seem to be important. One must not mistake griping for serious problem solving on topics of concern. In fact, there is a strict prohibition against griping in the presence of non-Israelis, like tourists, because outsiders do not understand the nature of griping and may take it literally, which would be embarrassing to the Israelis.

Griping follows a predictable pattern. It usually begins with an initial gripe, followed by an acknowledgment and a gripe by another person. The pattern of a griping session can go from general societal problems to local ones, or the other way around. Katriel found two interesting variants on the griping theme. *Metagriping* is griping about griping, or complaining that Israelis gripe too much. The other form is the *antigripe:* "Stop griping, and start doing something."

This study illustrates Hymes's categories of comparative ethnography very well. The griping session is a communication event, which consists of particular types of speech acts; it also has rules and serves particular functions. The example also illustrates the ethnographic problems of identity, meaning, and tension. Griping reflects a certain national identity in Israel. It is understood among Israelis according to particular meanings, and manages tensions around problems and what can be done about them. Griping is also a way that Israelis perform their culture, a topic considered n the following section.

Performance Ethnography

If you were to do fieldwork in a foreign culture, you would be observing what the people of the culture actually do—how they perform culture. The anthropologist Victor Turner is best known

for bringing our attention to the fact that culture is performed.[38] So much of ethnography focuses on what members of the culture say and not enough on what they do. Of course, saying is a kind of doing, but it needs to be put into a larger frame similar to a play in the theatre. In fact, Turner sees much in common between theatre and everyday cultural life. Like actors, we say our lines as we perform with our bodies.

Cultural performance involves not only the manipulation of the body itself but also the manipulation of various media that may be experienced by eyes, ears, nose, tongue, and touch. How these media are used both makes and reflects the meanings of the culture. Turner offers an example of the interplay of body and material artifacts in a performance:

> Different types of incense burned at different times in a performance communicate different meanings, gestures and facial expressions are assigned meanings with reference to emotions and ideas to be communicated. . . . Thus certain sensory codes are associated with each medium. The master-of-ceremonies, priest, producer, or director creates art from the ensemble of media and codes, just as a conductor in the single genre of classical music blends and opposes the sounds of the different instruments to produce an often unrepeatable effect.[39]

The public performances in a culture are like *social dramas,* in which the group works out their relationships and ideas. Such dramas are *liminal,* meaning that they mark a transition from one state to another or a border between one thing and another. A *limin* is like a threshold, or door between two places. Rites of passage are a good example, as they depict movement from one stage of life to another. Often rituals are liminal in the sense that they connect the sacred with the secular or symbolize the change of seasons.

Turner notes that social dramas tend to follow a certain process. The first stage is a *breach,* or some kind of violation or threat to community order. This is followed by a *crisis,* as members of the community become agitated and take various sides on the issues raised by the breach. In the third phase, consisting of *redressive or remedial procedures,* members of the culture make performances that mend the breach or in some way return to a state of acceptance. This stage of the social drama often involves the most self-examination and is the place where new meanings are created or old ones reproduced. There is, then, a fourth stage—*reintegration*—or restoration of peace. The way a community responds to a threat such as an attack or a natural disaster constitutes a kind of social drama. Or, on a smaller scale, certain groups might perform rituals that symbolize their understanding of threat and response.

Not all members of a group or culture participate in these social dramas and performances. Often certain members take the lead, and others may be selected to participate. Cultural performances, like presidential elections, are ways that "stars" show an audience its own culture. By seeing how the performers work things out through breach, crisis, redressive action, and reintegration, the culture is both formed and learned.

Sporting events are a good example of social dramas. The teams come together in competition, which creates a breach, or threat to order. As the teams play and make gains against one another, a spirit of crisis arises, and fans take sides, cheer, boo, feel elated, and then disappointed. Rules, officials, time-outs, halftime, huddles, and coaching offer moments of redressive action, as the teams and fans deal with the crisis in a variety of ways. And at the end of the game, reintegration occurs, as teams shake hands, fans tear down goalposts, people leave and turn on their car radios, or even tune in to another game. A major sporting event reproduces many aspects of the culture. It teaches us about competition, collaboration, loyalty, and a host of other values. It shows teamwork and expert coaching and play.

Performance ethnography is significant because it broadens the field beyond its traditional fixation on language and text to include *embodied practice*.[40] The performance ethnography movement is significant for the field of communication because communication itself is easily understood as performance, and indeed many communication scholars are primarily interested in performance.[41] This move—from text to performance—raises a number of interesting questions:[42]

1. Is *culture* better understood as a verb rather than a noun?
2. Is ethnographic fieldwork a joint performance between the researcher and the subject?
3. How does performance impact interpretation, and can performance be considered a kind of hermeneutics?
4. How should the results of performance ethnography be published, and how should scholarly representation itself make use of performance?
5. What is the relationship between performance and power?

◖● REFLECTIONS ON
The Sociocultural Tradition

Ethnographic theories clearly prioritize cultural conditions and tendencies over individual ones. Within this tradition, communication is never a simple tool for transmitting information and influence from one person to another, but a way in which culture itself is produced and reproduced. As a tradition, then, these theories place cultural forms at the center, showing how culture both influences and is influenced by our forms of communication.

Cultural productions are interesting in their own right, but they have serious personal and societal consequences, as we learn from the critical tradition.

● ● ●

◖● THE CRITICAL TRADITION

Many theories of communication have a tendency to "normalize" the institutions and structures constructed in social interaction. By this, we mean that theories often describe the outcomes of social interaction without questioning these outcomes. The critical tradition arose to counteract this tendency, which explains the term *critical*. Although diffuse and hard to organize, this tradition brings one thing in common to the table—the idea that social and cultural arrangements are loaded to enforce the power of certain stakeholders in ways that dominate and even oppress others. The work in this tradition, then, looks for the ways in which power imbalance, hegemony, and domination are constructed in social interaction, and this work imagines other possibilities that are humanizing and deeply democratic in orientation.[43]

Most critical theorists today view social processes as *overdetermined,* which means that they are caused by multiple sources. Critical scholars uncover oppressive forces through *dialectical analysis,* which exposes the underlying struggles between opposing forces.[44] Although the population generally perceives a kind of surface order to things, the critical scholar points out the contradictions that exist. Only by becoming aware of the dialectic of opposing forces in a struggle for power can individuals be liberated and free to change the existing order. Otherwise, they will remain alienated from one another and co-opted into their own oppression.

If you have lived your life as a member of a privileged group, it may be hard for you to see this point, because, as critical theories point out, power structures are invisible to groups well served by current social institutions. Everything looks normal and good to people of privilege. However, if you are a member of a marginalized group, you may see immediately the value that the critical tradition brings to bear. In many ways, the critical tradition is a consciousness-raising endeavor. It is very much mission driven in that critical theorists work to expose oppressive forces in society in ways that enable everyone to question the constructions of everyday communication.

Many critical theorists believe that contradiction, tension, and conflict are inevitable aspects of the social order and can never be eliminated. The ideal state is a social environment in which all voices can be heard so that no force dominates any other. Language is an important constraint on individual expression, for the language of the dominant class makes it difficult for working-class groups to understand their situation and to get out of it. In other words, the dominant language defines and perpetuates the oppression of marginalized groups. It is the job of the critical theorist to create new forms of language that will enable the predominant ideology to be exposed and competing ideologies to be heard.

Frankly, this section is difficult to organize, because the critical tradition itself is diffuse and wide-ranging. No scheme is perfect, but the use of four general categories of theory has been helpful to us in sorting out this body of work. These categories are (1) modernist theories; (2) postmodern theories; (3) poststructuralism; and (4) postcolonialism.

Modernism

The distinction between modern and postmodern movements marks a significant fault line within the critical tradition.[45] The modern version—often referred to as "structural"—centers on ongoing oppressive social structures, which are considered real and enduring, though they may be hidden from the consciousness of most people. Critical scholars in this group attempt to name and expose these oppressive arrangements. In contrast, the postmodern version teaches that there is no objectively real structure or central meaning and that oppressive "structures" are ephemeral. There is a struggle, but it is not a struggle between monolithic ideologies. It is a struggle between fluid interests and ideas.[46]

The structural tradition in critical social science is highly "theoretical" in the sense that it presents a standing version of social life to explain how oppressive structures work. The postmodern tradition is rather "antitheoretical" because it denies the existence of any particular structure over time.

In this section, we look at Marxism as the forebear of the modern branch of the critical tradition. We also look at the Frankfurt School and modernist approaches to feminist scholarship.

Marxism. One of the most important intellectual strands of the twentieth century was Marxist-based social theory. Originating with the ideas of Karl Marx and Friedrich Engels, who wrote in the nineteenth century, this movement consists of a number of loosely related theories challenging the dominant order of society. This line of thought has influenced virtually all branches of social science, including communication.[47]

Marx believed that a society's means of production determine the structure of that society.[48] Called the *base-superstructure* relationship, this notion is the idea that the economy is the base of all social structure. Marx was most concerned with the consequences of capitalism as an economic system, believing that profit drives production. Labor, then, becomes a mere tool to generate profit, to the ultimate harm of workers.

All institutions that perpetuate this form of domination are made possible by this economic system.[49] Economics drives politics, which is why classical Marxism is often called *the critique of political economy*. Marx's ultimate goal was revolution, in which workers—now aware of their plight—would rise up against the interests of capital to change the order of society. He believed that liberation would further the natural progress of history in which opposing forces come to clash. Few critical theorists today are Marxist, in the classical sense of this term, but there is no question that Marx had an immense influence on this school of thought, including concerns over dialectical conflict, domination, and oppression. For this reason much of this work is now labeled "neomarxist" or "marxist" (with a lowercase *m*).

As a movement, Marxism places great emphasis on the means of communication in society. Communication practices are an outcome of the tension between individual creativity and the social constraints on that creativity. Only when individuals are truly free to express themselves with clarity and reason will liberation occur, and that condition cannot come about in a class-based society.

The term *ideology* is important in most critical theories. An ideology is a set of ideas that structure a group's reality, a system of representations or a code of meanings governing how individuals and groups see the world.[50] In classical Marxism, an ideology is a false set of ideas perpetuated by the dominant political force. For the classical Marxist, science must be used to discover truth and to overcome the *false consciousness* of ideology.

More recent critical theorists tend to assert that there is no single dominant ideology but that the dominant classes in society are themselves constituted by a struggle among several ideologies. Many current thinkers reject the idea that an ideology is an isolated element in the social system; rather, it is deeply embedded in language and all other social and cultural processes.

A major theorist of ideology is the French Marxist Louis Althusser.[51] For Althusser, ideology is present in the structure of society itself and arises from the actual practices undertaken by institutions within society. As such, ideology actually forms the individual's consciousness and creates the person's subjective understanding of experience. In this model the superstructure (social organization) creates ideology, which in turn affects individuals' notions of reality.

For Althusser, this superstructure consists of *repressive state apparatuses*, such as the police and the military, and *ideological state apparatuses*, such as education, religion, and mass media. The repressive mechanisms enforce an ideology when it is threatened by deviant action, and the ideological apparatuses reproduce it more subtly in everyday activities of communication by making an ideology seem normal.

We live within a real set of material conditions, but we normally do not understand our relationship to actual conditions except through an ideology. The real conditions of existence can only be discovered through science, which Althusser poses in opposition to ideology. This idea has been highly controversial because it is based on a realist notion of truth, which most critical theorists now oppose.

Marxist theories tend to see society as the grounds for a struggle among interests through the domination of one ideology over another. *He-*

gemony is the process of domination, in which one set of ideas subverts or co-opts another—a process by which one group in society exerts leadership over all others. The Italian Marxist Antonio Gramsci originally elaborated the concept.[52]

The process of hegemony can occur in many ways and in many settings. In essence, it happens when events or texts are interpreted in a way that promotes the interests of one group over those of another. This can be a subtle process of co-opting the interests of a subordinate group into supporting those of a dominant one. For example, advertisers often play into the "women's liberation" theme, making it look as though the corporation supports women's rights. What is happening here is that women's interests are being reinterpreted or appropriated to promote the interests of the capital economy. Ideology plays a central role in this process because it structures the way people understand their experience, and it is therefore powerful in shaping how they interpret events.

Today, Marxist theory, in contrast with other branches of the critical tradition, is characterized by its identification of actual social structures that determine, or cause, domination and oppression to occur. This line of work, then, is highly *structuralist* in orientation. In communication, much of the recent work has focused less on the economic or materialist conditions that create oppression and more on the discursive formations that contribute to oppression and alienation. Whereas Marx conceived of economic forces as motivating or generating discourses that justify and hide the interests of domination, some communication scholars have made consciousness, speech, and text all-important determiners of social change, regardless of material conditions. Dana Cloud's work on "the materiality of discourse" offers a return to traditional Marxist foundations in her focus on the material within the rhetorical.[53]

Cloud argues that with the popularity of social constructionism—the line of thought that symbols construct our social worlds—critics are reluctant to argue that political and material conditions are implicated in texts. Instead, social constructionists are content to describe patterns in discourse and to see reality as a discursive formation, "rhetorically created and rhetorically altered."[54] The "material" is not physical conditions in the world but discourse or texts. According to Cloud, emancipation cannot be achieved "in 'mere talk,'"[55] and such an extreme constructionist position offers no guidance in evaluating different ideologies or for acting in the world. Disagreeing with this extreme social constructionist stance, Cloud asks: "If the discourse is the reality, would a critic of the 'freedom' inherent in the discourse around the war be forced to grant the nationalistic 1991 Super Bowl half-time an ontological status equal to the suffering of thousands of Iraqis as they were buried in the sand?"[56] While this example is extreme, she uses it to illustrate that "it is not only discourses and codes from which many people need liberation."[57]

Cloud's focus on materiality offers a return to a Marxist grounding in physical conditions without ignoring the role of discourse in influencing those conditions. She argues for viewing rhetorical texts as "symbolic resources within an ideological frame,"[58] so that the bodily reality is considered as it intersects with texts. Only when this intersection is considered, according to Cloud, does social change become a possibility. Otherwise, all the critic can do is simply describe the discourses present but cannot act on them to facilitate change in consciousness, action, or ideology.

Jürgen Habermas and the Frankfurt School. One of the longest and best-known Marxist traditions is the Frankfurt School. The *Frankfurt School* is such an important tradition in critical studies that it is often known simply as *Critical Theory*. These theorists originally based their ideas on Marxist thought, although it has gone far afield from that origin in the past eighty years. Communication takes a central place in this movement, and the study of mass communication has been especially important.[59]

This brand of critical theory began with the work of Max Horkheimer, Theodor Adorno,

TABLE **11.1**

Three Interests of Society

Type	Nature of Interest	Rationality	Associated Scholarship
Work	Technical	Instrumental	Empirical sciences
Interaction	Practical	Practical	History/hermeneutics
Power	Emancipatory	Self-reflection	Critical theory

Herbert Marcuse, and their colleagues at the Frankfurt Institute for Social Research in 1923.[60] The early Frankfurt scholars responded strongly to the classical ideals of Marxism and the success of the Russian revolution. They saw capitalism as an evolutionary stage in the development, first, of socialism and then of communism. Their ideas at that time formed a harsh critique of capitalism and liberal democracy. With the rise of the Nazis in Germany in the 1930s, the Frankfurt scholars immigrated to the United States and there became intensely interested in mass communication and the media as structures of oppression in capitalistic societies.

The best known contemporary Frankfurt scholar is Jürgen Habermas, whose theory of universal pragmatics and the transformation of society has had considerable influence in Europe and an increasing influence in the United States. Habermas is clearly the most important spokesperson for the Frankfurt School today.[61] His theory draws from a wide range of thought and presents a coherent critical view of communication and society.

Habermas teaches that society must be understood as a mix of three major interests—work, interaction, and power—all of which are necessary in a society. *Work,* the first interest, consists of the efforts to create material resources. Because of its highly instrumental nature—achieving tangible tasks and accomplishing concrete objectives—work is basically a "technical interest." It involves an instrumental rationality and is represented by the empirical-analytical sciences. In other words, technology is used as an instrument to accomplish practical results and is based on scientific research. This technical interest designs computers, builds bridges, puts satellites in orbit, administers organizations, and enables wondrous medical treatments.

The second major interest is *interaction,* or the use of language and other symbol systems of communication. Because social cooperation is necessary for survival, Habermas names this second item the "practical interest." It involves practical reasoning and is represented in historical scholarship and hermeneutics. The interaction interest can be seen in speeches, conferences, psychotherapy, family relations, and a host of other cooperative endeavors.

The third major interest is *power.* Social order naturally leads to the distribution of power, yet we are also interested in being freed from domination. Power leads to distorted communication, but by becoming aware of the ideologies that dominate in society, groups can themselves be empowered to transform society. Consequently, power is an "emancipatory interest." The rationality of power is self-reflection, and the branch of scholarship that deals with it is critical theory. For Habermas, the kind of work done by the critical theorists discussed thus far in this chapter is emancipatory because it can empower otherwise powerless groups. Table 11.1 summarizes the basic interests of work, interaction, and power.

As an example of these interests at work, consider Steven Ealy's study of a Georgia State job-classification survey in the 1970s.[62] At that time Georgia was strapped with the responsibility of reclassifying 45,000 state job positions, a monumental task; according to Ealy, the result was a serious communication breakdown. The state employed a consulting firm to conduct the necessary survey, and a plan was drafted to collect information about each position, develop job specifications, classify the positions, and then determine pay. A strong technical interest guided the reclassification study. There was a job to be done, and the consultants developed a method to achieve this goal. They proceeded as if the task could be solved by the use of "objective" or scientific procedures—gathering data, classifying jobs, and the like.

The employees and the departments, however, did not think of the study this way. They saw the study as a practical problem, one that affected their daily work and pay. For the departments, collecting data and implementing the results should have involved a good deal of interaction and consensus building, but it did not.

Because they held the power, the organizational decision makers' technical interests prevailed, the consultants' methods were imposed, and all practical interests were eliminated. In other words, the employees were expected simply to comply with the survey without much discussion about their needs and the practical problems like operational difficulties, management problems, and moral questions that reclassification might create.

In short, the participants were unequal in power and knowledge, and the interests of workers were subverted by those of management. The study lacked the kind of open communication that Habermas says is necessary in a free society. As a result the new classification system was not accepted by employees and was implemented only partially after many delays, new studies, lawsuits, and appeals.

As this case illustrates, human life cannot be properly conducted from the perspective of only one interest—work, interaction, or power. Any activity is likely to span all three categories. For example, the development of a new drug is a clear reflection of a technical interest, but it cannot be done without cooperation and communication, requiring an interaction interest as well. In a market economy, the drug is developed by a corporation to gain a competitive advantage, which is clearly a power interest too.

No aspect of life is interest free, even science. An emancipated society is free from unnecessary domination of any one interest, and everybody has equal opportunity to participate in decision making. Habermas believes that a strong public sphere, apart from private interests, is necessary to ensure this state of affairs.

Habermas is especially concerned with the domination of the technical interest in contemporary capitalistic societies.[63] In such societies, the public and private are intertwined to the point that the public sector cannot guard against the oppression of private, technical interests. Ideally, the public and private should be balanced, and the public sector should be strong enough to provide a climate for free expression of ideas and debate. In modern society, however, that climate is stifled.

It is clear from the foregoing discussion that Habermas values communication as essential to emancipation because language is the means by which the emancipatory interest is fulfilled. Communicative competence is therefore necessary for effective participation in decision making. Competence involves knowing how to use speech appropriately to accomplish goals, which requires compelling argumentation.[64]

Habermas's approach to communication is based largely on speech-act theory (see Chapter 5). Referring to his theory as *universal pragmatics*, Habermas establishes universal principles for the use of language. When communicating, you may assert a proposition (constative), seek to influence (regulative), or express a feeling (avowal). If you are asserting a proposition, you must demonstrate the truth of the claim. If you are trying to influence others, you must meet standards of appropriateness. If you are expressing feeling, you must show sincerity and truthfulness.

As an example, let's say that you give a speech to a labor group, claiming that labor unions today do not fight for their members' rights. Clearly, you want the audience to take some action on this problem. In this speech, you are combining all three types of speech acts. You are making a claim (constative), you are asserting your feelings about it (avowal), and you are trying to influence the audience (regulative). All three validity criteria must be met in order for your audience to take your speech seriously: (1) You must be truthful, (2) sincere, and (3) appropriate.

These validity claims are not always easy to secure, since people do not always believe that one's statements are valid. In the labor-management case, you might have some difficulty proving your case, as happened in the Georgia reclassification situation. Here, the management's validity claims about the new system were severely challenged in the form of objections, lawsuits, and individual appeals.

Habermas uses the term *discourse* to describe the special kind of communication required when a speaker's statements are challenged. Unlike normal communication, "discourse" is a systematic argument that makes special appeals to demonstrate the validity of a claim. So, for example, if your audience does not accept your speech at face value, you will need to engage in special argumentation, or *discourse*.

Again, there are different kinds of discourse, depending on the type of speech act being defended. Truth claims are argued with *theoretic discourse,* which emphasizes evidence. If the union denied your allegations about its role, you would be pressed to make a case by expanding your argument to include evidence showing that the union in fact did not participate in certain activities designed to benefit workers.

When appropriateness is being argued, *practical discourse* is used. This emphasizes norms. If the union resisted your attempts to begin bargaining, you would have to create practical discourse to demonstrate the appropriateness of negotiations. Challenges to one's sincerity also require special action to demonstrate genuine concern, but this is usually direct action rather than discourse.

Of course, there is no guarantee that the audience would agree with your evidence or the norms used to appeal for more union involvement. Where communicators do not share the same standards or concepts for evaluating the strength of an argument, they must move to a higher level of discourse, which Habermas calls *metatheoretical discourse.* Here, communicators argue about what constitutes good evidence for a claim or what norms are indeed appropriate in the given situation. This is the kind of thing the Supreme Court does, as one example.

An even higher level of discourse is sometimes necessary—*metaethical discourse.* Here, the very nature of knowledge itself is under contention and must be argued. Such discourse is a philosophical argument about what constitutes proper knowledge, which is precisely what critical theory does, for it challenges the assumed procedures for generating knowledge in society.

Habermas believes that free speech is necessary for productive normal communication and higher levels of discourse to take place. Although impossible to achieve, Habermas describes an *ideal speech situation* on which society should be modeled. First, the ideal speech situation requires freedom of speech; there must be no constraints on what can be expressed. Second, all individuals must have equal access to speaking. In other words, all speakers and positions must be recognized as legitimate. Finally, the norms and obligations of society are not one-sided but distribute power equally to all strata in society. Only when these requirements are met can completely emancipatory communication take place.

Emancipatory communication in the form of higher levels of discourse is essential to transform society so that the needs of the individual can be met. Habermas believes that people normally live in an unquestioned *life-world*—the ordinary, daily activities of life. This life-world, however, is constrained by certain aspects of the social system such as money, bureaucracy, and corporate power. We see here shades of Althusserian ideology in Habermas's theory: the idea that the superstructure creates an ideology that affects the ordinary understanding of citizens in their everyday lives. Habermas frames this problem as *colonization,* or the power of the system over individuals. When the life-world is colonized by the system, there is less opportunity to use language to achieve positive goals for individuals.

For Habermas, critical theory raises questions and calls attention to problems about the lifeworld that make critical reflection and resolution necessary. Only when we are aware of the problems of our life-world and the ways the system influences our view of life can we become emancipated from the entanglements of the system.

There is more opportunity to accomplish emancipation in modern society than in traditional society because of the relatively greater amount of conflict in modernity. In modern society we have the opportunity to hear a variety of viewpoints, but only if the system will allow free expression. Modern capitalistic societies have not yet achieved emancipation, and critical theorists have a responsibility to work toward making this possible.

Feminist Scholarship in the Modern Tradition. Another critical theory within the modernist tradition that also seeks society's emancipation is feminism. Feminist scholarship within the modernist tradition centers around two lines of inquiry: (1) feminisms that primarily work for the social, political, and economic equality of the sexes—that seek for women to gain equal status with men within existing power structures; and (2) feminisms that seek to dismantle and restructure the social system to make it more emancipatory for women and men. In the most general terms, these can be viewed as *liberal* and *radical* feminisms.

Liberal feminism, the foundation of the women's movement of the 1960s and 1970s, is based in liberal democracy, the idea that justice involves the assurance of equal rights for all individuals. Liberal feminists say that women have been oppressed as a group and that they have not had equal rights with men, as evidenced by women's lower average income, women's exclusion from centers of power and decision making, and women's lack of opportunity to advance in careers of their choice.

In contrast to the liberal school of thought, *radical feminism* believes that the oppression of women runs far deeper than political rights. For radical feminists, the problem goes to the heart of our social structure, which is patriarchal. The patriarchy perpetuates a set of gender-laden meanings that promote masculine interests and subordinate feminine ones. Women are oppressed because the very fabric of society is based on a constructed reality that devalues and marginalizes women's experience. If gender is a social construction, then in our present order of things it is a man-made construction. The term *radical* is appropriate for this movement because it goes to the root of social structure and demands *basic redefinitions* of all facets of society.

For example, instead of merely thinking that there should be more women physicians, society itself must redefine the whole nature of medicine, especially in regard to how it treats the experiences of women, how women as traditional healers have been displaced, and the like. Instead of limiting the struggle to overcoming the glass ceiling, women must strive to change the very definition of commerce and economy in society at large so that it better accommodates the interests and needs of women, children, and men. Feminist inquiry in this category seeks to transform society rather than simply just incorporate women's voices within it. [65]

The early work in terms of academic disciplines generally and communication in particular tended to focus on the first category of feminism—understanding sex and gender differences in order to move toward a valuing of the feminine on equal terms with the masculine. Women's discourse was seen, from this vantage point, as "different" from the position of white males and differently valued as a result. Feminist scholars sought to describe the different systems of realities that women's different discourse created, the different expectations of and patterns for women's communication, and the ways women accommodated, challenged, and subverted such expectations.[66] Feminist scholars sought, by means of these studies, to add women's communication practices to those of the discipline and to value the often-more-private and vernacular discourses that characterized much of women's experience.[67] They also argued that the inclusion of women and women's discourse—an elaborated range of communication behaviors—could be to everyone's benefit.

While such studies uncovered many important gendered patterns in society and created greater awareness of how gender functions, women and femininity often ended up constructed as unitary constructs—constructs that applied across the board to all women.[68] These essentializing tendencies have been forcefully and productively challenged by scholarship that seeks to emphasize individual standpoints as well as the necessary intersections of gender with other societal classifications.[69] With these developments, feminist scholarship moves from modernist to postmodern concerns, as we see in the next section.

Postmodernism

While the modern branch of the critical tradition identifies a variety of *a priori* oppressive social structures, the postmodern branch resists the idea that any one, enduring arrangement is responsible for power inequities. Postmodernism is based on the idea that social realities are constantly produced, reproduced, and changed through the use of language and other symbolic forms. We begin this section by describing cultural studies, the movement most frequently identified with postmodernism. We then turn to two important areas of application and extension—feminist cultural studies and critical race theory.

Cultural Studies. Cultural studies involves investigations of the ways culture is produced through a struggle among ideologies.[70] The most notable group of cultural scholars, British Cultural Studies, is associated with the Centre for Contemporary Cultural Studies at the University of Birmingham. The origins of this tradition are usually traced to the writings of Richard Hoggart and Raymond Williams in the 1950s, which examined the British working class after World War II.[71] Today, the name most associated with the movement is Stuart Hall.[72] Although influenced by Marxist thought, these scholars take a rather different direction in their thinking about oppressive communication.

The cultural studies tradition is distinctly reformist in orientation. These scholars want to see changes in Western society, and they view their scholarship as an instrument of socialist cultural struggle.[73] They believe that such change will occur in two ways: (1) by identifying contradictions in society, the resolution of which will lead to positive, as opposed to oppressive, change; and (2) by providing interpretations that will help people understand domination and the kinds of change that would be desirable. Samuel Becker describes their goal as "jarring both the audience and the workers in the media back from becoming too accepting of their illusions or existing practices so they will question them and their conditions."[74]

The study of mass communication is central to this work, for the media are perceived as powerful tools of dominant ideologies. In addition, media have the potential of raising the consciousness of the population about issues of class, power, and domination. We must be cautious in interpreting cultural studies in this light, however, because media are part of a much larger set of institutional forces. Media are important, but they are not the sole concern of these scholars, which is why they refer to their field as "cultural studies" rather than "media studies."

Cultural studies scholars speak of culture in two ways. The first definition is the common ideas on which a society or group rests, its ideology, or the collective ways by which a group understands its experience. The second definition is the practices or the entire way of life of a group—what individuals do materially from day to day. These two senses of culture cannot really be separated, for the ideology of a group is produced and reproduced in its practices. In fact, the general concern of cultural theorists is the link between the actions of society's institutions, such as the media and the culture. Practices and ideas always occur together within a historical context.

For example, people watch television every day, making them part of a television culture. The entire television industry is a cultural production as well because it is a means for creating, disputing, reproducing, and changing culture.

The concrete or material practices involved in producing and consuming television are a crucial mechanism in the establishment of ideology.

As members of a culture, we share a common sense about how things are. This shared understanding is an ideology determined by numerous, often subtle, influences that come together and make common experience seem real to us. In cultural studies, this process of having our realities reinforced from many sources is called *articulation.* Our shared understandings seem real because of the connection, or articulation, among several sources of verification.[75]

For example, it may seem absolutely essential to you to get a college degree. You think that a college education is good and leads to success in life. You think that you will get a good career by attending college and that you will be able to have a more meaningful life from what you learn in college. You think that a college education will make you more literate and able to participate more critically in our democratic society. These beliefs are commonly accepted by many people in our culture, but they are socially constructed ideas reinforced seemingly from every direction—from family, media, and school itself. Our acceptance of the superiority of higher education is a product of a very strong articulation.

Because some ideologies are more articulated than others, ideologies exist on an unequal footing in society. Cultural theory posits that capitalistic societies are dominated by a particular ideology of the elite. For certain stakeholder groups, the dominant ideology is false because it does not reflect their interests. Instead, the dominant ideology is involved in a hegemony against powerless groups.

Hegemony, however, is always a fluid process, what Hall calls a temporary state characterized by a "theatre of struggle." We must therefore "think of societies as complex formations, necessarily contradictory, always historically specific."[76] In other words, the struggle between contradictory ideologies is constantly changing.

As we saw earlier in the chapter, early Marxist theory taught that the infrastructure (economic system) determined superstructure.[77] In cultural studies, however, the relationship is believed to be more complex. The forces of society are considered to be *overdetermined,* or caused by multiple sources. Infrastructure and superstructure may therefore be mutually interdependent. Because of the complexity of causation in society, no one set of conditions is required for a particular outcome to occur.

The same is true of ideology. Multiple ideologies exist next to one another in dynamic tension. Hall puts the matter this way: "The important thing about systems of representation is that they are not singular. . . . As you enter an ideological field and pick out any one nodal representation or idea, you immediately trigger off a whole chain of connotative associations. Ideological representations connote—summon—one another."[78]

Communication, especially through the media, has a special role in affecting popular culture through the dissemination of information. The media are extremely important because they directly present a way of viewing reality. Even though the media portray ideology explicitly and directly, opposing voices will always be present as part of the dialectical struggle between groups in a society. Still the media are dominated by the prevailing ideology, and they therefore treat opposing views from within the frame of the dominant ideology, which has the effect of defining opposing groups as "fringe." The irony of media is that they present the illusion of diversity and objectivity, when in fact they are clear instruments of the dominant order.[79]

Producers control the content of media by particular ways of encoding messages. As Becker describes the process: "to be intelligible events must be put into symbolic form . . . the communicator has a choice of codes or sets of symbols. The one chosen affects the meaning of the events for receivers. Since every language—every symbol—coincides with an ideology, the choice of a set of symbols is, whether conscious or not, the choice of an ideology."[80] Advertisers, then, carefully design television commercials to create a certain image and thereby sell a product. Other kinds of programming such as news and comedy may seem less ideological, but they are every bit as much so.

At the same time, however, audiences may use their own categories to decode the message, and they often reinterpret media messages in ways never intended by the source.[81] As a result of alternative meanings, oppositional ideologies can and do arise in society. The intended meaning of a commercial may be completely lost on certain parts of the audience that interpret it in different ways. For example, an advertiser may use sex to make a product appealing to men, but feminist viewers see the image as demeaning to women. Or an image of wilderness may be used to sell SUVs, but it only irritates rather than persuades environmentalists.

For Hall and his colleagues, the interpretation of media texts always occurs within a struggle of ideological control. Ronald Lembo and Kenneth Tucker describe the process as "a competitive arena where individuals or groups express opposing interests and battle for cultural power."[82] Rap music is a good example of this struggle. Does it reflect the genuine values and interests of the black youth culture, or is it a sign of the degeneration of society? The answer depends on which interpretive community is asked. The chief aim of cultural studies, then, is to expose the ways ideologies of powerful groups are unwittingly perpetuated and the ways they can be resisted to disrupt the system of power that disfranchises certain groups.

Lawrence Grossberg's study of rock music is an especially interesting illustration of how cultural scholars work. He discusses a sweeping range of issues related to the meaning of rock and roll in contemporary culture, the role of punk, and the place of youth in society.[83] For Grossberg, rock and roll is an "apparatus" of culture, a movement unified by the feeling it engenders among its fans. Like any cultural text, rock and roll elicits a plethora of meanings in its various audiences and can be used for a variety of purposes.

Three characteristics demarcate rock and roll. First, it is associated with a particular group of fans, marking these individuals as somehow different from all other people. Second, the music is involved in the everyday lives of its listeners and is part of the larger context of their lives. Third, the entire rock apparatus provides intense pleasure to its fans, a pleasure of bodily sensation and emotional feeling. In short, it transforms the everyday lives of its fans: "The rock and roll apparatus is a kind of machine which, like a cookie cutter constantly changing its shape, produces or imprints a structure on the fans' desires and relations by organizing the material pieces of their lives."[84]

Rock music is also oppositional because it defines the youth culture as being different from "straight" and "boring." Grossberg points to the following evidence of rock and roll's oppositional nature, which he defines as its "attitude": "Rock and roll has, repeatedly and continuously, been attacked, banned, ridiculed and relegated to an insignificant cultural status. The fact that so much effort has been brought to bear in the attempt to silence it, makes it reasonable to assume that some struggle is going on, some opposition is being voiced."[85]

Grossberg also believes that the advent of punk has had a profound effect on the role of rock music as an oppositional force. Punk itself seems to say that anything goes and that nothing matters. Punk "deconstructed" all forms, including traditional rock and roll. As such, punk itself became an oppositional force. Punk, along with a host of other social and cultural factors, has led to a deconstruction of the youth culture, which had been the chief source of meaning for rock and roll among its fans: "Punk attacked rock and roll for having grown old and fat, for having lost that which puts it in touch with its audience and outside of the hegemonic reality."[86] Grossberg is confident that youth is currently under reconstruction, but he is uncertain how.

In the next two sections, we look at two applications of cultural studies—feminist cultural scholarship and critical race theory. And although each of these focuses on different aspects of culture, both exist within the postmodern tradition because they look at how categories such as gender and race are created in discourse and how these discourses create domination as well as opportunities for resistance and empowerment.

Feminist Cultural Studies. We saw in the previous section that modernist feminist studies identified a patriarchal system as the source of women's oppression. In contrast to this approach, feminist cultural studies suggests that power relations are constructed in social interaction of various types and that the language and symbolic forms are constantly creating categories of thought as well as social relationships. Specifically, feminist communication scholars examine the ways the male language bias affects the relations between the sexes, the ways male domination has constrained communication for females, and the ways women have both accommodated and resisted male patterns of speech and language. Although feminist scholarship has both modern and postmodern aspects, within the communication field, most current feminist work clearly aligns with cultural studies—and thus postmodernism—reflecting its interest in oppressive and emancipatory possibilities of discourse and other symbolic forms.[87] Indeed, Terry Lovell wrote that "Cultural studies, in locating a wide variety of types of text and of meaning as integral to contemporary society and culture, opened up a space where feminists could study women's lives as well as women's texts as part of the broad socio-cultural construction of gender in capitalist society."[88]

As an example of this kind of work, Fern L. Johnson and Karren Young looked at television commercials for children's toys aired in the 1990s in terms of the ways in which they embodied discourse codes linking products to gender stereotypes.[89] They found that in addition to outnumbering girl-oriented ads, boy-oriented commercials emphasized action, competition, destruction, and agency and control, while girl-oriented ads emphasized limited activity, feelings, and nurturing. In speaking roles, characters tended to polarize genders, and boy-ads included many power words, which were essentially absent in girl-ads. Based on this study,

then, children's television advertisements seem to reproduce cultural stereotypes by using them for marketing purposes and thus serve to socialize children into a pattern of gender relations that "undermine more nuanced cultural ideas about gender role changes."[90]

Feminist scholars do not just examine cultural texts out in the world; they have also become self-reflexive in treating scholarship and the scholarly enterprise itself as a cultural text. Feminist scholars have pointed out how research and theory building, like all aspects of life, are dominated not only by gender biases but by biases generally shared by Western discourse, including objectivity, Eurocentrism, and imperialism. Contemporary feminist scholars, then, seek to articulate the interrelated forms of oppression, realizing that working to end one kind of oppression is useless—and in fact impossible—if other oppressions remain entrenched and unaddressed.[91]

Accordingly, feminist scholars seek to devise methods of scholarship that take into account the shifting female subject and its related discourses while also situating it in lived experience. They explore how the so-called gender-neutral discourses of the academy have denied women voice, strategies by which women can "interrupt"[92] the academic conversation, and what the academy stands to lose and gain from such exclusions. Power relations are examined as they are manifest throughout society as well as in the very academic practices by which such investigations occur. In this sense, feminist scholarship undertakes the emancipatory aim of cultural studies, not only for culture generally but for its own scholarship.

Critical Race Theory. Critical race theory (CRT), another example of the cultural studies approach, has a foot in both the modernist and postmodern traditions. CRT dates its origins to the 1970s when a group of lawyers and legal scholars realized that the progress made by the civil rights movement had not continued and, in fact, that much racism had gone underground. Foundational to the movement was the idea of legal indeterminacy—the idea that not every legal decision has a single correct outcome. The movement also had activist origins as well: From the civil rights movement, CRT took the notion of social justice—that historic wrongs need to be addressed—and from radical feminism, it drew upon the idea that largely unrecognized patterns of social behavior constitute patriarchy and other forms of domination.[93] These origins point to a grounding in modernist approaches.

Proponents of critical race theory share several beliefs. The first two of these continue the modernist tradition within CRT. First, CRT scholars see racism as ordinary, common, or normal—it is "the usual way society does business" and thus difficult to address. Second, CRT scholars agree that white domination in the United States functions to serve the psychological and material advantage of dominant groups, which means there are relatively few people genuinely interested in eradicating racism.

CRT further posits, however, that race is a social construction—race and racism are products of social interaction that "society invents, manipulates, or retires when convenient."[94] This is where CRT makes a turn toward postmodernism. Critical race theorists understand that race is not only or merely or actually a structural category but a fluid and shifting one. Such scholars also attend to the different ways in which society racializes minority groups—a perspective that is very aligned with the postmodern tradition. A society may have, for example, little use for Chinese laborers at one time but does need Japanese workers. During another period, Japanese people may fall into disfavor—as was the case during World War II—while African Americans are "cultivated" for jobs in the Army and in factories. Finally, CRT advocates share a belief in the importance of blacks, Indians, Asians, and Latinos/Latinas telling their stories about race and racism as a way to bring their "unique perspectives" to the law's "master narratives," or widely accepted stories of what is normal and right.[95]

Within the communication discipline, critical race theory is still a relative newcomer. Mark McPhail suggests that "there has been scant discussion of race and rhetoric which incorporates contemporary perspectives."[96] Many intersections can be made, however, between race, language, and power. The tension between race as a social construction and race as a material condition is one that is, at the core, a matter of communication, each with different pragmatic implications. If race is seen as primarily material, then energies must be directed at physical conditions if racism is ever to be eradicated. If issues of race are considered as much social constructions as physical ones, as would be the case in a cultural-studies approach, then remedies can be found in language and social relations, ranging from curtailing racist speech, to hosting diversity seminars, to increasing the representations of underrepresented groups in media.

Another issue that also involves communication is the tension between the perspectives identified as color-blind and color-conscious. One position says that legal decisions should no longer take note of race—that decisions should be color-blind, a stance many CRT scholars dispute. They argue that if racism is indeed embedded in our thought processes, social structures, and discourse, then aggressive measures to address race are necessary in order to bring about change. So a paradox is constructed about race: In order to ameliorate race relations, we need to talk about race, but that conversation itself may reproduce existing patterns of racism. The insistence on attention to legal and civil rights—often the foundation upon which societal changes are predicated—is questioned by critical race theory because they often are procedural rather than substantive. "Rights" favor the interests of the powerful and can and are often changed to fit the interests of the dominant and elite. How rights are defined is a matter of interpretation, legally and socially, and language and communication are important factors in such definitions.[97]

Also of interest to communication scholars is the importance of telling one's story so that these personal stories can serve as counter-histories to many stock U.S. narratives about immigrants.[98] CRT's concern with introducing those narratives into legal discourse, and whether and how they will be heard are matters of communication. Thus, while CRT was modernist in its origins, contemporary concerns take a decidedly postmodernist stance as well as bringing communication issues to the fore.

A recent extension of critical race theory—and another line of work clearly within the postmodern tradition—is the study of whiteness. After many decades of studying race, "a generation of scholars is putting whiteness under the lens and examining the construction of the white race."[99] In general, these scholars examine what it means to be white, how whiteness became established legally, how certain groups moved into whiteness (Irish and Italians, for example, were originally seen as nonwhite, on par with blacks),[100] and the privileges that come with being white. Communication scholars have recognized the difficulty of studying whiteness, because whiteness is at once invisible and yet extremely important. Thomas Nakayama and Lisa Peñaloza note: "If whiteness is everything and nothing, if whiteness as a racial category does not exist except in conflict with others, how can we understand racial politics in a social structure that centers whites, yet has no center?"[101]

Thomas Nakayama and Robert Krizek attempt to make the cultural construction of whiteness visible by describing six strategies inherent to the discourse of whiteness.[102] They arrived at these strategies after interviewing people about what it means to be white. They found six different constructions of whiteness embedded in the answers they received: (1) white is equated with power—white means status, majority, and dominance; (2) white is a default position—if you are not another color, you are white; (3) white is a scientific classification—fairly meaningless and "drained of its social status";[103] (4) white means national origin—I'm an American; (5) white means the refusal to label self as any racialized category, whether white, black, or any other ethnic group; and (6) white means European ancestry. These varied and at times contradictory mappings of white discursive space suggest how expansive, central, and powerful the concept of whiteness is,

even when it is being downplayed. As Nakayama and Krizek summarize: "It garners its representational power through its ability to be many things at once, to be universal and particular; to be a source of identity and difference."[104]

In sum, critical race theory provides a postmodern example of how the careful examination of discourse can reveal ways in which society constructs categories that constrain and liberate various groups of people. We move now from the postmodern to the poststructural. As we make this transition, keep in mind that these two strands of the critical tradition support rather than oppose one another.

Poststructuralism and the Work of Michel Foucault

Originally, poststructuralism was a movement originating in France in reaction to traditional semiotic ideas about language.[105] Specifically, the poststructuralists objected to the idea that language structures are just natural forms to be used by individuals as a tool of communication. Their goal was to "deconstruct" language in order to show that language can be understood, used, and constructed in a limitless number of ways. When we normalize meanings and grammars, we are in fact privileging one form of discourse over another, which is ultimately and always oppressive. You can see that poststructuralism is also postmodern, because it resists any idea that posits a universal, normal structure or way of being in the world.

Within the communication field today, the most influential poststructuralist is Michel Foucault. Foucault is normally thought of as a poststructuralist but is, in fact, impossible to classify neatly.[106] Although he denied a structuralist bias in his work, his writings bridge poststructural and structural traditions within the critical tradition.

Foucault says that each period has a distinct worldview, or conceptual structure, that determines the nature of knowledge in that period. The character of knowledge in a given epoch Foucault calls the *episteme,* or *discursive formation.*

The vision of each age is exclusive and incompatible with visions from other ages, making it impossible for people in one period to think like those of another. The episteme, or way of thinking, is determined not by people but by the predominant discursive structures of the day. These discursive structures are deeply embedded ways of practicing or expressing ideas, and what people know cannot be separated from the structures of discourse used to express that knowledge. For Foucault, discourse includes written texts, but it also includes spoken language and nonverbal forms such as architecture, institutional practices and even charts and graphs.

An example of how discourse shapes knowledge is Richard Nixon's famous "Checkers" speech. Martha Cooper applied Foucault's ideas to this speech to show how the discourse made use of—indeed created—standards for responding to an accusation.[107] In the presidential campaign of 1952, vice-presidential candidate Richard Nixon was accused of harboring a secret campaign fund. He responded to this accusation by denying the charge, opening his private finances to public scrutiny, and claiming that the only possible illegitimate contribution he had received was a dog named Checkers.

This speech has been analyzed by several scholars of rhetoric, each looking at the ways this particular speaker used strategies to appeal to the national audience at that time. For Foucault, this kind of analysis is irrelevant. Cooper shows how this speech was an event that served to create and reinforce knowledge structures in our culture. In particular, the speech defined what it meant to respond to an accusation, reinforcing the rule that when accused, people should respond.

The structure of discourse is a set of inherent rules that determines the form and substance of discursive practice. Foucault's use of rules is not entirely like that of the other theories in this book, because for him, rules apply across the culture in a variety of types of discourse and function on a deep and powerful level. These are not merely rules for how to talk but rules that determine the very nature of our knowledge, power, and ethics. These rules control what can be talked or written about, who may talk or write, and whose talk is to be taken seriously. Such rules also prescribe the form that discourse must take. In our day, for example, "scientific authorities" are given great credibility, and in matters of "fact," most people prefer the form of "objective studies" over the form of conjecture or myth.

So in the "Checkers" speech, for instance, we see what counts as good evidence for a claim that a politician is corrupt (or not corrupt). We learn from this discourse that politicians must speak out when accused of wrongdoing, and the model of the honest, average American is created here as well.

Contrary to popular belief, according to Foucault, people are not responsible for establishing the conditions of discourse. Inversely, it is discourse that determines the place of the person in the scheme of the world. Our present discursive structure defines humans as the foundation and origin of knowledge, but people have never before achieved this status in any other period and will soon lose it. Foucault believes that the episteme will again shift, and humans will once again disappear from their central place in the world: "It is comforting . . . and a source of profound relief to think that man is only a recent invention, a figure not yet two centuries old, a new wrinkle in our knowledge, and that he will disappear again as soon as that knowledge has discovered a new form."[108]

This radical idea does not mean that humans do not produce discourse. Indeed, they do; but any number of individuals could have produced a given statement, and any speaker or writer is merely fulfilling a role in making a statement. That Nixon was the speaker of the "Checkers" address is unimportant. Nixon took the role of agent in this case, and since then any number of other politicians have done essentially the same thing. Discourse, then, does not require a knowing subject—a person who creates it, consumes it, understands it, and uses it. Rather, language itself prefigures personhood: Language creates the person. In other words, a Nixon-type person was created by the language in the "Checkers" speech.

In our era, persons are believed to obtain knowledge and have power, but this idea is a creation of the predominant discursive formation of our day, and the rules of expression with which we communicate establish this notion. In other times, entirely different ideas about knowledge and power emerge from the discourse in use.

Foucault's research on the penal system is a good example of this.[109] He found a dramatic shift in the eighteenth and nineteenth centuries away from torture and public punishment to incarceration and protection of the criminal from bodily harm. Prior to this period, convicts were publicly tortured or executed in a kind of spectacle. In the discursive formation of that day, the body was seen as the central object of political relations. It was very natural that power should be exerted against the body and that punishment should involve bodily pain. In the latter discursive formation, however, the body lost this status, as power became more a matter of the individual human psyche or soul. Thus locking people up came to be viewed as a more appropriate punishment than flogging them in public.

Foucault's work centers on analyzing discourse in a way that reveals its rules and structure. What he first called *archaeology* and later *genealogy*, this method seeks to uncover, through careful description, the regularities of discourse. It displays disparities or contradictions, rather than coherence, and reveals a succession of one form of discourse after another. For this reason, Foucault places emphasis on comparative descriptions of more than one piece of discourse. Interpretation, or establishing the meaning of a text, cannot be avoided in text analysis, but it should be minimized because interpretation does not reveal discursive structure and, in fact, may obscure it.

Foucault's writings center on the subject of power. He believes that power is an inherent part of all discursive formation. As such, it is a function of discourse or knowledge and not a human or institutional property. The episteme, as expressed in language, grants power. Thus, power and knowledge cannot be divided. Power, however, is a good, creative force that finds its zenith in "disciplinary power" or the prescription of standards of correct behavior. In sum, then, the discourse of our age will shape who we are and how we think.

One group of scholars is interested in looking at how colonialism embodies a discourse of oppression, in which the global truly becomes personal. We examine this work—the postcolonial—in the next section.

Postcolonialism

Postcolonial theory is postmodern in its critique of colonialism, which has been an important cultural structure of the modern period. Scholars working in the postcolonial movement are devoted to understanding Eurocentrism, imperialism, and the processes of colonization and decolonization—all of the ways in which the colonial experience can be understood as an ideology of domination. Postcolonial scholars seek to examine, understand, and ultimately undo the historical structures that created, maintain, and continue to reproduce the colonial experience. While many postcolonial scholars are themselves from nations that were subject to European colonization, their focus is not restricted to the literal colonization practices of these countries as empires. They also focus on what is called "neocolonialism" as it occurs in contemporary discourse about "others." *Neocolonialism* is present, for example, in the use of the terms *first* and *third* worlds to discuss "developing" nations, in the massive transference and "invasion" of U.S. culture into all parts of the world, and in treatments of nonwhite races as "other" in U.S. media.[110]

Edward Said's work on "otherness" is often considered the origins of postcolonial theory. In his book *Orientalism*, Said discusses the systems of discourse by which the "'world' is divided, administered, plundered, by which humanity is thrust into pigeonholes, by which 'we' are 'human' and 'they' are not."[111] These systems of discourses extend beyond the political realm to the academic world as well. Said points out how members of non-Western cultures are positioned as the "subjects" of study in the academy that then becomes a "learned" field. Then "others" become something to learn about, and thus they are turned into objects, making them dominated once again by the process of knowledge production.[112] The postcolonial project, then, is concerned generally with how the Western world, in all of its discourses, perceives and talks about itself and the rest of the world—talk that legitimizes certain power structures and reinforces the colonizing practices of those nations whose dominance continues to be reproduced.

The stance of postcolonialism is inherently political, seeing emancipation from oppressive structures as they continue to play out in Western discourses and in the material world. Postcolonial critics recognize, however, that the answer to Western domination is not simply retreating into a pre-Western past or indigenous tradition in order to preserve some kind of "native" identity. This is not only impractical but simply reproduces the "us" versus "them" ideology that is at work in the larger world.[113] Rather the postcolonial critic seeks to understand the world from a place between two cultures, to resist any singular form of cultural understanding, and to see cultural identities in more complicated ways.

An important theme in postcolonial work, then, is *hybridity*—the spaces between cultures.[114] Living between two cultures and not being truly part of either creates what Gloria Anzaldúa calls the borderlands,[115] a displaced position that carried with it a special consciousness and way of seeing that is valuable to understanding both cultures. Postcolonial theorists ask the discipline of communication to examine ways of communicating that take into account how all of us live, to some degree, in the borderlands.

Postcolonial theory is thus very much concerned with power—another basic component of the critical tradition. It provides an "international depth to the understanding of cultural power."[116] While offering a critical understanding of the power dynamics of imperialism in all of its forms, it also understands the difficulty of moving out of the ideological structures that dominate the academy and the world. Post-

colonial scholars suggest several ways to begin to grapple with the forms of domination in which we find ourselves. First is to unlearn privilege—to recognize and acknowledge the ways in which our daily practices connect to larger political, national, and international interests in the world.[117] Even simple things like being able to buy band-aids that match one's skin tone are signs of "privilege" that members of the dominant culture often do not even think about.

A second suggestion is to avoid essentializing others in the same way that others have been essentialized by Western discourses. The postcolonial critic who attempts to discuss the situation of a woman in Senegal, for instance, faces the problem of colonizing that woman by speaking with authority about and essentially defining the nature of her experience. Gayatri Spivak offers the idea of "strategic essentializing" as a way out of this bind. The critic recognizes that she or he will end up essentializing to some degree and thus constantly examines that stance, considering essentialism not as "the way things are" but "something one must adopt to produce a critique of anything."[118] The postcolonial critic, then, is constantly self-reflexive and considers how the processes of scholarship may be inscribing the very power relations and hegemonic structures she or he is seeking to resist.

The postcolonial project, in sum, brings the facets of the critical tradition—concerns with domination, ideology, and power—to the global scene. It seeks to offer ways that we can listen to those who have been colonized in all kinds of ways by Western discourses and can begin to bring them into the conversations about identities, politics, globalization, and power.

◖ REFLECTIONS ON
The Critical Tradition

Diverse as the critical tradition is, certain common themes are certainly apparent. The critical tradition is oppositional, it is conscious and proud of its values, and it holds a clear goal of consciousness raising. This tradition, too, includes assumptions and insights from all the other traditions, except the sociopsychological. The keen interest in signs and the effect of signs and symbols in establishing social domination shows a strong crossover with semiotics. The idea in post-modernism that patterns of influence and domination are overdetermined, or a product of the interaction of many forces, shows a certain kinship with cybernetics. Most critical studies are obviously influenced by the so-ciocultural, and because of their reliance on herme-neutic methods, the phenomenological as well.

Still, critical theories do resist many tendencies of the other traditions. They worry that other forms of scholarship are merely descriptive and participate in the normalizing of otherwise hegemonic forces. Post-structural theories especially resist the semiotic no-tions of language structure, and postmodern theorists would reject objective system descriptions often found in the cybernetic tradition. Finally, modernist critical theories would almost certainly reject phenomenology and especially its individualistic bias.

● ● ●

A P P L I C A T I O N S I M P L I C A T I O N S

The implications of communication theory in the broadest context are both grand and small, as they impact everyday life in society, culture, and individuals. We cap-ture these implications here in five propositions:

1. Difference is the soul of society.

Most psychologically oriented communication theory focuses not on difference, but on unity. When we look at the individual communicator from a psychological point of view, we seem most interested in the predictability and repeatability of an individ-ual's thinking and behavior. Once we move beyond the individual to look at larger social and cultural patterns, however, difference emerges as the defining character-istic of human life. Not only are cultures and social institutions diverse, but individual persons, because of their involvement in these larger social structures, are them-selves diverse.

The theories in this chapter say a great deal about difference—differences in language, cultural forms, class, gender, and power. Because people communicate within different circles of influence, because their cultures provide different linguistic forms, and because certain groups dominate others, society is like a tapestry of numerous threads, colors, and patterns, and the whole, composed of diversity, con-stitutes the largest context in which communication takes place.

Who you are as a person, then, is largely determined by the combination of so-cial formations impacting your life. For some of us, the forces that define our identi-ties are clear, especially in the case of race, class, gender, and other cultural forms. As any person who is lesbian, is an immigrant, or has a disability will tell you, group identity matters. For others, though equally important, the social categories affecting their lives are translucent. Though many of us fail to see the relevance of cultural factors, it would take only a few weeks in an intercultural communication course to realize the sociocultural nature of our lives.

The fact of difference is one of the most important things you can learn in life. Human beings are distinguished by difference, yet sometimes we have difficulty coping with it. Some resist it, some tolerate it, and others celebrate it. Each of these responses, however, is a matter of communication. Yet, we must manage our differences, and always we must do so through communication.

2. Social diversity is created and managed through communication.
Ordinary human beings make the arrangements that characterize the fabric of society in everyday communication. The people with whom we communicate, what we talk about, and how we communicate creates groups, organizations, cultures, and institutions. Dynamic social impact theory shows that mere clustering of people together into networks creates a kind of influence structure, ethnography provides rich descriptions of cultural forms, and cultural studies identifies the ways in which communication produces power and domination.

As we have seen in virtually all of the chapters of this book, communication is more than an odorless, tasteless, neutral tool for transmitting information. It is more than an instrument of influence. Communication is the environment in which social worlds are made, and we had better think about the kinds of worlds we want to make. The good news is that we have some power to determine what we want to achieve through communication; the bad news is we cannot do it alone. In other words, we are in this together, and we will together build a social world based on the communication forms we employ. Although we use a variety of visual, spatial, and tactile symbols in communication, language is especially important in the process of social construction.

3. Language and culture are inextricable.
The early work of Sapir and Whorf showed the power of language in influencing thought. Cultural difference, according to linguistic relativity, is determined in large measure by linguistic differences. Bernstein showed how language affects and reflects social class and family relationships, and the ethnography of communication broadens this analysis to show how cultural difference includes variation in expressive forms of all types. The conclusion is inescapable: Language and culture go hand in hand.

How you talk shows others who you are. Language use is a form of social bonding and identification. When you are "with" or "in" a group, your language says, "I am part of you, but not part of them," or, "I am with them, and not you." In other words, you perform culture every day.

It is true that "sticks and stones can break bones," but words matter too. A common belief is that words and deeds are different, that talking and doing are separate, and—more to the point—we should stop talking so much and start doing. But very little communication theory supports this idea. Indeed, communication scholars will almost universally tell you that doing and talking can never be separated, as each affects the other.

4. Social arrangements are consequential.
Your personal identity, what you think and do, your resources, and your privilege are all consequences of where you are positioned within the structure of society. For example, the theory of the diffusion of innovations says that the technologies you employ will depend in large measure on who you know and what technologies they use. The theory of elaborated and restricted codes suggests that how you think about yourself and other members of your family depends upon how you address one another.

Privilege is an especially important consequence of the organization of society. The privilege you enjoy or do not possess is determined, in part, by the opportunities you have had, and opportunity is very much a product of your own social status. For example, feminist theory shows that masculine values that permeate society can marginalize the experiences of women. Cultural studies takes a more complex view. These scholars do not see any single set of ideas as perpetually dominant. Although various interests may dominate at any particular time and certain classes of people are oppressed in this process, the field of ideological struggle is constantly in flux.

5. Contexts of communication are interlinked.
Because contexts are built up from interaction, no single context is ever sufficient to explain the communication process. Your communication may be affected largely by your sense of self (Chapter 4), the messages of others (Chapter 5), the conversations you are having at the moment (Chapter 6), your relationships (Chapter 7), the group (Chapter 8), the organization (Chapter 9), or the media (Chapter 10); but in the end all are part of a large social and cultural milieu that affects and is affected by all the others.

NOTES

1. Edward Sapir, *Language: An Introduction to the Study of Speech* (New York: Harcourt, Brace & World, 1921); Benjamin L. Whorf, *Language, Thought, and Reality*, ed. John B. Carroll (New York: Wiley, 1956). In the Whorf book, the following articles are most helpful: John B. Carroll, "Introduction," pp. 1–34; "The Relation of Habitual Thought and Behavior to Language," pp. 134–159; and "Language, Mind, and Reality," pp. 246–270.
2. Edward Sapir, quoted in Whorf, *Language, Thought, and Reality*, p. 134.
3. Carroll, "Introduction," in Whorf, *Language, Thought, and Reality*, p. 27.
4. Adapted from Whorf, *Language, Thought, and Reality*, p. 213.
5. Whorf, *Language, Thought, and Reality*, p. 158.
6. Basil Bernstein, *Class, Codes, and Control: Theoretical Studies Toward a Sociology of Language* (London: Routledge & Kegan Paul, 1971).
7. Bernstein, *Class, Codes, and Control*, p. 177.
8. Bernstein, *Class, Codes, and Control*, p. 175.
9. Bernstein, *Class, Codes, and Control*, pp. 76–117.
10. Bernstein, *Class, Codes, and Control*, p. 186.
11. Bernstein, *Class, Codes, and Control*, p. 186.
12. Bibb Latané, "Dynamic Social Impact: Robust Predictions from Simple Theory," in *Modelling and Simulation in the Social Sciences from the Philosophy of Science Point of View*, ed. R. Hegselmann, U. Mueller, and K. G. Troitzsch (Dordrecht, Netherlands: Kluwer Theory and Decision Library, 1996), pp. 287–310. See also the symposium on DSIT, Edward L. Fink, "Dynamic Social Impact Theory and the Study of Human Communication," *Journal of Communication* 46 (1996): 4–77.
13. Paul Lazarsfeld, Bernard Berelson, and H. Gaudet, *The People's Choice* (New York: Columbia University Press, 1948). See also Everett M. Rogers, *A History of Communication Study: A Biographical Approach* (New York: Free Press, 1994), pp. 244–315.
14. An excellent summary of this hypothesis is Elihu Katz, "The Two-Step Flow of Communication," *Public Opinion Quarterly* 21 (1957): 61–78.
15. Elihu Katz and Paul Lazarsfeld, *Personal Influence: The Part Played by People in the Flow of Mass Communications* (New York: Free Press, 1955).
16. Research on opinion leadership is summarized in Everett M. Rogers, *Diffusion of Innovations* (New York: Free Press, 1995), pp. 290–304.
17. Rogers, *Diffusion of Innovations*, pp. 281–334.
18. Rogers, *Diffusion of Innovations*. For a summary of this theory, see John F. Cragan and Donald C. Shields, *Understanding Communication Theory: The Communicative Forces for Human Action* (Boston: Allyn & Bacon, 1998), pp. 175–207.

19. Everett M. Rogers and D. Lawrence Kincaid, *Communication Networks: Toward a New Paradigm for Research* (New York: Free Press, 1981). The Korean case is discussed throughout the book. See especially pages 258–285.

20. Everett Rogers, personal communication, 2003.

21. The idea of critical mass is discussed in Alwin Mahler and Everett M. Rogers, "The Diffusion of Interactive Communication Innovations and the Critical Mass: The Adoption of Telecommunications Services by German Banks," *Telecommunications Policy* 23 (1999): 719–740; and Everett M. Rogers, "Diffusion Theory: A Theoretical Approach to Promote Community-Level Change," in *Handbook of HIV Prevention*, ed. John L. Peterson and Ralph J. DiClemente (New York: Kluwer Academic, 2000), pp. 57–65.

22. For a discussion of the role of culture in the communication field, see John H. Powers, "On the Intellectual Structure of the Human Communication Discipline," *Communication Education* 44 (1995): 191–222.

23. See Michael Agar, *Speaking of Ethnography* (Beverly Hills, CA: Sage, 1986); Paul Atkinson, *Understanding Ethnographic Texts* (Newbury Park, CA: Sage, 1992).

24. See especially Clifford Geertz, *The Interpretation of Cultures* (New York: Basic, 1973); and Clifford Geertz, *Local Knowledge: Further Essays in Interpretive Anthropology* (New York: Basic, 1983).

25. Geertz, *Local Knowledge*, p. 57.

26. Lyall Crawford, "Personal Ethnography," *Communication Monographs* 63 (1996): 158.

27. Donal Carbaugh and Sally Hastings, "A Role for Communication Theory in Ethnography and Cultural Analysis," *Communication Theory* 2 (1992): 156–165.

28. George Herbert Mead, *Mind, Self, and Society* (Chicago: University of Chicago Press, 1934); Herbert Blumer, *Symbolic Interactionism: Perspective and Method* (Englewood Cliffs, NJ: Prentice-Hall, 1969). For a summary of this work, see Barbara Ballis Lal, "Symbolic Interaction Theories," *American Behavioral Scientist* 38 (1995): 421–441.

29. Anthony Giddens, *Profiles and Critiques in Social Theory* (Berkeley: University of California Press, 1982).

30. For a description of this field, see Deborah Cameron, *Working with Spoken Discourse* (London: Sage, 2001), pp. 53–67.

31. Dell Hymes, *Foundations in Sociolinguistics: An Ethnographic Approach* (Philadelphia: University of Pennsylvania Press, 1974).

32. Hymes, *Foundations in Sociolinguistics*, pp. 29–66.

33. Gerry Philipsen, "An Ethnographic Approach to Communication Studies," in *Rethinking Communication: Paradigm Exemplars*, ed. Brenda Dervin, Lawrence Grossberg, Barbara J. O'Keefe, and Ellen Wartella (Newbury Park, CA: Sage, 1989), pp. 258–269.

34. See, for example, Gerry Philipsen, "A Theory of Speech Codes," in *Developing Communication Theories*, ed. Gerry Philipsen and Terrance L. Albrecht (Albany: SUNY Press, 1997), pp. 119–156.

35. Donal Carbaugh, "Culture Talking About Itself," in *Cultural Communication and Intercultural Contact*, ed. Donal Carbaugh (Hillsdale, NJ: Lawrence Erlbaum, 1990), pp. 1–9.

36. Donal Carbaugh, *Situating Selves: The Communication of Social Identities in American Scenes* (Albany: SUNY Press, 1996), p. 197.

37. Tamar Katriel, "'Griping' as a Verbal Ritual in Some Israeli Discourse," in *Cultural Communication and Intercultural Contact*, ed. Donal Carbaugh (Hillsdale, NJ: Lawrence Erlbaum, 1990), pp. 99–114.

38. Victor Turner, *The Anthropology of Performance* (New York: PAJ, 1987).

39. Turner, *Anthropology of Performance*, p. 23.

40. Dwight Conquergood, "Rethinking Ethnography: Toward a Critical Cultural Politics," *Communication Monographs* 58 (1991): 179–194; "Ethnography, Rhetoric, and Performance," *Quarterly Journal of Speech* 78 (1992): 80–97.

41. See, for example, the journal *Text and Performance Studies*.

42. Conquergood, "Rethinking Ethnography."

43. For a further elaboration on this aspect of the critical tradition, see Helene A. Shugart, "An Appropriating Aesthetic: Reproducing Power in the Discourse of Critical Scholarship," *Communication Theory* 13 (2003): 275–303.

44. See, for example, Robert Pryor, "On the Method of Critical Theory and Its Implications for a Critical Theory of Communication," in *Phenomenology in Rhetoric and Communication*, ed. Stanley A. Deetz (Washington, DC: Center for Advanced Research in Phenomenology/University Press of America, 1981), pp. 25–35; Jennifer Daryl Slack and Martin Allor, "The Political and Epistemological Constituents of Critical Communication Research," *Journal of Communication* 33 (1983): 128–218; Dallas W. Smythe and Tran Van Dinh, "On Critical and Administrative Research: A New Critical Analysis," *Journal of Communication* 33 (1983): 117–127; Everett M. Rogers, "The Empirical and the Critical Schools of Communication Research," in *Communication Yearbook 5*, ed. Michael Burgoon (New Brunswick, NJ: Transaction, 1982), pp. 125–144.

45. For more detailed discussions of these schools of thought see Mats Alvesson and Stanley A. Deetz, "Critical Theory and Postmodernism Approaches to Organizational Studies," in *Handbook of Organizational Studies*, ed. S. Clegg, C. Harding, and W. Nord (London: Sage, 1996), pp. 173–202; Douglas Kellner, *Media Culture: Cultural Studies, Identity and Politics Between the Modern and the Postmodern* (London: Routledge, 1995); Thomas McCarthy, *Ideals and Illusions: On Reconstruction and Deconstruction in Contemporary Critical Theory* (Cambridge, MA: MIT Press, 1993); Della Pollock and J. Robert Cox, "Historicizing 'Reason': Critical Theory, Practice, and Postmodernity," *Communication Monographs* 58 (1991): 170–178; Donald G. Ellis, "Poststructuralism and Language: Non-Sense," *Communication Monographs* 58 (1991): 213–224; and Michael Huspek, "Taking Aim on Habermas's Critical Theory: On the Road Toward a Critical Hermeneutics," *Communication Monographs* 58 (1991): 225–233.

46. For a good description and critique of postmodern media studies, see John B. Harms and David R. Dickens, "Postmodern Media Studies: Analysis or Symptom," *Critical Studies in Mass Communication* 13 (1996): 210–227.

47. For a brief overview of the movement, see Rogers, *A History of Communication Study*, pp. 102–128; Tom Bottomore and Armand Mattelart, "Marxist Theories of Communication," in *International Encyclopedia of Communications*, vol. 2, ed. Erik Barnouw (New York: Oxford University Press, 1989), pp. 476–483. For coverage of a variety of Marxist-based ideas, see Cary Nelson and Lawrence Grossberg, eds., *Marxism and the Interpretation of Culture* (Urbana: University of Illinois Press, 1988).

48. Karl Marx's best-known works are *The Communist Manifesto* (London: Reeves, 1888) and *Capital* (Chicago: Kerr, 1909).

49. For a discussion of capitalist oppression as the basis for critical theory, see Graham Murdock, "Across the Great Divide: Cultural Analysis and the Condition of Democracy," *Critical Studies in Mass Communication* 12 (1995): 89–95.

50. For a brief discussion of theories of ideology, see Stuart Hall, "Ideology," in *International Encyclopedia of Communications*, vol. 2, ed. Erik Barnouw (New York: Oxford University Press, 1989), pp. 307–311.

51. Louis Althusser, *For Marx*, trans. B. Brewster (New York: Vintage, 1970); and *Lenin and Philosophy*, trans. B. Brewster (New York: Monthly Review Press, 1971). Althusser's work is summarized by Stuart Hall, "Signification, Representation, Ideology: Althusser and the Post-Structuralist Debates," *Critical Studies in Mass Communication* 2 (1985): 91–114; Dennis K. Mumby, *Communication and Power in Organizations: Discourse, Ideology, and Domination* (Norwood, NJ: Ablex, 1988), pp. 74–78.

52. Antonio Gramsci, *Selections from the Prison Notebooks*, trans. Q. Hoare and G. Nowell Smith (New York: International, 1971). For a brief summary, see Joseph P. Zompetti, "Toward a Gramscian Critical Rhetoric," *Western Journal of Communication* 61 (1997): 66–86.

53. Dana L. Cloud, "The Materiality of Discourse as Oxymoron: A Challenge to Critical Rhetoric," *Western Journal of Communication* 58 (Summer 1994): 141–163. For a more general discussion of the "material," see Momim Rahman and Anne Witz, "What Really Matters? The Elusive Quality of the Material in Feminist Thought," *Feminist Theory* 4 (December 2003): 243–261.

54. Cloud, "The Materiality of Discourse," p. 152.

55. Cloud, "The Materiality of Discourse," p. 154.

56. Cloud, "The Materiality of Discourse," pp. 155–156.

57. Cloud, "The Materiality of Discourse," p. 157.

58. Cloud, "The Materiality of Discourse," p. 158.

59. Michael Huspek, "Toward Normative Theories of Communication with Reference to the Frankfurt School: An Introduction," *Communication Theory* 7 (1997): 265–276. See also Douglas Kellner, "Media Communications vs. Cultural Studies" pp. 162–177.

60. For a brief historical perspective, see Thomas B. Farrell and James A. Aune, "Critical Theory and Communication: A Selective Literature Review," *Quarterly Journal of Speech* 65 (1979): 93–120. See also Andrew Arato and Eike Gebhardt, eds., *The Essential Frankfurt School Reader* (New York: Continuum, 1982).

61. The important works of Habermas include *Postmetaphysical Thinking: Philosophical Essays*, trans. William Mark Hohengarten (Cambridge, MA: MIT Press, 1992); *Knowledge and Human Interests*, trans. J. J. Shapiro (Boston: Beacon, 1971); *Legitimation Crisis*, trans. T. McCarthy (Boston: Beacon, 1975); *The Theory of Communicative Action, Volume 1: Reason and the Rationalization of Society*, trans. T. McCarthy (Boston: Beacon, 1984). For critical commentary, see the special issue of *Communication Theory* 7 (November 1997). Excellent secondary summaries can be found in Thomas B. Farrell, *Norms of Rhetorical Culture* (New Haven, CT: Yale University Press, 1993); Sonja K. Foss, Karen A. Foss, and Robert Trapp, *Contemporary Perspectives on Rhetoric*, 3rd ed. (Prospect Heights, IL: Waveland, 2002); see also Sue Curry Jansen, "Power and Knowledge: Toward a New Critical Synthesis," *Journal of Communication* 33 (1983): 342–354; Mumby, *Communication and Power*, pp. 23–54; and Richard L. Lanigan, *Phenomenology of Communication: Merleau-Ponty's Thematics in Communicology and Semiology* (Pittsburgh: Duquesne University Press, 1988), pp. 75–99.

62. Steven D. Ealy, *Communication, Speech, and Politics: Habermas and Political Analysis* (Washington, DC: University Press of America, 1981).

63. See especially Habermas, *Legitimation Crisis*.

64. This emphasis on communication competence takes a major step away from the earlier Frankfurt scholars, who emphasized social and economic structure as the root of oppression. For a good discussion of the differences between Habermas and other members of the Frankfurt School in this regard, see William Fusfield, "Communication Without Constellation? Habermas's Argumentative Turn in (and Away from) Critical Theory," *Communication Theory* 7 (1997): 301–320.

65. For discussions of the transformative potential of feminism, see Sonja K. Foss, Cindy L. Griffin, and Karen A. Foss, "Transforming Rhetoric Through Feminist Reconstruction: A Response to the Gender-Diversity Perspective," *Women's Studies in Communication* 20 (1997): 117–136.

66. For some articulations of women's systems, see Carol Gilligan, *In a Different Voice* (Cambridge, MA: Harvard University Press, 1982); and Anne Wilson Schaef, *Women's Reality: An Emerging Female System in the White Male Society* (Minneapolis, MN: Winston Press, 1981). Although few would claim that there is an essential or monolithic female experience, a set of perspectives have been characterized as feminist in much of the literature. These include, for example, a sense of interdependence and relationship, the legitimacy of emotionality, fusion of public and private realms of experience, egalitarian values, concern for process over product, and openness to multiple ways of seeing and doing. For a discussion of women's forms of expression outside the traditional communication field, see Karen A. Foss and Sonja K. Foss, *Women Speak: The Eloquence of Women's Lives* (Prospect Heights, IL: Waveland, 1991).

67. Feminism has long been concerned with the exclusion of women's voices from virtually every aspect of society, both literally—as in the denial of the right to read, speak, vote, and the like—to more abstract denials implicit in a privileging of the masculine. For an early exploration of everyday discursive practices especially significant to women's lives, see Bettina Aptheker, *Tapestries of Life: Women's Work, Women's Consciousness, and the Meaning of Daily Experience* (Amherst: University of Massachusetts Press, 1989). A more contemporary essay that addresses marginalized discourses is John M. Sloop and Kent A. Ono, "Out-Law Discourse: The Critical Politics of Material Judgment," *Philosophy and Rhetoric* 30 (1997): 50–69; the authors define out-law discourses as "found in the vernacular, the practice of everyday life, and oppose or are separate from dominant discourses" (p. 60).

68. For a discussion of feminism and the issue of difference, see Bonnie J. Dow, "Feminism, Difference(s), and Rhetorical Studies," *Communication Studies* 46 (Spring-Summer 1995): 106–117.

69. As an example of a feminist/womanist challenge, see Marsha Houston and Olga Idriss Davis, eds., *Centering Ourselves: African American Feminist and Womanist Studies of Discourse* (Creskill, NJ: Hampton Press, 2002).

70. For a readable overview, see Ben Agger, *Cultural Studies as Critical Theory* (London: Falmer, 1992). See also the review essay by Thomas Rosteck, "Cultural Studies and Rhetorical Studies," *Quarterly Journal of Speech* 81 (1995): 386–421; Kellner, "Media Communications vs. Cultural Studies."

71. Richard Hoggart, *Uses of Literacy* (London: Chatto & Windus, 1957); Raymond Williams, *The Long Revolution* (New York: Columbia University Press, 1961).

72. For a good survey of the work of Hall and others at the Centre, see Stuart Hall, Dorothy Hobson, Andrew Lowe, and Paul Willis, eds., *Culture, Media, Language* (London: Hutchinson, 1981). See also Stuart Hall, "Cultural Studies: Two Paradigms," in *Media, Culture, and Society: A Critical Reader,* ed. R. Collins (London: Sage, 1986); and Hall, "Signification, Representation, Ideology." Four secondary treatments are especially helpful: Anne Makus, "Stuart Hall's Theory of Ideology: A Frame for Rhetorical Criticism," *Western Journal of Speech Communication* 54 (1990): 495–514; Ronald Lembo and Kenneth H. Tucker, "Culture, Television, and Opposition: Rethinking Cultural Studies," *Critical Studies in Mass Communication* 7 (1990): 97–116; Samuel L. Becker, "Marxist Approaches to Media Studies: The British Experience," *Critical Studies in Mass Communication* 1 (1984): 66–80; and Robert White, "Mass Communication and Culture: Transition to a New Paradigm," *Journal of Communication* 33 (1983): 279–301.

73. Murdock, "Across the Great Divide."

74. Becker, "Marxist Approaches," p. 67.

75. This point is explained in greater detail by Ian Angus, "The Politics of Common Sense: Articulation Theory and Critical Communication Studies," in *Communication Yearbook 15*, ed. Stanley Deetz (Newbury Park, CA: Sage, 1992), pp. 535–570.

76. Hall, "Cultural Studies," p. 36.

77. This problem and other issues facing the cultural studies program are discussed in Hall, "Cultural Studies," pp. 15–47.

78. Hall, "Signification, Representation, Ideology," p. 104.

79. This point is explored and challenged by Kevin M. Carragee, "A Critical Evaluation of the Media Hegemony Thesis," *Western Journal of Communication* 57 (1993): 330–348.

80. Becker, "Marxist Approaches," p. 72.

81. This idea is explored in more detail by Poonam Pillai, "Rereading Stuart Hall's Encoding/Decoding Model," *Communication Theory* 2 (1992): 221–233.
82. Lembo and Tucker, "Culture, Television, and Opposition," p. 100.
83. Lawrence Grossberg, "Is There Rock After Punk?" *Critical Studies in Mass Communication* 3 (1986): 50–73.
84. Grossberg, "Is There Rock After Punk?" p. 55.
85. Grossberg, "Is There Rock After Punk?" p. 53.
86. Grossberg, "Is There Rock After Punk?" p. 62.
87. See, for example, Sue Thornham, *Feminist Theory and Cultural Studies: Stories of Unsettled Relations* (London: Arnold, 2000).
88. Terry Lovell, "Introduction: Feminist Criticism and Cultural Studies," in *British Feminist Thought: A Reader*, ed. Terry Lovell (Oxford: Blackwell, 1990), pp. 271–280.
89. Fern L. Johnson and Karren Young, "Gendered Voices in Children's Television Advertising," *Critical Studies in Media Communication* 19 (2002): 461–480.
90. Johnson and Young, "Gendered Voices," p. 478.
91. bell hooks's definition of feminism is one example of the call to take interlocking oppressions into account: "to be 'feminist' in any authentic sense of the term is to want for all people, female and male, liberation from sexist role patterns, domination, and oppression." Thus feminism "directs our attention to systems of domination and the inter-relatedness of sex, race, and class oppression." See bell hooks, *Feminist Theory: From Margin to Center* (Boston: South End Press, 1984), p. 31.
92. For a discussion of feminism's "interruption" of cultural studies, see Thornham, *Feminist Theory and Cultural Studies*, pp. 184–186.
93. For a history of CRT, see Richard Delgado and Jean Stefancic, *Critical Race Theory: An Introduction* (New York: New York University Press, 2001), pp. 1–6.
94. Delgado and Stefancic, *Critical Race Theory*, p. 7.
95. Delgado and Stefancic, *Critical Race Theory*, pp. 8–9.
96. Mark L. McPhail, *The Rhetoric of Racism* (Lanham, MD: University Press of America, 1994), p. 8.
97. For a discussion of the color-blind/color-conscious dilemma and the "rights" dilemma, see Delgado and Stefancic, *Critical Race Theory*, pp. 20–24.
98. For a discussion of how contradictory narratives functioned in California's Proposition 187 debate and how they could be interpreted from a CRT perspective, see Marouf Hasian, Jr. and Fernando Delgado, "The Trials and Tribulations of Racialized Critical Rhetorical Theory: Understanding the Rhetorical Ambiguities of Proposition 187," *Communication Theory* 8 (August 1998): 245–270.
99. Delgado and Stefancic, *Critical Race Theory*, p. 75.
100. Delgado and Stefancic, *Critical Race Theory*, p. 77.
101. Thomas K. Nakayama and Lisa N. Peñaloza, "Madonna T/Races: Music Videos Through the Prism of Color," in *The Madonna Connection: Representational Politics, Subcultural Identities, and Cultural Theory*, ed. Cathy Schwichtenberg (Boulder, CO: Westview, 1993), p. 54.
102. Thomas K. Nakayama and Robert L. Krizek, "Whiteness: A Strategic Rhetoric," *Quarterly Journal of Speech* 81 (August 1995): 291–309. For other treatments of whiteness, see Thomas K. Nakayama and Judith N. Martin, eds., *Whiteness: The Communication of Social Identity* (Thousand Oaks, CA: Sage, 1999); Roberto Avant-Mier and Marouf Hasian, Jr., "In Search of the Power of Whiteness: A Genealogical Exploration of Negotiated Racial Identities in America's Ethnic Past," *Communication Quarterly* 50 (Summer/Fall 2002): 391–409; and Alberto González and JoBeth González, "The Color Problem in Sillyville: Negotiating White Identity in One Popular 'Kid-Vid,'" *Communication Quarterly* 50 (Summer/Fall 2002): 410–421.
103. Nakayama and Krizek, "Whiteness," p. 300.
104. Nakayama and Krizek, "Whiteness," p. 302.
105. For a good background discussion of this movement, see Jonathan Potter, *Representing Reality: Discourse, Rhetoric and Social Construction* (London: Sage, 1996), pp. 68–96.
106. Foucault's primary works on this subject include *The Archaeology of Knowledge,* trans. A. M. Sheridan Smith (New York: Pantheon, 1972); *The Order of Things: An Archaeology of the Human Sciences* (New York: Pantheon, 1970); and *Power/Knowledge: Selected Interviews and Other Writings 1927–1977,* trans. Colin Gordon and others, ed. Colin Gordon (New York: Pantheon, 1980). For an excellent short summary, see Foss, Foss, and Trapp, *Contemporary Perspectives on Rhetoric.* See also Carole Blair, "The Statement: Foundation of Foucault's Historical Criticism," *Western Journal of Speech Communication* 51 (1987): 364–383; Sonja K. Foss and Ann Gill, "Michel Foucault's Theory of Rhetoric as Epistemic," *Western Journal of Speech Communication* 51 (1987): 384–402; and Nancy Fraser, *Unruly Practices: Power, Discourse, and Gender in Contemporary Social Theory* (Minneapolis: University of Minnesota Press, 1989).
107. Martha Cooper, "Rhetorical Criticism and Foucault's Philosophy of Discursive Events," *Central States Speech Journal* 39 (1988): 1–17.
108. Foucault, *The Order of Things*, p. xxii.

109. Michel Foucault, *Discipline and Punish: The Birth of the Prison*, trans. A. Sheridan (New York: Vintage, 1979).

110. Raka Shome, "Postcolonial Interventions in the Rhetorical Canon: An 'Other' View," in *Contemporary Rhetorical Theory: A Reader*, ed. John Louis Lucaites, Celeste Michelle Condit, and Sally Caudill (New York: Guilford, 1999), p. 593.

111. Edward Said, *Orientalism* (New York: Random House, 1978), p. 41.

112. Said, *Orientalism*, p. 32.

113. Arif Dirlik, "Culturalism as Hegemonic Ideology and Liberating Practice," in A. JanMohamed and D. Lloyd, eds., *The Nature and Context of Minority Discourse* (New York: Oxford University Press, 1990), pp. 394–431.

114. Marwan M. Kraidy, "Hybridity in Cultural Globalization," *Communication Theory* 12 (2002): 316–339.

115. Gloria Anzaldúa, *Borderlands/La Frontera: The New Mestiza* (San Francisco: Aunt Lute, 1978), p. 9.

116. Raka Shome and Radha S. Hegde, "Postcolonial Approaches to Communication: Charting the Terrain, Engaging the Intersections," *Communication Theory* 12 (August 2002): 252.

117. Shome, "Postcolonial Interventions," p. 596.

118. Gayatri Spivak, *The Postcolonial Critic*, ed. S. Harasym (New York: Routledge, 1990), p. 51.

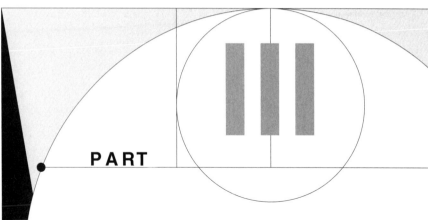

INTEGRATION

12 MAKING THEORIES PERSONAL

MAKING THEORIES PERSONAL

Upon finishing this book, you may feel that you have been assaulted by a limitless list of theories and a pile of names that boggle the mind and stuff the brain. Rather than using these unfortunate metaphors, we encourage you to take a different view, to find another metaphor that helps you put what you have read in some kind of larger perspective.

Try thinking about communication theory as a prism. Using this metaphor, communication becomes a multifaceted process that impacts and is understood in terms of many contexts, some narrow and some broad. You can look at a prism from any of its sides, peer into it, and watch various reflections come off the surface as you turn it at different angles. Like a prism, communication theory absorbs insight and reflects it back in colorful and interesting ways. Communication theory, then, can be a way to see many possibilities for how to think about and study communication, discover and understand how various theories correlate with and reflect one another, and gain insight into which facets of communication you prefer.

Or maybe a project metaphor works for you. Instead of thinking of communication theories as discrete bits of data produced by individual scholars, think of the field as a collaborative building effort. What may look now like a coherent structure—an edifice, a building—is in fact the result of decades of particular efforts to hammer out explanations for communication processes. But each of these efforts builds on other pieces and those connect to yet other structures. The end result is something that looks like a single whole. The project is really never finished, though, as much as we can make it appear to be a sturdy edifice through how we organize and talk about it at any given time. Even as you read this, scholars are contributing new ideas to the project that is communication theory, and these will ultimately change the shape of the edifice as the years go by.

A metaphor we particularly like for thinking about communication theory is the metaphor of exploration. Imagine all of the theories described in this book as having been discovered during an exploration or adventure. Think of communication—all of those aspects that make up the complicated processes involved in human symbol use—as a countryside with several major trails and many minor ones. These trails meander in many directions, looping around, crossing one another, diverging again and again. Each trail has numerous side pathways that also link up, creating a maze of possible paths to take. Over time, some pathways will eventually come to be marked by deep ruts caused by heavy traffic, while others are less traveled and even overgrown and hard to find any more.

As an explorer or scholar of communication, you set off on one pathway and may find you stay with that, not deviating much onto smaller trails. Or you may find yourself turning from your original path to take a less traveled trail that, for some reason, catches your attention. Or perhaps you choose to hike off-trail, forging new trails and pathways for others to follow.

As we wander around exploring, we notice features of each trail that tell us something about the countryside itself. Sometimes we stop and study one feature for a while, and sometimes we notice how features are connected to or reflect one another.

As a beginning scholar of communication—perhaps on your first visit to this countryside—you will probably start walking down whatever trail happens to be in front of you until you see something intriguing and turn off to see what it is. After some time, you will have favorite trails that you revisit often, and you may find that in a while, there are some parts of the landscape that you no longer enter. You will also find that you tend to focus on some features of the landscape and not others. Some of you will look at landforms and geological structures—larger parts of theory. Others of you will be concerned with specifics within the landscape itself—the flowers growing there, for instance. Yet others might choose to focus on how climate and weather affect the landscape and how the relationships among features affect one another.

Each of these choices is not unlike how scholars choose to focus within the grand landscape that is communication theory. Some study smaller

units, others larger ones, and yet others the connections among theories. Each of these kinds of investigations is necessary for understanding the landscape as a whole, but it is impossible for any one person to undertake them all.

If you come to love this countryside, you might even write a guidebook to help others explore this terrain. Maybe the best way to think of our book, *Theories of Human Communication*, is as just such a guidebook, offering a coherent look at the field. It becomes a metadiscourse—communication about communication—that identifies the major trails within the discipline, maps where the trails of the terrain cross and where they diverge, and indicates where the newest trails are likely to be found. In writing this guidebook, we had to make choices about how to approach that landscape.

After pursuing several trails, we ended up adopting Robert Craig's model of communication theory. Craig, in trying to find a way to organize the field as a whole, generated a perspective that incorporates dialogue about (1) the nature of communication; (2) what is important to the field; and (3) how we might examine the particulars about communication.[1] Craig provided a way to start this dialogue. He identified seven traditions that have contributed to our understanding of communication. Although this is certainly not the only way to think of the field, we found Craig's traditions a helpful starting point for identifying the similarities and differences among the assumptions, focal points, and methods that characterize communication as a field.[2] We have related Craig's traditions to various contexts for viewing communication, which, taken as a whole, can provide an excellent summary of theories, along with a better understanding of how to think about communication.

Indeed, the goal of this book is to provide a dual learning: (1) learning about communication; and (2) learning various ways to think about the subject. Table 12.1 is a sampler of ideas and the theories that have helped to develop those ideas; we hope it will serve as a reminder of the important aspects of communication landscape that we have covered. Table 12.2 summarizes important

TABLE **12.1**

An Idea Sampler

Topic	Semiotic	Phenomenological	Cybernetic	Sociopsychological	Sociocultural	Critical
Communicator			Information processing Information integration Cognitive dissonance Beliefs, attitudes, and values	Traits and factors Biological influences Attribution Social judgment Elaboration likelihood	Self	Identity politics Standpoint Gender and sex
Message	Signs and symbols Meaning Language Nonverbal behavior	Textual interpretation Text and tradition		Action assembly Planning Strategy choice Message design Connotative meaning	Speech acts Identification Gender	
Conversation			Coordinated meaning and action	Uncertainty and anxiety reduction Accommodation and adaptation Expectancy violations Interpersonal deception	Symbolic interaction Symbolic convergence Conversational maxims Conversational sequencing Conversational rationality Conversational argument Face negotiation	Language and culture Invitational rhetoric
Relationship		Congruence Dialogue	Relational patterns	Family schemas Family types Social penetration	Dialogics Dialectics Privacy management	
Group			Bona fide groups Input-process-output Interaction analysis Intercultural effectiveness	Interpersonal behavior	Structuration Group functions Groupthink	

Topic	Semiotic	Phenomenological	Cybernetic	Sociopsychological	Sociocultural	Critical
Organization			Organizing Equivocality Networks	Bureaucracy Participative management	Organizational text Structuration Concertive control Organizational culture	Organizational hegemony Managerialism Organizational democracy Gender and race
Media	Media signs Simulation		Public opinion Spiral of silence	Media effects Uses and gratifications Media dependency Cultivation	Medium Agenda-setting Media communities	Domination
Society and Culture	Linguistic relativity Elaborated and restricted codes	Cultural interpretation	Networks Diffusion		Speech community Cultural codes Cultural performance	Political economy Ideal speech situation Liberal and radical feminism Cultural productions Race Archeology Colonization

Thinking about Communication

Context	Approach	Description	Contributing Traditions	Key Questions
The communicator	The autonomous individual	The communicator is a unique individual with particular characteristics, determined partially by genetics. Individuals have complex minds that organize information into attitudes, beliefs, and values, which in turn affect behavior.	Cybernetic Sociopsychological	What mechanisms make a person think and act a certain way?
	Self identity	The communicator is a person with a conscious sense of identity, a "self" that is developed through interaction. Individuals are positioned in a social fabric of culture and power relations.	Sociocultural Critical	How does personal identity embody social affiliations and relationships?
The message	Interpretation of texts	Messages are texts, or organized sets of signs, that have meaning for communicators.	Semiotic Phenomenological	How does meaning arise?
	Message production	Individuals produce messages strategically to achieve goals.	Sociopsychological	How are messages formed in the minds of communicators?
	Social function	Messages accomplish social functions that bring people together into relationships of various kinds.	Sociocultural	What do messages achieve?
The conversation	Individual behavior	Conversations consist of individual social behavior.	Sociopsychological	How do individuals behave in social situations?
	Coordinated social action	Conversations are processes in which communicators coordinate, or organize, interaction in ways that create coherent patterns of meaning.	Cybernetic Sociocultural	What gets made in conversations?
	Cultural productions	Power relations are enacted through the use of language in conversations.	Critical	What are the consequences of conversational forms on the treatment of individuals and groups?

Context	Approach	Description	Contributing Traditions	Key Questions
The relationship	Patterns of interaction	Relationships are defined by patterns of interaction.	Cybernetic Sociopsychological	How is a relationship structured?
	Management of tension	Relationships involve the management of opposing forces in a way that provides a sense of coherence and wholeness.	Cybernetic Sociocultural	What makes a relationship dynamic?
	Dialogue	Good relationships are characterized by a healthy view of self and other.	Phenomenological	What is a healthy relationship?
Groups and organizations	Process of organizing	Groups and organizations are created through interaction.	Cybernetic Sociopsychological Sociocultural	How do groups and organizations develop?
	Structuration	Group and organizational action lead to unintended consequences that structure future effort	Cybernetic Sociocultural Critical	What are the consequences of inter-action in groups and organizations?
The media	Cultural production	Media create cultural forms and influence social structure.	Semiotic Sociocultural Critical	How do media influence society?
	Media participation	The media and the community respond to one another, leading to outcomes that are consequential to the media, to individuals, and to communities.	Cybernetic Sociocultural Sociopsychological	How do audiences and media affect one another?
	Individual effects	Media affect individual behavior.	Sociopsychological	What are the personal effects of media communication?
Society and culture	Power of symbols	Society and culture are largely shaped by the use of language and other symbolic forms.	Semiotic Sociocultural Critical	How does language affect culture?
	Personal networks	Society is organized by a complex system of personal networks.	Cybernetic	How are groups, institutions, and communities comprised?
	Cultural forms	Cultures are distinguished by unique ways of being, reflected in and produced by symbolic forms and cultural practices.	Phenomenological Sociocultural	What is culture?

core concepts within each of the traditions as they intersect with various contexts. We hope this table will serve as a reminder of the basic ideas that guide the theories within each section of the field. The first table, to continue our metaphor, tracks various trails that have been most often taken in the field; the second table develops some of the features of those trails—features that help distinguish one trail from another.

As you look at these tables, we offer some generalizations that may be helpful in looking at the terrain of the discipline as a whole:

1. **Notice that no tradition contributes to every aspect of communication.** For example, the sociopsychological tradition has been very powerful in addressing many aspects of communication, but it has said little about society and culture. The phenomenological tradition has been somewhat limited in its contribution to communication theory, at least directly; yet, its ideas about interpretation have been vital in helping us understand texts of all kinds and in the interpretation of culture.

2. **The traditions are not mutually exclusive.** Indeed, they have influenced one another and overlap in significant ways. Notice, for example, that the semiotic, phenomenological, sociocultural, and critical traditions seem to cluster together at points in their shared concern for the power of symbols, the importance of human experience and interpretation, and, at least in communication theory, their mutual regard for the centrality of social relations. Even unexpected affinities sometimes arise, so that, for example, the cybernetic and sociopsychological traditions occasionally merge.

3. **Still, each tradition does have its distinctive character, and in some cases, they even repel one another.** The sociopsychological and sociocultural occasionally touch, but rarely. The critical and sociopsychological traditions would certainly never be found on the same trail, and the cybernetic and semiotic rarely come together. In these cases, the basic assumptions that drive the traditions are essentially incompatible.

4. **As you switch contexts, different traditions assume value.** Because communication is multicontextual, each tradition has value in helping us understand similarities and differences across context. It is quite understandable, for example, why the context of the communicator is well dominated by the psychological perspective, at least in our highly individualized Western tradition. Yet, as the context broadens to include increasingly larger social structures, the sociopsychological begins to lose power.

5. **Even though traditions do not distribute themselves equally across contexts, neither are they limited to a narrow range of concerns.** Critical theory, for example, which has much to say about broad social structures, also contributes to our understanding of individual communicators as the embodiment of political identity. Even the sociopsychological tradition, which applies most clearly to individuals, has something to say about groups, organizations, and even the media in terms of the role of psychology in social entities.

In the end, then, we think it more productive for you to spend some time thinking about how to think about communication than to contemplate the long list of theories and concepts you have encountered in the previous chapters. We want you to realize that any time you think about communication, you must have a perspective, which will be influenced, in part, by the kinds of questions you are asking and the traditions that frame those questions, your academic aptitudes, your life experiences, and your goals. Once you begin to look through a certain lens, you reify what you see, you reproduce it, and you elaborate it.

This is exactly how traditions of communication theory are developed and sustained: Cadres of devoted scholars initially found a certain way of thinking attractive, assimilated this thinking into their way of working, and developed a way of understanding what they experienced. We know that as you explore communication theory, you will also make connections and contributions of your own as you navigate this terrain, come to appreciate some theories over others, and find they work for you in explaining how you see the world. And throughout this process, you will be collaborating with many others in helping to develop the field of communication.

▌◖ NOTES

1. Robert T. Craig, "Communication Theory as a Field," *Communication Theory* 9 (1999): 119–161.
2. As explained in Chapter 3, we do not pursue the rhetorical tradition in this book because it often forms a study of its own and is most frequently explored separately in other courses.

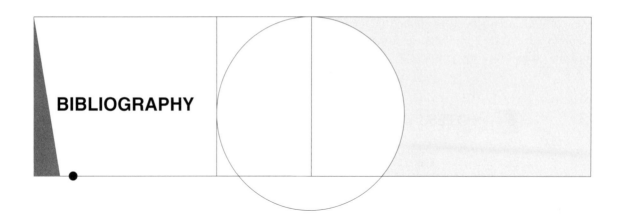

BIBLIOGRAPHY

Chapter 1: Communication Theory and Scholarship

Andersen, Peter A. "When One Cannot Not Communicate: A Challenge to Motley's Traditional Communication Postulates." *Communication Studies* 42 (1991): 309–325.

Anderson, James A. *Communication Theory: Epistemological Foundations.* New York: Guilford, 1996.

Asante, Molefi K. *Afrocentricity: The Theory of Social Change.* Trenton, NJ: Africa World Press, 1988.

Asante, Molefi K. "An Afrocentric Communication Theory." In *Contemporary Rhetorical Theory: A Reader*, edited by John L. Lucaites, Celeste M. Condit, and Sally Caudill, 552–562. New York: Guilford Press, 1999.

Atwater, Tony. "Communication Theory and Research: The Quest for Credibility in the Social Sciences." In *An Integrated Approach to Communication Theory*, edited by M. B. Salwen and D. W. Stacks, 539–549. Mahwah, NJ: Lawrence Erlbaum, 1996.

Barnlund, Dean. *Interpersonal Communication: Survey and Studies.* New York: Houghton Mifflin, 1968.

Bavelas, Janet Beavin. "Behaving and Communicating: A Reply to Motley." *Western Journal of Speech Communication* 54 (1990): 593–602.

Beach, Wayne A. "On (Not) Observing Behavior Interactionally." *Western Journal of Speech Communication* 54 (1990): 603–612.

Berelson, Bernard, and Gary Steiner. *Human Behavior.* New York: Harcourt, Brace, and World, 1964.

Berger, Charles R., and Steven H. Chaffee. "The Study of Communication as a Science." In *Handbook of Communication Science*, edited by Charles R. Berger and Steven H. Chaffee. Newbury Park, CA: Sage, 1987.

Blair, Carole, Julie R. Brown, and Leslie A. Baxter. "Disciplining the Feminine." *Quarterly Journal of Speech* 80 (1994): 383–409.

Blalock, Hubert M. *Basic Dilemmas in the Social Sciences.* Beverly Hills, CA: Sage, 1984.

Bormann, Ernest G. *Theory and Research in the Communicative Arts.* New York: Holt, Rinehart & Winston, 1965.

Bowers, John Waite, and James J. Bradac. "Issues in Communication Theory: A Metatheoretical Analysis." In *Communication Yearbook 5*, edited by Michael Burgoon, 1–28. New Brunswick, NJ: Transaction, 1982.

Brinberg, David, and Joseph E. McGrath. *Validity and the Research Process.* Beverly Hills, CA: Sage, 1985.

Bross, B. J. *Design for Decision.* New York: Macmillan, 1952.

Burrell, G., and G. Morgan. *Sociological Paradigms and Organizational Analysis.* London: Heinemann, 1979.

Cappella, Joseph N., ed. "Symposium on Mass and Interpersonal Communication." *Human Communication Research* 15 (1988): 236–318.

Chen, G-M. "Toward Transcultural Understanding: A Harmony Theory of Chinese Communication." In *Transcultural Realities: Interdisciplinary Perspectives on Cross-cultural Relations*, edited by V. H. Milhouse, M. K. Asante, and P. O. Nwosu, 55–70. Thousand Oaks, CA: Sage, 2001.

Clevenger, Jr., Theodore. "Can One Not Communicate? A Conflict of Models." *Communication Studies* 42 (1991): 340–353.

Cohen, Jonathan, and Miriam Metzger. "Social Affiliation and the Achievement of Ontological Security Through Interpersonal and Mass Communication." *Critical Studies in Mass Communication* 15 (1998): 41–60.

Craig, Robert T. "Communication as a Practical Discipline." In *Rethinking Communication: Paradigm Issues*, edited by Brenda Dervin, Lawrence Grossberg, Barbara J. O'Keefe, and Ellen Wartella, 97–122. Newbury Park, CA: Sage, 1989.

Craig, Robert T. "Communication Theory as a Field." *Communication Theory* 9 (1999): 119–161.

Craig, Robert T. "Why Are There So *Many* Communication Theories?" *Journal of Communication* 43 (1993): 26–33.

Craig, Robert T., and Karen Tracy. "Grounded Practical Theory: The Case of Intellectual Discussion." *Communication Theory* 5 (1995): 248–272.

Cronen, Vernon E. "Practical Theory, Practical Art, and the Pragmatic-Systemic Account of Inquiry." *Communication Theory* 11 (2001): 14–35.

Dallmayr, Fred R. *Language and Politics.* Notre Dame, IN: University of Notre Dame Press, 1984.

Dance, Frank E. X. "The 'Concept' of Communication." *Journal of Communication* 20 (1970): 201–210.

Dance, Frank E. X., and Carl E. Larson. *The Functions of Human Communication: A Theoretical Approach.* New York: Holt, Rinehart & Winston, 1976.

Deetz, Stanley A. "Future of the Discipline: The Challenges, the Research, and the Social Contribution." In *Communication Yearbook 17,* edited by Stanley A. Deetz, 565–600. Thousand Oaks, CA: Sage, 1994.

Deetz, Stanley A. "Describing Differences in Approaches to Organization Science." *Organization Science* 7 (1996): 191–207.

Delia, Jesse G. "Communication Research: A History." In *Handbook of Communication Science,* edited by Charles R. Berger and Steven H. Chaffee, 20–98. Newbury Park, CA: Sage, 1987.

DePaulo, Bella M., Matthew E. Ansfield, and Kathy L. Bell. "Theories About Deception and Paradigms for Studying It: A Critical Appraisal of Buller and Burgoon's Interpersonal Deception Theory and Research." *Communication Theory* 6 (1996): 297–311.

Deutsch, Karl W. "On Communication Models in the Social Sciences." *Public Opinion Quarterly* 16 (1952): 362–363.

Diefenbeck, James A. *A Celebration of Subjective Thought.* Carbondale: Southern Illinois University Press, 1984.

Dissanayake, Wimal. *Communication Theory: The Asian Perspective.* Singapore: Asian Mass Communication Research and Information Center, 1988.

Dissanayake, Wimal. "The Need for the Study of Asian Approaches to Communication," *Media Asia* 13 (1986): 6–13.

Ellis, Donald G. *Crafting Society: Ethnicity, Class, and Communication Theory.* Mahwah, NJ: Lawrence Erlbaum, 1999.

Farrell, Thomas B. "Beyond Science: Humanities Contributions to Communication Theory." In *Handbook of Communication Science,* edited by Charles R. Berger and Steven H. Chaffee, 123–139. Newbury Park, CA: Sage, 1987.

Fiske, Donald W., and Richard A. Shweder, eds. "Introduction: Uneasy Social Science." In *Metatheory in Social Science: Pluralisms and Subjectivities.* Chicago: University of Chicago Press, 1986.

Fortner, Robert. "Mediated Communication Theory." In *Building Communication Theories: A Socio/Cultural Approach,* edited by Fred L. Casmir, 209–240. Hillsdale, NJ: Lawrence Erlbaum, 1994.

Friedrich, Gustav W., and Don M. Boileau. "The Communication Discipline." In *Teaching Communication,* edited by Anita L. Vangelisti, John A. Daly, and Gustav Friedrich, 3–13. Mahwah, NJ: Lawrence Erlbaum, 1999.

Giddens, Anthony. *Profiles and Critiques in Social Theory.* Berkeley: University of California Press, 1983.

Glazer, Nathan. "The Social Sciences in Liberal Education." In *The Philosophy of the Curriculum,* edited by S. Hook, 145–158. Buffalo: Prometheus, 1975.

Grossberg, Lawrence. "Does Communication Theory Need Intersubjectivity? Toward an Immanent Philosophy of Interpersonal Relations." In *Communication Yearbook 6,* edited by Michael Burgoon, 171–205. Beverly Hills, CA: Sage, 1984.

Hall, Calvin S., and Lindzey Gardner. *Theories of Personality.* New York: Wiley, 1970.

Hanson, N. R. *Patterns of Discovery.* Cambridge: Cambridge University Press, 1961.

Harper, Nancy. *Human Communication Theory: The History of a Paradigm.* Rochelle Park, NJ: Hayden, 1979.

Hawkins, Robert P., John M. Wiemann, and Suzanne Pingree, eds. *Advancing Communication Science.* Newbury Park, CA: Sage, 1988.

Holton, Gerald. "Science, Science Teaching, and Rationality." In *The Philosophy of the Curriculum,* edited by S. Hook, 101–108. Buffalo: Prometheus, 1975.

Jarrett, James L. *The Humanities and Humanistic Education.* Reading, MA: Addison-Wesley, 1973.

Kincaid, Lawrence D. *Communication Theory: Eastern and Western Perspectives.* San Diego: Academic, 1987.

Krippendorff, Klaus. "Conversation or Intellectual Imperialism in Comparing Communication (Theories)." *Communication Theory* 3 (1993): 252–266.

Kuhn, Thomas S. *The Structure of Scientific Revolutions.* Chicago: University of Chicago Press, 1970.

Littlejohn, Stephen W. "An Overview of the Contributions to Human Communication Theory from Other Disciplines." In *Human Communication Theory: Comparative Essays,* edited by Frank E. X. Dance, 243–285. New York: Harper and Row, 1982.

Miike, Yoshitaka. "Japanese *Enryo-Sasshi* Communication and the Psychology of *Amae:* Reconsideration and Reconceptualization." *Keio Communication Review* 25 (2003): 3–25.

Miike, Yoshitaka. "Theorizing Culture and Communication in the Asian Context: An Assumptive Foundation." *Intercultural Communication Studies* 11 (2002): 1–21.

Miller, Gerald R., and Henry Nicholson. *Communication Inquiry.* Reading, MA: Addison-Wesley, 1976.

Monge, Peter R. "Communication Theory for a Globalizing World." In *Communication: Views from the Helm for the 21st Century,* edited by Judith S. Trent, 3–7. Boston: Allyn and Bacon, 1998.

Motley, Michael T. "Communication as Interaction: A Reply to Beach and Bavelas." *Western Journal of Speech Communication* 54 (1990): 613–623.

Motley, Michael T. "How One May Not Communicate: A Reply to Andersen." *Communication Studies* 42 (1991): 326–339.

Motley, Michael T. "On Whether One Can(not) Not Communicate: An Examination Via Traditional Communication Postulates." *Western Journal of Speech Communication* 54 (1990): 1–20.

O'Sullivan, Patrick B. "Bridging the Mass-Interpersonal Divide." *Human Communication Research* 25 (1999): 569–588.

Pearce, W. Barnett. *Communication and the Human Condition.* Carbondale: Southern Illinois University Press, 1989.

Pearce, W. Barnett. "Scientific Research Methods in Communication Studies and Their Implications for Theory and Research." In *Speech Communication in the 20th Century,* edited by Thomas W. Benson, 255–286. Carbondale: Southern Illinois University Press, 1985.

Pearce, W. Barnett, and Karen A. Foss. "The Historical Context of Communication as a Science." In *Human Communication: Theory and Research,* edited by G. L. Dahnke and G. W. Clatterbuck, 1–20. Belmont, CA: Wadsworth, 1990.

Peters, John Durham. "The Gaps of Which Communication Is Made." *Critical Studies in Mass Communication* 11 (1994): 117–140.

Peters, John Durham, "Tangled Legacies." *Journal of Communication* 46 (1996): 85–147.

Powers, John H. "On the Intellectual Structure of the Human Communication Discipline." *Communication Education* 44 (1995): 191–222.

Reardon, Kathleen K., and Emmeline G. dePillis. "Multichannel Leadership: Revisiting the False Dichotomy." In *An Integrated Approach to Communication Theory and Research,* edited by M. B. Salwen and D. W. Stacks, 399–407. Mahwah, NJ: Lawrence Erlbaum, 1996.

Rogers, Everett M. "Anatomy of the Two Subdisciplines of Communication Study." *Human Communication Research* 25 (1999): 618–631.

Rogers, Everett M. *A History of Communication Study: A Biographical Approach.* New York: Free Press, 1994.

Rosengren, Karl Erik. "Culture, Media, and Society: Agency and Structure, Continuity and Change." In *Media Effects and Beyond,* edited by Karl Erik Rosengren, 3–28. London: Routledge, 1994.

Rosengren, Karl Erik. "From Field to Frog Ponds." *Journal of Communication* 43 (1993): 6–17.

Ruesch, Jürgen. "Technology and Social Communication." In *Communication Theory and Research,* edited by L. Thayer. Springfield, IL: Thomas, 1957.

Sigman, Stuart J. "Do Social Approaches to Interpersonal Communication Constitute a Contribution to Communication Theory?" *Communication Theory* 2 (1992): 347–356.

Sholle, David. "Resisting Disciplines: Repositioning Media Studies in the University." *Communication Theory* 5 (1995): 130–143.

Smith III, Ted J. "Diversity and Order in Communication Theory: The Uses of Philosophical Analysis." *Communication Quarterly* 36 (1988): 28–40.

Snow, C. P. *The Two Cultures and a Second Look.* Cambridge: Cambridge University Press, 1964.

Sparks, Glenn G., W. James Potter, Roger Cooper, and Michel Dupagne. "Is Media Research Prescientific?" *Communication Theory* 5 (1995): 273–289.

Stacks, Don W., and Michael B. Salwen. "Integrating Theory and Research: Starting with Questions." In *An Integrated Approach to Communication Theory and Research,* edited by M. B. Salwen and D. W. Stacks, 3–14. Mahwah, NJ: Lawrence Erlbaum, 1996.

Stewart, John. *Language as Articulate Contact.* Albany: SUNY Press, 1995.

Stewart, John. "Speech and Human Being." *Quarterly Journal of Speech* 72 (1986): 55–73.

Stiff, James B. "Theoretical Approaches to the Study of Deceptive Communication: Comments on Interpersonal Deception Theory." *Communication Theory* 6 (1996): 289–296.

Streeter, Thomas. "Introduction: For the Study of Communication and Against the Discipline of Communication." *Communication Theory* 5 (1995): 117–129.

Winch, Peter. *The Idea of a Social Science and Its Relation to Philosophy.* London: Routledge and Kegan Paul, 1958.

Winter, Gibson. *Elements for a Social Ethic: Scientific and Ethical Perspectives on Social Process.* New York: Macmillan, 1966.

Chapter 2: The Idea of Theory

Achinstein, P. *Laws and Explanation.* New York: Oxford University Press, 1971.

Andersen, Peter A. "The Trait Debate: A Critical Examination of the Individual Differences Paradigm in the Communication Sciences." In *Progress in Communication Sciences,* edited by Brenda Dervin and M. J. Voigt. Norwood, NJ: Ablex, 1986.

Anderson, James A. *Communication Theory: Epistemological Foundations.* New York: Guilford, 1996.

Anderson, James A. "Thinking Qualitatively." In *An Integrated Approach to Communication Theory and Research,* edited by M. B. Salwen and D. W. Stacks, 45–59. Mahwah, NJ: Lawrence Erlbaum, 1996.

Austin, J. L. *How to Do Things with Words.* Cambridge, MA: Harvard University Press, 1962.

Austin, J. L. *Philosophy of Language.* Englewood Cliffs, NJ: Prentice-Hall, 1964.

Beatty, Michael J. "Thinking Quantitatively." In *An Integrated Approach to Communication Theory and Research,* edited by M. B. Salwen and D. W. Stacks, 33–44. Mahwah, NJ: Lawrence Erlbaum, 1996.

Beatty, Michael J., and James C. McCroskey. *The Biology of Communication: A Communibiological Perspective.* Cresskill, NJ: Hampton Press, 2001.

Berger, Charles R. "Evidence? For What?" *Western Journal of Communication* 58 (1994): 11–19.

Berger, Peter, and Thomas Luckmann. *The Social Construction of Reality.* Garden City, NY: Doubleday, 1966.

Boster, Franklin J. "On Making Progress in Communication Science." *Human Communication Research* 28 (2002): 473–490.

Bostrom, Robert, and Lewis Donohew. "The Case for Empiricism: Clarifying Fundamental Issues in Communication Theory." *Communication Monographs* 59 (1992): 109–129.

Bowers, John Waite, and James J. Bradac. "Issues in Communication Theory: A Metatheoretical Analysis." In *Communication Yearbook 5,* edited by Michael Burgoon, 1–28. New Brunswick, NJ: Transaction, 1982.

Brummett, Barry. "Some Implications of 'Process' or 'Intersubjectivity': Postmodern Rhetoric." *Philosophy and Rhetoric* 9 (1976): 21–51.

Casmir, Fred L. "The Role of Theory and Theory Building." In *Building Communication Theories: A Socio/Cultural Approach*, edited by Fred. L. Casmir, 7–45. Hillsdale, NJ: Lawrence Erlbaum, 1994.

Chaffee, Steven H. "Thinking About Theory." In *An Integrated Approach to Communication Theory and Research*, edited by M. B. Salwen and D. W. Stacks, 15–32. Mahwah, NJ: Lawrence Erlbaum, 1996.

Craig, Robert T., and Karen Tracy. "Grounded Practical Theory: The Case of Intellectual Discussion." *Communication Theory* 5 (1995): 248–272.

Cronen, Vernon, and Peter Lang. "Language and Action: Wittgenstein and Dewey in the Practice of Therapy and Consultation." *Human Systems: The Journal of Systemic Consultation and Management* 5 (1994): 4–43.

Cushman, Donald P., and W. Barnett Pearce. "Generality and Necessity in Three Types of Theory About Human Communication, with Special Attention to Rules Theory." *Human Communication Research* 3 (1977): 344–353.

Deetz, Stanley A. *Democracy in an Age of Corporate Colonization: Developments in Communication and the Politics of Everyday Life.* Albany: SUNY Press, 1992.

Fay, Brian. *Social Theory and Political Practice.* London: Allen and Unwin, 1975.

Fisher, B. Aubrey. *Perspectives on Human Communication.* New York: Macmillan, 1978.

Gergen, Kenneth J. "The Social Constructionist Movement in Modern Psychology." *American Psychologist* 40 (1985): 266–275.

Gergen, Kenneth J. *Toward Transformation in Social Knowledge.* New York: Springer-Verlag, 1982.

Hamelink, Cees J. "Emancipation or Domestication: Toward a Utopian Science of Communication." *Journal of Communication* 33 (1983): 74–79.

Hanson, N. R. *Patterns of Discovery.* Cambridge: Cambridge University Press, 1961.

Harré, Rom, and Paul F. Secord. *The Explanation of Social Behavior.* Totowa, NJ: Littlefield Adams, 1979.

Houna, Joseph. "Two Ideals of Scientific Theorizing." In *Communication Yearbook 5,* edited by Michael Burgoon, 29–48. New Brunswick, NJ: Transaction, 1982.

Jacobsen, Thomas L. "Theories as Communications." *Communication Theory* 2 (1991): 145–150.

Jensen, Joli. "The Consequences of Vocabularies." *Journal of Communication* 43 (1993): 67–74.

Kaplan, Abraham. *The Conduct of Inquiry.* San Francisco: Chandler, 1964.

Krippendorff, Klaus. "Conversation or Intellectual Imperialism in Comparing Communication (Theories)." *Communication Theory* 3 (1993): 252–266.

Krippendorff, Klaus. "The Past of Communication's Hoped-For Future." *Journal of Communication* 43 (1993) 34–44.

Kuhn, Thomas S. *The Structure of Scientific Revolutions.* 2nd ed. Chicago: University of Chicago Press, 1970.

Leeds-Hurwitz, Wendy, ed. *Social Approaches to Communication.* New York: Guilford, 1995.

Leeds-Hurwitz, Wendy. "Social Approaches to Interpersonal Communication." *Communication Theory* 2 (1992): 131–139.

Littlejohn, Stephen W. "Communication Theory." In *Encyclopedia of Rhetoric and Composition: Communication from Ancient Times to the Information Age,* edited by T. Enos, 117–121. New York: Garland, 1996.

Lustig, Myron W. "Theorizing About Human Communication. "*Communication Quarterly* 34 (1986): 451–459.

MacIntyre, Alasdair. "Ontology." *The Encyclopedia of Philosophy,* Vol. 5, edited by P. Edwards, 542–543. New York: Macmillan, 1967.

Macy, Joanna. *Mutual Causality in Buddhism and General System Theory.* Albany: SUNY Press, 1991.

McLuskie, Ed. "Ambivalence in the 'New Positivism' for the Philosophy of Communication: The Problem of Communication and Communicating Subjects." In *Communication Yearbook 24,* edited by William B. Gudykunst, 255–269. Thousand Oaks, CA: Sage, 2001.

Pavitt, Charles. "The Third Way: Scientific Realism and Communication Theory." *Communication Theory* 9 (1999): 162–188.

Pearce, W. Barnett. "A 'Camper's Guide' to Constructionisms." *Human Systems: The Journal of Systemic Consultation and Management* 3 (1992): 139–161.

Pearce, W. Barnett. "A Sailing Guide for Social Constructionists." In *Social Approaches to Communication,* edited by Wendy Leeds-Hurwitz, 88–113. New York: Guilford, 1995.

Pearce, W. Barnett. "On Comparing Theories: Treating Theories as Commensurate or Incommensurate." *Communication Theory* 2 (1991): 159–164.

Penman, Robyn. "Good Theory and Good Practice: An Argument in Progress." *Communication Theory* 3 (1992): 234–250.

Pepper, Stephen. *World Hypotheses.* Berkeley: University of California Press, 1942.

Polanyi, Michael. *Personal Knowledge.* London: Routledge and Kegan Paul, 1958.

Rapoport, Anatol. "Strategy and Conscience." In *The Human Dialogue: Perspectives on Communication,* edited by F. Matson and A. Montague. New York: Free Press, 1967.

Rorty, Richard. *Philosophy and the Mirror of Nature.* Princeton, NJ: Princeton University Press, 1979.

Rosengren, Karl Erik. "Substantive Theories and Formal Models—Bourdieu Confronted." *European Journal of Communication* 10 (1995): 7–39.

Schutz, Alfred. *The Phenomenology of the Social World.* Translated by George Walsh and Frederick Lehnert. Evanston, IL: Northwestern University Press, 1967.

Secord, Paul F., ed. *Explaining Human Behavior: Consciousness, Human Action, and Social Structure.* Beverly Hills, CA: Sage, 1982.

Shapiro, Michael A. "Generalizability in Communication Research." *Human Communication Research* 28 (2002): 491–500.

Shotter, John. "Before Theory and After Representationalism: Understanding Meaning 'From Within' a Dialogue Process." In *Beyond the Symbol Model: Reflections on the Representational Nature of Language,* edited by John Stewart, 103–134. Albany: SUNY Press, 1996.

Taylor, John R. *Linguistic Categorization: Prototypes in Linguistic Theory.* London: Clarendon Press, 1995.

VanderVoort, Lise. "Functional and Causal Explanations in Group Communication Research," *Communication Theory* 12 (2002): 469–486.

VanLear, C. Arthur. "Dialectical Empiricism: Science and Relationship Metaphors." In *Dialectical Approaches to Studying Personal Relationships,* edited by Barbara M. Montgomery and Leslie A. Baxter, 109–136. Mahwah, NJ: Lawrence Erlbaum, 1998.

von Wright, George H. *Explanation and Understanding.* Ithaca, NY: Cornell University Press, 1971.

Wallace, Walter L. *Sociological Theory: An Introduction.* Chicago: Aldine, 1969.

Williams, Kenneth. "Reflections on a Human Science of Communication." *Journal of Communication* 23 (1973): 239–250.

Chapter 3: Traditions of Communication Theory

Agar, Michael. *Speaking of Ethnography.* Beverly Hills, CA: Sage, 1986.

Aldoory, Linda, and Elizabeth L. Toth. "The Complexities of Feminism in Communication Scholarship Today." In *Communication Yearbook 24,* edited by William B. Gudykunst, 345–361. Thousand Oaks, CA: Sage, 2001.

Anderson, James A. *Communication Theory: Epistemological Foundations.* New York: Guilford, 1996.

Arato, Andrew, and Eike Gebhardt, eds. *The Essential Frankfurt School Reader.* New York: Continuum, 1982.

Ashby, W. Ross. "Principles of the Self-Organizing System." In *Principles of Self-Organization,* edited by H. von Foerster and G. Zopf, 255–278. New York: Pergamon, 1962.

Ashcroft, Bill, Gaareth Griffiths, and Helen Tiffin, eds. *The Post-Colonial Studies Reader.* London: Routledge, 1995.

Atkinson, Paul. *Understanding Ethnographic Texts.* Newbury Park, CA: Sage, 1992.

Bahg, Chang-Gen. "Major Systems Theories Throughout the World." *Behavioral Science* 35 (1990): 79–107.

Bauman, Zygmunt. *Hermeneutics and Social Science.* New York: Columbia University Press, 1978.

Bellah, Robert N., and others. *Habits of the Heart.* Berkeley: University of California Press, 1985.

Berger, Arthur Asa. *Signs in Contemporary Culture: An Introduction to Semiotics.* Salem, WI: Sheffield, 1989.

Berger, Peter L., and Thomas Luckmann. *The Social Construction of Reality: A Treatise in the Sociology of Knowledge.* New York: Doubleday, 1966.

Blumer, Herbert. *Symbolic Interactionism: Perspective and Method.* Englewood Cliffs: NJ: Prentice-Hall, 1969.

Bochner, Arthur P., and Eric M. Eisenberg. "Family Process: System Perspectives." In *Handbook of Communication Science,* edited by Charles R. Berger and Steven H. Chaffee, 540–563. Newbury Park, CA: Sage, 1987.

Bottomore, Tom, and Armand Mattelart. "Marxist Theories of Communication." In *International Encyclopedia of Communications,* Vol. 2, edited by Erik Barnouw, 476–483. New York: Oxford University Press, 1989.

Bourdieu, Pierre. *Language and Symbol Power.* Cambridge, MA: Harvard University Press, 1991.

Bryant, Donald C. "Rhetoric: Its Functions and Its Scope." *Quarterly Journal of Speech* 39 (1953): 401–424.

Burrell, G., and G. Morgan. *Sociological Paradigms and Organizational Analysis.* London: Heinemann, 1979.

Buttny, Richard. "The Ascription of Meaning: A Wittgensteinian Perspective." *Quarterly Journal of Speech* 72 (1986): 261–273.

Button, Graham, ed. *Ethnomethodology and the Human Sciences.* Cambridge: Cambridge University Press, 1991.

Charon, Joel M. *Symbolic Interactionism: An Introduction, an Interpretation, an Integration.* Englewood Cliffs, NJ: Prentice-Hall, 1992.

Craig, Robert T. "Communication Theory as a Field." *Communication Theory* 9 (1999): 119–161.

Dallmayr, Fred R. *Language and Politics.* Notre Dame, IN: University of Notre Dame Press, 1984.

Deetz, Stanley. "Describing Differences in Approaches to Organization Science." *Organization Science* 7 (1996): 191–207.

Deetz, Stanley. "Words Without Things: Toward a Social Phenomenology of Language." *Quarterly Journal of Speech* 59 (1973): 40–51.

Dick, Hugh C., ed. *Selected Writings of Francis Bacon.* New York: Modern Library, 1955.

Eco, Umberto. *A Theory of Semiotics.* Bloomington: Indiana University Press, 1976.

Ehninger, Douglas. *Contemporary Rhetoric: A Reader's Coursebook.* Glenview, IA: Scott, Foresman, 1972.

Ellis, Donald G. "Fixing Communicative Meaning: A Coherentist Theory." *Communication Research* 22 (1995): 515–544.

Ellis, Donald G. *From Language to Communication.* Mahwah, NJ: Lawrence Erlbaum, 1999.

Donaldson, Rodney E. "Cybernetics and Human Knowing: One Possible Prolegomenon." *Cybernetics and Human Knowing* 1 (1992): 1–4.

Farrell, Thomas B. *Norms of Rhetorical Culture.* New Haven, CT: Yale University Press, 1993.

Farrell, Thomas B., and James A. Aune. "Critical Theory and Communication: A Selective Literature Review." *Quarterly Journal of Speech* 65 (1979): 93–120.

Fay, Brian. *Social Theory and Political Practice.* London: Allen and Unwin, 1975.

Fine, Gary Alan. "The Sad Demise, Mysterious Disappearance, and Glorious Triumph of Symbolic Interactionism." *Annual Review of Sociology* 19 (1993): 61–87.

Fisch, Max H. *Peirce, Semiotic, and Pragmatism.* Bloomington: Indiana University Press, 1986.

Foss, Sonja K., Karen A. Foss, and Robert Trapp. *Contemporary Perspectives on Rhetoric.* 3rd ed. Prospect Heights, IL: Waveland, 2002.

Fraser, Nancy. *Unruly Practices: Power, Discourse, and Gender in Contemporary Social Theory.* Minneapolis: University of Minnesota Press, 1989.

Froman, Wayne. *Merleau-Ponty: Language and the Act of Speech.* Lewisburg, PA: Bucknell University Press, 1982.

Garfinkel, Harold. *Studies in Ethnomethodology.* Englewood Cliffs, NJ: Prentice-Hall, 1967.

Gergen, Kenneth J. "The Social Constructionist Movement in Modern Psychology." *American Psychologist* 40 (1985): 266–275.

Glenn, Cheryl. *Rhetoric Retold: Regendering the Tradition from Antiquity Through the Renaissance.* Carbondale: Southern Illinois University Press, 1997.

Goudge, Thomas A. *The Thought of Peirce.* Toronto: University of Toronto Press, 1950.

Gray-Rosendale, Laura, and Sibylle Gruber. *Alternative Rhetorics: Challenges to the Rhetorical Tradition.* Albany: State University of New York Press, 2001.

Grossberg, Lawrence. "Does Communication Theory Need Intersubjectivity?: Toward an Immanent Philosophy of Interpersonal Relations." In *Communication Yearbook 6,* edited by Michael Burgoon, 171–205. Beverly Hills, CA: Sage, 1984.

Habermas, Jürgen. *Communication and the Evolution of Society.* Translated by Thomas McCarthy. Boston: Beacon, 1979.

Habermas, Jürgen. *Knowledge and Human Interests.* Translated by J. J. Shapiro. Boston: Beacon, 1971.

Habermas, Jürgen. *Legitimation Crisis.* Translated by Thomas McCarthy. Boston: Beacon, 1975.

Habermas, Jürgen. *Postmetaphysical Thinking: Philosophical Essays.* Translated by William Mark Hohengarten. Cambridge, MA: MIT Press, 1992.

Habermas, Jürgen. *The Theory of Communicative Action, Volume 1: Reason and the Rationalization of Society.* Translated by Thomas McCarthy. Boston: Beacon, 1984.

Habermas, Jürgen. *The Theory of Communicative Action, Volume 2: Lifeworld and System.* Translated by Thomas McCarthy. Boston: Beacon, 1987.

Hall, A. D., and R. E. Fagen. "Definition of a System." In *Modern Systems Research for the Behavioral Scientist,* edited by W. Buckley, 81–92. Chicago: Aldine, 1968.

Harré, Rom. "Language Games and Texts of Identity." In *Texts of Identity,* edited by John Shotter and K. Gergen, 20–35. London: Sage, 1989.

Heidegger, Martin. *Being and Time.* Translated by J. Macquarrie and E. Robinson. New York: Harper and Row, 1962.

Heidegger, Martin. *An Introduction to Metaphysics.* Translated by R. Manheim. New Haven, CT: Yale University Press, 1959.

Heidegger, Martin. *On the Way to Language.* Translated by P. Hertz. New York: Harper and Row, 1971.

Harper, Nancy L. *Human Communication Theory: The History of a Paradigm.* Rochelle Park, NJ: Hayden, 1979.

Hewes, Dean E., and Sally Planalp. "The Individual's Place in Communication Science." In *Handbook of Communication Science,* edited by Charles R. Berger and Steven H. Chaffee, 146–183. Newbury Park, CA: Sage, 1987.

Hookway, Christopher. *Peirce.* London: Routledge and Kegan Paul, 1985.

Huspek, Michael. "Toward Normative Theories of Communication with Reference to the Frankfurt School: An Introduction." *Communication Theory* 7 (1997): 265–276.

Husserl, Edmund. *Ideas: General Introduction to Pure Phenomenology.* Translated by W. R. B. Gibson. New York: Collier, 1962.

Hyde, Michael J. "Transcendental Philosophy and Human Communication." In *Interpersonal Communication,* edited by J. J. Pilotta, 15–34. Washington, DC: Center for Advanced Research in Phenomenology, 1982.

Janik, Allan, and Stephen Toulmin. *Wittgenstein's Vienna.* New York: Simon and Schuster, 1973.

Jansen, Sue Curry. "Power and Knowledge: Toward a New Critical Synthesis." *Journal of Communication* 33 (1983): 342–354.

Kavoori, Anandam P. "Getting Past the Latest 'Post': Assessing the Term 'Post-Colonial.'" *Critical Studies in Mass Communication* 15 (1998): 195–202.

Kellner, Douglas. "Media Communications vs. Cultural Studies: Overcoming the Divide." *Communication Theory* 5 (1995): 162–177.

Kennedy, George A. *Comparative Rhetoric: An Historical and Cross-Cultural Introduction.* New York: Oxford University Press, 1998.

Koestler, Arthur. *The Ghost in the Machine.* New York: Macmillan, 1967.

Krippendorff, Klaus. "Cybernetics." In *International Encyclopedia of Communications,* vol. 1, edited by Erik

Barnouw and others, 443–446. New York: Oxford University Press, 1989.

Kwant, Remy C. *The Phenomenological Philosophy of Merleau-Ponty.* Pittsburgh: Duquesne University Press, 1963.

Lal, Barbara Ballis. "Symbolic Interaction Theories." *American Behavioral Scientist* 38 (1995): 421–441.

Lanigan, Richard L. *Phenomenology of Communication: Merleau-Ponty's Thematics in Communicology and Semiology.* Pittsburgh: Duquesne University Press, 1988.

Lannamann, John W. "Deconstructing the Person and Changing the Subject of Interpersonal Studies." *Communication Theory* 2 (1992): 139–148.

Lannamann, John W. "Interpersonal Communication Research as Ideological Practice." *Communication Theory* 1 (1991): 179–203.

Leeds-Hurwitz, Wendy. *Semiotics and Communication: Signs, Codes, Cultures.* Hillsdale, NJ: Lawrence Erlbaum, 1993.

Littlejohn, Stephen W. "An Overview of the Contributions to Human Communication Theory from other Disciplines." In *Human Communication Theory: Comparative Essays*, edited by Frank E. X. Dance, 243–285. Cambridge, MA: Harper and Row, 1982.

Lyne, John R. "Rhetoric and Semiotic in C. S. Peirce." *Quarterly Journal of Speech* 66 (1980): 155–168.

MacIntyre, Alasdair. *After Virtue.* Notre Dame, IN: University of Notre Dame Press, 1984.

Macey, David. *The Penguin Dictionary of Critical Theory.* London: Penguin Books, 2000.

Macy, Joanna. *Mutual Causality in Buddhism and General System Theory.* Albany: SUNY Press, 1991.

Mahmood, Saba. "Cultural Studies and Ethnic Absolutism: Comments on Stuart Hall's 'Culture, Community, and Nation.'" *Cultural Studies* 10 (1996): 1–11.

Mallin, Samuel B. *Merleau-Ponty's Philosophy.* New Haven, CT: Yale University Press, 1979.

Manis, Jerome G., and Bernard N. Meltzer, eds. *Symbolic Interaction.* Boston: Allyn and Bacon, 1978.

Martyna, Wendy. "What Does 'He' Mean?" *Journal of Communication* 28 (1978): 131–138.

Maruyama, Magoroh. *Mindscapes: The Epistemology of Magoroh Maruyama*, edited by Michael T. Caley and Daiyo Sawada. Amsterdam: Gordon and Breach, 1994.

Maruyama, Magoroh. "The Second Cybernetics: Deviation-Amplifying Mutual Causal Processes." *American Scientist* 51 (1963): 164–179.

Marx, Karl. *Capital.* Chicago: Kerr, 1909.

Marx, Karl. *The Communist Manifesto.* London: Reeves, 1888.

Matson, Floyd W. *The Idea of Man.* New York: Delacorte, 1976.

Mattelart, Armand, and Michèle Mattelart. *Theories of Communication: A Short Introduction.* London: Sage, 1998.

Mead, George H. *Mind, Self, and Society.* Chicago: University of Chicago Press, 1934.

Merleau-Ponty, Maurice. *The Phenomenology of Perception*, translated by C. Smith. London: Routledge and Kegan Paul, 1974.

Mertz, Elizabeth, and Richard J. Parmentier, eds. *Semiotic Mediation: Sociocultural and Psychological Perspectives.* Orlando: Academic, 1985.

Miike, Yoshitaka. "Theorizing Culture and Communication in the Asian Context: An Assumptive Foundation." *Intercultural Communication Studies* 11 (2002): 1–21.

Moriarty, Sandra E. "Abduction: A Theory of Visual Interpretation." *Communication Theory* 6 (1996): 167–187.

Morris, Charles. *Signification and Significance.* Cambridge, MA: MIT Press, 1964.

Morris, Charles. *Signs, Language, and Behavior.* New York: Braziller, 1946.

Mueller, Milton. "Why Communications Policy Is Passing 'Mass Communication' By: Political Economy as the Missing Link." *Critical Studies in Mass Communication* 12 (1995): 455–472.

Mumby, Dennis K. *Communication and Power in Organizations: Discourse, Ideology, and Domination.* Norwood, NJ: Ablex, 1988.

Murdock, Graham. "Across the Great Divide: Cultural Analysis and the Condition of Democracy." *Critical Studies in Mass Communication* 12 (1995): 89–95.

Nelson, Cary, and Lawrence Grossberg, eds. *Marxism and the Interpretation of Culture.* Urbana: University of Illinois Press, 1988.

Ogden, C. K., and I. A. Richards. *The Meaning of Meaning.* London: Kegan, Paul, Trench, Trubner, 1923.

Palmer, Richard E. *Hermeneutics: Interpretation Theory in Schleiermacher, Dilthey, Heidegger, and Gadamer.* Evanston, IL: Northwestern University Press, 1969.

Parmentier, Richard J. "'Signs' Place in Medias Res: Peirce's Concept of Semiotic Mediation." In *Semiotic Mediation: Sociocultural and Psychological Perspectives*, edited by Elizabeth Mertz and Richard Parmentier, 23–48. Orlando: Academic, 1985.

Peirce, Charles Saunders. *Charles S. Peirce: Selected Writings*, edited by P. O. Wiener. New York: Dover, 1958.

Planalp, Sally, and Dean E. Hewes. "A Cognitive Approach to Communication Theory: *Cogito Ergo Dico?*" In *Communication Yearbook 5*, edited by Michael Burgoon, 49–77. New Brunswick, NJ: Transaction Books, 1982.

Pollock, Della, and J. Robert Cox. "Historicizing 'Reason': Critical Theory, Practice, and Postmodernity." *Communication Monographs* 58 (1991): 170–178.

Potter, Jonathan, and Margaret Wetherell. *Discourse and Social Psychology: Beyond Attitudes and Behavior.* London: Sage, 1987.

Reynolds, Larry T. *Interactionism: Exposition and Critique.* Dix Hills, NY: General Hall, 1990.

Rogers, Everett M. *A History of Communication Study: A Biographical Approach.* New York: Free Press, 1994.

Rosengren, Karl Erik. "Culture, Media, and Society: Agency and Structure, Continuity and Change." In

Media Effects and Beyond, edited by Karl Erik Rosengren, 3–28. London: Routledge, 1994.

Rosengren, Karl Erik. "From Field to Frog Ponds." *Journal of Communication* 43 (1993): 6–17.

Sankoff, Gillian. *The Social Life of Language*. Philadelphia: University of Pennsylvania Press, 1980.

Schutz, Alfred. *The Phenomenology of the Social World*, translated by G. Walsh and F. Lehnert. Evanston, IL: Northwestern University Press, 1967.

Sebeok, Thomas. "The Doctrine of Sign." In *Frontiers in Semiotics*, edited by J. Deely, B. Williams, and F. E. Kruse. Bloomington: Indiana University Press, 1986.

Shapiro, Michael A., Mark A. Hamilton, Annie Lang, and Noshir S. Contractor. "Information Systems Division: Intrapersonal Meaning, Attitude, and Social Systems." In *Communication Yearbook 24*, edited by William B. Gudykunst, 17–50. Thousand Oaks, CA: Sage, 2001.

Silverman, David, and Brian Torode. *The Material Word: Some Theories of Language and Its Limits*. London: Routledge and Kegan Paul, 1980.

Silverman, Kaja. *The Subject of Semiotics*. New York: Oxford University Press, 1983.

Shome, Raka. "Caught in the Term 'Post-Colonial': Why the 'Post-Colonial' Still Matters." *Critical Studies in Mass Communication* 15 (1998): 203–212.

Shome, Raka. "Postcolonial Interventions in the Rhetorical Canon: An 'Other' View." *Communication Theory* 6 (1996): 40–59.

Shome, Raka, and Radha S. Hegde. "Postcolonial Approaches to Communication: Charting the Terrain, Engaging the Intersections." *Communication Theory* 12 (2002): 249–270.

Smith III, Ted J. "Diversity and Order in Communication Theory: The Uses of Philosophical Analysis." *Communication Quarterly* 36 (1988): 28–40.

Stewart, John. *Language as Articulate Contact: Toward a Post-Semiotic Philosophy of Communication*. Albany: SUNY Press, 1995.

Stewart, John. "One Philosophical Dimension of Social Approaches to Interpersonal Communication." *Communication Theory* 2 (1992): 337–347.

Stewart, John. "Speech and Human Being." *Quarterly Journal of Speech* 72 (1986): 55–73.

Stewart, John. "The Symbol Model vs. Language as Constitutive Articulate Contact." In *Beyond the Symbol Model: Reflections on the Representational Nature of Language*, edited by John Stewart, 9–63. Albany: SUNY Press, 1996.

Toda, Masanao, and Emir H. Shuford. "Logic of Systems: Introduction to a Formal Theory of Structure." *General Systems* 10 (1965): 3–27.

van Dijk, Teun A. "Discourse Semantics and Ideology." *Discourse and Society* 6 (1995): 243–289.

van Dijk, Teun A. "Principles of Critical Discourse Analysis." *Discourse and Society* 4 (1993): 249–283.

von Bertalanffy, Ludwig. "Ludwig von Bertalanffy." *General Systems* 17 (1972): 219–228.

von Foerster, Heinz. *Observing Systems: Selected Papers of Heinz von Foerster*. Seaside, CA: Intersystems, 1981.

Wander, Philip. "Review Essay: Marxism, Post-Colonialism, and Rhetoric of Contextualism." *Quarterly Journal of Speech*, 82 (1996): 402–435.

Wiener, Norbert. *The Human Use of Human Beings: Cybernetics in Society*. Boston: Houghton Mifflin, 1954.

Winter, Gibson. *Elements for a Social Ethic: Scientific and Ethical Perspectives on Social Process*. New York: Macmillan, 1966.

Wittgenstein, Ludwig. *Philosophical Investigations*. Oxford: Basil Blackwell, 1953.

Wittgenstein, Ludwig. *Tractatus Logico-Philosophicus*. London: Routledge and Kegan Paul, 1922.

Chapter 4: The Communicator

Ajzen, Icek, and Martin Fishbein. *Understanding Attitudes and Predicting Social Behavior*. Englewood Cliffs, NJ: Prentice-Hall, 1980.

Allen, Mike, and Rodney Reynolds. "The Elaboration Likelihood Model and the Sleeper Effect: An Assessment of Attitude Change over Time." *Communication Theory* 8 (1993): 73–82.

Andersen, Peter A. "The Trait Debate: A Critical Examination of the Individual Differences Paradigm in the Communication Sciences." In *Progress in Communication Sciences*, edited by Brenda Dervin and M. J. Voigt. Norwood, NJ: Ablex, 1986.

Andersen, Peter A., Laura K. Guerrero, David Buller, and Peter F. Jorgensen. "An Empirical Comparison of Three Theories of Nonverbal Immediacy Exchange." *Human Communication Research* 24 (1998): 501–535.

Anderson, Norman H. "Integration Theory and Attitude Change." *Psychological Review* 78 (1971): 171–206.

Anzaldúa, Gloria. *Borderlands/La Frontera: The New Mestiza*. San Francisco: Aunt Lute Books, 1987.

Anzaldúa, Gloria. "La Prieta." In *This Bridge Called My Back: Writings by Radical Women of Color*. 2nd ed., edited by Cherríe Moraga and Gloria Anzaldúa. New York: Kitchen Table: Women of Color, 1983.

Averill, J. "The Acquisition of Emotions During Adulthood." In *The Social Construction of Emotions*, edited by Rom Harré, 98–119. New York: Blackwell, 1986.

Averill, J. *Anger and Aggression: An Essay on Emotion*. New York: Springer-Verlag, 1982.

Averill, J. "A Constructivist View of Emotion." In *Theories of Emotion*, edited by K. Plutchik and H. Kellerman, 305–339. New York: Academic, 1980.

Averill, J. "On the Paucity of Positive Emotions." In *Assessment and Modification of Emotional Behavior*, edited by K. R. Blankstein, P. Pliner, and J. Polivy, 7–45. New York: Plenum, 1980.

Babrow, Austin S. "Communication and Problematic Integration: Milan Kundera's 'Lost Letters.'" *Communication Monographs* 62 (1995): 283–300.

Babrow, Austin S. "Communication and Problematic Integration: Understanding Diverging Probability and

Value, Ambiguity, Ambivalence, and Impossibility." *Communication Theory* 2 (1992): 95–130.

Babrow, Austin S. "Uncertainty, Value, Communication, and Problematic Integration." *Journal of Communication* 51 (2001): 553–573.

Beatty, Michael J., and James C. McCroskey. *The Biology of Communication: A Communibiological Perspective.* Cresskill, NJ: Hampton Press, 2001.

Beatty, Michael J., James C. McCroskey, and Alan D. Heisel. "Communication Apprehension as Temperamental Expression: A Communibiological Paradigm." *Communication Monographs* 65 (1998): 197–219.

Booth-Butterfield, Melanie, and Steve Booth-Butterfield. "The Role of Affective Orientation in the Five Factor Personality Structure." *Communication Research Reports* 19 (2002): 301–313.

Burgoon, Judee K., and Norah E. Dunbar. "An Interactionist Perspective on Dominance-Submission: Interpersonal Dominance as a Dynamic, Situationally Contingent Social Skill." *Communication Monographs* 67 (2000): 96–121.

Burgoon, Michael, Deborah A. Newton, and Thomas S. Birk. "A Theory of Belief, Attitude, Intention, and Behavior Extended to the Domain of Corrective Advertising." In *Communication Yearbook 15,* edited by Stanley A. Deetz, 263–286. Newbury Park, CA: Sage, 1992.

Burhans, David T. "The Attitude-Behavior Discrepancy Problem: Revisited." *Quarterly Journal of Speech* 57 (1971): 418–428.

Burleson, Brant R. "Attribution Schemes and Causal Inference in Natural Conversations." In *Contemporary Issues in Language and Discourse Processes,* edited by Donald G. Ellis and William A. Donohue, 63–86. Hillsdale, NJ: Lawrence Erlbaum, 1986.

Butler, Judith. *Gender Trouble: Feminism and the Subversion of Identity.* New York: Routledge, 1989.

Cahill, Spencer. "Erving Goffman." In *Symbolic Interactionism: An Introduction, an Interpretation, an Integration,* edited by Joel M. Charon, 185–200. Englewood Cliffs, NJ: Prentice-Hall, 1992.

Charon, Joel M. *Symbolic Interactionism: An Introduction, an Interpretation, an Integration.* Englewood Cliffs, NJ: Prentice-Hall, 1992.

Digman, J. "Personality Structure: Emergence of the Five-Factor Model." *Annual Review of Psychology* 41 (1990): 417–440.

Dillard, James Price, and Linda J. Marshall. "Persuasion as a Social Skill." In *Handbook of Communication and Social Interaction Skills,* edited by John O. Greene and Brant R. Burleson, 479–513. Mahwah, NJ: Lawrence Erlbaum, 2003.

Donnelly, J. H., and J. M. Ivancevich, "Post-Purchase Reinforcement and Back-Out Behavior." *Journal of Marketing Research* 7 (1970): 399–400.

Eysenck, H. J. "Biological Dimensions of Personality." In *Handbook of Personality,* edited by L. A. Pervin, 244–276. New York: Guilford, 1991.

Festinger, Leon. *A Theory of Cognitive Dissonance.* Stanford, CA: Stanford University Press, 1957.

Festinger, Leon, and James M. Carlsmith. "Cognitive Consequences of Forced Compliance." *Journal of Abnormal and Social Psychology* 58 (1959): 203–210.

Fishbein, Martin, ed. "A Behavior Theory Approach to the Relations Between Beliefs About an Object and the Attitude Toward the Object." In *Readings in Attitude Theory and Measurement.* New York: Wiley, 1967.

Fishbein, Martin, and Icek Ajzen. *Belief, Attitude, Intention, and Behavior.* Reading, MA: Addison-Wesley, 1975.

Gauntlett, David. *Media, Gender, and Identity: An Introduction.* London: Routledge, 2002.

Geertz, Clifford. *Local Knowledge: Further Essays in Interpretive Anthropology.* New York: Basic, 1983.

Gergen, Kenneth J., and Gün R. Semin. "Everyday Understanding in Science and Daily Life." In *Everyday Understanding: Social and Scientific Implications,* edited by Gün R. Semin and Kenneth J. Gergen, 1–18. London: Sage, 1990.

Giles, Howard, and Richard L. Street, Jr. "Communicator Characteristics and Behavior." In *Handbook of Interpersonal Communication,* 2nd ed., edited by Mark L. Knapp and Gerald R. Miller, 103–161. Thousand Oaks, CA: Sage, 1994.

Goffman, Erving. *Behavior in Public Places.* New York: Free Press, 1963.

Goffman, Erving. *Encounters: Two Studies in the Sociology of Interaction.* Indianapolis: Bobbs-Merrill, 1961.

Goffman, Erving. *Frame Analysis: An Essay on the Organization of Experience.* Cambridge, MA: Harvard University Press, 1974.

Goffman, Erving. *Interaction Ritual: Essays on Face-to-Face Behavior.* Garden City, NY: Doubleday, 1967.

Goffman, Erving. *The Presentation of Self in Everyday Life.* Garden City, NY: Doubleday, 1959.

Goffman, Erving. *Relations in Public.* New York: Basic, 1971.

Hamilton, Mark A., John E. Hunter, and Franklin J. Boster. "The Elaboration Likelihood Model as a Theory of Attitude Formation: A Mathematical Analysis." *Communication Theory* 8 (1993): 50–64.

Harding, Sandra. *Whose Science? Whose Knowledge? Thinking From Women's Lives.* Ithaca, NY: Cornell University Press, 1991.

Harré, Rom. "Is There Still a Problem About the Self?" In *Communication Yearbook 17,* edited by Stanley A. Deetz, 55–73. Thousand Oaks, CA: Sage, 1994.

Harré, Rom, "An Outline of the Social Constructionist Viewpoint." In *The Social Construction of Emotions,* edited by Rom Harré. New York: Blackwell, 1986.

Harré, Rom. *Personal Being: A Theory for Individual Psychology.* Cambridge, MA: Harvard University Press, 1984.

Harré, Rom. *Social Being: A Theory for Social Behavior.* Totowa, NJ: Littlefield, Adams, 1979.

Heider, Fritz. *The Psychology of Interpersonal Relations.* New York: Wiley, 1958.

Hickman, C. A., and Manford Kuhn. *Individuals, Groups, and Economic Behavior.* New York: Holt, Rinehart & Winston, 1956.

Hill Collins, Patricia. *Black Feminist Thought: Knowledge, Consciousness, and the Politics of Empowerment.* Boston: Unwin Hyman, 1990.

Houston, Marsha. "The Politics of Difference: Race, Class and Women's Communication." In *Women Making Meaning: New Feminist Directions in Communication,* edited by Lana Rakow, 45–59. New York: Routledge, 1992.

Houston, Marsha. "When Black Women Talk With White Women: Why the Dialogues Are Difficult." In *Our Voices: Essays in Culture, Ethnicity, and Communication.* 3rd ed., edited by Alberto González, Marsha Houston, and Victoria Chen, 98–104. Los Angeles, CA: Roxbury, 2000.

Houston, Marsha, and Olga Idriss Davis, eds. *Centering Ourselves: African American Feminist and Womanist Studies of Discourse.* Cresskill, NJ: Hampton Press, 2002.

Hovland, Carl I., O. J. Harvey, and Muzafer Sherif. "Assimilation and Contrast Effects in Reactions to Communication and Attitude Change." *Journal of Abnormal and Social Psychology* 55 (1957): 244–252.

Infante, Dominic A., Teresa A. Chandler, and Jill E. Rudd. "Test of an Argumentative Skill Deficiency Model of Interspousal Violence." *Communication Monographs* 56 (1989): 163–177.

Infante, Dominic A., and Andrew S. Rancer. "Argumentativeness and Verbal Aggressiveness: A Review of Recent Theory and Research." In *Communication Yearbook 19,* edited by Brant R. Burleson, 319–352. Thousand Oaks, CA: Sage, 1996.

Infante, Dominic A., Andrew S. Rancer, and Deanna F. Womack. *Building Communication Theory.* Prospect Heights, IL: Waveland, 1993.

Lal, Barbara Ballis. "Symbolic Interaction Theories." *American Behavioral Scientist* 38 (1995): 421–441.

Lutz, Catherine. "Morality, Domination, and Understandings of 'Justifiable Anger' Among the Ifaluk." In *Everyday Understanding: Social and Scientific Implications,* edited by Gün R. Semin and Kenneth J. Gergen, 204–226. London: Sage, 1990.

Manis, Jerome G., and Bernard N. Meltzer, eds. *Symbolic Interaction.* Boston: Allyn and Bacon, 1978.

Martin, Leonard, and Abraham Tesser, eds. *The Construction of Social Judgments.* Hillsdale, NJ: Lawrence Erlbaum, 1992.

McCroskey, James C. "The Communication Apprehension Perspective." In *Avoiding Communication: Shyness, Reticence, and Communication Apprehension,* edited by John A. Daly and James C. McCroskey, 13–38. Beverly Hills, CA: Sage, 1984.

McCroskey, James C., ed. *Personality and Communication: Trait Perspectives.* New York: Hampton Press, 1998.

McCroskey, James C., Alan D. Heisel, and Virginia Richmond. "Eysenck's BIG THREE and Communication Traits: Three Correlational Studies." *Communication Monographs* 68 (2001): 360–366.

Mendoza, S. Lily, Rona T. Halualani, and Jolanta A. Drzewiecka. "Moving the Discourse on Identities in Intercultural Communication: Structure, Culture, and Resignification." *Communication Quarterly,* 50 (2002): 312–327.

Metts, Sandra, and Erica Grohskopf. "Impression Management: Goals, Strategies, and Skills." In *Handbook of Communication and Social Interaction Skills,* edited by John O. Greene and Brant R. Burleson, 357–399. Mahwah, NJ: Lawrence Erlbaum, 2003.

Miller, Gerald R. "Some (Moderately) Apprehensive Thoughts on Avoiding Communication." In *Avoiding Communication: Shyness, Reticence, and Communication Apprehension,* edited by John A. Daly and James C. McCroskey, 237–246. Beverly Hills, CA: Sage, 1984.

Miller, Lynn C., Michael J. Cody, and Margaret L. McLaughlin. "Situations and Goals as Fundamental Constructs in Interpersonal Communication Research." In *Handbook of Interpersonal Communication,* 2nd ed., edited by Mark L. Knapp and Gerald R. Miller, 162–197. Thousand Oaks, CA: Sage, 1994.

O'Keefe, Daniel J. *Persuasion: Theory and Research.* Newbury Park, CA: Sage, 1990.

Patterson, Miles L., and Vicki Ritts. "Social and Communicative Anxiety: A Review and Meta-Analysis." *Communication Yearbook 20,* edited by Brant R. Burleson. Thousand Oaks, CA: Sage, 1997.

Petty, Richard E., and John T. Cacioppo. *Communication and Persuasion: Central and Peripheral Routes to Attitude Change.* New York: Springer-Verlag, 1986.

Petty, Richard E., John T. Cacioppo, and R. Goldman. "Personal Involvement as a Determinant of Argument-Based Persuasion." *Journal of Personality and Social Psychology* 41 (1981): 847–855.

Petty, Richard E., Duane T. Wegener, Leandre R. Fabrigar, Joseph R. Priester, and John T. Cacioppo. "Conceptual and Methodological Issues in the Elaboration Likelihood Model of Persuasion: A Reply to the Michigan State Critics." *Communication Theory* 3 (1993): 336–362.

Phelan, Shane. *Getting Specific: Postmodern Lesbian Politics.* Minneapolis: University of Minnesota Press, 1994.

Ponse, Barbara. *Identities in the Lesbian World: The Social Construction of Self.* Westport, CT: Greenwood Press, 1978.

Reynolds, Larry T. *Interactionism: Exposition and Critique.* Dix Hills, NY: General Hall, 1990.

Rokeach, Milton. *Beliefs, Attitudes, and Values: A Theory of Organization and Change.* San Francisco: Jossey-Bass, 1969.

Rokeach, Milton. *The Nature of Human Values.* New York: Free Press, 1973.

Sedgwick, Eve Kosofsky. *Tendencies.* Durham, NC: Duke University Press, 1993.

Seibold, David R., and Brian H. Spitzberg. "Attribution Theory and Research: Formalization, Review, and Implications for Communication." In *Progress in Communication Sciences.* Vol. 3, edited by Brenda Dervin and M. J. Voigt. Norwood, NJ: Ablex, 1981.

Shapiro, Michael A., Mark A. Hamilton, Annie Lang, and Noshir S. Contractor. "Information Systems Division: Intrapersonal, Meaning, Attitude, and Social Systems." In *Communication Yearbook 24,* edited by William B. Gudykunst, 17–50. Thousand Oaks, CA: Sage, 2001.

Sherif, Muzafer. *Social Interaction—Process and Products.* Chicago: Aldine, 1967.

Sherif, Muzafer, and Carl I. Hovland. *Social Judgment.* New Haven, CT: Yale University Press, 1961.

Sherif, Muzafer, Carolyn Sherif, and Roger Nebergall. *Attitude and Attitude Change: The Social Judgment-Involvement Approach.* Philadelphia: Saunders, 1965.

Sigman, Stuart J. *A Perspective on Social Communication.* Lexington, MA: Lexington Books, 1987.

Sillars, Alan L. "Attribution and Communication." In *Social Cognition and Communication,* edited by Michael E. Roloff and Charles R. Berger, 73–106. Beverly Hills, CA: Sage, 1982.

Slater, Michael D. "Persuasion Processes Across Receiver Goals and Message Genres." *Communication Theory* 7 (1997): 125–148.

Smith, Eliot R. "Social Cognition Contributions to Attribution Theory and Research." In *Social Cognition: Impact on Social Psychology,* edited by Patricia G. Devine, David L. Hamilton, and Thomas M. Ostrom, 77–108. San Diego: Academic, 1994.

Stiff, James B. *Persuasive Communication.* New York: Guilford, 1994.

Tucker, Charles. "Some Methodological Problems of Kuhn's Self Theory." *Sociological Quarterly* 7 (1966): 345–358.

Vangelisti, Anita L., Mark L. Knapp, and John A. Daly. "Conversational Narcissism." *Communication Monographs* 57 (1990): 251–274.

Verhoeven, Jef. "Goffman's Frame Analysis and Modern Micro-Sociological Paradigms." In *Micro-Sociological Theory: Perspectives on Sociological Theory,* Vol. 2, edited by H. J. Helle and S. N. Eisenstadt, 71–100. Beverly Hills, CA: Sage, 1985.

Wilson, Steven R., and Christina M. Sabee. "Explicating Communication Competence as a Theoretical Term." In *Handbook of Communication and Social Interaction Skills,* edited by John O. Greene and Brant R. Burleson, 3–50. Mahwah, NJ: Lawrence Erlbaum, 2003.

Wood, Julia T. "Gender and Moral Voice: Moving from Woman's Nature to Standpoint Epistemology." *Women's Studies in Communication* 15 (1992): 1–24.

Wyer, Robert S. *Cognitive Organization and Change.* Hillsdale, NJ: Lawrence Erlbaum, 1974.

Young, Stacey. "Dichotomies and Displacement: Bisexuality in Queer Theory and Politics." In *Playing With Fire: Queer Politics, Queer Theories,* edited by Shane Phelan, 55–56. New York: Routledge, 1997.

Chapter 5: The Message

Akmajian, Adrian, Richard A. Demers, Ann K. Farmer, and Robert M. Harnish. *An Introduction to Language and Communication.* Cambridge, MA: MIT Press, 1994.

Applegate, James L. "The Impact of Construct System Development on Communication and Impression Formation in Persuasive Messages." *Communication Monographs* 49 (1982): 277–289.

Applegate, James L., and Howard E. Sypher. "A Constructivist Theory of Communication and Culture." In *Theories in Intercultural Communication,* edited by Young Y. Kim and William B. Gudykunst, 41–65. Newbury Park, CA: Sage, 1988.

Babrow, Austin. "The Advent of Multiple-Process Theories of Communication." *Journal of Communication* 43 (1993): 110–118.

Berger, Charles R. "Message Production Skill in Social Interaction." In *Handbook of Communication and Social Interaction Skills,* edited by John O. Greene and Brant R. Burleson, 257–290. Mahwah, NJ: Lawrence Erlbaum, 2003.

Berger, Charles R. "Planning Strategic Interaction." *Communication Theory* 4 (1994): 3–6.

Berger, Charles R. *Planning Strategic Interaction: Attaining Goals Through Communicative Action.* Mahwah, NJ: Lawrence Erlbaum, 1997.

Berger, Charles R., Susan H. Karol, and Jerry M. Jordan. "When a Lot of Knowledge Is a Dangerous Thing: The Debilitating Effects of Plan Complexity on Verbal Fluency." *Human Communication Research* 16 (1989): 91–119.

Bernstein, Richard J. *Beyond Objectivism and Relativism: Science, Hermeneutics, and Praxis.* Philadelphia: University of Pennsylvania Press, 1983.

Birdwhistell, R. *Introduction to Kinesics.* Louisville, KY: University of Louisville Press, 1952.

Birdwhistell, R. *Kinesics and Context.* Philadelphia: University of Pennsylvania Press, 1970.

Blankenship, Jane, and Deborah C. Robson. "A 'Feminine Style' in Women's Political Discourse: An Exploratory Essay." *Communication Quarterly* 43 (1995): 353–366.

Bloomfield, Leonard. *Language.* New York: Holt, Rinehart & Winston, 1933.

Brock, Bernard L. "Evolution of Kenneth Burke's Criticism and Philosophy of Language." In *Kenneth Burke and Contemporary European Thought: Rhetoric in Transition,* edited by Bernard L. Brock, 1–33. Tuscaloosa: University of Alabama Press, 1995.

Brown, Penelope, and Stephen Levinson. *Politeness: Some Universals in Language Usage.* Cambridge: Cambridge University Press, 1987.

Brown, Roger. "Politeness Theory: Exemplar and Exemplary." In *The Legacy of Solomon Asch: Essays in Cognition and Social Psychology,* edited by Irvin Rock, 23–38. Hillsdale, NJ: Lawrence Erlbaum, 1990.

Buck, Ross. "From DNA to MTV: The Spontaneous Communication of Emotional Messages." In *Message Production: Advances in Communication Theory,* edited by John O. Greene, 313–340. Mahwah, NJ: Lawrence Erlbaum, 1997.

Buck, Ross, and C. Arthur VanLear. "Verbal and Nonverbal Communication: Distinguishing Symbolic, Spontaneous, and Pseudo-Spontaneous Nonverbal Behavior." *Journal of Communication* 52 (2002): 522–541.

Burgoon, Judee K. "Nonverbal Signals." In *Handbook of Interpersonal Communication*, edited by Mark L. Knapp and Gerald R. Miller, 229–285. Thousand Oaks, CA: Sage, 1994.

Burgoon, Judee K., and Aaron E. Bacue. "Nonverbal Communication Skills." In *Handbook of Communication and Social Interaction Skills*, edited by John O. Greene, and Brant R. Burleson, 179–219. Mahwah, NJ: Lawrence Erlbaum, 2003.

Burke, Kenneth. *Attitudes Toward History*. New York: New Republic, 1937.

Burke, Kenneth. *Counter-Statement*. New York: Harcourt, Brace, 1931.

Burke, Kenneth. *A Grammar of Motives*. Englewood Cliffs, NJ: Prentice-Hall, 1945.

Burke, Kenneth. *Language as Symbolic Action*. Berkeley: University of California Press, 1966.

Burke, Kenneth. *Permanence and Change*. New York: New Republic, 1935.

Burke, Kenneth. *The Philosophy of Literary Form*. Baton Rouge: Louisiana State University Press, 1941.

Burke, Kenneth. "Prologue in Heaven," *The Rhetoric of Religion Studies in Logology*. Berkeley, CA: University of California Press, 1979.

Burke, Kenneth. *A Rhetoric of Motives*. Englewood Cliffs, NJ: Prentice-Hall, 1950.

Burke, Kenneth. *A Rhetoric of Religion*. Boston: Beacon, 1961.

Burleson, Brant R. "Comforting Messages: Significance, Approaches, and Effects." In *Communication of Social Support: Messages, Interactions, Relationships, and Community*, edited by Brant R. Burleson, Terrance L. Albrecht, and Irwin G. Sarason, 3–28. Thousand Oaks, CA: Sage, 1994.

Burleson, Brant R. "The Constructivist Approach to Person-Centered Communication: Analysis of a Research Exemplar." In *Rethinking Communication: Paradigm Exemplars*, edited by Brenda Dervin, Lawrence Grossberg, Barbara J. O'Keefe, and Ellen Wartella, 29–46. Newbury Park, CA: Sage, 1989.

Burleson, Brant R. "Emotional Support Skill." In *Handbook of Communication and Social Interaction Skills*, edited by John O. Greene and Brant R. Burleson, 551–594. Mahwah, NJ: Lawrence Erlbaum, 2003.

Burleson, Brant R., and Sally Planalp. "Producing Emotion(al) Messages." *Communication Theory* 10 (2000): 221–250.

Cameron, Deborah. *Working with Spoken Discourse*. London: Sage, 2001.

Campbell, John Angus. "Hans-Georg Gadamer's Truth and Method." *Quarterly Journal of Speech* 64 (1978): 101–122.

Campbell, Karlyn Kohrs. *Man Cannot Speak For Her: A Critical Study of Early Feminist Rhetoric*. Vol. 1. Westport, CT: Greenwood, 1989.

Cheney, George, and Phillip K. Tompkins. "On the Facts of the Text as the Basis of Human Communication Research." In *Communication Yearbook 11*, edited by James A. Anderson, 455–481. Newbury Park, CA: Sage, 1988.

Chomsky, Noam. *Language and Mind*. New York: Harcourt, Brace, Jovanovich, 1975.

Cragan, John F., and Donald C. Shields. *Symbolic Theories in Applied Communication Research: Bormann, Burke, and Fisher*. Cresskill, NJ: Hampton, 1995.

Crockett, Walter H. "Cognitive Complexity and Impression Formation." In *Progress in Experimental Personality Research*. Vol. 2, edited by B. A. Maher. New York: Academic, 1965.

Dallmayr, Fred. *Language and Politics*. Notre Dame, IN: University of Notre Dame Press, 1984.

Deetz, Stanley. "Conceptualizing Human Understanding: Gadamer's Hermeneutics and American Communication Studies." *Communication Quarterly* 26 (1978): 12–23.

Delia, Jesse G. "Interpersonal Cognition, Message Goals, and Organization of Communication: Recent Constructivist Research." In *Communication Theory: Eastern and Western Perspectives*, edited by D. L. Kincaid, 255–274. San Diego: Academic, 1987.

Delia, Jesse G., Susan L. Kline, and Brant R. Burleson. "The Development of Persuasive Communication Strategies in Kindergartners Through Twelfth-Graders." *Communication Monographs* 46 (1979): 241–256.

Delia, Jesse G., Barbara J. O'Keefe, and Daniel J. O'Keefe. "The Constructivist Approach to Communication." In *Human Communication Theory: Comparative Essays*, edited by Frank E. X. Dance, 147–191. New York: Harper and Row, 1982.

de Saussure, Ferdinand. *Course in General Linguistics*. London: Peter Owen, 1960.

Dilthey, Wilhelm. "The Rise of Hermeneutics," translated by F. Jameson. *New Literary History* 3 (1972): 229–244.

Ekman, Paul, and Wallace Friesen. *Emotion in the Human Face: Guidelines for Research and an Integration of Findings*. New York: Pergamon, 1972.

Ekman, Paul, and Wallace Friesen. "Nonverbal Behavior in Psychotherapy Research." In *Research in Psychotherapy*. Vol. 3, edited by J. Shlien, 179–216. Washington, DC: American Psychological Association, 1968.

Ekman, Paul, and Wallace Friesen. "The Repertoire of Nonverbal Behavior: Categories, Origins, Usage, and Coding." *Semiotica* 1 (1969): 49–98.

Ekman, Paul, and Wallace Friesen. *Unmasking the Face*. Englewood Cliffs, NJ: Prentice-Hall, 1975.

Ellis, Donald G. "Fixing Communicative Meaning: A Coherentist Theory." *Communication Research*, 22 (1995): 515–544.

Ellis, Donald G. *From Language to Communication*. Mahwah, NJ: Lawrence Erlbaum, 1999.

Fish, Stanley. *Is There a Text in This Class?* Cambridge, MA: Harvard University Press, 1980.

Fodor, J. A., T. G. Bever, and M. F. Garrett. *The Psychology of Language: An Introduction to Psycholinguistics and Generative Grammar*. New York: McGraw-Hill, 1974.

Foss, Karen A., Sonja K. Foss, and Cindy L. Griffin. "Cheris Kramarae," *Feminist Rhetorical Theories*. Thousand Oaks, CA: Sage, 1999.

Foss, Sonja K., Karen A. Foss, and Robert Trapp. *Contemporary Perspectives on Rhetoric*. 3rd ed. Prospect Heights, IL: Waveland, 2002.

Fries, Charles. *The Structure of English*. New York: Harcourt, Brace and World, 1952.

Gadamer, H. G. *Truth and Method*. New York: Seabury, 1975.

Garko, Michael G. "Perspectives on and Conceptualizations of Compliance and Compliance-Gaining." *Communication Quarterly* 38 (1990): 138–157.

Gastil, John. "An Appraisal and Revision of the Constructivist Research Program." In *Communication Yearbook 18*, edited by Brant R. Burleson, 83–104. Thousand Oaks, CA: Sage, 1995.

Giddens, Anthony. *Central Problems in Social Theory: Action, Structure, and Contradiction in Social Analysis*. Berkeley: University of California Press, 1979.

Goldsmith, Daena J. "The Role of Facework in Supportive Communication." In *Communication of Social Support: Messages, Interactions, Relationships, and Community*, edited by Brant R. Burleson, Terrance L. Albrecht, and Irwin G. Sarason, 29–49. Thousand Oaks, CA: Sage, 1994.

Graddol, David, Jenny Cheshire, and Joan Swann. *Descriptive Language*. Buckingham, UK: Open University Press, 1994.

Greene, John O. "Action Assembly Theory: Metatheoretical Commitments, Theoretical Propositions, and Empirical Applications." In *Rethinking Communication: Paradigm Exemplars*, edited by Brenda Dervin, Lawrence Grossberg, Barbara J. O'Keefe, and Ellen Wartella, 117–128. Newbury Park, CA: Sage, 1989.

Greene, John O. "A Cognitive Approach to Human Communication: An Action Assembly Theory." *Communication Monographs* 51 (1984): 289–306.

Greene, John O., and Deanna Geddes. "An Action Assembly Perspective on Social Skill." *Communication Theory* 3 (1993): 26–49.

Hale, Claudia. "Cognitive Complexity-Simplicity as a Determinant of Communication Effectiveness." *Communication Monographs* 47 (1980): 304–311.

Hall, Edward T. *The Hidden Dimension*. New York: Random House, 1966.

Hall, Edward T. *The Silent Language*. Greenwich, CT: Fawcett, 1959.

Hall, Edward T. "A System for the Notation of Proxemic Behavior." *American Anthropologist* 65 (1963): 1003–1026.

Harris, Zellig. *Structural Linguistics*. Chicago: University of Chicago Press, 1951.

Harrison, Randall. *Beyond Words: An Introduction to Nonverbal Communication*. Englewood Cliffs, NJ: Prentice-Hall, 1974.

Hodge, Robert, and Gunther Kress. *Social Semiotics*. Ithaca, NY: Cornell University Press, 1988.

Jacobs, Scott. "Language and Interpersonal Communication." In *Handbook of Interpersonal Communication*, edited by Mark L. Knapp and Gerald R. Miller, 199–228. Thousand Oaks, CA: Sage, 1994.

Jones, Stanley E., and Curtis D. LeBaron. "Research on the Relationship Between Verbal and Nonverbal Communication: Emerging Integrations." *Journal of Communication* 52 (2002): 499–521.

Kelly, George. *The Psychology of Personal Constructs*. New York: North, 1955.

Kline, Susan L., and Janet M. Ceropski. "Person-Centered Communication in Medical Practice." In *Emergent Issues in Human Decision Making*, edited by Gerald M. Phillips and Julia T. Wood, 120–141. Carbondale: Southern Illinois University Press, 1984.

Knapp, Mark L., and Judith Hall. *Nonverbal Communication in Human Interaction*. New York: Holt, Rinehart & Winston, 1992.

Kramarae, Cheris. "Gender and Dominance." *Communication Yearbook 15*, edited by Stanley A. Deetz. Newbury Park, CA: Sage, 1992.

Kramarae, Cheris. *Women and Men Speaking: Frameworks for Analysis*. Rowley, MA: Newbury House, 1981.

Kramarae, Cheris. "Words on a Feminist Dictionary." In *A Feminist Dictionary*, edited by Cheris Kramarae, Paula A. Treichler, with Ann Russo. Boston: Pandora, 1985.

Langer, Susanne. *Mind: An Essay on Human Feeling*. 3 vols. Baltimore: Johns Hopkins University Press, 1967, 1972, 1982.

Langer, Susanne. *Philosophy in a New Key*. Cambridge, MA: Harvard University Press, 1942.

Leeds-Hurwitz, Wendy. *Semiotics and Communication: Signs, Codes, Cultures*. Hillsdale, NJ: Lawrence Erlbaum, 1993.

Marwell, Gerald, and David R. Schmitt. "Dimensions of Compliance-Gaining Strategies: A Dimensional Analysis." *Sociometry* 30 (1967): 350–364.

Miller, Gerald R. "Persuasion." In *Handbook of Communication Science*, edited by Charles R. Berger and Steven H. Chaffee, 446–483. Newbury Park, CA: Sage, 1987.

Motley, Michael T. "Facial Affect and Verbal Context in Conversation." *Human Communication Research* 20 (1993): 3–40.

Motley, Michael T., and Carl T. Camden. "Facial Expression of Emotion: A Comparison of Posed Expressions Versus Spontaneous Expressions in an Interpersonal Communication Setting." *Western Journal of Speech Communication* 52 (1988): 1–22.

Nicotera, Anne Maydan. "The Constructivist Theory of Delia, Clark, and Associates." In *Watershed Research Traditions in Human Communication Theory*, edited by Donald P. Cushman and Branislav Kovačić, 45–66. Albany: SUNY Press, 1995.

O'Keefe, Barbara J. "The Logic of Message Design: Individual Differences in Reasoning About Communication." *Communication Monographs* 55 (1988): 80–103.

O'Keefe, Barbara J. "Variation, Adaptation, and Functional Explanation in the Study of Message Design." In *Developing Communication Theories*, edited by Gerry Philipsen, 85–118. Albany: SUNY Press, 1997.

O'Keefe, Barbara J., and Gregory J. Shepherd. "The Pursuit of Multiple Objectives in Face-to-Face Persuasive Interactions: Effects of Construct Differentiation on Message Organization." *Communication Monographs* 54 (1987): 396–419.

O'Keefe, Daniel J. "From Strategy-Based to Feature-Based Analyses of Compliance Gaining Message Classification and Production." *Communication Theory* 4 (1994): 61–69.

Osgood, Charles. *Cross Cultural Universals of Affective Meaning.* Urbana: University of Illinois Press, 1975.

Osgood, Charles. "The Nature of Measurement of Meaning." in *The Semantic Differential Technique*, edited by J. Snider and C. Osgood, 9–10. Chicago: Aldine, 1969.

Osgood, Charles. "On Understanding and Creating Sentences." *American Psychologist* 18 (1963): 735–751.

Osgood, Charles. "Semantic Differential Technique in the Comparative Study of Cultures." In *The Semantic Differential Technique,* edited by J. Snider and C. Osgood, 303–323. Chicago: Aldine, 1969.

Osgood, Charles, and Meredith Richards. "From *Yang* and *Yin* to *And* or *But.*" *Language* 49 (1973): 380–412.

Ricoeur, Paul. *The Conflict of Interpretations: Essays in Hermeneutics,* edited by Don Ihde. Evanston, IL: Northwestern University Press, 1974.

Ricoeur, Paul. *Hermeneutics and the Human Sciences: Essays on Language, Action, and Interpretation,* translated and edited by J. B. Thompson. Cambridge: Cambridge University Press, 1981.

Ricoeur, Paul. *Interpretation Theory: Discourse and the Surplus of Meaning.* Fort Worth: Texas University Press, 1976.

Roskill, Mark. "'Public' and 'Private' Meanings: The Paintings of van Gogh." *Journal of Communication* 29 (1979): 157–169.

Rueckert, William, ed. *Critical Responses to Kenneth Burke.* Minneapolis: University of Minnesota Press, 1969.

Sanders, Robert E., and Kristine L. Fitch. "The Actual Practice of Compliance Seeking." *Communication Theory* 11 (2001): 263–289.

Schleiermacher, Friedrich. *Hermeneutik,* edited by H. Kimmerle. Heidelberg. Germany: Carl Winter, Universitaetsverlag, 1959.

Searle, John. *Speech Acts: An Essay in the Philosophy of Language.* Cambridge: Cambridge University Press, 1969.

Seibold, David R., James G. Cantrill, and Renee A. Meyers. "Communication and Interpersonal Influence." In *Handbook of Interpersonal Communication.* 2nd ed., edited by Mark L. Knapp and Gerald R. Miller, 542–588. Thousand Oaks, CA: Sage, 1994.

Simons, Herbert W., and Trevor Melia, ed. *The Legacy of Kenneth Burke.* Madison: University of Wisconsin Press, 1989.

Snider, James, and Charles Osgood, eds. *The Semantic Differential Technique.* Chicago: Aldine, 1969.

Stewart, John. *Language as Articulate Contact: Toward a Post-Semiotic Philosophy of Communication.* Albany: SUNY Press, 1995.

Stewart, John. "The Symbol Model vs. Language as Constitutive Articulate Contact." In *Beyond the Symbol Model: Reflections on the Representational Nature of Language,* edited by John Stewart, 9–63. Albany: SUNY Press, 1996.

Stiff, James B. *Persuasive Communication.* New York: Guilford, 1994.

Swartz, Omar. *Conducting Socially Responsible Research.* Thousand Oaks, CA: Sage, 1997.

Tracy, David. "Interpretation (Hermeneutics)." In *International Encyclopedia of Communications,* Vol. 2, edited by Erik Barnouw, George Gerbner, Wilbur Schramm, Tobia L. Worth, and Larry Gross, 343–348. New York: Oxford University Press, 1989.

Warnick, Barbara. "A Ricoeurian Approach to Rhetorical Criticism." *Western Journal of Speech Communication* 51 (1987): 227–244.

Weiser, Irwin. "Linguistics." In *Encyclopedia of Rhetoric and Composition,* edited by Theresa Enos, 386–391. New York: Garland, 1996.

Wheeless, Lawrence R., Robert Barraclough, and Robert Stewart. "Compliance-Gaining and Power in Persuasion." In *Communication Yearbook 7,* edited by R. N. Bostrom, 105–145. Beverly Hills, CA: Sage, 1983.

Wilson, Steven R. "Developing Theories of Persuasive Message Production: The Next Generation." In *Message Production: Advances in Communication Theory,* edited by John O. Greene, 15–46. Mahwah, NJ: Lawrence Erlbaum, 1997.

Wyer, Jr., Robert S., and Rashmi Adaval. "Message Reception Skills in Social Communication." In *Handbook of Communication and Social Interaction Skills,* edited by John O. Greene and Brant R. Burleson, 291–355. Mahwah, NJ: Lawrence Erlbaum, 2003.

Chapter 6: The Conversation

Affifi, Walid A., ed. "Colloquy on Information Seeking." *Human Communication Research* 28 (2002): 207–312.

Alvy, K. T. "The Development of Listener-Adapted Communication in Grade-School Children from Different Social Class Backgrounds." *Genetic Psychology Monographs* 87 (1973): 33–104.

Andersen, Peter A. "Nonverbal Immediacy in Interpersonal Communication." In *Multichannel Integrations of Nonverbal Behavior,* edited by A. W. Siegman and S. Feldstein, 1–36. Hillsdale, NJ: Lawrence Erlbaum, 1985.

Babrow, Austin S., ed. "Special Issue: Uncertainty, Evaluation, and Communication." *Journal of Communication* 51 (2001).

Becker, Howard. "Becoming a Marihuana User." *American Journal of Sociology* 59 (1953): 235–242.

Berger, Charles R. "Producing Messages Under Uncertainty." In *Message Production: Advances in Communication Theory*, edited by John O. Greene, 221–244. Mahwah, NJ: Lawrence Erlbaum, 1997.

Berger, Charles R., and James J. Bradac. *Language and Social Knowledge: Uncertainty in Interpersonal Relations.* London: Arnold, 1982.

Berger, Charles R., and R. J. Calabrese. "Some Explorations in Initial Interaction and Beyond: Toward a Developmental Theory of Interpersonal Communication." *Human Communication Research* 1 (1975): 99–112.

Berger, Charles R., and William Douglas. "Thought and Talk: "Excuse Me, But Have I Been Talking to Myself?" In *Human Communication Theory,* edited by Frank E. X. Dance, 42–60. New York: Harper and Row, 1982.

Berger, Charles R., R. R. Gardner, M. R. Parks, L. Schulman, and Gerald R. Miller. "Interpersonal Epistemology and Interpersonal Communication." In *Explorations in Interpersonal Communication,* edited by Gerald R. Miller, 149–171. Beverly Hills, CA: Sage, 1976.

Berger, Charles R., and Katherine Ann Kellermann. "To Ask or Not to Ask: Is That a Question?" In *Communication Yearbook 7,* edited by R. N. Bostrom, 342–368. Beverly Hills, CA: Sage, 1983.

Blumer, Herbert. *Symbolic Interactionism: Perspective and Method.* Englewood Cliffs: NJ: Prentice-Hall, 1969.

Bormann, Ernest G. *Communication Theory.* New York: Holt, Rinehart & Winston, 1980.

Bormann, Ernest G. "Fantasy and Rhetorical Vision: The Rhetorical Criticism of Social Reality. *Quarterly Journal of Speech* 58 (1972): 396–407.

Bormann, Ernest G. "Fantasy and Rhetorical Vision: Ten Years Later." *Quarterly Journal of Speech* 68 (1982): 288–305.

Bormann, Ernest G. *The Force of Fantasy: Restoring the American Dream.* Carbondale: Southern Illinois University Press, 1985.

Bormann, Ernest G., John F. Cragan, and Donald C. Shields. "An Expansion of the Rhetorical Vision Component of the Symbolic Convergence Theory: The Cold War Paradigm Case." *Communication Monographs* 63 (1996): 1–28.

Bormann, Ernest G., John F. Cragan, and Donald C. Shields. "Three Decades of Developing, Grounding, and Using Symbolic Convergence Theory (SCT)." In *Communication Yearbook 25,* edited by William B. Gudykunst, 271–313. Mahwah, NJ: Lawrence Erlbaum, 2001.

Branham, Robert J., and W. Barnett Pearce. "Between Text and Context: Toward a Rhetoric of Contextual Reconstruction." *Quarterly Journal of Speech* 71 (1985): 19–36.

Buller, David B., and Judee K. Burgoon. "Another Look at Information Management: A Rejoinder to McCornack, Levine, Morrison, and Lapinski." *Communication Monographs* 63 (1996): 92–98.

Buller, David B., and Judee K. Burgoon. "Interpersonal Deception Theory." *Communication Theory* 6 (1996): 203–242.

Burgoon, Judee K. "Communicative Effects of Gaze Behavior: A Test of Two Contrasting Explanations." *Human Communication Research* 12 (1986): 495–524.

Burgoon, Judee K. "It Takes Two to Tango: Interpersonal Adaptation and Implications for Relational Communication." In *Communication: Views from the Helm for the 21st Century,* edited by Judith S. Trent. Boston, 53–59. Boston: Allyn and Bacon, 1998.

Burgoon, Judee K., "Nonverbal Signals." In *Handbook of Interpersonal Communication,* edited by Mark L. Knapp and Gerald R. Miller, 253–255. Thousand Oaks, CA: Sage, 1994.

Burgoon, Judee K., David B. Buller, Laura K. Guerrero, Walid A. Afifi, and Clyde M. Feldman. "Interpersonal Deception: XII. Information Management Dimensions Underlying /Deceptive and Truthful Messages." *Communication Monographs* 63 (1996): 50–69.

Burgoon, Judee K., Leesa Dillman, and Lesa A. Stern. "Adaptation in Dyadic Interaction: Defining and Operationalizing Patterns of Reciprocity and Compensation." *Communication Theory* 3 (1993): 295–316.

Burgoon, Judee K., and Jerold L. Hale. "Nonverbal Expectancy Violations: Model Elaboration and Application." *Communication Monographs* 55 (1988): 58–79.

Burgoon, Judee K., Lesa A. Stern, and Leesa Dillman. *Interpersonal Adaptation: Dyadic Interaction Patterns.* New York: Cambridge University Press, 1995.

Burgoon, Judee K., and Cindy H. White. "Researching Nonverbal Message Production: A View from Interaction Adaptation Theory." In *Message Production: Advances in Communication Theory,* edited by John O. Greene, 279–312. Mahwah, NJ: Lawrence Erlbaum, 1997.

Button, Graham, ed. *Ethnomethodology and the Human Sciences.* Cambridge: Cambridge University Press, 1991.

Cameron, Deborah. *Working with Spoken Discourse.* London: Sage, 2001.

Cappella, Joseph N. "The Management of Conversational Interaction in Adults and Infants." In *Handbook of Interpersonal Communication,* edited by Mark L. Knapp and Gerald R. Miller, 406–407. Thousand Oaks, CA: Sage, 1994.

Cappella, Joseph N. "The Management of Conversations." In *Handbook of Interpersonal Communication,* edited by Mark L. Knapp and Gerald R. Miller, 393–439. Beverly Hills, CA: Sage, 1985.

Cappella, Joseph N., and John O. Greene. "A Discrepancy-Arousal Explanation of Mutual Influence in Expressive Behavior for Adult-Adult and Infant-Adult Interaction." *Communication Monographs* 49 (1982): 89–114.

Chimombo, Moira, and Robert L. Roseberry. *The Power of Discourse: An Introduction to Discourse Analysis.* Mahwah, NJ: Lawrence Erlbaum, 1998.

Cragan, John F., and Donald C. Shields. *Applied Communication Research: A Dramatistic Approach.* Prospect Heights, IL: Waveland, 1981.

Cragan, John F., and Donald C. Shields, *Symbolic Theories in Applied Communication Research: Bormann, Burke, and Fisher*. Cresskill, NJ: Hampton, 1995.

Cragan, John F., and Donald C. Shields. *Understanding Communication Theory: The Communicative Forces for Human Action*. Boston: Allyn and Bacon, 1998.

Craig, Robert T., and Karen Tracy, ed. *Conversational Coherence: Form, Structure, and Strategy*. 3rd ed. Beverly Hills, CA: Sage, 1983.

Cronen, Vernon E., Kenneth M. Johnson, and John W. Lannamann. "Paradoxes, Double Binds, and Reflexive Loops: An Alternative Theoretical Perspective," *Family Process* 20 (1982): 91–112.

Cronen, Vernon, W. Barnett Pearce, and Linda Harris. "The Coordinated Management of Meaning." In *Comparative Human Communication Theory*, edited by Frank E. X. Dance. New York: Harper and Row, 1982.

Cronen, Vernon, W. Barnett Pearce, and Linda Harris. "The Logic of the Coordinated Management of Meaning." *Communication Education* 28 (1979): 22–38.

Cronen, Vernon, Victoria Chen, and W. Barnett Pearce. "Coordinated Management of Meaning: A Critical Theory." In *Theories in Intercultural Communication*, edited by Young Y. Kim and William B. Gudykunst, 66–98. Newbury Park, CA: Sage, 1988.

Cushman, Donald P. "The Rules Approach to Communication Theory: A Philosophical and Operational Perspective." In *Communication Theory: Eastern and Western Perspectives*, edited by D. L. Kincaid, 223–234. San Diego: Academic, 1987.

Cushman, Donald P. "The Rules Perspective as a Theoretical Basis for the Study of Human Communication." *Communication Quarterly* 25 (1977): 30–45.

Delia, Jesse G. "Communication Research: A History." In *Handbook of Communication Science*, edited by Charles R. Berger and Steven H. Chaffee, 30–37. Newbury Park, CA: Sage, 1987.

Ellis, Donald G. *Crafting Society: Ethnicity, Class, and Communication Theory*. Mahwah, NJ: Lawrence Erlbaum, 1999.

Ellis, Donald G. "Fixing Communicative Meaning: A Coherentist Theory." *Communication Research* 22 (1995): 515–544.

Ellis, Donald G. *From Language to Communication*. Mahwah, NJ: Lawrence Erlbaum, 1999.

Ellis, Donald G., and William A. Donohue, ed. *Contemporary Issues in Language and Discourse Processes*. Hillsdale, NJ: Lawrence Erlbaum, 1986.

Foss, Karen A., and Sonja K. Foss. *Inviting Transformation: Presentational Speaking for a Changing World*. 2nd ed. Prospect Heights, IL: Waveland, 2003.

Foss, Sonja K., and Cindy L. Griffin. "Beyond Persuasion: A Proposal for an Invitational Rhetoric." *Communication Monographs*, 62 (March 1995): 2–18.

Garfinkel, Harold. *Studies in Ethnomethodology*. Englewood Cliffs, NJ: Prentice-Hall, 1967.

Giles, Howard, Justine Coupland, and Nikolas Coupland. "Accommodation Theory: Communication, Context, and Consequence." In *Contexts of Accommodation: Developments in Applied Sociolinguistics*, edited by Howard Giles, Justine Coupland, and Nikolas Coupland, 1–68. Cambridge: Cambridge University Press, 1991.

Giles, Howard, Anthony Mulac, James J. Bradac, and Patricia Johnson. "Speech Accommodation Theory: The First Decade and Beyond." In *Communication Yearbook 10*, edited by M. L. McLaughlin, 13–48. Newbury Park, CA: Sage, 1987.

Grice, H. Paul. "Logic and Conversation." In *Syntax and Semantics*. Vol. 3, edited by P. Cole and J. Morgan. New York: Academic, 1975.

Gudykunst, William B. "Culture and the Development of Interpersonal Relationships." In *Communication Yearbook 12*, edited by James A. Anderson, 315–354. Newbury Park, CA: Sage, 1989.

Gudykunst, William B. "Uncertainty and Anxiety." In *Theories in Intercultural Communication*, edited by Young Y. Kim and William B. Gudykunst, 123–156. Newbury Park, CA: Sage, 1988.

Gudykunst, William B. "The Uncertainty Reduction and Anxiety-Uncertainty Reduction Theories of Berger, Gudykunst, and Associates." In *Watershed Research Traditions in Human Communication Theory*, edited by Donald P. Cushman and Branislav Kovačić, 67–100. Albany: SUNY Press, 1995.

Hall, Edward T. *Beyond Culture*. New York: Doubleday, 1976.

Harré, Rom, and Paul Secord. *The Explanation of Social Behavior*. Totowa, NJ: Rowman and Littlefield, 1972.

Holtgraves, Thomas. "Comprehending Speaker Meaning." In *Communication Yearbook 26*, edited by William B. Gudykunst, 2–35. Mahwah, NJ: Lawrence Erlbaum, 2002.

Jackson, Sally, and Scott Jacobs. "Conversational Relevance: Three Experiments on Pragmatic Connectedness in Conversation." In *Communication Yearbook 10*, edited by M. L. McLaughlin, 323–347. Newbury Park, CA: Sage, 1987.

Jacobs, Scott. "Language." In *Handbook of Interpersonal Communication*, edited by Mark L. Knapp and Gerald R. Miller, 330–335. Beverly Hills, CA: Sage, 1985.

Jacobs, Scott. "Language and Interpersonal Communication." In *Handbook of Interpersonal Communication*, edited by Mark L. Knapp and Gerald R. Miller, 199–228. Thousand Oaks, CA: Sage, 1994.

Jacobs, Scott, Dale Brashers, and Edwin J. Dawson. "Truth and Deception." *Communication Monographs* 63 (1996): 98–103.

Jacobs, Scott, Edwin J. Dawson, and Dale Brashers. "Information Manipulation Theory: A Replication and Assessment." *Communication Monographs* 63 (1996): 70–82.

Jacobs, Scott, and Sally Jackson. "Building a Model of Conversational Argument." in *Rethinking Communica-*

tion: Paradigm Exemplars. Vol. 2, edited by Brenda Dervin, Lawrence Grossberg, Barbara J. O'Keefe, and Ellen Wartella, 153–171. Newbury Park, CA: Sage, 1989.

Jacobs, Scott, and Sally Jackson. "Speech Act Structure in Conversation: Rational Aspects of Pragmatic Coherence." In *Conversational Coherence: Form, Structure, and Strategy.* 3rd ed., edited by Robert T. Craig and Karen Tracy, 47–66. Beverly Hills, CA: Sage, 1983.

Jacobs, Scott, and Sally Jackson. "Strategy and Structure in Conversational Influence Attempts." *Communication Monographs* 50 (1983): 285–304.

Johnson, C. David, and J. Stephen Picou. "The Foundations of Symbolic Interactionism Reconsidered." In *Micro-Sociological Theory: Perspectives on Sociological Theory.* Vol. 2, edited by H. J. Helle and S. N. Eisenstadt, 54–70. Beverly Hills, CA: Sage, 1985.

Johnson, Fern L. *Speaking Culturally: Language Diversity in the United States.* Thousand Oaks, CA: Sage, 2000.

LeBaron, Curtis D., Jenny Mandelbaum, and Phillip J. Glenn. "An Overview of Language and Social Interaction Research." In *Studies in Language and Social Interaction in Honor of Robert Hopper,* edited by P. J. Glenn, C. D. LeBaron, and J. Mandelbaum, 1–44. Mahwah, NJ: Lawrence Erlbaum, 2003.

Leeds-Hurwitz, Wendy. "A Social Account of Symbols." In *Beyond the Symbol Model: Reflections on the Representational Nature of Language,* edited by John Stewart, 257–278. Albany: SUNY Press, 1996.

LePoire, Beth A. "Two Contrasting Explanations of Involvement Violations: Expectancy Violations Theory Versus Discrepancy Arousal Theory." *Human Communication Research* 20 (1994): 560–591.

Mandelbaum, Jenny. "Interpersonal Activities in Conversational Storytelling." *Western Journal of Speech Communication* 53 (1989): 114–126.

McCornack, Steven A. "Information Manipulation Theory." *Communication Monographs* 59 (1992): 1–17.

McCornack, Steven A., Timothy R. Levine, Kelly Morrison, and Maria Lapinski. "Speaking of Information Manipulation: A Critical Rejoinder." *Communication Monographs* 63 (1996): 83–92.

McCornack, Steven A., Timothy R. Levine, Kathleen Solowczuk, Helen I. Torres, and Dedra M. Campbell. "When the Alteration of Information Is Viewed as Deception: An Empirical Test of Information Manipulation Theory." *Communication Monographs* 59 (1992): 17–29.

McLaughlin, Margaret L. *Conversation: How Talk Is Organized.* Beverly Hills, CA: Sage, 1984.

Mead, G. H. *Mind, Self, and Society.* Chicago: University of Chicago Press, 1934.

Meltzer, Bernard N. "Mead's Social Psychology." In *Symbolic Interaction,* edited by J. G. Manis and B. N. Meltzer, 4–22. Boston: Allyn and Bacon, 1972.

Mokros, Hartmut B., and Mark Aakhus. "From Information-Seeking Behavior to Meaning Engagement Practice: Implications for Communication Theory and Research." *Human Communication Research* 28 (2002): 298–312.

Morris, Charles. "Introduction to George H. Mead as Social Psychologist and Social Philosopher." In *Mind, Self, and Society.* Chicago: University of Chicago Press, 1934.

Mura, Susan Swan. "Licensing Violations: Legitimate Violations of Grice's Conversational Principle." In *Conversational Coherence: Form, Structure, and Strategy,* edited by Robert T. Craig and Karen Tracy, 101–115. Beverly Hills, CA: Sage, 1983.

Nofsinger, Robert. *Everyday Conversation.* Newbury Park, CA: Sage, 1991.

O'Keefe, Daniel J. "Two Concepts of Argument." *Journal of the American Forensic Association* 13 (1977): 121–128.

Patterson, M. L. *Nonverbal Behavior: A Functional Perspective.* New York: Springer-Verlag, 1983.

Pearce, W. Barnett. "The Coordinated Management of Meaning: A Rules Based Theory of Interpersonal Communication." In *Explorations in Interpersonal Communication,* edited by Gerald R. Miller, 17–36. Beverly Hills, CA: Sage, 1976.

Pearce, W. Barnett. "Rules Theories of Communication: Varieties, Limitations, and Potentials." Paper presented at the meeting of the Speech Communication Association, New York, 1980.

Pearce, W. Barnett, and Vernon Cronen. *Communication, Action, and Meaning.* New York: Praeger, 1980.

Pearce, W. Barnett, and Kimberly A. Pearce. "Extending the Theory of the Coordinated Management of Meaning (CMM) Through a Community Dialogue Process." *Communication Theory* 10 (2000): 405–423.

Philipsen, Gerry. "The Coordinated Management of Meaning Theory of Pearce, Cronen, and Associates." In *Watershed Research Traditions in Human Communication Theory,* edited by Donald P. Cushman and Branislav Kovačić, 13–43. Albany: SUNY Press, 1995.

Pomerantz, Anita, and B. J. Fehr. "Conversation Analysis: An Approach to the Study of Social Action as Sense Making Practices." In *Discourse as Social Interaction,* edited by T. A. van Dijk, 64–91. Thousand Oaks, CA: Sage, 1997.

Potter, Jonathan. *Representing Reality: Discourse, Rhetoric and Social Construction.* London: Sage, 1996.

Potter, Jonathan, and Margaret Wetherell. *Discourse and Social Psychology: Beyond Attitudes and Behavior.* London: Sage, 1987.

Psathas, George. *Conversation Analysis: The Study of Talk-in-Interaction.* Thousand Oaks, CA: Sage, 1995.

Rogers, Everett M. *A History of Communication Study: A Biographical Approach.* New York: Free Press, 1994.

Sacks, Harvey, Emanuel Schegloff, and Gail Jefferson. "A Simplest Systematics for the Organization of Turn Taking for Conversation." *Language* 50 (1974): 696–735.

Shimanoff, Susan B. *Communication Rules: Theory and Research.* Beverly Hills, CA: Sage, 1980.

Sigman, Stuart J. "On Communication Rules from a Social Perspective." *Human Communication Research* 7 (1980): 37–51.

Stenstrøm, Anna-Brita. *An Introduction to Spoken Interaction.* London: Longman, 1994.

Stillar, Glenn F. *Analyzing Everyday Texts: Discourse, Rhetoric, and Social Processes.* Thousand Oaks, CA: Sage, 1998.

Sunnafrank, Michael. "Predicted Outcome Value and Uncertainty Reduction Theories: A Test of Competing Perspectives." *Human Communication Research* 17 (1990): 76–103.

Sunnafrank, Michael. "Predicted Outcome Value During Initial Interactions." *Human Communication Research* 13 (1986): 3–33.

Tannen, Deborah. *The Argument Culture: Stopping America's War of Words.* New York: Ballantine, 1998.

Taylor, James R., Francois Cooren, Nicole Giroux, and Daniel Robichaud. "The Communicational Basis of Organization: Between the Conversation and the Text." *Communication Theory* 6 (1996): 1–39.

Tracy, Karen. "Discourse Analysis in Communication." In *Handbook of Discourse Analysis,* edited by Deborah Schiffrin, Deborah Tannen, and Heidi Hamilton. Oxford, UK: Blackwell, 2002.

Tracy, Karen. *Everyday Talk: Building and Reflecting Identities.* New York: Guildford Press, 2002.

van Eemeren, Frans H., and Rob Grootendorst. *Argumentation, Communication, and Fallacies: A Pragma-Dialectical Perspective.* Hillsdale, NJ: Lawrence Erlbaum, 1992.

van Eemeren, Frans H., Rob Grootendorst, Sally Jackson, and Scott Jacobs. *Reconstructing Argumentative Discourse.* Tuscaloosa: University of Alabama Press, 1993.

Walton, Douglas N. *Plausible Argument in Everyday Conversation.* Albany: SUNY Press, 1992.

Wiley, Norbert. *The Semiotic Self.* Chicago: University of Chicago Press, 1994.

Woodward, Wayne. "Triadic Communication as Transactional Participation." *Critical Studies in Mass Communication* 13 (1996): 155–174.

Chapter 7: The Relationship

Altman, Irwin. "Dialectics, Physical Environments, and Personal Relationships." *Communication Monographs* 60 (1993): 26–34.

Altman, Irwin, and Dalmas Taylor. *Social Penetration: The Development of Interpersonal Relationships.* New York: Holt, Rinehart & Winston, 1973.

Altman, Irwin, A. Vinsel, and B. Brown. "Dialectic Conceptions in Social Psychology: An Application to Social Penetration and Privacy Regulation." In *Advances in Experimental Social Psychology.* Vol. 14, edited by L. Berkowitz, 76–100. New York: Academic, 1981.

Andersen, Peter A. "When One Cannot Not Communicate: A Challenge to Motley's Traditional Communication Postulates." *Communication Studies* 42 (1991): 309–325.

Anderson, Rob, Leslie A. Baxter, and Kenneth N. Cissna, eds. *Dialogic Approaches to Communication.* Thousand Oaks, CA: Sage, in press.

Anderson, Rob, and Kenneth N. Cissna. *The Martin Buber-Carl Rogers Dialogue: A New Transcript With Commentary.* Albany: SUNY Press, 1997.

Arnett, Ronald C. *Communication and Community: Implications of Martin Buber's Dialogue.* Carbondale: Southern Illinois University Press, 1986.

Arnett, Ronald C. "Rogers and Buber: Similarities, Yet Fundamental Differences." *Western Journal of Speech Communication* 45 (1981): 358–372.

Arnett, Ronald C., and Pat Arneson. *Dialogic Civility in a Cynical Age: Community, Hope, and Interpersonal Relationships.* Albany: SUNY Press, 1999.

Bakhtin, Mikhail M. *The Dialogic Imagination: Four Essays,* edited by Michael Holquist and translated by Caryl Emerson and Michael Holquist. Austin: University of Texas Press, 1981.

Bakhtin, Mikhail M. "Discourse in the Novel." In *The Dialogic Imagination: Four Essays,* edited by Michael Holquist and translated by Caryl Emerson and Michael Holquist, 276. Austin: University of Texas Press, 1981.

Bakhtin, Mikhail M. "Toward a Methodology for the Human Sciences." In Michael M. Bakhtin, *Speech Genres and Other Late Essays,* edited by Caryl Emerson and Michael Holquist and translated by Vern W. McGee. Austin: University of Texas Press, 1986.

Bakhtin, Mikhail M. "Toward a Reworking of the Dostoevsky Book." In *Problems of Dostoevsky's Poetics,* edited and translated by Caryl Emerson. Minneapolis: University of Minnesota Press, 1984.

Bavelas, Janet Beavin. "Behaving and Communicating: A Reply to Motley." *Western Journal of Speech Communication* 54 (1990): 593–602.

Baxter, Leslie A. "Relationships as Dialogues." *Personal Relationships,* in press.

Baxter, Leslie A. "The Social Side of Personal Relationships: A Dialectical Perspective." In *Social Context and Relationships: Understanding Relationship Processes.* Vol. 3, edited by Steve Duck, 139–169. Newbury Park, CA: Sage, 1993.

Baxter, Leslie A., and Dawn O. Braithwaite. "Social Dialectics: The Contradictions of Relating." In *Contemporary Communication Theories and Exemplars,* edited by Bryan Whaley and Wendy Samter. Mahwah, NJ: Lawrence Erlbaum, in press.

Baxter, Leslie A., and Barbara M. Montgomery. "A Guide to Dialectical Approaches to Studying Personal Relationships." In *Dialectical Approaches to Studying Personal Relationships,* edited by Barbara Montgomery and Leslie Baxter, 1–15. Mahwah, NJ: Lawrence Erlbaum, 1998.

Berger, Charles R. "Interpersonal Communication." In *An Integrated Approach to Communication Theory and Research,* edited by Michael B. Salwen and Don W. Stacks, 277–296. Mahwah, NJ: Lawrence Erlbaum, 1996.

Buber, Martin. *I and Thou,* translated by Walter Kaufmann. New York: Charles Scribner, 1958.

Cissna, Kenneth N., and Rob Anderson. "The Contributions of Carl R. Rogers to a Philosophical Praxis of

Dialogue." *Western Journal of Speech Communication* 54 (1990): 125–147.

Clevenger, Jr., Theodore. "Can One Not Communicate? A Conflict of Models." *Communication Studies* 42 (1991): 340–353.

Cozby, P. W. "Self-Disclosure: A Literature Review." *Psychological Bulletin* 79 (1973): 73–91.

Fiske, A. P., and S. E. Taylor. *Social Cognition.* New York: McGraw-Hill, 1991.

Fitzpatrick, Mary Anne. *Between Husbands and Wives: Communication in Marriage.* Newbury Park, CA: Sage, 1988.

Fitzpatrick, Mary Anne. "Interpersonal Communication on the Starship Enterprise: Resilience, Stability, and Change in Relationships in the Twenty-First Century." In *Communication: Views from the Helm for the 21st Century*, edited by Judith S. Trent, 41–46. Boston: Allyn and Bacon, 1998.

Fletcher, G. J. O. "Cognition in Close Relationships." *New Zealand Journal of Psychology* 22 (1993): 69–81.

Friedman, Maurice, ed. *Martin Buber and the Human Sciences.* Albany: SUNY Press, 1996.

Friedman, Maurice. "Reflections on the Buber-Rogers Dialogue: Thirty-Five Years After." In *Martin Buber and the Human Sciences*, edited by Maurice Friedman, 357–370. Albany: SUNY Press, 1996.

Gilbert, Shirley J. "Empirical and Theoretical Extensions of Self-Disclosure." In *Explorations in Interpersonal Communication*, edited by Gerald R. Miller, 197–216. Beverly Hills, CA: Sage, 1976

Jourard, Sidney. *Disclosing Man to Himself.* New York: Van Nostrand, 1968.

Jourard, Sidney. *Self-Disclosure: An Experimental Analysis of the Transparent Self.* New York: Wiley, 1971.

Jourard, Sidney. *The Transparent Self.* New York: Van Nostrand Reinhold, 1971.

Kantor, David, and William Lehr. *Inside the Family.* New York: Harper and Row, 1975.

Kelley, Harold H., and John W. Thibaut. *Interpersonal Relations: A Theory of Interdependence.* 3rd ed. New York: Wiley, 1989.

Knapp, Mark L., and Gerald R. Miller, eds. *Handbook of Interpersonal Communication.* Thousand Oaks, CA: Sage, 1994.

Knapp, Mark L., Gerald R. Miller, and Kelly Fudge. "Background and Current Trends in the Study of Interpersonal Communication." In *Handbook of Interpersonal Communication*, edited by Mark L. Knapp and Gerald R. Miller, 3–20. Thousand Oaks, CA: Sage, 1994.

Koerner, Ascan F., and Mary Anne Fitzpatrick. "Toward a Theory of Family Communication." *Communication Theory* 12 (2002): 70–91.

Koerner, Ascan F., and Mary Anne Fitzpatrick. "Understanding Family Communication Patterns and Family Functioning: The Roles of Conversation Orientation and Conformity Orientation." In *Communication Yearbook 26*, edited by William B. Gudykunst, 36–68. Mahwah, NJ: 2002.

Millar, Frank E., and L. Edna Rogers. "Power Dynamics in Marital Relationships." In *Perspectives on Marital Interaction*, edited by P. Noller and M. Fitzpatrick, 78–97. Clevedon, UK: Multilingual Matters, 1988.

Millar, Frank E., and L. Edna Rogers. "A Relational Approach to Interpersonal Communication." In *Explorations in Interpersonal Communication*, edited by Gerald R. Miller, 87–105. Beverly Hills, CA: Sage, 1976.

Millar, Frank E., and L. Edna Rogers. "Relational Dimensions of Interpersonal Dynamics." In *Interpersonal Processes: New Directions in Communication Research*, edited by Michael E. Roloff and Gerald R. Miller, 117–139. Newbury Park, CA: Sage, 1987.

Montgomery, Barbara M., and Leslie A. Baxter. "Dialogism and Relational Dialectics." In *Dialectical Approaches to Studying Personal Relationships*, edited by Barbara Montgomery and Leslie Baxter. Mahwah, NJ: Lawrence Erlbaum, 1998.

Morson, Gary Saul, and Caryl Emerson. *Mikhail Bakhtin: Creation of a Prosaics.* Stanford, CA: Stanford University Press, 1990.

Motley, Michael T. "Forum: Can One Not Communicate?" *Western Journal of Speech Communication* 54 (1990): 593–623.

Motley, Michael T. "How One May Not Communicate: A Reply to Andersen." *Communication Studies* 42 (1991): 326–339.

Motley, Michael T. "On Whether One Can(not) Not Communicate: An Examination via Traditional Communication Postulates." *Western Journal of Speech Communication* 54 (1990): 1–20.

Petronio, Sandra. *Balancing the Secrets of Private Disclosures.* Mahwah, NJ: Lawrence Erlbaum, 2000.

Petronio, Sandra. *Boundaries of Privacy: Dialectics of Disclosure.* Albany: SUNY Press, 2002.

Rawlins, William. *Friendship Matters: Communication, Dialectics, and the Life Course.* Hawthorne, NY: Aldine, 1992.

Rogers, Carl. *Client-Centered Therapy.* Boston: Houghton-Mifflin, 1951.

Rogers, Carl. *On Becoming a Person.* Boston: Houghton-Mifflin, 1961.

Rogers, Carl. "A Theory of Therapy, Personality, and Interpersonal Relationships, as Developed in the Client-Centered Framework." In *Psychology: A Study of Science.* Vol. 3, edited by S. Koch, 184–256. New York: McGraw-Hill, 1959.

Rogers, Carl. *A Way of Being.* Boston: Houghton Mifflin, 1980.

Roloff, Michael E. *Interpersonal Communication: The Social Exchange Approach.* Beverly Hills, CA: Sage, 1981.

Taylor, Dalmas A., and Irwin Altman. "Communication in Interpersonal Relationships: Social Penetration Theory." In *Interpersonal Processes: New Directions in Communication Research*, edited by Michael E. Roloff and Gerald R. Miller, 257–277. Newbury Park, CA: Sage, 1987.

Thibaut, John W., and Harold H. Kelley. *The Social Psychology of Groups.* New York: Wiley, 1959.

Watzlawick, Paul, Janet Beavin, and Don Jackson. *Pragmatics of Human Communication: A Study of Interactional Patterns, Pathologies, and Paradoxes.* New York: Norton, 1967.

Werner, Carol M., and Baxter, Leslie A. "Temporal Qualities of Relationships: Organismic, Transactional, and Dialectical Views." In *Handbook of Interpersonal Communication,* edited by Mark L. Knapp and Gerald R. Miller, 323–279. Thousand Oaks, CA: Sage.

VanLear, C. Arthur. "Testing a Cyclical Model of Communicative Openness in Relationship Development: Two Longitudinal Studies." *Communication Monographs* 58 (1991): 337–361.

Chapter 8: The Group

Bales, Robert F. *Interaction Process Analysis: A Method for the Study of Small Groups.* Reading, MA: Addison-Wesley, 1950.

Bales, Robert F. *Personality and Interpersonal Behavior.* New York: Holt, Rinehart & Winston, 1970.

Bales, Robert F., Stephen P. Cohen, and Stephen A. Williamson. *SYMLOG: A System for the Multiple Level Observation of Groups.* London: Collier, 1979.

Banks, Stephen P., and Patricia Riley. "Structuration Theory as an Ontology for Communication Research." *Communication Yearbook 16,* edited by Stanley A. Deetz, 167–196. Newbury Park, CA: Sage, 1993.

Barge, J. Kevin, and Randy Y. Hirokawa. "Toward a Communication Competency Model of Group Leadership." *Small Group Behavior* 20 (1989): 167–189.

Billingsley, Julie M. "An Evaluation of the Functional Perspective in Small Group Communication." In *Communication Yearbook 16,* edited by Stanley A. Deetz, 615–622. Newbury Park, CA: Sage, 1993.

Bormann, Ernest. "Symbolic Convergence and Communication in Group Decision Making." In *Communication and Group Decision-Making,* edited by Randy Y. Hirokawa and Marshall Scott Poole, 219–236. Beverly Hills, CA: Sage, 1986.

Cattell, Raymond. "Concepts and Methods in the Measurement of Group Syntality." *Psychological Review* 55 (1948): 48–63.

Collins, Barry, and Harold Guetzkow. *A Social Psychology of Group Processes for Decision-Making.* New York: Wiley, 1964.

Courtright, John A. "A Laboratory Investigation of Groupthink." *Communication Monographs* 45 (1978): 229–246.

Cragan, John F., and David W. Wright. "Small Group Communication Research of the 1980s: A Synthesis and Critique." *Communication Studies* 41 (1990): 212–236.

Dewey, John. *How We Think.* Boston: Heath, 1910.

Fisher, B. Aubrey. "Decision Emergence: Phases in Group Decision Making." *Speech Monographs* 37 (1970): 53–60.

Fisher, B. Aubrey. "The Process of Decision Modification in Small Discussion Groups." *Journal of Communication* 20 (1970): 51–64.

Fisher, B. Aubrey. *Small Group Decision Making: Communication and the Group Process.* New York: McGraw-Hill, 1980.

Fisher, B. Aubrey, and Leonard Hawes. "An Interact System Model: Generating a Grounded Theory of Small Groups." *Quarterly Journal of Speech* 57 (1971): 444–453.

Follett, Mary Parker. *Creative Experience.* New York: Longman, Green, 1924.

Frey, Lawrence R., ed. *Group Communication in Context: Studies of Bona Fide Groups.* Mahwah, NJ: Lawrence Erlbaum, 2003.

Frey, Lawrence R., ed. *The Handbook of Group Communication Theory and Research.* Thousand Oaks, CA: Sage, 1999.

Giddens, Anthony. *New Rules of Sociological Method.* New York: Basic, 1976.

Giddens, Anthony. *Profiles and Critiques in Social Theory.* Berkeley: University of California Press, 1982.

Giddens, Anthony. *Studies in Social and Political Theory.* New York: Basic, 1977.

Gouran, Dennis S. "Communication in Groups: The Emergence and Evolution of a Field of Study." In *The Handbook of Group Communication Theory and Research,* edited by Lawrence R. Frey, 3–36. Thousand Oaks, CA: Sage, 1999.

Gouran, Dennis S. "Communication Skills for Group Decision Making." In *Handbook of Communication and Social Interaction Skills,* edited by John O. Greene and Brant R. Burleson, 834–870. Mahwah, NJ: Lawrence Erlbaum, 2003.

Gouran, Dennis S. "The Paradigm of Unfulfilled Promise: A Critical Examination of the History of Research on Small Groups in Speech Communication." In *Speech Communication in the 20th Century,* edited by Thomas W. Benson. Carbondale: Southern Illinois University Press, 1985.

Gouran, Dennis S., and Randy Y. Hirokawa. "Counteractive Functions of Communication in Effective Group Decision-Making." In *Communication and Group Decision-Making,* edited by Randy Y. Hirokawa and Marshall Scott Poole, 81–92. Beverly Hills, CA: Sage, 1986.

Gouran, Dennis S., Randy Y. Hirokawa, Kelly M. Julian, and Geoff B. Leatham. "The Evolution and Current Status of the Functional Perspective on Communication in Decision-Making and Problem-Solving Groups." In *Communication Yearbook 16,* edited by Stanley A. Deetz, 573–600. Newbury Park, CA: Sage, 1993.

Gouran, Dennis S., Randy Y. Hirokawa, Michael Calvin McGee, and Laurie L. Miller "Communication in Groups: Research Trends and Theoretical Perspectives." In *Building Communication Theories: A Socio/Cultural Approach,* edited by Fred L. Casmir, 241–268. Hillsdale, NJ: Lawrence Erlbaum, 1994.

Hirokawa, Randy Y. "Group Communication and Decision Making Performance: A Continued Test of the

Functional Perspective." *Human Communication Research* 14 (1988): 487–515.

Hirokawa, Randy Y. "Group Communication and Problem-Solving Effectiveness: An Investigation of Group Phases." *Human Communication Research* 9 (1983): 291–305.

Hirokawa, Randy Y. "Group Communication and Problem-Solving Effectiveness I: A Critical Review of Inconsistent Findings." *Communication Quarterly* 30 (1982): 134–141.

Hirokawa, Randy Y. "Group Communication and Problem-Solving Effectiveness II." *Western Journal of Speech Communication* 47 (1983): 59–74.

Hirokawa, Randy Y., Abran J. Salazar, Larry Erbert, and Richard J. Ice. "Small Group Communication." In *An Integrated Approach to Communication Theory and Research*, edited by Michael B. Salwen and Don W. Stacks, 359–382. Mahwah, NJ: Lawrence Erlbaum, 1996.

Hirokawa, Randy Y., and Dirk R. Scheerhorn. "Communication in Faulty Group Decision-Making." In *Communication and Group Decision-Making*, edited by Randy Y. Hirokawa and Marshall Scott Poole, 63–80. Beverly Hills, CA: Sage, 1986.

Janis, Irving. *Crucial Decisions: Leadership in Policy Making and Crisis Management*. New York: Free Press, 1989.

Janis, Irving. *Groupthink: Psychological Studies of Policy Decisions and Fiascoes*. Boston: Houghton Mifflin, 1982.

Janis, Irving, and Leon Mann. *Decision Making: A Psychological Analysis of Conflict, Choice, and Commitment*. New York: Free Press, 1977.

Jarboe, Susan. "A Comparison of Input-Output, Process-Output, and Input-Process-Output Models of Small Group Problem-Solving Effectiveness." *Communication Monographs* 55 (1988): 121–142.

Lewin, Kurt. *Resolving Social Conflicts: Selected Papers on Group Dynamics*. New York: Harper and Row, 1948.

Littlejohn, Stephen W., and Kathy Domenici. *Engaging Communication in Conflict: Systemic Practice*. Thousand Oaks, CA: Sage, 2001.

Oetzel, John G. "Culturally Homogeneous and Heterogeneous Groups: Explaining Communication Processes through Individualism-Collectivism and Self-Construal." *International Journal of Intercultural Relations* 22 (1998): 135–161.

Oetzel, John G. "Effective Intercultural Work Group Communication Theory." In *Theorizing about Communication and Culture*, edited by William B. Gudykunst. Thousand Oaks, CA: Sage, in press.

Oetzel, John G. "Explaining Individual Communication Processes in Homogeneous and Heterogeneous Groups through Individualism-Collectivism and Self-Construal." *Human Communication Research* 25 (1998): 202–224.

Oetzel, John G. "Intercultural Small Groups: An Effective Decision-Making theory." In *Intercultural Communication Theories*, edited by R. L. Wiseman, 247–270. Thousand Oaks, CA: Sage, 1995.

Oetzel, John G. "Self-Construals, Communication Processes, and Group Outcomes in Homogeneous and Heterogeneous Groups." *Small Group Research* 32 (2001): 19–54.

Oetzel, John G., Trudy E. Burtis, Martha I. Chew Sanchez, and Frank G. Pérez. "Investigating the Role of Communication in Culturally Diverse Work Groups: A Review and Synthesis." *Communication Yearbook 25*, edited by William B. Gudykunst, 237–270. (Mahwah, NJ: Lawrence Erlbaum, 2001.

Poole, Marshall Scott. "Do We Have Any Theories of Group Communication?" *Communication Studies* 41 (1990): 237–247.

Poole, Marshall Scott, and Jonelle Roth. "Decision Development in Small Groups IV: A Typology of Group Decision Paths." *Human Communication Research* 15 (1989): 323–356.

Poole, Marshall Scott, and Jonelle Roth. "Decision Development in Small Groups V: Test of a Contingency Model." *Human Communication Research* 15 (1989): 549–589.

Poole, Marshall Scott, David R. Seibold, and Robert D. McPhee. "Group Decision-Making as a Structurational Process." *Quarterly Journal of Speech* 71 (1985): 74–102.

Poole, Marshall Scott, David R. Seibold, and Robert D. McPhee. "A Structurational Approach to Theory-Building in Group Decision-Making Research." In *Communication and Group Decision-Making*, edited by Randy Y. Hirokawa and Marshall Scott Poole, 238–240. Beverly Hills, CA: Sage, 1986.

Putnam, Linda L. "Revitalizing Small Group Communication: Lessons Learned from a Bona Fide Group Perspective." *Communication Studies* 45 (1994): 97–102.

Putnam, Linda L., and Cynthia Stohl. "Bona Fide Groups: An Alternative Perspective for Communication and Small Group Decision Making." In *Communication and Group Decision Making*, edited by Randy Y. Hirokawa and Marshall Scott Poole, 147–178. Thousand Oaks, CA: Sage, 1996.

Putnam, Linda L., and Cynthia Stohl. "Bona Fide Groups: A Reconceptualization of Groups in Context." *Communication Studies* 41 (1990): 248–265.

Rogers, Everett M. *A History of Communication Study: A Biographical Approach*. New York: Free Press, 1994.

Scott, Craig R. "Communication Technology and Group Communication." In *The Handbook of Group Communication Theory and Research*, edited by Lawrence R. Frey, 432–474. Thousand Oaks, CA: Sage, 1999.

Seibold, David R. "Groups and Organizations: Premises and Perspectives." In *Communication: Views from the Helm for the 21st Century*, edited by Judith S. Trent, 162–168. Boston: Allyn and Bacon, 1998.

Stohl, Cynthia, and Michael E. Holms. "A Functional Perspective for Bona Fide Groups." In *Communication Yearbook 16*, edited by Stanley A. Deetz, 601–614. Newbury Park, CA: Sage, 1993.

Stohl, Cynthia, and Linda L. Putnam. "Communication in Bona Fide Groups: A Retrospective and Prospective Account." In *Group Communication in Context: Studies of Bona Fide Groups*, edited by Lawrence R. Frey, 399–414. Mahwah, NJ: Lawrence Erlbaum, 2003.

Stohl, Cynthia, and Linda L. Putnam. "Group Communication in Context: Implications for the Study of Bona Fide Groups." In *Group Communication in Context: Studies of Natural Groups*, edited by Lawrence Frey, 284–292. Hillsdale, NJ: Lawrence Erlbaum, 1994.

VanderVoort, Lise. "Functional and Causal Explanations in Group Communication Research," *Communication Theory* 12 (2002): 469–486.

Chapter 9: The Organization

Ashcroft, Karen Lee, and Brenda J. Allen. "The Racial Foundation of Organizational Communication." *Communication Theory* 13 (February 2003): 5–38.

Banks, Stephen P., and Patricia Riley. "Structuration Theory as an Ontology for Communication Research." *Communication Yearbook 16*, edited by Stanley A. Deetz, 167–196. Newbury Park, CA: Sage, 1993.

Barker, James R., and George Cheney. "The Concept and the Practices of Discipline in Contemporary Organizational Life." *Communication Monographs* 61 (1994): 19–43.

Bell, Elizabeth, and Linda C. Forbes. "Office Folklore in the Academic Paperwork Empire: The Interstitial Space of Gendered (Con)Texts." *Text and Performance Quarterly* 14 (July 1994): 181–196.

Carlone, David, and Bryan Taylor. "Organizational Communication and Cultural Studies: A Review Essay." *Communication Theory* 8 (August 1998): 337–367.

Cheney, George. *Rhetoric in an Organizational Society: Managing Multiple Identities.* Columbia: University of South Carolina Press, 1991.

Cheney, George. "The Rhetoric of Identification and the Study of Organizational Communication." *Quarterly Journal of Speech* 69 (1983): 143–158.

Cheney, George, and Lars Thøger Christensen. "Organizational Identity: Linkages Between Internal and External Communication." In *The New Handbook of Organizational Communication: Advances in Theory, Research, and Methods*, edited by Fredric M. Jablin and Linda L. Putnam, 231–269. Thousand Oaks, CA: Sage, 2001.

Cheney, George, Joseph Straub, Laura Speirs-Glebe, Cynthia Stohl, Dan DeGooyer, Jr., Susan Whalen, Kathy Garvin-Doxas, and David Carole. "Democracy, Participation, and Communication at Work: A Multidisciplinary Review." In *Communication Yearbook 21*, edited by Michael E. Roloff, 35–91. Thousand Oaks, CA: Sage, 1998.

Cheney, George, and Phillip K. Tompkins. "Coming to Terms with Organizational Identification and Commitment." *Central States Speech Journal* 38 (1987): 1–15.

Clair, Robin Patric. *Organizing Silence: A World of Possibilities.* Albany: SUNY Press, 1998.

Clair, Robin Patric. "Organizing Silence: Silence as Voice and Voice as Silence in the Narrative Exploration of the Treaty of New Echota." *Western Journal of Communication* 61 (Summer 1997): 315–337.

Deetz, Stanley A. *Democracy in an Age of Corporate Colonization: Developments in Communication and the Politics of Everyday Life.* Albany: SUNY Press, 1992.

Deetz, Stanley A. "Disciplinary Power in the Modern Corporation." In *Critical Management Studies*, edited by M. Alvesson and H. Willmott, 21–45. Newbury Park, CA: Sage, 1992.

Deetz, Stanley A. "The New Politics of the Workplace: Ideology and Other Unobtrusive Controls." In *After Postmodernism: Reconstructing Ideology Critique*, edited by H. W. Simons and M. Billig, 172–199. Thousand Oaks, CA: Sage, 1994.

Deetz, Stanley A. *Transforming Communication, Transforming Business: Building Responsive and Responsible Workplaces.* Cresskill, NJ: Hampton, 1995.

Edwards, R. "The Social Relations of Production at the Point of Production." In *Complex Organizations: Critical Perspectives*, edited by M. Zey-Ferrell and M. Aiken. Glenview, IL: Scott, Foresman, 1981.

Eisenberg, Eric M., and Patricia Riley. "Organizational Culture." In *The New Handbook of Organizational Communication: Advances in Theory, Research, and Methods*, edited by Fredric M. Jablin and Linda L. Putnam, 291–322. Thousand Oaks, CA: Sage, 2001.

Eisenstadt, S. N. *Max Weber on Charisma and Institution Building.* Chicago: University of Chicago Press, 1968.

Etzioni, Amatai. *Modern Organizations.* Englewood Cliffs, NJ: Prentice-Hall, 1964.

Everett, James L. "Communication and Sociocultural Evolution in Organizations and Organizational Populations." *Communication Theory* 4 (1994): 93–110.

Fayol, Henri. *General and Industrial Management.* New York: Pitman, 1949. Originally published in 1925.

Habermas, Jürgen. *Knowledge and Human Interests*, translated by J. Shapiro. Boston: Beacon Press, 1971.

Habermas, Jürgen. *Legitimation Crisis*, translated by Thomas McCarthy. Boston: Beacon Press, 1975.

Habermas, Jürgen. *Theory and Practice*, translated by Thomas McCarthy. Boston: Beacon Press, 1973.

Habermas, Jürgen. *The Theory of Communicative Action, Volume 1: Reason and the Rationalization of Society*, translated by Thomas McCarthy. Boston: Beacon Press, 1984.

Habermas, Jürgen. *The Theory of Communicative Action, Volume 2: Lifeworld and System*, translated by Thomas McCarthy. Boston: Beacon Press, 1987.

Jablin, Fredric M., and Linda L. Putnam, eds. *The New Handbook of Organizational Communication: Advances in Theory, Research, and Methods.* Thousand Oaks, CA: Sage, 2001.

Johnson, H. "A New Conceptualization of Source of Organizational Climate." *Administrative Science Quarterly* 3 (1976): 275–292.

Likert, Rensis. *The Human Organization*. New York: McGraw-Hill, 1967.

Likert, Rensis. "New Patterns in Sales Management." In *Changing Perspectives in Marketing Management,* edited by Martin Warshaw. Ann Arbor: Bureau of Business Research, University of Michigan, 1972.

Likert, Rensis. *New Patterns of Management*. New York: McGraw-Hill, 1961.

Marshall, Judi. "Viewing Organizational Communication from a Feminist Perspective: A Critique and Some Offerings." In *Communication Yearbook 16,* edited by Stanley A. Deetz, 122–14. Newbury Park, CA: Sage, 1993.

McPhee, Robert D. "Formal Structure and Organizational Communication." In *Organizational Communication: Traditional Themes and New Directions,* edited by Robert D. McPhee and Phillip K. Tompkins, 149–178. Beverly Hills, CA: Sage, 1985.

McPhee, Robert D. "Organizational Communication: A Structurational Exemplar." In *Rethinking Communication: Paradigm Exemplars,* edited by Brenda Dervin, Lawrence Grossberg, Barbara J. O'Keefe, and Ellen Wartella, 199–212. Beverly Hills, CA: Sage, 1989.

McPhee, Robert D., and Marshall Scott Poole. "Organizational Structures and Configurations." In *The New Handbook of Organizational Communication: Advances in Theory, Research, and Methods,* edited by Fredric M. Jablin and Linda L. Putnam, 503–543. Thousand Oaks, CA: Sage, 2001.

Monge, Peter R. "The Network Level of Analysis." In *Handbook of Communication Science,* edited by Charles R. Berger and Steven H. Chaffee, 239–270. Newbury Park, CA: Sage, 1987.

Monge, Peter R., and Noshir S. Contractor. "Emergent Communication Networks." *The New Handbook of Organizational Communication: Advances in Theory, Research, and Methods,* edited by Fredric M. Jablin and Linda L. Putnam, 440–502. Thousand Oaks, CA: Sage, 2001.

Monge, Peter R., and Noshir S. Contractor. *Theories of Communication Networks*. Oxford: Oxford University Press, 2003.

Morgan, Gareth. *Images of Organization*. Beverly Hills, CA: Sage, 1986.

Mumby, Dennis K. "Critical Organizational Communication Studies: The Next 10 Years." *Communication Monographs* 60 (March 1993): 18–25.

Mumby, Dennis K. "The Problem of Hegemony: Rereading Gramsci for Organizational Communication Studies." *Western Journal of Communication* 61 (1997): 343–375.

Pacanowsky, Michael E. "Creating and Narrating Organizational Realities." In *Rethinking Communication: Paradigm Exemplars,* edited by Brenda Dervin, Lawrence Grossberg, Barbara J. O'Keefe, and Ellen Wartella, 250–257. Newbury Park, CA: Sage, 1989.

Pacanowsky, Michael E., and Nick O'Donnell-Trujillo. "Communication and Organizational Cultures." *Western Journal of Speech Communication* 46 (1982): 115–130.

Pacanowsky Michael E., and Nick O'Donnell-Trujillo. "Organizational Communication as Cultural Performance." *Communication Monographs* 50 (1983): 129–145.

Papa, Michael J., Mohammad A. Auwal, and Arvind Singhal. "Organizing for Social Change Within Concertive Control Systems: Member Identification, Empowerment, and the Masking of Discipline." *Communication Monographs* 64 (1997): 219–249.

Perrow, Charles. *Complex Organizations: A Critical Essay*. Glenview, IL: Scott, Foresman, 1972.

Poole, Marshall Scott. "Communication and Organizational Climates: Review, Critique, and a New Perspective." In *Organizational Communication: Traditional Themes and New Directions,* edited by Robert D. McPhee and Phillip K. Tompkins, 79–108. Beverly Hills, CA: Sage, 1985.

Poole, Marshall Scott, and Robert D. McPhee. "A Structural Analysis of Organizational Climate." In *Communication and Organizations: An Interpretive Approach,* edited by Linda L. Putnam and Michael E. Pacanowsky, 195–220. Beverly Hills, CA: Sage, 1983.

Putnam, Linda L. "Metaphors of Communication and Organization." In *Communication: Views from the Helm for the 21st Century,* edited by Judith S. Trent, 145–152. Boston: Allyn and Bacon, 1998.

Richmond, Virginia, and James C. McCroskey. "Management Communication Style, Tolerance for Disagreement, and Innovativeness as Predictors of Employee Satisfaction: A Comparison of Single-Factor, Two-Factor, and Multiple-Factor Approaches." In *Communication Yearbook 3,* edited by D. Nimmo, 359–373. New Brunswick, NJ: Transaction, 1979.

Sackmann, Sonja A. "Managing Organizational Culture: Dreams and Possibilities." In *Communication Yearbook 13,* edited by James Anderson, 114–148. Newbury Park, CA: Sage, 1990.

Sass, James S., and Daniel J. Canary. "Organizational Commitment and Identification: An Examination of Conceptual and Operational Convergence." *Western Journal of Speech Communication* 55 (1991): 275–293.

Senge, Peter. *The Fifth Discipline: The Art and Practice of the Learning Organization*. New York: Currency-Doubleday, 1994.

Simon, Herbert. *Administrative Behavior*. New York: Free Press, 1976.

Stohl, Cynthia. *Organizational Communication: Connectedness in Action*. Thousand Oaks, CA: Sage, 1995.

Taylor, Frederick. *Principles of Scientific Management*. New York: Harper Brothers, 1947. Originally published in 1912.

Taylor, James, R. *Rethinking the Theory of Organizational Communication: How to Read an Organization*. Norwood, NJ: Ablex, 1993.

Taylor, James R. "Shifting from a Heteronomous to an Autonomous Worldview of Organizational Communication: Communication Theory on the Cusp." *Communication Theory* 5 (1995): 1–35.

Taylor, James R., Francois Cooren, Nicole Giroux, and Daniel Robichaud. "The Communicational Basis of Organization: Between the Conversation and the Text." *Communication Theory* 6 (1996): 1–39.

Taylor, James R., Andrew J. Flanagin, George Cheney, and David R. Seibold. "Organizational Communication Research: Key Moments, Central Concerns, and Future Challenges." In *Communication Yearbook 24*, edited by William B. Gudykunst, 99–138. Thousand Oaks, CA: Sage, 2001.

Taylor, James R., and Elizabeth J. Van Every. *The Emergent Organization: Communication as Its Site and Surface.* Mahwah, NJ: Lawrence Erlbaum, 2000.

Tompkins, Phillip K., and George Cheney. "Account Analysis of Organizations: Decision Making and Identification." In *Communication and Organizations: An Interpretive Approach*, edited by Linda L. Putnam and Michael E. Pacanowsky, 123–146. Beverly Hills, CA: Sage, 1983.

Tompkins, Phillip K., and George Cheney. "Communication and Unobtrusive Control in Contemporary Organizations." In *Organizational Communication: Traditional Themes and New Directions*, edited by Robert D. McPhee and Phillip K. Tompkins, 179–210. Beverly Hills, CA: Sage, 1985.

Trethewey, Angela. "Disciplined Bodies: Women's Embodied Identities at Work." *Organizational Studies* 20 (1999): 423–450.

Trethewey, Angela. "Isn't It Ironic: Using Irony to Explore the Contradictions of Organizational Life." *Western Journal of Communication* 63 (Spring 1999): 140–167.

Trethewey, Angela. "Resistance, Identity, and Empowerment: A Postmodern Feminist Analysis of Clients in a Human Service Organization." *Communication Monographs* 64 (1977): 281–301.

Van Maanen, John, and Stephen R. Barley. "Cultural Organization: Fragments of a Theory." In *Organizational Culture*, edited by P. J. Frost, and others, 31–54. Beverly Hills, CA: Sage, 1985.

Weber, Max. *The Theory of Social and Economic Organizations*, translated by A. M. Henderson and T. Parsons. New York: Oxford University Press, 1947.

Weick, Karl. *The Social Psychology of Organizing*, 2nd ed. Reading, MA: Addison-Wesley, 1979.

Chapter 10: The Media

Allor, Martin. "Relocating the Site of the Audience." *Critical Studies in Mass Communication* 5 (1988): 217–233.

Ball-Rokeach, Sandra J., and Muriel G. Cantor, eds. *Media, Audience, and Social Structure.* Beverly Hills, CA: Sage, 1986.

Ball-Rokeach, Sandra J., and Melvin L. DeFleur. "A Dependency Model of Mass-Media Effects." *Communication Research* 3 (1976): 3–21.

Baudrillard, Jean. *The Illusion of the End*, translated by Chris Turner. Cambridge: Polity, 1994.

Baudrillard, Jean. *Simulations*, translated by Paul Foss, Paul Patton, and Philip Beitchman. New York: Semiotext(e), 1983.

Baudrillard, Jean. *Symbolic Exchange and Death*, translated by Iain Hamilton Grant. Thousand Oaks, CA: Sage, 1993.

Bauer, Raymond. "The Audience." In *Handbook of Communication*, edited by I. de sola Pool and others, 141–152. Chicago: Rand McNally, 1973.

Bauer, Raymond. "The Obstinate Audience: The Influence Process from the Point of View of Social Communication." *American Psychologist* 19 (1964): 319–328.

Bineham, Jeffery L. "A Historical Account of the Hypodermic Model in Mass Communication." *Communication Monographs* 55 (1988): 230–246.

Biocca, Frank A. "Opposing Conceptions of the Audience: The Active and Passive Hemispheres of Mass Communication Theory." In *Communication Yearbook 11*, edited by James A. Anderson, 51–80. Newbury Park, CA: Sage, 1988.

Blumler, Jay, and Elihu Katz, eds. *The Uses of Mass Communication.* Beverly Hills, CA: Sage, 1974.

Boulding, Kenneth. "The Medium Is the Massage." In *McLuhan: Hot and Cool*, edited by G. E. Stearn, 56–64. New York: Dial, 1967.

Brantlinger, Patrick. *Bread and Circuses: Theories of Mass Culture as Social Decay.* Ithaca, NY: Cornell University Press, 1983.

Brookey, Robert Alan, and Robert Westerfelhaus. "Pistols and Petticoats, Piety and Purity: *To Wong Foo*, the Queering of the American Monomyth, and the Marginalizing Discourse of Deification." In *Critical Studies in Media Communication*, 18 (2001): 141–155.

Burrowes, Carl Patrick. "From Functionalist to Cultural Studies: Manifest Ruptures and Latent Continuities." *Communication Theory* 6 (1996): 88–103.

Carey, J. W. "Harold Adams Innis and Marshall McLuhan." *Antioch Review* 27 (1967): 5–39.

Carragee, Kevin M. "A Critical Evaluation of Debates Examining the Media Hegemony Thesis." *Western Journal of Communication* 57 (Summer 1993): 330–348.

Carragee, Kevin M. "Interpretive Media Study and Interpretive Social Science." *Critical Studies in Mass Communication* 7 (1990): 81–96.

Childs, M., and J. Reston, eds. *Walter Lippmann and His Times.* New York: Harcourt Brace, 1959.

Davis, Dennis K., and Stanley J. Baran, *Mass Communication and Everyday Life: A Perspective on Theory and Effects.* Belmont, CA: Wadsworth, 1981.

Davis, Dennis K., and Thomas F. N. Puckett. "Mass Entertainment and Community: Toward a Culture-Centered Paradigm for Mass Communication Research." In *Communication Yearbook 15*, edited by Stanley A. Deetz, 3–34. Newbury Park, CA: Sage, 1992.

DeFleur, Melvin L., and Sandra J. Ball-Rokeach, *Theories of Mass Communication*. New York: Longman, 1982.

Elliott, Philip. "Uses and Gratifications Research: A Critique and Sociological Alternative." In *The Uses of Mass Communication*, edited by J. Blumler and E. Katz, 249–268. Beverly Hills, CA: Sage, 1974.

Ellis, Donald G. *Crafting Society: Ethnicity, Class, and Communication Theory*. Mahwah, NJ: Lawrence Erlbaum, 1999.

Emmers-Sommer, Tara M., and Mike Allen. "Surveying the Effect of Media Effects: A Meta-Analytic Summary of the Media Effects Research." *Human Communication Research* 25 (1999): 478–497.

Fiske, John. *Introduction to Communication Studies*. New York: Methuen, 1982.

Fiske, John. *Reading the Popular*. Winchester, MA: Unwin Hyman, 1989.

Fiske, John. *Television Culture*. New York: Methuen, 1987.

Fiske, John. *Understanding Popular Culture*. Winchester, MA: Unwin Hyman, 1989.

Fortner, Robert S. "Mediated Communication Theory." In *Building Communication Theories: A Socio/Cultural Approach*, edited by Fred L. Casmir, 209–240. Hillsdale, NJ: Lawrence Erlbaum, 1994.

Foss, Sonja K., Karen A. Foss, and Robert Trapp, *Contemporary Perspectives on Rhetoric*, 3rd ed. Prospect Heights, IL: Waveland, 2002.

Fry, Donald L., and Virginia H. Fry. "A Semiotic Model for the Study of Mass Communication." In *Communication Yearbook 9*, edited by M. L. McLaughlin, 443–462. Beverly Hills, CA: Sage, 1986.

Gauntlett, David. *Media, Gender, and Identity*. London: Routledge, 2002.

Gerbner, George. "Living with Television: The Dynamics of the Cultivation Process." In *Perspectives on Media Effects*, edited by Jennings Bryant and Dolf Zillmann, 17–40. Hillsdale, NJ: Lawrence Erlbaum, 1986.

Gerbner, George. "Mass Media and Human Communication Theory." In *Human Communication Theory*, edited by Frank E. X. Dance. New York: Holt, Rinehart & Winston, 1967.

Gerbner, George, Larry Gross, Michael Morgan, and Nancy Signorielli. "Living with Television." In *Perspectives on Media Effects*, edited by Jennings Bryant and Dolf Zillmann. Hillsdale, NJ: Lawrence Erlbaum, 1986.

Greenberg, Bradley S., and Michael B. Salwen. "Mass Communication Theory and Research: Concepts and Models." In *An Integrated Approach to Communication Theory and Research*, edited by Michael B. Salwen and Don W. Stacks, 63–78. Mahwah, NJ: Lawrence Erlbaum, 1996.

Gronbeck, Bruce. "McLuhan as Rhetorical Theorist." *Journal of Communication* 31 (1981): 117–128.

Huesca, Robert, and Brenda Dervin. "Theory and Practice in Latin American Alternative Communication Research." *Journal of Communication* 44 (1994): 53–73.

Innis, Harold Adams. *The Bias of Communication*. Toronto: University of Toronto Press, 1951.

Innis, Harold Adams. *Empire and Communications*, 2nd ed. Toronto: University of Toronto Press, 1972.

Jensen, Klaus Bruhn. "When Is Meaning? Communication Theory, Pragmatism, and Mass Media Reception." In *Communication Yearbook 14*, edited by James A. Anderson, 3–32. Newbury Park, CA: Sage, 1991.

Katz, Elihu, Jay Blumler, and Michael Gurevitch. "Uses of Mass Communication by the Individual." In *Mass Communication Research: Major Issues and Future Directions*, edited by W. P. Davidson and F. Yu, 11–35. New York: Praeger, 1974.

Klapper, Joseph T. *The Effects of Mass Communication*. Glencoe, IL: Free Press, 1960.

Lasswell, Harold. "The Structure and Function of Communication in Society." In *The Communication of Ideas*, edited by L. Bryson. New York: Institute for Religious and Social Studies, 1948.

Lazarsfeld, Paul, and Robert K. Merton. "Mass Communication, Popular Taste, and Organized Social Action." In *The Process and Effects of Mass Communication*, edited by W. Schramm and D. F. Roberts. Urbana: University of Illinois Press, 1971.

Leeds-Hurwitz, Wendy. *Semiotics and Communication: Signs, Codes, Cultures*. Hillsdale, NJ: Lawrence Erlbaum, 1993.

Lindlof, Thomas R. "Media Audiences as Interpretive Communities." In *Communication Yearbook 11*, edited by James A. Anderson, 81–107. Newbury Park, CA: Sage, 1988.

Lindlof, Thomas R., and Timothy P. Meyer. "Mediated Communication as Ways of Seeing, Acting, and Constructing Culture: The Tools and Foundations of Qualitative Research." In *Natural Audiences: Qualitative Research of Media Uses and Effects*, edited by Thomas R. Lindlof, 1–32. Norwood, NJ: Ablex, 1987.

Lippmann, Walter. *Public Opinion*. New York: Macmillan, 1921.

Lull, James. "The Social Uses of Television." *Human Communication Research* 6 (1980): 197–209.

McCombs, Maxwell. "New Frontiers in Agenda Setting: Agendas of Attributes and Frames." *Mass Communication Review* 24 (1997): 4–24.

McCombs, Maxwell, and Tamara Bell. "The Agenda Setting Role of Mass Communication." In *An Integrated Approach to Communication Theory and Research*, edited by Michael B. Salwen and Don W. Stacks, 93–110. Mahwah, NJ: Lawrence Erlbaum, 1996.

McLuhan, Marshall. *The Gutenberg Galaxy: The Making of Typographic Man*. Toronto: University of Toronto Press, 1962.

McLuhan, Marshall. *The Mechanical Bride*. New York: Vanguard, 1951.

McLuhan, Marshall. *Understanding Media*. New York: McGraw-Hill, 1964.

McLuhan, Marshall, and Quentin Fiore, *The Medium Is the Massage.* New York: Bantam, 1967.

McQuail, Denis. *Mass Communication Theory: An Introduction.* London: Sage, 1987.

Meyrowitz, Joshua. "Images of Media: Hidden Ferment—and Harmony—in the Field." *Journal of Communication* 43 (1993): 55–67.

Moores, Shaun. *Interpreting Audiences: The Ethnography of Media Consumption.* London: Sage, 1993.

Morgan, Michael, and James Shanahan. "Two Decades of Cultivation Research: An Appraisal and Meta-Analysis." *Communication Yearbook 20,* edited by Brant R. Burleson, 1–45. Thousand Oaks, CA: Sage, 1997.

Newhagen, John E. "Colloquy: Information Processing: A More Inclusive Paradigm for the Study of Mass Media Effects." *Human Communication Research* 26 (2000): 99–103.

Noelle-Neumann, Elisabeth. "The Effect of Media on Media Effects Research." *Journal of Communication* 33 (1983): 157–165.

Noelle-Neumann, Elisabeth. "Return to the Concept of Powerful Mass Media." In *Studies of Broadcasting,* edited by H. Eguchi and K. Sata, 67–112. Tokyo: Nippon Hoso Kyokii, 1973.

Noelle-Neumann, Elisabeth. *The Spiral of Silence: Public Opinion—Our Social Skin.* Chicago: University of Chicago Press, 1984.

Noelle-Neumann, Elisabeth. "The Theory of Public Opinion: The Concept of the Spiral of Silence." In *Communication Yearbook 14,* edited by James A. Anderson, 256–287. Newbury Park, CA: Sage, 1991.

Palmgreen, Philip. "Uses and Gratifications: A Theoretical Perspective." In *Communication Yearbook 8,* edited by R. N. Bostrom, 20–55. Beverly Hills, CA: Sage, 1984.

Pietilä, Veikko. "Perspectives on Our Past: Charting the Histories of Mass Communication Studies." *Critical Studies in Mass Communication* 11 (1994): 346–361.

Potter, W. James. *On Media Violence.* Thousand Oaks, CA: Sage, 1999.

Power, Paulo, Robert Kubey, and Spiro Kiousis. "Audience Activity and Passivity: An Historical Taxonomy." *Communication Yearbook 26,* edited by William B. Gudykunst. Mahwah, NJ: Lawrence Erlbaum, 2002.

Protess, David, and Maxwell McCombs, *Agenda Setting: Readings on Media, Public Opinion, and Policymaking.* Hillsdale, NJ: Lawrence Erlbaum, 1991.

Rayburn, II, J. D. "Uses and Gratifications." In *An Integrated Approach to Communication Theory and Research,* edited by Michael B. Salwen and Don W. Stacks, 145–163. Mahwah, NJ: Lawrence Erlbaum, 1996.

Reese, Stephen D. "Setting the Media's Agenda: A Power Balance Perspective." In *Communication Yearbook 14,* edited by James A. Anderson, 309–340. Newbury Park, CA: Sage, 1991.

Rogers, Everett M. *A History of Communication Study: A Biographical Approach.* New York: Free Press, 1994.

Rogers, Everett M., and James W. Dearing. "Agenda-Setting Research: Where Has It Been, Where Is It Going?" in *Communication Yearbook 11,* edited by James A. Anderson, 555–593. Newbury Park, CA: Sage, 1988.

Rosengren, Karl Erik, L. Wenner, and P. Palmgreen, eds. *Media Gratifications Research: Current Perspectives.* Beverly Hills, CA: Sage, 1985.

Rubin, Alan M. "Audience Activity and Media Use." *Communication Monographs* 60 (1993): 98–105.

Rubin, Alan M., and Paul M. Haridakis. "Mass Communication Research at the Dawn of the 21st Century." In *Communication Yearbook 24,* edited by William B. Gudykunst, 73–99. Thousand Oaks, CA: Sage, 2001.

Rubin, Alan M., and Sven Windahl. "The Uses and Dependency Model of Mass Communication." *Critical Studies in Mass Communication* 3 (1986): 193.

Salmon, Charles T., and Carroll J. Glynn. "Spiral of Silence: Communication and Public Opinion as Social Control." In *An Integrated Approach to Communication Theory and Research,* edited by Michael B. Salwen and Don W. Stacks, 165–180. Mahwah, NJ: Lawrence Erlbaum, 1996.

Scheufele, Dietram A. "Framing as a Theory of Media Effects." *Journal of Communication* 49 (1999): 103–122.

Schoening, Gerard T., and James A. Anderson. "Social Action Media Studies: Foundational Arguments and Common Premises." *Communication Theory* 5 (1995): 93–116.

Sears, David O., and Jonathan I. Freedman. "Selective Exposure to Information: A Critical Review." In *The Process and Effects of Mass Communication,* edited by W. Schramm and D. F. Roberts, 209–234. Urbana: University of Illinois Press, 1971.

Severin, Werner J., and James W. Tankard, *Communication Theories: Origins, Methods, Uses.* New York: Hastings House, 1979.

Shaw, Donald L., and Maxwell E. McCombs, *The Emergence of American Political Issues.* St. Paul, MN: West, 1977.

Shoemaker, Pamela J. "Media Gatekeeping." In *An Integrated Approach to Communication Theory and Research,* edited by Michael B. Salwen and Don W. Stacks, 79–91. Mahwah, NJ: Lawrence Erlbaum, 1996.

Shugart, Helene A. "Reinventing Privilege: The New (Gay) Man in Contemporary Popular Media." *Critical Studies in Media Communication* 20 (2003): 67–91.

Shugart, Helene A., Catherine Egley Waggoner, and D. Lynn O'Brien Hallstein. "Mediating Third-Wave Feminism: Appropriation as Postmodern Media Practice." *Critical Studies in Media Communication* 18 (2001): 194–210.

Signorielli, Nancy. "Television's Mean and Dangerous World: A Continuation of the Cultural Indicators Perspective." In *Cultivation Analysis: New Directions in Media Effects Research,* edited by Nancy Signorielli and Michael Morgan, 85–106. Newbury Park, CA: Sage, 1990.

Signorielli, Nancy, and Michael Morgan, eds. *Cultivation Analysis: New Directions in Media Effects Research.* Newbury Park, CA: Sage, 1990.

Signorielli, Nancy, and Michael Morgan. "Cultivation Analysis: Research and Practice." In *An Integrated Approach to Communication Theory and Research,* edited by Michael B. Salwen and Don W. Stacks, 111–126. Mahwah, NJ: Lawrence Erlbaum, 1996.

Siune, Karen, and Ole Borre. "Setting the Agenda for a Danish Election." *Journal of Communication* 25 (1975): 65–73.

Sproule, J. Michael. "Progressive Propaganda Critics and the Magic Bullet Myth." *Critical Studies in Mass Communication* 6 (1989): 225–246.

Steiner, Linda. "Oppositional Decoding as an Act of Resistance." *Critical Studies in Mass Communication* 5 (1988): 1–15.

Swanson, David L. "Political Communication Research and the Uses and Gratifications Model: A Critique." *Communication Research* 6 (1979): 36–53.

Swanson, David L., and Austin S. Babrow. "Uses and Gratifications: The Influence of Gratification-Seeking and Expectancy-Value Judgments on the Viewing of Television News." In *Rethinking Communication: Paradigm Exemplars,* edited by Brenda Dervin, Lawrence Grossberg, Barbara J. O'Keefe, and Ellen Wartella, 361–375. Newbury Park, CA: Sage, 1989.

Wolfe, Tom. "The New Life Out There." In *McLuhan: Hot and Cool,* edited by G. E. Stearn, 34–56. New York: Dial, 1967.

Zhu, Jian-Hua, and Deborah Blood. "Media Agenda-Setting Theory: Telling the Public What to Think About." In *Emerging Theories of Human Communication,* edited by Branislav Kovaĉić, 88–114. Albany: SUNY Press, 1997.

Chapter 11: Culture and Society

Agar, Michael. *Speaking of Ethnography.* Beverly Hills, CA: Sage, 1986.

Agger, Ben. *Cultural Studies as Critical Theory.* London: Falmer, 1992.

Althusser, Louis. *For Marx,* translated by B. Brewster. New York: Vintage, 1970.

Althusser, Louis. *Lenin and Philosophy,* translated by B. Brewster. New York: Monthly Review Press, 1971.

Alvesson, Mats, and Stanley A. Deetz. "Critical Theory and Postmodernism Approaches to Organizational Studies." In *Handbook of Organizational Studies,* edited by S. Clegg, C. Harding, and W. Nord, 173–202. London: Sage, 1996.

Angus, Ian. "The Politics of Common Sense: Articulation Theory and Critical Communication Studies." In *Communication Yearbook 15,* edited by Stanley A. Deetz, 535–570. Newbury Park, CA: Sage, 1992.

Anzaldúa, Gloria. *Borderlands/La Frontera: The New Mestiza.* San Francisco: Aunt Lute, 1978.

Aptheker, Bettina. *Tapestries of Life: Women's Work, Women's Consciousness, and the Meaning of Daily Experience.* Amherst: University of Massachusetts Press, 1989.

Arato, Andrew, and Eike Gebhardt, eds. *The Essential Frankfurt School Reader.* New York: Continuum, 1982.

Atkinson, Paul. *Understanding Ethnographic Texts.* Newbury Park, CA: Sage, 1992.

Avant-Mier, Roberto, and Marouf Hasian, Jr. "In Search of the Power of Whiteness: A Genealogical Exploration of Negotiated Racial Identities in America's Ethnic Past." *Communication Quarterly* 50 (2002): 391–409.

Becker, Samuel L. "Marxist Approaches to Media Studies: The British Experience," *Critical Studies in Mass Communication* 1 (1984): 66–80.

Bernstein, Basil. *Class, Codes, and Control: Theoretical Studies Toward a Sociology of Language.* London: Routledge & Kegan Paul, 1971.

Blair, Carole. "The Statement: Foundation of Foucault's Historical Criticism," *Western Journal of Speech Communication* 51 (1987): 364–383.

Blumer, Herbert. *Symbolic Interactionism: Perspective and Method.* Englewood Cliffs, NJ: Prentice-Hall, 1969.

Bottomore, Tom, and Armand Mattelart. "Marxist Theories of Communication." In *International Encyclopedia of Communications,* Vol. 2, edited by Erik Barnouw, 476–483. New York: Oxford University Press, 1989.

Cameron, Deborah. *Working with Spoken Discourse.* London: Sage, 2001.

Carbaugh, Donal, ed. "Culture Talking About Itself." In *Cultural Communication and Intercultural Contact,* edited by Donal Carbaugh, 1–9. Hillsdale, NJ: Lawrence Erlbaum, 1990.

Carbaugh, Donal. *Situating Selves: The Communication of Social Identities in American Scenes.* Albany: SUNY Press, 1996.

Carbaugh, Donal, and Sally Hastings. "A Role for Communication Theory in Ethnography and Cultural Analysis," *Communication Theory* 2 (1992): 156–165.

Carragee, Kevin M. "A Critical Evaluation of the Media Hegemony Thesis," *Western Journal of Communication* 57 (1993): 330–348.

Cloud, Dana L. "The Materiality of Discourse as Oxymoron: A Challenge to Critical Rhetoric," *Western Journal of Communication* 58 (Summer 1994): 141–163.

Conquergood, Dwight. "Ethnography, Rhetoric, and Performance," *Quarterly Journal of Speech* 78 (1992): 80–97.

Conquergood, Dwight. "Rethinking Ethnography: Toward a Critical Cultural Politics," *Communication Monographs* 58 (1991): 179–194.

Cooper, Martha. "Rhetorical Criticism and Foucault's Philosophy of Discursive Events," *Central States Speech Journal* 39 (1988): 1–17.

Cragan, John F., and Donald C. Shields, *Understanding Communication Theory: The Communicative Forces for Human Action.* Boston: Allyn and Bacon, 1998.

Crawford, Lyall. "Personal Ethnography," *Communication Monographs* 63 (1996): 158–170.

Delgado, Richard, and Jean Stefancic, *Critical Race Theory: An Introduction*. New York: New York University Press, 2001.

Dirlik, Arif. "Culturalism as Hegemonic Ideology and Liberating Practice." In *The Nature and Context of Minority Discourse*, edited by A. Jan Mohamed and D. Lloyd, 394–431. New York: Oxford University Press, 1990.

Dow, Bonnie J. "Feminism, Difference(s), and Rhetorical Studies," *Communication Studies* 46 (Spring-Summer 1995): 106–117.

Ealy, Steven D. *Communication, Speech, and Politics: Habermas and Political Analysis*. Washington, DC: University Press of America, 1981.

Ellis, Donald G. "Poststructuralism and Language: Non-Sense," *Communication Monographs* 58 (1991): 213–224.

Farrell, Thomas B. *Norms of Rhetorical Culture*. New Haven, CT: Yale University Press, 1993.

Farrell, Thomas B., and James A. Aune. "Critical Theory and Communication: A Selective Literature Review," *Quarterly Journal of Speech* 65 (1979): 93–120.

Fink, Edward L. "Dynamic Social Impact Theory and the Study of Human Communication," *Journal of Communication* 46 (1996): 4–77.

Foss, Karen A., and Sonja K. Foss, *Women Speak: The Eloquence of Women's Lives*. Prospect Heights, IL: Waveland, 1991.

Foss, Sonja A., Karen A. Foss, and Robert Trapp, *Contemporary Perspectives on Rhetoric*, 2nd ed. Prospect Heights, IL: Waveland, 1991.

Foss, Sonja K., and Ann Gill. "Michel Foucault's Theory of Rhetoric as Epistemic," *Western Journal of Speech Communication* 51 (1987): 384–402.

Foss, Sonja K., Cindy L. Griffin, and Karen A. Foss. "Transforming Rhetoric Through Feminist Reconstruction: A Response to the Gender-Diversity Perspective," *Women's Studies in Communication* 20 (1997): 117–136.

Foucault, Michel. *The Archaeology of Knowledge*, translated by A. M. Sheridan Smith. New York: Pantheon, 1972.

Foucault, Michel. *Discipline and Punish: The Birth of the Prison*, translated by A. Sheridan. New York: Vintage, 1979.

Foucault, Michel. *The Order of Things: An Archaeology of the Human Sciences*. New York: Pantheon, 1970.

Foucault, Michel. *Power/Knowledge: Selected Interviews and Other Writings 1927–1977*, translated by Colin Gordon, and others. New York: Pantheon, 1980.

Fusfield, William. "Communication Without Constellation? Habermas's Argumentative Turn in (and Away from) Critical Theory," *Communication Theory* 7 (1997): 301–320.

Geertz, Clifford. *The Interpretation of Cultures*. New York: Basic, 1973.

Geertz, Clifford. *Local Knowledge: Further Essays in Interpretive Anthropology*. New York: Basic, 1983.

Giddens, Anthony. *Profiles and Critiques in Social Theory*. Berkeley: University of California Press, 1982.

Gilligan, Carol. *In a Different Voice*. Cambridge, MA: Harvard University Press, 1982.

González, Alberto, and JoBeth González. "The Color Problem in Sillyville: Negotiating White Identity in One Popular "Kid-Vid." *Communication Quarterly* 50 (2002): 410–421.

Gramsci, Antonio. *Selections from the Prison Notebooks*, translated by Q. Hoare and G. Nowell Smith. New York: International, 1971.

Grossberg, Lawrence. "Is There Rock After Punk?" *Critical Studies in Mass Communication* 3 (1986): 50–73.

Habermas, Jürgen. *Knowledge and Human Interests*, translated by J. J. Shapiro. Boston: Beacon, 1971.

Habermas, Jürgen. *Legitimation Crisis*, translated by Thomas McCarthy. Boston: Beacon, 1975.

Habermas, Jürgen. *Postmetaphysical Thinking: Philosophical Essays*, translated by William Mark Hohengarten. Cambridge, MA: MIT Press, 1992.

Habermas, Jürgen. *The Theory of Communicative Action, Volume 1: Reason and the Rationalization of Society*, translated by Thomas McCarthy. Boston: Beacon, 1984.

Hall, Stuart. "Cultural Studies and the Centre: Some Problematics and Problems." In *Culture, Media, Language*, edited by S. Hall, D. Hobson, A. Lowe, and P. Willis, 15–47. London: Hutchinson, 1981.

Hall, Stuart. "Cultural Studies: Two Paradigms." In *Media, Culture, and Society: A Critical Reader*, edited by R. Collins. London: Sage, 1986.

Hall, Stuart. "Ideology." In *International Encyclopedia of Communications*. Vol. 2, edited by Erik Barnouw, 307–311. New York: Oxford University Press, 1989.

Hall, Stuart. "Signification, Representation, Ideology: Althusser and the Post-Structuralist Debates," *Critical Studies in Mass Communication* 2 (1985): 91–114.

Hall, Stuart, Dorothy Hobson, Andrew Lowe, and Paul Willis, eds. *Culture, Media, Language*. London: Hutchinson, 1981.

Harms, John B., and David R. Dickens. "Postmodern Media Studies: Analysis or Symptom," *Critical Studies in Mass Communication* 13 (1996): 210–227.

Hasian, Jr., Marouf, and Fernando Delgado. "The Trials and Tribulations of Racialized Critical Rhetorical Theory: Understanding the Rhetorical Ambiguities of Proposition 187," *Communication Theory* 8 (August 1998): 245–270.

Hoggart, Richard. *Uses of Literacy*. London: Chatto and Windus, 1957.

hooks, bell. *Feminist Theory: From Margin to Center*. Boston: South End Press, 1984.

Houston, Marsha, and Olga Idriss Davis, eds. *Centering Ourselves: African American Feminist and Womanist Studies of Discourse*. Creskill, NJ: Hampton Press, 2002.

Huspek, Michael. "Taking Aim on Habermas's Critical Theory: On the Road Toward a Critical Hermeneutics," *Communication Monographs* 58 (1991): 225–233.

Huspek, Michael. "Toward Normative Theories of Communication with Reference to the Frankfurt School: An Introduction," *Communication Theory* 7 (1997): 265–276.

Hymes, Dell. *Foundations in Sociolinguistics: An Ethnographic Approach.* Philadelphia: University of Pennsylvania Press, 1974.

Jansen, Sue Curry. "Power and Knowledge: Toward a New Critical Synthesis," *Journal of Communication* 33 (1983): 342–354.

Johnson, Fern L., and Karren Young. "Gendered Voices in Children's Television Advertising," *Critical Studies in Media Communication* 19 (2002): 461–480.

Katriel, Tamar. "'Griping' as a Verbal Ritual in Some Israeli Discourse." In *Cultural Communication and Intercultural Contact,* edited by Donal Carbaugh, 99–114. Hillsdale, NJ: Lawrence Erlbaum, 1990.

Katz, Elihu. "The Two-Step Flow of Communication," *Public Opinion Quarterly* 21 (1957): 61–78.

Katz, Elihu, and Paul Lazarsfeld. *Personal Influence: The Part Played by People in the Flow of Mass Communications.* New York: Free Press, 1955.

Kellner, Douglas. "Media Communications vs. Cultural Studies: Overcoming the Divide," *Communication Theory* 5 (1995): 162–177.

Kellner, Douglas. *Media Culture: Cultural Studies, Identity and Politics Between the Modern and the Postmodern.* London: Routledge, 1995.

Kraidy, Marwan M. "Hybridity in Cultural Globalization," *Communication Theory* 12 (2002): 316–339.

Lal, Barbara Balas. "Symbolic Interaction Theories," *American Behavioral Scientist* 38 (1995): 421–441.

Lanigan, Richard L. *Phenomenology of Communication: Merleau-Ponty's Thematics in Communicology and Semiology.* Pittsburgh: Duquesne University Press, 1988.

Latané, Bibb. "Dynamic Social Impact: Robust Predictions from Simple Theory." In *Modelling and Simulation in the Social Sciences from the Philosophy of Science Point of View,* edited by R. Hegselmann, U. Mueller, and K. G. Troitzsch, 287–310. Dordrecht, Netherlands: Kluwer Theory and Decision Library, 1996.

Lazarsfeld, Paul, Bernard Berelson, and H. Gaudet, *The People's Choice.* New York: Columbia University Press, 1948.

Lembo, Ronald, and Kenneth H. Tucker. "Culture, Television, and Opposition: Rethinking Cultural Studies," *Critical Studies in Mass Communication* 7 (1990): 97–116.

Lovell, Terry. "Introduction: Feminist Criticism and Cultural Studies." In *British Feminist Thought: A Reader,* edited by Terry Lovell, 271–280. Oxford: Blackwell, 1990.

Mahler, Alwin, and Everett M. Rogers. "The Diffusion of Interactive Communication Innovations and the Critical Mass: The Adoption of Telecommunications Services by German Banks," *Telecommunications Policy* 23 (1999): 719–740.

Makus, Anne. "Stuart Hall's Theory of Ideology: A Frame for Rhetorical Criticism," *Western Journal of Speech Communication* 54 (1990): 495–514.

Marx, Karl. *Capital.* Chicago: Kerr, 1909.

Marx, Karl. *The Communist Manifesto.* London: Reeves, 1888.

McCarthy, Thomas. *Ideals and Illusions: On Reconstruction and Deconstruction in Contemporary Critical Theory.* Cambridge, MA: MIT Press, 1993.

McPhail, Mark. *The Rhetoric of Racism.* Lanham, MD: University Press of America, 1994.

Mead, George Herbert. *Mind, Self, and Society.* Chicago: University of Chicago Press, 1934.

Mumby, Dennis K. *Communication and Power in Organizations: Discourse, Ideology, and Domination.* Norwood, NJ: Ablex, 1988.

Murdock, Graham. "Across the Great Divide: Cultural Analysis and the Condition of Democracy," *Critical Studies in Mass Communication* 12 (1995): 89–95.

Nakayama, Thomas K., and Robert L. Krizek. "Whiteness: A Strategic Rhetoric," *Quarterly Journal of Speech* 81 (August 1995): 291–309.

Nakayama, Thomas K., and Judith N. Martin, eds. *Whiteness: The Communication of Social Identity.* Thousand Oaks, CA: Sage, 1999.

Nakayama, Thomas K., and Lisa N. Peñaloza, "Madonna T/Races: Music Videos Through the Prism of Color." In *The Madonna Connection: Representational Politics, Subcultural Identities, and Cultural Theory,* edited by Cathy Schwichtenberg. Boulder, CO: Westview, 1993.

Nelson, Cary, and Lawrence Grossberg, eds. *Marxism and the Interpretation of Culture.* Urbana: University of Illinois Press, 1988.

Philipsen, Gerry. "An Ethnographic Approach to Communication Studies." In *Rethinking Communication: Paradigm Exemplars,* edited by Brenda Dervin, Lawrence Grossberg, Barbara J. O'Keefe, and Ellen Wartella, 258–269. Newbury Park, CA: Sage, 1989.

Philipsen, Gerry. "A Theory of Speech Codes." In *Developing Communication Theories,* edited by Gerry Philipsen and Terrance L. Albrecht, 119–156. Albany: SUNY Press, 1997.

Pillai, Poonam. "Rereading Stuart Hall's Encoding/Decoding Model," *Communication Theory* 2 (1992): 221–233.

Potter, Jonathan. *Representing Reality: Discourse, Rhetoric and Social Construction.* London: Sage, 1996.

Powers, John H. "On the Intellectual Structure of the Human Communication Discipline," *Communication Education* 44 (1995): 191–222.

Pryor, Robert. "On the Method of Critical Theory and Its Implications for a Critical Theory of Communication." In *Phenomenology in Rhetoric and Communication,* edited by Stanley A. Deetz, 25–35. Washington, DC: Center for Advanced Research in Phenomenology/University Press of America, 1981.

Rahman, Momim, and Anne Witz, "What Really Matters? The Elusive Quality of the Material in Feminist Thought." *Feminist Theory* 4 (Dec., 2003): 243–261.

Rogers, Everett M. *Diffusion of Innovations.* New York: Free Press, 1995.

Rogers, Everett M. "Diffusion Theory: A Theoretical Approach to Promote Community-Level Change." In

Handbook of HIV Prevention, edited by John L. Peterson and Ralph J. DiClemente, 57–65. New York: Kluwer Academic, 2000.

Rogers, Everett M. "The Empirical and the Critical Schools of Communication Research." In *Communication Yearbook 5*, edited by Michael Burgoon, 125–144. New Brunswick, NJ: Transaction, 1982.

Rogers, Everett M. *A History of Communication Study: A Biographical Approach*. New York: Free Press, 1994.

Rogers, Everett M., and D. Lawrence Kincaid, *Communication Networks: Toward a New Paradigm for Research*. New York: Free Press, 1981.

Rosteck, Thomas. "Cultural Studies and Rhetorical Studies," *Quarterly Journal of Speech* 81 (1995): 386–421.

Said, Edward. *Orientalism*. New York: Random House, 1978.

Sapir, Edward. *Language: An Introduction to the Study of Speech*. New York: Harcourt, Brace and World, 1921.

Schaef, Anne Wilson. *Women's Reality: An Emerging Female System in the White Male Society*. Minneapolis, MN: Winston Press, 1981.

Shome, Raka. "Postcolonial Interventions in the Rhetorical Canon: An 'Other' View." In *Contemporary Rhetorical Theory: A Reader*, edited by John Louis Lucaites, Celeste Michelle Condit, and Sally Caudill. New York: Guilford, 1999.

Shome, Raka, and Radha S. Hegde. "Postcolonial Approaches to Communication: Charting the Terrain, Engaging the Intersections," *Communication Theory* 12 (August 2002): 249–270.

Shugart, Helene A. "An Appropriating Aesthetic: Reproducing Power in the Discourse of Critical Scholarship," *Communication Theory* 13 (2003): 275–303.

Slack, Jennifer Daryl, and Martin Allor. "The Political and Epistemological Constituents of Critical Communication Research," *Journal of Communication* 33 (1983): 128–218.

Sloop, John M., and Kent A. Ono. "Out-Law Discourse: The Critical Politics of Material Judgment," *Philosophy and Rhetoric* 30 (1997): 50–69.

Smythe, Dallas W., and Tran Van Dinh. "On Critical and Administrative Research: A New Critical Analysis," *Journal of Communication* 33 (1983): 117–127.

Spivak, Gayatri. *The Postcolonial Critic*, edited by S. Harasym. New York: Routledge, 1990.

Thornham, Sue. *Feminist Theory and Cultural Studies: Stories of Unsettled Relations*. London: Oxford University Press, 2000.

Turner, Victor. *The Anthropology of Performance*. New York: PAJ, 1987.

White, Robert. "Mass Communication and Culture: Transition to a New Paradigm," *Journal of Communication* 33 (1983): 279–301.

Whorf, Benjamin L. *Language, Thought, and Reality*, edited by John B. Carroll. New York: Wiley, 1956.

Williams, Raymond. *The Long Revolution*. New York: Columbia University Press, 1961.

Zompetti, Joseph P. "Toward a Gramscian Critical Rhetoric," *Western Journal of Communication* 61 (1997): 66–86.

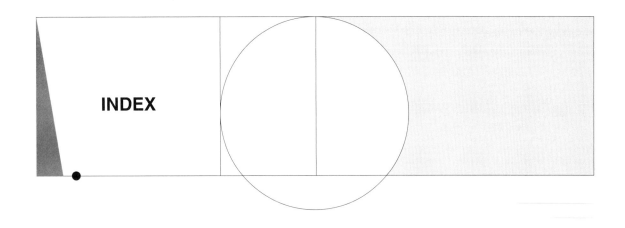

INDEX